INSTRUCTOR'S RESOURCE MANUAL

Ways of the World

A Brief Global History

ERIC W. NELSON
Missouri State University

PHYLLIS G. JESTICE
University of Southern Mississippi

Bedford/St. Martin's
Boston ◆ New York

Manufactured in the United States of America.

3 2 1 0 9 8
f e d c b a

For information, write: Bedford/St. Martin's, 75 Arlington Street, Boston, MA 02116 (617-399-4000)

ISBN-10: 0-312-48710-X
ISBN-13: 978-0-312-48710-2

Instructors who have adopted *Ways of the World* as a textbook for a course are authorized to duplicate portions of this manual for their students.

Preface

We have written this Instructor's Resource Manual as an aid for new world history instructors and for veteran teachers looking for fresh ideas as they make a transition to the distinctive approach to world history found in *Ways of the World*. This manual offers both support material and concrete suggestions for getting the most out of the textbook, which privileges big ideas over learning lots and lots of facts. Since every instructor teaches history differently, the resources in this manual have been designed to be flexible, giving you many options for designing and redesigning a course to focus on specific topics or areas of interest.

Features in Each Chapter

For the Volume 1 prologue and each chapter in the textbook, this manual includes the following elements:

Chapter Overview

The **Chapter Objectives** that open the first section of each chapter offer an overview of the chapter's main themes in a bulleted-list format for easy reference.

The **Chapter Outline** gives an in-depth review of each chapter, covering major topics and themes. It is also annotated with cross-references to the teaching ideas located in the Using *Ways of the World* in the Classroom section of each chapter of the manual.

Using *Ways of the World* in the Classroom

The **Lecture Strategies** for each chapter engage directly with the central themes of the textbook chapter. Each strategy is designed both to give students a more detailed understanding of a topic and to offer suggestions on how a theme might be taken in different directions in the classroom. While the lecture strategies do not amount to full lecture outlines, they should provide enough specifics to ease lecture preparation.

The **Discussion Topics** are designed to challenge students to explore, through classroom interaction, key textbook themes from new and stimulating perspectives. The three discussion ideas in each chapter emphasize contextualization, comparison, and ways to address misconceptions or difficult topics.

The **Classroom Activities** section includes three activities designed to engage students in active learning in the classroom. For ease of reference, each of these ideas is identified as suitable for small groups, for large groups, or for both small and large groups. A wide variety of assignments is suggested, including close-reading, analysis, role-playing, and timeline activities. Many of these draw on special features of *Ways of the World,* including activities that require students to analyze maps and illustrations from the textbook. The final classroom activity is a "clicker question," designed to elicit a personal response from each student about a key topic explored in the textbook. Instructors who use a computer to project these questions at the front of the classroom and who use the i>clicker personal response system can get an instant tally of answers to these multiple-choice questions. These and other questions designed for use with i>clicker are available on the instructor side of the book companion site at bedfordstmartins.com/strayer and on the Instructor's Resource CD-ROM.

The **Key Terms** section provides an easy reference for definitions to all terms found in the "What's the Significance?" section at the end of each textbook chapter. Pronunciation keys are included for challenging terms.

Answer Guidelines for Chapter Questions

The **Big Picture Questions** section in the manual repeats the questions found at the end of the textbook chapter and provides answer guidelines in bulleted-list format. These answers offer an outline of what a student can reasonably be expected to draw from *Ways of the World,* and they can be used to grade quizzes on chapter reading or to guide discussion sections.

The **Margin Review Questions** section includes bullet-point answers to each question that appears in the margins of the textbook chapter. As with the answers to the Big Picture questions, these provide a quick reference to what a student could reasonably be expected to draw from their reading, and they can be used for quizzing or discussion. Wherever possible, the answer draws directly on the wording of the chapter.

Additional Resources

The **Additional Bedford/St. Martin's Resources** section appears near the end of each chapter of this manual. This detailed guide correlates to the chapter-specific material from all the supplements available from the publisher for use with Ways of the World (see "Also Available with *Ways of the World*" below).

The annotated **Further Reading** list offers an up-to-date selection of books and Web sites chosen specifically to provide instructors with short scholarly introductions to topics covered in each chapter of the textbook and in the lecture strategies.

The annotated **Literature** section lists both full-text and extract primary source readings available in print or online. In addition, the list includes a selection of fictional works, both modern and contemporaneous to the period covered in the chapter, that are particularly well suited for classroom use.

The annotated **Film** list suggests easily accessible and up-to-date academic videos for classroom use, along with historical fiction films appropriate to the chapter.

Appendices

The six appendices located at the end of this manual offer resources to help both veteran and first-time world history instructors build and reinvigorate their courses using *Ways of the World* and other useful works.

Sample class plans, which appear in Appendices I and II, offer suggestions for structuring courses that meet three times a week using *Ways of the World*. The plan for each day of class integrates textbook reading assignments with teaching suggestions from this manual. These class plans can easily be adapted for courses that meet twice a week as well.

Discussing *Ways of the World*: A Survival Guide for First-Time Teaching Assistants appears in Appendix III of this manual. This resource supplements the instructor's materials with practical advice for teaching with *Ways of the World*, working with professors, overcoming problems with students, running discussion sections, designing assignments, grading tests and papers, relating thesis and dissertation work to classroom teaching, and more.

The New World History Instructor: Thirty Books to Get You Started in Appendix IV offers a short, annotated bibliography of essential books for first-time world history instructors.

A World History Reference Library in Appendix V offers a short bibliography of reference books to which every world history instructor should have access.

Useful Web Sites for the World History Instructor in Appendix VI provides an up-to-date list of Web sites that may be particularly useful to a world history instructor.

Also Available with *Ways of the World*

The comprehensive collection of ancillaries available with *Ways of the World: A Brief Global History*, provides an integrated support system for veteran teachers, first-time teaching assistants, and instructors who lecture to large and small classes alike.

For Instructors

New Media Resources

Instructor's Resource CD-ROM. This disc provides instructors with ready-made and customizable PowerPoint multimedia presentations built around chapter outlines, maps, figures, and all images from the textbook, plus jpeg versions of all maps, figures, and images. The disc also contains chapter related multiple-choice questions that can be used with the i>clicker personal response system.

Computerized Test Bank. The test bank provides more than thirty exercises per chapter, including multiple-choice, fill-in-the-blank, short-answer, and full-length essay questions.

Instructors can customize quizzes, add or edit both questions and answers, and export questions and answers to a variety of formats, including WebCT and Blackboard. The disc includes correct answers and essay outlines.

Book Companion Site at bedfordstmartins.com/ strayer. The companion Web site gathers all the Web-based resources for *Ways of the World*, including the Online Study Guide and related Quiz Gradebook, at a single Web address and provides convenient links to lecture, assignment, and research materials, such as PowerPoint chapter outlines and the digital libraries at Make History.

Make History at bedfordstmartins.com/strayer. Comprising the content of Bedford/St. Martin's five acclaimed online libraries—Map Central, the Bedford History Image Library, DocLinks, HistoryLinks, and PlaceLinks—Make History provides one-stop access to relevant digital content, including maps, images, documents, and Web links. Students and instructors alike can search this free, easy-to-use database by keyword, topic, date, or specific chapter of *Ways of the World* and download the content they find. Instructors can also create entire collections of content and store them online for later use or post them to the Web to share with students.

Content for Course Management Systems. A variety of student and instructor resources developed for this textbook is ready for use in course management systems such as Blackboard, WebCT, and other platforms. This e-content includes nearly all of the offerings from the book's Online Study Guide as well as the book's test bank.

Videos and Multimedia. A wide assortment of videos and multimedia CD-ROMs on various topics in world history is available to qualified adopters.

For Students

Print Resources

World History Matters: A Student Guide to World History Online. Based on the popular "World History Matters" Web site produced by the Center for History and New Media, this unique resource, written by Kristin Lehner (The Johns Hopkins University), Kelly Schrum (George Mason University), and T. Mills Kelly, (George Mason University), combines reviews of 150 of the most useful and reliable world history Web sites, with an introduction that guides students in locating, evaluating, and correctly citing online sources. The Web sites offer opportunities for researching broad themes as well as special topics and regions and feature a range of sources, including primary documents, maps, art,

photographs, statistics, and audio and video recordings. This resource is available free when packaged with the text.

Bedford Series in History and Culture. More than 100 titles in this highly praised series combine first-rate scholarship, historical narrative, and important primary documents for undergraduate courses. Each book is brief, inexpensive, and focused on a specific topic or period. Package discounts are available.

Trade Books. Titles published by sister companies Farrar, Straus and Giroux; Henry Holt and Company; Hill and Wang; Picador; and St. Martin's Press are available at a 50 percent discount when packaged with Bedford/St. Martin's textbooks. For more information, visit bedfordstmartins .com/tradeup.

New Media Resources

Online Study Guide at bedfordstmartins.com/strayer. The Online Study Guide helps students synthesize the material covered in *Ways of the World*. For each chapter, it provides a multiple choice self-test that focuses on important conceptual ideas; an identification quiz that helps students remember key people, places, and events; a flashcard activity that tests students' knowledge of key terms; and two interactive map activities intended to strengthen students' geographic skills. Instructors can monitor students' progress through an online Quiz Gradebook or receive e-mail updates.

Benjamin, A Student's Online Guide to History Reference Sources at bedfordstmartins.com/strayer. This Web site provides links to history-related databases, indexes, and journals, plus contact information for state, provincial, local, and professional history organizations.

The Bedford Bibliographer at bedfordstmartins.com/ strayer. The *Bedford Bibliographer*, a simple but powerful Web-based tool, assists students with the process of collecting sources and generates bibliographies in four commonly used documentation styles.

The Bedford Research Room at bedfordstmartins .com/strayer. The Research Room, drawn from Mike Palmquist's *The Bedford Researcher*, offers a wealth of resources—including interactive tutorials, research activities, student writing samples, and links to hundreds of other places online—to support students in courses across the disciplines. The site also offers instructors a library of helpful instructional tools.

Diana Hacker's Research and Documentation Online at bedfordstmartins.com/strayer. This Web site provides clear advice on how to integrate primary and secondary sources into research papers, how to cite sources correctly, and how to format in MLA, APA, *Chicago*, or CBE style.

The St. Martin's Tutorial on Avoiding Plagiarism at bedfordstmartins.com/strayer. This online tutorial reviews the consequences of plagiarism and explains what sources to acknowledge, how to keep good notes, how to organize research, and how to organize research, and how to integrate sources appropriately. The tutorial includes exercises to help students practice integrating sources and recognize acceptable summaries.

Acknowledgments

We would like to thank Dr. Robert Strayer, the author of *Ways of the World*, for his very quick and very helpful feedback on drafts of this Instructor's Resource Manual. We would also like to thank Heidi Hood and Jack Cashman at Bedford/St. Martin's for all their help in producing this volume.

Eric W. Nelson
Missouri State University

Phyllis G. Jestice
University of Southern Mississippi

Prologue
From Cosmic History to Human History

Outline

I. **Opening Vignette**
   A. Different peoples have believed that the world was created in different ways.
      1. myths of origin try to answer a fundamentally human question: what happened in the beginning?
      2. try to provide a larger context to anchor particular societies
   B. World historians also try to puzzle out beginnings.
      1. modern creation stories depend heavily on fields that developed during and after the Scientific Revolution (astronomy, physics, geology, biology)
      2. but modern models are better at answering *how* things began than *why*
      3. many modern people have tried to reconcile scientific and religious understandings of beginnings

II. **The History of the Universe**
   A. The largest modern framework for understanding beginnings is "big history."
      1. "history of everything" from the big bang to the present (around 13.7 billion years)
      2. the largest possible context for understanding the human journey
         a. the idea of the cosmic calendar: whole history of the cosmos as a single year

   B. The study of cosmic history is disturbing to many.
      1. gives a sense of the insignificance of human life
      2. but human awareness of the universe makes us unique and can inspire awe

III. **The History of a Planet**
   A. Our solar system emerged around 4.7 billion years ago.
   B. Life first appeared on earth about 600 million years after the earth itself was formed.
      1. remained at the level of single-celled organisms for about 3 billion years
      2. all multicelled creatures have evolved over the past 600 million years
   C. Each species has had its own history.
      1. but history books and courses focus on our own species, *Homo sapiens*
      2. *Homo sapiens* only appeared in the last few minutes of December 31 on the cosmic calendar
   D. The short history of *Homo sapiens* has had more consequences for the planet than the history of any other species.
      1. human communication skills allow us to learn from each other
      2. ability to accumulate knowledge and pass it on to future generations
      3. humans have had a massive impact on the earth

IV. **The History of the Human Species . . . in a Single Paragraph: A Preview**
   A. The history of *Homo sapiens* has occupied roughly the last 250,000 years and is typically divided into three major phases.
      1. Paleolithic age was very long; 95 percent of human history
         a. settlement of every major landmass
         b. construction of the first human societies
      2. agricultural era began about 12,000 years ago
         a. domestication of plants and animals
         b. dependence on domestic plants and animals to sustain life fundamentally shaped the human experience
      3. modern industrial era: from around 1750 to the present
         a. massive increase in the rate of technological change
         b. massive increase in human control over nature
         c. rise of "modern" societies

V. **Why World History?**
   A. As recently as the mid-twentieth century, almost all college-level history courses were focused on particular civilizations or nations.
   B. Since then, education has moved toward world history.
      1. the world wars revealed the evils of unchecked nationalism
      2. economic and cultural globalization has emphasized the interdependence of the world's peoples and their unequal positions
      3. new awareness that many human problems are global in scope
      4. third world peoples wanted to have their histories known, too
   C. The "world history movement" has tried to create global understanding of the past by highlighting broad patterns that transcend particular civilizations.
      1. also tries to include the distinctive histories of many peoples
      2. this is a massive task that has generated much controversy

VI. **Comparison, Connection, and Change: The Three Cs of World History**
   A. Most world historians agree on three major issues that define their field of study.
      1. the need for constant **comparison**
         a. world history is comparative
         b. comparison is a recurring theme throughout this text
         c. comparison is useful in fighting Eurocentrism
         d. the art of comparison must be learned and is a matter of careful choice
      2. awareness of **connections**
         a. effort to counteract the habit of thinking about peoples or states as self-contained and isolated
         b. no societies developed in a vacuum
         c. cross-cultural connections have existed for a very long time
      3. examination of "big picture" **changes**
         a. What caused both large and small transformations?
   B. Change and comparison in particular help to counteract "essentialism" or "stereotyping."
      1. it's too easy to define particular groups of people as having unchanging characteristics
      2. in reality, every category of people has endless divisions and conflicts
         a. human communities are in a constant state of flux
      3. but human existence also has broad continuities

USING *WAYS OF THE WORLD* IN THE CLASSROOM

Key Terms

big history: The "history of everything" is a recent historiographical approach that provides an enormous context for history—from the creation of the universe to the present—rather than just focusing on the history of humankind.

comparative history: Recent historiographical approach that emphasizes the examination of issues that cross the bounds of a single culture, hoping by comparison to identify characteristics that are fundamental to a phenomenon as well as how different cultures respond differently to similar stimuli, and to sort out what is distinctive about a region's historical development.

cosmic calendar: The recent scholarly notion of charting the history of the cosmos as if it were a single 365-day year, with the big bang occurring on January 1 and the history of *Homo sapiens* fitting entirely within the last few hours of December 31; such an approach helps drive home the shortness of the human experience within the context of the age of the universe.

myths of origin: Traditional stories told by most of the earth's peoples in which they seek to explain where they came from as a people, or how humankind or the world itself came into being; these stories often express a religious sense of place and purpose that transcends more scientific explanations.

three Cs, the: The three most fundamental elements of the study of world history: comparison (between cultures), connection (among different peoples), and change.

ANSWER GUIDELINES FOR PROLOGUE QUESTIONS

The two sets of questions that follow appear in the textbook at the end of the Prologue and in the margins of the reading. They are also provided in the Computerized Test Bank with answer guidelines, for your convenience.

The Big Picture Questions

1. What is the difference between religiously based myths of origin and creation stories derived from scientific accounts?

- Religiously based stories or myths of origin seek to anchor particular societies in a larger context, providing their people with a sense of place, purpose, and belonging.
- Scientific accounts claim to be truer and more certain, at least in a literal sense, for they can be checked and verified rather than simply accepted and believed.

- Scientific accounts are stronger on how things began than on why.

2. How do you respond personally to modern notions of the immense size and age of the universe?

- This question by its very nature has no right answer.
- However, the Prologue does note that many in the past have found it disturbing to contemplate the scope of the universe, as it gives a sense of the insignificance of human life.
- The Prologue also notes that human awareness of the vast mystery of the universe makes us unique and can inspire in many people a sense of awe.

3. What examples of comparison, connection, and change in world history would you like to explore further as your course unfolds?

- This question by its very nature has no right answer, and thus responses will vary from student to student.

Margin Review Questions

Q. *What have been the major turning points in the prehuman phases of "big history"?*

- The big bang occurred 13.7 billion years ago.
- Stars and galaxies began to form 12 billion years ago.
- The Milky Way galaxy formed 10 billion years ago.
- The origin of the solar system dates to 4.7 billion years ago.
- Formation of the earth took place 4.5 billion years ago.
- The earliest life on earth appeared 4 billion years ago.
- Oxygen formed on earth 1.3 billion years ago.
- The first worms appeared 658 million years ago.
- The first fish and the first vertebrates emerged 534 million years ago.
- The first reptiles and the first trees appeared 370 million years ago.
- The age of dinosaurs lasted from 329 million to 164 million years ago.
- The first humanlike creatures appeared 2.7 million years ago.

Q. *Why has world history achieved an increasingly prominent place in American education in recent decades?*

• The world wars of the twentieth century revealed the evils of unchecked nationalism.

• Economic and cultural globalization has emphasized the interdependence of the world's peoples as well as their unequal positions within the world.

• There is a new awareness that many human problems are global in scope.

• Third world peoples wanted to have their histories known.

Prologue to Volume 2
Considering World History

Outline

I. **Opening Vignette**
   A. The history of the human species goes back 250,000–300,000 years and is usually divided into three phases.
      1. Paleolithic age constitutes 95 percent of that time
         a. gathering and hunting
         b. settlement of every major landmass
         c. construction of the first human societies
      2. age of agriculture began about 12,000 years ago
         a. domesticated plants and animals became the main source of human food
         b. fundamentally reshaped human experience
      3. modern industrial age began around 1750 C.E.
         a. vast increase in productivity, wealth, and human control over nature
         b. has also fundamentally reshaped the human experience
   B. Volume 2 of *Ways of the World* focuses on the last centuries of the agricultural era and on the modern industrial age.
   C. The planetary/global/world history perspective has become increasingly prominent among those who study the past.

II. **Why World History?**
   A. As recently as the mid-twentieth century, almost all college-level history courses were focused on particular civilizations or nations.
   B. Since then, education has moved toward world history.
      1. the world wars revealed the evils of unchecked nationalism
      2. economic and cultural globalization has emphasized the interdependence of the world's peoples and their unequal positions
      3. new awareness that many human problems are global in scope
      4. third world peoples wanted to have their histories known, too
   C. The "world history movement" has tried to create global understanding of the past by highlighting broad patterns that transcend particular civilizations.
      1. also tries to include the distinctive histories of many peoples
      2. this is a massive task that has generated much controversy

III. **Comparison, Connection, and Change: The Three Cs of World History**
   A. Most world historians agree on three major issues that define their field of study.
      1. the need for constant **comparison**
         a. world history is comparative
         b. comparison is a recurring theme throughout this text
         c. comparison is useful in fighting Eurocentrism
         d. the art of comparison must be learned and is a matter of careful choice

2. awareness of **connections**
    a. effort to counteract the habit of thinking about peoples or states as self-contained and isolated
    b. no societies developed in a vacuum
    c. cross-cultural connections have existed for a very long time
3. examination of "big picture" **changes**
    a. What caused both large and small transformations?

B. Change and comparison in particular help to counteract "essentialism" or "stereotyping."
    1. it's too easy to define particular groups of people has having unchanging characteristics
    2. in reality, every category of people has endless divisions and conflicts
        a. human communities are in a constant state of flux
    3. but human existence also has broad continuities

Contents

FIRST THINGS FIRST
Beginnings in History, to 500 B.C.E.

Outline: The Big Picture: Turning Points in Early World History

I. **The Emergence of Humankind**
   A. Most scholars in the post-Darwinian world regard human beginnings in the context of biological change.
      1. archeologists and anthropologists believe that the lines of descent leading to *Homo sapiens* and chimpanzees diverged around 5 million–6 million years ago
      2. hominid family emerged in eastern and southern Africa, with 20–30 different related species
         a. they were bipedal (walked on two legs)
   B. The hominids developed over time.
      1. brain size increased
      2. around 2.3 million years ago, *Homo habilis* began to use stone tools
      3. by 1 million years ago, some hominid species, especially *Homo erectus*, began to migrate from Africa
         a. knew how to use fire

   C. Of the hominid species, only *Homo sapiens* still survives.
      1. emerged in Africa around 250,000 years ago
      2. began to migrate beyond Africa after 100,000 years ago

II. **The Globalization of Humankind**
   A. Initial migrations from Africa took place in the Paleolithic Era.
      1. gatherers and hunters
      2. Paleolithic era continued until around 11,000 years ago
         a. the Paleolithic era accounts for over 90 percent of human time on earth
         b. accounts for about 12 percent of the total number of people who have lived
   B. No other large species created homes in every environmental niche as *Homo sapiens* did.
      1. slowly developed technology
      2. slowly imposed meaning through art, ritual, and religion

III. **The Revolution of Farming and Herding**
   A. 6.2 billion people in the world today; almost all live from domesticated plants and animals.
   B. Domestication first occurred in several regions about 11,000 years ago.
      1. it was the most significant and enduring transformation of humankind
      2. provided the foundation for almost all subsequent change
      3. the period from 11,000 years ago to around 1750 C.E. can be regarded as a single age—the age of agriculture

4. allowed for a large increase in the human population

C. Food production laid the foundation for enduring divisions within human communities.

1. some regions were luckier in terms of climate and plants/animals available for domestication

2. the Americas were disadvantaged by the lack of large animals to be domesticated

3. in the Afro-Eurasian world, conflicts between agriculturalists and pastoralists became an enduring pattern

IV. The Turning Point of Civilization

A. The most prominent human communities that emerged were "civilizations": societies based in cities and governed by powerful states.

B. Almost everyone in the world now lives in a state with a formal political authority.

1. state-based societies give prominence to cities

2. around half of the world's population now lives in urban centers

C. The first cities and states emerged around 3500 B.C.E.

1. state- and city-based societies have been the most powerful and innovative human communities

a. they have given rise to empires

b. they have created enduring cultural and religious traditions

c. they have created new technologies

d. they have bred sharp class inequalities, patriarchy, and large-scale warfare

V. A Note on Dates

A. A recent convention encourages dating by B.C.E. and C.E., not B.C. and A.D.

1. B.C.E. = before the Common Era = B.C. (before Christ)

2. C.E. = the Common Era = A.D. (*Anno Domini*, Latin for "year of the Lord")

B. B.C.E./C.E. dating is an effort to get away from Christian-centered and Eurocentric thinking.

C. Societies have reckoned time in many different ways.

1. China: dated by the reign of particular emperors

2. Muslim calendar: Year 1 marks Muhammad's emigration to Medina in 622 C.E.

First Peoples
Populating the Planet, to 10,000 B.C.E.

CHAPTER OVERVIEW

Chapter Objectives

- To familiarize students with the spread of human societies in the Paleolithic era
- To explore the conditions of life in gathering and hunting societies
- To examine factors that eventually led to change in the gathering and hunting societies

Chapter Outline

I.   **Opening Vignette**
  A. The Hazda of Tanzania are one of the last gathering and hunting societies on earth.
    1. likely to disappear soon
    2. will mark the end of what was universal human existence until 10,000–12,000 years ago
  B. For 95 percent of human history, the means of life was gathering and hunting.
    1. food collection, not food production
    2. has been labeled "Paleolithic" (old stone age) era
  C. It's wrong to ignore the first 200,000 years of human experience.
    1. archaeology reveals a great deal about these peoples

    2. they settled the planet
    3. they created the earliest human societies
    4. they were the first to reflect on issues of life and death

II. **Out of Africa to the Ends of the Earth: First Migrations**
  A. *Homo sapiens* emerged in eastern and southern Africa 250,000 years ago.
    1. stayed there exclusively for about 150,000 years
    2. Africa was home to the "human revolution," in which culture became more important than biology in shaping human behavior
    3. humans began to inhabit environments not touched by earlier hominids
    4. technological innovation: use of stone and bone tools
    5. hunting and fishing, not just scavenging
      a. settlements planned around movement of game and fish
    6. patterns of exchange
    7. use of ornaments, perhaps planned burials
    8. around 100,000 years ago: beginning of migrations out of Africa
      a. adapted to nearly every environment on earth
      b. much took place in the difficulties of the last Ice Age
        i. ice lowered sea levels, created land bridges
  B. Into Eurasia

1. humans started migrating into the Middle East around 40,000 years ago
2. the best evidence of early European settlement comes from southern France and northern Spain
   a. settlers in northern Europe were pushed southward into warmer areas around 20,000 years ago
   b. developed new hunting habits, new hunting technologies
3. the earliest Europeans left hundreds of cave paintings: depictions of animals and humans and abstract designs (maybe early form of writing)
   a. scholars debate the meaning of cave images
      i. perhaps examples of "totemic" thinking—the belief that particular people are associated with or descended from particular animals
      ii. perhaps "hunting magic" to enhance success
      iii. perhaps part of religious practice or rites of passage
      iv. perhaps showed division of male and female realms
4. development of new technologies in Ukraine and Russia
   a. needles, multilayered clothing, weaving, nets, baskets, pottery, etc.
   b. partially underground dwellings made from mammoth remains
   c. suggests semipermanent settlement
   d. creation of female figurines ("Venus figurines")
      i. have been found all across Europe

C. Into Australia
1. humans reached Australia about 60,000 years ago from Indonesia
   a. first known use of boats
2. very sparse settlement; estimated 300,000 people in 1788
3. development of some 250 languages
4. still completely a gathering and hunting economy when Europeans arrived in 1788
5. complex worldview: the Dreamtime
   a. stories, ceremonies, and art tell of ancestral beings

b. everything in the natural order is an echo of ancient happenings
   c. current people are intimately related to places and events in past
6. major communication and exchange networks
   a. included stones, pigments, wood, *pituri* (psychoactive drug)
   b. also included songs, dances, stories, and rituals

D. Into the Americas
1. when settlement of the Americas began is still argued over (somewhere between 30,000 and 15,000 years ago)
   a. mode of migration (Bering Strait or by sea down west coast of North America) also still argued about
   b. how many migrations and how long they took also argued over
   c. evidence of humans in southern Chile by 12,500 years ago
2. Clovis: the first clearly defined and widespread culture of the Americas
   a. name comes from the Clovis point, a kind of projectile point
   b. flourished 12,000–11,000 years ago
   c. hunted large mammals (mammoths, bison)
   d. disappeared about 10,900 years ago, at the same time as the extinction of a number of large mammals
3. next stage: much greater cultural diversity, as people adapted to the end of the Ice Age in different ways

E. Into the Pacific
1. the last phase of the great human migration, started ca. 3,500 years ago
2. migration by water from the Bismarck and Solomon islands and the Philippines
3. very quick migration over very long distances
4. migrants spoke Austronesian languages (can be traced to southern China)
5. settled every habitable area of the Pacific basin within 2,500 years
   a. also settled the island of Madagascar
   b. made Austronesian the most widespread language family

c. completed initial human settlement of the world ca. 900 C.E. with occupation of Aotearoa (New Zealand)

6. Pacific settlers
   a. took agriculture with them, unlike other migrations
   b. apparently followed a deliberate colonization plan
   c. created highly stratified societies or chiefdoms (e.g., Hawaii)
   d. massive environmental impact on previous uninhabited lands
      i. many animals became extinct
      ii. deforestation of Rapa Nui (Easter Island) in fifteenth to seventeenth centuries nearly destroyed society there

III. The Ways We Were

A. The First Human Societies
   1. societies were small, bands of 25–50 people
      a. relationships defined by kinship
   2. very low population density (because of available technology)
      a. very slow population growth
      b. perhaps 10,000 people in world 100,000 years ago
      c. grew to 500,000 by 30,000 years ago
      d. reached 6 million 10,000 years ago
   3. Paleolithic bands were seasonally mobile or nomadic
      a. moved in regular patterns to exploit wild plants and animals
      b. since they moved around, they couldn't accumulate goods
   4. societies were highly egalitarian
      a. perhaps the most free people in human existence
         i. no formal chiefs, kings, bureaucrats, soldiers, priests
      b. did not have specialists, so most people had the same skills
         i. male and female tasks often differed sharply
      c. relationships between women and men were far more equal than in later societies
         i. women as gatherers provided the bulk of family food, perhaps 70 percent of diet
   5. James Cook described the gathering and hunting peoples of Australia as tranquil and socially equal

a. but European settlers found physical competition among Australian males, wife beating

6. Paleolithic societies had clearly defined rules
   a. men hunted, women gathered
   b. clear rules about distribution of meat from a kill
   c. rules about incest and adultery

B. Economy and the Environment
   1. gathering and hunting peoples used to be regarded as "primitive" and impoverished
      a. modern studies point out that they worked fewer hours
      b. wanted or needed little
      c. but life expectancy was low (35 years on average)
   2. alteration of natural environments
      a. deliberately set fires to encourage growth of certain plants
      b. extinction of many large animals shortly after humans arrived
      c. gradual extinction of other hominids, like the Neanderthals (Europe) and Flores man (Indonesia)

C. The Realm of the Spirit
   1. it is difficult to decipher the spiritual world of Paleolithic peoples
      a. lack of written sources
      b. art is subject to interpretation
      c. contemporary gathering and hunting peoples may not reflect ancient experience
   2. Paleolithic peoples had a rich ceremonial life
      a. led by part-time shamans (people especially skilled at dealing with the spirit world)
      b. frequent use of psychoactive drugs to contact spirits
   3. apparent variety of beliefs
      a. some societies were seemingly monotheistic
      b. others saw several levels of supernatural beings
      c. still others believed in an impersonal force running throughout the natural order
         i. could be accessed by shamans in a trance dance

d. Venus figurines make some scholars think that Paleolithic religion was strongly feminine, with a Great Goddess

e. many peoples probably had a cyclical view of time

D. Settling Down: "The Great Transition"

1. gradual change as populations grew, climates changed, and peoples interacted

2. collection of wild grains started in northeastern Africa around 16,000 years ago

3. last Ice Age ended 16,000–10,000 years ago

a. followed by a "global warming" period

b. richer and more diverse environment for human societies

c. population rise

d. beginnings of settlement

4. settlement led to societal change

a. larger and more complex societies

b. storage and accumulation of goods led to inequality

5. settling-down process occurred in many areas 12,000–4,000 years ago

a. Jomon culture in Japan

b. Scandinavia, Southeast Asia, North America, Middle East

c. bows and arrows were invented independently in Europe, Africa, and Middle East

6. the process of settlement was a major turn in human history

a. placed greater demand on the environment, led to agriculture

IV. **Comparing Paleolithic Societies**

A. Both the San and the Chumash preserved their ancient way of life into modern times.

B. The San of Southern Africa

1. northern fringe of the Kalahari Desert (present-day Angola, Namibia, Botswana)

2. 50,000–80,000 San still live in the region

3. part of the Khoisan language family, inhabited southern Africa at least 5,000 years

a. gathering and hunting way of life, with stone tools

b. remarkable rock art, going back 26,000 years

i. tradition persisted into the nineteenth century

ii. perhaps reflected the religious experience of trance healers

c. most of the Khoisan peoples were absorbed or displaced by Bantu-speaking peoples

4. The San (Ju/'hoansi) still practiced their ancient life with few borrowings when anthropologists started studying them in the 1950s and 1960s

a. use some twenty-eight tools, including digging stick, leather garment for carrying things, knife, spear, bow and poisoned arrows, ropes, and nets

b. men hunt, women do most of gathering

c. adequate diet

d. short workweek, with even labor division between men and women

e. uncertain and anxious life, dependent on nature

5. San society characterized by mobility, sharing, and equality

a. basic unit is band of 10–30 people, connected to other bands

b. many people claimed membership in more than one band

c. frequent movement to new territory

d. no formal leaders, priests, or craft specialists

e. very complex social relations

f. high value given to modesty, cooperation, equality

i. e.g., "insulting the meat": a hunter is expected to disparage his accomplishment

g. complex system of unequal gift exchange

6. relative equality between the sexes

a. free sex play between teenagers

b. most marriages are monogamous

c. frequent divorce among young couples

7. frequent conflict over distribution of meat; rivalries over women

8. belief system:

a. Creator God, *Gao Na*, is capricious

b. lesser god *Gauwa* is destructive but sometimes assists humans

c. *gauwasi* (spirits of dead ancestors) are most serious threat to human welfare

d. evil influences can be counteracted with *n/um*, a spiritual potency that can be activated in "curing dances"

e. state of warfare with the divine

C. The Chumash of Southern California

1. show a later Paleolithic stage than the San, with permanent villages

2. Chumash lived near present-day Santa Barbara, California

   a. richer environment than the San

   b. perhaps 20,000 when the Spaniards arrived in the sixteenth century

   c. Chumash created new society after 1150 C.E. in response to violence and food shortages

3. central technological innovation: the planked canoe (*tomol*)

   a. ability to make and own tomol led to social inequality

   b. stimulated trade between the coast and islands

   c. made deep-sea fishing possible

4. living conditions were more elaborate than the San

   a. round, permanent, substantial houses (for up to 70 people)

   b. a market economy, despite being gathering and hunting peoples

      i. use of money (stringed beads)

      ii. regulation of the money supply to prevent inflation

      iii. specialized production

      iv. payment for services of dancers, healers, and buriers

      v. some private ownership

   c. beginning of class distinctions (e.g., bearskin capes, burials)

   d. emergence of a permanent, hereditary political elite

      i. chiefs (some were women) led in war and rituals, regulated trade

      ii. periodic feasts for the poor

5. Chumash largely solved the problems of violence in the region

V. **Reflections: The Uses of the Paleolithic**

A. The study of history is about those who tell it today, not just about the past.

1. views of the past reflect our own smugness or disillusionment

2. Paleolithic era is sometimes regarded as a golden age

   a. admired by feminists, environmentalists, antimaterialists

3. scholars have looked to the Paleolithic era in questioning explosive population and economic growth of recent past

4. gathering and hunting peoples of today have looked to Paleolithic era in an effort to maintain or recover their identities

B. A basic question: "What have we lost in the mad rush to modernity?"

C. Nobody can be completely detached when studying the past.

1. but passionate involvement is a good thing

USING *WAYS OF THE WORLD* IN THE CLASSROOM

Lecture Strategies

Lecture Strategy 1

"Looking at the 'losers': Neanderthals and other failed branches of the human bush."

Anthropologists now regard the development of our species less as a family "tree" of evolution than as a family "bush" in which, at each level, several branches evolved independently in different regions. Two of the most fascinating of these dead-end branches are recent ones within the genus of *Homo sapiens*: the Neanderthals of Europe and the Near East and the recently discovered Flores man of Indonesia. This lecture strategy is to compare these Paleolithic peoples to the "winners"—*Homo sapiens*. Its objectives are:

- to explore the late stages of human evolution and speculate on why modern humans were the "winners"
- to introduce students to Neanderthals and Flores man
- to drive home the basic lesson of the fundamental similarities of all modern humans as members of the single species *Homo sapiens*

A good place to start is with the first discovery of Neanderthal fossils in the nineteenth century and the endless debate the discovery caused in scientific circles. The lecture will probably focus on Neanderthal/modern human interaction, since material on the Neanderthals is more readily available than material on Flores man. Other points to consider in a possible lecture are:

- the habitat of the Neanderthals (much of Europe and the Near East)
- how Neanderthals (and Flores man) are different from our modern species (be sure to read recent materials; recent discoveries include that Neanderthals were probably fully capable of speech)
- discussion of the significance of those differences
- the nature of Neanderthal life, comparing it to that of "Cro-Magnon man" (modern humans)—you won't find much difference between the two
- the long cohabitation of Neanderthals and modern humans
- discussion of what the existence of Neanderthals and Flores man can teach us about human evolution and early human societies

Lecture Strategy 2

"The world of the last Ice Age."
The purpose of this lecture strategy is to explore in greater detail the challenges that faced human beings as they migrated in the conditions of the last Ice Age and how they overcame those challenges. Its objectives are to:

- teach students about the Ice Age, including presentation of the natural warming and cooling trends of the planet
- discuss what it *meant* that the earth had an Ice Age—the geographical, biological, and human effects
- present early human beings as problem solvers who managed to survive and adapt themselves to Ice Age environmental challenges

A good place to begin is with a map that shows the extent of the last Ice Age (readily available on the Internet). Go over the main species extinctions that occurred with the changing climate, how glaciation shaped much of the landscape, and the land bridges that were created by the lower sea level of the period. Then back up and discuss the earth's natural pattern of

warming and cooling (this is of course a good place to bring up the current global-warming trend and why scientists think it is different than the natural cycles of the past). From there, go on to consider humans and the Ice Age. Some points to include are:

- the need for teamwork in hunting large mammals (mammoths, bison)
- what sort of tools or weapons would have been developed to deal with the challenges
- the more pressing need for shelter (whether people in this age were really "cavemen," and the other sorts of shelters they created)
- the need for clothing (and thus for means to fasten animal hides around themselves with fastening pins or sewing)
- what sort of adaptation must have taken place when the Ice Age *ended*

Lecture Strategy 3

"How do we know? Digging up *Homo sapiens*."
Many world civ. classes start with human evolution. While this text begins (rather more logically) with the Paleolithic era, this lecture strategy is an opportunity to give a brief overview of evolution, while keeping the focus on the modern human species. This lecture strategy's objectives are:

- to examine how we know what we know about Paleolithic communities—what archaeology has discovered and the problems of interpretation
- to explore the evolution of modern *Homo sapiens* and how the process of discovering earlier hominid species provoked a firestorm of debate about human origins that continues today

The story of how archaeologists discovered human origins is an exciting one. There are two basic ways to tell it: (1) chronologically by human species, thus starting with early *australopithicenes* and working your way to modern *Homo sapiens*; or (2) chronologically by discovery, starting with the discovery of the Neanderthal in 1856 and how that find provoked a search for human origins that is still turning up interesting discoveries today (a particularly handy Web site is Hominid Transitionals at www.wdd2.net/hominidtrans.html).

Especially when it comes to the Paleolithic era, images will come in handy to encourage discussion of how scholars have interpreted human artifacts. Some images to consider are:

- a typical Paleolithic tool—often indistinguishable from a rock, except to professionals
- an "advanced" Paleolithic tool—one that shows clear signs of human shaping
- a burial layout, showing careful positioning of the body, perhaps covered with ochre
- Paleolithic ornaments—beads, shells with a hole bored for hanging, etc.
- an image of a reconstructed hut made of mammoth bones and tusks
- the Willendorf Venus or another of the early Venus figurines
- cave art, such as that painted at Lascaux or Chauvet

Arm yourself with some of the current scholarly views on the meaning of these artifacts, and then encourage a discussion among the students about their meaning.

Things to Do in the Classroom

Discussion Topics

1. **Misconception/Difficult Topic, large or small group.** "Cavemen dragged women around by their hair."
This would have just *hurt* and is a rather silly image perpetrated by cartoons. Encourage students to discuss why this hairy, grunting, dominant caveman image might have come about and why it is still popular. Students should be encouraged in this way to consider modern stereotypes and what they have to say about contemporary society. Some questions to ask are:

What contemporary images have you seen of grunting cavemen waving clubs, dragging women around, etc.?
What were the contexts of those images? What point was the creator or creators of those images trying to make?
Is there any evidence that Paleolithic humans actually behaved that way?
What evidence is there that they *didn't*?

2. **Comparison, large or small group.** "Why were Paleolithic women relatively equal?"

The starting point for this discussion is biology: the average woman is simply not as strong as the average man. Yet modern scholars believe that the Paleolithic era was a golden age of relative equality for women. Ask students to discuss the reasons for this equal status and to consider its limitations.

3. **Contextualization, large or small group.** "The *best* sort of Paleolithic."
Ask students to discuss the following question: Would you rather be a member of the San or the Chumash? Why?

Classroom Activities

1. **Map analysis, large or small group.** "Tracing human migrations." Using either a modern physical map or a map that shows the extent of the last Ice Age, ask students to trace out the probable lines of human migration from Africa. Emphasize the role of land bridges and where they lay during the Ice Age.

2. **Role-playing exercise, small group.** "Paleolithic life." Divide the class into small groups, each of which is a Paleolithic band. Ask each group to pick a climate area and to decide what items they absolutely need for survival.

3. **Clicker question.** Would you like living in a Paleolithic society?

Key Terms

Austronesian migrations: The last phase of the great human migration that established a human presence in every habitable region of the earth. Austronesian-speaking people settled the Pacific islands and Madagascar in a series of seaborne migrations that began around 3,500 years ago. (*pron.* aws-troe-NEEZH-an)

Brotherhood of the Tomol: A prestigious craft guild that monopolized the building and ownership of large oceangoing canoes, or *tomols* (*pron.* toe-mole), among the Chumash people (located in what is now southern California).

Chumash culture: Paleolithic culture of southern California that survived until the modern era.

Clovis culture: The earliest widespread and distinctive culture of North America; named from the Clovis point, a particular kind of projectile point.

Dreamtime: A complex worldview of Australia's Aboriginal people that held that current humans live in a vibration or echo of ancestral happenings.

Flores man: A recently discovered hominid species of Indonesia.

"gathering and hunting peoples": As the name suggests, people who live by collecting food rather than producing it. Recent scholars have turned to this term instead of the older "hunter-gatherer" in recognition that such societies depend much more heavily on gathering than on hunting for survival.

Great Goddess: According to one theory, a dominant deity of the Paleolithic era.

Hadza: A people of northern Tanzania, almost the last surviving Paleolithic society. (*pron.* HAHD-zah)

"human revolution": The term used to describe the transition of humans from acting out of biological imperative to dependence on learned or invented ways of living (culture).

Ice Age: Any of a number of cold periods in the earth's history; the last Ice Age was at its peak around 20,000 years ago.

"insulting the meat": A San cultural practice meant to deflate pride that involved negative comments about the meat brought in by a hunter and the expectation that a successful hunter would disparage his own kill.

Jomon culture: A settled Paleolithic culture of prehistoric Japan, characterized by seaside villages and the creation of some of the world's earliest pottery. (*pron.* JOE-mahn)

megafaunal extinction: Dying-out of a number of large animal species, including the mammoth and several species of horses and camels, that occurred around 11,000–10,000 years ago, at the end of the Ice Age. The extinction may have been caused by excessive hunting or by the changing climate of the era. (*pron.* meg-ah-FAWN-al)

Neanderthals: *Homo sapiens neanderthalensis*, a European variant of *Homo sapiens* that died out about 25,000 years ago.

n/um: Among the San, a spiritual potency that becomes activated during "curing dances" and protects humans from the malevolent forces of gods or ancestral spirits.

"the original affluent society": Term coined by the scholar Marshall Sahlins in 1972 to describe Paleolithic societies, which he regarded as affluent not because they had so much but because they wanted or needed so little.

Paleolithic: Literally "old stone age"; the term used to describe early *Homo sapiens* societies in the period before the development of agriculture.

Paleolithic rock art: While this term can refer to the art of any gathering and hunting society, it is typically used to describe the hundreds of Paleolithic paintings discovered in Spain and France and dating to about 20,000 years ago; these paintings usually depict a range of animals, although human figures and abstract designs are also found. The purpose of this art is debated.

Paleolithic "settling down": The process by which some Paleolithic peoples moved toward permanent settlement in the wake of the last Ice Age. Settlement was marked by increasing storage of food and accumulation of goods as well as growing inequalities in society.

San, or Jo/'hoansi: A Paleolithic people still living on the northern fringe of the Kalahari desert in southern Africa; a sample of their language can be found at http://ling.cornell.edu/plab/amanda/juspeech.html. (*pron.* ZHUN-twasi)

shaman: In many early societies, a person believed to have the ability to act as a bridge between living humans and supernatural forces, often by means of trances induced by psychoactive drugs.

trance dance: In San culture, a nightlong ritual held to activate a human being's inner spiritual potency (*n/um*) to counteract the evil influences of gods and ancestors. The practice was apparently common to the Khoisan people, of whom the Jo/'hoansi are a surviving remnant.

Venus figurines: Paleolithic carvings of the female form, often with exaggerated breasts, buttocks, hips, and stomachs, which may have had religious significance.

ANSWER GUIDELINES FOR CHAPTER QUESTIONS

The two sets of questions that follow appear in the textbook at the end of the chapter and in the margins of the reading. They are also provided in the Computerized Test Bank with answer guidelines, for your convenience.

The Big Picture Questions

1. What is the significance of the Paleolithic era in world history?

• During the Paleolithic era, humans created a way of life that sustained humankind over 95 percent of the time that our species has inhabited the earth and was not challenged by alternatives until 10,000 to 12,000 years ago.
• Paleolithic humans spread across the globe successfully, settling almost every habitable region on the planet.
• Paleolithic humans began reflection on the great questions of life and death.
• The changes that Paleolithic humans wrought provided the foundation on which all subsequent human history was constructed.

2. In what ways did various Paleolithic societies differ from one another, and how did they change over time?

• While all Paleolithic humans shared a lifestyle of gathering and hunting, different variations in their environments and their different food supplies did create differences among groups that became increasingly pronounced as humankind spread across the globe. For instance, the spread of humankind into the Pacific islands required the development of seaworthy canoe technologies that other Paleolithic groups did not develop, and the cold and lack of caves in parts of Eastern Europe spurred the development of multilayered clothing and partially underground dwellings constructed from the bones and tusks of mammoths.
• A key differentiation occurred after the end of the last Ice Age between 16,000 and 10,000 years ago. As many plants and animals thrived, providing humans with a larger and more secure food source, some Paleolithic groups were able to settle down in more permanent settlements or villages. Others continued their nomadic existences. Those societies that settled down became larger and more complex. Settlement meant the ability of households to store and accumulate goods

to a greater degree than their nomadic ancestors. This accumulation of goods led to inequality and a wearing away of the egalitarianism found in more nomadic Paleolithic groups.

3. What statements in this chapter seem to be reliable and solidly based on facts, and which ones are more speculative and uncertain?

• From a general perspective, the chapter is most solidly based when it discusses subjects that can be explored through material remains. Thus, the arrival of humans in regions, the material life of Paleolithic humans, and the evolution of technologies (such as the emergence of smaller stone blades) are substantiated by clear archeological evidence.
• The chapter is also on solid ground when it examines relatively contemporary groups that eyewitnesses have described, such as the San and the Chumash, whose lifestyles were similar to those of much earlier Paleolithic societies.
• In general, those passages that discuss the earliest emergence of humankind are more speculative because of lack of evidence.
• The author also had to rely on speculation when he touched on the meaning of artistic expressions and the beliefs of Paleolithic societies. A good example of this is when he speculates on the meaning of cave paintings in southern France and their role in Paleolithic society or when he discusses the religious or spiritual aspects of Paleolithic culture.

4. How might our attitudes toward the modern world influence our assessment of Paleolithic societies?

• Some modern people are likely to work from the assumption that the urban civilized culture in which we live is superior to the primitive world of Paleolithic societies. Modern people might regard our ancestors as superstitious, unevolved, unable to exercise control over nature, and ignorant of the workings of nature.
• Others, disillusioned with modernity, might look to the Paleolithic era for material with which to criticize contemporary life. For instance, some feminists have found in gathering and hunting peoples a much more gender-equal society, and environmentalists have sometimes identified peoples of the Paleolithic period as uniquely in tune with their natural environment rather than seeking to dominate it.

Margin Review Questions

Q. *What was the sequence of human migration across the planet?*

• The earliest *Homo sapiens* emerged in Africa 250,000 years ago
• The first human migration out of Africa occurred 100,000 years ago
• Human entry into eastern Asia took place 70,000 years ago
• Human entry into Australia happened 60,000–40,000 years ago
• Human entry into Europe occurred 40,000 years ago
• Human entry into the Americas took place 30,000–15,000 years ago
• Austronesian migration to the Pacific islands and Madagascar occurred 3,500–1,000 years ago
• Human entry into New Zealand happened 1,000 years ago

Q. *How did Austronesian migrations differ from other early patterns of human movement?*

• They occurred quite recently, beginning only about 3,500 years ago.
• They were waterborne migrations, making use of oceangoing canoes and remarkable navigational skills.
• They happened very quickly, over the course of about 2,500 years, and over a huge area of the planet.
• Unlike other migrations, they were undertaken by people with an agricultural technology who carried both domesticated plants and animals in their canoes.

Q. *In what ways did a gathering and hunting economy shape other aspects of Paleolithic societies?*

• Because gathering and hunting did not allow for the accumulation of much surplus, Paleolithic societies were highly egalitarian, lacking the inequalities of wealth and power found in later agricultural and urban life.
• Paleolithic societies also lacked specialists, with most people possessing the same set of skills, although male and female tasks often differed sharply.
• Relationships between women and men were usually far more equal than in later societies. This was in part the result of gathering women bringing in more of the food consumed by the family than hunting men.

Q. *Why did some Paleolithic peoples abandon earlier, more nomadic ways and begin to live a more settled life?*

• Climatic warming allowed many plants and animals upon which humans relied to flourish. The increased food stocks allowed some groups of humans to settle down and live in more permanent settlements.

Q. *What are the most prominent features of San life?*

• They practice a gathering and hunting way of life.
• They use stone-age tools and technology.
• Their society is characterized by mobility, sharing, and equality.
• The basic unit of social organization is a band or camp of ten to thirty people who are connected by ties of exchange and kinship with similar camps across a wide area.
• Membership in a camp fluctuates over time, with many people claiming membership in more than one band.
• They are seminomadic, seldom staying in one place for more than a few months and living in quickly built grass huts.
• There are no formal leaders, chiefs, headmen, priests, or craft specialists. Decisions are made by individual families and camps after much discussion.
• However, there is a strong sense of relationships through biological kinship, marriage, and a naming system that creates a bond between otherwise unrelated individuals.
• They use exchange not to accumulate goods but to establish and reinforce social relationships. Wealth is calculated in terms of friends or people with obligations to oneself, rather than in possessing goods.
• Relations between men and women are more equal than in most societies.
• The San believe that both their ancestors and the gods visit misfortune on humankind but that humans can defend themselves through *n/um*, a sort of spiritual potency that lies in the stomach and becomes activated during "curing dances."

Q. *In what ways, and why, did Chumash culture differ from that of the San?*

• The San are representative of a seminomadic gathering and hunting society; the Chumash are more representative of the later, post–Ice Age Paleolithic peoples who settled in permanent villages and constructed more complex gathering and hunting societies.

- The Chumash experienced remarkable technological innovation that led to the creation of a planked oceangoing canoe some twenty to thirty feet long; the San maintained only stone-age technologies.
- Knowing how to construct or possessing an oceangoing canoe brought wealth and power into Chumash society and with it greater social inequality than found in San society.
- The canoes also stimulated trade on a scale unseen in San society.
- The material life of the Chumash was far more elaborate than that of the San. The Chumash lived in permanent, substantial houses and possessed soapstone bowls, wooden plates, and reed baskets, among other items. These items reflected a pattern of technological innovation far beyond that of the San.
- The Chumash developed a market economy and the private ownership of many goods, unlike the San system of exchange, which was more about the establishment of relationships than the accumulation of goods. As part of this evolution, the Chumash developed a bead-based currency without parallel in San society.
- The Chumash established permanent villages that ranged in size from several hundred to a thousand people, whereas the San set up mobile villages of twenty-five to fifty people.
- The Chumash established greater specialization of skills and more social differentiation, including the emergence of chiefs as rulers, than did their San counterparts.

ADDITIONAL RESOURCES FOR CHAPTER 1

Additional Bedford/St. Martin's Resources

FOR INSTRUCTORS

Computerized Test Bank

This test bank provides over thirty exercises per chapter, including multiple-choice, fill-in-the-blank, short-answer, and full-length essay questions. Instructors can customize quizzes, add or edit both questions and answers, and export questions and answers to a variety of formats, including WebCT and Blackboard. The disc includes correct answers and essay outlines.

Instructor's Resource CD-ROM

This disc provides instructors with ready-made and customizable PowerPoint multimedia presentations built around chapter outlines, maps, figures, and all images from the textbook, plus JPEG versions of all maps, figures, and images.

The following maps and images from Chapter 1 are available in both JPEG and PowerPoint format on the Instructor's Resource CD-ROM:

- Map 1.1: The Global Dispersion of Humankind (pp. 14–15)
- Map 1.2: Migration of Austronesian-Speaking People (p. 19)
- Paleolithic Art (p. 10)
- The Lascaux Caves (p. 16)
- Native Australians (p. 21)
- The Willendorf Venus (p. 22)
- Jomon Figurines (p. 24)
- A Chumash Tomol (p. 30)

FOR STUDENTS

Online Study Guide at bedfordstmartins.com/strayer

The Online Study Guide helps students synthesize the material from the text as well as practice the skills historians use to make sense of the past. Each chapter of the Online Study Guide contains specific testing exercises, including a multiple-choice self-test that focuses on important conceptual ideas; an identification quiz that helps students remember key people, places, and events; a flashcard activity that tests students on their knowledge of key terms; and two interactive map activities intended to strengthen students' geographic skills. Instructors can monitor students' progress through an online Quiz Gradebook or receive email updates.

Further Reading

Art History Resources on the Web: Prehistoric Art, http://witcombe.sbc.edu/ARTHprehistoric.html.

This page has links to a vast assortment of Paleolithic, Mesolithic, and Neolithic art.

The Cave of Chauvet-Pont-d'Arc, http://www.culture .gouv.fr/culture/arcnat/chauvet/en/index.html. This is a wonderful site about the Chauvet Cave, home to one of the finest collections of early cave art. It includes information about the cave's discovery and a complete virtual tour of the cave with high-quality images.

Guthrie, R. Dale. *The Nature of Paleolithic Art*. Chicago: University of Chicago Press, 2006. A large and detailed study of the subject.

Hovers, Erella, and Steven L. Kuhn, eds. *Transitions Before the Transition: Evolution and Stability in the Middle Paleolithic and Middle Stone Age*. New York: Springer, 2006. A collection of conference proceedings, with the latest scholarly understanding of important Paleolithic issues.

Rudgley, Richard. *The Lost Civilizations of the Stone Age*. New York: Free Press, 1999. Despite its provocative title, this highly readable book devotes considerable space to the Paleolithic era.

Schrenk, Friedemann, and Stephanie Müller. *The Neanderthals*. Trans. Phyllis G. Jestice. London: Routledge, 2008. A short handbook that lays out clearly the current scholarly understanding of Neanderthals, as well as the development of hominids more generally.

Smith, Andrew, et al. *The Bushmen of Southern Africa: A Foraging Society in Transition*. Athens: Ohio University Press, 2000. An interesting examination of the San culture.

Literature

Paleolithic cultures have left us no literary tradition, but modern fiction authors have attempted to fill in the gap, creating a whole genre of "paleofiction." Here are some popular modern novels about life in the Paleolithic era.

Auel, Jean M. *The Clan of the Cave Bear*. New York: Crown Publishers, 1980. The first and by far the best volume in a series that tells of a *Homo sapiens* girl taken in by a clan of Neanderthals.

Kurtén, Björn. *Dance of the Tiger: A Novel of the Ice Age*. 2nd ed. Berkeley: University of California Press, 1995. A very interesting and vivid story about western Europeans 35,000 years ago, written by a leading scholar of Ice Age animals.

Sarabande, William. *Beyond the Sea of Ice: The First Americans*. New York: Bantam Books, 1987. The first volume in an extended series.

Film

First Contact. Roadshow Home Entertainment, 1984. 52 minutes. Film footage and commentary on the first contact that Australian prospectors made with the Stone Age peoples of Papua New Guinea in 1930.

Homo Sapiens: A Look into a Distant Mirror. Films for the Humanities and Sciences, 1999. 53 minutes. A good overview of early *Homo sapiens* and their spread across the globe.

Nova. "In Search of Human Origins." Three-part series. PBS Home Videos, 1994. 60 minutes each. Part III deals with Neanderthals and early *Homo sapiens*.

Origins of Homo Sapiens: East African Roots. Films for the Humanities and Sciences, 1997. 47 minutes. A look at the emergence of the earliest *Homo sapiens* in Africa.

First Farmers

The Revolutions of Agriculture, 10,000 B.C.E.–3000 B.C.E.

CHAPTER OVERVIEW

Chapter Objectives

- To make students aware that agriculture evolved independently in several regions of the world
- To trace the development of agriculture and its local variations
- To consider the social implications of the Agricultural Revolution

Chapter Outline

I. **Opening Vignette**
  A. In the past two centuries, there has been a dramatic decline in the number of farmers worldwide.
    1. the United States is an extreme case: only around 5 percent of Americans, many of them over 65 years old, were still on farms in 2000
    2. great increase in the productivity of modern agriculture
  B. The modern retreat from the farm is a reversal of humanity's first turn to agriculture.

II. **The Agricultural Revolution in World History**
  A. Agriculture is the second great human process after settlement of the globe.
    1. started about 12,000 years ago
    2. often called the Neolithic or Agricultural Revolution
    3. deliberate cultivation of plants and domestication of animals
    4. transformed human life across the planet
  B. Agriculture is the basis for almost all human developments since.
  C. Agriculture brought about a new relationship between humans and other living things.
    1. actively changing what they found in nature rather than just using it
    2. shaping the landscape
    3. selective breeding of animals
  D. "Domestication" of nature created new mutual dependence. **[see Classroom Activity 1]**
    1. many domesticated plants and animals came to rely on humans
    2. humans lost gathering and hunting skills
      a. population increase: too many humans to live by gathering and hunting

E. "Intensification" of living: getting more food and resources from much less land.
  1. more food led to more people
  2. more people led to greater need for intensive exploitation

III. **Comparing Agricultural Beginnings**
  A. The Agricultural Revolution happened independently in several world regions.**[see Classroom Activity 2]**
   1. Fertile Crescent of Southwest Asia
   2. several areas in sub-Saharan Africa
   3. China
   4. New Guinea
   5. Mesoamerica
   6. the Andes
   7. eastern North America
   8. all happened at about the same time, 12,000–4000 years ago
   9. scholars have struggled with the question of why agriculture developed so late in human history
  B. Common Patterns
   1. Agricultural Revolution coincided with the end of the last Ice Age
    a. global warming cycle started around 16,000 years ago
    b. Ice Age was over by about 11,000 years ago
    c. end of Ice Age coincided with human migration across earth
    d. extinction of some large mammals: climate change and hunting
    e. warmer, wetter weather allowed more wild plants to flourish
   2. gathering and hunting peoples had already learned some ways to manage the natural world
    a. "broad spectrum diet"
    b. development of sickles, baskets, and other tools to make use of wild grain in the Middle East
    c. Amazon: peoples had learned to cut back some plants to encourage growth of the ones they wanted
    d. Australians had elaborate eel traps
   3. women were probably the agricultural innovators
    a. men perhaps led in domesticating animals

   4. gathering and hunting peoples started to establish more permanent villages
    a. especially in resource-rich areas
    b. population growth perhaps led to a "food crisis"
     i. motivation to increase the food supply
   5. agriculture developed in a number of regions, but with variation
    a. depended on the plants and animals that were available
    b. only a few hundred plant species have been domesticated
     i. five (wheat, corn, rice, barley, sorghum) supply over half the calories that sustain humans
    c. only 14 large mammal species were domesticated
  C. Variations
   1. the Fertile Crescent was the first to have a full Agricultural Revolution **[see Lecture Strategy 1]**
    a. presence of large variety of plants and animals to be domesticated
    b. transition to agriculture triggered by a cold and dry spell between 11,000 and 9500 B.C.E.
    c. transition apparently only took about 500 years
     i. much larger settlements
    d. much more societal sophistication (mud bricks, monuments and shrines, more elaborate burials, more sophisticated tools)
   2. at about the same time, domestication started in the eastern Sahara (present-day Sudan)
    a. the region was much more hospitable 10,000–5,000 years ago
    b. domestication of cattle there about 1,000 years before Middle East and India
     i. the donkey was domesticated nearer the Red Sea
    c. in Africa, animals were domesticated first; elsewhere, plants were domesticated first
    d. emergence of several widely scattered farming practices
     i. sorghum in eastern Sahara region
     ii. teff and enset in Ethiopian highlands
     iii. yams, oil palm trees, okra, and the kola nut in West Africa

e. African agriculture was less productive than agriculture in the Fertile Crescent

3. separate development of agriculture at several places in the Americas

   a. absence of animals available for domestication

      i. only one of the 14 domesticated large mammals existed in the Americas: the llama/alpaca

      ii. so Americans lacked protein, manure, and power of large animals

      iii. Americans continued to rely on hunting for meat

   b. only cereal grain available was maize or corn

      i. required thousands of years of selective adaptation to reach a size sufficient for productive agriculture

      ii. nutritionally poorer than cereals of the Fertile Crescent

   c. result: replacement of gathering and hunting with agriculture took 3,500 years in Mesoamerica

   d. Americas are oriented north/south, so agricultural practices had to adapt to distinct climate zones to spread

      i. east/west axis of Eurasia helped the spread of innovation

      ii. domesticated plants and animals took much longer to spread in the Americas

IV. **The Globalization of Agriculture**

   A. Agriculture spread in two ways:

      1. diffusion: gradual spread of techniques and perhaps plants and animals, but without much movement of human population

      2. colonization or migration of agricultural peoples

         a. conquest, absorption, or displacement of gatherers and hunters

      3. often both processes were involved

   B. Triumph and Resistance

      1. language and culture spread with agriculture

         a. Indo-European languages probably started in Turkey, are spoken today from Europe to India

         b. similar process with Chinese farming

   c. spread of Bantu language in southern Africa

      i. Bantu speakers originated in southern Nigeria or Cameroon ca. 3000 B.C.E.

      ii. moved south and east over several millennia, taking agriculture with them

   d. similar spread of Austronesian-speaking peoples to Philippines and Indonesian islands, then to Pacific islands

   2. the globalization of agriculture took about 10,000 years

      a. did not spread beyond its core region in New Guinea

      b. did not spread in a number of other regions

      c. was resisted where the land was unsuitable for farming or where there was great natural abundance

         i. some peoples apparently just didn't *want* agriculture

   3. by the beginning of the Common Era, gathering and hunting peoples were a small minority of humankind

      a. expansion of agriculture destroyed gathering and hunting societies

         i. process was sometimes peaceful, sometimes violent

   C. The Culture of Agriculture [see **Discussion Topic 1**]

      1. agriculture led to much greater populations

         a. e.g., early settlement near Jericho had about 2,000 people

      2. changes in world population

         a. 10,000 years ago: around 6 million people

         b. 5,000 years ago: around 50 million people

         c. beginning of Common Era: around 250 million people

      3. farming did not necessarily improve life for ordinary people

         a. meant much more hard work

         b. health deteriorated in early agricultural societies

         c. new diseases from interaction with animals [see **Discussion Topic 2**]

         d. the first epidemics, thanks to larger communities

         e. new vulnerability to famine, because of dependence on a small number of plants or animals

4. new constraints on human communities
   a. all agricultural people settled in permanent villages
   b. the case of BanPo in China (settled ca. 7,000 years ago)
5. explosion of technological innovation
   a. pots
   b. textiles
      i. textile work, like horticultural farming, was especially suitable for women with children
   c. metallurgy
6. "secondary products revolution" started ca. 4000 B.C.E.: a new set of technological changes
   a. new uses for domesticated animals, including milking, riding, hitching them to plows and carts
   b. only available in the Eastern Hemisphere
7. deliberate alteration of the natural ecosystem
   a. removal of ground cover, irrigation, grazing
   b. evidence of soil erosion and deforestation in the Middle East within 1,000 years after beginning of agriculture

V. Social Variation in the Age of Agriculture
A. Pastoral Societies **[see Lecture Strategy 2 and Discussion Topic 2]**
   1. some regions relied much more heavily on animals, because farming was difficult or impossible there
   2. pastoral nomads emerged in central Asia, the Arabian Peninsula, the Sahara desert, parts of eastern and southern Africa
   3. relied on different animals in different regions
      a. horses were domesticated by 4000 B.C.E.; encouraged the spread of pastoral peoples on Central Asian steppes
      b. domesticated camels allowed human life in the inner Asian, Arabian, and Saharan deserts
   4. no pastoral societies emerged in the Americas
B. Agricultural Village Societies **[see Lecture Strategy 3]**
   1. most characteristic form of early agricultural societies, like Banpo or Jericho
   2. maintenance of equality and freedom (no kings, chiefs, bureaucrats, aristocrats)
   3. the case of Çatalhüyük, in southern Turkey
      a. population: several thousand
      b. dead buried under their houses
      c. no streets; people moved around on rooftops
      d. many specialized crafts, but little sign of inherited social inequality
      e. no indication of male or female dominance
         i. men hunted; women were involved in agriculture
   4. village-based agricultural societies were usually organized by kinship, group, or lineage
      a. performed the functions of government
      b. the Tiv of central Nigeria organized nearly a million people this way in the late nineteenth century
   5. sometimes modest social/economic inequality developed
      a. elders could win privileges
      b. control of female reproductive powers
C. Chiefdoms
   1. chiefs, unlike kings, usually rely on generosity, ritual status, or charisma to govern, not force
   2. chiefdoms emerged in Mesopotamia sometime after 6000 B.C.E.
   3. anthropologists have studied recent chiefdoms in the Pacific islands
   4. chiefdoms such as Cahokia emerged in North America
   5. distinction between elite and commoner was first established
      a. based on birth, not age or achievement

VI. Reflections: The Legacies of Agriculture
[see Classroom Activity 3]
A. Agriculture is a recent development in world history.
   1. was an adaptation to the unique conditions of the latest interglacial period
   2. has radically transformed human life and life on the planet more generally
B. One species, *Homo sapiens*, was given growing power over other animals and plants.
C. Agriculture also gave some people the power to dominate others.

USING *WAYS OF THE WORLD* IN THE CLASSROOM

Lecture Strategies

Lecture Strategy 1

"The Fertile Crescent then and now."
Modern Americans are more familiar with the territory known as the Fertile Crescent than ever before, thanks to U.S. involvement in Iraq. This modern familiarity can cause students confusion: except for oil, present-day Iraq and surrounding countries are poor and appear to be anything but "fertile." So, why is the area called the "Fertile Crescent"? The objectives of this lecture strategy are:

- to explore the land and climate of the Fertile Crescent
- to investigate how conditions might have been different there at the time of the Neolithic Revolution
- to examine whether the conditions that are good for an agricultural revolution are the same as those that make modern states prosperous
- to discuss the deterioration of the land that has been caused by millennia of agriculture

A good place to start is to identify the Fertile Crescent clearly on a map and to go over what modern states are in the region. Then go over the following points:

- examine the weather and climate of the Fertile Crescent (access to water, lack of natural resources except soil, the need for irrigation in most areas)
- ask students to review the reasons given in the chapter for why conditions were good for an early agricultural revolution in the region (wild grains, large variety of animals to be domesticated, and a natural crisis to encourage innovation)
- consider what makes modern states prosperous: Can a state be prosperous without a strong underpinning of agriculture? Are economies that rely heavily on agriculture as their most significant element prosperous in modern terms?
- discuss what happened to lower the fertility of the Fertile Crescent over the centuries; some

points to consider are salinization caused by excessive irrigation, erosion, the problem of overgrazing, and the role of political systems in undermining the agricultural capabilities of the region (the Mongols usually get a lot of the blame for letting the ancient irrigation system of Iraq fall into ruin, with permanent consequences)

Lecture Strategy 2

"The great Neolithic monuments: where, why, and how."
The most mysterious thing about early Neolithic societies in Europe is that they sometimes liked to build *big*, despite the lack of many other features that historians regard as "civilization." The purpose of this lecture strategy is to explore some of the megaliths (big stone monuments) of Europe and what they can teach about Neolithic society. Its objectives are:

- to familiarize students with several of the major Neolithic sites of Europe
- to explore the level of organization and the amount of labor it would have taken to build them
- to discuss the possible purposes of these structures

The megaliths of the British Isles are the best-known. Unfortunately, many of these Neolithic monuments were broken up over the centuries, perhaps because they are in areas that have long had high population densities. A good place to begin is Stonehenge in England, since most of your students will have heard about it before. Discuss the scale of labor involved in creating Stonehenge: the weight of the stones, their source, and the skills needed to raise them. Then pick three or four other Neolithic monuments and do the same. Some possibilities are:

- Avesbury Stone Circles, England
- Knock, Ireland (Neolithic burial mound)
- Newgrange, Ireland (Neolithic burial mound)
- Megaliths of Carnac, France (long lines of hundreds of stones)
- Neolithic Temples of Malta

After dealing with the main features of the sites you have chosen, go on to consider the common ground between them, such as:

- the astonishing scale of the work considering the available labor force

- astronomical alignments
- how they later entered legend (e.g., Newgrange as the home of the gods in Celtic Irish myth)

Lecture Strategy 3

"Farmers and herders: the two models of Neolithic life."

In most accounts, the term "Agricultural Revolution" is used only in terms of farming, with a brief nod to the domesticated animals that pulled the plows. One of the most interesting points in this chapter is the presentation of both pastoralists and village settlers as products of the Agricultural Revolution. This lecture strategy is intended to explore the differences and common ground between the groups in more detail than the chapter could provide. Its objectives are:

- to dispel the notion that nomads are gatherers and hunters
- to explore how people who wander from place to place can be compared to village-dwellers
- to examine the common ground between Neolithic pastoralists and farmers

A good place to start is with a closer examination of Neolithic farming life. Choose one or two Neolithic village sites. Some particularly interesting sites can be found in the northern British Isles, such as Skara Brae in the Orkneys (an outstanding site because the houses were built of stone and several have been preserved) and the Céide Fields in Ireland (particularly interesting for the walls between the long strip fields). Links to quite a few Neolithic farming sites can be found at archaeology.about.com/od/neolithic/Neolithic_Revolution.htm. Be sure to discuss the issues of how people lived, such as the division of labor, means of protection from the elements, storage of food, etc. Encourage a student discussion of which of these elements were part of an essential definition of life in the wake of the Agricultural Revolution.

Next, consider the lifestyle of pastoralists. Clearly, some of the elements regarded as typical of the Neolithic Revolution do not apply to them, such as fixed settlements, food storage, and farming. This is a starting point to discuss how they *did* live, and how a lifestyle based on herding animals is every bit as artificial as one based on making particular kinds of plants grow in particular places. Nonetheless, pastoralists continued to rely more heavily on gathering and hunting for part of their food supply. It is more difficult to find materials on the early pastoralists, but nomadic life has changed little over the centuries, so it is possible to use material on the ancient peoples of the steppe as a starting place.

Things to Do in the Classroom

Discussion Topics

1. **Comparison, large or small group.** "Daily life in the Paleolithic and Neolithic eras."
Divide the students into four groups, and ask each group to make an outline of one of the following:

   the daily life of a Paleolithic woman
   the daily life of a Paleolithic man
   the daily life of a Neolithic (sedentary) woman
   the daily life of a Neolithic (sedentary) man

Then bring the groups together and ask the class to discuss essential similarities and differences.

2. **Historical Analysis, large or small group.**
"Disease, the domestication of animals, and the human connection"
The domestication of animals, particularly of large mammals that live in herds, was one of the driving forces of the Agricultural Revolution, but for the people who domesticated them, these animals were both great assets and the bringers of new and deadly diseases.

   Open the discussion by asking students to identify the advantages that the peoples of the Fertile Crescent received from their domestication of animals as compared to Mesoamerica, where no such large mammals were domesticated. Once students have laid out the advantages in terms of meat, milk, wool, fertilizer, and animal power, ask them if there were any drawbacks to the domestication of animals. Students might note the problems of animal-borne diseases that are mentioned at several points in the chapter. Take this opportunity to discuss the nature of human disease in order to emphasize that the Agricultural Revolution also brought a revolution in human disease. Both William McNeill, *Plagues and Peoples* (New York: Anchor, 1976), and Jared Diamond, *Guns, Germs, and Steel* (New York: Norton, 1997), provide useful overviews of human disease and its impact on human history.

Two key developments with important implications for disease occurred during the Agricultural Revolution. The first was true of all agricultural societies: living in higher concentrations of population facilitated the spread of some diseases. The second was true only of societies that domesticated animals, especially large herd mammals: humans first caught many of the most deadly and destructive diseases, including small pox, flu, measles, chicken pox, malaria, tuberculosis, and rabies, from their domesticated animals. While humans at the time were probably unaware of this linkage, the emergence of these diseases was a heavy price to pay for the domestication of animals. It is useful at the end of the discussion to point ahead by noting how Mesoamerica largely escaped the worst human diseases until first contact with Europeans, when smallpox in particular spread among the populations of the Americas with devastating effect.

3. Misconception/Difficult Topic, large or small group. "What, aren't nomads gatherers and hunters?"

Ask students to list the characteristics of gathering and hunting societies and then to consider the ways in which typical nomads fit or do not fit this list.

Classroom Activities

1. Role-playing exercise, small group. "How to domesticate a plant."

You are gatherers and hunters, thinking that there *has* to be an easier way of getting food than wandering around looking for plants. There's a great bulbous tuber that you like to eat; how would you go about making it grow where you want it, when you want it?

2. Map analysis, large or small group. "Environment and the first agriculturalists."

Using a physical map, identify the main regions that independently developed agriculture. Then encourage a discussion of the physical characteristics that made these regions likely candidates for an agricultural revolution. (Don't forget the fact that the Sahara was still green back when agriculture developed there.)

3. Clicker question. Taken as a whole, do you think the Agricultural Revolution was a good thing?

Key Terms

Agricultural Revolution: Also known as the Neolithic Revolution, this is the transformation of human (and world) existence caused by the deliberate cultivation of particular plants and the deliberate taming and breeding of particular animals.

Austronesian: An Asian-language family whose speakers gradually became the dominant culture of the Philippines, Indonesia, and the Pacific islands, thanks to their mastery of agriculture.

Banpo: A Chinese archeological site, where the remains of a significant Neolithic village have been found. (*pron.* bahn-poe)

Bantu: An African-language family whose speakers gradually became the dominant culture of eastern and southern Africa, thanks to their agricultural techniques and, later, their ironworking skills. (*pron.* BAHN-too)

Bantu migration: The spread of Bantu-speaking peoples from their homeland in what is now southern Nigeria or Cameroon to most of Africa, in a process that started ca. 3000 B.C.E. and continued for several millennia.

broad spectrum diet: Archeologists' term for the diet of gathering and hunting societies, which included a wide array of plants and animals.

Cahokia: An important agricultural chiefdom of North America that flourished around 1100 C.E.). (*pron.* cah-HOKE-ee-ah)

Çatalhüyük: An important Neolithic site in what is now Turkey. (*pron.* cha-TAHL-hoo-YOOK)

chiefdom: A societal grouping governed by a chief who typically relies on generosity, ritual status, or charisma rather than force to win obedience from the people.

diffusion: The gradual spread of agricultural techniques without extensive population movement.

domestication: The taming and changing of nature for the benefit of humankind.

end of the last Ice Age: A process of global warming that began around 16,000 years ago and ended about 5,000 years later, with the earth enjoying a climate similar to that of our own time; the end of the Ice Age changed conditions for human beings, leading to increased population and helping to pave the way for agriculture.

Fertile Crescent: Region sometimes known as Southwest Asia that includes the modern states of

Iraq, Syria, Israel/Palestine, and southern Turkey; the earliest home of agriculture.

horticulture: Hoe-based agriculture, typical of early agrarian societies.

intensification: The process of getting more in return for less; e.g., growing more food on a smaller plot of land.

Jericho: Site of an important early agricultural settlement of perhaps 2,000 people in present-day Israel.

Mesopotamia: The valley of the Tigris and Euphrates rivers in present-day Iraq.

native Australians: Often called "aboriginals" (from the Latin *ab origine*, the people who had been there "from the beginning"), the natives of Australia continued (and to some extent still continue) to live by gathering and hunting, despite the transition to agriculture in nearby lands.

pastoral society: A human society that relies on domesticated animals rather than plants as the main source of food; pastoral nomads lead their animals to seasonal grazing grounds rather than settling permanently in a single location.

"secondary products revolution": A term used to describe the series of technological changes that began ca. 4000 B.C.E., as people began to develop new uses for their domesticated animals, exploiting a revolutionary new source of power.

stateless societies: Village-based agricultural societies, usually organized by kinship groups, that functioned without a formal government apparatus.

teosinte: The wild ancestor of maize. (*pron.* tay-oh-SIN-tay)

ANSWER GUIDELINES FOR CHAPTER QUESTIONS

The two sets of questions that follow appear in the textbook at the end of the chapter and in the margins of the reading. They are also provided in the Computerized Test Bank with answer guidelines, for your convenience.

The Big Picture Questions

1. The Agricultural Revolution marked a decisive turning point in human history. What evidence might you offer to support this claim, and how might you argue against it?

• In support of the claim, one might note the ability of humankind after the Agricultural Revolution to support much larger populations;

• the beginning of the dominance of the human species over other forms of life on the planet;

• an explosion of technological innovation, including techniques for making pottery and weaving textiles and metallurgy;

• and the growing impact of humans on their environments.

• In opposition to the claim, one might argue that the Agricultural Revolution was a long-term process rather than a turning point and that even today it is not practiced universally by all humankind.

• One might also argue that the Agricultural Revolution was part of a longer process of more intense human exploitation of the earth that began long before the first permanent agricultural settlements took shape.

2. How did early agricultural societies differ from those of the Paleolithic era? How does the example of settled gathering and hunting peoples such as the Chumash complicate this comparison?

• Agricultural societies experienced greater social inequality than those of the Paleolithic era.

• Agricultural societies were larger and more densely settled than gathering and hunting societies.

• Agricultural societies, with the exception of pastoral societies, were less mobile than their Paleolithic counterparts.

• Agricultural societies developed more advanced technologies than did Paleolithic societies, including techniques for making pottery and weaving textiles and metallurgy.

• Everyday life and health was not necessarily better in agricultural societies than in Paleolithic societies. Farming involved more and harder work than gathering and hunting. Agricultural diets were often nutritionally poorer than those of Paleolithic societies, and agricultural societies were often more vulnerable to famine should their crops fail.

• The Chumash complicate the comparison, as their sedentary lifestyle allowed them to develop more advanced technologies.

• They are exceptional because they lived in a region in which fishing could support a large population.

• In Chumash society, acquisition of goods led to greater social inequality, so that, in terms of social structure, Chumash society with its chiefs resembled more closely an agricultural chiefdom than a typical gathering and hunting society.

3. Was the Agricultural Revolution inevitable? Why did it occur so late in the story of humankind?

• Only after more favorable climatic conditions emerged following the last Ice Age did the Agricultural Revolution begin. While it is impossible to discount the possibility that an agricultural revolution would have happened even without improved weather conditions, the revolution as it occurred required favorable climatic conditions and therefore cannot be seen as inevitable.

• Aside from climatic conditions, the Agricultural Revolution was part of a longer process of more intense human exploitation of the earth that began long before the first permanent agricultural settlements took shape. The development of techniques and technologies during this process proved important for the transition to settled agriculture, and the need to develop these new techniques and technologies also explains in part why the Agricultural Revolution occurred so late in human history.

4. "The Agricultural Revolution provides evidence for 'progress' in human affairs." Do you agree with this statement?

• One can point to a number of developments that could be considered "progress," including the growth of population;

• the beginning of the dominance of the human species over other forms of life on the planet;

• and an explosion of technological innovation, including techniques for making pottery and weaving textiles and metallurgy.

• However, one could also point to a number of developments associated with the Agricultural Revolution that less clearly were "progress," including growing social inequality;

• the emergence of the payment of tribute;

• a general decline in nutrition;

• and the emergence of new and deadly diseases.

Margin Review Questions

Q. *What accounts for the emergence of agriculture after countless millennia of human life without it?*

• The end of the last Ice Age brought a process of global warming around 16,000 years ago that by about 11,000 years ago made agriculture possible. The warmer, wetter, and more stable climatic conditions permitted the flourishing of more wild plants, especially cereal grasses, which humans would come to rely on.

• At the same time, this climate change, along with human hunting, pushed various species of large mammals, on which Paleolithic people relied, into extinction, adding to the need for new food sources.

• Humans were able to take advantage of favorable climatic changes because they had already developed a deep knowledge of the natural world and, in some cases, an ability to manage it actively. They had learned to make use of a large number of plants and animals. Moreover, they had developed techniques and technologies to encourage the growth of favored plants and to harvest wild plants and animals more easily.

• The need to increase food supplies to feed growing populations of humans also contributed to the emergence of agriculture.

Q. *In what different ways did the Agricultural Revolution take shape in various parts of the world?*

• In the Fertile Crescent of Southwest Asia, an extraordinary variety of wild plants and animals capable of domestication provided a rich array of species on which the now largely settled gathering and hunting people could draw. A cold and dry spell between 11,000 and 9500 B.C.E. seems to have forced the population toward agriculture. During the period, people domesticated figs, wheat, barley, rye, peas, lentils, sheep, goats, pigs, and cattle. Archeological evidence indicates that the transition in this region from gathering and hunting to a fully agricultural way of life occurred quickly, within as little as 500 years.

• At roughly the same time in Africa, domestication unfolded in the eastern part of what is now the Sahara Desert in present-day Sudan. During this period, rainfall was much higher. In this region, animal domestication preceded plant domestication, with cattle and donkeys being the first animals brought under human control. In Africa, different plants were domesticated in several different regions, including sorghum (eastern Sahara), teff and enset (Ethiopia), and yams, oil palm trees, okra, and kola nuts (West Africa). The more scattered nature of domestication in sub-Saharan Africa led to a less productive agriculture than in the more favored and compact Fertile Crescent.

• By 4000 to 3000 B.C.E., another pattern of domestication took shape in the Americas. As in Africa, domestication of plants in the Americas occurred separately in a number of locations. But what makes domestication most distinctive in the Americas was the absence of animals: the llama/alpaca was the only large mammal to be domesticated. This shaped how farming was conducted in the Americas, as farmers lacked animal power for plows or their manure for fertilizer. It also meant that hunting and fishing remained more important to agricultural people of the Americas. Moreover, the Americas lacked the rich cereal grains available elsewhere. Instead, maize was the key crop. But it required thousands of years of selective adaptation to become a productive crop in terms of calories and even then was nutritionally poorer than the protein-rich cereals of the Fertile Crescent. Because of the north-south orientation of the Americas and the relative isolation of agricultural regions, crops spread less successfully. The result was that full dependence on agriculture came more slowly in Mesoamerica, taking some 3,500 years.

• In China between 6500 and 5000 B.C.E. several key breakthroughs took place, with rice, millet, and soybeans being grown and pigs, chickens, and water buffalo being domesticated.

• In highland New Guinea between 7000 and 4000 B.C.E., taro, bananas, and yams were domesticated.

Q. *In what ways did agriculture spread? Where and why was it sometimes resisted?*

• Agriculture spread in two ways: through diffusion and through colonization. Diffusion refers to the gradual spread of the techniques of agriculture, and perhaps of the plants and animals themselves, but without the extensive movement of agricultural peoples. Colonization refers to the migration of agricultural peoples as growing populations and pressures to expand pushed them outward. Often this meant the conquest, absorption, or displacement of earlier gatherers and hunters.

• Successful resistance to the encroachment of agriculture occurred in areas that were unsuitable to farming or in regions of particular natural abundance where the population did not need to farm intensively.

It also helped to not be in the direct line of advance of a more powerful agricultural people. Many gathering and hunting peoples knew of the farming practices of their nearby neighbors but chose to resist them, preferring the freer life of their Paleolithic ancestors.

Q. *What was revolutionary about the Agricultural Revolution?*

• the ability to support much larger populations
• the beginning of the dominance of the human species over other forms of life on the planet
• an explosion of technological innovation, including techniques for making pottery and weaving textiles and metallurgy
• the growing impact of humans on their environments

Q. *What different kinds of societies emerged out of the Agricultural Revolution?*

• Pastoral societies were societies that relied far more extensively on domesticated animals than on crops. Pastoral societies were common in regions where farming was difficult or impossible—arctic tundra, some grasslands, and deserts. Wherever pastoral societies arose, they were mobile, as they relied on moving seasonally, following the changing patterns of vegetation, in order to feed their animals.

• Village-based agricultural societies consisted of settled farmers. Such societies retained much of the equality and freedom of gathering and hunting communities, as they continued to do without kings, chiefs, bureaucrats, or aristocracies. Instead they were usually organized in terms of kinship groups or lineages, within which large numbers of people could make and enforce rules, maintain order, and settle disputes. These societies sometimes developed modest social and economic inequalities.

• Chiefdoms were those societies in which agricultural communities were ruled by figures who inherited positions of power and privilege. These chiefs ruled through their generosity or gift giving, their ritual status, or their personal charisma. Only rarely could they use force to compel obedience. Chiefs typically led important rituals and ceremonies, organized the community for warfare, directed its economic life, and sought to resolve internal conflicts. They collected tribute from commoners in the form of food, manufactured goods, and raw material, which they redistributed to subordinates after keeping enough to maintain their prestige.

Q. *How did chiefdoms differ from stateless agricultural village societies?*

• Chiefdoms were ruled by figures who inherited positions of power and privilege. Chiefs ruled through their generosity or gift giving, their ritual status, or their personal charisma. Only rarely did they rule through force. Chiefs led important rituals and ceremonies, organized the community for warfare, directed its economic life, and sought to resolve internal conflicts.

• Agricultural village societies possessed no such figure conducting their affairs as a full-time ruler. They often organized themselves in terms of kinship groups or lineages. The lineage system provided the framework within which large numbers of people could make and enforce rules, maintain order, and settle disputes.

• Chiefdoms possessed more well-defined and pronounced social inequalities, some of which were inherited. Agricultural villages developed modest social and economic inequalities, but they were not as well defined as those of chiefdoms and were not hereditary.

• Unlike members of agricultural village societies, commoners in chiefdoms provided tribute to their chief in the form of food, manufactured goods, and raw materials.

ADDITIONAL RESOURCES FOR CHAPTER 2

Additional Bedford/St. Martin's Resources

FOR INSTRUCTORS

Computerized Test Bank

This test bank provides over thirty exercises per chapter, including multiple-choice, fill-in-the-blank, short-answer, and full-length essay questions. Instructors can customize quizzes, add or edit both questions and answers, and export questions and answers to a variety of formats, including WebCT and Blackboard. The disc includes correct answers and essay outlines.

Instructor's Resource CD-ROM

This disc provides instructors with ready-made and customizable PowerPoint multimedia presentations built around chapter outlines, maps, figures, and all images from the textbook, plus JPEG versions of all maps, figures, and images.

The following maps and images from Chapter 2 are available in both JPEG and PowerPoint format on the Instructor's Resource CD-ROM:

• Map 2.1: The Fertile Crescent (p. 40)
• Map 2.2: The Global Spread of Agriculture (pp. 44–45)
• Chinese Neolithic Pottery (p. 34)
• Teosinte and Maize/Corn (p. 42)
• Women and Weaving (p. 48)
• The Domestication of Animals (p. 49)
• Çatalhüyük (p. 50)
• Cahokia (p. 52)

FOR STUDENTS

Documents and Essays from *Worlds of History: A Comparative Reader,* Third Edition

The following documents, essays, and illustrations to accompany Chapter 2 are available in Chapter 1 of this reader by Kevin Reilly:

• Natalie Angier, "Furs for Evening, but Cloth Was the Stone Age Standby"
• Marjorie Shostak, From *Nisa: The Life and Words of a !Kung Woman*
• Elise Boulding, "Women and the Agricultural Revolution"
• Gerda Lerner, "The Urban Revolution: Origins of Patriarchy"

Online Study Guide at bedfordstmartins.com/strayer

The Online Study Guide helps students synthesize the material from the text as well as practice the skills historians use to make sense of the past. Each chapter of the Online Study Guide contains specific testing exercises, including a multiple-choice self-test that focuses on important conceptual ideas; an identification quiz that helps students remember key people, places, and events; a flashcard activity that tests students on their knowledge of key terms; and two interactive map activities intended to strengthen students' geographic skills. Instructors can monitor students' progress through an online Quiz Gradebook or receive email updates.

Further Reading

Edmonds, Mark. *Ancestral Geographies of the Neolithic: Landscapes, Monuments and Memory.* London: Routledge, 1999. A vivid portrait of life in Neolithic Britain in the fourth millennium B.C.E.

Keeley, Lawrence H. *War Before Civilization: The Myth of the Peaceful Savage.* New York: Oxford University Press, 1996. A very interesting study of warfare in the Neolithic era.

Neolithic Revolution, http://archaeology.about.com/od/neolithic/Neolithic_Revolution.htm. A useful Web page with links to many Neolithic sites.

Orkneyjar: The Heritage of the Orkney Islands— Skara Brae, http://www.orkneyjar.com/history/skarabrae/. An excellent Web site about the best-preserved Neolithic settlement in the world.

Scarre, Chris. *Exploring Prehistoric Europe.* New York: Oxford University Press, 1999. An interesting and highly readable book that covers both Paleolithic and Neolithic Europe. It has especially good coverage of the monumental structures of Neolithic Europe.

Scarre, Chris, ed. *The Seventy Wonders of the Ancient World.* London: Thames and Hudson, 1999. Good discussion of how the great Neolithic monuments were built, along with much more.

Simmons, Alan H. *The Neolithic Revolution in the Near East: Transforming the Human Landscape.* University of Arizona Press, 2007. A very clear and interesting study of the phenomenon.

Stonehenge, http://www.english-heritage.org.uk/server/show/nav.876. A detailed site on Stonehenge, with reconstruction drawings, good photos, and details about how the monument was constructed, provided by English Heritage.

Film

Agricultural and Urban Revolutions. Insight Media, 2004. 30 minutes. Examines the social, technological, and cultural developments associated with the establishment of permanent human settlements.

The Agricultural Revolution, 8000 B.C.–5000 B.C. Insight Media, 1985. 26 minutes. Examines how the domestication of plants and animals across the world led to unprecedented population growth.

Ancient Britons. Films for the Humanities and Sciences, 1996. 48 minutes. Includes a useful segment about the Neolithic "Dawn People" from the Orkneys to Wessex.

Guns, Germs, and Steel. Three-part series. National Geographic Video, 2005. 60 minutes each. A provocative explanation of regional economic differences based on variations among early agricultural revolutions.

First Civilizations

Cities, States, and Unequal Societies, 3500 B.C.E.–500 B.C.E.

CHAPTER OVERVIEW

Chapter Objectives

- To establish the relationship between the First Civilizations and the Agricultural Revolution
- To contrast civilizations with other forms of human communities
- To explore when, where, and how the First Civilizations arose in human history
- To explore how the emergence of civilizations transformed how humans lived and how human societies were structured
- To show the various ways in which civilizations differed from one another
- To explore the outcomes of the emergence of civilizations, both positive and negative, for humankind

Chapter Outline

I. **Opening Vignette**
    A. The contrast between "artificial" life as a "civilized" city dweller and the spacious freedom and imagined simplicity of earlier times still resonates today.
    B. "Civilizations" are a relatively recent phenomenon in human history made possible by the surpluses produced by the Agricultural Revolution.
    C. The distinctive features of civilizations are:
       1. cities with monumental architecture and populations in the tens of thousands
       2. powerful states that could compel obedience and wage large-scale warfare
       3. much greater inequality in economic function, wealth, and social status

II. **Something New: The Emergence of Civilizations** [see Classroom Activity 1]
    A. Civilization was a global phenomenon
       1. six major civilizations and some smaller manifestations
       2. scattered around world
       3. developed after 3500 B.C.E.
    B. Introducing the First Civilizations
       1. one of the earliest civilizations emerged in Sumer (in southern Mesopotamia) between 3500 and 3000 B.C.E.
          a. first written language
          b. appearance of Egyptian civilization in Nile River Valley (northeast Africa) and smaller Nubian civilization to its south at about the same time
       2. Norte Chico (central coastal Peru), emerged between 3000 and 1800 B.C.E.
          a. twenty-five urban centers

b. Norte Chico differed in several ways from Mesopotamia and Egypt:
   i. smaller cities without walls or signs of pervasive warfare
   ii. less evidence of economic specialization
   iii. no grain-based agriculture
   iv. did not develop certain technologies like pottery
   v. developed an accounting system based on the *quipu* (a series of knotted cords) but no writing system
c. unusually self-contained; only import was maize, derived from Mesoamerica

3. Indus Valley civilization in Indus and Saraswati river valleys of present-day Pakistan arose between 3000 and 2000 B.C.E.
   a. elaborately planned cities and standardized weights, measures, architectural styles, and brick sizes
   b. written script that remains thus far undeciphered
   c. unlike other civilizations, it generated no palaces, temples, elaborate graves, kings, or warrior classes
   d. scholars remain uncertain as to how society was organized; theories include a series of small republics, rule by priests, or an early form of the caste system
   e. environmental degradation led to the collapse of this civilization by about 1700 B.C.E., but several aspects of its culture shaped later Indian societies

4. around 2200 B.C.E., a First Civilization took shape in China
   a. from the start, China was defined by the ideal of a centralized state
   b. the Xia, Shang, and Zhou dynasties enlarged the Chinese state
   c. ruler was the "Son of Heaven," an intermediary between heaven and earth
   d. early written language with oracle bones as early documents
   e. China has maintained impressive cultural continuity into modern times

5. the Olmec produced a First Civilization much later (around 1200 B.C.E.) on coast of Gulf of Mexico, near present-day Veracruz

a. cities arose from competing chiefdoms and produced elaborate ceremonial centers
b. created the first written language in the Americas by about 900 B.C.E.
c. culture influenced later civilizations in Mesoamerica, including the Maya and Teotihuacán

6. other smaller civilizations also flourished
   a. Nubian civilization south of Egypt was distinctive and independent
   b. city of Sanxingdui in China arose separately from the more well-known Shang Dynasty

C. The Question of Origins
   1. First Civilizations had their roots in Agricultural Revolution
   2. First Civilizations tended to develop from earlier, competing chiefdoms that already had some social rank and economic specialization
   3. process was gradual and evolutionary
   4. why did some chiefdoms develop into civilizations and others did not?
      a. one argument: the need to organize large-scale irrigation projects (archeologists have found that these projects appeared long after civilizations began)
      b. another argument: the needs of elite groups, warfare, and trade all played roles as well
      c. Robert Carneiro's argument: population density created competition, especially when agricultural land was limited
         i. tensions sparked innovations such as irrigation and plows and also intense competition that led to repeated warfare
         ii. winners absorbed losing populations into their societies as subordinated workers
   5. the creation of the first civilizations was quick by world history standards but was an unconscious undertaking for those involved
   6. all First Civilizations relied on highly productive agriculture

D. An Urban Revolution [see Lecture Strategy 1]
   1. cities were one of the most distinctive features of First Civilizations

2. the scale, layout, and specialized industries of cities would have impressed visitors from villages
3. cities lay at the heart of all First Civilizations because they were:
   a. political/administrative capitals
   b. centers of cultural production—art, architecture, literature, ritual, and ceremony
   c. places of local and long-distance exchange
   d. centers of manufacturing activity
4. cities produced new societies with greater specialization and inequality

III. **The Erosion of Equality** [see Classroom Activity 2]
  A. Professional and craft specialization marked early urban life.
  B. Hierarchies of Class
     1. First Civilizations had vast inequalities in wealth, status, and power
     2. civilizations multiplied and magnified inequalities that already existed in complex gathering and hunting societies and agricultural chiefdoms
     3. these new levels of inequality represent one of the major turning points in the social history of humankind
     4. upper classes:
        a. enjoyed great wealth
        b. avoided physical labor
        c. had the finest in everything
        d. occupied the top positions in political, military, and religious life
        e. and were frequently distinguished by their
           i. clothing
           ii. houses
           iii. manner of burial
           iv. treatment under the law
     5. free commoners formed the vast majority of the population and included artisans of all kinds, lower-level officials, soldiers and police, servants, and farmers
        a. their surplus production was appropriated to support the upper classes
        b. some members of these classes recognized and resented their situation

6. slaves were at the bottom of social hierarchies everywhere **[see Discussion Topic 1]**
   a. slavery and civilization seem to have emerged together
   b. first-generation slaves were prisoners of war, criminals, and debtors
   c. worked in fields, mines, homes, and shops
   d. more rarely, they were sacrificed
   e. slavery varied from place to place
      i. Egypt and the Indus Valley civilizations initially had fewer slaves than the more militarized Mesopotamia
      ii. later, the Greeks and Romans employed slaves far more extensively than did the Chinese or Indians
   f. most ancient slavery differed from the recent American variety
      i. slaves were not a primary agricultural labor force
      ii. many children of slaves were freed
      iii. slavery was not defined by race or skin color
C. Hierarchies of Gender
   1. civilizations everywhere undermined the earlier and more equal relationships between men and women
   2. women in horticultural societies remained relatively equal to men
   3. but patriarchy gradually emerged in First Civilizations
      a. more intensive agriculture with animal-drawn plows and large dairy herds favored male labor over female
      b. patriarchy also developed in civilizations without plow agriculture, such as Mesoamerica and the Andes
      c. David Christian: the declining position of women was a product of growing social complexity
         i. men were less important in the household, so may have been more available to assume powerful and prestigious specialist roles
         ii. men used this authority to shape the values and practices of their societies in ways that benefited them at the expense of women

d. the association of women with nature because of their role in reproduction may also have played a role
   i. civilizations highlight human mastery over nature
   ii. women may have become associated with an inferior dimension of human life (nature)
e. warfare may also have contributed to patriarchy
   i. large-scale military conflict was a feature of most First Civilizations
   ii. military service was largely restricted to men
f. private property and commerce also may have played a role
   i. need to restrict female sexual activities to assure inheritance by *father's* offspring
   ii. exchange of female slaves, concubines, and wives became part of male commerce

D. Patriarchy in Practice
   1. Gerda Lerner: emergence of patriarchy in Mesopotamia
      a. written law codes codified patriarchal family life
      b. regulation of female sexuality was central
      c. women in Mesopotamia were sometimes divided into two sharply distinguished categories, depending on protection of one man
      d. powerful goddesses of Mesopotamia were gradually replaced by male deities
   2. Egyptian patriarchy gave women greater opportunities than in most First Civilizations, including ability to:
      a. own property and slaves
      b. administer and sell land
      c. make their own wills
      d. sign their own marriage contracts
      e. initiate divorce
   3. royal women occasionally wielded political power as regents for their sons or, more rarely, as queens in their own right
   4. Egyptian statues and love poetry suggest affection between sexes

IV. **The Rise of the State**
   A. States were central to the organization and stability of First Civilizations.
   B. Coercion and Consent
      1. the state fulfilled a variety of roles in coordinating and regulating the first civilizations, including:
         a. organizing irrigation systems
         b. adjudicating conflicts
         c. defense
      2. the state served the needs of the upper classes by:
         a. protecting the privileges of the elites
         b. requiring farmers to give up a portion of their product to support city people
         c. demanding labor on large public projects
      3. the state frequently used force to secure its will
      4. force was not always necessary because the state often claimed that its authority was normal, natural, and ordained by the gods
         a. rule by divine right
         b. deference to religion restrained or even undermined the right to rule as in the rule of Chinese emperors by the Mandate of Heaven
   C. Writing and Accounting **[see Discussion Topic 2]**
      1. writing provided support for the state and emerged in all of the First Civilizations except the Andes (though some scholars now regard their knotted strings, or quipus, as a kind of writing)
      2. writing sustained the First Civilizations by:
         a. defining elite status and conveying prestige on those who wrote
         b. allowing some commoners to join the elite through literacy
         c. providing a means for propaganda
         d. providing a means to keep accurate accounts and complex calendars
         e. giving weight to regulations and laws
      3. writing also served functions beyond the state
         a. fostered literature, philosophy, astronomy, mathematics, and history
         b. sometimes threatened rulers
   D. The Grandeur of Kings
      1. source of state authority

2. monumental residences and temples
3. luxurious dress
4. elaborate burials
V. **Comparing Mesopotamia and Egypt**
   A. Environment and Culture
      1. both depended on rivers, but were very different
         a. erratic and destructive flooding in Mesopotamia
         b. Nile flooded more predictably and less destructively
      2. Mesopotamia was less geographically isolated than Egypt
         a. Mesopotamia was vulnerable to external attack
         b. Egypt was usually protected from external attack
      3. many scholars see a relationship between physical setting and culture
         a. more negative Mesopotamian worldview seems to reflect its precarious and violent environment
         b. Egyptian worldview reflected the more stable, predictable, and beneficent environment in which it took shape
      4. Environmental impact of rising population
         a. in southern Mesopotamia, deforestation, soil erosion, and salinization of the soil weakened Sumerian city-states, leading to foreign conquest and the northward shift of Mesopotamia's cultural centers
         b. Egypt built a more sustainable agricultural system that contributed to the remarkable continuity of its civilization
   B. Cities and States **[see Lecture Strategy 2]**
      1. the political systems of Mesopotamia and Egypt differed sharply
      2. Mesopotamia for its first thousand years was organized into a dozen or more separate city-states
         a. each city-state was ruled by a king
         b. 80 percent of the population lived in city-states for protection
         c. environmental devastation and endemic warfare ultimately led to conquest by outside forces after about 2350 B.C.E.
         d. these outside powers built large territorial states or bureaucratic empires

encompassing all or most of Mesopotamia
      3. Egypt
         a. around 3100 B.C.E., several earlier states or chiefdoms merged into a unified territory that stretched some 1,000 miles along the Nile
         b. for 3,000 years, Egypt maintained its unity and independence with few interruptions
            i. unity was reinforced by ease of travel along Nile
         c. most Egyptians lived in agricultural villages, perhaps because of greater security
         d. the pharaoh, a god in human form, was the focus of the Egyptian state
            i. the pharaoh ensured the annual flooding of the Nile
            ii. the pharaoh defined the law of the land
            iii. access to the afterlife was linked to proximity to the pharaoh
            iv. pharaohs were most powerful before 2400 B.C.E.
            v. local officials gained in power over time
            vi. pharaohs were discredited by Nile's failure to flood around 2200 B.C.E.
         e. from 2200 to 2000 B.C.E., anarchy; when state was restored, pharaohs never regained their old power
   C. Interaction and Exchange
      1. Egypt and Mesopotamia frequently interacted
      2. Egypt's agriculture benefited from interaction
      3. Mesopotamian models may have influenced Egypt's step pyramids and system of writing
      4. Egypt's "divine kingship" seems to have been derived from central or eastern Sudan
      5. both Mesopotamia and Egypt carried on extensive long-distance trade
         a. Mesopotamian sea trade with the Indus Valley civilization as early as 2300 B.C.E.
         b. Mesopotamian trade with Anatolia, Egypt, Iran, and Afghanistan
         c. Egyptian trade in the Mediterranean and Middle East

d. Egyptian trade in Nubia and along the East African coast

6. Mesopotamian and Egyptian cultural influences moved along trade routes

   a. Hebrews migrated from Mesopotamia to Palestine and Egypt early in their history

      i. Mesopotamian influence on Hebrew laws and flood story

      ii. emerging conception of a merciful and single deity, Yahweh, who demanded an ethical life from his people, was unique

   b. Phoenicians (in present-day Lebanon) were commercially active in the Mediterranean basin

      i. adopted the Mesopotamian fertility goddess

      ii. adapted Mesopotamian writing into simpler alphabetic system

   c. some Indo-European peoples settled in north-central Anatolia

      i. adopted deities, bronze metallurgy, and the wheel from Mesopotamia

      ii. spread them with further migrations

   d. sustained contact between Nubia and Egypt

      i. Nubians built Egyptian-style pyramids

      ii. Nubians worshipped Egyptian gods and goddesses

      iii. Nubians used Egyptian hieroglyphic writing

      iv. but Nubia maintained its distinctiveness

         a) developed an alphabetic script

         b) retained many of its own gods

         c) developed a major ironworking industry by 500 B.C.E.

         d) asserted political independence whenever possible

   e. in the Mediterranean basin:

      i. Egyptian influence can be seen in Minoan art (emerged in Crete around 2500 B.C.E.)

      ii. Martin Bernal: the Greeks drew heavily upon both Egyptian and Mesopotamian precedents in art, religion, philosophy, and language

7. Mesopotamia and Egypt were also influenced by their neighbors

   a. Indo-Europeans brought horse-and-chariot-based armies to Mesopotamia; Indo-European Hittites conquered the Babylonian empire in 1595 B.C.E.

   b. the Hyksos invaded using chariot-based armies and ruled Egypt between 1650 and 1535 B.C.E.

   c. Mesopotamians and Egyptians adopted chariot technology

   d. arrival of the Hyksos spurred further innovations in Egypt:

      i. new armor and weaponry

      ii. new methods of spinning and weaving

      iii. new musical instruments

      iv. olive and pomegranate trees

8. by 1500 B.C.E., Egypt had become an imperial state

   a. rule over non-Egyptian peoples in both Africa and Asia

   b. regular diplomatic correspondence with Middle Eastern empires

VI. **Reflections: "Civilization": What's in a Word?** [see Lecture Strategy 3 and Discussion Topic 3]

A. Some scholars have reservations about the use of the word "civilizations" to describe the cultures studied in this chapter.

   1. implication of superiority: "civilization" in popular usage suggests refined behavior, a "higher" form of society, something unreservedly positive; using this word implies that other ways of living are "uncivilized," which normally implies inferiority

B. Modern assessments of the First Civilizations reveal a profound ambiguity.

   1. They gave us inspiring art, profound reflections on life, more productive technologies, increased control over nature, and writing

   2. but they also produced massive inequalities, state oppression, slavery, large-scale warfare, the subordination of women, and epidemic disease

   3. Some scholars prefer more neutral terms, such as complex societies, urban-based societies, or state-organized societies.

C. Scholars object to the term "civilization," as it implies more clear-cut boundaries from other societies than was actually the case.
1. aside from elites, most of the people living in the First Civilizations probably defined themselves more by occupation, clan, village, city, or region than as a member of some larger "civilization"
2. First Civilizations lacked clear borders
3. unclear line between civilizations and other kinds of societies
D. This book continues to use the term because:
1. it is so deeply embedded in our way of thinking about the world
2. no alternative concept has achieved widespread usage
3. we need to make distinctions among different kinds of human communities
E. But in using this term, we must remember:
1. historians use "civilization" as a purely descriptive term designating a particular type of human society—one with cities and states—without implying any judgment or assessment, any sense of superiority or inferiority
2. it is used to define broad cultural patterns in particular geographic regions while recognizing that many people living in those regions may have been more aware of differences and conflicts than of those commonalities

USING *WAYS OF THE WORLD* IN THE CLASSROOM

Lecture Strategies

Lecture Strategy 1

"The monumental nature of First Civilizations."
The objectives of this lecture strategy are to:

- help students visualize the physical culture of First Civilizations in a comparative way
- aid comprehension of societal organization

This lecture strategy requires access to PowerPoint or to an overhead projector.

Start with images of one or two major Neolithic building projects, such as Newgrange, Stonehenge, or one of the Neolithic Temples of Malta. Discuss the amount of organized, skilled labor involved in such projects—the amount of earth moved at Newgrange, the difficulties in lifting the lintel stones at Stonehenge, etc. As much as possible, call on students for information covered in earlier reading assignments or lectures.

Continue with monumental images from at least four of the First Civilizations covered in Chapter 3. The textbook has several interesting images; you might also consider:

- Egypt: the Great Pyramid is the most obvious, but you might also consider the temple of Hatshepsut at Luxor, the Ramesseum, the Colossi of Memnon, or Abu Simbel
- Mesopotamia: the ziggurat of Ur
- Teotihuicán: the pyramid to the sun and the pyramid to the moon
- Olmec: the monumental heads (an image search for the site La Venta will come up with interesting images)
- Norte Chico: pyramid at Caral
- Indus Valley: citadel at Harappa, Lothal Harbor, Great Bath at Mohenjo Daro

Ask students questions that will encourage a discussion of physical remains that might not have survived (e.g., Was wood for building available in the region? What is the likelihood of water or wind damage over the centuries? Might there have been reuse of building materials by later civilizations?). In this context, contrasting images of the current remains of these sites with artist reconstructions of their original form can be very useful.

Help the students make a list entitled "To produce works like these, a civilization needed . . . ," encouraging discussion of kings strong enough to force their people to do unpaid labor for the state, specialized sculptors, ability to move building materials long distances, and so on.

Lecture Strategy 2

"Unification in the First Civilizations."
The objectives of this lecture strategy are to:

- review material covered in the chapter
- fill in some of the history of Mesopotamia

- develop material about the Indus Valley
- aid students in directed examination of what archeological material *means*

Start with the issue of how Egypt became a single political entity. Key issues are the political division between Upper and Lower Egypt (don't forget to remind students that "lower" means "downstream"—thus, Lower Egypt is *north* of Upper Egypt) and the unification under Menes (Narmer). A good visual resource is the "Narmer Palette" commemorating the unification. Include the point that early pharaohs had two tombs—one in Upper Egypt and one in Lower Egypt—and that the royal crown incorporates the symbols of both north and south.

Move from Egypt to the more drawn-out process of unification in Mesopotamia, paying special attention to the role of city-states with strong self-identities in *hindering* the process of unification. Students respond well to a narrative history of ancient Mesopotamia organized around the question, "What got in the way of unification?" Start with Sumer and its city-states, then explore what made it possible for Sargon of Agade to establish the Akkadian Empire (military, administration, use of religious institutions—such as making his daughter Enheduanna, the world's first named author, priestess of the moon god at Ur). Discuss internal and external factors that made the Akkadian Empire dissolve after only two generations, comparing the Akkadian experience to the relative stability of Egypt (use, for instance, the Gutian invasion to examine the resentment of "foreign" rule). Then explore the rise of the more stable Old Babylonian Empire, best represented by the rule of Hammurabi, again discussing why it enjoyed greater longevity.

Finally, lead the students in speculating about the much more mysterious Indus Valley civilization. Review the basic facts about this civilization (Web searches for "Harappa" or "Harappan India" will yield better material on the whole than searches for "Indus Valley"). Ask the students whether, based on the archeological evidence, they think this civilization consisted of a unified territorial state (like Egypt) or independent city-states (like Sumer).

Lecture Strategy 3

"How 'now' affects 'then'—modern prejudice and understanding the past."

The objectives of this lecture strategy are to:

- build from the discussion of the term "civilization" at the end of the chapter
- help students understand how crucial *interpretation* is in understanding the past
- encourage students to think objectively about the past
- encourage students to recognize their own prejudices about other cultures

This strategy provides an opportunity to talk about archeology—who conducts it, methodology, and the prejudices that affect the interpretation of archeological evidence. It can be approached in a variety of ways. Some basic points to consider are:

- the development of archeology as a branch of science in the nineteenth century
- the role of the Bible and romantic views of ancient Greece in the development of the discipline
- nineteenth-century attitudes about the "colored peoples" of the world

Discuss some notorious cases of bias by archeologists, such as Heinrich Schliemann and the destruction of the level of Troy he was looking for. You might also consider feminist interpretations of Çatalhüyük, or even "proofs" that Europeans (or even the Chinese!) created the early civilizations of the Americas.

Three other central issues are:

1. civilizations that have still not been systematically excavated (such as Norte Chico and Nubia) because of political climate, lack of funding, or lack of interest
2. odd interpretations based on assumptions about a culture's potential (a good example is the fact that scholars of ancient Egypt have translated a word as "king" while scholars of ancient Nubia have interpreted the same word as "chief")
3. evidence for diffusion versus independent invention

Conclude by showing some archeological finds from the First Civilizations for which we do not have deciphered written records, and encourage the class to discuss what their significance *might* be, especially encouraging comparison to materials from the cultures we understand more deeply thanks to writing. For example, is the statuette of a dancing girl from Mohenjo Daro erotic, religious, or decorative?

Things to Do in the Classroom

Discussion Topics

1. Comparison, large or small group. "Slavery in human societies."

The passage on pages 65–66 offers an ideal opportunity to engage with the history of slavery. Add to this passage by asking students to read outside of class—or alternatively bring into the classroom—extracts of Hammurabi's law code:

- How did slavery in Mesopotamia compare to slavery in the United States?
- Why did slavery first emerge with civilization?
- Hammurabi's law code also provides an ideal opportunity to compare and contrast the status of free women and slaves in Mesopotamia and the impact of "class" on Mesopotamian society.

2. Contextualization, large or small group. "Studying First Civilizations versus studying societies before civilizations."

This chapter offers an ideal opportunity to discuss the importance of writing to the study of the past:

- What questions can now be answered, thanks to the development of writing?
- Does the existence of deciphered writing from one First Civilization help in understanding them all?
- What questions would you most like to ask an inhabitant of the Olmec civilization? the Norte Chico civilization? the Indus Valley civilization?
- What do you think the answers would be?

3. Misconception/Difficult Topic, large or small group. "That 'civilization' is necessarily a good thing."

The whole chapter, and especially the Reflections section, provides fertile ground for class discussion of the deep-seated assumption that civilization was necessarily a good thing in human history. Such a discussion provides an ideal opportunity to ask students to assess the positive and negative implications for humankind of the emergence of civilizations. Possible approaches:

- Break students into small groups to report back, or require groups of students to present the cases "for" and "against" civilization.

- Ask students to assess deep-seated assumptions in Western society today, including that civilization is a product of Western culture and that the Americas were "uncivilized" before Europeans arrived.
- Should historians be in the business of making these kinds of judgments about the past? Is it enough to understand what happened and why? Should we move on to issues of moral assessment? Or are such issues unavoidable?
- Would the students prefer to live in a First Civilization rather than in a gathering and hunting band, agricultural village, or chiefdom? If so, under what circumstances? Would the student's gender or class status make a difference in that judgment?
- To what extent do the experiences of First Civilizations reflect the experiences of civilization today?

Classroom Activities

1. Map analysis, large or small group. Using a physical map of the world, ask students to identify the location of the main civilizations discussed in this chapter. Then encourage the students to make lists of

1. physical conditions (mountains, oceans, deserts, and so on) that would simplify or hinder contact with other regions
2. similarities (longitude, river valleys, etc.) and differences (relative size and so on) between the geographic settings of the first civilizations

2. Role-playing exercise, small group. You and your family have just migrated from an agricultural/nomadic/chiefdom society to one of the newly established cities of Sumer.

- How would your life change?
- What would stay the same?
- How would your gender impact your experience?
- Would your experience be different if you had migrated to Egypt? the Indus Valley? China?

3. Clicker question. On the whole, was the emergence of First Civilizations a positive or negative development for humankind?

Key Terms

Code of Hammurabi: A series of laws publicized at the order of King Hammurabi of Babylon (d. 1750 B.C.E.). Not actually a code, but a number of laws that proclaim the king's commitment to social order.

cradle of civilization: Commonly used term for southern Mesopotamia (in present-day Iraq).

cuneiform: Wedge-shaped writing in the form of symbols incised into clay tablets; used in Mesopotamia from around 3100 B.C.E. to the beginning of the Common Era.

Egypt: "the gift of the Nile": Egypt is often known as "the gift of the Nile" because the region would not have been able to support a significant human population without the Nile's annual inundation, which provided rich silt deposits and made agriculture possible.

Epic of Gilgamesh: The most famous extant literary work from ancient Mesopotamia, it tells the story of one man's quest for immortality.

Harappa: A major city of the Indus Valley civilization; flourished around 2000 B.C.E. (*pron.* hah-RAHP-uh)

Hatshepsut: Ancient Egypt's most famous queen; reigned 1472–1457 B.C.E. (*pron.* hat-shep-soot)

Hebrews: A smaller early civilization whose development of a monotheistic faith that provided the foundation of modern Judaism, Christianity, and Islam assured them a significant place in world history.

hieroglyphs: Ancient Egyptian writing system; literally, "sacred carvings"—so named because the Greeks saw them prominently displayed in Egyptian temples.

Hittites: An Indo-European civilization established in Anatolia in the eighteenth century B.C.E.

Hyksos: A pastoral group of unknown ethnicity that invaded Egypt and ruled in the north from 1650 to 1535 B.C.E. Their dominance was based on their use of horses, chariots, and bronze technology. (*pron.* HICK-sose)

Indus Valley: home of a major civilization that emerged in what is now Pakistan during the third millennium B.C.E., in the valleys of the Indus and Saraswati rivers, noted for the uniformity of its elaborately planned cities over a large territory

Mandate of Heaven: The ideological underpinning of Chinese emperors, this was the belief that a ruler held authority by command of divine force as long as he ruled morally and benevolently.

Mesopotamia: The "land between the rivers" Tigris and Euphrates, in what is now Iraq.

Minoan civilization: An advanced civilization that developed on the island of Crete around 2500 B.C.E.

Mohenjo Daro: A major city of the Indus Valley civilization; flourished around 2000 B.C.E. (*pron.* moe-hen-joe DAHR-oh)

Norte Chico/Caral: Norte Chico is a region along the central coast of Peru, home of a civilization that developed in the period 3000–1800 B.C.E. Caral was the largest of some twenty-five urban centers that emerged in the area at that time.

Nubia: A civilization to the south of Egypt in the Nile Valley, noted for development of an alphabetic writing system and a major ironworking industry by 500 B.C.E.

Olmec civilization: An early civilization that developed along the coast of the Gulf of Mexico around 1200 B.C.E.

oracle bones: In Chinese civilization, animal bones that were heated and the cracks then interpreted as prophecies. The prophecies were written on the bone and provide our earliest written sources for ancient China.

patriarchy: Literally "rule of the father"; a social system of male dominance.

pharaoh: A king of Egypt. The term literally means "the palace" and only came into use in the New Kingdom, but it is generally employed in reference to all ancient Egyptian rulers.

Phoenicians: A civilization in the area of present-day Lebanon, creators of the first alphabetic writing system.

pyramid: Monumental tomb for an Egyptian pharaoh; mostly built during the Old Kingdom (2663–2195 B.C.E.). Pyramids are also found in Meroë to the south of Egypt.

quipu: A series of knotted cords, used for accounting and perhaps as a form of writing in the Norte Chico civilization.

rise of the state: A process of centralization that took place in the First Civilizations, growing out of the greater complexity of urban life in recognition of the need for coordination, regulation, adjudication, and military leadership.

salinization: The buildup of minerals in soil, decreasing its fertility; can be caused by long-term irrigation.

Sanxingdui: An ancient city of China that developed independently from the Shang dynasty. (*pron.* sahn-shing-dwee)

Shang dynasty: Period of Chinese history from 1766 to 1122 B.C.E. (*pron.* shahng)

Son of Heaven: Title of the ruler of China, first known from the Zhou dynasty. It acknowledges the ruler's position as intermediary between heaven and earth.

Teotihuacán: The largest city of ancient Mesoamerica; flourished around 500 C.E. (*pron.* teh-o-tee-WAH-kahn)

Uruk: The largest city of ancient Mesopotamia. (*pron.* OOH-rook)

Xia dynasty: A legendary series of monarchs of early China, traditionally dated to 2200–1766 B.C.E. (*pron.* shah)

Zhou dynasty: Period of Chinese history from 1122 to 256 B.C.E. (*pron.* joe)

ziggurat: A Mesopotamian stepped pyramid. Unlike an Egyptian pyramid, a ziggurat was a solid structure of baked brick, an artificial hill at the summit of which stood a temple.

ANSWER GUIDELINES FOR CHAPTER QUESTIONS

The two sets of questions that follow appear in the textbook at the end of the chapter and in the margins of the reading. They are also provided in the Computerized Test Bank with answer guidelines, for your convenience.

The Big Picture Questions

1. What distinguishes civilizations from other forms of human community?

• Larger populations than previous human communities
• Sizeable cities that were political/administrative capitals, centers for production of culture, marketplaces for both local and long-distance exchange, and centers of manufacturing
• Cultural developments including monumental architecture and systems of writing

• Rule by powerful states whose rulers could use force to compel obedience
• Profound social differentiation by economic function, skill, wealth, and status that led to greater inequality and greater oppression than in earlier agricultural villages, pastoral societies, and chiefdoms
• The emergence of patriarchy and with it the undermining of more equal relationships between men and women found in earlier agricultural villages, pastoral societies, and chiefdoms
• Emergence of large-scale warfare

2. How does the use of the term "civilization" by historians differ from that of popular usage? How do you use the term?

• In popular usage, "civilization" implies superiority; refined behavior of a "higher" form of society is seen as unreservedly positive. This idea suggests that other forms of living must be "uncivilized," which normally implies inferiority.
• Scholars have also opposed the term "First Civilizations" because it implies more clearly demarcated boundaries from other units than was actually the case. The earlier civilizations lacked clear borders, and identification with the civilization probably faded as distance from its core region increased. The line between civilizations and other kinds of societies is not always clear.
• Historians continue to use the term "civilizations" because the term is deeply embedded in our way of thinking about the world; there is no alternative term; and we need to make distinctions among different kinds of human communities. Historians, though, use "civilization" purely as a descriptive term designating a particular type of human society—one with cities and states—without implying any judgment or assessment, any sense of superiority or inferiority. Instead, "civilization" is used to define broad cultural patterns in particular geographic regions, recognizing that many people living in those regions may have been more aware of differences and conflicts than of those commonalities.

3. "Civilizations were held together largely by force." Do you agree with this assessment, or were there other mechanisms of integration as well?

• Force played a role in holding the First Civilizations together. The state used coercion or the threat of coercion to extract surplus product from farmers to support city people. The First Civilizations used officials, soldiers, police, and "attendants" to accumulate resources.

• Other mechanisms also helped to hold the First Civilizations together. The state solved certain widely shared problems such as the organization of irrigation networks, the adjudication of disputes, and defense. These roles earned First Civilizations a measure of voluntary support among the population. States were also able to secure voluntary support by generating the idea that class and gender inequalities were normal, natural, and ordained by the gods. States also used grandeur displayed through lavish lifestyles, impressive rituals, and imposing structures. Grandeur was intended to overwhelm the common people and reinforce the sense that it was natural that the ruling elites were in charge.

4. In the development of the First Civilizations, what was gained for humankind, and what was lost?

• First Civilizations gained urban living, writing, complex calendars, monumental architecture, trade specialists who helped to drive technological innovation, a wider variety of consumer goods, and greater overall wealth.

• Humankind also experienced less desirable developments, such as greater class and wealth differentiation, slavery, patriarchy, and large-scale warfare.

Margin Review Questions

Q. *When and where did the First Civilizations emerge?*

• Emergence of the First Civilizations was a global phenomenon that happened independently in six major locations around the world and in a number of smaller expressions as well.
• The six major locations were:

1. Sumer in Mesopotamia, by 3000 B.C.E.
2. Egypt in the Nile River valley, by 3000 B.C.E.
3. Norte Chico along the coast of central Peru, by 3000 B.C.E.
4. Indus Valley civilization in the Indus and Saraswati river valleys of present-day Pakistan, by 2000 B.C.E.
5. China, by 2200 B.C.E.

6. The Olmec along the coast of the Gulf of Mexico near present-day Veracruz in southern Mexico, around 1200 B.C.E.

• In addition, other smaller civilizations also flourished, including the Nubian civilization that emerged south of Egypt in the Nile River valley, and the large city in China known as Sanxingdui, which arose separately but at the same time as the more well-known Shang dynasty.

Q. *What accounts for the initial breakthroughs to civilization?*

• Civilizations had their roots in the Agricultural Revolution, which allowed communities to produce sufficient food surpluses to support large populations and the specialized or elite minorities who did not themselves produce food.
• Scholars have posited many theories as to why some agricultural societies formed into civilizations and other did not, including: a need to organize for large-scale irrigation projects; the efforts of favored groups to protect their privileges; the needs of warfare; and the influence of trade.
• Robert Carneiro combines several of these factors to argue that:

1. The growing density of population, producing more congested and competitive societies, was a fundamental motor of change, especially where rich agricultural land was limited either by geography or by powerful competing societies.
2. Such settings provided incentives for innovations, such as irrigation or plows that could produce more food, because opportunities for territorial expansion were not readily available.
3. These same environments generated intense competition among rival groups that led to repeated warfare. A strong and highly organized state was a decided advantage in such competition.
4. Since losers could not easily flee to new lands, they were absorbed into the winner's society as a lower class.
5. Successful leaders of the winning side emerged as an elite with an enlarged base of land, a class of subordinated workers, and a powerful state at their disposal.

Q. *What was the role of cities in the early civilizations?*

• political and administrative centers
• centers of culture including art, architecture, literature, ritual, and ceremony
• marketplaces for both local and long-distance exchange
• centers of manufacturing activity

Q. *In what ways was social inequality expressed in early civilizations?*

• wealth
• avoidance of physical labor
• clothing
• houses
• manner of burial
• class-specific treatment in legal codes

Q. *In what ways have historians tried to explain the origins of patriarchy?*

• Transition from hoe and digging-stick agriculture (mostly women) to more intensive agriculture with animal-drawn plows and more intensive large-herd pastoralism (tasks that men were better able to perform)
• The growing population of civilizations meant that women were more often pregnant and even more deeply involved in child care than before.
• Men, because they were less important in the household, were available to take on positions of economic, religious, and political authority as societies grew more complex. From these positions men shaped the values and practices of their societies in a manner that benefited them at the expense of women. In this development lay the origin of the ancient distinction between the realm of the home, defined as the domain of women, and the world of public life, associated with men.
• Women had long been identified with nature because of their intimate involvement in reproduction, but civilization valued culture and the human mastery of nature through agriculture, through monumental art and architecture, and through the creation of large-scale cities and states. Some scholars have suggested that, as civilizations developed, women became associated with an inferior dimension of human life (nature), while men assumed responsibility for the higher order of culture.
• Large-scale military conflict with professionally led armies was a central feature of the First Civilizations.

With military service largely restricted to men, the needs of warfare served to enhance the power and prestige of a male warrior class.
• The emergence of private property and commerce also may have shaped the status of women. Restrictions on women's sexual activity became central to ensuring that offspring of the male head of household inherited family property. Moreover, the buying and selling associated with commerce was soon applied to male rights over women, whether as slaves, concubines, or wives.

Q. *How did Mesopotamian and Egyptian patriarchy differ from each other?*

• In Mesopotamia by the second millennium B.C.E., written law codified and sought to enforce a patriarchal family life. The law supported unquestioned authority of men while offering women a measure of paternalistic protection. Central to these laws was the regulation of female sexuality by men.
• Women in Mesopotamian civilization were sometimes divided into two sharply distinguished categories: (1) respectable women, those under the protection and sexual control of one man, who were often veiled outside the home; and (2) nonrespectable women, such as slaves and prostitutes, who were often forbidden to wear a veil.
• Powerful goddesses of early Mesopotamian civilization were gradually relegated to home and hearth, to be replaced by male deities, who were credited with the power of creation and fertility and viewed as the patrons of wisdom and learning.
• While Egypt was still a patriarchal society, it afforded women greater opportunities than did Mesopotamia.
• Women in Egypt were recognized as legal equals to men. They were able to own property, sell land, make their own wills, sign their own marriage contracts, and initiate their own divorces.
• Royal women occasionally exercised significant political power as regents for their young sons or, more rarely, as queens in their own right.
• Women were not veiled in Egypt, and art depicting married couples showed women and men in affectionate poses as equal partners.

Q. *What were the sources of state authority in the First Civilizations?*

• Citizens recognized that the complexity of life in cities or densely populated territories required some

the authority to coordinate and regulate the community enterprises such as defense and irrigation.

• State authorities frequently used force to compel obedience.

• Authority in early civilizations was often associated with divine sanction.

• Writing and accounting augmented state authority by defining elite status, conveying prestige on the literate, providing a means to disseminate propaganda, strengthening the state by making accurate record keeping possible, and giving added weight to orders, regulations, and laws.

• Grandeur in the form of lavish lifestyles of elites, impressive rituals, and the building of imposing structures added to the perception of state authority and power.

Q. *In what ways did Mesopotamian and Egyptian civilizations differ from each other?*

• The Mesopotamian outlook on life viewed humankind as caught in an inherently disorderly world, subject to the whims of capricious and quarreling gods, and facing death without much hope of a life beyond. By contrast, Egypt produced a more cheerful and hopeful outlook on the world, wherein the rebirth of the sun each day and of the river every year assured Egyptians that life would prevail over death.

• Mesopotamian civilization adversely affected its environment through deforestation, soil erosion, and salinization of the soil. This ecological deterioration weakened Sumerian city-states, facilitating their conquest and the shift of Mesopotamian civilization permanently north from its original heartland. By contrast, Egypt produced a more sustainable agricultural system that lasted for thousands of years and contributed to the continuity of its civilization.

• Mesopotamia and Egypt also differed in settlement patterns. Some 80 percent of the population of Sumer lived in urban environments because of the need for protection in an unstable world. In Egypt, cities were primarily political, religious, and market centers, with most people living in agricultural villages along the river. This was possible in part because Egypt's greater security made it less necessary for people to gather in fortified towns.

• The political system in Sumer, the first Mesopotamian civilization, consisted of independent city-states that frequently warred among themselves and were subject to unexpected attack from the outside.

This instability, along with environmental degradation, weakened the civilization and led to its ultimate conquest by outside powers. By contrast, Egypt unified early in its history under the pharaoh, the head of a strong divine right monarchical system. While over time the pharaohs declined in real power, the political tradition helped Egypt to maintain unity and independence with only occasional interruptions for 3,000 years.

• Underlying these contrasts were the very different rivers along which the two civilizations developed and the geographic locations in which they emerged. The Nile proved a more predictable river, one whose yearly floods facilitated agricultural production. Meanwhile, the Tigris and Euphrates were more unpredictable, bringing fertility but also on occasion destruction through flooding. Moreover, the Nile River valley was more protected from invasion than was Mesopotamia. The Nile was surrounded by deserts, mountains, seas, and cataracts that limited the possibility of outside invasion, while Mesopotamia lacked any serious obstacles to travel and suffered from frequent invasions. The certainty and security enjoyed by Egyptians had an impact on their civilization, just as the uncertainty and insecurity experienced by Mesopotamians influenced *their* civilization.

Q. *In what ways were Mesopotamian and Egyptian civilizations shaped by their interactions with near and distant neighbors?*

• Egyptian agriculture relied on wheat and barley adopted from Mesopotamia as well as gourds, watermelon, domesticated donkeys, and cattle from Sudan.

• Some scholars argue that Egypt's step pyramids and system of writing were stimulated by Mesopotamian models.

• The practice of "divine kingship" most likely derived from traditions in central or eastern Sudan.

• Indo-European pastoralists influenced both Mesopotamia and Egypt as they migrated into the region. They brought with them the domesticated horse and chariot technology, which proved effective on the battlefield. Both Mesopotamian and Egyptian armies rapidly incorporated both the horse and chariot into their armies.

• With the invasion of the Hyksos into Egypt, Egyptian civilization also adopted new kinds of armor, bows, daggers, and swords; improved methods of spinning and weaving; new musical instruments; and olive and pomegranate trees.

ADDITIONAL RESOURCES FOR CHAPTER 3

Additional Bedford/St. Martin's Resources

FOR INSTRUCTORS

Computerized Test Bank

This test bank provides over thirty exercises per chapter, including multiple-choice, fill-in-the-blank, short-answer, and full-length essay questions. Instructors can customize quizzes, add or edit both questions and answers, and export questions and answers to a variety of formats, including WebCT and Blackboard. The disc includes correct answers and essay outlines.

Instructor's Resource CD-ROM

This disc provides instructors with ready-made and customizable PowerPoint multimedia presentations built around chapter outlines, maps, figures, and all images from the textbook, plus JPEG versions of all maps, figures, and images.

The following maps and images from Chapter 3 are available in both JPEG and PowerPoint format on the Instructor's Resource CD-ROM:

- Map 3.1: First Civilizations (pp. 58–59)
- Map 3.2: Mesopotamia (p. 75)
- Map 3.3: An Egyptian Empire (p. 82)
- Raherka and Mersankh (p. 54)
- Shang Dynasty Bronze (p. 61)
- A Mesopotamian Ziggurat (p. 63)
- Mohenjo Daro (p. 64)
- Olmec Head (p. 73)
- Egypt and Nubia (p. 80)

FOR STUDENTS

Documents and Essays from *Worlds of History: A Comparative Reader,* Third Edition

The following documents, essays, and illustrations to accompany Chapter 3 are available in Chapter 2 of this reader by Kevin Reilly:

- Kevin Reilly, "Cities and Civilization"
- From *The Epic of Gilgamesh*
- From *Hammurabi's Code*
- "Advice to the Young Egyptian: 'Be a Scribe'"
- Images from Egypt

Online Study Guide at bedfordstmartins.com/strayer

The Online Study Guide helps students synthesize the material from the text as well as practice the skills historians use to make sense of the past. Each chapter of the Online Study Guide contains specific testing exercises, including a multiple-choice self-test that focuses on important conceptual ideas; an identification quiz that helps students remember key people, places, and events; a flashcard activity that tests students on their knowledge of key terms; and two interactive map activities intended to strengthen students' geographic skills. Instructors can monitor students' progress through an online Quiz Gradebook or receive email updates.

Further Reading

The Ancient Indus Cvilization, http://www.harrappa.com/har/har0.html. Hundreds of vivid pictures and several brief essays on Indus Valley civilization.

Bridging World History: Order and Early Societies, http://www.learner.org/channel/courses/world-history/unit_main_6.html. An interesting and useful site, with video clips, teaching suggestions, and even an audio glossary for those hard-to-pronounce words.

Dillehay, Thomas D. *The Settlement of the Americas: A New Prehistory.* New York: Basic Books, 2000. This book is an interesting and readable study of archeology in the Americas and what it teaches and contains much detail about how persistent prejudice has hampered scholarship.

Gabriel, Richard A., and Karen S. Metz. *From Sumer to Rome: The Military Capabilities of Ancient Armies.* Westport, CT: Greenwood Press, 1991. This study is particularly useful for its information about war in Mesopotamia.

Mesopotamia—Internet Resources, http://www.wsu.edu/~dee/MESINRES.HTM. This Web site includes links to primary sources and studies of Mesopotamia, as well as works of art.

National Geographic, Egypt: Secrets of an Ancient World, http://www.nationalgeographic.com/pyramids/. This is an entertaining site with interactive displays on important matters like how to make a mummy.

Scarre, Chris, ed. *The Seventy Wonders of the Ancient World*. London: Thames and Hudson, 1999. A quick read that is full of useful information about such things as pyramids and ziggurats.

Scarre, Christopher, and Brian M. Fagan. *Ancient Civilizations*, 2nd ed. Upper Saddle River, NJ: Prentice Hall, 2003. This is a book that every world civ. instructor should have on her or his shelf. It starts with background on the rediscovery of the ancient world and concepts of the state, going on to short presentations on Mesopotamia, Egypt, Indus Valley, early Chinese civilizations, Near Eastern kingdoms, the early states in northeast Africa, early civilizations in the Americas, and more.

Art History Resources on the Web: Art of the Ancient Near East, http://witcombe.sbc.edu/ARTHmesopotamian.html. An impressive collection of good-quality images for classroom use, assembled by Christopher L. C. E. Witcombe, a professor of art history at Sweet Briar College.

Art History Resources on the Web: Ancient Egyptian Art, http://witcombe.sbc.edu/ARTHegypt.html. Links to an impressive number of images for all periods of ancient Egyptian history, assembled by Christopher L. C. E. Witcombe, a professor of art history at Sweet Briar College.

Literature

Book of Songs: The Ancient Chinese Classic of Poetry. Translated by Arthur Waley. New York: Grove, 1987. A collection of lyrics compiled around 600 B.C.E. that, according to tradition, Confucius selected from a larger corpus because they exemplified models for statecraft and personal relationships.

Dalley, Stephanie, trans. *Myths from Mesopotamia*. Oxford: Oxford University Press, 1998. A useful and accessible study of Mesopotamian myths.

Enheduanna. *Inanna, Lady of Largest Heart*. Translated by Betty de Shong Meador. Austin: University of Texas Press, 2001. A collection of Mesopotamian hymns to the goddess Inanna by Enheduanna, the earliest known author of written literature.

Norton, Andre. *Shadow Hawk*. Harcourt, 1960 (and later editions). An enjoyable novel, set in Egypt during the period of the Hyksos intrusion and told by a master storyteller.

Parkinson, R. B., ed. and trans. *The Tale of Sinuhe and Other Ancient Egyptian Poems, 1940–1640 BC*. Oxford: Oxford World Classics, 1997.

Sandars, N. K., trans. *The Epic of Gilgamesh*. Middlesex: Penguin, 1972.

Film

The First Egyptians. Films for the Humanities and Sciences, 2004. 25 minutes. Explores the archeological evidence from Egypt that predates the building of the pyramids by thousands of years in order to discover whether the dynasties of the pharaohs were directly linked to the early inhabitants of Egypt.

Indus: The Unvoiced Civilization. Insight Media, 2000. 59 minutes. Explores the language, customs, and beliefs of the Indus River civilization.

Mari, Part 1: Sumerian City on the Euphrates. Films for the Humanities and Sciences, 2005. 26 minutes. Explores the emergence of urban living and Mesopotamian culture through a study of the ancient city of Mari.

Mari, Part 2: The Palace of Zimri-Lim. Films for the Humanities and Sciences, 2005. 27 minutes. Provides insight into life at the center of power in a Sumerian city through the archeological excavation of the Palace of Zimri-Lim.

Mesopotamia: I Have Conquered the River. Insight Media, 2000. 58 minutes. Explores ancient Mesopotamian civilization, with particular emphasis given to the emergence of writing and law and the impact of the wheat crop's collapse on the agricultural economy of Sumerian city-states.

Messages from the Past: Reassessing Ancient Civilizations. Four-part series. Films for the Humanities and Sciences, 2000. 59 minutes each. Examines the histories of ancient Egypt, Mesopotamia, the

Indus Valley, and China by focusing on the rivers that sustained them.

Writing and Civilization. Insight Media, 1998. 23 minutes. Explores the shift from oral to written communication in China, Mesopotamia, and Egypt, paying particular attention to the connection of writing to religious, political, and economic developments. The film also considers the development of phonetic writing in Phoenicia.

PART TWO

THE CLASSICAL ERA IN WORLD HISTORY,
500 B.C.E.–500 C.E.

Outline: The Big Picture: After the First Civilizations: What Changed and What Didn't?

I. This is a good point at which to pull back and look broadly at the age of agricultural civilizations (ca. 3500 B.C.E.–ca. 1750 C.E.)

A. The most prominent large-scale trend in this phase of human history was the globalization of civilization.

1. the first wave—the First Civilizations—was already global (see Ch. 3)

2. First Civilizations proved to be fragile and vulnerable

a. Mesopotamian city-states were absorbed into larger empires

b. Egypt suffered a series of foreign conquests

c. Indus Valley civilization declined in face of desertification and political collapse

d. Norte Chico civilization faded away by 1800 B.C.E.

e. the Olmecs apparently razed and abandoned their major cities around 400 B.C.E.

f. China fragmented into warring states

B. There was no going back from the civilization model of human society.

1. new urban-centered and state-based societies emerged to replace the First Civilizations

2. smaller civilizations emerged elsewhere

3. "second wave" civilizations were followed by a "third wave" in roughly 500–1500 C.E. (see Part Three)

C. Sometimes historians focus on civilizations and neglect other cultures, but societies that were not state- or city-centered remained important.

II. Continuities in Civilization

A. The second and third waves of civilization didn't differ much from the first ones, if regarded from a panoramic view.

1. little fundamental change from one to the next

2. no technological or economic breakthrough that would allow new kinds of human societies to emerge

B. The age of agricultural civilizations was marked by fluctuation, repetitive cycles, and minor changes, not by fundamental transformations.

III. **Changes in Civilization**
   A. Looked at more closely, many things of great importance took place during the second and third waves of civilization.
      1. more rapid population growth (with important fluctuations)
         a. but no fundamental economic breakthrough that could support much larger numbers
      2. states and empires grew in size, dwarfing the First Civilizations
         a. brought together many diverse peoples in a single political system
         b. in the seventeenth century C.E., only a third of the world's land area (but a majority of the world's population) was controlled by a state-based system
      3. the rise and fall of empires had an enormous impact on their peoples
   B. Second- and third-wave civilizations saw innovations in many spheres.
      1. enduring cultural and religious systems, including Confucianism, Daoism, Hinduism, Buddhism, Greek rationalism, Judaism, Zoroastrianism, Christianity, and Islam
      2. no fundamental technological break-through, but innovations still increased

human ability to manipulate the environment
         a. China was a major source of technological change
   C. More elaborate, widespread, and dense communications and exchange networks emerged after the end of the First Civilizations.
      1. spread of technologies, such as sugar production
      2. long-distance trade routes developed, carrying goods, culture, and disease

IV. **Classical Civilizations**
   A. The next four chapters focus on the major second-wave civilizations of the period 500 B.C.E.–500 C.E.
   B. The period is frequently called the "classical era" of world history.
      1. term emphasizes the enduring traditions that developed in this period
      2. modern identities of many countries, regions, and civilizations are still linked to classical-era achievements
   C. The "classical era" definition is based largely on Eurasian experience.
      1. the largest, most influential civilizations took shape on the outer rim of Eurasia during the classical era
      2. around 80 percent of the world's population resided on the Eurasian continent

Eurasian Empires

500 B.C.E.–500 C.E.

CHAPTER OVERVIEW

Chapter Objectives

- To consider the nature of imperial systems in the classical era
- To explore why empires developed in some regions but not in others
- To show the important similarities and differences between imperial systems and the reasons behind them
- To reflect on the significance that classical empires have for us today

Chapter Outline

I. **Opening Vignette**
    A. The 2007 book *Are We Rome?* asked if the United States has become the new Roman Empire.
       1. collapse of the Soviet Union
       2. overextension of the United States
       3. sense of unique, global mission
       4. commitment to military dominance
       5. reminder of continuing relevance of a long-dead empire
    B. Modern fascination with empires **[see Discussion Topic 1]**
       1. earliest empires developed in era of First Civilizations

          a. Akkadian Empire
          b. Babylonian Empire
          c. Assyrian Empire
       2. empires have been central to world history for 4,000 years
    C. What is an empire?
       1. simple answer: empires are political systems with coercive power
       2. more typical: larger, more aggressive states
          a. conquer other states
          b. use their resources
          c. usually include multiple peoples and cultures under a single political system
       3. no clear line between empires and small multiethnic states
          a. can have a common culture without a unified political system
    D. Eurasian empires of the classical era include:
       1. Persian Empire
       2. Greek empire of Alexander the Great
       3. Roman Empire
       4. Chinese empire (Qin and Han dynasties)
       5. India (Mauryan and Gupta empires)
    E. Common problems of classical empires:
       1. Would they try to impose their culture on varied subjects?
       2. Would they rule conquered peoples directly or through local elites?
       3. How should they extract wealth while maintaining order?
       4. all eventually collapsed
    F. Why have empires always been so fascinating?

1. size was imposing
2. blood and violence of conquest
3. satisfaction in witnessing the fall of the mighty when they collapse
4. contrast to nonimperial civilizations
5. empires were *important*
   a. majority of humans before twentieth century lived in empires
   b. stimulated exchange of ideas, cultures, and values
      i. e.g., Roman Empire as vehicle for spread of Christianity
   d. peace and security encouraged development, commerce, and cultural mixing

II. **Empires and Civilizations in Collision: The Persians and the Greeks**
   A. The Eurasian classical era saw a flowering of second-wave civilizations.
      1. civilizations did not usually encounter each other directly
      2. Mediterranean world and Middle East were the important exceptions
         a. Persians and Greeks were neighbors
         b. very important cultural encounter
   B. The Persian Empire
      1. in 500 B.C.E., it was the largest and most impressive empire
         a. Persians were Indo-Europeans, homeland on the Iranian plateau
         b. imperial system drew on Mesopotamian prototypes
         c. much larger and more splendid
         d. Cyrus (r. 557–530 B.C.E.) and Darius (r. 522–486 B.C.E.) expanded empire from Egypt to India
         e. diverse empire with population of around 35 million people
      2. elaborate cult of kingship
         a. rule by will of the god Ahura Mazda
         b. absolute monarchy
      3. holding the empire together
         a. violent punishments by king
         b. effective administrative system
            i. *satraps* governed the empire's twenty-three provinces
            ii. lower-level officials were local
            iii. system of imperial spies ("eyes and ears of the King")

c. respect for non-Persian cultural traditions
   i. Cyrus allowed Jews to return from Babylonian exile and rebuild Jerusalem temple
   ii. Herodotus: Persians adopt foreign customs readily
d. standardized coinage, predictable taxes
e. encouragement of communication and commerce
   i. canal dug between Nile and Red Sea
   ii. "royal road" 1,700 miles long across empire
   iii. imperial courier service
      4. immense wealth and power
         a. elaborate imperial centers (especially Susa, Persepolis)
   C. The Greeks [see Lecture Strategy 1]
      1. Indo-Europeans
      2. classical Greece emerged ca. 750 B.C.E., flourished for about 400 years
      3. distinctiveness of Hellenistic civilization
         a. population of Greece and the Aegean basin was 2 million to 3 million people
         b. geography of mountains, valleys encouraged development of hundreds of city-states and small settlements
            i. most had 500–5,000 male citizens
            ii. fierce independence, frequent conflict with neighbors
         c. shared common language and common gods
            i. common participation in Olympic Games (founded 776 B.C.E.)
      4. between 750 and 500 B.C.E., colonization around Mediterranean basin and Black Sea
      5. most distinctive feature: popular participation in political life of city-states [see Discussion Topic 2]
         a. equality of all citizens before the law
         b. extent of citizenship varied depending on time and city
            i. early Greek history: only wealthy and well-born were citizens
            ii. gradually expanded to middle- and lower-class men
            iii. an important element was ability to afford armor and weapons to fight as *hoplites* for the city-state

  c. *tyrants* (dictators) emerged in many areas, supported by the poorer classes against the rich

  d. Sparta gave most political authority to Council of Elders

  e. Athens: most distinctive expression of political participation

   i. period of intense class conflict

   ii. Solon's reforms began in 594 B.C.E.

   iii. extension of citizens' rights by Cleisthenes and Pericles

   iv. by 450 B.C.E., holders of public office chosen by lot, paid

   v. The Assembly was open for participation by all citizens, was center of political life

  f. differences between Athenian and modern democracy

   i. direct, not representative

   ii. women, slaves, and foreigners were excluded

D. Collision: The Greco-Persian Wars **[see Discussion Topic 3]**

 1. point of collision was Ionia (Greek settlements on Anatolian seacoast)

  a. in 499 B.C.E., some Ionian Greeks revolted against Persia

  b. were supported by Athens

 2. Persia responded with expeditions against Greeks in 490 and 480 B.C.E.

  a. Greeks astonishingly defeated Persians on land and sea

  b. Greeks believed they won Battle of Marathon (490 B.C.E.) because they were motivated by Greek freedoms

 3. notion of East/West divide as dominant theme in European thought

  a. Greece = Europe, freedom

  b. Persia = Asia, despotism

 4. victory radicalized Athenian democracy: poor rowers received full citizenship

  a. fifty-year Golden Age of Greek culture after Persian Wars

   i. construction of Parthenon

   ii. birth of Greek theatre (Aeschylus, Sophocles, Euripides)

   iii. early career of philosopher Socrates

  b. beginnings of imperialism

   i. Athenian naval power led to dominance over allies

  c. Peloponnesian War (431–404 B.C.E.)

   i. Sparta led resistance to Athenian imperialism

   ii. Athens defeated

   iii. Greek states were exhausted, distrusted each other

   iv. opened the way to takeover by Macedonia (frontier region on northern edge of Greece)

E. Collision: Alexander and the Hellenistic Era **[see Lecture Strategy 2]**

 1. Philip II of Macedon completed conquest of Greece by 338 B.C.E.

  a. political unification of Greece by force

  b. plan for great Greek expedition against Persia

 2. Alexander's expedition against Persia (333–323 B.C.E.)

  a. created a massive Greek empire that reached from Egypt and Anatolia to Afghanistan and India

  b. defeat of Persian Empire, destruction of Persepolis

  c. Alexander anointed as pharaoh of Egypt, declared to be "son of the gods"

 3. Alexander died in 323 B.C.E.; empire divided into three kingdoms, ruled by Macedonian generals

 4. Alexander's conquests were most important in world history terms for creation of the Hellenistic era (323–30 B.C.E.)

  a. dissemination of Greek culture through much of Asia and Egypt

  b. role of cities in spread of Greek culture

   i. Alexander and successors established many cities

   ii. many thousands of Greek settlers

   iii. Greek public centers and government

   iv. Alexandria (Egypt) as great cosmopolitan center

  a. library of 700,000 volumes

  b. the Museum: sponsorship of scholars

 5. A simplified form of Greek was widely spoken from Mediterranean to India

  a. Indian monarch Ashoka published some of his decrees in Greek

b. many Jews were attracted to Greek culture; Pharisees developed their own school system to counter the influence

6. Hellenistic cities were much more culturally diverse than original Greek city-states
   a. were not independent, but part of conquest states
   b. Macedonians and Greeks formed the elite
      i. efforts to remain separate from the natives
      ii. periodic rebellions against Greek exploitation
   c. cultural interaction and blending were still possible
      i. Alexander encouraged intermarriage
      ii. Greek rulers supported native cults
      iii. many natives became Greek citizens by adopting Greek education and culture
      iv. in India, Greeks became part of Ksatriya (warrior) caste
      v. some Bactrian Greeks converted to Buddhism, including King Menander
      vi. depiction of the Buddha in human form, Greek style

7. Roman rule replaced that of Greeks in western part of Hellenistic world
   a. continued to spread Greek culture and ideas

III. **Comparing Empires: Roman and Chinese**
[see Classroom Activity 1]
A. The Roman and Chinese empires had little direct contact but interesting similarities.
   1. both flourished ca. 200 B.C.E.–200 C.E.
   2. were of similar size (about 1.5 million square miles)
   3. both had 50 million to 60 million people
   4. between them, they controlled nearly half the world's population
   5. interesting variations on imperial theme
B. Rome: From City-State to Empire
   1. started as small, unimportant city-state in central Italy in eighth century B.C.E.
   2. overthrew monarchy and established a republic ca. 509 B.C.E.
      a. dominance of wealthy patricians

b. rule by two consuls, with advice from Senate

3. conflict with plebeians (poorer classes)
   a. developed into political role for the plebeians
   b. tribunes represented plebeians, could veto legislation
4. pride in republican values: rule of law, citizens' rights, lack of pretension, morality—"the way of the ancestors"
5. creation of the empire
   a. began in 490s B.C.E. with wars to control Italian peninsula
   b. 264–146 B.C.E.: Punic Wars with Carthage
      i. gave Rome control over western Mediterranean
      ii. made Rome a naval power
   c. conquest of Greece, Egypt, Mesopotamia, and present-day Spain, France, and Britain
   d. reached greatest geographical extent in early second century C.E.
   e. gradual, unplanned pursuit of opportunities
   f. skill and brutality of Roman army
   g. usually generous treatment of conquered peoples
6. political crisis of first century B.C.E.
   a. rise of military leaders (Marius, Sulla, Pompey, Julius Caesar)
   b. decline of republican values
   c. Caesar Augustus (r. 27 B.C.E.–14 C.E.) was first emperor
      i. maintenance of republican forms
      ii. reality: emperor as sole authority
7. establishment of *pax Romana* (Roman peace)
   a. security
   b. relative prosperity
C. China: From Warring States to Empire
   1. creation of empire regarded as a restoration
      a. Xia, Shang, and Zhou dynasties had created a Chinese state
      b. system fell apart by 500 B.C.E.
      c. age of warring states: seven competing kingdoms
      d. multiple states were regarded as unnatural

2. unification by Shihuangdi, ruler of Qin (r. 221–210 B.C.E.)
   a. adopted Legalism as political philosophy: clear rules and harsh punishments to enforce state authority
   b. Shihuangdi means "first emperor"
3. expansion of empire into northern Vietnam and Korea and into steppes to northwest
4. creation of empire was brutal
   a. military force
   b. execution of scholars, book burning
   c. hundreds of thousands of laborers built Great Wall
   d. Shihuangdi's monumental tomb, with about 7,500 life-size ceramic statues
   e. standardized weights, measures, currency, written Chinese, and even axle lengths for carts
5. Qin dynasty collapsed in 206 B.C.E.; followed by Han dynasty (206 B.C.E.– 220 C.E.)
   a. kept Qin centralization
   b. less harsh
D. Consolidating the Roman and Chinese Empires
1. both empires defined themselves in universal terms
2. both invested heavily in public works
3. both claimed supernatural sanctions
   a. deceased Roman emperors as gods
      i. persecution of Christians for nonparticipation in cult
   b. Chinese emperor as Son of Heaven
      i. rule by Mandate of Heaven
      ii. dependent on just rule
      iii. heavy ritual duties to maintain relationship between earth and heaven
      iv. moral government spelled out by writings of Confucius and his followers
4. both absorbed a foreign religious tradition
   a. development of Christianity in Roman Empire
      i. eventually became dominant religion of Europe
   b. introduction of Buddhism into China by traders
      i. not very popular until collapse of Han dynasty
      ii. temporary state support under Sui dynasty
      iii. never dominated in China
5. relationships with societies they governed
   a. Romans were always a minority in empire
      i. gradual expansion of Roman citizenship; was granted to nearly all free people of empire in 212 C.E.
      ii. did not imply cultural assimilation
      iii. some Roman culture was attractive to western Europeans
      iv. Greek culture continued to dominate eastern empire
   b. ethnic Chinese had much larger cultural heartland
      i. active assimilation of "barbarians"
6. role of language differed in the two empires
   a. Latin (alphabetic language) gave rise to Spanish, Portuguese, French, Italian, Romanian
   b. Chinese characters (represented words or ideas) could not be transferred easily to other languages
      i. but all literate people could understand written Chinese
      ii. more important than Latin in assimilating the elites
7. Roman Empire's peoples maintained separate cultural identities far more than in China
8. Bureaucracy was much more elaborate in China than in Roman Empire
   a. Chinese emperor Wudi (r. 141–87 B.C.E.) established an academy to train officials based on works of Confucius
      i. developed into civil service system
      ii. lasted until twentieth century
   b. Roman administration relied on regional elites and army
      i. unlike China, developed major body of law that was applicable equally to all people of the realm
E. The Collapse of Empires
1. Why do they fall?
   a. Han dynasty ended in 220 C.E.

b. traditional date for fall of western Roman Empire is 476 C.E.; eastern half survived as Byzantine Empire

2. common factors

   a. excessive size, overextension, too expensive for available resources

   b. no great technological breakthrough to enlarge resources

   c. tax evasion by large landowning families

   d. tax burden fell heavily onto the poor

      i. provoked Yellow Turban Rebellion, peasant revolt in China in 184 C.E.

   e. rivalry between elite factions created instability

   f. epidemic disease

   g. threat from nomadic or semi-agricultural peoples on frontier

      i. China had dealt with Xiongnu for centuries

         a) as state weakened, nomadic peoples breached frontier defenses

         b) establishment of "barbarian states" in north

         c) gradual adoption of Chinese culture

      ii. Rome: Germanic-speaking peoples

         a) began to enter empire in fourth century C.E.

         b) establishment of independent kingdoms

         c) only partially adopted Roman culture

         d) creation of Latin/Germanic hybrid culture

3. effects of imperial collapse

   a. decline of urban life

   b. population decline

   c. reduction of international trade

   d. vast insecurity

4. most important difference between collapse of Han and Roman Empires: what happened next

   a. China: about 350 years of disorder, then creation of a similar imperial state (Sui, Tang, and Song dynasties)

   b. Europe: no large-scale imperial system has *ever* been successfully established in western Europe since Romans

      i. division into large number of states with weak rulers

      c. Why was China more successful in restoration?

         i. greater cultural homogeneity

         ii. stronger bureaucratic tradition

         iii. Confucianism valued state; Christianity often at odds with the state

         iv. China had more advanced agriculture and metallurgy

IV. **Intermittent Empire: The Case of India**

   A. The idea of empire was much less prominent in India than in Persia, the Mediterranean, or China.

      1. fall of Indus Valley civilization by 1500 B.C.E.

      2. creation of new civilization along Ganges River

         a. debate continues over role of Aryan invaders

      3. establishment in northern India of classic civilization of South Asia by 600 B.C.E.

         a. enormous political, ethnic, cultural, and linguistic diversity

         b. Indian civilization as a whole shaped by political fragmentation and cultural diversity

         c. identity provided by distinctive religious tradition and social organization

            i. Hinduism

            ii. caste system

   B. **Mauryan Empire (326–184 B.C.E.)**

      1. stimulated by Persian and Greek penetration of northwest

      2. ruled all but southern tip of India

      3. population of around 50 million

      4. large military and civilian bureaucracy

      5. state-operated industries

      6. Ashoka (r. 268–232 B.C.E.) is best-known emperor, thanks to edicts

         a. conversion to Buddhism

         b. effort to rule empire peacefully

         c. effort to develop a moral code for whole empire

      7. Mauryan Empire broke apart after Ashoka's death

   C. **Gupta Empire (320–550 C.E.) and other short-lived** empires followed

   D. **Why couldn't India maintain an empire?**

      1. states **failed** to command loyalty

      2. **great cultural diversity**

3. frequent invasions from Central Asia
4. caste system encouraged local loyalties
   E. Indian trade flourished despite the lack of unity.
   1. merchants and artisans patronized public buildings and festivals
   2. Hinduism and Buddhism spread through much of Asia
   3. Indian mathematics and astronomy flourished
V. **Reflections: Classical Empires and the Twentieth Century** [see Lecture Strategy 3 and Classroom Activities 2 and 3]
   A. Classical empires continue to be used as models and inspirations.
   1. Mao Zedong compared himself to Shihuangdi
   2. modern Indians pride themselves on Ashoka's nonviolence and tolerance
   3. Great Britain celebrated its empire as a modern Roman Empire
   4. Mussolini regarded Italian expansion as the creation of a new Roman Empire
   5. recent question: are Americans the new Romans?
   B. There is a danger of misusing historical analogies, but history is vital to understanding the complexities of contemporary life.

USING *WAYS OF THE WORLD* IN THE CLASSROOM

Lecture Strategies

Lecture Strategy 1

"The shadow of the Parthenon."
The objectives of this lecture strategy are:

- to explore in greater depth the legacy of ancient Greece
- to drive home the lesson of the political diversity of classical Greece
- to consider why the golden age of Athens has been so important to all subsequent western civilization

This lecture strategy requires access to PowerPoint or to another sort of image projection system.

A good place to start a lecture is the Athenian historian Thucydides' claim that in later years, people would never believe, looking at the physical remains, that Sparta was as important as it was—but that they would think that Athens was twice as great. Show images of the physical impact of the two cities, such as:

- a general view of the ruins of ancient Sparta
- the Athenian Acropolis
- the Parthenon
- the Parthenon Frieze
- the Theatre of Dionysus (rebuilt in stone in the fourth century B.C.E. but on the site of an earlier wooden structure)

Move from these images to a discussion of why democracies (by contrast with empires) would indulge in monumental art. Be sure to consider the problem of survival (the Parthenon itself only survived because it became a church dedicated to the Virgin Mary, but then it was nearly destroyed when gunpowder stored in it exploded). Clearly, buildings alone are not enough to explain greatness, but they are an expression of Athens's cultural pride in the fifth century B.C.E.

The end of Athenian political greatness was its defeat in the Peloponnesian War and again by Philip II of Macedon in 338 B.C.E. Yet the physical remains of Athens after that time suggest a different story—for example:

- the Temple of Olympian Zeus (major construction by Hellenistic king Antiochus IV Epiphanes; completion by Roman emperor Hadrian)
- Stoa of Attalos (built by King Attalus II of Pergamon)
- Odeon of Herodes Atticus (built in 161 C.E.)
- Parliament House in Syntagma Square (built in the nineteenth century C.E.)

Consider the lessons of these images: that foreign rulers patronized Athens heavily for centuries; that Athens continued to be regarded as a center of culture; and that, when Greece won its independence from Turkey in the nineteenth century, Athens was the natural capital of the new state.

Discuss cultural transmission: how the Macedonians admired Athenian learning (even hiring the Athenian-trained Aristotle to tutor Alexander the Great) and carried it with them, and how Athenian works were preserved by Hellenistic education and libraries. It might be a good opportunity to look ahead, too, at how Boethius in the sixth century C.E. translated some of the works of Aristotle, and how most of the other works of the Aristotelian corpus were rediscovered in the Middle Ages.

But it is important to recognize that much Greek culture did *not* emanate directly from Athens—for example:

- the historian Herodotus was from Halicarnassus in Ionia
- the historian Thucydides spent much of his life in exile from Athens
- Aristotle was from Stagira, not Athens, and never headed a school in Athens
- Euripides spent the last years of his life in Macedonia

Lecture Strategy 2

"The conquests of Alexander the Great."
Many students have an interest in military history and have already heard of Alexander the Great. Thus it makes sense to use Alexander as a convenient hook to draw your students' interest to the exploration of Greek military history, Persian political organization, and both Greek and Persian culture. There are many ways to approach such a lecture. Possible points to include are:

- the development of Greek hoplite armies, and their further evolution in Macedon (with special attention to cavalry and the phalanx)
- the big question of whether Alexander won because the Persians were really "barbarians, fit only to be slaves" (as Aristotle would have it)
- Darius III's slow response to Alexander's invasion, and possible reasons for it (Darius's shaky claim to the throne, contempt for Greeks, and impediments caused by the sheer scale of Darius's empire)
- Alexander as founder of cities (it's important to note that Persia had major cities, such as Susa, Persepolis, Babylon, and the cities of the eastern Mediterranean, before Alexander came along) and the role those cities played
- Alexander's military genius (perhaps best seen in sieges such as that of Tyre, rather than the pitched battles at Granicus or Issus)

- why the Persians doubtless thought that the Greeks were a bunch of barbarians (lack of personal modesty, lack of court etiquette, the burning of Persepolis)
- why the Greeks doubtless thought that the Persians were a bunch of barbarians (inability to speak Greek, servile fawning toward rulers, large numbers of eunuchs, the wearing of trousers and long sleeves)
- how willing Persian subject peoples were to accept Greek rule and the reasons why attitudes varied in different parts of the empire

Lecture Strategy 3

"Tying it all together: Identity and governance in classical empires."
The primary objectives of this lecture strategy are to:

- reinforce the chapter's points about the nature of empires, both good and ill
- consider the modern notion of nationalism and whether it has any place in a discussion of classical empires

An interesting way to begin a lecture on this topic is with a video clip from Monty Python's *Life of Brian*, that wonderful spoof of Judean resistance against Roman oppression. I'd recommend the scene in which members of the People's Front of Judea raise the question: "What have the Romans ever done for us?"—only to come up with a lengthy list of benefits ranging from sanitation to peace. That would provide a natural introduction to a presentation of the tangible benefits that major empires provided to their subjects. You might include:

- Roman aqueducts (the Pont du Gard is a great illustration for this point)
- Roman roads
- the Persian royal road (maps of the route are readily available)
- an excerpt or two from Ashoka's Rock Edicts or Pillar Edicts, in which he orders the planting of shade trees for travelers or legislates other benefits
- the influence of the Library and Museum of Alexandria
- the Great Wall of China and governmental defense against the Xiongnu
- the Roman *limes* (fortification system against the Germans) or Hadrian's Wall in northern England (defense against the Scots and Picts)

- the general issue of how an imperial system encourages commerce, thanks to peace, standardized coinage and weights, and so on

Yet it cannot be denied that imperial governance was frequently resented. Choose 2–3 examples of revolt from different empires, describing them briefly to the class. Then ask the question: how did each empire fail its subject population? Could the same sort of revolt have occurred in one of the other empires? Some possible revolts to consider are:

- In the Roman Empire: the revolt of Boudica in Britain; the assassination of Nero; the Bar Kochba rebellion
- In the Chinese empire: the Yellow Turban Rebellion; Liu Bang's revolt against the Qin in 206 B.C.E.
- In the Persian Empire: noble revolts against Darius I; Egypt's willing acceptance of Alexander the Great
- In the Hellenistic empire: the Maccabee revolt against Antiochus IV Epiphanes

Finally, work out a definition of "nationalism" with the class, and consider whether a nationalist sentiment was an important factor in these subjects' relations with their conquerors.

Things to Do in the Classroom

Discussion Topics

1. Contextualization, large or small group.
"What makes classical empires different from First Civilizations?"
This is an opportunity to review what Chapter 3 had to say about First Civilizations while reinforcing the lessons of Chapter 4.

- Ask students to list the differences between classical empires and First Civilizations.
- Ask students to discuss the significance of those differences.
- Would an imperial system have made life different for the average person in a First Civilization?
- How would life have been different for members of the elite in a classical empire, compared to a First Civilization?

2. Comparison, large or small group.
"Government of the people, by the people, and for the people."
This chapter includes two major examples of popular government, Roman republicanism and Greek democracy. They provide an excellent opportunity for students to consider the meaning of the terms, the strengths and weaknesses of the two systems, and lessons that could be applied to the present-day United States. Encourage students to discuss the following questions:

- What is the difference between a republic (Roman) and a democracy (Greek)?
- What are the important strengths of each form of government?
- What are the weaknesses?
- Is the present-day United States a republic or a democracy? (Be sure that referendums and recall elections are mentioned.)
- Why did Greek democracy fail? Does the United States have safeguards against a similar fall?
- Why did the Roman republic fall, giving place to an imperial system? Does the United States have safeguards against a similar fall?

3. Misconception/Difficult Topic, large or small group. "The Persians were a bunch of barbarian savages."
The recent movie *300* presented Persians as an odd cross between orcs and demented ninjas; the purpose of this discussion is to allow the students to weigh the evidence on the subject. There is ample evidence in the chapter for a comparison of Greek and Persian civilizations. Possible approaches:

- Divide the class into two camps, Persian and Greek. Each side should prepare debating points on why they should be regarded as the most civilized (be sure to put some strong students on the Persian side, because the evidence is more difficult to extract).
- Divide students into small groups to discuss whether they think democracy is inherently superior to monarchy, and if so, why.
- Project or distribute images of two examples of Persian monumental architecture (such as the tomb of Cyrus or the ruins of Persepolis), and ask the students, in small groups, to come up with points that the images can teach them about the Persian Empire.

Classroom Activities

1. **Role-playing exercise, small group.** You are Chinese officials in the service of Wangdi, sent on an embassy to Rome.

   - What do you think would most surprise you about the Roman Empire?
   - What would seem most familiar?
   - How would your visit be different from a visit to India?

2. **Map analysis, large or small group.** Ask the students to examine the maps provided in Chapter 4 and then to discuss the following questions:

   - Which classical empire had a geographical setting that was most conducive to empire?
   - Can geography explain the failure of the Mauryan Empire in India?
   - Are there geographical reasons that can explain why democracy evolved in Greece but not in the areas where classical empires developed?

3. **Clicker question.** On the whole, did classical empires do more good or more harm?

Key Terms

Ahura Mazda: In Zoroastrianism, the good god who rules the world. (*pron.* ah-HOOR-a MAZ-dah)

Alexander the Great: Alexander III of Macedon (356–323 B.C.E.), conqueror of the Persian Empire and part of northwest India.

Aryans: Indo-European pastoralists who moved into India about the time of the collapse of the Indus Valley civilization; their role in causing this collapse is still debated by historians.

Ashoka: The most famous ruler of the Mauryan Empire (r. 268–232 B.C.E.), who converted to Buddhism and tried to rule peacefully and with tolerance. (*pron.* ah-SHOKE-uh)

Athenian democracy: A radical form of direct democracy in which much of the free male population of Athens had the franchise and officeholders were chosen by lot.

Caesar Augustus: The great-nephew and adopted son of Julius Caesar who emerged as sole ruler of the Roman state at the end of an extended period of civil war (r. 31 B.C.E.–14 C.E.).

Cyrus (the Great): Founder of the Persian Empire (r. 557–530 B.C.E.); a ruler noted for his conquests, religious tolerance, and political moderation.

Darius I: Great king of Persia (r. 522–486 B.C.E.) following the upheavals after Cyrus's death; completed the establishment of the Persian Empire. (*pron. most commonly in American English* DAHR-ee-us)

Greco-Persian Wars: Two major Persian invasions of Greece, in 490 B.C.E. and 480 B.C.E., in which the Persians were defeated on both land and sea.

Gupta Empire: An empire of India (320–550 C.E.). (*pron.* GHOOP-tuh)

Han dynasty: Dynasty that ruled China from 206 B.C.E. to 220 C.E., creating a durable state based on Shihuangdi's state-building achievement. (*pron.* hahn)

Hellenistic era: The period from 323 to 30 B.C.E. in which Greek culture spread widely in Eurasia in the kingdoms ruled by Alexander's political successors.

Herodotus: Greek historian known as the "father of history" (ca. 484–ca. 425 B.C.E.). His *Histories* enunciated the Greek view of a fundamental divide between East and West, culminating in the Greco-Persian Wars of 490–480 B.C.E. (*pron.* hair-ODD-uh-tus)

hoplite: A heavily armed Greek infantryman. Over time, the ability to afford a hoplite panoply and to fight for the city came to define Greek citizenship.

Ionia: The territory of Greek settlements on the coast of Anatolia; the main bone of contention between the Greeks and the Persian Empire.

Mandate of Heaven: The ideological underpinning of Chinese emperors, this was the belief that a ruler held authority by command of divine force as long as he ruled morally and benevolently.

Marathon, Battle of: Athenian victory over a Persian invasion in 490 B.C.E.

Mauryan Empire: A major empire (322–185 B.C.E.) that encompassed most of India.

Olympic Games: Greek religious festival and athletic competition in honor of Zeus; founded in 776 B.C.E. and celebrated every four years.

patricians: Wealthy, privileged Romans who dominated early Roman society.

pax Romana: The "Roman peace," a term typically used to denote the stability and prosperity of the early Roman Empire, especially in the first and second centuries C.E. (*pron.* pox roh-MAHN-uh)

Peloponnesian War: Great war between Athens (and allies) and Sparta (and allies), lasting from 431 to 404 B.C.E. The conflict ended in the defeat of Athens and the closing of Athens's Golden Age.

Persepolis: The capital and greatest palace-city of the Persian Empire, destroyed by Alexander the Great. (*pron.* per-SEP-oh-lis)

Persian Empire: A major empire that expanded from the Iranian plateau to incorporate the Middle East from Egypt to India; flourished from around 550 to 330 B.C.E.

plebeians: Poorer, less privileged Romans who gradually won a role in Roman politics.

Punic Wars: Three major wars between Rome and Carthage in North Africa, fought between 264 and 146 B.C.E., that culminated in Roman victory and control of the western Mediterranean.

Qin dynasty: A short-lived (221–206 B.C.E.) but highly influential Chinese dynasty that succeeded in reuniting China at the end of the Warring States period. (*pron.* chin)

Qin Shihuangdi: Literally "first emperor from the Qin"; Shihuangdi (r. 221–210 B.C.E.) forcibly reunited China and established a strong and repressive state. (*pron.* chin shee-hwang-dee)

Solon: Athenian statesman and lawmaker (fl. 594–560 B.C.E.) whose reforms led the Athenians toward democracy.

Wudi: Han emperor (r. 141–86 B.C.E.) who began the Chinese civil service system by establishing an academy to train imperial bureaucrats. (*pron.* woo-dee)

Xiongnu: Nomadic peoples to the north of the Great Wall of China who were a frequent threat to the stability of the Chinese state. (*pron.* shong-noo)

Yellow Turban Rebellion: A major Chinese peasant revolt that began in 184 C.E. and helped cause the fall of the Han dynasty.

ANSWER GUIDELINES FOR CHAPTER QUESTIONS

The two sets of questions that follow appear in the textbook at the end of the chapter and in the margins of the reading. They are also provided in the Computerized Test Bank with answer guidelines, for your convenience.

The Big Picture Questions

1. What common features can you identify in the empires described in this chapter?

• All empires controlled large areas and populations.
• All empires were brought together by conquest and funded in part by extracting wealth from conquered peoples.
• All empires stimulated the exchange of ideas, cultures, and values amongst the peoples that they conquered.
• All empires sought to foster an imperial identity that transcended more local identities and loyalties.
• All empires ultimately collapsed.

2. In what ways did these empires differ from one another? What accounts for those differences?

• Some empires sought to rule through local elites; other empires sought to rule with a more centralized power structure.
• Some empires were new; others drew on older traditions.
• Some empires lasted for considerably longer periods than others.
• Some empires assimilated conquered peoples more quickly and completely than others.

3. Are you more impressed with the "greatness" of empires or with their destructive and oppressive features? Why?

• This question can reasonably be answered either way.
• Empires were impressive because of the impact they had on regions that they conquered.
• They were impressive because of their sheer size and the number of subjects over which they ruled.
• Their military conquests were often impressive.
• Their monumental architecture, often associated with the promotion of political authority, could be impressive.
• The use of force in the creation of empires offers a strong argument that they were destructive and oppressive.
• Their use of coercion to extract resources, particularly from conquered peoples, also adds to the case for their destructive and oppressive nature.

4. Do you think that the classical empires hold "lessons" for the present, or are contemporary circumstances sufficiently unique as to render the distant past irrelevant?

• This question can be answered successfully from several perspectives, although in order to argue that the classical empires are irrelevant a student would have to deal with the arguments made in the Reflections section.

• A student might focus on the cultural memory of empires being used in the modern world. The Reflections section offers examples of Mao Zedong, the modern Indian nonviolence movement, the British imperial education system, and Mussolini all using the examples of previous empires as models for their own societies.

• As prompted by the opening and closing of the chapter, a student might draw potential lessons for the United States today, especially from the model of Rome, whose conquests led to a political shift from a republican to an imperial political system.

• A student could also argue that basic problems of classical empires, such as overextension and the creation of a unified identity that redefines conquered peoples, are timeless issues that still have relevance today.

Margin Review Questions

Q. *How did Persian and Greek civilizations differ in their political organization and values?*

• The Persians built an imperial political system that drew upon previous Mesopotamian polities, including the Babylonian and Assyrian empires. The Persian Empire was far larger than its predecessors, stretching from Egypt to India, and ruled over some 35 million subjects.

• The Persian system was centered on an elaborate cult of kingship in which the emperor was secluded in royal magnificence and was approachable only through an elaborate ritual.

• Persian emperors were considered absolute in their power and possessed a divine right to rule by the will of the Persian god Ahura Mazda.

• The Persian Empire was ruled through an effective administrative system that placed Persian governors, called *satraps*, in each of twenty-three provinces,

while lower-level officials were drawn from local authorities. This system was monitored by a system of imperial spies.

• Persia's rule of its many conquered peoples was strengthened by a policy of respect for the empire's non-Persian cultural traditions.

• In contrast, Greek political organization was based on hundreds of independent city-states or small settlements of between 500 and 5,000 male citizens.

• The Greeks did not build an empire but did expand through the establishment of colonies around the Mediterranean and Black seas.

• The most distinctive feature of Greek political culture lay in the extent of popular participation in political life that occurred within the city-states. This participation was based on the unique ideas of "citizenship," of free people running the affairs of state, and of equality for all citizens before the law. Political participation in Greek city-states was much wider than in Persia, but it varied considerably between city-states and over time. Early in Greek history, only the wealthy and well-born had the rights of full citizenship, but middle- and lower-class men gradually obtained these rights in some city-states.

• Nowhere was participation universal. The widest participation occurred in Athens beginning in 594 B.C.E., when the reforming leader Solon took Athenian politics in a more democratic direction, breaking the hold of a small group of aristocratic families. Debt slavery was abolished, access to public office was opened to a wider group of men, and all citizens were allowed to take part in the Assembly. Later, all holders of public office were chosen by lot and were paid, so that even the poorest could serve. Athenian democracy was direct rather than representative. Even at its height, it was far from universal, with well over half the population, including women, slaves, and foreigners, excluded from participation.

Q. *Why did semi-democratic governments emerge in some of the Greek city-states?*

• Growing numbers of men were able to afford the armor and weapons that would allow them to serve in the armies of the city-states.

• In many places, dictators known as tyrants emerged for a time, usually with the support of the poorer classes, to challenge the prerogatives of the wealthy. The Athenian leader Solon, who emerged in

594 B.C.E., is a good example of a tyrant. During his rule, he broke the hold on power of a small group of aristocratic families in Athens. At the same time, he abolished debt slavery, increased access to public office to a wider group of men, and allowed all citizens to take part in the Assembly.

Q. *What were the consequences for both sides of the encounter between the Persians and the Greeks?*

• While no doubt embarrassing, the failure of the Persian invasions of Greece had very little impact on the Persian Empire.

• Defeat of the Persian armies was a source of enormous pride for Greece. For the Greeks (especially the Athenians), it confirmed their view that Greek freedoms strengthened their will to fight, while Persia came to represent despotism. This view persisted into the twentieth century in European thinking in the notion of an East/West divide in which Europe (the West) represented freedom and Asia (the East) represented despotism.

• Greek victory radicalized Athenian democracy, because service by poorer Athenians as rowers in the navy placed them in a position to insist on full citizenship. The fifty years following the Greco-Persian Wars were the high point for participation in Athenian democracy.

• The fifty years following the defeat of the Persians also witnessed the Golden Age of Greek (and especially Athenian) culture, a period when monumental buildings like the Parthenon in Athens were built, Greek theatre was born, and Socrates was beginning his career as a philosopher.

• But the Greco-Persian Wars also led to an era of incipient empire. After the war, Athens tried to solidify its dominant position among the Greeks who had allied against Persia, and this led to intense resentment and finally to a bitter civil war known as the Peloponnesian War. Athens was defeated, while the Greeks exhausted themselves and magnified their distrust of one another. This infighting ultimately opened the way for Macedonia to conquer the Greek city-states.

Q. *What changes did Alexander's conquests bring in their wake?*

• Alexander's conquests led to the widespread dissemination of Greek culture into Egypt, Mesopotamia, and India. The major avenue for this spread lay in the many cities established by the Greeks throughout the Hellenistic world.

Q. *How did Rome grow from a single city to the center of a huge empire?*

• The values of the Roman republic, including rule of law, the rights of citizens, absence of pretension, upright moral behavior, and keeping one's word—along with a political system that offered some protection to the lower classes—provided a basis for Rome's empire-building enterprise.

• Victory in the Punic Wars with Carthage (264–146 B.C.E.) extended Roman control over the western Mediterranean and made Rome a naval power.

• As the empire grew, each addition of territory created new vulnerabilities that drove further conquests.

• Poor soldiers hoped for land, loot, or salaries.

• The well-to-do or well-connected gained great estates, earned promotion, and sometimes achieved public acclaim and high political office by participating in empire building.

• The wealth of long-established societies in the eastern Mediterranean spurred Roman conquests, as did the resources and food supplies of the less developed western Mediterranean.

• Rome's central location in the Mediterranean basin made empire building easier.

• Rome's army was a key to its success. It was drawn from the growing population of Italy and was renowned for being well trained, well fed, and well rewarded.

• As the empire grew, so did political support in Rome for its continued expansion. This ensured that the necessary manpower and resources were committed to empire building.

Q. *How and why did the making of the Chinese empire differ from that of the Roman Empire?*

• Unlike the Roman Empire (which was new), the Chinese empire represented an effort to revive an imperial tradition that already existed under the Xia, Shang, and Zhou dynasties. Because of the preexisting imperial tradition in China, the process of creating the empire was quicker, though it was no less reliant on military force and no less brutal than the centuries-long Roman effort.

• Unlike Rome's transition from republic to empire, the creation of the Chinese empire had only brief and superficial domestic repercussions.

Q.   *In comparing the Roman and Chinese empires, which do you find more striking—their similarities or their differences?*

• The Roman and Chinese empires shared many common features, though they did also differ in important ways. In general, the Chinese empire was able to foster greater cultural homogeneity and more centralized political control than did its Roman counterpart.

• Both defined themselves in universal terms.

• Both invested heavily in public works designed to integrate their respective domains militarily and commercially.

• Both invoked supernatural sanctions to support their rule.

• Both absorbed foreign religious traditions, though the process unfolded somewhat differently. In the case of Rome, Christianity was born as a small sect of a small province in a remote corner of the empire. From there, it spread slowly for several centuries, mostly among the poor and lower classes, suffering from intermittent persecution. In the fourth century C.E., it obtained state support from the emperors and thereafter spread quite rapidly, becoming the dominant religious tradition throughout Europe in the centuries after the fall of Rome. In the case of China, Buddhism came from India, far beyond the Chinese world. It was introduced by Central Asian traders and received little support from Chinese rulers until the Sui dynasty emperor Wendi (589–618 C.E.). Even then it became only one of several religious strands in a complex Chinese mix.

• The Roman and Chinese empires also had a different relationship to the societies that they governed. The Romans ruled as a distinct minority within the empire. Over time, the empire did assimilate conquered peoples by granting them Roman citizenship for service to the empire or in recognition of their adoption of Roman culture. In 212 C.E., Roman citizenship was bestowed on all free people of the empire. The Chinese empire, by contrast, grew out of a much larger cultural heartland that was already ethnically Chinese. Moreover, as the Chinese empire expanded to the south, it actively assimilated non-Chinese people.

• The Roman Empire assimilated more cultural traditions, with Roman and Greek culture freely mixing and other non-Roman cultural traditions—including the cult of the Persian god Mithra, the cult of the Egyptian goddess Isis, and the Judaism-derived religion of

Christianity—spreading throughout the empire. In China, with the exception of Buddhism, Chinese culture was widely recognized as the model to which others should conform. It experienced little competition from an older, venerated, or foreign tradition.

• Language served the two empires in important but contrasting ways. Latin, an alphabetic language depicting sounds, gave rise to distinctive languages—Spanish, Portuguese, French, Italian, Romanian. Chinese did not, in part because Chinese written characters, which represented words or ideas more than sounds, were not easily transferable to other languages. But written Chinese could be understood by all literate people no matter which spoken dialect of the language they used. So Chinese, more than Latin, served as an instrument of elite assimilation.

• Politically, both empires established effective centralized control over vast regions and huge populations. But the Chinese, far more than the Romans, developed an elaborate bureaucracy to hold the empire together. The Chinese relied on a civil service system, complete with examinations and selection by merit; the Romans relied more on regional elites and the army to provide cohesion. The Romans, though, unlike the Chinese, developed an elaborate body of law applicable equally to all people of the realm.

Q.   *How did the collapse of empire play out differently in the Roman world and in China?*

• While the Han Empire came to an end in 220 C.E., only the western half of the Roman Empire collapsed, leaving the eastern half (subsequently known as the Byzantine Empire) to maintain the tradition of imperial Rome for another thousand years.

• Nomadic or semi-agricultural peoples occupying the frontier regions of both empires became growing threats that ultimately conquered portions of both empires. However, the nomads who successfully invaded and settled in north China assimilated culturally, while the nomads who invaded and settled in Western Europe developed their own ethnic identities, even as they drew on Roman law and adopted Roman Christianity. Thus, the collapse of the western portion of the Roman Empire produced greater cultural changes that ultimately provided the foundation for the hybrid Latin and Germanic civilization that would arise in Western Europe.

• The most significant difference between the collapse of the Roman world and the Chinese world is that, after 350 years, a Chinese imperial state was reassembled under the Sui (589–618 C.E.), Tang (618–907 C.E.), and Song (960–1279 C.E.) dynasties. In the western part of the Roman Empire, no large-scale, centralized, imperial authority, encompassing all of Western Europe, has ever been successfully reestablished for any length of time.

Q. *Why were centralized empires so much less prominent in India than in China?*

• Indian empires failed to command the kind of loyalty or exercise the degree of influence that Chinese empires did.

• India's unparalleled cultural diversity made a centralized empire less easy to construct than in more culturally united China.

• The frequency of invasions from Central Asia in comparison to China also made centralized empire less likely, because Indian states, which otherwise might have provided the nucleus for an all-India empire, were repeatedly smashed by invaders.

• In contrast to the situation in China, India's social structure, embodied in a caste system linked to occupational groups, made for intensely local loyalties at the expense of wider identities that might have fostered empires.

ADDITIONAL RESOURCES FOR CHAPTER 4

Additional Bedford/St. Martin's Resources

FOR INSTRUCTORS

Computerized Test Bank

This test bank provides over thirty exercises per chapter, including multiple-choice, fill-in-the-blank, short-answer, and full-length essay questions. Instructors can customize quizzes, add or edit both questions and answers, and export questions and answers to a variety of formats, including WebCT and Blackboard. The disc includes correct answers and essay outlines.

Instructor's Resource CD-ROM

This disc provides instructors with ready-made and customizable PowerPoint multimedia presentations built around chapter outlines, maps, figures, and all images from the textbook, plus JPEG versions of all maps, figures, and images.

The following maps and images from Chapter 4 are available in both JPEG and PowerPoint format on the Instructor's Resource CD-ROM:

• Map 4.1: The Persian Empire (p. 100)
• Map 4.2: Classical Greece (p. 102)
• Map 4.3: Alexander's Empire and Successor States (p. 106)
• Map 4.4: The Roman Empire (p. 110)
• Map 4.5: Classical China (p. 113)
• Map 4.6: Empire in South Asia (p. 120)
• China's Terra-Cotta Army (p. 96)
• Persepolis (p. 101)
• Alexander the Great (p. 107)
• Queen Boudica (p. 112)
• Meeting of Attila and Pope Leo I (p. 118)
• Ashoka of India (p. 121)

FOR STUDENTS

Documents and Essays from *Worlds of History: A Comparative Reader,* Third Edition

The following documents, essays, and illustrations to accompany Chapter 4 are available in Chapter 4 of this reader by Kevin Reilly:

• S. A. M. Adshead, "China and Rome Compared" from *China in World History*
• Confucius, from *The Analects*
• Plutarch, "On Education"
• G. E. R. Lloyd, "Chinese and Greco-Roman Innovation"
• "The Salt and Iron Debates"
• Cicero, "Against Verres"

Online Study Guide at bedfordstmartins.com/strayer

The Online Study Guide helps students synthesize the material from the text as well as practice the skills historians use to make sense of the past. Each chapter of the Online Study Guide contains specific testing exercises, including a multiple-choice self-test that focuses on important conceptual ideas; an identification quiz that helps students remember key people, places, and events; a flashcard activity that tests students on their knowledge of key terms; and two interactive map activities intended to strengthen students' geographic skills. Instructors can monitor students' progress through an online Quiz Gradebook or receive email updates.

Further Reading

Alexander the Great on the Web, http://www.isidore-of-seville.com/alexander/. An excellent collection of Web links for, and information about, Alexander the Great.

Allen, Lindsay. *The Persian Empire*. Chicago: University of Chicago Press, 2005.

The Ancient City of Athens, http://www.stoa.org/athens/. This is a great photographic archive of the remains of ancient Athens.

De Imperatoribus Romanis: An Online Encyclopedia of Roman Rulers and Their Families, http://www.roman-emperors.org/. An excellent site that includes many good images of Roman emperors.

East & Southeast Asia: An Annotated Directory of Internet Resources, http://newton.uor.edu/Departments&Programs/AsianStudiesDept/. This useful page provides links to anything you are likely to want to know about China and the states of Southeast Asia.

Gabriel, Richard A., and Karen S. Metz. *From Sumer to Rome: The Military Capabilities of Ancient Armies*. Westport, CT: Greenwood Press, 1991. Full of useful facts about the military establishment of early empires.

India: Internet Resources, http://www.wsu.edu/~dee/INDINRES.HTM. This site includes a large number of links to information on Indian history and culture.

Persepolis: Ancient Capital of the Achaemenian Kings, http://www.art-arena.com/persepolis.htm. A photographic tour of the city of Persepolis.

Twitchett, Denis, and Michael Loewe, eds. *The Cambridge History of China*. Vol. 1, *The Ch'in and Han Empires, 221 BC–AD 220*. Cambridge: Cambridge University Press, 1986. A comprehensive study of Qin and Han China.

Warry, John. *Alexander 334–323 BC: Conquest of the Persian Empire*. London: Osprey, 1991.

Literature

There is a very large assortment of ancient Greek and Roman literature available in translation and published in inexpensive editions by Penguin and Oxford World Classics. The following list includes only a few suggestions.

Aristotle. *The Athenian Constitution*. Trans. P. J. Rhodes. Middlesex: Penguin, 1984. Although written in the second half of the fourth century B.C.E., this treatise includes much valuable information about democracy in Athens's Golden Age.

Ashoka. *The Edicts of King Ashoka*. Trans. Ven. S. Dhammika. http://www.cs.colostate.edu/~malaiya/ashoka.html. The Mauryan emperor Ashoka had these edicts carved on rocks and pillars throughout his empire. They express his attempt to establish a nonviolent empire ruled by *dharma*.

Crump, James, ed. and trans. *Legends of the Warring States: Persuasions, Romances, and Stories from Chan-kuo Ts'e*. Ann Arbor, MI: Center for Chinese Studies, 1998. These selections brilliantly demonstrate China's longing for unity and political order during the Warring States period.

Herodotus. *The Histories*. Trans. Aubrey de Selincourt. London: Penguin, 2003. A magnificent view of the Persian Wars and a treasure trove of information about Greek attitudes in the fifth century B.C.E. by the "father of history."

Juvenal. *The Satires*. Trans. Niall Rudd. Oxford: Oxford World Classics, 1999. A text that works very well, especially with honors sections, the *Satires* are a racy look at life in the early Roman Empire.

Kalidasa. *The Recognition of Sakuntala*. Trans. W. J. Johnson. Oxford: Oxford World Classics, 2001. This is

India's first great dramatic work, telling of romance between a king and the daughter of an ascetic.

Plutarch. *Fall of the Roman Republic.* Trans. Rex Warner. Middlesex: Penguin, 1958. Biographies of great figures of the first century B.C.E., such as Julius Caesar and Cicero, that tend to work well with classes.

Sima Qian. *Records of the Grand Historian: Qin Dynasty.* Trans. Burton Watson. 3rd ed. Columbia: Columbia University Press, 1995. Sima Qian became Wudi's official historian in 108 B.C.E.; his work is an outstanding source for the Qin and early Han dynasties.

Suetonius. *The Twelve Caesars.* Trans. Robert Graves. London: Penguin, 2003. These early second-century C.E. biographies are among our best sources for the early Roman Empire.

Tacitus. *The Agricola and the Germania.* Trans. H. Mattingly. Middlesex: Penguin, 1971. The *Agricola* tells the story of Rome's final conquest of Britain; the *Germania* is a romanticized view of life beyond the Roman border, advocating a return to old Roman morality.

Thucydides. *Peloponnesian War.* Trans. Rex Warner. Middlesex: Penguin, 1954. A deeply insightful history of Athens's hubris and its destruction in the Peloponnesian War, written by an Athenian general in exile.

Film

Empire: The Romans. Four-part series. Discovery Channel, 2003. 46–52 minutes each. Focuses on all aspects of the Roman Empire, from high politics to the everyday life of soldiers and citizens.

Empires: The Greeks: Crucible of Civilization. Three-part series. PBS Home Video, 2000. 50 minutes each. Examines the rise and decline of classical Greece with particular emphasis on Athens.

The Immortal Emperor: Shihuangdi. BBC, 1996. 50 minutes. Uses Shihuangdi's famous tomb to examine the political, philosophical, and religious structure of Chinese society during the Qin dynasty.

Maurya. Insight Media, 1998. 26 minutes. Explores the Mauryan Empire with particular emphasis on its army.

The Search for Alexander the Great. Four-part series. Time-Life Video, 1981. 60 minutes each. Explores the life of Alexander the Great and the creation of the Hellenistic Empire.

Eurasian Cultural Traditions
500 B.C.E.–500 C.E.

CHAPTER OVERVIEW

Chapter Objectives

• To point out the enormous influence on world history of the religious and cultural traditions developed in the classical world

• To examine the reasons behind the development of these religious and cultural traditions

• To consider the common ground and significant differences between these religious and cultural traditions and examine possible reasons behind them

Chapter Outline

I. **Opening Vignette**
   A. In 2004, China celebrated the 2,555th birthday of Confucius, despite Communism.
      1. Buddhism and Christianity also growing rapidly in China
      2. part of enduring legacy of the classical world
   B. In the period around 500 B.C.E., there was a great emergence of durable cultural traditions that have shaped the world ever since. **[see Classroom Activity 1]**
      1. China: Kong Fuzi (Confucius) and Laozi
      2. India: *Upanishads* defined Hinduism
         a. Siddhartha Gautama founded Buddhism
      3. Middle East: development of monotheism
         a. Persia: Zoroastrianism (prophet Zarathustra)

b. Israel: Judaism (prophets such as Isaiah)
      4. Greece: rational humanism (Socrates, Plato, Aristotle, et al.)
      5. all sought an alternative to polytheism, placating of gods through ritual and sacrifice
         a. quest for source of order and meaning in the universe
         b. guide humans to personal moral or spiritual transformation (especially development of compassion)
         c. the questions they pose still trouble and inspire humankind
         d. they defined their distinctive cultures
   C. Why did all these traditions emerge at about the same time? **[see Classroom Activity 2]**
      1. some historians point to major social changes
         a. iron-age technology led to higher productivity and deadlier war
         b. growing cities, increasing commerce
         c. emergence of new states and empires
         d. new contacts between civilizations
      2. it's a mystery why particular societies developed particular answers

II. **China and the Search for Order** [see Lecture Strategy 1 and Discussion Topic 2]
   A. China had a state-building tradition that went back to around 2000 B.C.E.
      1. idea of Mandate of Heaven was established by 1122 B.C.E. (foundation of the Zhou dynasty)

2. breakdown into the chaos of the "age of warring states" (403–221 B.C.E.)
    a. chaos made the quest for order urgent
A. The Legalist Answer
    1. Han Feizi was a leading Legalist philosopher
    2. principle: strict rules, clearly defined and strictly enforced, are the answer to disorder
    3. pessimistic view of human nature; only the state can act in people's long-term interest
    4. promotion of farmers and soldiers, who performed the only essential functions in society
    5. Legalism inspired the Qin dynasty reunification of China
        a. the philosophy was discredited by Qin brutality
B. The Confucian Answer
    1. Confucius (551–479 B.C.E.) was an educated, ambitious aristocrat
        a. spent much of life looking for a political position to put his ideas into practice
        b. Confucius's ideas had enormous impact on China and the rest of East Asia
        c. his teachings were collected by students as the *Analects*
        d. elaboration and commentary on his ideas by later scholars, creating Confucianism as a body of thought
    2. principle: the moral example of superiors is the answer to disorder
        a. society consists of unequal relationships
        b. duty of the superior member to be sincere and benevolent
        c. will inspire deference and obedience from the inferior member
    3. humans have capacity for improvement: education is the key
        a. advocated a broad liberal arts education
        b. application of liberal arts education to government problems
        c. need for ritual and ceremonies
    4. after Legalism was discredited, Confucianism became the official ideology of the Chinese state
        a. Confucianism became central part of education system in the Han dynasty
    5. the family as a model for political life, with focus on filial piety

    a. defined role of women as being humble, serving husbands
    b. woman writer Ban Zhao (45–116 C.E.): *Lessons for Women*
    6. emphasized the great importance of history
        a. ideal good society was a past golden age
        b. "superior men" had outstanding moral character and intellect; not just aristocrats
            i. added a "democratic" element: poor boys could rise through talent and education
            ii. modest social mobility
        c. created expectations for government: emperors to keep taxes low, give justice, and provide for material needs
    7. Confucianism was nonreligious in character
        a. emphasis was practical, focused on this world
        b. did not deny existence of gods and spirits, but the educated elite had little to do with them
C. The Daoist Answer
    1. associated with the legendary Laozi (sixth century B.C.E.), author of the *Daodejing* (*The Way and Its Power*)
        a. Daoist ideas later spelled out more clearly by Zhuangzi (369–286 B.C.E.)
    2. Daoism was in many ways the opposite of Confucianism
        a. education and striving for improvement was artificial and useless
        b. urged withdrawal into the world of nature
    3. central concept: *dao*: the way of nature, the underlying principle that governs all natural phenomena
        a. encouraged simple living, disengagement from public life
    4. elite Chinese often regarded Daoism as a complement to Confucianism
        a. helped by the concept of yin and yang (the unity of opposites)
    5. Daoism entered popular religion
        a. sought to tap the power of the dao for practical purposes (magic, the quest for immortality)

      b. provided the ideology for peasant rebellions (e.g., Yellow Turbans)

III. Cultural Traditions of Classical India

  A. Indian cultural development was different

    1. elite culture was enthusiastic about the divine and about spiritual matters

    2. Hinduism (the Indian religious tradition) had no historical founder

      a. developed along with Indian civilization

      b. spread into Southeast Asia, but remained associated with India and the Indians above all

      c. was never a single tradition; "Hinduism" is a term invented by outsiders

  B. South Asian Religion: From Ritual Sacrifice to Philosophical Speculation **[see Discussion Topic 3]**

    1. widely recognized sacred texts provided some common ground within the diversity of Indian culture and religion

    2. the *Vedas* (poems, hymns, prayers, rituals)

      a. compiled by *Brahmins* (priests), transmitted orally

      b. were not written down (in Sanskrit) until around 600 B.C.E.

      c. provide a glimpse of Indian civilization in 1500–600 B.C.E.

      d. role of Brahmins in practicing elaborate ritual sacrifices gave them power and wealth

        i. Brahmin power generated growing criticism

    3. the *Upanishads* (mystical, philosophical works) developed in response to dissatisfaction with Brahmins

      a. composed between 800 and 400 B.C.E.

      b. probe inner meaning of Vedic sacrifices—introspection

      c. central idea: *Brahman* (the World Soul) as ultimate reality

        i. individual human soul (*atman*) as part of Brahman

        ii. final goal of humans is union with Brahman (*moksha* or "liberation")

        iii. achieving moksha takes many lifetimes

        iv. centrality of rebirth (*samsara*) to Hindu thinking

        v. law of *karma*: reincarnation depends on one's actions

        vi. caste system as a register of spiritual progress

      d. Brahmin priests and especially wandering ascetics spread ideas

  C. The Buddhist Challenge

    1. developed side by side with philosophical Hinduism

    2. Siddhartha Gautama (ca. 566–ca. 486 B.C.E.)

      a. spiritual journey led to "enlightenment" (insight) at age 35

      b. his followers saw him as the Buddha, the Enlightened One

    3. central Buddhist teaching: life is suffering

      a. sorrow's cause is craving for individual fulfillment, attachment to self

      b. "cure" it with modest and moral life, meditation

      c. goal is achievement of enlightenment or *nirvana* (extinguishing of individual identity)

        i. serenity

        ii. immense compassion for all beings

    4. large elements of Hinduism are present in Buddhist teaching

      a. life as an illusion

      b. karma and rebirth

      c. overcoming demands of the ego

      d. practice of meditation

      e. hope for release from the cycle of rebirth

    5. much of Buddhism challenged Hinduism

      a. rejection of Brahmins' religious authority

      b. lack of interest in abstract speculation

      c. need for individuals to take responsibility for their own spiritual development

      d. strong influence of Indian patriarchy

        i. but thousands of women became Buddhist nuns

        ii. position was inferior, but offered more independence than did Hindus

    6. appealed especially to lower castes and women in India

      a. teaching was in local language, not classical Sanskrit

      b. linked to local traditions with establishment of monasteries and *stupas* (shrines with relics of the Buddha)

 c. state support from Ashoka (268–232
 B.C.E.)
 7. the split within Buddhism
  a. early Buddhism (*Theravada*, the Teaching
  of the Elders)
   i. the Buddha was a great teacher, but
   not divine
   ii. set of practices rather than set of
   beliefs
   iii. the gods are relatively unimportant
  b. by early in the Common Era,
  development of *Mahayana* (Great
  Vehicle)
   i. *bodhisattvas* provide help on journey
   to enlightenment
   ii. the Buddha developed divine
   qualities; earlier and future Buddhas
   could offer help in spiritual path
   iii. Buddhism became a popular religion
   of salvation
   iv. winning religious merit through acts
   of piety
 D. Hinduism as a Religion of Duty and
 Devotion
  1. Buddhism was gradually reincorporated
  into Hinduism in India
  2. Mahayana Buddhism in particular spread
  elsewhere in Asia
  3. first millennium C.E.: development of a
  more popular Hinduism
   a. expressed in epic poems, the *Mahabharata* and the *Ramayana*
   b. action in the world and performance of
   caste duties provide a path to liberation
   c. *bhakti* (worship) movement began in
   south India
    i. intense devotion to a particular deity
    ii. Vishnu and Shiva were the most
    popular
    iii. proliferation of gods and goddesses

**IV. Moving toward Monotheism: The Search
 for God in the Middle East**
 A. The radical notion of a single supreme Deity
 developed in Zoroastrianism and Judaism and
 became the basis for both Christianity and
 Islam.
 B. Zoroastrianism
  1. Persian prophet Zarathustra traditionally
  dated to sixth or seventh century B.C.E.

 2. some state support during Achaemenid
 dynasty (558–330 B.C.E.)
 3. single god Ahura Mazda is source of truth,
 light, goodness
  a. cosmic struggle with Angra Mainyu
  (force of evil)
  b. Ahura Mazda will eventually win, aided
  by a final savior
  c. judgment day: restoration of world to
  purity and peace
   i. followers of Ahura Mazda will have
   eternal life in Paradise
   ii. followers of the "Lie" will have
   everlasting punishment
  d. need for the individual to choose good
  or evil
 4. Zoroastrianism did not spread widely
 beyond Persia
  a. Alexander and the Seleucid dynasty
  were disastrous for it
  b. flourished in Parthian (247 B.C.E.–
  226 C.E.) and Sassanid (224– 651 C.E.)
  empires
  c. final decline caused by arrival of Islam;
  some Zoroastrians fled to India, became
  known as Parsis ("Persians")
 5. Jews in the Persian Empire were influenced
 by Zoroastrian ideas
  a. idea of God vs. Satan
  b. idea of a last judgment and bodily
  resurrection
  c. belief in the final defeat of evil, with
  help of a savior (Messiah)
  d. remaking of the world at the end of time
 C. Judaism **[see Lecture Strategy 2]**
  1. developed among the Hebrews, recorded
  in the Old Testament
   a. early tradition of migration to Palestine,
   led by Abraham
   b. early tradition of enslavement in Egypt
   and escape
   c. establishment of state of Israel ca. 1000
   B.C.E.
    i. soon divided into Israel (north) and
    Judah (south)
    ii. precarious existence thanks to great
    empires
    iii. Assyrian conquest of Israel in
    722 B.C.E.

    iv. Babylonian conquest of Judah in 586 B.C.E.

  2. Judean exiles in Babylon retained their cultural identity, returned to homeland

    a. centerpiece of their identity was their unique religious ideas

  3. distinctive conception of God

    a. Yahweh demanded exclusive loyalty

    b. relationship with Yahweh as a covenant (contract)

      i. role as chosen people in return for sole devotion

    c. lofty, transcendent deity—but communication was possible

      i. divine action in the historical process

      ii. transformed into a god of social justice and compassion

  4. foundation for both Christianity and Islam

V. The Cultural Tradition of Classical Greece: The Search for a Rational Order

A. Classical Greece did not create an enduring religious tradition.

  1. system of polytheism, fertility cults, etc. remained

  2. Greek intellectuals abandoned mythological framework

    a. world is a physical reality governed by natural laws

    b. humans can understand those laws

    c. human reason can work out a system for ethical life

  3. perhaps was caused by diversity and incoherence of mythology

    a. intellectual stimulation of great civilizations

    b. possible influence of growing role of law in Athenian political life

B. The Greek Way of Knowing

  1. flourished 600–300 B.C.E. (same time as city-states flourished)

  2. key element: the way questions were asked (argument, logic, questioning of received wisdom)

  3. best example: Socrates (469–399 B.C.E.) of Athens

    a. constant questioning of assumptions

    b. conflict with city authorities over Athenian democracy

    c. accused of corrupting the youth, executed

  4. earliest classical Greek thinkers

    a. applied rational questioning to nature

      i. Thales—water as basic stuff of universe

      ii. Democritus—world made up of atoms

      iii. Pythagoras—mathematical order beneath all

    b. application to medicine

      i. Hippocrates—theory of "humors" that are balanced in a healthy body

  5. application of Greek rationalism to understand human behavior

    a. Herodotus: why did Greeks and Persians fight each other?

    b. Plato (429–348 B.C.E.) outlined design for a good society (*Republic*) led by a "philosopher-king"

    c. Aristotle (384–322 B.C.E.)

      i. student of Plato, teacher of Alexander the Great

      ii. most complete expression of Greek way of knowing

      iii. emphasis on empirical observation

C. The Greek Legacy

  1. many people continued traditional religious beliefs and practices

  2. Greek rationalism spread widely

    a. helped by Roman Empire

    b. Christian theology was expressed in Greek philosophical terms

    c. classical Greek texts preserved in Byzantine Empire

    d. Western Europe: neglect of classical scholarship after fall of Roman Empire

      i. rediscovery beginning in twelfth century

      ii. Greek legacy as central to "Western" civilization

    e. part of Islamic culture

      i. rediscovery in West was largely through Arabic translations

VI. Comparing Jesus and the Buddha [see Lecture Strategy 3]

A. The Lives of the Founders

  1. Gautama was royal, Jesus was from a lower-class family

2. both became spiritual seekers
   a. both were mystics: claimed personal experience of another level of reality
   b. based life's work on their religious experience
3. both were "wisdom teachers"
   a. challenged conventional values
   b. urged renunciation of wealth
   c. stressed love or compassion as the basis of morality
   d. called for personal transformation of their followers
4. important differences
   a. Jesus had Jewish tradition of single personal deity
     i. Gautama largely ignored the supernatural
   b. Jesus' teaching was more social and political than Gautama's
   c. Jesus was active for about three years; Gautama for over forty
   d. Jesus was executed as a criminal; Gautama died of old age

B. Establishing New Religions
1. probably neither intended to create a new religion, but both did
2. followers transformed both into gods
3. how Christianity became a world religion
   a. process began with Paul (10–65 C.E.)
     i. missionary journeys
     ii. inclusion of non-Jews
   b. women had more opportunities (but early years still reflected patriarchy of time)
   c. early converts were typically urban lower class and women
   d. attraction of miracle stories
   e. attraction of Christian care for each other
4. Roman persecution of Christians as "atheists" for their antagonism to all divine powers except their one god
   a. ended with conversion of Emperor Constantine in early fourth century C.E.
   b. later Roman emperors tried to use Christianity as social glue
   c. Theodosius ordered closure of all polytheistic temples
   d. spread of Christianity throughout Europe, parts of Africa, Middle East, Asia

5. Buddhism: Ashoka's support helped, but Buddhism was never promoted as India's sole religion

C. Creating Institutions
1. Christianity developed a male hierarchical organization to replace early "house churches"
   a. women were excluded from priesthood
   b. concern for uniform doctrine and practice
   c. emergence of bishop of Rome (pope) as dominant leader in Western Europe
     i. eventual split between Catholic and Orthodox branches of Christendom
   d. doctrinal controversies
     i. nature of Jesus
     ii. nature of the Trinity
     iii. series of church councils to define correct views
2. Buddhism clashed over interpretation of the Buddha's teachings
   a. series of councils did not prevent divisions
   b. less sense of "right" and "wrong" than with Christian conflicts
3. Buddhism did not develop an overall church hierarchy
   a. did develop carefully regulated monastic communities

VII. Reflections: Religion and Historians [see Classroom Activity 3]
A. Religion is a sensitive subject for historians, too.
1. for believers, religion goes beyond earthly evidence
B. There are important points of tension between believers and historians.
1. change: religions present selves as timeless, but historians see development over time, as a human phenomenon
2. experience of a divine reality: historians have trouble dealing with believers' experiential claims
   a. need for historians to take spiritual claims seriously
3. which group within a religion is "authentic": historians usually refuse to take sides

C. It can be difficult to reconcile personal religious belief with historical scholarship.

D. Classical religious traditions are enormously important in world history.

USING *WAYS OF THE WORLD* IN THE CLASSROOM

Lecture Strategies

Lecture Strategy 1

"Religion and government."
The purpose of this lecture strategy is to give deeper consideration to the ways in which governments in the ancient world could use religion—and how religion could use government to further its own ends. The main objectives are:

- to consider religion as a tool of state control
- to examine the symbiotic relationship between religions and states, and the reasons why that symbiosis sometimes fails to take place
- to review the material covered in the chapter

Try to avoid excessive cynicism.

Start the class by soliciting points from the students, including:

- Ask students to rate the religious and cultural systems covered in this chapter on a line that ranges from "most closely integrated with the state" to "least closely integrated with the state." This should encourage some discussion in cases of change over time or in cases where a religion did not win state support in one region but did in another.
- Ask students to come up with cases in which they think the religion or cultural system "took advantage of" a state. With luck, this will spark at least some debate, especially for traditions that lack a clear hierarchy or "mastermind" to direct policy, such as Confucianism, Greek rationalism, or Buddhism (don't let the students get away with thinking of any of these traditions as a single corporate entity that is centrally controlled).

Go over some of the advantages of a symbiotic relationship between a religion and a state. Some examples you might find useful are:

- the Roman Empire's adoption of Christianity in the fourth century C.E.
- Hellenistic rulers' patronage of Greek rationalism
- Han support of Confucianism
- Sassanian Persian sponsorship of Zoroastrianism
- Qin support of Legalism
- Israel (during the Monarchy) and Judaism

Lay out (or encourage the students to discuss, if you have a small enough class for interaction) possible reasons *why* states supported a particular religion/cultural tradition in these cases. Then consider some cases of state persecution of a religion/cultural tradition and discuss the common ground between those cases. Some possibilities for consideration:

- Roman persecution of Christians
- Christian persecution of Greco-Roman philosophers (the case of Hypatia of Alexandria is a good example that is easy to research)
- Sassanian Persian persecution of Christians
- Qin persecution of Confucian scholars
- the Seleucid king Antiochus IV Epiphanes' attempt to suppress Judaism

Lecture Strategy 2

"Digging in the past: The hidden roots of the great monotheisms."
The purpose of this lecture strategy is to delve more deeply than the chapter can go into the historical roots of the three great monotheistic religions (Judaism, Christianity, and Islam). It has several objectives:

- to emphasize the point that few ideas in world civ. spring fully developed from nothing
- to review and add further detail to earlier material about the First Civilizations and classical empires
- to explore how religious tradition can be shaped by individual genius (or enlightenment) from diverse strands

This is a topic that must be approached carefully and with sensitivity, but when approached gently it can help teach students the ways of historical analysis without insulting their faith.

The most convenient place to start is with the Hebrews and their wanderings. Abraham is described in Genesis as coming from "Ur of the Chaldeans"—in other words, ancient Mesopotamia. Consider what Hebrew pastoralists would have seen in the states of Mesopotamia and what would have impressed them. It is also important to note that this was a selective process; the Hebrews adopted elements of belief and social organization that resonated with their own beliefs in a highly selective process. Possible points to consider:

- Mesopotamian ziggurats as the inspiration behind the "Tower of Babel"
- the similarity of the Genesis flood story to that told in the *Epic of Gilgamesh* (reading an excerpt from each is a good idea, as is going over handouts of both in class)
- the many points of close kinship between Old Testament law and Mesopotamian law codes like the Code of Hammurabi

Move from there to a discussion of how Jews would have become familiar with Zoroastrianism, asking the class to provide the main points at which Zoroastrianism influenced Judaism.

Finally, consider the large number of cultural influences that were present in Palestine at the beginning of the Common Era. Points to consider:

- the strong influence of Greek rationalism on Judaism
- reaction against Greek rationalism within Judaism (the pharisees)
- Greco-Roman polytheism
- heaps of Greco-Roman mystery religions
- Zoroastrianism
- perhaps some Buddhism
- and, of course, the teachings of Jesus

Lecture Strategy 3

"The rise of Christianity."
If approached carefully, this is a very good topic to introduce issues of social dislocation in cities, hybridization of traditions (in this case, Judaism with Greek rationalism), and the power of emperors (most notably Constantine, Julian the Apostate, and Theodosius the Great). The objectives of this lecture strategy are:

- to examine how Christianity became a major religion in the period between the apostles and around 400 C.E.

- to consider the cultural and social conditions of the Roman Empire
- to engage in a frank discussion of historical method vs. belief

A good place to start is by carefully reminding students of how historians cannot take a stand (in their professional work) on issues of religious truth. It is also useful to point out that the divine is rather beyond scholarship, but that *religion* by contrast is the way human societies have tried to understand the divine and is thus subject to historical analysis. This lecture could be approached in a number of ways. Some points to consider:

- the existence of noncanonical gospels (reading an excerpt from the Gospel of Mary or the Acts of Paul and Thekla can definitely open up discussion)
- the problem that even the canonical gospels were written forty to seventy years after the events described
- how conversion to Christianity worked (rarely with public preaching; usually via friends or relatives who had already converted)
- the atrocious conditions of life in the great cities of the Roman Empire (and the realization that it took Christianity centuries to penetrate deeply into the countryside)
- the problem of sporadic persecution
- the two "great" persecutions under Decius and Diocletian
- the question of whether Constantine converted out of pragmatism or faith
- how much Roman sponsorship of Christianity in the fourth century encouraged conversion
- the case of Julian the Apostate and the effort to stop Christianity
- Theodosius and the edicts against traditional polytheism
- the question of how voluntary the conversion process was for a majority of people in the fourth century

Things to Do in the Classroom

Discussion Topics

1. **Comparison, large or small group.**
"Reflections on Human Love from Mediterranean Civilizations" (Snapshot 5-2).

Snapshot 5-2 (p. 145) includes several statements from different classical cultures on the nature of love. They provide an excellent starting point for students to consider both common ground and differences between the classical cultural systems. Some possible questions to ask:

- Which of the excerpts appeals to you the most?
- Which of the excerpts seems most alien to modern American culture?
- How much do you think each is a reflection of their parent society's cultural system, as outlined in this chapter?

2. **Contextualization, large or small group.** "Disaster and cultural creation."
Encourage students to use material from both Chapter 4 and Chapter 5 to consider in greater depth the suggestion that the great religious/cultural traditions were born from the crucible of disaster, social dislocation, and uncertainty. Possible approaches include making a timeline of the great thinkers whose work is outlined in Chapter 5 and superimposing on it major events, such as:

- the Peloponnesian War
- the creation of the Persian Empire
- the conquests of Alexander the Great
- the Warring States period
- the Roman Empire's conquest of the eastern Mediterranean
- the creation of the Mauryan Empire

3. **Analysis, large or small group.** "The language of religion."
One of the challenges of teaching classical belief systems is the unfamiliar terminology that students must master in order to understand the system. Nowhere is this more difficult than with the Indian religious tradition, where students must come to grip with terms like *Brahman, atman, moksha, samsara,* and *karma* in order to understand the Hindu and Buddhist faiths. A good approach to the mastery of these terms is to place the following sentence on the board and ask students to translate the key terms into their own words: "Through *samsara,* the *atman* seeks *moksha* to escape from the material world and become one with *Brahman,* but the pace of this process depends on *karma.*" A discussion structured around this sentence offers excellent possibilities for helping students compare ideas that they are familiar with to eastern ideas that bear some resemblance to

them—like, for instance, whether "heaven" or "God" can constructively be used in a translation for Brahman. One might also find it useful to use a Buddhist Wheel of Life as a visual "sentence" to explore the basic teachings of the Buddha.

Classroom Activities

1. **Image analysis, large or small group.** Ask students to examine two of the illustrations provided in this chapter, one each from two different cultures, and to discuss

- whether they believe the image expresses in some way the essence of the religion/cultural tradition it illustrates
- whether the artistic tradition followed affects how much meaning they can get from the image
- how the artist of one of the two images would have depicted the scene in the other.

2. **Role-playing exercise, small group.** The class is a group of Ethiopian royal counselors in the third century C.E. Select three groups of students to play the roles of missionaries from Buddhism, Christianity, and Zoroastrianism (this isn't as silly as it may sound, since India had regular trade contact with eastern Africa by this time and the Persian Gulf isn't that far away). Have each group make a short presentation on why the king of Ethiopia should convert to *their* religion, then allow the rest of the class to vote, based on the quality of the presentations.

3. **Clicker question.** Do you believe that the textbook has done a good job outlining the classical religious/cultural traditions in a way that is fair to all of them?

Key Terms

Ahura Mazda: In Zoroastrianism, the good god who rules the world. (*pron.* ah-HOOR-ah MAHZ-dah)
Angra Mainyu: In Zoroastrianism, the evil god, engaged in a cosmic struggle with Ahura Mazda. (*pron.* AHN-grah MINE-you)
Aristotle: A Greek polymath philosopher (384–322 B.C.E.); student of Plato and teacher of Alexander the Great.

atman: The human soul, which in classic Hindu belief seeks union with *Brahman*. (*pron.* AHT-mahn)

Ban Zhao: A major female Confucian author of Han dynasty China (45–116 C.E.) whose works give insight into the implication of Confucian thinking for women. (*pron.* bahn joe)

Bhagavad Gita: A great Hindu epic text, part of the much larger *Mahabharata*, which affirms the performance of caste duties as a path to religious liberation. (*pron.* BAH-gah-vahd GHEE-tah)

bhakti movement: An immensely popular development in Hinduism, advocating intense devotion toward a particular deity. (*pron.* BAHK-tee)

Brahman: The "World Soul" or final reality in upanishadic Hindu belief. (*pron.* BRAH-mahn)

Brahmins: The priestly caste of India. (*pron.* BRAH-min)

Buddhism: The cultural/religious tradition first enunciated by Siddhartha Gautama (the Buddha).

Confucianism: The Chinese philosophy first enunciated by Confucius, advocating the moral example of superiors as the key element of social order.

Confucius (Kong Fuzi): The founder of Confucianism (551–479 B.C.E.); an aristocrat of northern China who proved to be the greatest influence on Chinese culture in its history. (*pron. of Chinese form of name:* kuhng fuh-tzuh)

Constantine: Roman emperor (r. 306–337 C.E.) whose conversion to Christianity paved the way for the triumph of Christianity in Europe.

Daodejing: The central text of Daoism; translated as *The Way and Its Power*. (*pron.* dow-day-jing)

Daoism: A Chinese philosophy/popular religion that advocates simplicity and understanding of the world of nature, founded by the legendary figure Laozi. (*pron.* dow-ism)

filial piety: The honoring of one's ancestors and parents, a key element of Confucianism.

Greek rationalism: A secularizing system of scientific and philosophic thought that developed in classical Greece in the period 600 to 300 B.C.E.; it emphasized the power of education and human reason to understand the world in nonreligious terms.

Hinduism: A word derived from outsiders to describe the vast diversity of indigenous Indian religious traditions.

Hippocrates: A very influential Greek medical theorist (ca. 460–ca. 370 B.C.E.); regarded as the father of medicine.

Isaiah: One of the most important prophets of Judaism, whose teachings show the transformation of the religion in favor of compassion and social justice (eighth century B.C.E.).

Jesus of Nazareth: The prophet/god of Christianity (ca. 4 B.C.E.–ca. 30 C.E.).

Judaism: The monotheistic religion developed by the Hebrews, emphasizing a sole personal god (Yahweh) with concerns for social justice.

karma: In Hinduism, the determining factor of the level at which the individual is reincarnated, based on purity of action and fulfillment of duty in the prior existence.

Laozi: A legendary Chinese philosopher of the sixth century B.C.E.; regarded as the founder of Daoism. (*pron.* low-tzuh)

Legalism: A Chinese philosophy distinguished by an adherence to clear laws with vigorous punishments.

Mahayana: "Great Vehicle," the popular development of Buddhism in the early centuries of the Common Era, which gives a much greater role to supernatural beings and proved to be more popular than original (Theravada) Buddhism. (*pron.* mah-hah-YAH-nah)

moksha: In Hindu belief, liberation from separate existence and union with Brahman. (*pron.* moke-shuh)

nirvana: The end goal of Buddhism, in which individual identity is "extinguished" into a state of serenity and great compassion. (*pron.* neer-VAH-nah)

Plato: A disciple of Socrates whose *Dialogues* convey the teachings of his master while going beyond them to express Plato's own philosophy; lived from 429 to 348 B.C.E.

Pythagoras: A major Greek philosopher (ca. 560–ca. 480 B.C.E.) who believed that an unchanging mathematical order underlies the apparent chaos of the world. (*pron.* pith-AG-or-us)

Saint Paul: The first great popularizer of Christianity (10–65 C.E.).

Siddhartha Gautama (the Buddha): The Indian prince turned ascetic (ca. 566–ca. 486 B.C.E.) who founded Buddhism. (*pron.* sidd-ARTH-uh gow-TAHM-uh)

Socrates: The first great Greek philosopher to turn rationalism toward questions of human existence (469–399 B.C.E.).

Thales of Miletus: A Greek natural philosopher (ca. 624–ca. 547 B.C.E.), noted for his application of reason to astronomy and for his questioning of the fundamental nature of the universe. (*usually pron.* THAY-lees)

Theodosius: Roman emperor (r. 379–395 C.E.) who made Christianity the official religion of the Roman state, banning all polytheistic rituals.

Theravada: "The Teaching of the Elders," the early form of Buddhism according to which the Buddha was a wise teacher but not divine and which emphasizes practices rather than beliefs. (*pron.* THAIR-ah-VAH-dah)

Upanishads: Indian mystical and philosophical works, written between 800 and 400 B.C.E. (*pron.* ooh-PAHN-ish-ahds)

Vedas: The earliest religious texts of India, a collection of ancient poems, hymns, and rituals that were transmitted orally before being written down ca. 600 B.C.E. (*pron.* VAY-dahs)

Warring States period: Period in China from 403 to 221 B.C.E. that was typified by disorder and political chaos.

yin and yang: Expression of the Chinese belief in the unity of opposites.

Zarathustra: A Persian prophet, traditionally dated to the sixth or seventh century B.C.E. (but perhaps much older), who founded Zoroastrianism. (*pron.* zah-rah-THOOS-trah)

Zhuangzi: A Chinese philosopher (369–286 B.C.E.) who spelled out the teachings of Daoism. (*pron.* jwang-tzuh)

Zoroastrianism: Persian monotheistic religion founded by the prophet Zarathustra. (*pron.* zor-oh-AST-ree-an-ism)

ANSWER GUIDELINES FOR CHAPTER QUESTIONS

The two sets of questions that follow appear in the textbook at the end of the chapter and in the margins of the reading. They are also provided in the Computerized Test Bank with answer guidelines, for your convenience.

The Big Picture Questions

1. "Religions are fundamentally alike." Does the material of this chapter support or undermine this idea?

• This question can constructively be answered either way.

• In support of the thesis that religions are fundamentally alike, one could point to influences like that of Zoroastrianism on Judaism, Christianity, and Islam or the influence of Judaism on Christianity and Islam.

• One could also note similarities across traditions like those between Buddhism and Christianity highlighted in the chapter.

• If one wished to emphasize differences, one could point to differences even within cultural traditions, such as the beliefs that separate the Hindu and Buddhist faiths.

• One could also point to important differences across cultural traditions, such as the difference between the conception of God in the Jewish and Christian traditions and Brahman in the Indian tradition or the dao in the Chinese tradition.

• One could also note the difference between Greek and Confucian philosophy and the traditions that focus on the supernatural.

2. Is a secular outlook on the world an essentially modern phenomenon, or does it have precedents in the classical era?

• In answering this question, the philosophical systems of both China and Greece are central.

• In China, Legalism possessed several features of a modern secular political philosophy in its reliance on law and the enforcement of law to secure a stable society.

• Also from the Chinese tradition, the thrust of Confucian teaching was distinctly this-worldly and practical. Confucianism was primarily concerned with human relationships, with effective government, and with social harmony.

• Greek thought, with its emphasis on argument and logic, relentless questioning of received wisdom, confidence in human reason, and enthusiasm for puzzling out the world without much reference to the gods, also provides a precedent for modern secular outlooks on the world.

3. "Religion is a double-edged sword, both supporting and undermining political authority and social elites." How would you support both sides of this statement?

• In answering this question one must deal with the problem of what is and what is not a religion. In doing so, Legalist and Confucian ideas along with

Greek rationalism would have to be placed to one side, although one could note that (like religions) philosophies can both support and threaten political authorities and social elites. Both Legalist and Confucian traditions are largely supportive of political authorities and social elites, while Greek rationalism, as seen in Socrates' death, could threaten the political and social elites.

• In support of political and social authority, one can readily point to individual instances where new and popular religions were adopted by elites. Ashoka's conversion to Buddhism in Mauryan India provides one example, the support of the Achaemenid dynasty for Zoroastrianism another. Finally, the adoption of Christianity by Constantine and the ultimate reinforcement of patriarchy by the Christian church speak to the political and social support that a new religion could provide to established power structures.

• On a more general front, the tendency of several religions to focus the believer's attention away from action in this world also served to support political authority and social elites. This was true of Daoism in China, Buddhism in India, and Christianity in the Roman Empire.

• However, if followed, the teachings of many religions put real constraints on political and social authorities. For instance, Ashoka's adoption of Buddhism limited the scope for his legitimate use of violence, while dictates about the treatment of the poor and the equality of all believers in the Christian faith brought into question the social norms of Roman society.

• Religious leaders could prove subversive to the current system, as the execution of Jesus by the Roman authorities indicates. Also, the teachings of a faith could potentially challenge established authorities. For instance, the strict monotheism practiced by early Christians effectively precluded the worship of Roman gods, which traditionally was seen as a sign of obedience and loyalty to the Roman Empire.

4. How would you define the appeal of the religious/cultural traditions discussed in this chapter? To what groups were they attractive, and why?

• Each religious/cultural tradition was unique in its appeal, but some generalizations can constructively be made.

• Some religious/cultural traditions, including Legalism and Confucianism, found widespread appeal among the elite because they reinforced the established social structure that defined the elites.

• Other traditions, like Buddhism and Christianity, appealed to the lower strata of society because they offered universal salvation to all believers regardless of class or gender.

• Traditions such as Judaism appealed to all strata of one ethnic group because they defined a special relationship between that group and a powerful divine entity.

• However, each cultural and religious tradition explored in this chapter appealed to its adherents because it brought guidance for living along with meaning and order to life.

Margin Review Questions

Q. What different answers to the problem of disorder arose in classical China?

• There were three major schools of thought that emerged from the Warring States period.

• Legalism was a hardheaded practical philosophy based on a rather pessimistic view of human nature that assumed that people were stupid and shortsighted. Supporters of Legalism argued that only the state could act in the long-term interests of society as a whole. They advocated a system of clearly defined laws and rules, strictly enforced through rewards and punishments, as the best means of securing desirable behavior from subjects.

• Confucianism argued that social harmony could only be restored through the moral example of superiors. Confucius emphasized that, because human society (both within the family and in public life) consisted primarily of unequal relationships, social harmony relied on the superior party in these relationships behaving with sincerity, benevolence, and genuine concern for others. Only then would the inferior party be motivated to respond with deference and obedience.

• Daoism provided a third alternative, arguing that disorder stemmed from human actions and that order could return to life if people withdrew from the world of political and social activism and instead aligned themselves with *dao*, the way of nature. In practice, this meant simplicity in living, small self-sufficient communities, limited government, and the abandonment of education and active efforts at self-improvement.

Q. Why has Confucianism been defined as a "humanistic philosophy" rather than a supernatural religion?

• The thrust of Confucian teaching was distinctly this-worldly and practical, concerned with human relationships, with effective government, and with social harmony.

• Confucianism is based on the cultivation of *ren*—translated as human-heartedness, benevolence, goodness, nobility of heart. *Ren* is not achieved through divine intervention but rather is nurtured within the person through personal reflection, education, and a willingness to strive continuously to perfect one's moral character.

• Ritual and ceremonies nurture *ren*, not because of contact with the supernatural but because they convey rules of appropriate behavior in the many and varying circumstances of life.

Q. *How did the Daoist outlook differ from that of Confucianism?*

• Daoists found Confucian emphasis on education and the earnest striving for moral improvement and good government artificial and useless. Instead, Daoists urged withdrawal into the world of nature and encouraged behavior that was spontaneous, individualistic, and natural.

• Daoists turned the spotlight onto the immense realm of nature and its mysterious unfolding patterns, while Confucians focused on the world of human relationships.

Q. *In what ways did the religious traditions of South Asia change over the centuries?*

• It is difficult to generalize about religious tradition in South Asia because of the variety of religious patterns in the region. However, there was a general evolution away from a religion based on external sacrifice and ritual to one of philosophical speculation, and finally to one of devotional worship and detached action in the world.

Q. *In what ways did Buddhism reflect Hindu traditions, and in what ways did it challenge them?*

• Buddhism reflected Hindu traditions in the idea that ordinary life is an illusion, the concepts of karma and rebirth, the goal of overcoming the incessant demands of the ego, the practice of meditation, and the hope for final release from the cycle of rebirth.

• Buddhism challenged Hindu traditions through its rejection of the religious authority of the Brahmins, the lack of interest in abstract speculation about the creation of the world or the existence of gods, and its rejection of the inequalities of a Hindu-based caste system through its belief that neither caste position nor gender was a barrier to enlightenment.

Q. *What is the difference between the Theravada and Mahayana expressions of Buddhism?*

• The Theravada expression was championed by monks and nuns who withdrew from society to devote themselves fully to the quest for nirvana. It portrayed the Buddha as an immensely wise teacher and model, but certainly not divine. It was more psychological than religious, a set of practices rather than a set of beliefs. And the gods, while never completely denied, played little role in assisting believers in their search for enlightenment.

• The Mahayana expression proclaimed that help was available to reach enlightenment. Within this expression, *bodhisattvas*, spiritually developed people who postponed their own entry into nirvana in order to assist those who were still suffering, could help the believer. The Buddha himself could also help. The Buddha became something of a god, and both earlier and future Buddhas were available to offer their help on the path to enlightenment. The Mahayana expression developed elaborate descriptions of these supernatural beings, together with various levels of heavens and hells that ultimately transformed Buddhism into a popular religion of salvation. As part of this development, religious merit leading to salvation might now be earned by acts of piety and devotion, and merit might be transferred to others.

Q. *What new emphases characterized Hinduism as it responded to the challenges of Buddhism?*

• Hinduism emphasized more clearly that action in the world and the detached performance of caste duties might provide a path to salvation.

• Another emphasis was on devotion to one or another of India's many gods and goddesses. One manifestation of this emphasis was the *bhakti* movement, which involved intense adoration of and identification with a particular deity through songs, prayers, and rituals associated with the many cults that emerged throughout India. The most popular deities were Vishnu and Shiva.

Q. *What aspects of Zoroastrianism and Judaism subsequently found a place in Christianity and Islam?*

• Zoroastrian concepts of the conflict between God and an evil counterpart, the notion of a last judgment and resurrected bodies, a belief in the final defeat of evil, the arrival of a savior, and the remaking of the world at the end of time all influenced Judaism. Some of these teachings, especially the concepts of heaven and hell and of a coming savior, also became prominent in Christianity and Islam through this influence on Judaism.

• From Judaism, both Christianity and Islam drew a distinctive conception of the divine as singular, transcendent, personal, separate from nature, engaged in history, and demanding social justice and moral righteousness above sacrifices and rituals.

Q. *What was distinctive about the Jewish religious tradition?*

• Unlike other Mesopotamian peoples, the Jewish people through time came to believe in a single god, whom they called Yahweh.

• The Jews came to understand their relationship with Yahweh as a contract or covenant. In return for their sole devotion and obedience, Yahweh would consider the Jews his chosen people.

• Unlike other gods in Mesopotamia, Yahweh was increasingly seen as a lofty, transcendent deity of utter holiness and purity, set far above the world of nature, which he had created.

• Unlike the impersonal conceptions of ultimate reality found in Daoism and Hinduism, Yahweh was encountered as a divine person with whom people could actively communicate. He was also a god who acted within the historical process.

• Yahweh was also distinctive in that he was transformed from a god of war into a god of social justice and compassion for the poor and marginalized.

Q. *What are the distinctive features of the Greek intellectual tradition?*

• Emphasis on argument and logic
• Relentless questioning of received wisdom
• Confidence in human reason
• Enthusiasm for puzzling out the world without much reference to the gods

Q. *How would you compare the lives and teachings of Jesus and the Buddha? In what different ways did the two religions evolve after the death of their founders?*

• Their backgrounds were very different. Jesus was a rural or small-town worker from a distinctly lower-class family, while Gautama was born into a ruling family and was surrounded by luxury.

• Both became spiritual seekers, mystics in their own traditions, who claimed to have personally experienced another level of reality. Those powerful religious experiences provided the motivation for their life's work and the personal authenticity that attracted their growing band of followers.

• Both were "wisdom teachers," challenging the conventional values of their time, urging the renunciation of wealth, and emphasizing the supreme importance of love or compassion as the basis for a moral life.

• Both called for the personal transformation of their followers.

• Jesus inherited from his Jewish tradition an intense devotion to a single personal deity with whom he was on intimate terms. According to the New Testament, the miracles Jesus performed reflected the power of God available to him as a result of that relationship. The Buddha's original message largely ignored the supernatural, involved no miracles, and taught a path of intense self-effort aimed at ethical living and "mindfulness" as a means of ending suffering.

• Jesus' teachings had a sharper social and more political edge than those of the Buddha.

• Jesus' public life was very brief, probably less than three years compared to over forty years for the Buddha.

• Neither Jesus nor the Buddha probably planned to found new religions.

• Both the Buddha's and Jesus' messages emerged soon after their deaths as separate religions proclaimed to much wider and more inclusive audiences.

• Both the Buddha and Jesus were transformed from teachers into gods by their followers.

• The Christian faith was ultimately promoted as the single legal faith in the Roman Empire. Buddhism, while supported by some rulers, was never promoted to the exclusion of other faiths in India.

• Both Buddhist and Christian followers clashed over interpretation of their respective founder's teachings. However, Buddhist disagreements generally lacked the clear-cut distinctions defined by "right" and "wrong" that Christian disagreements developed.

Q. *In what ways was Christianity transformed in the five centuries following the death of Jesus?*

• Jesus became divine in the eyes of his followers.

• It developed from a small Jewish sect into a world religion that included non-Jews.

• It spread throughout the Roman Empire, first largely among the "lower stratum" of people in the towns and cities, but as it gained in popularity, Roman rulers sought to use its popularity as a glue to hold together a very diverse population in a weakening imperial state.

• In the fourth century, Christianity became the official religion of the Roman Empire, and all polytheistic religions were banned.

• Christianity adopted elements of religious practice in the Roman world as it spread and converted the population.

• It developed a hierarchical organization, with patriarchs, bishops, and priests.

• It ultimately developed a patriarchal, male-dominated clergy.

• It sought unity in matters of doctrine and practice, but ultimately permanent divisions formed.

ADDITIONAL RESOURCES FOR CHAPTER 5

Additional Bedford/St. Martin's Resources

FOR INSTRUCTORS

Computerized Test Bank

This test bank provides over thirty exercises per chapter, including multiple-choice, fill-in-the-blank, short-answer, and full-length essay questions. Instructors can customize quizzes, add or edit both questions and answers, and export questions and answers to a variety of formats, including WebCT and Blackboard. The disc includes correct answers and essay outlines.

Instructor's Resource CD-ROM

This disc provides instructors with ready-made and customizable PowerPoint multimedia presentations built around chapter outlines, maps, figures, and all images from the textbook, plus JPEG versions of all maps, figures, and images.

The following maps and images from Chapter 5 are available in both JPEG and PowerPoint format on the Instructor's Resource CD-ROM:

• Map 5.1: The Spread of Early Christianity and Buddhism (p. 149)
• China's Cultural Traditions (p. 124)
• Filial Piety (p. 129)
• Chinese Landscape Paintings (p. 131)
• Hindu Ascetics (p. 134)
• The Mahabodhi Temple (p. 135)
• Zoroastrian Fire Altar (p. 139)
• *The Death of Socrates* (p. 142)
• Women in the Early Church (p. 147)

FOR STUDENTS

Documents and Essays from *Worlds of History: A Comparative Reader,* Third Edition

The following documents, essays, and illustrations to accompany Chapter 5 are available in Chapter 6 of this reader by Kevin Reilly:

• *Svetasvatara Upanishad*
• Buddhism: *Gotama's Discovery*
• *The Buddha's First Sermon*
• Buddhism and Caste
• The Bible: History, Laws, and Psalms
• The Bible: Prophets and Apocalypse
• Christianity: Jesus According to Matthew

Online Study Guide at bedfordstmartins.com/strayer

The Online Study Guide helps students synthesize the material from the text as well as practice the skills historians use to make sense of the past. Each chapter of the Online Study Guide contains specific testing exercises, including a multiple-choice self-test that focuses on important conceptual ideas; an identification quiz that helps students remember key people, places, and events; a flashcard activity that tests students on their knowledge of key terms; and two interactive map activities intended to strengthen students' geographic skills. Instructors can monitor students' progress through an online Quiz Gradebook or receive email updates.

Further Reading

Berthrong, John H., and Evelyn N. Berthrong. *Confucianism: A Short Introduction*. Oxford: Oneworld, 2000. Part of an excellent series, this volume gives a straightforward overview of Confucian beliefs.

Buddhist Studies WWW Virtual Library, http://www. ciolek.com/WWWVL-Buddhism.html. This top-ranking Web site for Buddhist studies has been in business for over twelve years and includes links to Buddhist texts, doctrine, history, and art.

Cohen, Norman. *Cosmos, Chaos and the World to Come: The Ancient Roots of Apocalyptic Faith*. New Haven: Yale University Press, 1993. A fascinating study of Zoroastrianism and its impact on the world religions.

Fredriksen, Paula. *From Jesus to Christ*. 2nd ed. New Haven: Yale University Press, 2000. An important study of how the authors of the New Testament interpreted Jesus as they established a durable church.

Hindu Traditions, http://www.religiousworlds.com/ hindu.html. Gateway to a number of interesting sites about both historical and contemporary Hinduism.

Jacobs, Louis. *Oxford Concise Companion to the Jewish Religion*. Oxford: Oxford University Press, 1999. A very handy guide to both historic Judaism and to modern practice.

Klostermaier, Klaus K. *Hinduism: A Short History*. Oxford: Oneworld, 2000. A readable, practical study of a complex subject.

Nystrom, Bradley P., and David P. Nystrom. *The History of Christianity: An Introduction*. Boston: McGraw-Hill, 2004. An excellent and readable overview of Christianity.

Reat, Noble Ross. *Buddhism: A History*. Fremont, CA: Jain Publishing Company, 1996. A useful guide to the major developments of Buddhism.

Stark, Rodney. *The Rise of Christianity*. Princeton, NJ: Princeton University Press, 1996. A thought-provoking analysis of why Christianity became a major world religion, from the perspective of modern sociology.

Literature

Confucius. *The Analects*. Trans. D. C. Lau. London: Penguin, 1989. Confucius's teachings, as written down by his disciples.

Lao Tzu (Laozi). *Tao Te Ching*. Trans. D. C. Lau. Harmondsworth: Penguin, 1963. The principal classic of Daoism.

Mascaró, Juan, trans. *The Bhagavad Gita*. London: Penguin, 1962. The most-read section of the *Mahabharata*, with a very powerful presentation of duty and the nature of the divine.

Miller, Robert J., ed. *The Complete Gospels*. San Francisco: HarperSanFrancisco, 1992. A collection of all twenty-one early Christian gospels.

O'Flaherty, Wendy Doniger, trans. *The Rig Veda*. Harmondsworth: Penguin, 1982. This is the oldest of the Vedas, a collection of 108 hymns.

Roebuck, Valerie, trans. *The Upanishads*. Rev. ed. London: Penguin, 2003.

Film

Ashes in the River: Four Religions of India. Five-part series. Films for the Humanities and Sciences, 1995. 50 to 52 minutes each. Includes episodes on Buddhism, Hinduism, and Jainism.

The Birth of a New Religion: Christianity in the First and Second Centuries. Films for the Humanities and Sciences, 1999. 48 minutes. Chronicles the life of Jesus in the context of first-century Judea and the evolution and spread of his message by Paul and other early missionaries.

Buddhism. Insight Media, 1999. 50 minutes. Provides an overview of Buddha and the faith that he founded.

Classical Greek Philosophy. Insight Media, 2004. 51 minutes. Explores core Greek philosophical topics in a brief format.

Confucianism. Films for the Humanities and Sciences, 1996. 56 minutes. Explores Confucianism in the context of Daoism and Buddhism.

Confucius. Insight Media. 1998. 50 minutes. Explores Confucius's life and teaching in the context of China during the Warring States period.

Hinduism. Insight Media, 1999. 55 minutes. Explores the diversity of traditions within Hinduism.

The Roots of Belief: Animism to Abraham, Moses, and Buddha. Films for the Humanities and Sciences, 1998. 51 minutes. Explores the path toward the institutionalization of religious practice in the Jewish and Buddhist traditions.

Trials and Triumphs in Rome: Christianity in the Third and Fourth Centuries. Films for the Humanities and Sciences, 1999. 47 minutes. Explores the establishment of Christianity as the official religion of the Roman Empire.

The Voice of Zarathustra. Insight Media, 1990. 40 minutes. Explains the philosophy of the prophet Zarathustra and examines the tenets of Zoroastrianism.

Eurasian Social Hierarchies
500 B.C.E.–500 C.E.

CHAPTER OVERVIEW

Chapter Objectives

- To explore social structures in classical Eurasia
- To consider what made social structures different in different civilizations
- To explore the nature of classical patriarchy and its variations

Chapter Outline

I. **Opening Vignette**
   A. Caste continues to be central to present-day India.
   B. The period 1750–present has challenged many social structures once thought to be immutable.
      1. series of revolutions destroyed monarchies and class hierarchies
      2. abolition of slavery
      3. women's movement
      4. Gandhi's effort to raise status of "untouchables"
   C. Patterns of inequality generated social tensions during the "second wave" civilizations, too.
      1. were justified and challenged by religious and cultural traditions

   D. Classical civilizations were hierarchical and patriarchal, but they varied in how they organized their societies.

II. **Society and the State in Classical China**
   [see Lecture Strategy 1 and Classroom Activity 1]
   A. Chinese society was more shaped by state actions than were other societies.
      1. immense social prestige and political power of state officials
      2. officials as cultural and social elite
   B. An Elite of Officials
      1. world's first professional civil service
      2. 124 B.C.E.: Wudi established an imperial academy for officials
         a. around 30,000 students by end of Han dynasty
         b. written examinations used to select officials
         c. system lasted until early twentieth century
      3. favored the wealthy, who could educate sons
         a. closeness to the capital, family connections important
         b. it was possible for commoners to rise via education
      4. system developed further in later dynasties
         a. example of Po Chu-I (772–846 C.E.) passing his exam
      5. bureaucrats had great prestige and privileges

C. The Landlord Class
1. by first century B.C.E., small-scale peasant farmers had been displaced by large landowners and tenant farmers
2. state opposed creation of large estates throughout Chinese history, without much success
   a. large landowners could often evade taxes
   b. large landowners sometimes kept independent military forces that could challenge imperial authority
   c. reforms by usurper Wang Mang (r. 8–23 C.E.)
      i. nationalized private estates and distributed them to the landless
      ii. limited amount of land a family could own
      iii. ended private slavery
      iv. reforms collapsed, Wang Mang was assassinated
3. landowner prestige was based on both wealth and prestige of membership in the bureaucracy ("scholar-gentry")
   a. lives of luxury
D. Peasants [see Classroom Activity 2]
1. in Chinese history, most of population have been peasants
   a. some relatively prosperous, some barely surviving
      i. natural disasters
      ii. taxes, state labor, and military service
   b. tenant farmers in Han dynasty owed as much as two-thirds of crop to landowners
      i. some were driven to begging or banditry
2. periodic peasant rebellions
   a. Yellow Turban Rebellion in 184 C.E. provoked by flooding and epidemics
      i. unified by popular Daoism
      ii. effort to create a golden age of equality (the "Great Peace")
   b. peasant revolts devastated the economy and contributed to overthrow of Han dynasty
   c. Chinese peasant movements were often expressed in religious terms
E. Merchants
1. Chinese cultural elite disliked merchants

a. stereotyped as greedy and profiting from work of others
b. seen as a social threat that impoverished others
2. periodic efforts to control merchants
   a. sumptuary laws
   b. forbidden to hold public office
   c. state monopolies on important industries (salt, iron, alcohol)
   d. forced to make loans to the state
3. merchants often prospered anyway
   a. won their way to respectability by purchasing estates or educating their sons
   b. many officials and landlords were willing to work with them

III. **Class and Caste in India**
A. Caste as *Varna*
1. the word "caste" comes from Portuguese word meaning "race" or "purity of blood"
2. caste may have evolved from encounter between Aryans (light-skinned) and natives (dark-skinned)
   a. certainly grew from interaction of culturally diverse peoples
   b. development of economic and social differences between them
   c. economic specialization and culture apparently more important than notions of race
3. ca. 500 B.C.E., there was clear belief that society was divided into four great classes (*varna*), with position determined by birth
   a. three segments of pure Aryans (the "twice-born")
      i. *Brahmins*: priests
      ii. *Ksatriyas*: warriors and rulers
      iii. *Vaisyas*: originally peasants
   b. *Sudras*: native peoples, in very subordinate positions
      i. could not take part in Aryan rituals
      ii. very low value
4. varna theory: the four groups were formed from the body of the god Purusha; immutable
   a. reality: considerable social change in ancient India
   b. frequent conflict between Brahmin and Ksatriya groups

c. absorption of "tribal peoples" within Aryan groups

d. Vaisya varna evolved into business class

e. Sudra varna became peasant farmers

f. creation of untouchables below Sudras

    i. people who did most unclean, polluting work

B. Caste as *Jati*

1. social distinctions based on specific occupations, organized as guilds (*jatis*)

    a. blended with varna system to create full caste system

    b. thousands of jatis as primary cell of social life

    c. each of four great classes divided into many jatis (sub-castes)

2. clearly defined social position

    a. marriage and eating together only permitted within individual's jati

    b. each jati has particular duties, rules, obligations

3. ideas of ritual purity and pollution applied to caste groups

4. inherent inequality supported by idea of *karma, dharma,* and rebirth

    a. birth into a caste determined by good or bad deeds (karma) of a previous life

    b. rebirth in a higher caste is determined by performance of present caste duties (dharma)

5. threat of social ostracism for violating rules of the jati

6. individuals couldn't raise social status, but whole jatis could improve social standing

C. The Functions of Caste

1. caste was very local, so it focused loyalties on a restricted territory

    a. made empire building very difficult

    b. caste as a substitute for the state

2. caste provided some social security and support (care for widows, orphans, the destitute)

3. caste was a means to accommodate migrants and invaders

4. made it easier for the wealthy and powerful to exploit the poor

    a. multitude of castes made organized resistance nearly impossible

IV. **Slavery in the Classical Era: The Case of the Roman Empire** [see Lecture Strategy 2 and Discussion Topic 1]

A. Why did slavery emerge in the First Civilizations? There are various theories:

1. domestication of animals provided a model for human slavery

2. war, patriarchy, and private property ideas encouraged slavery

3. women captured in war were probably the first slaves

4. patriarchal "ownership" of women may have encouraged slavery

B. Slavery and Civilization

1. slavery as "social death": lack of rights or independent personal identity

2. slavery was long-established tradition by the time of Hammurabi (around 1750 B.C.E.)

3. almost all civilizations had some form of slavery

    a. varied considerably over place and time

    b. classical Greece and Rome: manumission was common

    c. Aztec Empire: children of slaves were considered to be free

    d. labor of slaves varied widely

4. minor in China (maybe 1 percent of population)

    a. convicts and their families were earliest slaves

    b. poor peasants sometimes sold their children into slavery

5. India: criminals, debtors, war captives were slaves

    a. largely domestic

    b. religion and law gave some protections

    c. society wasn't economically dependent on slavery

C. The Making of a Slave Society: The Case of Rome

1. Mediterranean/Western civilization: slavery played immense role

    a. Greco-Roman world was a slave society

    b. one-third of population of classical Athens was enslaved

    c. Aristotle: some people are "slaves by nature"

2. at beginning of Common Era, Italy's population was 33 to 40 percent slaves
   a. wealthy Romans owned hundreds or thousands of slaves
   b. people of modest means often owned two or three slaves
3. how people became slaves:
   a. massive enslavement of war prisoners
   b. piracy
   c. long-distance trade for Black Sea, East African, and northwest European slaves
   d. natural reproduction
   e. abandoned/exposed children
4. not associated with a particular ethnic group
5. little serious social critique of slavery, even within Christianity
6. slavery was deeply entrenched in Roman society
   a. slaves did all sorts of work except military service
   b. both highly prestigious and degraded tasks
7. slaves had no legal rights
   a. could not marry legally
   b. if a slave murdered his master, all of the victim's slaves were killed
   c. manumission was common; Roman freedmen became citizens
D. Resistance and Rebellion
   1. cases of mass suicide of war prisoners to avoid slavery
   2. "weapons of the weak": theft, sabotage, poor work, curses
   3. flight
   4. occasional murder of owners
   5. rebellion
      a. most famous was led by Spartacus in 73 B.C.E. **[see Discussion Topic 2]**
         i. attracted perhaps 120,000 rebellious slaves
         ii. eventual military defeat, crucifixion of 6,000 rebels
      b. nothing on similar scale occurred in the West until Haiti in the 1790s
      c. Roman slave rebellions did not attempt to end slavery; participants just wanted freedom for themselves

V. **Comparing Patriarchies of the Classical Era** [see Lecture Strategy 3, Discussion Topic 3, and Classroom Activity 3]
   A. Every human community has created a gender system.
      1. at least since the First Civilizations, the result has been patriarchy
      2. men regarded as superior to women
      3. men had greater legal and property rights
      4. public life as male domain
      5. polygamy was common, with sexual control of females of family
      6. notion that women need male protection and control
      7. patriarchy varied in different civilizations
         a. urbanization and empires restricted women more
      8. interaction of patriarchy and class: greatest restrictions on upper-class women
   B. A Changing Patriarchy: The Case of China
      1. in the Han dynasty, elite ideas became more patriarchal and linked to Confucianism
         a. thinking about pairs of opposites applied in unequal terms
            i. *yang*: masculine, related to Heaven, strength, rationality
            ii. *yin*: feminine, related to Earth, weakness, emotion
         b. men's sphere is public; women's sphere is domestic
         c. "three obediences": woman is subordinated to father, then husband, then son
      2. woman writer Ban Zhao (45–116 C.E.): female inferiority reinforced by birth rituals
      3. subordination wasn't the whole story
         a. a few women had considerable political authority
            i. provoked antifemale hostility from officials
         b. some writers praised virtuous women as wise counselors
         c. honor given to the mothers of sons
            i. significant authority as mother-in-law
         d. **dowry** was regarded as woman's own **property**
         e. **value** of women as textile producers
         f. a **wife** had much higher status than a concubine

4. changes following the collapse of the Han dynasty
   a. cultural influence of nomadic peoples/less restriction
   b. by Tang dynasty (618–907), elite women regarded as capable of handling legal and business affairs, even of riding horses
      i. right of a married daughter to inherit family property
   c. major sign of weakening patriarchy: reign of Empress Wu (r. 690–705 C.E.)
      i. only woman ever to rule China as "emperor"
      ii. worked to improve position of women
      iii. bitterly criticized by Confucians
   d. growing popularity of Daoism opened new women's roles
      i. Daoism encouraged "feminine" virtues of passivity
      ii. often had female priests, nuns, recluses
      iii. establishment of a variety of goddesses
      iv. women also became Buddhist nuns

C. Contrasting Patriarchies in Athens and Sparta
   1. Athens and Sparta were substantially different in views about women
   2. Athens: increasing limitations on women 700–400 B.C.E.
      a. completely excluded from public life
      b. represented by a guardian in law; not even named in court proceedings
      c. Aristotle: position justified in terms of women's natural "inadequacy" compared to males
      d. restricted to the home
         i. within home, lived separately from men
      e. married in mid-teens to men 10–15 years older
      f. role in life: domestic management and bearing sons
      g. land normally passed through male heirs
      h. women could only negotiate small contracts
      i. most notable exception: Aspasia (ca. 470–400 B.C.E.)
         i. mistress of Pericles
         ii. noted for learning and wit
   3. Sparta: militaristic regime very different from Athens
      a. need to counter permanent threat of *helot* rebellion
      b. Spartan male as warrior above all
      c. situation gave women greater freedom
      d. central female task was reproduction
         i. women encouraged to strengthen their bodies
         ii. were not secluded like Athenian women
         iii. married men about their own age (about 18)
      e. men were often preparing for or waging war, so women had larger role in household
   4. Sparta, unlike Athens, discouraged homosexuality
      a. other Greek states approved homoerotic relationships
      b. Greek attitude toward sexual choice was quite casual

VI. **Reflections: Arguing with Solomon and the Buddha**
A. What is more impressive about classical Eurasian civilizations: change or enduring patterns?
   1. Ecclesiastes—basic changelessness and futility of human life
   2. Buddhism—basic impermanence of human life
B. Clearly, some things changed.
   1. Greek conquest of the Persian Empire
   2. unification of the Mediterranean world by the Roman Empire
   3. emergence of Buddhism and Christianity as universal religions
   4. collapse of dynasties, empires, and civilizations
C. But the creations of the classical era have been highly durable.
   1. China's scholar-gentry class
   2. India's caste system
   3. slavery largely unquestioned until nineteenth century
   4. patriarchy has been most fundamental, durable, and taken-for-granted feature of all civilizations
      a. not effectively challenged until twentieth century

b. still shapes lives and thinking of vast majority of people

5. religious and cultural traditions started in the classical age still practiced or honored by hundreds of millions of people

USING *WAYS OF THE WORLD* IN THE CLASSROOM

Lecture Strategies

Lecture Strategy 1

"Popular religion in East and West."
This lecture strategy seeks to draw themes from Chapters 5 and 6 together by exploring issues of popular religion only touched upon in the text. To do so, it focuses upon the comparison of Greco-Roman polytheism and mystery religions to Chinese ancestor worship and Daoism and to Indian popular practices. The objectives are to:

- explore popular religion by comparison to the elite systems described in Chapter 5
- consider what popular religion meant in social, class, and gender terms

A handy place to start is with gods and goddesses. Again, Greco-Roman polytheism is mostly likely to be familiar to your students, so it is a good place to start. Go on from there to consider Hindu polytheism, and then China. Some major issues:

- the gendering of the divine: whether gods or goddesses are associated with various powers (the Indian/Chinese Guan Yin is particularly interesting, since he was transformed over time from a male into a female figure)
- the role of religious festivals in controlling the masses
- the role of holy figures and holy places (the *stupas* of India, which contain relics of the Buddha, are an interesting example)
- the connection (if there is one) between popular religion and elite religious/cultural systems

Lecture Strategy 2

"A closer look at Greco-Roman slavery."
The purpose of this lecture strategy is to develop material provided in the text, allowing a closer look at social issues in the Mediterranean world. Its objectives are to:

- help students imagine their way into a "slave society"
- reinforce the differences (and similarities) between ancient Mediterranean and relatively modern American slavery
- emphasize the difference between the classical Mediterranean society and other classical societies in terms of slavery

A good place to start is with some numbers. Review the figures given in the textbook for the approximate numbers of slaves in classical China, Athens, and Italy. There are many ways to approach this topic:

- Discuss the use of slave labor for major state building projects, and the limitations of that use (e.g., Hadrian's Wall was built by legionaries, and much of the labor on Greek temples was undertaken by free skilled artisans, but Rome had large numbers of state-owned laborers to build aqueducts, palaces, ports, etc.). Compare it to the Chinese use of slaves or "voluntary" peasant labor for major state projects.
- Compare the lot of slave gangs working on *latifundia* or in mines to that of household slaves. Develop with material about Roman mining and productivity.
- Modern conveniences have made domestic servants pretty unnecessary. Discuss what domestic slaves *did*—the portrayals of rich men's slaves standing around looking respectful in the recent miniseries *Rome* give a very false image of the average slave's life.
- It is important to discuss the casual attitude of Greco-Roman society toward sex, and the likelihood that domestic slaves (both female and male) would be sexually used by their masters. Compare to India, where laws existed discouraging such activity, and ask whether the caste system would allow such a degree of sexual freedom.
- Encourage an open discussion of what slavery would be like in a society in which slaves

worked side by side with free people at many crafts and where slaves were not clearly identified by race, clothing, or other markers.

Lecture Strategy 3

"Women . . . and men . . . of the classical world." This lecture strategy requires access to PowerPoint or to another type of image projection system. This lecture strategy has several objectives:

- to sensitize students to the use of images as primary sources
- to deepen students' understanding of the relative position of women and men in the ancient world
- to examine comparatively gender issues in several classical civilizations

A good place to start is ancient Greece, since it's most likely to be familiar to students. Try some of these images/issues:

- the *kouros* figures of Archaic Greece (undraped male figures)
- the caryatids of the Erechtheum (pillars carved in the shape of draped women)
- a scene from the Parthenon Frieze (naked horsemen)
- the Aphrodite of Cnidus (undraped female, Hellenistic)

Be sure to point out the changes in male/female depiction over time. Encourage a discussion of what the different representations of a given time suggest about cultural values (admiration of the male body, female immobility, more open attitude toward the female form in the Hellenistic period).

Once the basis for comparison has been established, do the same for two or three other civilizations discussed in this chapter. The illustrations in the text are a good starting point.

- A convenient site for India is Image India: Indian Sculpture and Temple Ornamentation at members.tripod.com/%7EIMAGE_INDIA/ sculpture.html.
- Art History Resources on the Web: Chinese Art at witcombe.sbc.edu/ARTHchina.html has a good selection of Chinese images.
- For Rome, a good starting point is Art History Resources on the Web: Roman Art at witcombe.sbc.edu/ARTHrome.html.

Encourage discussion of the significance of whether the male or female figure is undraped, the relationship between women and men when both are depicted in an artwork, coloring of male and female figures and what it might mean, and the representation of female deities.

Things to Do in the Classroom

Discussion Topics

1. **Comparison, large or small group.** "Why did empires vary in their approach to slavery?" This is an opportunity to review what Chapter 4 had to say about the empires of the classical age, as well as the religious/cultural systems outlined in Chapter 5. Some possible questions to consider:

- The Mauryan Empire, just like the Roman Empire, was created by conquest, yet it had fewer slaves. Why?
- Classical Greeks prided themselves on their democracy, yet they had nearly as many slaves as the Romans did. What can this teach you about the relationship between or attitudes of the two societies?
- Slavery was relatively unimportant in China. Why?
- Can we draw any general lessons about why slavery flourished in some classical societies but not in others?

2. **Contextualization, large or small group.** "Modern views of Roman slavery." Show a clip from the classic movie *Spartacus* (1960), preferably one in which Spartacus (Kirk Douglas) makes an impassioned speech in favor of liberty. Then ask students to discuss the following questions:

- Do you think the real Spartacus acted this way? Why or why not?
- What did Spartacus want?
- In 1960, what societal influences affected the way the movie was conceived?

3. **Misconception/Difficult Topic, large or small group.** "Only women are 'oppressed' in a patriarchy." It is very easy to see world history as one long history of oppression of women. The textbook provides good examples of how some civilizations were less

oppressive than others, and how there were always exceptions. This is a good starting point for a discussion of patriarchy and social dominance more generally.

- Ask the students to identify common threads of female subordination in the various civilizations covered in this chapter.
- Then ask the students to use these common threads as a starting point to ask the question, "What percentage of the male population do you think suffered similar limitations?" Encourage the students to consider how "free" peasants, commoners, and slaves were. Try to go beyond that to a consideration of how sons were usually subject to their fathers (including in matters such as marriage) and the lot of the poor, whether male or female.

Classroom Activities

1. **Clicker question.** Where would you rather have lived, classical China or classical India?

2. **Role-playing exercise, large or small group.** "Peasant life."
Imagine what life would be like as a peasant in one of the classical civilizations detailed in this chapter.

3. **Close-reading exercise, large or small group.** "Analyzing gender issues."
Distribute a 1–2 page primary source that deals with the issue of gender. Some possible texts are:

   a. a selection from Juvenal, *Satire* 6, available at stoa.org/diotima/anthology/wlgr/wlgr-mensopinions69.shtml (Roman)
   b. Xenophon on men and women, easily found at fordham.edu/halsall/ancient/xenophon-genderroles.html (Greek)
   c. Kautilya on gender issues, available at fordham.edu/halsall/india/kautilya2.html (Indian)
   d. Fu Xuan on women, at academic.brooklyn.cuny.edu/core9/phalsall/texts/c-poet2.html (Chinese)

Review with the class the basic method of close analysis of the reading, using an example from the first few lines of the text you have distributed. Then have the students divide into groups, and ask each group to come up with at least three particular points from the reading that add to their insight on women's position in that culture.

Key Terms

Aspasia: A foreign woman resident in Athens (ca. 470–400 B.C.E.) and partner of the statesman Pericles who was famed for her learning and wit.

Ban Zhao: A Chinese woman writer and court official (45–116 C.E.) whose work provides valuable insight on the position of women in classical China. (*pron.* bahn joe)

Brahmins: The Indian social class of priests. (*pron.* BRAH-min)

caste as varna and jati: The system of social organization in India that has evolved over millennia; it is based on an original division of the populace into four inherited classes (*varna*), with the addition of thousands of social distinctions based on occupation (*jatis*), which became the main cell of social life in India. (*pron.* VAR-nah / JAH-tee)

dharma: In Indian belief, performance of the duties appropriate to an individual's caste; good performance will lead to rebirth in a higher caste.

Greek and Roman slavery: In the Greek and Roman world, slaves were captives from war and piracy (and their descendants), abandoned children, and the victims of long-distance trade; manumission was common. Among the Greeks, household service was the most common form of slavery, but in parts of the Roman state, thousands of slaves were employed under brutal conditions in the mines and on great plantations.

helots: The dependent, semi-enslaved class of ancient Sparta whose social discontent prompted the militarization of Spartan society.

karma: In Indian belief, the force generated by one's behavior in a previous life that decides the level at which an individual will be reborn.

Ksatriya: The Indian social class of warriors and rulers. (*pron.* kshah-TREE-yah)

latifundia: Huge estates operated by slave labor that flourished in parts of the Roman Empire (singular *latifundium*).

Pericles: A prominent and influential statesman of ancient Athens (ca. 495–429 B.C.E.); presided over Athens's Golden Age. (*pron.* PEAR-ih-klees)

"ritual purity" in Indian social practice: In India, the idea that members of higher castes must adhere to strict regulations limiting or forbidding their contact with objects and members of lower castes to preserve their own caste standing and their relationship with the gods.

scholar-gentry class: A term used to describe members of China's landowning families, reflecting their wealth from the land and the privilege that they derived as government officials.

Spartacus: A Roman gladiator who led the most serious slave revolt in Roman history from 73 to 71 B.C.E.).

Sudra: The lowest Indian social class of varna; regarded as servants of their social betters. The Sudra varna eventually included peasant farmers. (*pron.* SHOOD-rah)

the "three obediences": In Chinese Confucian thought, the notion that a woman is permanently subordinate to male control: first that of her father, then of her husband, and finally of her son.

untouchables: An Indian social class that emerged below the Sudras and whose members performed the most unclean and polluting work.

Vaisya: The Indian social class that was originally defined as farmers but eventually comprised merchants. (*pron.* VIESH-yah)

Wang Mang: A Han court official who usurped the throne and ruled from 8 C.E. to 23 C.E.; noted for his reform movement that included the breakup of large estates. (*pron.* wahng mahng)

Wu, Empress: The only female "emperor" in Chinese history (r. 690–705 C.E.), Empress Wu patronized scholarship, worked to elevate the position of women, and provoked a backlash of Confucian misogynist invective.

Wudi: The Chinese emperor (r. 141–87 B.C.E.) who started the Chinese civil service system with the establishment in 124 B.C.E. of an imperial academy for future officials. (*pron.* woo-dee)

Yellow Turban Rebellion: A massive Chinese peasant uprising inspired by Daoist teachings that began in 184 C.E. with the goal of establishing a new golden age of equality and harmony.

ANSWER GUIDELINES FOR CHAPTER QUESTIONS

The two sets of questions that follow appear in the textbook at the end of the chapter and in the margins of the reading. They are also provided in the Computerized Test Bank with answer guidelines, for your convenience.

The Big Picture Questions

1. What is the difference between class and caste?

• Both systems are used to define social hierarchy.

• But the caste system defined social groups more rigidly and with less opportunity for social mobility than in many class-based systems.

• The caste system defined the social order in terms of religious ideas about the creation of the universe more explicitly and more closely than many class-based systems.

2. Why was slavery so much more prominent in Greco-Roman civilization than in India or China?

• There were far more slaves in the Greco-Roman world.

• Slaves played a critical role in the economy of the Greco-Roman civilization.

• Slaves participated in a more diverse array of occupations in the Roman Empire than they did in other classical civilizations—from among the highest and most prestigious positions to the lowest and most degraded ones.

3. What philosophical, religious, or cultural ideas served to legitimate the class and gender inequalities of classical civilizations?

• Every classical system drew on ideas to legitimate class and gender inequalities.

• In China, Confucian philosophy was used to justify both the class system and patriarchy, although peasants successfully used Daoism when rebelling against established authorities.

• Religious beliefs underpinned the caste system in India—where the varnas (the four classes of society) were described as being formed from the body of the god Purusha; where one's current place in the caste system was explained through the concepts of karma and rebirth; and where one's future lives were determined in part by dharma or the fulfillment of one's caste duties.

• Greek rationalism underpinned key ideas about class and gender in the Mediterranean world. Aristotle developed the notion that some people were "slaves by nature" and should be enslaved for their own good and for that of the larger society. This idea helped to justify large-scale slave ownership in classical Athens, where perhaps one-third of the population were slaves, and continued to justify slave ownership in ancient Rome. Greek philosophers, including Aristotle, also provided a set of ideas that justified the exclusion of women from public life and their general subordination to men. According to Aristotle, women were infertile men who were inadequate because they could not generate sperm (which contained the "form" or "soul" of a new human being). From this understanding of women came further ideas, such as that women, like children or domesticated animals, were influenced unduly by instinct and passion and lacked the rationality to take part in public life.

4. "Social inequality was both accepted and resisted in classical civilizations." What evidence might support this statement?

• Support for this statement can be found in the successful maintenance of social structures based on inequality in every classical civilization. Thus one could point to the reality of a slave-based society in the classical Mediterranean world, the caste system in India, or the class system in China.

• Support for this statement can also be found in the philosophical and religious systems of classical civilizations, including Greek rationalism, the Hindu faith, and Confucian philosophy.

• While much resistance in the form of small-scale theft, sabotage, or other acts of defiance have left no historical trace, more dramatic and widespread forms of resistance to social inequality in the form of Spartacus's slave revolt in the Roman Empire or the Yellow Turban peasant rebellion in China show that, when given the chance, those at the bottom end of the social structure could and did oppose the social order.

5. What changes in the patterns of social life of the classical era can you identify? What accounts for these changes?

• The classical era brought no dramatic changes in the social structures of societies. Rather, it brought further strengthening of cultural traditions and institutions that reinforced social inequality and patriarchy.

• Strong states like that of China or Rome served to strengthen social inequality and patriarchy.

• Also underpinning these changes lay the development of classical belief systems, including the caste system in India, Confucian and Legalist philosophies in China, and Greek rationalism in the Mediterranean region.

6. "Cultural and social patterns of civilizations seem to endure longer than the political framework of states and empires." Based on Chapters 4, 5, and 6, would you agree with this statement?

• Chapters 4, 5, and 6 offer much evidence to support this statement.

• Chapter 4 traces the rise and collapse of classical Eurasian empires, none of which survived beyond 550 C.E.

• Meanwhile, Chapter 5 explores the creation of a number of cultural traditions that continue to have relevance and attract followings even today, including Confucian and Daoist ideas from China; Buddhist and Hindu traditions from India; and Zoroastrian, Jewish, Greek rational, and Christian traditions from the Near East and Eastern Mediterranean.

• Moreover, Chapter 6 explores several features of classical social hierarchies that persisted long after the collapse of the classical empires. Key here are the social hierarchy of China, which persisted into the twentieth century, and the caste system of India, which continues to influence Indian society today. Slavery also continued to be a major social phenomenon in many regions into the late nineteenth century. Finally, some elements of patriarchies that evolved during the classical era remain influential today.

Margin Review Questions

Q. *How would you describe the social hierarchy of classical China?*

• At the top of the social hierarchy in China were the emperor's officials, who represented the cultural and social elite.

• Officials were in large part drawn from wealthy landowning families. Despite the efforts of Chinese emperors, landowners remained a central feature of Chinese society, especially since many members of this group also served the emperor as his officials.

• Peasants made up the largest part of the Chinese population. By the first century B.C.E., population growth, taxation, and indebtedness had resulted in many peasants becoming tenant farmers rather than farmers who owned their own land. There was significant differentiation between peasant families; some worked or owned enough land to feed themselves and perhaps sell something at the local market, while others could barely survive.

• The elite in Chinese society possessed a largely negative view of merchants, who were viewed as unproductive people who made a shameful profit by selling the work of others. The authorities made periodic efforts to rein in merchant activity, but despite active discrimination, merchants frequently became quite wealthy, and some tried to achieve respectable elite status by purchasing landed estates and educating their sons to become civil servants.

Q. *What class conflicts disrupted Chinese society?*

• One conflict was between the emperor and wealthy landowners; the emperor worked to limit the accumulation of estates by large landowners, who could potentially threaten his power.

• Another class conflict in Chinese society had elite officials and landowners on one side and peasants on the other. Landowners often extracted high rents of up to two-thirds of the harvest from the peasants who worked the land. Meanwhile, the state required payment of taxes and about a month's labor each year. Particularly after a series of bad harvests, peasants frequently abandoned their land, forming bandit gangs or rising up against their social superiors, as was the case with the Yellow Turban Rebellion, which reached its peak in the 180s C.E.

• A final conflict had landowners and officials on one side and merchants on the other. Merchants did not enjoy a favorable reputation in the eyes of China's cultural elite. They were widely viewed as unproductive and as making a shameful profit from selling the work of others. Merchants were also seen as a social threat, as their ill-gained wealth impoverished others, deprived the state of needed revenues, and fostered resentments. The authorities made periodic efforts to rein in merchant activity, but despite active discrimination, merchants frequently became quite wealthy, and some tried to achieve respectable elite status by purchasing landed estates and educating their sons to become civil servants.

Q. *What set of ideas underlay India's caste-based society?*

• India's caste-based society grew out of the interaction of culturally diverse peoples and the development of economic and social differences between them.

• By 500 B.C.E., there was a clear belief that society was organized into four great classes (*varnas*), with one's position in this system determined by birth.

• Three classes were pure Aryans: the *Brahmins* (priests); the *Ksatriyas* (warriors and rulers); and the *Vaisyas* (peasants).

• The final class was not of Aryan heritage and was known as the *Sudras*; they were native peoples who served in very subordinate positions.

• According to varna theory, the four segments were formed from the body of the god Purusha and were immutable.

• In reality, there was considerable social change in ancient India. For instance, the Vaisya varna developed into a merchant class, while the Sudra varna became the peasants. A new group known as the untouchables emerged below the Sudras; they undertook the most polluting and unclean tasks.

• As the varna system took shape, another system of occupationally based groups known as *jatis* emerged and blended with the varna system. The jatis became the primary cell of social life in India beyond the family or household. Each jati was associated with one of the great classes or with the untouchables. Within a particular village or region, the jatis were ranked in a hierarchy. Each jati was associated with a particular set of duties, rules, and obligations that defined its members' position in the wider society.

Q. *What is the difference between varna and jati as expressions of classical India's caste system?*

• The varna system was older. It provided broad categories in a social hierarchy that explained social inequality.

• The jatis were occupationally based groups that split the varnas and the untouchables into thousands of smaller social groupings based on occupation. Jatis became the primary cells of social life in India beyond the family or household. Each jati was associated with one of the great classes or with the untouchables. Marriage and eating together were permitted only within one's own jati, and each jati was associated with its own particular set of duties, rules, and obligations, which defined its members' unique and separate place in the larger society.

Q. *How did India's caste system differ from China's class system?*

• India's caste system gave priority to religious status and ritual purity, while China elevated political officials to the highest of elite positions.

• The caste system divided Indian society into a vast number of distinctive social groups compared to the broader categories of Chinese society.

• The caste system defined social groups far more rigidly and with even less opportunity for social mobility than did China's class system.

Q. *How did the inequalities of slavery differ from those of caste?*

• Slaves possessed the status of outsiders, whereas each jati possessed a recognized position in the social hierarchy.

• Slaves were owned and sold, unlike members of the caste system.

• Slaves worked without pay, unlike members of the caste system.

• Slaves lacked any rights or independent personal identity, unlike individuals in the caste system.

• In some traditions, slaves could transform their status by being freed by their master or by purchasing their freedom. Also in some traditions, children of slaves were considered free at birth. These traditions offered more opportunities for social mobility than did the caste system.

Q. *How did Greco-Roman slavery differ from that of other classical civilizations?*

• Greco-Roman society depended more upon slaves than did other classical civilizations.

• There were far more slaves in the Greco-Roman world than in other classical civilizations.

• Slaves participated in a greater number and range of occupations than other classical civilizations, from the highest and most prestigious positions to the lowest and most degraded. Slaves were excluded only from military service.

Q. *In what ways did the expression of Chinese patriarchy change over time, and why did it change?*

• Long-established patterns of thinking in terms of pairs of opposites were now described in gendered and unequal terms, with the superior symbol of *yang* (associated with heaven, rulers, strength, rationality, and light) viewed as masculine and *yin* (associated with the earth, subjects, weakness, emotion, and darkness) viewed as feminine.

• Thinkers emphasized the distinction between the public and political roles of men and the private domain of women.

• The idea of the "three obediences" was also emphasized; it described a woman's subordination first to her father, then to her husband, and finally to her son.

• The Chinese woman writer Ban Zhao recorded how women were taught from birth that they were inferior and subordinated to men and should be passive and subservient in their relations with men.

• Emerging Confucian ideology played an important role in the evolving ideas about patriarchy in Chinese society.

Q. *How did the patriarchies of Athens and Sparta differ from each other?*

• Athens placed increasing limitations on women between 700 and 400 B.C.E.

• Athens completely excluded women from public life.

• Athens required that women be represented by a guardian in legal matters, and women were not even referred to by name in court proceedings.

• Athens restricted women to the home, where they lived separately from men.

• In Athens, marriage customarily saw a woman in her mid-teens marry a man ten to fifteen years her senior.

• In Athens, land passed through male heirs.

• Spartan women possessed more freedom.

• Sparta's fear of helot rebellion meant that great value was placed on male warriors.

• In this context, the central task for women in Spartan society was reproduction—specifically, the bearing of strong healthy sons.

• To secure strong sons, women were encouraged to strengthen their bodies, and they even participated in public sporting events.

• Spartan women were not secluded or segregated like their Athenian counterparts.

• Spartan women married men about their own age, putting the new couple on a more equal basis.

• Men were often engaged in or preparing for war, so women in Sparta had more authority in the household.

• However, as in Athens, women in Sparta lacked any formal public role.

ADDITIONAL RESOURCES FOR CHAPTER 6

Additional Bedford/St. Martin's Resources

FOR INSTRUCTORS

Computerized Test Bank

This test bank provides over thirty exercises per chapter, including multiple-choice, fill-in-the-blank, short-answer, and full-length essay questions. Instructors can customize quizzes, add or edit both questions and answers, and export questions and answers to a variety of formats, including WebCT and Blackboard. The disc includes correct answers and essay outlines.

Instructor's Resource CD-ROM

This disc provides instructors with ready-made and customizable PowerPoint multimedia presentations built around chapter outlines, maps, figures, and all images from the textbook, plus JPEG versions of all maps, figures, and images.

The following maps and images from Chapter 6 are available in both JPEG and PowerPoint format on the Instructor's Resource CD-ROM:

- Indian Society (p. 154)
- Chinese Peasants (p. 159)
- India's Untouchables (p. 161)
- Roman Slavery (p. 167)
- Chinese Women Musicians (p. 171)
- Chinese Women at Work (p. 172)
- Women of Athens (p. 174)
- A Girl of Sparta (p. 176)

FOR STUDENTS

Documents and Essays from *Worlds of History: A Comparative Reader,* Third Edition

The following documents, essays, and illustrations to accompany Chapter 6 are available in Chapter 3 and Chapter 5 of this reader by Kevin Reilly:
From Chapter 3

- William H. McNeill, *Greek and Indian Civilization*
- From the *Rig Veda*: Sacrifice as Creation
- From the Upanishads: Karma and Reincarnation
- From the Upanishads: Brahman and Atman
- From the *Bhagavad Gita*: Caste and Self
- Aristotle, from *The Athenian Constitution: Territorial Sovereignty*
- Thucydides, *The Funeral Oration of Pericles*
- Plato, from *The Republic*

From Chapter 5

- Sarah Shaver Hughes and Brady Hughes, *Women in the Classical era*
- K. Narayan, from *The Ramayana*
- Ban Zhao, *Lessons for Women*
- Aristophanes, from *Lysistrata*
- Livy, *Women Demonstrate against the Oppian Law*
- Fayum Portraits

Online Study Guide at bedfordstmartins.com/strayer

The Online Study Guide helps students synthesize the material from the text as well as practice the skills historians use to make sense of the past. Each chapter of the Online Study Guide contains specific testing exercises, including a multiple-choice self-test that focuses on important conceptual ideas; an identification quiz that helps students remember key people, places, and events; a flashcard activity that tests students on their knowledge of key terms; and two interactive map activities intended to strengthen students' geographic skills. Instructors can monitor students' progress through an online Quiz Gradebook or receive email updates.

Further Reading

Ancient India: Contents, http://www.wsu.edu:8080/~dee/ANCINDIA/CONTENTS.HTM. Links to useful resources.

Bradley, K. R. *Slaves and Masters in the Roman Empire: A Study in Social Control.* New York: Oxford University Press, 1987. An in-depth look at Rome as a "slave society."

Desika Char, S. V. *Caste, Religion, and Country: A View of Ancient and Medieval India*. New Delhi: Orient Longman, 1993. An interesting study of the interaction of caste and religion in India.

Gross, Susan Hill. *Women in Traditional China: Ancient Times to Modern Reform*. Hudson, WI: G. E. McCuen, 1980. A useful study of the topic.

McKeown, Niall. *The Invention of Ancient Slavery*. London: Duckworth, 2007. A useful short introduction to slavery in the Greco-Roman world.

Pomeroy, Sarah B. *Spartan Women*. Oxford: Oxford University Press, 2002. A highly readable study whose comparisons shed light on women elsewhere in the Greek world.

Women in the Ancient and Medieval Worlds, http://www.faculty.de.gcsu.edu/~dvess/ids/women/chinawom.html. Links to interesting texts and images regarding Chinese women, compiled by Dr. Deborah Vess.

Literature

Halsall, Paul, ed. *Internet Women's History Sourcebook*. http://www.fordham.edu/halsall/women/womensbook.html. A large number of links to both primary sources and studies of gender issues in history.

Johnson, W. J., trans. *The Sauptikaparvan of the Mahabharata: The Massacre at Night*. Oxford: Oxford World Classics, 1998. This is the tenth book of the *Mahabharata*, famous for its exploration of the role of dharma in Hindu belief.

Juvenal. *The Sixteen Satires*. Trans. Peter Green. 3rd ed. London: Penguin, 1999. An acid look at Roman society, including the issue of slavery.

Petronius. *The Satyricon*. Trans. P. G. Walsh. Oxford: Oxford World Classics, 1999. The only Roman "novel"; the section known as "Trimalchio's Feast" presents a coarse portrait of a Roman freedman and his wife.

Film

Ancient China. Films for the Humanities and Sciences, 1996. 50 minutes. A useful overview that contextualizes China's social structure.

Ancient Civilizations: Greece. Films for the Humanities and Sciences, 1996. 50 minutes. An overview that includes an examination of daily life in Greece.

Ancient India. Films for the Humanities and Sciences, 1996. 48 minutes. A useful overview that examines the Indian caste system in the context of wider social, religious, and political developments.

Gladiators. Insight Media, 1998. 20 minutes. Short introduction to gladiators, their lives, and their sport.

The Surprising History of Rome. Films for the Humanities and Sciences, 2002. 51 minutes. Focuses on daily life in the Roman Empire and is particularly strong on the issue of slavery.

CHAPTER

7

Classical Era Variations:
Africa and the Americas, 500 B.C.E.–1200 C.E.

CHAPTER OVERVIEW

Chapter Objectives

• To make students aware of classical civilizations that evolved outside of the more well-known civilizations of Eurasia
• To explore the development of civilizations in Africa and the Americas
• To consider the factors that make civilizations develop in some regions but not in others
• To raise the possibility of complex civilizations without any recognizable centralized control

Chapter Outline

I.   **Opening Vignette**
  A. Maya language and folkways still survive among about 6 million people.
    1. recent Maya revival
       a. 1994 uprising
  B. Classical-era civilizations aren't just Eurasian.
    1. the Americas: Maya and Moche
    2. Africa: Meroë, Axum, Niger River valley
  C. There are basic similarities in the development of human cultures everywhere.
    1. part of great process of human migration

  2. Agricultural Revolutions took place independently in Eurasia, Africa, and the Americas
  3. resultant development of civilizations
  D. The world's population at the beginning of the Common Era was about 250 million people.
    1. more than 80 percent were in Eurasia
  E. There were important differences between civilizations in different regions.
    1. the Americas lacked nearly all animals suitable for domestication
    2. Africa imported previously domesticated sheep, goats, chickens, horses, camels
    3. metallurgy was less developed in the Americas
    4. writing
       a. limited in the Americas to Mesoamerica; most highly developed among the Maya
       b. in Africa, was confined to north and northeast
    5. fewer and smaller classical civilizations in the Americas and Africa

II. **The African Northeast** [see Classroom Activity 2]
  A. Africa had no common cultural identity in the classical era. **[see Lecture Strategy 1, Discussion Topic 1, and Classroom Activity 1]**

95

1. great environmental variation within the continent
2. enormous size of the continent
3. most distinctive: Africa is the most tropical of world's supercontinents
    a. climate means poorer soils and less productive agriculture
    b. more disease-carrying insects and parasites
4. Africa also shaped by interaction with nearby Eurasia and Arabia
    a. North Africa as part of the Roman Empire
    b. Arabia as source of the domesticated camel

B. Meroë: Continuing a Nile Valley Civilization
1. Nubian civilization was almost as old as Egyptian civilization
    a. constant interaction
    b. remained a distinct civilization
2. with decline of Egypt, Nubian civilization came to focus on Meroë
    a. civilization there flourished 300 B.C.E.–100 C.E.
3. ruled by an all-powerful sacred monarch (usually female)
    a. buried with human sacrifices
4. city of Meroë had craft specialization
    a. ironworking was especially important
5. rural areas had combination of herding and farming
    a. paid tribute to the ruler
    b. farming was based on rainfall, not irrigation
    c. so population was less concentrated on the Nile, less directly controlled by the capital
6. major long-distance trade was the source of much of wealth and military power
    a. had contact with the Mediterranean
    b. also traded to east and west by means of camel caravans
    c. less Egyptian influence than earlier times
        i. new prominence of local lion god Apedemek
        ii. Egyptian writing was replaced by a new Meroitic script
7. decline of Meroë after 100 C.E.
    a. deforestation (too much wood used in iron industry)

b. conquest in 340s C.E. by Axum
c. penetration of Coptic Christianity; Christian dominance for 1,000 years
d. penetration of Islam after about 1300

C. Axum: The Making of a Christian Kingdom
1. Axum was located in present-day Eritrea and northern Ethiopia
2. kingdom's economic foundation was highly productive agriculture
    a. plow-based farming (not reliant on hoe or digging stick like most of Africa)
    b. high production of wheat, barley, millet, teff
3. substantial state emerged by about 50 C.E.
    a. stimulated by Red Sea and Indian Ocean trade (port of Adulis)
    b. commerce taxes were major source of state revenue
4. capital city Axum (in the interior) was center of monumental building
    a. huge stone obelisks (probably mark royal graves)
        i. some over 100 feet tall
    b. town language was Geez, written in South Arabian–derived script
    c. most of rural populace spoke Agaw
    d. capital exerted loose control, mostly collection of tribute
5. Christianity arrived in fourth century C.E.
    a. King Ezana adopted Christianity about the time of Constantine
    b. Coptic Christianity is still the religion of half the region
6. fourth to sixth centuries C.E.: imperial expansion into Meroë and Yemen
    a. reached gates of Mecca by 571
    b. decline followed
        i. soil exhaustion, erosion, deforestation
        ii. rise of Islam altered trade routes
    c. revival of state several centuries later, but further south
7. both Meroë and Axum paralleled Eurasian developments and had direct contact with Mediterranean civilizations

IV. **Along the Niger River: Cities without States**
A. There was major urbanization along the middle stretches of the Niger River between 300 B.C.E. and 900 C.E.

1. migration of peoples from the southern Sahara during long dry period
2. but no evidence of a state structure, either imperial or city-state
3. archeologists have not found evidence of despotic power, widespread war, or deep social inequality (like Indus Valley civilization)

B. Cities like Jenne-jeno were clusters of economically specialized settlements.
   1. iron smithing was earliest and most prestigious occupation
   2. villages of cotton weavers, potters, praise-singers (griots) grew up around central towns
      a. artisan communities became occupational castes
      b. rural populace also specialized (fishing, rice cultivation, etc.)

C. The middle Niger cities were stimulated by a network of West African commerce.

D. Large-scale states emerged in West Africa in the second millennium C.E.
   1. stimulated by trans-Saharan commerce

V. **South of the Equator: The World of Bantu Africa**

A. Movement of Bantu-speaking peoples into Africa south of equator
   1. over time, 400 distinct Bantu languages developed
   2. by the first century C.E., Bantu agriculturalists occupied forest regions of equatorial Africa; some had probably reached East African coast
   3. spread to most of eastern and southern Africa
   4. the movement wasn't a conquest or self-conscious migration

B. Cultural Encounters
   1. Bantu-speaking peoples interacted with established societies
   2. most significant interaction: agricultural Bantu and gathering and hunting peoples
   3. Bantu advantages
      a. numbers: agriculture supports more people
      b. disease: Bantu brought new diseases to people with little immunity
      c. iron

      d. so gathering and hunting peoples were largely displaced, absorbed, eliminated
   4. survival of a few gathering and hunting peoples like the San to modern times
      a. Bantu peoples have preserved some of language and ways of people they displaced
      b. the Batwa (Pygmy) people became "forest specialists" and interacted with the Bantu
   5. Bantu culture changed because of encounter with different peoples
      a. in East Africa, shifted from yam-based agriculture to grains
         i. also adopted Southeast Asian crops
   6. Bantu peoples spread their skills and culture through eastern and southern Africa

C. Society and Religion
   1. creation of many distinct societies and cultures in 500–1500 C.E.
      a. Kenya: decision-making by kinship and age structures
      b. Zimbabwe and Lake Victoria region: larger kingdoms
      c. East African coast after 1000 C.E.: rival city-states
      d. development depended on large number of factors
   2. religion placed less emphasis on a remote High God and more on ancestral or nature spirits
      a. sacrifices (especially cattle) to access power of dead ancestors
      b. power of charms was activated by proper rituals
      c. widespread belief in witches
      d. diviners could access world of the supernatural
      e. based on the notion of "continuous revelation": new messages still come from the world beyond
      f. no missionary impulse

VI. **Civilizations of Mesoamerica** [see Lecture Strategy 2]

A. There was a lack of interaction with other major cultures, including with other cultures in the Americas.
   1. development without large domesticated animals or ironworking

2. important civilizations developed in Mesoamerica and the Andes long before Aztec and Inca empires
3. extraordinary diversity of Mesoamerican civilizations
    a. but shared an intensive agricultural technology
    b. shared economies based on market exchange
    c. similar religions
    d. frequent interaction
B. The Maya: Writing and Warfare **[see Lecture Strategy 3]**
    1. Maya ceremonial centers developed as early as 2000 B.C.E. in present-day Guatemala and Yucatán
    2. classical phase of May civilization: 250–900 C.E.
        a. development of advanced mathematical system
        b. elaborate calendars
        c. creation of most elaborate writing system in the Americas **[see Discussion Topic 2]**
        d. large amount of monumental architecture (temples, pyramids, palaces, public plazas)
    3. Maya economy
        a. agriculture had large-scale human engineering (swamp drainage, terracing, water management system)
        b. supported a substantial elite and artisan class
    4. political system of city-states and regional kingdoms was highly fragmented
        a. frequent warfare; capture and sacrifice of prisoners
        b. densely populated urban and ceremonial centers
            i. ruled by "state shamans" who could mediate with divine
            ii. Tikal's population was around 50,000 people, with 50,000 more in hinterland
        c. no city-state ever succeeded in creating a unified empire
    5. rapid collapse in the century after a long-term drought began in 840
        a. population dropped by at least 85 percent

b. elements of Maya culture survived, but not the great cities
c. reasons posited for the collapse:
    i. extremely rapid population growth after 600 C.E. outstripped resources
    ii. political disunity and rivalry prevented a coordinated response to climatic catastrophe
    iii. warfare became more frequent
C. Teotihuacán: America's Greatest City **[see Discussion Topic 3]**
    1. city was begun ca. 150 B.C.E.
    2. by 550 C.E., population was 100,000–200,000
    3. much about Teotihuacán is unknown
    4. city was centrally planned on a gridlike pattern
    5. specialized artisans
    6. little evidence of rulers or of tradition of public inscriptions
        a. may have been ruled by an oligarchy
    7. deep influence on Mesoamerica, especially in 300–600 C.E.
        a. directly administered perhaps 10,000 square miles
        b. influence of Teotihuacán armies spread further
        c. apparently also had diplomatic connections with other areas
        d. trade
        e. copying of Teotihuacán art and architecture
    8. mysterious collapse ca. 650 C.E.
    9. Aztecs named the place Teotihuacán: "city of the gods"
VII. Civilizations of the Andes
A. The rich marine environment possessed an endless supply of seabirds and fish.
    1. most well-known civilization of the region was the Incas
    2. central Peruvian coast was home to one of the First Civilizations: Norte Chico
    3. classical era of Andean civilization is 1000 B.C.E.–1000 C.E.
B. Chavín: A Pan-Andean Religious Movement
    1. numerous ceremonial centers uncovered, dating to 2000–1000 B.C.E.
    2. ca. 900 B.C.E., Chavín de Huántar became focus of a religious movement

a. Chavín de Huántar was in good location along trade routes

b. elaborate temple complex

c. beliefs apparently drew on both desert region and rain forests

d. probably used hallucinogenic San Pedro cactus

3. widespread imitation across Peru and beyond

a. Chavín became a pilgrimage center

4. did not become an empire

5. faded by 200 B.C.E.

C. Moche: A Regional Andean Civilization

1. flourished between about 100 and 800 C.E. along 250 miles of Peru's north coast

2. agriculture based on complex irrigation system

3. rule by warrior-priests

a. some lived on top of huge pyramids

i. Pyramid of the Sun was made of 143 million bricks

b. rituals mediated between humans and gods

c. use of hallucinogenic drugs

d. human sacrifice

e. rulers had elaborate burials

4. superb craftsmanship of elite objects

5. ecological disruption in sixth century C.E. undermined the civilization

6. many other civilizations grew up in the Andes (Nazca, Huari, Chimu)

VIII. North America in the Classical Era: From Chaco to Cahokia

A. "Semi-sedentary" peoples were established in the eastern woodlands of North America, Central America, the Caribbean islands, and the Amazon basin.

1. gathering and hunting peoples still populated much of Americas

B. Pit Houses and Great Houses: The Ancestral Pueblo

1. southwestern North America began maize cultivation in second millennium B.C.E.

a. only became the basis of settled agriculture ca. 600–800 C.E.

b. gradual adaptation of maize to desert environment

2. establishment of permanent villages

a. pit houses in small settlements

b. by 900 C.E., many villages also had larger ceremonial structures (kivas)

3. local trading networks, some long-distance exchange

4. development of larger settlements (pueblos)

a. most spectacular was in Chaco canyon

i. five major pueblos emerged between 860 and 1130 C.E.

ii. about 70 outlying settlements linked to main centers

b. largest "great house" or town (Pueblo Bonito) was five stories high with over 600 rooms

c. hundreds of roads radiated out from Chaco (maybe were a sacred landscape)

5. Chaco was a center for turquoise production

6. warfare increased with extended drought after 1130

7. great houses abandoned by 1200

C. The Mound Builders of the Eastern Woodlands

1. Mississippi River valley: Agricultural Revolution by 2000 B.C.E.

a. agriculture as a supplement to gathering and hunting diet

2. creation of societies marked by large earthen mounds

a. earliest built ca. 2000 B.C.E.

b. most elaborate of mound-building cultures (Hopewell culture) was established between 200 B.C.E. and 400 C.E.

3. Hopewell: large burial mounds and geometric earthworks

a. many artifacts found in them—evidence of extensive trade

b. careful astronomical orientation

4. Cahokia (near present-day St. Louis, MO) flourished between 900 and 1250 C.E.

a. introduction of maize agriculture allowed larger population

b. central mound: terraced pyramid of four levels

i. occupied 15 acres

ii. was over 100 feet high

c. community of about 10,000 people

d. widespread trade network

e. apparently had stratified class system

5. sixteenth-century Europeans encountered similar chiefdom among the Natchez in southwestern Mississippi
   a. paramount chiefs ("Great Suns") lived in luxury
   b. clear social elite
   c. but upper-class people were required to marry commoners
   d. significant military capacity

IX. **Reflections: Deciding What's Important: Balance in World History** [see Classroom Activity 3]
   A. Teachers and writers of world history have to decide what to include.
   B. Several possible standards can be used in decision making:
      1. durability (which would make the Paleolithic section enormous)
      2. change
      3. population (Eurasia, with 80 percent of population, gets more space)
      4. influence (impact of Buddhism, Christianity, and Islam)
      5. the historian's location and audience
         a. What's wrong with being "Eurocentric" with a Western audience?
   C. Historians do not agree on the "proper" balance when teaching world civ.

USING *WAYS OF THE WORLD* IN THE CLASSROOM

Lecture Strategies

Lecture Strategy 1

"How we know: Rewriting African history."
Nearly every year, what we know about the early history of Africa changes. A thirty-year-old textbook, for example, shows no awareness that sub-Saharan Africans had any knowledge of ironworking technology before European contact—the contrast to our current text is obvious. Similarly, the recent discovery of book caches in Timbuktu promises to transform our understanding of medieval West Africa. This lecture strategy calls for some research, but its basic question of

"how do we know" what we now know about African history is a useful introduction to archeological, linguistic, and historical analysis of the formerly "Dark Continent." Its objectives are:

- to give students a basic introduction to archeology and linguistic research in Africa
- to explore how archeologists wrest meaning from physical remains
- to explore what we can know—and what we *can't* know—about complex societies that have left us no written records

A good place to start is with European stereotypes about Africa. Try reading the class some excerpts from Paul du Chaillu's account of his travels in Africa in 1868–1870 (available at fordham.edu/halsall/mod/1870chaillu-africa.html), emphasizing the ways in which du Chaillu assumes European superiority. Go on from that point to discuss how archeology has transformed our understanding but still has to fight stereotypes, using cases like the following (in each of the following cases, any good account includes a section on excavation):

- Great Zimbabwe (and the decades-long argument that it must have been constructed by Europeans)
- the rediscovery of Meroë and Axum (a handy source is the Nubia Salvage Project at oi.uchicago.edu/OI/PROJ/NUB/NUBX92/NUBX92_brochure.html)
- the ongoing excavation of Jenne-jeno (a useful starting point is Jenne-jeno, an Ancient African City, at www.ruf.rice.edu/~anth/arch/brochure/)
- the Nok Culture of Nigeria, whose existence was only recognized in 1943
- how linguists have teased out evidence of cultural change, especially from the many strands of Bantu (see Christopher Ehret, *An African Classical Age*, in the Further Reading section for approaches)

Lecture Strategy 2

"Diversity in the Americas."
This lecture strategy is intended to explore the variety of human experience in the Americas during the classical period. Its objectives are to:

- encourage students to think about the types of culture that developed in the Americas

in relation to the cultures discussed in
Chapters 3–6
- discuss the role of religion in state formation
- explore the various classical-era cultures of the Americas
- explore why only a few small regions developed civilizations, while a few others established agricultural villages

A good way to start a lecture on this topic is to review the stages of social development already seen in Eurasia—from gathering and hunting societies to Neolithic villages, to First Civilizations, to empires. Ask students to schematize, as much as they can, what makes progression to the next step possible or desirable.

Now, apply these lessons to the Americas. Consider the following issues:

- "Neolithic village society": the case of the Ancestral Pueblo. How well does Chaco canyon culture fit the image of Neolithic life laid out in Chapter 2? Discuss not only the important similarities but also the points of difference. A key element is the number of Chaco canyon settlements. Are they better described as a First Civilization, like Sumer or the Indus Valley? Most people would say "no"; discuss the level of sophistication of the Ancestral Pueblo culture as a way to pin down what makes it different from the First Civilizations, such as evidence of social stratification, monumental public works, trade specialization, and written language.
- We already saw two American First Civilizations, those of the Olmecs and Norte Chico. Can the Mound Builders, especially the people of Cahokia, be regarded as having reached a similar stage of social development? Provide more details about the Hopewell and Cahokia people, including the artifacts that have been found in their mounds, the complexity of their geometrical earthworks, the size of the Cahokia pyramids, the settlement patterns around Cahokia, and the evidence available about social stratification.
- "Empires." The Americas did not create any classical-era empires, in the political sense, of the size and scale seen in Eurasia, but they *did* produce areas of broad cultural hegemony that can perhaps be compared to classical-age

Greece. This is a great place to explore the creation of cities—or even empires—in terms of ceremonial or ritual centers. Develop the material the text has provided about Chavín culture, and use it as a starting point to consider *why* urbanization occurred in Mesoamerica and the Andes. Explore theories that American cities originated as cultic space, a view borne out by the centrality of great ritual spaces at Teotihuacán, in Maya cities, and elsewhere.

Lecture Strategy 3

"Life among the Maya."
This lecture strategy allows the instructor to delve more deeply into the most well known and accessible of the cultures covered in this chapter. Its objectives are to:

- give students a sense of the texture of daily life in classical-era Mesoamerica
- provide material for comparison with the more well-known civilizations of Europe
- pose questions about what elements are common to all organized urban life, and what elements are dependent on a particular culture

Images of Maya architecture and art are readily available, so the use of PowerPoint or another image projection system is recommended for this lecture strategy.

This lecture strategy can be approached in a variety of ways. Here are some suggestions:

- give an archeology-based lecture, focusing heavily on interpretation of physical remains that you show to the class
- make your lecture more comparative, contrasting life in a single Maya city (such as Tikal) to a single city of another culture (a readily accessible contrasting city is Pompeii, the Roman town preserved by ash from Mt. Vesuvius's eruption in 79 C.E.)
- put your emphasis on social values, which will give you an opportunity to discuss Maya religion and come to grips with human sacrifice (it is useful to remind students that they have seen other cultures that practiced human sacrifice, and to discuss the theological underpinnings of the practice, using, for example, the Maya creation myth *Popol Vuh*)

Things to Do in the Classroom

Discussion Topics

1. **Misconception/Difficult Topic, large or small group.** "Africa is the 'Dark Continent.'"
Ask students to discuss what they knew about African history before taking this class and where they learned it. Some supplemental questions are:

- Was the history of Africa covered in any detail in high school? junior high? grade school?
- Were they taught any misinformation about classical-era Africa, such as that all Africans lived in tribes or were ignorant of iron technology?
- What do they know about *present-day* Africa? What African issues receive American news coverage?

2. **Comparison, large or small group.** "Maya writing."
Distribute or project an example of Maya glyphs (writing), and ask students to compare it to the ancient writing systems already introduced in Chapter 3. Some questions to ask are:

- How would you rank Maya glyphs on a scale of "difficult" to "easy" compared to systems like hieroglyphs or cuneiform?
- What does the nature of the writing (complex pictographs and symbols representing syllables) suggest to you about who in society would have been able to write?

3. **Contextualization, large or small group.**
"America's great city: Teotihuacán."
Distribute a plan of Teotihuacán to the class (several maps are available online, including one at archaeology .la.asu.edu/teo/intro/citymp1.htm), and ask students to list everything they can tell or surmise about the city's society by studying the map closely. They should note:

- the number of pyramids and the centrality of the Feathered Serpent Pyramid
- the dominance of the central north-south street
- the different sizes of houses, suggesting social hierarchy
- the sheer mass of the place
- the regularity of the layout

With the lack of solid information about Teotihuacán in mind, what conclusions about the society and culture of the city do the students feel can be drawn from their observations?

Classroom Activities

1. **Map analysis, large or small group.** "Establishing African civilizations." Display a *physical* map of Africa. Ask students:

- to identify the location of the major African civilizations covered in this chapter
- to discuss the question of why these civilizations developed where they did, taking into account the physical characteristics of the African landscape

2. **Role-playing exercise, large or small group.** "Indian merchants and the African trade."
You are a merchant from the west coast of India at the time of the Gupta Empire. You are planning a voyage to trade along the eastern coast of Africa. Imagine your way into the challenges involved. You might divide the class into groups and ask students within each group to research:

- the role of monsoons in the Indian Ocean trade
- the sort of goods that would be traded
- what the Indian merchant would encounter in East Africa

3. **Clicker question.** Do you think that the author has struck a good balance so far in his efforts to cover world civilizations?

Key Terms

Ancestral Pueblo: Formerly known as the Anasazi, this people established a mixed agricultural and gathering/hunting society in the southwestern part of North America. (*pron.* PWAY-blow)

Apedemek: The lion god of classical Meroë; his popularity shows a turn away from Egyptian cultural influence. (*pron.* ah-PED-eh-mek)

Axum: Classical-era kingdom of East Africa, in present-day Eritrea and northern Ethiopia; flourished from 100 to 600 C.E. (*pron.* AX-uhm)

Bantu expansion: Gradual migration of Bantu-speaking peoples from their homeland in what is now southern Nigeria and the Cameroons into most of eastern and southern Africa, a process that began around 3000 B.C.E. and continued for several millennia. The agricultural techniques and ironworking technology of Bantu-speaking farmers gave them an advantage over the gathering and hunting peoples they encountered. (*pron.* BAHN-too)

Batwa: Forest-dwelling people of Central Africa who adopted some of the ways of their Bantu neighbors while retaining distinctive features of their own culture; also known as "Pygmies." (*pron.* BAHT-wah)

Cahokia: The dominant center of an important Mississippi valley mound-building culture, located near present-day St. Louis, Missouri; flourished from about 900 to 1250 C.E. (*pron.* cah-HOKE-ee-ah)

Chaco Phenomenon: Name given to a major process of settlement and societal organization that occurred in the period 860–1130 C.E. among the peoples of Chaco canyon, in what is now northwestern New Mexico; the society formed is notable for its settlement in large pueblos and for the building of hundreds of miles of roads (the purpose of which is not known). (*pron.* CHAH-koh)

Chavín: Andean town that was the center of a large Peruvian religious movement from around 900 to 200 B.C.E. (*pron.* cha-BEAN)

Coptic Christianity: The Egyptian variety of Christianity, distinctive in its belief that Christ has only a single, divine nature.

Ezana: King of Axum in the early fourth century C.E. who established Christianity in his state. (*pron.* eh-TZAHN-ah)

Hopewell culture: Named from its most important site (in present-day Ohio), this is the most elaborate and widespread of the North American mound-building cultures; flourished from 200 B.C.E. to 400 C.E.

Jenne-jeno: Largest and most fully studied of the cities of the Niger Valley civilization. (*pron.* JENN-ay JENN-oh)

Maya: The major classical civilization of Mesoamerica; flourished from 250 to 900 C.E.

Meroë: City in southern Nubia that was the center of Nubian civilization between 300 B.C.E. and 100 C.E. (*pron.* MER-oh-ee)

Moche: An important regional civilization of Peru, governed by warrior-priests; flourished from around 100 to 800 C.E. (*pron.* MO-che)

Mound Builders: Members of any of a number of cultures that developed east of the Mississippi River in what is now the United States and that are distinguished by their large earthen mounds, built during the period 2000 B.C.E.–1250 C.E.

Nazca: A civilization of southern coastal Peru, the Nazca became famous for their underground irrigation channels and their gigantic and mysterious lines in the desert in the form of monkeys, birds, spiders, and other designs. (*pron.* NAHZ-kah)

Niger Valley civilization: Distinctive city-based civilization that flourished from about 300 B.C.E. to about 900 C.E. in the floodplain of the middle Niger and that included major cities like Jenne-jeno; the Niger Valley civilization is particularly noteworthy for its apparent lack of centralized state structures, having been organized instead in clusters of economically specialized settlements.

pueblo: "Great house" of the Ancestral Pueblo people; a large, apartment building–like structure that could house hundreds of people.

"semi-sedentary": Term frequently used to describe the peoples of the eastern woodlands of the United States, Central America, the Amazon basin, and the Caribbean islands who combined partial reliance on agriculture with gathering and hunting.

Teotihuacán: The largest city of pre-Columbian America, with a population between 100,000 and 200,000; seemingly built to a plan in the Valley of Mexico, Teotihuacán flourished between 300 and 600 C.E., during which time it governed or influenced much of the surrounding region. The name *Teotihuacán* is an Aztec term meaning "city of the gods." (*pron.* teh-o-tee-WAH-kahn)

Tikal: Major Maya city, with a population of perhaps 50,000 people. (*pron.* TEE-kal)

ANSWER GUIDELINES FOR CHAPTER QUESTIONS

The two sets of questions that follow appear in the textbook at the end of the chapter and in the margins of the reading. They are also provided in the Computerized Test Bank with answer guidelines, for your convenience.

The Big Picture Questions

1. "The histories of Africa and the Americas during the classical era largely resemble those of Eurasia." Do you agree with this statement? Explain why or why not.

• There is evidence to support both an affirmative and a negative answer to this question.

• In support of the statement, one could point to the emergence of powerful states, especially in Axum and Teotihuacán, which sought to create empires.

• One could also point to the parallels between the Maya civilization and classical Greece.

• One could also point to the spread of the Chavín cult as being in some ways a parallel development to the emergence of widespread religious traditions in Eurasia.

• However, there are many differences as well.

• The Ancestral Pueblo and mound-building societies of North America and regional civilizations such as the Moche of South America more closely resemble the Neolithic villages and First Civilizations of Eurasia than they do their classical counterparts.

2. "The particular cultures and societies of Africa and the Americas discussed in this chapter developed largely in isolation from one another." What evidence would support this statement, and what might challenge it?

• Evidence in support of this statement includes the complete physical separation and lack of contact between the African and American cultures and societies discussed in this chapter;

• the geographic and cultural separation between Meroë and Axum on the one hand and the Niger Valley civilization on the other;

• and the significant physical distances that separated Andean, North American, and Mesoamerican civilizations, along with the lack of sustained contact between these three regions.

• Evidence to challenge this statement includes the extensive interaction between the Maya and Teotihuacán civilizations;

• the conquest of Meroë by Axum;

• the encounters between Bantu-speaking peoples and gathering and hunting groups, including the Batwa, as the Bantu-speaking peoples migrated into Africa south of the equator;

• the Chavín religious cult, which provided for the first time and for several centuries a measure of economic and cultural integration to much of the Peruvian Andes;

• and the critical arrival of maize from Mesoamerica into the Ancestral Pueblo and mound-building societies.

3. What generated change in the histories of Africa and the Americas during the classical era?

• In Africa, driving forces of change included the migration of the Bantu peoples into Africa south of the equator, the emergence of Niger Valley urban centers, and the rise and fall of both Axum and Meroë.

• Contact with the trade networks of Eurasia also generated change in Africa. Through contact along these networks, Christianity arrived in northeastern Africa, including Axum. Axum derived its written script from South Arabia. The Bantu-speaking peoples adopted new crops, including coconuts, sugarcane, and especially bananas, which Indonesian sailors and immigrants brought to East Africa early in the first millennium C.E.

• In the Americas, the emergence of the Maya and Teotihuacán civilizations pushed Mesoamerican civilization toward new levels of complexity.

• The Chavín religious cult provided for the first time and for several centuries a measure of economic and cultural integration to much of the Peruvian Andes.

• The spread of maize into North America made it possible for the Ancestral Pueblo society to take shape and allowed Cahokia to achieve a higher degree of sophistication than did the mound-building societies that preceded it.

Margin Review Questions

Q. *How did the history of Meroë and Axum reflect interaction with neighboring civilizations?*

• Both Meroë and Axum traded extensively with neighboring civilizations. Meroë's wealth and military power were in part derived from this trade. The formation of a substantial state in Axum was at least in part stimulated by Axum's participation in Red Sea and Indian Ocean commerce and the taxes that flowed from this commerce.

• Both Meroë and Axum developed their own distinct writing scripts. A Meroitic script eventually took the place of Egyptian-style writing, while Axum's script, Geez, was derived from South Arabian models.

• Axum adopted Christianity from the Roman world in the fourth century C.E., primarily through Egyptian influence, and the region once controlled by Meroë also adopted Christianity in the 340s C.E. following the decline of Meroë.

Q. *How does the experience of the Niger Valley challenge conventional notions of "civilization"?*

• The Niger River region witnessed the creation of large cities with the apparent absence of a corresponding state structure. These cities were not like the city-states of ancient Mesopotamia, nor were they encompassed within some larger imperial system. Instead, they resemble most closely the early cities of the Indus Valley civilization, where complex urban centers also apparently operated without the coercive authority of a centralized state.

Q. *In what ways did the arrival of Bantu-speaking peoples stimulate cross-cultural interaction?*

• The Bantu-speaking peoples brought agriculture to regions of Africa south of the equator, enabling larger numbers of people to live in a smaller area than was possible before their arrival.

• The Bantu-speaking peoples brought parasitic and infectious diseases, to which the gathering and hunting peoples had little immunity.

• The Bantu-speaking peoples brought iron.

• Many Bantu languages of southern Africa retain to this day distinctive "clicks" in their local dialects that they adopted from the now vanished gathering and hunting peoples that preceded them in the region.

• Bantu-speaking peoples participated in networks of exchange with forest-dwelling Batwa (Pygmy) peoples. The Batwa adopted Bantu languages, while maintaining a nonagricultural lifestyle and a separate identity. The Bantu farmers regarded their Batwa neighbors as firstcomers to the region and therefore closest to the ancestral and territorial spirits that determined the fertility of the land and the people. As forest-dwelling Bantu peoples grew in numbers and created chiefdoms, those chiefs appropriated the Batwa title of "owners of the land" for themselves, claimed Batwa ancestry, and portrayed the Batwa as the original "civilizers" of the earth.

• Bantu farmers in East Africa increasingly adopted grains as well as domesticated sheep and cattle from the already-established people of the region.

• They also acquired a variety of food crops from Southeast Asia, including coconuts, sugarcane, and especially bananas, which were brought to East Africa by Indonesian sailors and immigrants early in the first millennium C.E.

Q. *With what Eurasian civilizations might the Maya be compared?*

• Because of its fragmented political structure, classical Maya civilization more closely resembled the competing city-states of Mesopotamia or classical Greece than the imperial structures of Rome, Persia, or China.

Q. *In what ways did Teotihuacán shape the history of Mesoamerica?*

• Its military conquests brought many regions into its political orbit and made Teotihuacán a presence in the Maya civilization.

• Teotihuacán was at the center of a large trade network.

• The architectural and artistic styles of the city were imitated across Mesoamerica.

Q. *What kind of influence did Chavín exert in the Andes region?*

• Chavín-style architecture, sculpture, pottery, religious images, and painted textiles were widely imitated in the region.

• Chavín became a pilgrimage site and perhaps a training center for initiates from distant corners of the region.

• At locations three weeks or more away by llama caravan, temples were remodeled to resemble that of Chavín, although in many cases with locally inspired variations.

• The Chavín religious cult provided for the first time and for several centuries a measure of economic and cultural integration to much of the Peruvian Andes.

Q. *What supports scholars' contention that Moche represented a regional civilization in the Andes?*

- The Moche civilization dominated a 250-mile stretch of Peru's northern coast, incorporated thirteen river valleys, and flourished for seven hundred years beginning in 100 C.E.
- The Moche economy was rooted in a complex irrigation system that required constant maintenance.
- Politically, the Moche civilization was governed by warrior-priests.
- The warrior-priests sometimes lived atop huge pyramids, the largest of which was constructed out of 143 million sun-dried bricks.
- The wealth of the warrior-priest elite and the remarkable artistic skills of Moche craftspeople are reflected in the elaborate burials accorded the rulers. The Moche craftspeople are renowned for their metal-working, pottery, weaving, and painting.

Q. *In what ways were the histories of the Ancestral Pueblo and the Mound Builders similar to each other, and how did they differ?*

- The Ancestral Pueblo and Mound Builders were similar in a number of ways.
- Their settlements were linked into trading networks, and they also participated in long-distance exchange.
- Both groups created structures to track the heavens.
- Both ultimately adopted maize from Mesoamerica.
- They also differed in a number of ways.
- The Mound Builders participated in an independent Agricultural Revolution and continued to supplement their diets by gathering and hunting until maize arrived from Mesoamerica after 800 C.E. The Ancestral Pueblo peoples acquired maize from Mesoamerica much earlier and settled into a more full-time agricultural culture earlier in their development.
- The Mound Builders created larger monumental architecture both in their burial mounds and in their geometrical earthworks than did Ancestral Pueblo peoples, although the Ancestral Pueblo people did create kivas as ceremonial centers and networks of roads that may have had religious significance.
- The largest mound-building settlements, like Cahokia, were far larger urban centers than those of the Ancestral Pueblo.
- In comparison to the mound-building cultures, the Ancestral Pueblo society started later and did not last as long.

ADDITIONAL RESOURCES FOR CHAPTER 7

Additional Bedford/St. Martin's Resources

FOR INSTRUCTORS

Computerized Test Bank

This test bank provides over thirty exercises per chapter, including multiple-choice, fill-in-the-blank, short-answer, and full-length essay questions. Instructors can customize quizzes, add or edit both questions and answers, and export questions and answers to a variety of formats, including WebCT and Blackboard. The disc includes correct answers and essay outlines.

Instructor's Resource CD-ROM

This disc provides instructors with ready-made and customizable PowerPoint multimedia presentations built around chapter outlines, maps, figures, and all images from the textbook, plus JPEG versions of all maps, figures, and images.

The following maps and images from Chapter 7 are available in both JPEG and PowerPoint format on the Instructor's Resource CD-ROM:

- Map 7.1: Africa in the Classical Era (p. 185)
- An Elite Maya Woman (p. 180)
- A Bracelet from Meroë (p. 186)
- The Columns of Axum (p. 187)
- Khoikhoi of South Africa (p. 191)
- A Mural of Teotihuacán (p. 196)
- The Lord of Sipan (p. 200)
- Pueblo Bonito (p. 202)

FOR STUDENTS

Online Study Guide at bedfordstmartins.com/strayer

The Online Study Guide helps students synthesize the material from the text as well as practice the skills historians use to make sense of the past. Each chapter of the Online Study Guide contains specific testing exercises, including a multiple-choice self-test that focuses on important conceptual ideas; an identification quiz that helps students remember key people, places, and events; a flashcard activity that tests students on their knowledge of key terms; and two interactive map activities intended to strengthen students' geographic skills. Instructors can monitor students' progress through an online Quiz Gradebook or receive email updates.

Further Reading

Davidson, Basil. *Africa in History.* 4th ed. London: Orion Books, 1991. An excellent study that should be on every world historian's bookshelf, *Africa in History* provides an overview of African history and many insights into how Western assumptions have gotten in the way of interpreting the African past.

Ehret, Christopher. *An African Classical Age: Eastern and Southern Africa in World History, 1000 B.C. to A.D. 400.* Charlottesville: University Press of Virginia, 1998. Probably too detailed when cramming to put a lecture together, this study is a fairly difficult but rewarding look at Bantu history that incorporates the work of linguists in its interpretations.

Jenne-jeno, an Ancient African City, http://www.ruf.rice.edu/~anth/arch/brochure/. A detailed account of the city of Jenne-jeno, including the history of its discovery, authored by Susan Keech McIntosh and Roderick J. McIntosh.

MayaRuins.com, http://www.mayaruins.com/. A great photographic overview of the Mayan sites.

Newman, James L. *The Peopling of Africa: A Geographic Interpretation.* New Haven: Yale University Press, 1995. This book reaches from the first spread of *homo sapiens* to modern times.

Pohl, John M. D. *Exploring Mesoamerica.* New York: Oxford University Press, 2000. A very attractive recent study of the Maya and other peoples of Mesoamerica.

Scarre, Chis, ed. *The Seventy Wonders of the Ancient World.* London: Thames and Hudson, 1999. Includes good discussion of Chavín, the Pyramid of the Sun in Teotihuacán, Cahokia, the Hopewell earthworks at Newark, Ohio, and the Chaco road system of New Mexico, as well as much else.

Literature

Burstein, Stanley, ed. *Ancient African Civilizations: Kush and Axum.* Princeton: Marcus Wiener, 1998. A collection of ancient and medieval accounts of Kush and Axum, with a good introduction.

Halsall, Paul, ed. *Internet African History Sourcebook.* http://www.fordham.edu/halsall/africa/africasbook.html. Includes links to both ancient and modern views of Africa.

Tedlock, Dennis, trans. *Popol Vuh: The Definitive Edition of the Mayan Book of the Dawn of Life and the Glories of Gods and Kings.* Rev. ed. New York: Touchstone, 1996. The great Maya creation epic.

Film

Ancient Mysteries. "The Secret Burial Mounds of Pre-Historic America." History Channel, 1995. 50 minutes. Explores the mound-building societies of the eastern United States, including Cahokia.

Archaeology: Fall of the Maya. Insight Media, 1992. 30 minutes. Explores the rise and fall of the Maya civilization.

Sudan: Black Kingdoms of the Nile. Films for the Humanities and Sciences, 1997. 53 minutes. An exploration of archeological sites in the Sudan.

The Sun Dagger. Insight Media, 1983. 58 minutes. Explores the Ancestral Pueblo society that was centered on Chaco canyon.

Teotihuacán: The City of the Gods. Insight Media, 2001. 30 minutes. Explores the city of Teotihuacán and its impact on subsequent Mesoamerican societies.

PART THREE

AN AGE OF ACCELERATING CONNECTIONS
500–1500

Outline: The Big Picture: Defining a Millennium

I. **It is difficult to see when one phase of human history ends and another begins.**
   A. Between about 200 and 850 C.E., many classical states and civilizations were disrupted, declined, or collapsed.
   B. Columbus's transatlantic voyages around 1500 mark a new departure in world history for most people.

C. How should we understand the millennium that stretches from the end of the classical era to the beginning of modern world history?
   1. it has proven hard to define a distinct identity for this period
      a. some call it "postclassical," but that doesn't mean much
      b. some call it "medieval," but that's very Eurocentric and also suggests it was just a run-up to modernity
      c. this textbook sometimes uses the concept of "third-wave civilizations"

II. **Third-Wave Civilizations: Something New, Something Old, Something Blended**
   A. Various regions followed different trajectories in this era.
   B. There were several distinct patterns of development:
      1. some areas saw creation of new but smaller civilizations where none had existed before
         a. East African Swahili civilization
         b. Kievan Rus
         c. new civilizations in East and Southeast Asia

2. all were part of the pattern of increasing globalization of civilization
   a. the new civilizations were distinctive, but similar to earlier civilizations
   b. all borrowed heavily from earlier or more established centers
3. the most expansive and influential third-wave civilization was Islam
   a. creation of a new civilization defined by its religion
4. some older civilizations persisted or were reconstructed (e.g., Byzantium, China, India, Niger Valley)
   a. collapse of classical Maya civilization and Teotihuacán opened the way to a reshaping of an ancient civilization
   b. the Inca formed an empire out of various centers of Andean civilization
5. Western Europe: successor states tried to maintain links to older Greco-Roman-Christian traditions
   a. but far more decentralized societies emerged, led by Germans
   b. hybrid civilization was created of classical and Germanic elements
   c. development of highly competitive states after 1000 C.E.

III. The Ties That Bind: Transregional Interaction in the Postclassical Era

A. An important common theme is the great increase in interaction between the world's regions, cultures, and peoples.
   1. increasingly, change was caused by contact with strangers and/or their ideas, armies, goods, or diseases
   2. cosmopolitan regions emerged in a variety of places—"miniglobalizations"

B. Part Three highlights the accelerating pace of interaction in the third-wave era, giving special attention to three major mechanisms of interaction:
   1. trade, especially the growth of long-distance commerce
      a. trade led to the establishment of many new states or empires
      b. religious ideas, technologies, and germs also moved along trade routes
   2. large empires, incorporating many distinct cultures under a single political system
      a. provided security for long-distance trade
      b. many of the third-wave civilizations were larger than earlier ones (Arab, Mongol, and Inca empires)
      c. the largest empires were created by nomadic or pastoral peoples (Arabs, Turks, Mongols, Aztecs), who ruled over agriculturalists
   3. large-scale empires and long-distance trade worked together to facilitate the spread of ideas, technologies, crops, and germs
      a. wide diffusion of religions
      b. wide diffusion of technologies, many from China and India
      c. devastating epidemic disease (e.g., Black Death) linked distant communities

C. A focus on accelerating connections puts a spotlight on travelers rather than on those who stayed at home.

D. A focus on interaction raises questions for world historians about how much choice individuals or societies had in accepting new ideas or practices and about how they made those decisions.

Commerce and Culture
500–1500

CHAPTER OVERVIEW

Chapter Objectives

- To consider the significance of trade in human history
- To explore the interconnections created by long-distance trade in the period of third-wave civilizations
- To examine the full range of what was carried along trade routes (goods, culture, disease)
- To explore the differences between the commerce of the Eastern Hemisphere and that of the Western Hemisphere and the reasons behind those differences

Chapter Outline

I. **Opening Vignette**
  A. Modern highways are being built across Africa and Asia.
    1. part of modern process of globalization
    2. but also evoke older patterns of global commerce
  B. The roots of modern globalization lie deep in the past.
    1. exchange of goods between people of different ecological zones is a major feature of human history
    2. at times, some societies have monopolized desirable products (like silk)

  3. long-distance trade became more important than ever in 500–1500 C.E.
    a. most trade was indirect
    b. creation of a network of communication and exchange across the Afro-Eurasian world; a separate web in parts of the Americas
  C. Why was trade significant? **[see Discussion Topic 1]**
    1. altered consumption
    2. encouraged specialization
    3. diminished economic self-sufficiency of local societies
    4. traders often became a distinct social group
    5. sometimes was a means of social mobility
    6. provided prestige goods for elites
    7. sometimes the wealth from trade motivated state creation
    8. religious ideas, technological innovations, plants and animals, and disease also spread along trade routes
  D. The network of long-distance commerce is a notable feature of the third-wave civilizations.

II. **Silk Roads: Exchange across Eurasia**
  A. The Growth of the Silk Roads
    1. Eurasia is often divided into inner and outer zones with different ecologies
      a. outer Eurasia: relatively warm, well-watered (China, India, Middle East, Mediterranean)

b. inner Eurasia: harsher, drier climate, much of it pastoral (eastern Russia, Central Asia)

c. steppe products were exchanged for agricultural products and manufactured goods

2. creation of classical civilizations and imperial states in 500–0 B.C.E. included efforts to control pastoral peoples

a. by early centuries of the Common Era, there was a network of transcontinental exchange, often brokered by pastoral peoples

3. trading networks did best when large states provided security for trade

a. when Roman and Chinese empires anchored commerce

b. in seventh and eighth centuries, the Byzantine Empire, Abbasid dynasty, and Tang dynasty created a belt of strong states

c. in thirteenth and fourteenth centuries, Mongol Empire controlled almost the entirety of the Silk Roads

B. Goods in Transit **[see Discussion Topic 2]**

1. a vast array of goods traveled along the Silk Roads, often by camel

a. mostly luxury goods for the elite

b. high cost of transport did not allow movement of staple goods

2. silk symbolized the Eurasian exchange system

a. at first, China had a monopoly on silk technology

i. led to drain of resources from Roman Empire to east

ii. Romans regarded silk as morally decadent

b. by the sixth century C.E., other peoples produced silk

i. Byzantine Empire, Korea, Japan, India, Persia

c. silk was used as currency in Central Asia

d. silk was a symbol of high status

i. sumptuary laws restricted silk clothing to the elite in China and the Byzantine Empire

ii. silk was linked to the sacred in Buddhism and Christianity

e. silk industry only developed in Western Europe in twelfth century

3. volume of trade was small, but of economic and social importance

a. peasants in the Yangzi River delta of southern China produced market goods (silk, paper, porcelain, etc.) instead of crops

b. well-placed individuals could make enormous profits

C. Cultures in Transit **[see Lecture Strategy 1]**

1. cultural transmission was more important than exchange of goods

2. the case of Buddhism **[see Classroom Activity 1]**

a. spread along Silk Roads through Central and East Asia

b. had always appealed to merchants

c. conversion was heavy in the oasis cities of Central Asia

d. conversion was voluntary

i. link to the civilization of India

ii. winning religious merit by founding monasteries

iii. monasteries provided rest stops for merchants

e. many of the Central Asian cities became centers of learning and commerce

i. Buddhist texts and cave temples of Dunhuang

f. spread much more slowly among Central Asian pastoralists

i. pastoralists didn't have a written language

ii. monasticism is central to Buddhism, but pastoralists are nomads

iii. Shi Le, ruler of the nomadic Jie people (ruled northern China after collapse of Han), accepted conversion along with thousands of others, thanks to the monk Fotudeng

g. in China, was the religion of foreign merchants or rulers for centuries

h. Buddhism was transformed during its spread

i. monasteries became rich and involved in secular affairs

ii. Mahayana form of Buddhism flourished

iii. picked up Greek influences

D. Disease in Transit
  1. the major population centers of the Afro-Eurasian world developed characteristic disease patterns and ways to deal with them
  2. long-distance trade meant exposure to unfamiliar diseases
     a. early case: great epidemic in Athens in 430–429 B.C.E.
     b. during the Roman and Han empires, smallpox and measles devastated both populations
     c. in 534–750 C.E., bubonic plague from India ravaged Mediterranean world
        i. kept the Byzantine Empire from regaining Italy
        ii. made it harder for Christendom to resist spread of Islam
  3. the Black Death spread thanks to the Mongol Empire's unification of much of Eurasia (thirteenth–fourteenth centuries)
     a. could have been bubonic plague, anthrax, or collection of epidemic diseases
     b. killed one-third of European population between 1346 and 1350
     c. similar death toll in China and parts of the Islamic world
     d. Central Asian steppes were badly affected (undermined Mongol power)
  4. disease exchange gave Europeans an advantage when they reached the Western Hemisphere after 1500
     a. peoples of the Americas had little immunity to European and African diseases

III. **Sea Roads: Exchange across the Indian Ocean** [see Lecture Strategy 2 and Classroom Activity 2]
  A. The Mediterranean Sea was an avenue for commerce from the time of the Phoenicians.
     1. Venice was a center of commerce by 1000 C.E.
     2. controlled trade of imports from Asia
     3. linked Europe to the much greater trade network of the Indian Ocean
  B. The Indian Ocean network was the world's most important until after 1500.
     1. trade grew from environmental and cultural diversity
     2. transportation was cheaper by sea than by land
     3. made transportation of bulk goods possible (textiles, pepper, timber, rice, sugar, wheat)
     4. commerce was possible thanks to monsoons (alternating wind currents)
     5. commerce was between towns, not states
  C. Weaving the Web of an Indian Ocean World
     1. Indian Ocean trade started in the age of the First Civilizations
        a. Indus Valley writing may have been stimulated by cuneiform
        b. ancient Egyptians and Phoenicians traded down the Red Sea
        c. Malay sailors reached Madagascar in the first millennium B.C.E.
           i. introduced language and crops (bananas, coconuts, cocoyams)
     2. tempo of commerce increased in early centuries C.E. with greater understanding of monsoons
        a. merchants from Roman Empire settled in southern India and East African coast
           i. introduced Christianity
        b. growing trade in eastern Indian Ocean and South China Sea
           i. Chinese traders reached India by 100 C.E.
     3. fulcrum of trade was India
        a. spread of Hinduism and Buddhism in Southeast Asia
     4. two great encouragers for the Indian Ocean exchange:
        a. economic and political revival of China
           i. Tang and Song dynasties (618–1279) reestablished an effective and unified state
           ii. Chinese products flooded into Indian Ocean network
           iii. China provided a vast market for Indian and Southeast Asian goods
           iv. China developed larger ships and the magnetic compass
        b. rise of Islam in seventh century C.E.
           i. Islam was friendly to trade (Muhammad was a trader)
           ii. Arab Empire reached from Atlantic Ocean to India

iii. Muslims (and Jewish and Christian subjects) established trade communities from East Africa to southern China

iv. large-scale East African slave trade to work Iraqi plantations and salt mines

v. creation of international maritime culture by 1000 C.E.

vi. widespread conversion to Islam made trade easier

D. Sea Roads as a Catalyst for Change: Southeast Asia and Srivijaya

1. ocean commerce transformed Southeast Asia and East Africa

    a. trade stimulated political change

    b. introduction of foreign religious ideas

2. Southeast Asia: location between China and India made it important

    a. Malay sailors opened an all-sea route between India and China through the Straits of Malacca ca. 350 C.E.

    b. led many small ports to compete to attract traders

3. Malay kingdom of Srivijaya emerged from competition, dominated trade from 670 to 1025 C.E.

    a. gold, access to spices, and taxes on ships provided resources to create a state

    b. local belief: chiefs possessed magical powers

    c. also used Indian political ideas and Buddhism

        i. multitude of Indian merchants and teachers settled

        ii. Srivijaya became a major Buddhist center

4. Sailendras kingdom (central Java) was also influenced by India

    a. massive building of Hindu and Buddhist centers (eighth–tenth centuries)

    b. shows Buddhist cultural grounding in Javanese custom

5. Burma, the Khmer state of Angkor, etc., also show Indian culture

6. Islam penetrated later

E. Sea Roads as a Catalyst for Change: East Africa and Swahili Civilization **[see Lecture Strategy 3 and Discussion Topic 3]**

1. Swahili civilization of East Africa developed from blend of Bantu with commercial life of the Indian Ocean (especially Islamic)

    a. growing demand for East African products (gold, ivory, quartz, leopard skins, some slaves, iron, wood products)

    b. African merchant class developed, with towns and kingships

2. Swahili civilization flourished on East African coast between 1000 and 1500 C.E.

    a. very urban, with cities of 15,000–18,000 people

    b. each city was politically independent, ruled by a king

    c. accumulated goods from the interior and traded for Asian goods

    d. sharp class distinctions

3. most of trade was in Arab ships; Swahili craft traveled coastal waterways

4. deep participation in the Indian Ocean world

    a. regular visits by Arab and Indian (perhaps Persian) merchants; some settled

    b. many ruling families claimed Arab or Persian origins

    c. Swahili was written in Arabic script, with Arabic loan words

    d. widespread conversion to Islam

        i. society was heavily Islamicized (account of Ibn Battuta)

5. Islam and Swahili culture didn't reach much beyond coast until the nineteenth century

    a. but Swahili region traded with the interior, had an impact

    b. trade with interior for gold led to emergence of Great Zimbabwe (flourished in 1250–1350 C.E.)

IV. **Sand Roads: Exchange across the Sahara**

A. Commercial Beginnings in West Africa

1. trans-African trade was also based on environmental variation

    a. North Africa manufactured goods

    b. Sahara had copper and salt deposits, dates

    c. agricultural peoples further south grew crops, mined gold

2. earliest trade in the region was among agricultural peoples in the Sudan

a. emergence of urban clusters in the early centuries C.E.

b. most famous was Jenne-jeno (Niger Valley civilization)

B. Gold, Salt, and Slaves: Trade and Empire in West Africa

1. introduction of the camel in early centuries C.E. was a turning point

a. camels can go 10 days without water

b. made it possible to cross the Sahara

2. regular trans-Saharan commerce by 300–400 C.E.

3. merchants especially wanted gold from West Africa (along with ivory, kola nuts, slaves)

a. peoples of Sudan received horses, cloth, dates, manufactured goods, salt in return

4. the Sahara became a major international trade route

a. huge caravans (as many as 5,000 camels)

b. caravans traveled the desert for over 1,000 years

5. trade encouraged new and larger political structures

a. creation of a series of states in western and central Sudan between 500 and 1600 C.E., including Ghana, Mali, Songhay, Kanem, and Hausa city-states

b. all were monarchies with elaborate court life and at least some administration and military forces

c. all had a reputation for great riches

6. slavery was present in West Africa

a. at first, most slaves were women

b. with development of civilization, male slaves were used as officials, porters, craftsmen, miners, agricultural laborers

c. most slaves came from societies raided farther south

d. some 5,500 slaves a year came from across the Sahara between 1100 and 1400

i. most were sold in North Africa

ii. a few ended up in Europe

iii. Slavic-speaking slaves were much more common in Europe (origin of word "slave")

iv. African slaves only became common in Europe starting in 1440s (Atlantic slave trade)

7. substantial urban/commercial centers (such as Koumbi-Saleh, Jenne, Timbuktu)

a. some became manufacturing centers

b. Islam was established in towns

V. **An American Network: Commerce and Connection in the Western Hemisphere**
[see Discussion Topic 3]

A. There was no sustained interaction between the Western and Eastern hemispheres before the voyages of Columbus.

B. American trade networks were not as dense as Afro-Eurasian ones.

1. important limitations:

a. lack of domesticated large mammals, wheeled vehicles, large oceangoing ships

b. geographical or environmental obstacles, including north/south orientation

2. local and regional commerce flourished, but not long-distance trade

3. cultural traditions did not spread as widely as in Eastern Hemisphere

C. But there was a "loosely interactive web" from the Great Lakes to the Andes.

1. cultural elements spread gradually

2. evidence of at least indirect contact

3. Cahokia was at center of a widespread trading network

4. Chaco canyon culture also interacted with Mesoamerica

5. Amazon and Orinoco river exchange networks

6. Caribbean peoples conducted interisland trade

7. Chincha people traded along Pacific coast of South America

D. There was a major trade network in Mesoamerica.

1. Maya and Teotihuacán traded by land

2. Maya traded by sea on both coasts (with dugout canoes)

3. Aztecs of fifteenth century had professional merchants (*pochteca*)

E. There was a major trade network in the Andes.

1. Inca trade during fifteenth century was run by the state

VI. **Reflections: Economic Globalization— Ancient and Modern**

A. The interconnections of the modern era have their roots in much earlier patterns.

B. But premodern networks had important differences:
1. most people still produced for their own consumption
2. a much smaller range of goods was exchanged
3. far fewer wageworkers
4. trade was in luxury goods
5. circuits of commerce were more limited
6. had no single center; units were much more equivalent
C. The world of third-wave civilizations was more balanced and multicentered than that of the modern era.
1. relationships among major civilizations were much more equal
2. perhaps the twenty-first century is returning to that pattern

USING *WAYS OF THE WORLD* IN THE CLASSROOM

Lecture Strategies

Lecture Strategy 1

"Cultural mingling: A cross-cultural look at East Africa and Southeast Asia."
This lecture strategy will work best with PowerPoint or with another type of image projection system. Its objectives are to:

- help students *see* the cultural influences that worked upon East Africa and Southeast Asia
- compare the ways in which that cultural influence manifested itself
- review the material in the text on cultural influences in East Africa and Southeast Asia

Start the lecture with an image of the Borobudur temple complex (Java), such as the photo on page 230 of the textbook. Ask your students what, by itself, this image suggests (size, complexity, ability to work in stone). Then show a number of Hindu and Buddhist temples from India that were built at about the same time, and ask the students again what they can understand about the culture of the Sailendras kingdom by looking at an image of

Borobudur. Go on to show other Indian-influenced structures that can be found in Southeast Asia. Encourage discussion both of similarities to the architecture of India and of elements likely to be indigenous to the region in which the building was located.

It is much more difficult to find images of Swahili architecture before Vasco da Gama and his successors influenced the region; try the Gede ruins near the port city of Malindi, Kenya. Points of Islamic influence include arches, courtyards, special women's quarters, mihrabs, and elements of orientation.

As you deal with the physical remains of these two cultures, include discussion of the impact of foreign elements on language, religion, and culture more generally.

Lecture Strategy 2

"World transport among the third-wave civilizations." The purpose of this lecture strategy is to explore in greater detail how goods (and people) were transported in the premodern world. Its objectives are:

- to make students aware of the great difficulty and risks of long-distance trade
- to explore the technologies available that eased transport
- to consider how much infrastructure was available to ease the problems of transport

A good place to start is with the notion of the Silk and Sand Roads. What *actual* roads existed in the period 500 to 1500 C.E.? There was still the system of Roman roads (examine briefly how complex their construction was); Andean roads had been established with protective walls and bridges; and many other communities provided some sort of paved roads and bridges. But for interstate commerce, what we are talking about is *routes*, unpaved and undeveloped, for which a traveler needed to hire a guide or follow the traces left by earlier travelers. Wheeled carts could not travel on most of these long-distance routes; what was needed was pack animals or human bearers. Go on from this point to consider:

- How heavy a load can a horse carry?
- How heavy a load can a camel carry?
- How about a donkey?
- How about a human?
- On a good road, how heavily laden a cart can a horse pull (with the advantage of a horse collar, rather than a horse yoke)?

- How much can a ship carry?
- A common measure is that the reasonable load for one man to transport on foot is 50 pounds, but the same energy will move around 500 pounds on wheels on a road, 5,000 pounds on rails, and 50,000 pounds on water.

Go on to consider naval technology. It's a fascinating history that is only touched upon by the text. Some points to include:

- regions mentioned in the text that relied on dugout canoes or rafts
- the limitations of dugout canoes or rafts
- how dangerous various bodies of water are to sail on (the Indian Ocean is probably the safest, followed by the Mediterranean and then the Pacific; the Atlantic and North seas are pretty nasty)
- the advantages of sails over rowing
- Arab contributions to maritime history (such as lateen sails)
- the complexity of shipbuilding (e.g., the difficulty of making a North Sea–style clinker-built ship compared to the mortise-and-tenon construction of the Mediterranean)
- the advantage of rudders compared to steering oars
- the inventions that aided navigation (astrolabe, magnetic compass, etc.)
- you might also want to consider the importance of naval warfare in world history

Lecture Strategy 3

"The world of merchants."
What were trade towns really like in this period? This lecture strategy is to examine that question, drawing particularly on the writings of the fourteenth-century Arab traveler Ibn Battuta for information. The strategy's objectives are to:

- help students imagine the urban environments created by premodern trade
- consider how much those towns would have varied depending on region

The writings of Ibn Battuta are readily available in English (see the Further Reading section of this chapter for some suggestions). You will need to familiarize yourself with at least representative sections of his

work that deal with towns in Asia and in West, North, and East Africa. Use these writings as the basis for a lecture on the quality of life in trade towns, perhaps adding more familiar material about the trading cities of late medieval Italy. Some points to consider are:

- the lack of sanitation systems almost everywhere
- the extreme poverty of some of the population
- the ostentatious wealth of the elite
- the presence or absence of building codes
- the prevalence of disease
- the degree of government control of traders
- differences between trading cities in different parts of the world, and possible reasons for those differences

Things to Do in the Classroom

Discussion Topics

1. **Comparison, large or small group.** "The impact of long-distance trade."
Ask students to make a list of the ways in which people and regions can be affected, directly or indirectly, by commerce. Then distribute world maps and ask students to identify which regions of the earth *weren't* affected in a significant way by long-distance trade in the period 5–1500 C.E.

2. **Misconception/Difficult Topic, large or small group.** "What was traded in the long-distance trade of the premodern world?"
Modern trade includes astonishingly large and heavy commodities, ranging from millions of barrels of crude oil to every sort of food product—to the point that the average distance that a food item has traveled to reach an American plate is about 1,000 miles. Students often assume that the same trade in bulky items has always been the norm. To try to dispel this notion, ask students to consider the difficulties in transporting the following items in premodern times:

- wine (transported in barrels or pottery vessels, usually by ship because of the weight)
- beer (couldn't have been transported long distances, because it would spoil after a few days on the road)
- wheat (occasionally profitable to ship, but only by sea; consider the problem of it getting wet)

- horses or cattle (I'll leave you to imagine the problems with this one)
- porcelain
- spices
- silk

3. **Contextualization, large or small group.**
"What makes trade tick?"
Encourage a discussion of the necessary preconditions for long-distance trade to develop. The textbook provides considerable material for this question, especially in the case of the Americas, but the purpose of this discussion is to get students to reason out the answer for themselves based on what they have learned in class already. Some points that should emerge are:

- the need for a societal elite to consume the luxury goods that were traded
- the need for relative peace for traders to travel
- the need for some sort of accepted system of exchange (coinage, silk as currency, etc.)
- the need for camels or other draft animals if trading by land
- the need for a relatively advanced shipbuilding technology if trading by sea
- the need for a certain amount of capital for a trader to start business
- the need for a system that collects or produces goods and brings them to a central location, where traders can purchase them

Classroom Activities

1. **Close-reading exercise, large or small group.**
"A Chinese traveler to India."
Distribute an excerpt from the Chinese Buddhist monk Fa-Hsien's account of his travel to India (available at acc6.its.brooklyn.cuny.edu/~phalsall/texts/faxian.html). Discuss what this early fifth-century account can add to our understanding of cultural interaction. Encourage students to look at *details* (close reading) and to consider their significance.

2. **Clicker question.** Which do you think was more significant to world history, the Silk Roads or the Sea Roads?

3. **Role-playing exercise, small group.** "Crossing the world."

You are the followers of Ibn Battuta in the fourteenth century C.E. You want to travel from Timbuktu (West Africa) to Cholas (India). How would you do it? Consider:

- the various means of transportation you would need
- your probable route
- how long your journey would probably take

Key Terms

American web: A term used to describe the network of trade that linked parts of the pre-Columbian Americas; although less intense and complete than the Afro-Eurasian trade networks, this web nonetheless provided a means of exchange for luxury goods and ideas over large areas.

Black Death: The name given to the massive epidemic that swept Eurasia in the fourteenth century C.E.; it may have been bubonic plague, anthrax, or a collection of epidemic diseases.

Borobudur: The largest Buddhist monument ever built, Borobudur is a mountainous ten-level monument with an elaborate carving program, probably built in the ninth century C.E. by the Sailendras rulers of central Java; it is an outstanding example of cultural exchange and syncretism. (*pron.* BORE-ah-boo-DOOR)

bubonic plague: A highly fatal disease transmitted by fleas; it devastated the Mediterranean world between 534 and 750 C.E. and again in the period 1346–1350 C.E.

Ghana, Mali, Songhay: A series of important states that developed in western and central Sudan in the period 500–1600 C.E. in response to the economic opportunities of trans-Saharan trade (especially control of gold production). (*pron.* GAH-nah, MAH-lee, song-GAH-ee)

Great Zimbabwe: A powerful state in the African interior that apparently emerged from the growing trade in gold to the East African coast; flourished between 1250 and 1350 C.E.

Ibn Battuta: A famous Muslim traveler who visited much of the Islamic world in the fourteenth century and wrote a major account of what he saw. (*pron.* ibn bat-TOOT-ah)

Indian Ocean trading network: The world's largest sea-based system of communication and exchange before 1500 C.E., Indian Ocean commerce stretched from southern China to eastern Africa and included not only the exchange of luxury and bulk goods but also the exchange of ideas and crops.

Jie people: A nomadic people who controlled much of northern China in the third and fourth centuries; many converted to Buddhism. (*pron.* gee)

Malaysians: Speakers of Austronesian languages from what is now Indonesia who became major traders in Southeast Asia and Madagascar.

monsoons: Alternating wind currents that blew eastward across the Indian Ocean in the summer and westward in the winter, facilitating trade.

oasis cities of Central Asia: Cities such as Merv, Samarkand, Khotan, and Dunhuang that became centers of trans-Eurasian trade.

pochteca: Professional merchants among the Aztecs.

Sailendras: A kingdom of central Java that flourished from the eighth century to the tenth century C.E.; noted for being deeply influenced by Indian culture. (*pron.* sigh-LEN-drahs)

Sand Roads: A term used to describe the routes of the trans-Sahara trade in Africa.

Silk Roads: Land-based trade routes that linked Eurasia.

Srivijaya: A Malay kingdom that dominated the Straits of Malacca between 670 and 1025 C.E.; noted for its creation of a native/Indian hybrid culture. (*pron.* sree-vih-JUH-yah)

Sudan: From the Arabic term for "land of black people," a large region of West Africa that became part of a major exchange circuit.

Swahili civilization: An East African civilization that emerged in the eighth century C.E. from a blending of Bantu, Islamic, and other Indian Ocean trade elements. (*pron.* swah-HEE-lee)

third-wave civilizations: Civilizations that emerged between 500 and 1500 C.E. and were typified by intensifying trade networks.

trans-Saharan slave trade: A fairly small-scale trade that developed in the twelfth century C.E., exporting West African slaves captured in raids across the Sahara for sale mostly as household servants in Islamic North Africa; the difficulty of travel across the desert limited the scope of this trade.

Venice: An Italian city that by 1000 C.E. emerged as a major center of Mediterranean trade.

ANSWER GUIDELINES FOR CHAPTER QUESTIONS

The two sets of questions that follow appear in the textbook at the end of the chapter and in the margins of the reading. They are also provided in the Computerized Test Bank with answer guidelines, for your convenience.

The Big Picture Questions

1. What motivated and sustained the long-distance commerce of the Silk Roads, Sea Roads, and Sand Roads?
   - as far as motivation: the desire of elites for hard-to-find luxury items from distant parts of the Eurasian network
   - also, the accumulation of wealth, especially among merchants who participated in the trade
   - as far as sustaining the commerce: the support of empires and smaller states that benefited directly from the trade
   - the spread of religious traditions, including Islam and Buddhism, that through shared beliefs tied merchants and sometimes whole societies together over wide regions
   - the development of technologies like larger ships and the magnetic compass

2. Why did the Eastern Hemisphere develop long-distance trade more extensively than did the societies of the Western Hemisphere?
   - the absence of large domesticated mammals in the Americas
   - the absence of large oceanic vessels
   - the geographical realities of the Americas, especially the narrow bottleneck of Panama, which was largely covered by dense rain forests
   - the north/south orientation of the Americas, which required agricultural practices to move through, and adapt to, quite distinct climatic and vegetation zones

3. In what ways did commercial exchange foster other changes?
   - It frequently provided the incentives and resources for the creation of larger, more powerful states.

• It provided sustained contact through which cultural influences were also exchanged, as was the case with the spread of Buddhism and Islam.

• It facilitated the spread of epidemic diseases beyond local regions, with sometimes devastating effects.

• It resulted in the spread of plants and animals along with technological innovations.

• It altered consumption patterns.

• It encouraged specialization and diminished the economic self-sufficiency of local societies.

• Sometimes it was a means of social mobility, with traders often becoming a distinct social group.

4. In what ways was Afro-Eurasia a single interacting zone, and in what respects was it a vast region of separate cultures and civilizations?

• In support of the position that it was a single interacting zone: it was a network of exchange that stretched all across the Afro-Eurasian world;

• it altered consumption and encouraged peoples across the zone to specialize in producing particular products for sale rather than being self-sufficient;

• the spread of ideas and diseases across large parts of the interacting zone provides evidence of extensive and sustained contact across long distances.

• In support of the position that it was a vast region of separate cultures: none of the participants knew the full extent of the zone, for it was largely a "relay trade" in which goods were passed down the line, changing hands many times before reaching their final destination;

• numerous distinct cultural traditions existed side by side across the zone throughout the period.

Margin Review Questions

Q. *What lay behind the emergence of Silk Road commerce, and what kept it going for so many centuries?*

• the exchange of products of the forest and of the semi-arid northern grasslands of inner Eurasia, which were controlled by pastoral peoples, for the agricultural products and manufactured goods of the warmer, well-watered lands of outer Eurasia, including the Mediterranean, the Middle East, India, and China

• the construction of classical civilizations and their imperial states during the last five centuries

B.C.E.; classical civilizations invaded the territory of pastoral peoples, securing sections of the Silk Roads and providing security for merchants and travelers

• the continued support of later states, including the Byzantine, Abbasid, and Mongol empires, which also benefited from the trade

• the demand for hard-to-find luxury goods among elites across Eurasia

Q. *What made silk such a highly desired commodity across Eurasia?*

• It was used as currency and as a means of accumulating wealth in Central Asia.

• It became a symbol of high status in China and the Byzantine Empire.

• It became associated with the sacred in the expanding world religions of Buddhism and Christianity.

Q. *What were the major economic, social, and cultural consequences of Silk Road commerce?*

• In some regions, long-distance trade profoundly affected the lives of peasant farmers. For instance, peasants in the Yangzi River delta of southern China sometimes gave up the cultivation of food crops, choosing to focus instead on producing silk, paper, porcelain, lacquerware, or iron tools, much of which was destined for the markets of the Silk Roads.

• Favorably placed individuals could benefit enormously from long-distance trade; some merchants accumulated considerable fortunes.

Q. *What accounted for the spread of Buddhism along the Silk Roads?*

• Buddhism appealed to Indian merchants, who preferred its universal message to that of a Brahmin-dominated Hinduism that privileged the higher castes.

• Many inhabitants of the sophisticated and prosperous oasis cities of Central Asia that engaged in long-distance trade found in Buddhism a link to the larger, wealthy, and prestigious civilization of India. This resulted in many voluntary conversions.

• Well-to-do Buddhist merchants built monasteries and supported monks to earn religious merit. These monasteries in turn provided convenient and culturally familiar places of rest and resupply for merchants making the trek across Central Asia.

• Buddhism progressed only slowly among pastoral peoples of Central Asia. It had its greatest success when pastoralists engaged in long-distance trade or came to rule settled peoples.

• In China, Buddhism remained for many centuries a religion of foreign merchants or foreign rulers. Only slowly did it become popular among the Chinese themselves.

• As it spread, Buddhism changed, and some of these changes may have made it more appealing to local populations. In particular, the Mahayana form of Buddhism flourished, its emphasis on compassion and the possibility of earning merit making it more appealing than the more austere psychological teachings of the original Buddha.

• As it spread, Buddhism picked up elements of other cultures, including Greek influences, and the gods of many peoples along the Silk Roads were incorporated into Buddhist practice as bodhisattvas.

Q. *What was the impact of disease along the Silk Roads?*

• Contact led to peoples being exposed to unfamiliar diseases to which they had little immunity or effective methods of coping.

• The spread of some particularly virulent epidemic diseases could lead to deaths on a large scale. The worst example of this occurred in the fourteenth century, when the Black Death, identified variously with bubonic plague, anthrax, or a package of epidemic diseases, swept away nearly one-third of the population in Europe, China, and the Middle East.

• In the long run, the exchange of diseases gave Europeans a certain advantage when, after 1500, they confronted the peoples of the Western Hemisphere, who had little natural protection from the diseases of the Eastern Hemisphere.

Q. *How did the operation of the Indian Ocean trading network differ from that of the Silk Roads?*

• Transportation costs were lower on the Sea Roads than the Silk Roads, because ships could accommodate larger and heavier cargoes than camels. This meant that the Sea Roads could eventually carry more bulk goods and products destined for a mass market—textiles, pepper, timber, rice, sugar, wheat—whereas the Silk Roads were limited largely to luxury goods for the few.

• The Sea Roads relied on alternating wind currents known as monsoons.

• India was the center of the Sea Roads but not of the Silk Roads.

Q. *What lay behind the flourishing of Indian Ocean commerce in the postclassical millennium?*

• One important factor was the economic and political revival of China, especially during the Tang and Song dynasties (618–1279).

• China both supplied products for and consumed the products of the Indian Ocean trading network.

• China also provided technological innovations, including larger ships and the magnetic compass, which facilitated trade.

• A second important factor was the sudden rise of Islam in the seventh century C.E. and its subsequent spread across much of the Afro-Eurasian world.

• Islam was friendly to commercial life. The creation of an Arab Empire, stretching from the Atlantic Ocean through the Mediterranean basin and all the way to India, brought together in a single political system an immense range of economies and cultural traditions and provided a vast arena for trade.

• Middle Eastern gold and silver purchased pepper, textiles, and gemstones in India.

• Merchants from the Arab Empire established communities from East Africa to the China coast.

• Opportunities for trade led to the production of sugar and dates in Mesopotamia and stimulated a slave trade from East Africa to provide labor for the growing and refining of these products.

• Widespread conversion to Islam among traders in the Indian Ocean underpinned an international maritime culture and also helped to facilitate commercial transactions.

Q. *What is the relationship between the rise of Srivijaya and the world of Indian Ocean commerce?*

• Srivijaya emerged from the intense competition between small ports along the Straits of Malacca, the critical choke point of Indian Ocean commerce. It came to dominate the straits, which controlled the key all-sea route between India and China.

• Srivijaya's plentiful supply of gold, its access to the source of highly sought-after spices, and the taxes it levied on passing ships provided the resources to attract supporters, to fund an embryonic bureaucracy, and to create the military and naval forces that brought some security to the area.

• Srivijaya monarchs made use of imported Indian political ideas and Buddhist religious concepts (in addition to local beliefs about the magical powers of chiefs) to construct their government.

• They employed Indian merchants as advisers, clerks, and officials, even assigning them Sanskrit titles.

• The capital city of Palembang was a cosmopolitan city with cultural influences from the Indian Ocean trading network.

• The rulers of Srivijaya sponsored the creation of images of the Buddha and various bodhisattvas. Srivijaya ultimately became a major center of Buddhist observance and teaching.

Q. *What was the role of Swahili civilization in the world of Indian Ocean commerce?*

• Economically, Swahili cities provided commercial centers that accumulated goods from the interior of sub-Saharan Africa and exchanged them for the products of the Indian Ocean trading network.

• Culturally, Swahili civilization also participated in the larger Indian Ocean world. Most important, Swahili civilization rapidly and voluntarily became Islamic. Moreover, Arab, Indian, and perhaps Persian merchants visited and sometimes permanently settled in Swahili cities.

• Swahili rulers often claimed Arab or Persian origins to bolster their authority.

• In terms of material culture, Swahili elite dined off Chinese porcelain and dressed in Indian cottons.

• The Swahili language was grammatically a Bantu African tongue, but it was written in Arabic script and contained a number of Arabic loan words.

Q. *What changes did trans-Saharan trade bring to West Africa?*

• It provided both incentives and resources for the construction of new and larger political structures, including the city-states of the Hausa people and the empires of Ghana, Mali, Songhay, and Kanem.

• These Sudanic states established substantial urban and commercial centers where traders congregated and goods were exchanged. Some also became manufacturing centers, creating finely wrought beads, iron tools, or cotton textiles for trade.

• Islam accompanied trade and became an important element in the urban culture of West Africa.

Q. *In what ways did networks of interaction in the Western Hemisphere differ from those in the Eastern Hemisphere?*

• Direct connections among the civilizations and cultures of the Americas were less densely woven than in the Afro-Eurasian region. There was no equivalent in the Western Hemisphere to the long-distance trade of the Silk, Sea, or Sand Roads of the Eastern Hemisphere.

• The spread of agricultural products was slower and less pronounced in the Americas than in Eurasia. The north/south orientation of the Americas required agricultural practices to adapt to various and distinct climatic and vegetation zones, whereas the east/west orientation of Eurasia made crop dissemination easier and quicker there.

• The Americas had no equivalent to the spread of distinct cultural traditions like Buddhism, Christianity, or Islam that ultimately helped to integrate distant peoples in the Afro-Eurasian web.

• Nevertheless, the Americas did have zones of interaction, as reflected in the slow spread of cultural elements.

• Commerce did play an important role in regions where contact was possible—for instance, along the river networks of North America, in the Amazon basin, and between the islands of the Caribbean. But the most active and dense networks of communication and exchange lay within, rather than between, the regions that housed the two great civilizations of the Western Hemisphere—Mesoamerica and the Andes.

ADDITIONAL RESOURCES FOR CHAPTER 8

Additional Bedford/St. Martin's Resources

FOR INSTRUCTORS

Computerized Test Bank

This test bank provides over thirty exercises per chapter, including multiple-choice, fill-in-the-blank, short-answer, and full-length essay questions. Instructors can customize quizzes, add or edit both questions and answers, and export questions and answers to a variety of formats, including WebCT and Blackboard. The disc includes correct answers and essay outlines.

Instructor's Resource CD-ROM

This disc provides instructors with ready-made and customizable PowerPoint multimedia presentations built around chapter outlines, maps, figures, and all images from the textbook, plus JPEG versions of all maps, figures, and images.

The following maps and images from Chapter 8 are available in both JPEG and PowerPoint format on the Instructor's Resource CD-ROM:

- Map 8.1: The Silk Roads (p. 219)
- Map 8.2: The Sea Roads (p. 226)
- Map 8.3: The Sand Roads (p. 234)
- Map 8.4: The American Web (p. 236)
- Travels on the Silk Road (p. 216)
- Dunhuang (p. 223)
- Borobudur (p. 230)
- The Gold of Mali (p. 235)
- Inca Roads (p. 237)

FOR STUDENTS

Documents and Essays from *Worlds of History: A Comparative Reader,* Third Edition (Volume 1)

The following documents, essays, and illustrations to accompany Chapter 8 are available in Chapter 7 of this reader by Kevin Reilly:

- Jerry H. Bentley, *The Spread of World Religions*
- *Pliny Consults the Emperor Trajan*
- Eusebius, from *Life of Constantine*
- Buddhism in China: from *The Disposition of Error*
- From *The Lotus Sutra*
- From the *Koran*
- Islamic Expansion, Peace Terms with Jerusalem (636)
- *The Glorious Victories of 'Amda Seyon, King of Ethiopia*

Online Study Guide at bedfordstmartins.com/strayer

The Online Study Guide helps students synthesize the material from the text as well as practice the skills historians use to make sense of the past. Each chapter of the Online Study Guide contains specific testing exercises, including a multiple-choice self-test that focuses on important conceptual ideas; an identification quiz that helps students remember key people, places, and events; a flashcard activity that tests students on their knowledge of key terms; and two interactive map activities intended to strengthen students' geographic skills. Instructors can monitor students' progress through an online Quiz Gradebook or receive email updates.

Further Reading

African Empires to 1500 C.E., http://www.fsmitha.com/h3/h15-af.htm. An extensive article on African states (not just empires) before 1500, with links to helpful maps.

Civilizations in Africa, http://www.wsu.edu:8080/~dee/CIVAFRCA/CIVAFRCA.HTM. Resources for the study of Africa before 1500.

Curtin, Philip D. *Cross-Cultural Trade in World History.* Cambridge: Cambridge University Press, 1984. A far-reaching and thought-provoking study.

Dunn, Ross E. *The Adventures of Ibn Battuta: A Muslim Traveler of the Fourteenth Century.* Berkeley: University of California Press, 1987. Perhaps the most accessible work on the great Muslim traveler Ibn Battuta, with lengthy excerpts from his travel account.

Foltz, Richard C. *Religions of the Silk Road: Overland Trade and Cultural Exchange from Antiquity to the Fifteenth Century.* New York: St. Martin's Press, 1999. An insightful short book on the topic.

Horton, Mark, and John Middleton. *The Swahili: The Social Landscape of a Mercantile Society.* Oxford: Blackwell, 2000. An interesting and up-to-date study of Swahili history and culture.

Hourani, George F. *Arab Seafaring in the Indian Ocean in Ancient and Early Medieval Times.* 2nd ed. Princeton, NJ: Princeton University Press, 1995. A useful account of the importance of the Arab world in naval history.

McGrail, Seán. *Boats of the World: From the Stone Age to Medieval Times.* 2nd ed. New York: Oxford University Press, 2004. A wealth of information about ships and shipping.

The Spice Routes, http://asiapacificuniverse.com/pkm/spiceroutes.htm. A very interesting article on the international spice trade.

Literature

Dawson, Christopher, trans. *Mission to Asia*. Toronto: University of Toronto Press, 1980. This volume includes accounts by the friars John of Plano Carpini and William of Rubreck of their missions to the Mongol court in the thirteenth century. Both give a fine sense of travel along the Silk Roads, as well as much material about the Mongols.

Ibn Battutah. *The Travels of Ibn Battutah*. Ed. Tim Mackintosh-Smith. London: Picador, 2002. A good selection from Ibn Battuta's account of his travels (note that "Battuta" is the more common transliteration of his name).

Mandeville, John. *The Travels of Sir John Mandeville*. Trans. C. W. R. D. Moseley. London: Penguin, 2005. A frequently hilarious fourteenth-century account by a European who claimed to have traveled to the East. More useful for European assumptions than for factual content, the book nonetheless shows well the misconceptions that can arise in a world of indirect trade.

Polo, Marco. *The Travels*. Trans. Ronald Latham. London: Penguin, 1958. The most famous of all travel accounts.

Film

Ancient Trade Routes of the Arab World. Insight Media, 2002. 38 minutes. Looks at Arab trade routes across the Sahara, in East Africa, and across the Indian Ocean.

History of Trade in China. Insight Media, 2000. 26 minutes. The opening parts of this video discuss the growth of both the Silk Roads and the Sea Roads from China to the West.

The Silk Road. Six-part series. PBS Home Video, 2000. 55 minutes each. This series explores key sites along the Silk Roads.

Thailand and Cambodia: Temples of Glory. Insight Media, 2006. 30 minutes. Compares and contrasts the early histories of Thailand and Cambodia, including the temples at Ayutthaya, Siam, and Angkor.

China and the World
East Asian Connections, 500–1300

CHAPTER OVERVIEW

Chapter Objectives

- To explore the role of China as "superpower" among the third-wave civilizations
- To examine China's deep influence on East Asia
- To consider the ways in which interaction with other peoples had an impact on China
- To encourage students to question modern assumptions about China

Chapter Outline

I. Opening Vignette
   A. Many believe that China will be the next superpower.
      1. this is nothing new in Chinese history
   B. China was a major player among the "third-wave" civilizations.
      1. a China-centered "world order" encompassed most of eastern Asia
      2. China's borders reached far into Central Asia
      3. its wealthy and cosmopolitan culture attracted visitors from afar
      4. all of China's neighbors felt its gravitational pull
      5. China's economy and technological innovation had effects throughout Eurasia

   C. China was also changed by its interactions with non-Chinese peoples.
      1. nomadic military threat
      2. international trade as catalyst of change

II. The Reemergence of a Unified China
   A. The Han dynasty collapsed around 220 C.E.
      1. led to 300 years of political fragmentation
      2. nomadic incursion from the north
      3. conditions discredited Confucianism in many eyes
      4. Chinese migration southward to Yangzi River valley began
         a. beginning of vast environmental change
   B. A "Golden Age" of Chinese Achievement
      [see Lecture Strategy 1]
      1. the Sui dynasty (589–618) reunified China
         a. Sui rulers vastly extended the canal system
         b. but their ruthlessness and failure to conquer Korea alienated people, exhausted state's resources
         c. dynasty was overthrown, but state didn't disintegrate
      2. Tang (618–907) and Song (960–1279) dynasties built on Sui foundations
         a. established patterns of Chinese life that lasted into twentieth century
         b. regarded as a "golden age" of arts and literature
            i. poetry, landscape painting, ceramics of high order

ii. birth of Neo-Confucianism
   (Confucian revival with added
   elements of Buddhism and Daoism)
3. Tang and Song politics
   a. six major ministries were created, along
      with the Censorate for surveillance over
      government
   b. examination system revived to staff the
      bureaucracy
      i. encouraged by first printing of books
   c. proliferation of schools and colleges
   d. a large share of official positions went
      to sons of the elite
   e. large landowners continued to be
      powerful, despite state efforts to
      redistribute land to the peasants
4. "economic revolution" under the Song
   a. great prosperity
   b. rapid population growth (from 50
      million–60 million people during Tang
      dynasty to 120 million by 1200)
   c. great improvement in agricultural
      production
   d. China was the most urbanized region
      in the world
      i. dozens of cities with population over
         100,000
      ii. capital Hangzhou had more than
         a million people
   e. great network of internal waterways
      (canals, rivers, lakes)
      i. provided a cheap transport system that
         bound China together
   f. great improvements in industrial
      production
      i. iron industry greatly increased
         output
   g. invention of print (both woodblock and
      movable type)
   h. best navigational and shipbuilding
      technology in the world
   i. invention of gunpowder
5. production for the market rather than
   for local consumption was very
   widespread
   a. cheap transportation allowed peasants to
      grow specialized crops
   b. government demanded payment of taxes
      in cash, not in kind

c. growing use of paper money and
   financial instruments
C. Women in the Song Dynasty
   1. the era wasn't very "golden" for women
   2. during the Tang dynasty, elite women in
      the north had had greater freedom
      (influence of steppe nomads)
   3. Song: tightening of patriarchal restrictions
      on women
   4. literature highlighted the subjection of
      women
   5. foot binding started in tenth or eleventh
      century C.E.
      a. was associated with images of female
         beauty and eroticism
      b. kept women restricted to the house
   6. textile production became larger scale,
      displacing women from their traditional
      role in the industry
      a. women found other roles in cities
      b. prosperity of the elite created demand
         for concubines, entertainers, courtesans,
         prostitutes
   7. in some ways the position of women
      improved
      a. property rights expanded
      b. more women were educated, in order
         to raise sons better

III. **China and the Northern Nomads:**
   A Chinese World Order in the Making
   A. There have been two enduring misconcep-
      tions of Chinese history:
      1. the idea that Chinese civilization was
         impressive but largely static **[see
         Discussion Topic 1]**
      2. the idea that China was a self-contained
         civilization
   B. For most of its history, China's most enduring
      interaction with foreigners was in the north,
      with the peoples of the steppes. **[see
      Discussion Topic 2]**
      1. northern nomads typically lived in small
         kinship-based groups
      2. occasional creation of powerful states or
         confederations
      3. pastoral societies needed grain and other
         farm products from China
      4. leaders wanted Chinese manufactured and
         luxury goods

5. steppe pressure and intrusion was a constant factor in Chinese history for 2,000 years
6. nomads often felt threatened by the Chinese
   a. Chinese military attacks on the steppes
   b. Great Wall
7. China needed the nomads
   a. steppes provided horses and other goods
   b. nomads controlled much of the Silk Roads

C. The Tribute System in Theory **[see Lecture Strategy 2]**
   1. the Chinese understood themselves as the center of the world ("middle kingdom"), far superior to the "barbarian" outsiders
      a. believed that barbarians could become civilized Chinese
   2. establishment of "tribute system" to manage relations with non-Chinese peoples
      a. non-Chinese authorities must acknowledge Chinese superiority
      b. present tribute to the emperor
      c. would receive trading privileges and "bestowals" in return (often worth more than the tribute)
   3. the system apparently worked for centuries

D. The Tribute System in Practice
   1. but the system disguised contradictory realities
   2. some nomadic empires could deal with China on at least equal terms
      a. Xiongnu confederacy (established around 200 B.C.E.)
         i. Chinese emperor had to recognize political equality of the Xiongnu
         ii. had to pay Xiongnu what amounted to tribute
      b. Turkic empires of Mongolia were similar
         i. Uighurs rescued Tang dynasty from an internal revolt in the 750s
   3. steppe nomads usually did not want to conquer and rule China
      a. preferred extortion
      b. but nomads moved in when the Chinese state broke down
      c. several steppe states took over parts of northern China
         i. Khitan (907–1125)
         ii. Jurchen (1115–1234)

E. Cultural Influence across an Ecological Frontier
   1. nomads who ruled parts of China often adopted Chinese ways
      a. especially the Jurchen
   2. but Chinese culture did not have great impact on steppe nomads
      a. pastoral societies retained their own cultural patterns
      b. most lived where Chinese-style agriculture was impossible
   3. interaction took the form of trade, military conflict, negotiations, extortion, and some cultural influence
   4. steppe culture influenced the parts of northern China that were ruled frequently by nomads
      a. founders of Sui and Tang dynasties were of mixed blood
      b. Tang dynasty: fad among northern Chinese elites for anything connected to "western barbarians"
         i. growing backlash against foreign influence

IV. **Coping with China: Comparing Korea, Vietnam, and Japan** [see Classroom Activity 1]
   A. The emerging states and civilizations of Korea, Vietnam, and Japan also had tributary relationships with China.
      1. agricultural, sedentary societies
      2. their civilizations were shaped by proximity to China but did not *become* Chinese
      3. similar to twentieth-century Afro-Asian societies that accepted elements of Western culture while maintaining political/cultural independence
   B. Korea and China
      1. interaction with China started with temporary Chinese conquest of northern Korea during the Han dynasty, with some colonization
      2. Korean states emerged in fourth–seventh centuries C.E.
         a. the states were rivals; also resisted Chinese political control
         b. seventh century: the Silla kingdom allied with Tang dynasty China to bring some political unity

i. but Chinese interference provoked military resistance

ii. China made do with a tributary relationship after 688

3. Korea generally maintained political independence under the Silla (688–900), Koryo (918–1392), and Yi (1392–1910) dynasties

   a. but China provided legitimacy for Korean rulers

   b. efforts to replicate Chinese court life and administration

   c. capital city Kumsong modeled on Chinese capital Chang'an

4. acceptance of much Chinese culture

   a. Chinese luxury goods, scholarship, and religious influence

   b. Confucianism had negative impact on Korean women, especially after 1300

      i. ended "free choice" marriages

      ii. discouraged practice of a woman raising her children in her parents' home, often joined by husband

      iii. ended practice of plural marriage for men—so some wives were reduced in rank to concubinage

5. Korea maintained its Korean culture

   a. Chinese cultural influence had little effect on Korea's serflike peasants or large slave population

   b. only Buddhism moved beyond the Korean elite

   c. examination system for bureaucrats never won prominence

   d. in 1400s, Korea developed a phonetic alphabet (*hangul*)

C. Vietnam and China

1. the experience of Vietnam was broadly similar to that of Korea

2. but Vietnam's cultural heartland in the Red River valley was part of the Chinese state from 111 B.C.E. to 939 C.E.

   a. real effort at cultural assimilation of elite

   b. provoked rebellions

      i. great rebellion of Trung sisters (39–43 C.E.)

      ii. rebellion in early tenth century C.E. established Vietnam as separate state

      iii. remained tributary to China

3. Vietnamese rulers adopted the Chinese approach to government

   a. examination system helped undermine established aristocrats

   b. elite remained deeply committed to Chinese culture

4. much of distinctive Vietnamese culture remained in place

   a. language, cockfighting, betel nuts, greater roles for women

   b. kept nature goddesses and a "female Buddha" in popular belief

   c. developed a variation of Chinese writing, *chu nom* ("southern script")

D. Japan and China [see Lecture Strategy 3 and Classroom Activity 2]

1. Japan was never invaded or conquered by China, so borrowing of Chinese culture was voluntary

2. main period of cultural borrowing was seventh–ninth centuries C.E., when first unified Japanese state began to emerge

   a. creation of Japanese bureaucratic state modeled on China began with Shotoku Taishi (572–622)

   b. large-scale missions to China to learn

   c. Seventeen Article Constitution:

      i. proclaimed Japanese ruler as Chinese-style emperor

      ii. encouraged Buddhism and Confucianism

      iii. identified moral rulers as foundation for social harmony

   d. two capital cities (Nara and then Heian) were founded, both modeled on Chinese capital (Chang'an)

3. elements of Chinese culture took root in Japan

   a. several schools of Chinese Buddhism

   b. art, architecture, education, medicine, religious views

   c. Chinese writing system

4. Japanese borrowings were selective

   a. deliberate borrowings stopped after tenth century

5. Japan never created an effective centralized and bureaucratic state

   a. political power became decentralized

  b. local authorities developed their own military forces (*samurai*)
    i. *bushido*: samurai set of values
    ii. celebration of military values, unlike China
  6. religious distinctiveness
    a. Buddhism never replaced native belief system
    b. the way of the *kami* (sacred spirits), later called Shinto
  7. distinctive literary and artistic culture
    a. unique writing system mixed Chinese characters with phonetic symbols
    b. early development of *tanka* (highly stylized poetry)
    c. highly refined aesthetic court culture, especially in Heian period (794–1192)
      i. much is known from women writers who used vernacular script
      ii. Murasaki Shikibu's *Tale of Genji* (ca. 1000) shows court life particularly well
  8. elite women escaped most of Confucian oppression
    a. only began to lose status in the twelfth century, with rise of warrior culture

V. China and the Eurasian World Economy
  A. Spillovers: China's Impact on Eurasia
    1. many of China's technological innovations spread beyond its borders
      a. salt production through solar evaporation
      b. papermaking
      c. printing (though resisted by the Islamic world)
      d. gunpowder invented ca. 1000, but used differently after it reached Europe
      e. Chinese textile, metallurgical, and naval technologies also stimulated imitation and innovation (e.g., magnetic compass)
    2. Chinese prosperity stimulated commercial life all over Eurasia
  B. On the Receiving End: China as Economic Beneficiary
    1. China learned cotton and sugar cultivation and processing from India
    2. China was transformed around 1000 by introduction of new rice strains from Vietnam

  3. technological creativity was spurred by cross-cultural contact
    a. printing was stimulated by Buddhism (first printed book, in 868 C.E., was the Diamond Sutra, a Buddhist text)
  4. growing participation in Indian Ocean trade
    a. foreign merchant settlements in southern Chinese ports by Tang era
    b. sometimes brought violence, e.g., massive massacre of foreigners in Canton in the 870s
    c. transformation of southern China to production for export instead of subsistence

VI. China and Buddhism
  A. Buddhism was India's most important gift to China
    1. China's only large-scale cultural borrowing until Marxism
    2. China was the base for Buddhism's spread to Korea and Japan
  B. Making Buddhism Chinese
    1. Buddhism entered China via Silk Roads in first–second centuries C.E.
      a. had little appeal at first
      b. Indian culture was too different from Chinese
        i. Buddhist monasticism seemed to dishonor Chinese family values
        ii. concern for individual salvation seemed selfish
        iii. China's philosophy was "this-worldly"
    2. Buddhism took root 300–800 C.E.
      a. collapse of the Han dynasty ca. 200 C.E. brought chaos and discrediting of Confucianism
      b. nomadic rulers in northern China favored Buddhism
      c. Buddhism was comforting
      d. monasteries provided increasing array of social services
      e. Buddhists appeared to have access to magical powers
      f. serious effort to present Buddhism in a form accessible to the Chinese
        i. *dharma* was translated as *dao*
        ii. "morality" was translated as filial submission

g. it was Mahayana form of Buddhism that became popular
   i. Pure Land School was especially popular
3. Sui and early Tang dynasties gave state support to Buddhism
   a. Sui emperor Wendi (r. 581–604) had monasteries built at base of China's five sacred mountains
      i. used Buddhism to justify his military campaigns
   b. monasteries became very wealthy
   c. Buddhism was never independent from state authorities
C. Losing State Support: The Crisis of Chinese Buddhism [see Discussion Topic 3]
1. growth of Chinese Buddhism provoked resistance and criticism
   a. deepening resentment of the Buddhist establishment's wealth
   b. it was *foreign*, thus offensive
   c. monastic celibacy and withdrawal undermined the Confucian-based family system
2. new xenophobia perhaps started with An Lushan rebellion (755–763), led by foreign general
3. Chinese state began direct action against foreign religions in 841–845
   a. 260,000 monks and nuns forced to return to secular life
   b. thousands of monasteries, temples, and shrines confiscated or destroyed
   c. Buddhists forbidden to use precious metals or gems for their images
4. Buddhism did not vanish from China; it remained an important element of popular religion

VII. Reflections: Why Do Things Change? [see Classroom Activity 3]
A. Change and transformation are constants in human history.
   1. explaining why and how societies change is historians' most central issue
   2. there is often disagreement about what is the most important catalyst of change
B. The case of China illustrates the range of factors that drive change.
   1. world historians tend to find contact with strangers to be the primary source of change

2. the history of China and East Asia helps illustrate this view
3. but perhaps it's misleading to distinguish between internal and external sources of change

USING *WAYS OF THE WORLD* IN THE CLASSROOM

Lecture Strategies

Lecture Strategy 1

"China's golden age."
This chapter devotes some space to the issue of Song-era China as a "golden age" of prosperity and cultural achievement. This theme is worth exploring in greater detail, adding comparisons to other states that the class has already studied. The objectives of this lecture strategy are to:

- explore the cultural richness of the Song dynasty in China
- consider what part of the population was affected by this "golden age"
- examine in greater detail the ideological and economic underpinnings of this "golden age"
- investigate whether any society examined thus far in this class had a comparable cultural efflorescence

This lecture can be approached in a variety of ways. One might start with a political history of the Song dynasty (including the fact that there were *two* Song dynasties, one in the north and one in the south). Another way to begin is with a brief review of the factors that make a cultural golden age possible, such as a tradition that values scholarly achievement, the existence of a leisure class, and an elite that values "higher" culture (by reading its works, buying its products, and patronizing writers and artists). Some major points you might want to include in a lecture are:

- the great inventions of the Song period and how they were applied in China (movable type, the magnetic compass, gunpowder)
- the massive encyclopedic works of the era, such as the universal history *Zizhi Tongjian*

- the outstanding literary figures of the Song period (Zhuxi, Ouyang, Xiu, Su Shi, Sima Guang, Shen Kuo): the sort of material they produced, common themes, etc.
- civil officials who were also poets (e.g., Su Dongpo and Fan Zhongyan)
- painting (e.g., "Riverside Scene at the Qing Ming Festival" by the painter Zhang Zeduan)
- new government policies attempted by the Song dynasty
- the Jin takeover of the northern Song territory and its significance for art and culture
- the physical remains of Song dynasty culture (metalwork, silk weaving, porcelain)
- the introduction of tea drinking
- the development of Neo-Confucianism (especially the philosophers Cheng Yi and Zhu Xi)
- advances in mathematics (e.g., the work of Yang Hui and Qin Jiushao)
- advances in architecture (e.g., the Lingxiao Pagoda, the Liaodi Pagoda of Hebei, and the Song imperial tombs at Gongxian)

Lecture Strategy 2

"Is geography destiny? The case of East Asia."
This chapter discusses two important points at which geography affected the development of East Asian societies: the presence of the steppes along China's northern border and the one hundred miles of sea that lie between mainland Asia and the Japanese archipelago. The purpose of this lecture is to extend coverage of this issue. Its objectives are:

- to make students aware of the importance of geography in human historical processes
- using the case of East Asia, to examine what cultural or political factors can surmount the difficulties posed by geography

You will need a good physical map of East Asia for this lecture strategy.

Start by making sure that students are familiar with the location of the various states of East Asia that are discussed in this chapter. We know that China dominated the history of East Asia, so it makes sense to use China as the focal point. Consider its boundaries one by one, discussing Tang and Song relations with peoples on the other side of the border, attempts at conquest, or other forms of cultural interaction, as well as the geographical features that helped or hindered the process. Some points to consider are:

- the role of the Himalayas in shaping history, though Buddhist monks still made their way between China and India
- the steppes as both an aid and a hindrance to expansion
- Chinese penetration into Central Asia
- the presence of major river valleys along which agriculture could develop easily
- the role of the sea (especially noting the nature of the South China Sea, with its shallows and unappealing coastline)

Lecture Strategy 3

"Medieval Japan: Why unification failed."
Japan in the period ca. 600–ca. 1300 is another topic covered in this chapter that is worth developing into a full lecture. The material is interesting in the light it sheds on world political systems and the theme of cultural interaction. Students tend to be particularly interested in the samurai and how they came to dominate Japan. The objectives of this lecture strategy are:

- to teach the history of Heian and Kamakura Japan
- to explore why the Japanese state, apparently so promising, failed to hold onto the centralization of the early unification period
- to examine the features of samurai culture and its relationship to Japanese culture more generally

Any lecture on a period or region of history will work better if there is a single organizing theme, which is why we suggest the theme of failed unification. A useful approach to laying out the material is to use excerpts from contemporary Japanese sources to help you tell the story. For example, you might incorporate the following into your lecture (see the Further Reading section of this chapter for readily available editions of these works):

- *Jimmu Tenno* (the tale of the first emperor)
- the Seventeen Article Constitution
- the Taika Reform Edicts
- *The Diary of Lady Sarashina (1009–1059)*
- Taira Shigesuke's *Code of the Samurai*

Some main points to be sure to cover in your lecture are:

- the foundation myth of the sun goddess Amaterasu and her gifts to the emperors
- imperial descent from Amaterasu
- competition between great clans to unify Japan, and the importance of Japan as an archipelago in that process
- the strong ritual element of Japanese imperial rule
- Prince Shotoku
- the Taika reform movement
- the power of regents as a decentralizing force (especially the Fujiwara family)
- the rise of the *shoen* (great estates)
- the period of "cloister government"
- the role of the powerful monasteries in weakening the government
- recruitment of warriors to protect *shoen* and monasteries and to coerce the government
- the great power struggle that ended with the beginning of the Kamakura period (1185–1333)
- creation of a parallel administration, ruled by the *shogun*
- the development of the samurai ethos

Things to Do in the Classroom

Discussion Topics

1. **Misconception Topic/Difficult Topic, large or small group.** "China never changed."
This chapter provides a great deal of evidence that China *did* change. Ask students to review the major elements of that change and the reasons behind it. Then draw them into a general discussion of how that misconception of an unchanging Chinese culture could have evolved in Western society. Some supplementary questions to ask are:

- What sort of impression of China and the Chinese do you have from movies?
- What impression do American news services give of China and the Chinese?
- How were Americans first exposed to China, and what role could that first contact have played in creating the stereotype of an unchanging China?

- Is there any sense in which the stereotype still seems true to you? Why?

2. **Comparison, large or small group.** "Compare China's interaction with its northern 'barbarians' to U.S. interaction with the Plains Indians in the nineteenth century."
Many members of your class will be much more familiar with the history of the American "Wild West" than they are with the history of China. Thus this discussion segment provides an opportunity for them to compare the familiar with the unfamiliar and to explore important differences and similarities.

Ask the students to outline briefly the main points that they know of U.S. interaction with western Indians (try to keep them from dealing with the "First Contact" period on the East Coast in the colonial period). Then ask them to discuss the following questions:

- What basic similarities are there between China's northern nomads and the Indians of the Great Plains?
- What important differences are there?
- Are there points at which the U.S. government's relations with the Plains Indians were similar to that of the Tang and Song Chinese government with the nomads?
- In what ways were the responses different? Why?

3. **Contextualization, large or small group.** "The Chinese and xenophobia."
While this chapter shows that the Chinese were, in important ways, open to foreign influence, it also reveals a frequent strain of fear or hatred of foreigners (xenophobia). The purpose of this discussion module is to pull together disparate material in the chapter into an overarching consideration of this Chinese xenophobia.

Start by asking students to list the main reasons why the Chinese state turned against Buddhism in the ninth century. Then ask them to consider the following questions:

- At what other times can one see a strand of xenophobia in Chinese history?
- Besides the reasons for the reaction against Buddhism, what other reasons for this xenophobia can you identify?
- In the class so far, where else have we seen examples of widespread xenophobia?
- Were xenophobic incidents outside of China caused by the same factors?

- What can consideration of this topic teach you about Chinese society by comparison with other world societies we have studied?

Classroom Activities

1. **Analysis exercise, large or small group.** "The big picture."
With the class, lay out in chart form the key similarities and differences between Korea, Vietnam, and Japan. This will schematize material in the chapter and will also model an effective study technique for students. On the chart, be sure to include at least the following elements:

- when each state was unified
- the degree to which the government was centralized
- the degree of Chinese influence on government
- influence of Chinese scholarship on the elite
- influence of other cultural elements on the elite
- position of women in society before Chinese influence
- position of women in society after Chinese influence began
- main religious beliefs
- degree of Chinese influence on popular religious beliefs

2. **Close-reading exercise, small group.** "The Seventeen Article Constitution."
Distribute copies of Shotoku's Seventeen Article Constitution to the class (available at www.wsu.edu:8080/~dee/ANCJAPAN/CONST.HTM). Ask the students to look for particular points in the reading that they think reveal particularly well what Shotoku's agenda was, listing those points for further discussion with the whole class.

3. **Clicker question.** In this chapter, the author was at some pains to show China as a more "open" society than it is often believed to be. In your opinion, did he succeed in his goal?

Key Terms

An Lushan: Foreign-born general who led a major revolt against the Tang dynasty in 755–763, perhaps provoking China's turn to xenophobia. (*pron.* ahn loo-shahn)

bushido: The "way of the warrior," referring to the military virtues of the Japanese samurai, including bravery, loyalty, and an emphasis on death over surrender. (*pron.* boo-SHEE-doh)

Chinese Buddhism: Buddhism was China's only large-scale cultural borrowing before the twentieth century; Buddhism entered China from India in the first and second centuries C.E. but only became popular in 300–800 C.E. through a series of cultural accommodations. At first supported by the state, Buddhism suffered persecution during the ninth century but continued to play a role in Chinese society.

chu nom: A variation of Chinese writing developed in Vietnam that became the basis for an independent national literature; "southern script." (*pron.* choo nom)

foot binding: Chinese practice of tightly wrapping girls' feet to keep them small, begun in the Tang dynasty; an emphasis on small size and delicacy was central to views of female beauty.

hangul: A phonetic alphabet developed in Korea in the fifteenth century C.E. (*pron.* HAHN-gool)

Hangzhou: China's capital during the Song dynasty, with a population of more than a million people. (*pron.* hong-joe)

Heian: Japan's second capital city (now known as Kyoto), modeled on the Chinese capital of Chang'an; also used to describe the period of Japanese history from 794 to 1192 C.E. (*pron.* HIGH-an)

Jurchen: A nomadic people who established a state that included parts of northern China (1115–1234).

kami: Sacred spirits of Japan, whether ancestors or natural phenomena; their worship much later came to be called Shinto. (*pron.* KAHM-ee)

Khitan: A nomadic people who established a state that included parts of northern China (907–1125). (*pron.* kee-tahn)

Koryo: Korean dynasty (918–1392). (*pron.* KAW-ree-oh)

Kumsong: The capital of Korea in the medieval era, modeled on the Chinese capital of Chang'an. (*pron.* KOOM-song)

Murasaki Shikibu: Perhaps Japan's greatest author, a woman active at the Heian court who is best known for *The Tale of Genji,* which she wrote around 1000 C.E. (*pron.* moo-rah-SAH-kee shee-KEE-boo)

Nara: Japan's first capital city, modeled on the Chinese capital of Chang'an. (*pron.* NAH-rah)

Neo-Confucianism: A philosophy that emerged in Song-dynasty China; it revived Confucian thinking while adding in Buddhist and Daoist elements.

Pure Land Buddhism: A school of Buddhism that proved to be immensely popular in China; emphasized salvation by faith in the Amitabha Buddha.

samurai: Members of Japan's warrior class, which developed as political power became increasingly decentralized. (*pron.* SAM-ooh-rye)

Shotoku Taishi: Japanese statesman (572–622) who launched the drive to make Japan into a centralized bureaucratic state modeled on China; he is best known for the Seventeen Article Constitution, which lays out the principles of this reform. (*pron.* show-TOE-koo tie-EESH-ah)

Silla dynasty: The first ruling dynasty to bring a measure of political unity to the Korean peninsula (688–900 C.E.). (*pron.* SILL-ah or SHILL-ah)

Song dynasty economic revolution: A major economic quickening that took place in China under the Song dynasty (960–1279 C.E.); marked by rapid population growth, urbanization, economic specialization, the development of an immense network of internal waterways, and a great increase in industrial production and innovation. (*pron.* soong)

Sui dynasty: Ruling dynasty of China (581–618 C.E.) that effectively reunited the country after several centuries of political fragmentation. (*pron.* sway)

Tang dynasty: Ruling dynasty of China from 618 to 907 C.E.; noted for its openness to foreign cultural influences. (*pron.* tahng)

tanka: Highly stylized form of Japanese poetry that has been a favored means of expression for centuries. (*pron.* TAHN-kah)

tribute system: Chinese method of dealing with foreign lands and peoples that assumed the subordination of all non-Chinese authorities and required the payment of tribute—produce of value from their countries—to the Chinese emperor (although the Chinese gifts given in return were often much more valuable).

Trung sisters: Two Vietnamese sisters who launched a major revolt against the Chinese presence in Vietnam in 39 C.E.; the rebellion was crushed and the sisters committed suicide, but they remained symbols of Vietnamese resistance to China for centuries. (*pron.* troong)

Uighurs: Turkic empire of the steppes; flourished in eighth century C.E. (*pron.* WEE-gers)

Wendi, Emperor: Sui emperor (r. 581–604 C.E.) who particularly patronized Buddhism. (*pron.* WEN-dee)

Xiongnu: Major nomadic confederacy that was established ca. 200 B.C.E. and eventually reached from Manchuria to Central Asia. (*pron.* SHE-OONG-noo)

Yi: Korean dynasty (1392–1910). (*pron.* yee)

ANSWER GUIDELINES FOR CHAPTER QUESTIONS

The two sets of questions that follow appear in the textbook at the end of the chapter and in the margins of the reading. They are also provided in the Computerized Test Bank with answer guidelines, for your convenience.

The Big Picture Questions

1. In what ways did Tang and Song dynasty China resemble the classical Han dynasty period, and in what ways had China changed?

• Tang and Song dynasty China resembled the Han dynasty period in a number of ways, including the maintenance of the imperial political system;

• the importance of a professional bureaucracy formally trained and subject to competitive exams;

• a focus on establishing a dominant political position in East Asia that was recognized by China's neighbors;

• an interest in and support for long-distance trade;

• and the continued importance of the Confucian tradition in elite society.

• China also experienced important changes following the Han dynasty period, including tighter unification of northern and southern China through a vast waterway system;

• the long-term migration of Chinese populations south into the Yangzi River valley after 220 C.E.;

• an economic revolution that made it the richest empire on earth;

• and rapid population growth, from 50 million to 60 million people during the Tang dynasty to 120 million people by 1200, that was spurred in part by a remarkable growth in agricultural production.

• Also, the economy of China became the most highly commercialized in the world and became more active in long-distance trade than during the Han dynasty.

2. Based on this chapter, how would you respond to the idea that China was a self-contained or isolated civilization?

• There are many developments noted in this chapter that oppose this idea, including China's active participation in long-distance trade;
    • the tribute system, which established ties with China's neighbors;
    • the influence of Buddhism on Chinese society;
    • the popularity for a time during the Tang dynasty of "western barbarian" music, dancing, clothing, foods, games, and artistic styles among the upper classes;
    • the influence of pastoral and nomadic peoples on China;
    • the spread of Chinese technological innovations to other parts of the world;
    • China's adoption of outside crops and technology, including cotton, sugar, and the processing techniques for these crops from India, as well as fast-ripening rice from Vietnam;
    • and the cosmopolitan nature of China's port cities.
• However, in defense of the idea, one could point to the perception of the educated Chinese elite that China was self-sufficient, requiring little from the outside world.

3. In what different ways did nearby peoples experience their giant Chinese neighbor, and how did they respond to it?

• China's neighbors did not experience China in one uniform way, but in general nearby peoples experienced their Chinese neighbor as a trade partner, cultural influence, and political influence. China could also be a military threat at times.
• Some neighbors, such as Korea and Vietnam, experienced China as a military conqueror; others, such as the pastoral peoples to the north of China, were at different times both the conquerors and rulers of parts of China and subject to attack by the Chinese. Japan had no military conflict with China.
• As far as their responses, neighbors such as Korea and Vietnam, and sometimes the pastoral peoples and Japan as well, participated in the tribute system promoted by China.

• Some, such as Japan, voluntarily adopted Chinese intellectual, cultural, and religious traditions. Other neighbors, such as Vietnam, both willingly adopted some Chinese intellectual, cultural, and religious traditions and had others imposed upon them while under Chinese rule.
• Responses to Chinese influence varied from outright rebellion in Vietnam under the Trung sisters to the active embrace of Chinese influence by the Japanese under Shotoku Taishi.

4. How can you explain the changing fortunes of Buddhism in China?

• Buddhism first grew in influence in China during a period of disorder following the collapse of the Han dynasty, a time when many in China had lost faith in Chinese systems of thought.
• Buddhism also benefited from the support of foreign nomadic rulers who during this period governed portions of northern China.
• Once established, Buddhism grew for a number of reasons: Buddhist monasteries provided an array of social services to ordinary people; Buddhism was associated with access to magical powers; there was a serious effort by Buddhist monks and scholars to present this Indian religion in terms that the Chinese could relate to; and under the Sui and Tang dynasties, Buddhism received growing state support.
• However, it declined during the ninth century because some perceived the Buddhist establishment as a challenge to imperial authority.
• There was also a deepening resentment of the enormous wealth of Buddhist monasteries.
• Buddhism was offensive to some Confucian and Daoist thinkers because Buddhism was clearly of foreign origin and because the practices of Buddhist monks undermined the ideal of the family.
• Imperial decrees in the 840s shut down Buddhist monasteries, and the state confiscated Buddhist resources.

5. How did China influence the world beyond East Asia? How was China itself transformed by its encounters with a wider world?

• Chinese products, especially silk, were key to the Afro-Eurasian trade networks.
• Chinese technologies, including those related to shipbuilding, navigation, gunpowder, and printing, spread to other regions of Eurasia.

• Buddhism from South Asia had a profound impact on China.

• China's growing trade with the rest of the world made it the richest country in the world.

• It also became the most highly commercialized society in the world, with regions, especially in the south, producing for wider markets rather than for local consumption.

• China adopted cotton and sugar crops and the processes for refining them from South Asia.

Margin Review Questions

Q. *Why are the centuries of the Tang and Song dynasties in China sometimes referred to as a "golden age"?*

• During this period, China reached a cultural peak, setting standards of excellence in poetry, landscape painting, and ceramics.

• Particularly during the Song dynasty, there was an explosion of scholarship that gave rise to Neo-Confucianism.

• Politically, the Tang and Song dynasties built a state structure that endured for a thousand years.

• Tang and Song dynasty China experienced an economic revolution that made it the richest empire on earth.

• Population grew rapidly, from 50 million–60 million people during the Tang dynasty to 120 million by 1200, spurred in part by a remarkable growth in agricultural production.

• During this period, China possessed dozens of cities of over 100,000 people and a capital at Hangzhou with a population of over a million people.

• Industrial production soared during the period, and technological innovation flourished, including the invention of printing and gunpowder, along with innovations in navigation and shipbuilding that led the world.

• The economy of China became the most highly commercialized in the world, producing for the market rather than for local consumption.

Q. *In what ways did women's lives change during the Tang and Song dynasties?*

• Chinese women of the Tang dynasty era, at least in the north, had participated in social life with greater freedom than in classical times. This was because of the influence of steppe nomads, whose women led less restricted lives.

• But the revival of Confucianism and rapid economic growth during the Song dynasty resulted in the tightening of patriarchal restrictions on women. These new restrictions were perhaps most strikingly on display in the practice of foot binding.

• In the textile industry, urban workshops and state factories increasingly took over the skilled tasks of weaving textiles that had previously been the work of rural women.

• Growing wealth and urban environments offered women opportunities as restaurant operators, sellers of vegetables and fish, maids, cooks, or dressmakers.

• The growing prosperity of elite families funneled increasing numbers of women into roles as concubines, entertainers, courtesans, and prostitutes. This trend reduced the ability of wives to negotiate as equals with their husbands, and it set women against one another.

• Some positive trends in the lives of women occurred during the Song dynasty. Women saw their property rights expanded, and in some quarters, the education of women was advocated as a way to better prepare their sons for civil service exams.

Q. *How did the Chinese and their nomadic neighbors to the north view each other?*

• The nomadic neighbors saw China as the source of grain, other agricultural products, and luxury goods.

• They also viewed China as a threat, because the Chinese periodically directed their military forces deep into the steppes, built the Great Wall to keep the nomads out, and often proved unwilling to allow pastoral peoples easy access to trading opportunities within China.

• The Chinese saw the nomads as a military threat.

• But they also needed the nomads, whose lands were the source of horses, which were essential to the Chinese military, and of other products, including skins, furs, hides, and amber.

• Also, the nomads controlled much of the Silk Road trading network, which funneled goods from the West into China.

Q. *What assumptions underlay the tribute system?*

• Several assumptions underlay the tribute system, such as that China was the "middle kingdom," the center of the world, infinitely superior to the "barbarian" peoples beyond its borders;

• that China was self-sufficient, requiring little from the outside world, while barbarians sought access to China's wealth and wisdom;

• and that the Chinese might provide access to their wealth and wisdom under certain controlled conditions in the hope that it would help to civilize the barbarians.

• The tribute system was a set of practices designed to facilitate this civilizing contact. It required non-Chinese authorities to acknowledge Chinese superiority and their own subordinate place in a Chinese-centered world order. In exchange for expressions of submission, the Chinese emperor would grant foreigners permission to trade in China and provide them with gifts, which were often worth more than the tribute offered by the foreigners.

• The system was an effort to regulate relations with neighboring states and groups of nomads on the borders of the empire.

Q. *How did the tribute system in practice differ from the ideal Chinese understanding of its operation?*

• Often, China was in reality confronting powerful nomadic empires that were able to deal with China on at least equal terms.

• At times, the Chinese emperors negotiated arrangements that recognized nomadic states as political equals.

• They promised Chinese princesses as wives,

• sanctioned exchanges of goods that favored the nomads,

• and agreed to supply the nomads annually with large quantities of grain, wine, and silk. While these goods were officially termed "gifts," granted in accord with the tribute system, they were in fact tribute in reverse or even protection money.

Q. *In what ways did China and the nomads influence each other?*

• When nomadic peoples actually ruled over parts of China, some of them adopted Chinese ways. But on the whole, Chinese culture had only a modest impact on the nomadic people of the northern steppes. Few of these pastoral societies were incorporated into the Chinese state for any significant length of time, and most lived in areas where Chinese-style agriculture was simply impossible.

• On the Chinese side, elements of steppe culture had some influence on those parts of northern China that were periodically conquered and ruled by

nomadic peoples; for example, some high-ranking members of the Chinese imperial family led their troops in battle in the style of Turkic warriors.

Q. *In what different ways did Korea, Vietnam, and Japan experience and respond to Chinese influence?*

• Both Korea and Vietnam achieved political independence while participating fully in the tribute system as vassal states. Japan was never conquered by the Chinese but did participate for some of its history in the tribute system as a vassal state.

• The cultural elite of Korea, Vietnam, and Japan borrowed heavily from China—Confucianism, Daoism, Buddhism, administrative techniques, the examination system, artistic and literary styles—even as their own cultures remained distinct.

• Both Korea and Vietnam experienced some colonization by ethnic Chinese settlers.

• Unlike Korea or Japan, the cultural heartland of Vietnam was fully incorporated into the Chinese state for over a thousand years, far longer than corresponding parts of Korea. This political dominance led to cultural changes in Vietnam such as the adoption of Chinese-style irrigated agriculture, the education of the Vietnamese elite in Confucian-based schools and their inclusion in the local bureaucracy, Chinese replacing the local language in official business, and the adoption of Chinese clothing and hairstyles.

• Unlike Korea or Vietnam, Japan was physically separated from China, and thus its adoption of elements of Chinese civilization from the seventh to the ninth centuries was wholly voluntary. The high point of that cultural borrowing occurred when the first Japanese state emerged and deliberately sought to transform Japan into a centralized bureaucratic state on the Chinese model. In doing so, Japan voluntarily embraced, among other things, a Chinese-style emperor, Buddhism, Confucianism, Chinese court and governmental structures, and the Chinese calendar. But because the adoptions were voluntary, the Japanese could be selective. By the tenth century, Japan's tribute missions to China stopped. In the long run, Japanese political, religious, literary, and artistic cultures evolved in distinctive ways despite much borrowing from China.

Q. *In what different ways did Japanese and Korean women experience the pressures of Confucian orthodoxy?*

• Elite Japanese women, unlike those in Korea, largely escaped the more oppressive features of Chinese

Confucian culture, such as the prohibition of remarriage for widows,

  • seclusion within the home,
  • and foot binding.
  • Moreover, elite Japanese women continued to inherit property,
  • Japanese married couples often lived apart or with the wife's family,
  • and marriages in Japan were made and broken easily.

Q. *In what ways did China participate in the world of Eurasian commerce and exchange, and with what outcomes?*

  • China actively participated in commerce, with its export products—silk, porcelain, lacquerware—in high demand.
  • Several Chinese ports became cosmopolitan centers of commerce and trade and points of contact between Chinese and other Afro-Eurasian cultures.
  • The size of the Chinese domestic economy provided a ready market for hundreds of commodities from afar.
  • One key outcome was the diffusion of many Chinese technological innovations, including techniques for producing salt, papermaking, and printing.
  • Chinese innovations in explosives, textiles, metallurgy, and naval technologies also often sparked further innovations. For instance, the arrival of gunpowder in Europe spurred the development of cannons.
  • China learned about the cultivation and processing of both cotton and sugar from India and gained access to new, fast-ripening, and drought-resistant strains of rice from Vietnam. Outside influences also helped inspire Chinese innovation, such as Buddhism spurring the development of printing.

Q. *What facilitated the rooting of Buddhism within China?*

  • The chaotic, violent, and politically fragmented centuries that followed the collapse of the Han dynasty discredited Confucianism and opened the door to alternative understandings of the world.
  • Nomadic rulers who governed much of northern China after the fall of the Han dynasty found Buddhism useful in part because it was foreign. Their support led to the building of many Buddhist monasteries and works of art.
  • In southern China, Buddhism provided some comfort to the elite in the face of a collapsing society.
  • Once established, Buddhist monasteries provided an array of social services to ordinary people.
  • Buddhism was associated with access to magical powers.
  • There was a serious effort by Buddhist monks, scholars, and translators to present this Indian religion in terms that Chinese could relate to.
  • Under the Sui and Tang dynasties, Buddhism received growing state support.

Q. *What were the major sources of opposition to Buddhism within China?*

  • Some perceived the Buddhist establishment as a challenge to imperial authority.
  • There was a deepening resentment of the enormous wealth of the Buddhist establishment.
  • Buddhism was clearly of foreign origin and therefore offensive to some Confucian and Daoist thinkers.
  • For some Confucian thinkers, the celibacy of monks and their withdrawal from society undermined the Confucian-based family system of Chinese tradition.
  • After 800 C.E., a growing resentment of foreign culture took hold, particularly among the literate classes. Ultimately, a series of imperial decrees between 841 and 845 C.E. ordered some 260,000 monks and nuns to return to secular life, and thousands of monasteries, temples, and shrines were destroyed or turned to public use.

ADDITIONAL RESOURCES FOR CHAPTER 9

Additional Bedford/St. Martin's Resources

FOR INSTRUCTORS

Computerized Test Bank

This test bank provides over thirty exercises per chapter, including multiple-choice, fill-in-the-blank, short-answer, and full-length essay questions. Instructors can customize quizzes, add or edit both questions and answers, and export questions and answers to a variety of formats, including WebCT and Blackboard. The disc includes correct answers and essay outlines.

Instructor's Resource CD-ROM

This disc provides instructors with ready-made and customizable PowerPoint multimedia presentations built around chapter outlines, maps, figures, and all images from the textbook, plus JPEG versions of all maps, figures, and images.

The following maps and images from Chapter 9 are available in both JPEG and PowerPoint format on the Instructor's Resource CD-ROM:

- Map 9.1: Tang and Song Dynasty China (p. 243)
- Map 9.2: The World of Asian Buddhism (p. 262)
- Chinese Astronomy (p. 240)
- Kaifeng (p. 245)
- Foot Binding (p. 247)
- The Tribute System (p. 250)
- The Trung Sisters (p. 255)
- The Samurai of Japan (p. 258)

FOR STUDENTS

Documents and Essays from *Worlds of History: A Comparative Reader,* Third Edition (Volume 1)

The following documents, essays, and illustrations to accompany Chapter 9 are available in Chapters 7, 8, and 9 of this reader by Kevin Reilly:

From Chapter 7

- "Buddhism in China": from *The Disposition of Error*
- From *The Lotus Sutra*

From Chapter 8

- Ichisada Miyazaki, *The Chinese Civil Service Exam System*
- Liu Tsung-Yuan, *Camel Kuo the Gardener*
- *Rules for the Fan Lineage's Charitable Estate*

From Chapter 9

- Kevin Reilly, *Love in Medieval Europe, India, and Japan*
- Murasaki Shikibu, from *The Tale of Genji*

Online Study Guide at bedfordstmartins.com/strayer

The Online Study Guide helps students synthesize the material from the text as well as practice the skills historians use to make sense of the past. Each chapter of the Online Study Guide contains specific testing exercises, including a multiple-choice self-test that focuses on important conceptual ideas; an identification quiz that helps students remember key people, places, and events; a flashcard activity that tests students on their knowledge of key terms; and two interactive map activities intended to strengthen students' geographic skills. Instructors can monitor students' progress through an online Quiz Gradebook or receive email updates.

Further Reading

China: Tang and Song Dynasties, http://www.newtrier.k12.il.us/library/teacher_assignments/dynasties.htm. An interesting collection of links to Tang and Song history and literature.

China the Beautiful, http://www.chinapage.com/main2.html. This page has hundreds of links to Web sites that deal with Chinese culture and history.

East & Southeast Asia: An Annotated Directory of Internet Resources, http://newton.uor.edu/Departments&Programs/AsianStudiesDept/index.html. This is a *great* place to find information about China, Korea, Japan, Vietnam, and other Asian countries.

Ebrey, Patricia Buckley. *The Cambridge Illustrated History of China.* Rev. ed. Cambridge: Cambridge University Press, 1999. An excellent (and beautiful) overview of Chinese history and culture.

Friday, Karl F. *Samurai, Warfare and the State in Early Medieval Japan.* London: Routledge, 2003.

Pratt, Keith. *Everlasting Flower: A History of Korea.* London: Reaktion, 2006. An interesting recent account.

Literature

Carter, Steven, trans. *Traditional Japanese Poetry: An Anthology.* Stanford, CA: Stanford University Press, 1993. A large selection of Japanese poetry ranging from the earliest-known works to works of the twentieth century.

Ebrey, Patricia Buckley, ed. *Chinese Civilization: A Sourcebook.* 2nd ed. New York: Free Press, 1993.

Halsall, Paul, ed. *Internet East Asian History Sourcebook.* http://www.fordham.edu/halsall/eastasia/eastasiasbook.html. This site offers access to a good selection of texts for this period, most of them Chinese but with some Japanese and a few Korean sources. They vary in length, from selections that are easy to use in class to whole works.

Li Po and Tu Fu. *Poems.* Trans. Arthur Cooper. Harmondsworth: Penguin, 1973. Selected works of two great eighth-century Chinese poets.

McCann, David, trans. *Early Korean Literature.* New York: Columbia University Press, 2000. Texts from the twelfth to the eighteenth century with interpretive analysis.

Murasaki Shikibu. *Diary of Lady Murasaki.* Trans. Richard Bowring. London: Penguin, 1999. At 144 pages, Lady Murasaki's diary is more accessible for classroom use than her famous novel *The Tale of Genji* but also gives an interesting look at life in eleventh-century Heian court circles.

Red Pine, trans. *Poems of the Masters: China's Classic Anthology of T'ang and Sung Dynasty Verse.* Port Townsend, WA: Copper Canyon Press, 2003. A large collection of great Chinese poetry.

Yohannan, John D., ed. *A Treasury of Asian Literature.* New York: New American Library, 1956. A useful collection of works from India, China, Japan, and the Arab world.

Yuzan Daidoji. *Code of the Samurai: A Modern Translation of the Bushido Shoshinshu of Taira Shigesuke.* Trans. Thomas Cleary. Boston: Tuttle Publishing, 1999. Although not written until the late seventeenth century, this book is the best view we have of the code of *bushido* in Japan.

Film

Buddha in the Land of the Kami. Films for the Humanities and Sciences, 1989. 53 minutes. Explores the arrival of Buddhism in Japan between the seventh and twelfth centuries.

Buddhism in China. Insight Media, 1983. 30 minutes. Offers an overview of Buddhism from its arrival in China to the twentieth century.

Budo Sai: The Spirit of the Samurai. Films for the Humanities and Sciences, 1992. 70 minutes. Explores the world of the Japanese samurai.

China: The Age of Maturity. Insight Media, 1977. 23 minutes. Examines Chinese society during the Song dynasty.

Early Japan. Insight Media, 1976. 28 minutes. Offers an overview of Japanese history from prehistory to the Heian period.

Religions in China. Insight Media, 1999. 57 minutes. Examines the various religions of China, including Buddhism.

The Tale of Genji. Films for the Humanities and Sciences, 1993. 60 minutes. Follows the plot of this milestone in world literature through the panels of hand-painted twelfth-century scrolls. In doing so, the film explores Japanese culture and society.

Two-Way Traffic: China, the Hub of the East. Films for the Humanities and Sciences, 2000. 58 minutes. Looks at the travelers, ideas, inventions, and goods that have flowed from and come to China since ancient times. It tests the perception of China as an isolated society.

The Worlds of European Christendom
Connected and Divided, 500–1300

CHAPTER OVERVIEW

Chapter Objectives

• To examine European society after the breakup of the Roman Empire
• To compare the diverse legacies of Rome in Western Europe and the Byzantine Empire
• To explore medieval European expansion
• To present the backwardness of medieval Europe relative to other civilizations, and the steps by which it caught up

Chapter Outline

I. **Opening Vignette**
A. In 1964, the Eastern Orthodox patriarch Athenagoras and Pope Paul VI met and rescinded the mutual excommunication decrees imposed by their respective churches in 1054.
1. Christianity had provided common ground for postclassical societies in western Eurasia
2. but Christendom was deeply divided: Byzantine Empire and West
a. Byzantium continued Roman imperial traditions

b. West tried to maintain links to classical world
c. but Roman imperial order disintegrated in the West
3. Roman Catholic Church of the West established independence from political authorities; Eastern Orthodox Church did not
4. Western church was much more rural than Byzantium
5. Western Europe emerged, at an increasing pace after 1000, as a very dynamic third-wave civilization
6. Western Europe was a hybrid civilization: classical, Germanic, Celtic
7. in 500 C.E., only about one-third of all Christians lived in Europe
a. many distinct forms of Christianity in other regions
b. many branches have survived throughout Afro-Eurasia; other branches were eliminated by spread of alternative religions

II. **Eastern Christendom: Building on the Past**
A. The Byzantine Empire has no clear starting point.
1. continuation of the Roman Empire
2. some scholars date beginning to 330 C.E., with foundation of Constantinople

a. formal division of Roman Empire into eastern and western halves in late fourth century C.E.

3. western empire collapsed in fifth century; eastern half survived another 1,000 years

4. eastern empire contained ancient civilizations: Egypt, Greece, Syria, and Anatolia

5. Byzantine advantages over western empire
   a. wealthier and more urbanized
   b. more defensible capital (Constantinople)
   c. shorter frontier
   d. access to the Black Sea; command of eastern Mediterranean
   e. stronger army, navy, and merchant marine
   f. continuation of late Roman infrastructure
   g. conscious effort to preserve Roman ways

B. The Byzantine State

1. the Byzantine Empire was much smaller than the Roman Empire

2. but it remained a major force in eastern Mediterranean until around 1200
   a. reformed administrative system: generals had civil authority in the provinces, raised armies from peasants

3. political authority was tightly centralized in Constantinople
   a. emperor ruled as God's representative on earth
   b. awesome grandeur of court (based on ancient Persian style)
   c. was mostly concerned with tax collection and keeping order

4. territory shrank after 1085, as western Europeans and Turks attacked
   a. 1453: Ottoman Turks conquered Constantinople, ended empire

C. The Byzantine Church and Christian Divergence **[see Discussion Topic 1]**

1. the Church was closely tied to the state: *caesaropapism*
   a. Byzantine emperor was head of both the state and the Church
   b. emperor appointed the patriarch, sometimes made doctrinal decisions, called church councils

2. Orthodox Christianity deeply influenced all of Byzantine life
   a. legitimated imperial rule
   b. provided cultural identity
   c. pervasiveness of churches, icons
   d. even common people engaged in theological disputes

3. Eastern Orthodoxy increasingly defined itself in opposition to Latin Christianity
   a. Latin Christianity was centered on the pope, Rome
   b. growing rift between the two parts of Christendom
   c. sense of religious difference reflected East/West political difference
   d. with rise of Islam, Constantinople and Rome remained as sole hubs of Christendom
   e. important East/West cultural differences (language, philosophy, theology, church practice)
      i. iconoclast movement in Byzantium from 726 to 843
      ii. issues like priests shaving, celibacy, leavened bread
      iii. issue of authority: growing claims of popes to be final authority for all Christians
   f. schism in 1054, with mutual excommunication
   g. Crusades (from 1095 on) worsened the situation
   h. during Fourth Crusade, Westerners sacked Constantinople (1204) and ruled Byzantium for next 50 years

D. Byzantium and the World

1. Byzantium had a foot in both Europe and Asia, interacted intensively with neighbors

2. continuation of long Roman fight with Persian Empire
   a. weakened both states, left them open to Islamic conquests
   b. Persia was conquered by Islam; Byzantium lost territory
      i. invention of "Greek fire" helped Byzantines survive

3. Byzantium was a central player in long-distance Eurasian trade

a. Byzantine gold coins (bezants) were a major Mediterranean currency for over 500 years

b. Byzantine crafts (jewelry, textiles, purple dyes, silk) were in high demand

4. important cultural influence of Byzantium

a. transmitted ancient Greek learning to Islamic world and West

b. transmission of Orthodox Christianity to Balkans and Russia

   i. missionaries Cyril and Methodius created a written language for the Slavs (Cyrillic script) to aid transmission

E. The Conversion of Russia [see Classroom Activity 1]

1. most important conversion was that of Prince Vladimir of Kiev

2. Orthodoxy transformed state of Rus; became central to Russian identity

3. Moscow finally declared itself to be the "third Rome," assuming role of protector of Christianity after fall of Constantinople

III. **Western Christendom: Constructing a Hybrid Civilization** [see Lecture Strategy 1]

A. Western Europe was on the margins of world history for most of the postclassical millennium.

1. it was far removed from the growing world trade routes

2. European geography made political unity difficult

3. coastlines and river systems facilitated internal exchange

4. moderate climate enabled population growth

B. In the Wake of Roman Collapse: Political Life in Western Europe, 500–1000

1. traditional date for fall of western Roman Empire is 476 C.E.

2. with Roman collapse: [see Discussion Topic 2]

a. large-scale centralized rule vanished

b. Europe's population fell by 25 percent because of war and disease

c. contraction of land under cultivation

d. great diminution of urban life

e. long-distance trade outside of Italy shriveled up

f. great decline in literacy

g. Germanic peoples emerged as the dominant peoples in West

h. shift in center of gravity from Mediterranean to north and west

3. survival of much of classical and Roman heritage

a. Germanic peoples who established new kingdoms had been substantially Romanized already

   i. had established distinct ethnic identities and had militarized thanks to contact with Rome

   ii. had picked up Roman culture while serving in Roman army

b. high prestige of things Roman

c. Germanic rulers adopted Roman-style written law

4. several Germanic kingdoms tried to recreate Roman-style unity [see Lecture Strategy 2]

a. Charlemagne (r. 768–814) acted "imperial"

b. revival of Roman Empire on Christmas Day 800 (coronation of Charlemagne); soon fragmented

c. another revival of Roman Empire with imperial coronation of Otto I of Saxony (r. 936–973)

   i. his realm was later known as the Holy Roman Empire

   ii. largely limited to Germany

C. In the Wake of Roman Collapse: Society and the Church, 500–1000

1. within these new kingdoms:

a. highly fragmented, decentralized society

b. great local variation

c. landowning warrior elite exercised power

2. social hierarchies

a. lesser lords and knights became vassals of kings or great lords

b. serfdom displaced slavery

   i. serfs owed services and goods to lords

   ii. lived on their own small farms

3. Catholic Church was a major element of stability

a. hierarchy modeled on that of the Roman Empire

b. became very rich

c. conversion of Europe's non-Christians

    i. top-down conversion was the norm

    ii. similar process to spread of Buddhism among nomads

    iii. occasional coercion (e.g., Charlemagne and the Saxons)

    iv. considerable cultural accommodation

      a) Pope Gregory's instructions to missionaries in England

      b) amulets, sacred wells, and festivals were preempted by Christianity

d. most of Europe was Christian (with pagan elements) by 1100

4. Church and ruling class usually reinforced each other

    a. also an element of competition as rival centers of power

    b. right to appoint bishops and the pope was controversial (the Investiture conflict)

D. Accelerating Change in the West: 1000–1300

1. a series of invasions in 700–1000 hindered European development

    a. Muslims, Magyars, Vikings

    b. largely ended by 1000

2. weather improved with warming trend that started after 750

3. High Middle Ages: time of clear growth and expansion

    a. European population in 1000 was about 35 million; about 80 million in 1340

    b. opening of new land for cultivation

4. growth of long-distance trade, from two major centers

    a. northern Europe

    b. northern Italian towns

      i. commerce with Islam and Byzantium

    c. great trading fairs (especially in Champagne area of France) enabled exchange between northern and southern merchants

5. European town and city populations rose

    a. Venice by 1400 had around 150,000 people

    b. still smaller than great cities elsewhere in the world

c. new specializations, organized into guilds

6. new opportunities for women

    a. a number of urban professions were open to women

    b. widows of great merchants could continue husbands' business

    c. opportunities declined by the fifteenth century

      i. technological progress may have harmed women

    d. religious life: nuns, Beguines, anchoresses (e.g., Hildegard of Bingen and Julian of Norwich)

7. growth of territorial states with better-organized governments

    a. kings consolidated their authority in eleventh–thirteenth centuries

    b. appearance of professional administrators

    c. some areas did not develop territorial kingdoms (Italian city-states, small German principalities)

E. Europe Outward Bound: The Crusading Tradition [see Lecture Strategy 3]

1. medieval expansion of Christendom after 1000

    a. occurred at the same time that Byzantium declined

    b. clearance of land, especially on eastern fringe of Europe

    c. Scandinavian colonies in Newfoundland, Greenland, Iceland

    d. Europe had direct, though limited, contact with East and South Asia by thirteenth–fourteenth centuries

2. Crusade movement began in 1095

    a. wars at God's command, authorized by the pope, for which participants received an indulgence (release from penalty for confessed sins)

    b. amazingly popular; were religious wars at their core

3. most famous Crusades aimed to regain Jerusalem and holy places

    a. many waves of Crusaders to the Near East

    b. creation of four small Christian states (last fell in 1291)

      c. showed Europe's growing organizational ability

   4. Iberian Peninsula Crusade

   5. Baltic Crusade

   6. attacks on Byzantine Empire and Russia

   7. Crusades had little lasting political or religious impact in the Middle East

      a. Turkic and Mongol invasions are more important in Islamic history

   8. Crusades had a significant impact on Europe

      a. conquest of Spain, Sicily, Baltic region

      b. Crusaders weakened Byzantium

      c. popes strengthened their position for a time

      d. tens of thousands of Europeans made contact with the Islamic world

         i. stimulated demand for Asian goods

         ii. learned how to produce sugar

         iii. Muslim/Greek scholarship entered Europe

      e. hardened cultural barriers

         i. deepened the Catholic/Orthodox divide

         ii. development of anti-Semitism in Europe

         iii. memory of the Crusades still affects dealings between Western civilization and Islam

IV. The West in Comparative Perspective
[see Classroom Activity 2]

  A. Catching Up

   1. the hybrid civilization of Western Europe was less developed than Byzantium, China, India, or the Islamic world

      a. Muslims regarded Europeans as barbarians

      b. Europeans recognized their own backwardness

   2. Europeans were happy to exchange with/borrow from more advanced civilizations to the east

      a. European economies reconnected with the Eurasian trading system

      b. Europeans welcomed scientific, philosophical, and mathematical concepts from Arabs, classical Greeks, and India

      c. the most significant borrowing was from China

         i. borrowing was usually indirect

         ii. the compass, papermaking, gunpowder, etc.

         iii. in thirteenth–fourteenth centuries, many Europeans went to China

         iv. European voyages of exploration were in search of the sources of African and Asian wealth

   3. Europe was a developing civilization like others of the era

   4. by 1500, Europe had caught up with China and the Islamic world; surpassed them in some areas

   5. 500–1300 was a period of great innovation

      a. agriculture

         i. development of heavy-wheeled plow

         ii. greater dependence on horses, use of better equipment

         iii. three-field system of crop rotation

      b. new reliance on nonanimal sources of energy

         i. new type of windmill

         ii. water-driven mills

         iii. water and wind power were applied to several industries

      c. technological borrowing for warfare, with further development

         i. Europeans were probably the first to use Chinese gunpowder in cannons

         ii. at sea: borrowed compass, rudder, lateen sail

      d. Europe developed a passion for technology

  B. Pluralism in Politics **[see Classroom Activity 3]**

   1. Europe crystallized into a system of competing states

   2. political pluralism shaped Western European civilization

      a. led to frequent wars and militarization

      b. stimulated technological development

   3. states still were able to communicate economically and intellectually

   4. rulers were generally weaker than those to the east

a. royal-noble-ecclesiastical power struggle allowed urban merchants to win great independence

b. perhaps paved the way for capitalism

c. development of representative institutions (parliaments)

C. Reason and Faith **[see Discussion Topic 3]**

1. distinctive intellectual tension between faith and reason developed

2. intellectual life flourished in the centuries after 1000

a. creation of universities from earlier cathedral schools

b. scholars had some intellectual freedom at universities

3. in the universities, some scholars began to emphasize the ability of human reason to understand divine mysteries

a. also applied reason to law, medicine, and world of nature

b. development of "natural philosophy" (scientific study of nature)

4. search for classical Greek texts (especially Aristotle)

a. were found in Byzantium and the Arab world

b. twelfth–thirteenth centuries: access to ancient Greek and Arab scholarship

5. deep impact of Aristotle

a. his writings were the basis of university education

b. dominated Western European thought between 1200 and 1700

6. no similar development occurred in the Byzantine Empire

a. focus of education was the humanities

b. suspicion of classical Greek thought

7. Islamic world had deep interaction with classical Greek thought

a. massive amount of translation in ninth–tenth centuries

b. encouraged a flowering of Arab scholarship between 800 and 1200

c. caused a debate among Muslim thinkers on faith and reason

d. Islamic world eventually turned against natural philosophy

V. **Reflections: Remembering and Forgetting: Continuity and Surprise in the Worlds of Christendom**

A. Many features of medieval Christendom have extended into the modern era.

1. crusading motivated Spanish and Portuguese explorers

2. merchants' freedom helped lead to capitalism and industrialization

3. endemic military conflict

4. ongoing "faith and reason" controversy

5. Eastern Orthodox/Roman Catholic division of Christianity remains

6. universities were a medieval creation

B. We need to beware of the notion that the course of medieval European civilization determined the future.

1. some historians have argued that Europe's global domination in the nineteenth century grew from its unique character after 1000

2. in reality: Europe's recent development was a great surprise

3. such a view minimizes the way people at the time understood their world

USING *WAYS OF THE WORLD* IN THE CLASSROOM

Lecture Strategies

Lecture Strategy 1

"The fall of Rome and creation of the Germanic successor states."

Students tend to be very interested in the fall of the (western) Roman Empire, and since exploration of the matter provides an excellent opportunity to look more deeply at the factors that make empires fall, this is a topic that can be expanded very profitably from the textbook coverage.

A good place to start is with two maps of Europe, ca. 300 C.E. and ca. 500 C.E. (excellent maps of Europe for each century from 1 to 2000 can be found at www.euratlas.com), which will show more clearly than mere words could that the eastern Roman Empire survived but that the western empire was carved into a number of states labeled with various Germanic ethnic names (Kingdom of the Franks, etc.). Thus you may pose the basic question, "What happened to change the picture between 300 and 500?"

People have written very large books on this topic, so one must of course be selective. As much as possible, though, it is useful to compare what happened to the Roman Empire to circumstances in other empires (comparison to the fall of the Han dynasty is particularly useful). Some issues to consider:

- Edward Gibbons's classic argument that it was all the fault of the Christians, who drained top talent from the administration and were too fond of "turning the other cheek" (it's important to note that a number of fourth-century bishops, such as Ambrose, actually spent part of their career as administrators and that Christians in fact have always had an extremely poor track record when it comes to cheek-turning). A comparison to the implication of Daoists in the fall of the Han dynasty is instructive.
- The issue of hiring mostly Germanic mercenaries to staff the armies of Rome (important to note that this was not a new phenomenon)
- The theory that, as soon as the empire stopped expanding, its fall began (which cannot be supported if one looks at a basic chronological chart)
- The weakness of Roman bureaucracy (especially compared to that of Han China), with very few bureaucrats and a system that was largely militarized and that gave much of the responsibility for governance to unpaid members of the elite
- The role of Germanic pressure in bringing down the empire, especially considering that Roman-trained armies could easily defeat Germanic tribal forces
- The great Visigothic crisis of 375–378, with the Visigothic defeat of Emperor Valens at Adrianople, and consideration of how badly this issue really affected the empire
- The division of the empire into eastern and western units, finalized in 395 C.E.

- You may care to include, if you have time, some sense of why the eastern empire survived (shorter frontiers, higher population and thus larger tax base, military reforms).
- And of course you should include at least one of the "silly" reasons sometimes given for the fall of Rome. My personal favorite is that, thanks to lead-based glaze for storage containers, all of the Roman upper class was suffering from lead poisoning.

It is very important to note the ways in which the Germanic peoples who eventually established successor states had already adopted Roman ways and perspectives.

Lecture Strategy 2

"Charlemagne and the last wave of 'barbarian' invasions."

Recently, the historian Pierre Riché subtitled a book on the Carolingians (Charlemagne's dynasty) "a family who forged Europe." Charlemagne, his immediate predecessors, and his successors as kings of the Franks do indeed stand out in the history of the early Middle Ages for their bold efforts at state building, creating an amalgam of Christian, Germanic, and Roman practices to create a surprisingly strong state that influenced all later European states. This consolidated Kingdom of the Franks suffered heavily under the onslaught of the last wave of invasions of Europe (by Vikings, Magyars, and Muslims), but much of what these figures created survived.

A useful place to start this lecture is with a discussion of conditions in the early Germanic successor states—low literacy, gradually dissolving vestiges of Roman administration, and a high degree of decentralization. From there, follow the story of the Carolingians, emphasizing that this was only the most successful example of a phenomenon that occurred elsewhere in Europe (such as Mercia under King Offa or Visigothic Spain). Important points to include:

- Charles Martel's consolidation of power in Francia as protector of the Church and leader against Muslim invasions from Spain
- The role of Anglo-Saxon missionaries and an alliance with the papacy in consolidating the Carolingian hold on power
- Pepin the Short's usurpation of the Frankish throne

- Charlemagne's highly successful military campaigns, which made him so wealthy that he could experiment with governmental reform
- The Carolingian renaissance: what it set out to do, its scope, and its impact on society
- Charlemagne's coronation as emperor on December 25, 800
- Charlemagne's efforts to build a Christian empire modeled on that of Constantine
- The civil wars during the reign of Charlemagne's son Louis the Pious, including both reasons for this centrifugal pull and its effects
- Why Vikings liked to raid, what real damage they did, and why they were difficult to fight
- The effect of the larger-scale Viking attacks on England in encouraging centralization
- The effect of the large-scale Magyar raids on East Francia in encouraging the emergence of a strong German state
- The role of Muslim raids on Italy in creating strong Italian city-states
- A comparison of this last wave of invasions with the Germanic invasions that brought the western Roman Empire to an end

Lecture Strategy 3

"The medieval expansion of Europe."
This lecture would examine in more detail the remarkable expansion of French-influenced Western Christendom in the period after the year 1000. A good place to start is with an examination of Europe's "core lands" (most notably France) at the turn of the millennium. Important points to include are:

- the preeminence of heavy cavalry ("knights")
- economic recovery
- beginnings of significant population growth
- religion around the year 1000

Time is always limited in a world civ. class, so this lecture certainly would not be able to include all the major expansion areas, such as:

- the English conquest of Ireland and Wales
- Scandinavian efforts to conquer Finland
- the Christian conquest of Spain (*reconquista*)
- the conquest of Prussia and much of the Baltic, especially by the Teutonic Knights and their allies
- the maritime expansion in the Mediterranean

- the Holy Land Crusades and establishment of the Crusader principalities
- Western efforts to seize Byzantine territories

For a short lecture, a thematic approach may serve you better. For example, consider a lecture using some of the following themes as your organizational base:

- the militarism of later medieval Europe (including the high level of training of knights, the social importance of knights, the integrated nature of medieval armies with heavy reliance on infantry), and comparison to the military capability of their enemies
- the role of political decentralization in encouraging expansion by private entrepreneurship (e.g., Strongbow's original plan to carve out a state in Ireland, the role of nobles in carving out states in the Near East, the Teutonic Knights' seizure of Prussia), and how kings could take advantage of this private enterprise (most notably when the king of France gained control of Languedoc in the wake of the Albigensian Crusade)
- the role of a rising merchant class (essential to the story of the Italian trading states in the Mediterranean, the Crusades, and the European expansion into the Baltic)
- the role of religion as a catalyst in the various crusading movements

Things to Do in the Classroom

Discussion Topics

1. Comparison, large or small group.
"Caesaropapism or ecclesiastical independence?"
This chapter presented two styles of Christian Church development—the caesaropapism of the Byzantine Empire and the greater independence of spiritual authorities in Western Europe. Choose two teams, and ask them to debate with each other which system has the greatest advantages. Make sure they stay medieval as much as possible!

2. Misconception/Difficult Topic, large or small group. "That the era of the Middle Ages in Europe was a 'Dark Age.'"
Few things annoy scholars of medieval Europe more than calling their era a "Dark Age." Yet one still finds

the term in the realm of popular history, no matter how hard we try to discourage it. The purpose of this discussion is to consider what truth, if any, there is in that old stereotype.

Begin with a brief explanation of how the term "Dark Ages" came into use for Europe during the period of third-wave civilizations (it was invented by Renaissance scholars who had a strong stake in implying that nothing worthwhile had happened between antiquity and their own glorious time). Then ask students to discuss:

- What are various reasons why a civilization could be called "dark"?
- Using those criteria, are there any civilizations we have studied that fit the description?
- Are there *parts* of the European Middle Ages that could be defined as "dark"?
- If you were to draw a timeline, which part of the period covered in this chapter would fit your definition?

3. Contextualization, large or small group.

"Faith or reason—the longest argument."
This chapter presents the development of tension between faith and reason in medieval Europe. Ask students to:

- lay out the main reasons why this tension developed in the medieval context
- discuss which medieval factors are still part of the modern faith/reason debate
- discuss which factors are unique to the modern world

Classroom Activities

1. Role-playing exercise, small group. "Converting Russia."

Most of the class consists of advisers to Grand Prince Vladimir of Kiev, who has decided that the time has come to align his state with one of the dominant religions of the tenth century. Select groups of students to enact delegations from the four religions he is considering—Judaism, Islam, Catholicism, and Eastern Orthodoxy. Let each delegation try to convince the class that its religion is the best. Make sure that the students performing the reenactment (1) do some research beyond the textbook and (2) remain true to their tenth-century context (i.e., not presenting modern Reform Judaism

or any other religious branch that had not yet been invented).

2. Clicker question. Would you rather live in Song China or in later medieval Europe?

3. Map-analysis exercise, large or small group. "A fragmented Europe."

If possible, display to the class a physical map of Europe that includes modern political borders. Ask your students to:

- identify the geographical elements that contributed to European political fragmentation (mountains, major rivers, etc.—but be sure to remind them that rivers and bodies of water can often facilitate contact)
- identify the regions where separate states formed for no clear geographical reason (look especially at Eastern Europe for this)
- discuss what other factors made for fragmentation in regions where no physical reason is apparent

Key Terms

Aristotle and classical Greek learning: Some works of the Greek philosopher Aristotle (384–322 B.C.E.) had always been known in Western Europe, but beginning in the eleventh century, medieval thought was increasingly shaped by a great recovery of Aristotle's works and a fascination with other Greek authors; this infusion of Greek rationalism into Europe's universities shaped intellectual development for several centuries.

Byzantine Empire: Term used by modern historians to refer to the surviving eastern Roman Empire during the medieval centuries; named after the ancient Greek city Byzantium, on the site of which the Roman emperor Constantine founded a new capital, Constantinople, in 330 C.E. (*pron.* BIZ-an-teen)

caesaropapism: A political-religious system in which the secular ruler is also head of the religious establishment, as in the Byzantine Empire. (*pron.* SEEZ-ar-oh-PAPE-ism)

Charlemagne: Ruler of the Carolingian Empire (r. 768–814) who staged an imperial revival in Western Europe. (*pron.* SHAHR-leh-mane)

Christianity, Eastern Orthodox: Branch of Christianity that developed in the eastern part of the Roman Empire and gradually separated, mostly on matters of practice, from the branch of Christianity dominant in Western Europe; noted for the subordination of the Church to political authorities, a married clergy, the use of leavened bread in the Eucharist, and insistence on church councils as the ultimate authority in Christian belief and practice.

Christianity, Roman Catholic: Western European branch of Christianity that gradually defined itself as separate from Eastern Orthodoxy, with a major break in 1054 C.E. that has still not been healed; "Roman Catholic" was not commonly used until after the Protestant Reformation, but the term is just since, by the eleventh century, Western Christendom defined itself in centralized terms, with the bishop of Rome (the pope) as the ultimate authority in matters of doctrine.

Constantinople: New capital for the eastern half of the Roman Empire, established by Emperor Constantine in 330 C.E. on the site of the ancient Greek city of Byzantium; Constantinople's highly defensible and economically important site helped assure the city's cultural and strategic importance for many centuries. (*pron.* con-stan-tih-NO-pul)

Crusades: Modern term meaning "ventures of the cross," used to describe the "holy wars" waged by Western Christendom from 1095 until the end of the Middle Ages and beyond; Crusades could only be declared by the pope and were marked by participants swearing a vow and receiving an indulgence in return.

Cyril and Methodius: Ninth-century Byzantine missionaries to the Slavs whose development of Cyrillic script made it possible to write Slavic languages. (*pron.* SIR-uhl, meth-ODE-ee-us)

Cyrillic: Alphabet based on Greek letters that was developed by two Byzantine missionaries, Cyril and Methodius, to write Slavic languages. (*pron.* sih-RIL-ik)

European cities: Western Europe saw a major process of urbanization beginning in the eleventh century, with towns that created major trade networks and that were notable for the high degree of independence they often enjoyed.

Greek fire: Form of liquid fire that could be sprayed at the enemy; invented by the Byzantines and very important in their efforts to halt the Arab advance into Byzantine territory.

guild: An association formed by people pursuing the same line of work that regulates their professions and also provides a social and religious network for members.

Holy Roman Empire: Term invented in the twelfth century to describe the Germany-based empire founded by Otto I in 962 C.E.

"hybrid civilization," the West as a: The distinctive path of Western Europe in the centuries following the fall of the western Roman Empire, leading to a society that included elements of ancient Rome, the practices of Germanic invaders who formed new states, Christianity, and elements of pre-Roman culture that still survived.

iconoclasm: The destruction of holy images; a term most often used to describe the Byzantine state policy of image destruction from 726 to 843. (*pron.* eye-KON-oh-klasm)

indulgence: A remission of the penalty (penance) for confessed sin that could be granted only by a pope, at first to Crusaders and later for a variety of reasons.

Justinian: Byzantine emperor (r. 527–565 C.E.), noted for his short-lived reconquest of much of the former western Roman Empire and for his codification of Roman law.

Kievan Rus: State that emerged around the city of Kiev in the ninth century C.E.; a culturally diverse region that included Vikings as well as Finnic and Baltic peoples. The conversion of Vladimir, the grand prince of Kiev, to Orthodox Christianity in 988 had long-term implications for Russia. (*pron.* key-YEV-an ROOS)

natural philosophy: The scientific study of nature, which developed, especially in Europe, in the later Middle Ages.

Otto I: King of Germany (r. 936–973) who built a consolidated German–northern Italian state and was crowned emperor in 962, creating what became known in time as the "Holy Roman Empire."

system of competing states: The distinctive organization of Western European political life that developed after the fall of the western Roman Empire in the fifth century C.E. in which the existence of many small, independent states encouraged military and economic competition.

Vikings: Scandinavian raiders who had an impact on much of Western Europe in the late eighth to eleventh centuries; their more peaceful cousins also founded colonies, including Newfoundland, Greenland, and Iceland.

Vladimir, prince of Kiev: Grand prince of Kiev (r. 978–1015 C.E.) whose conversion to Orthodox Christianity led to the incorporation of Russia into the sphere of Eastern Orthodoxy. (*pron.* vlad-IH-mir)

ANSWER GUIDELINES FOR CHAPTER QUESTIONS

The two sets of questions that follow appear in the textbook at the end of the chapter and in the margins of the reading. They are also provided in the Computerized Test Bank with answer guidelines, for your convenience.

The Big Picture Questions

1. How did the histories of the Byzantine Empire and Western Europe differ during the era of third-wave civilizations?

• Western Europe collapsed politically in the fifth century, never to come together again as a single political entity, whereas Byzantium survived as a single political entity throughout the period.

• The Byzantine emperor exerted greater control over the Orthodox Church than political authorities in Western Europe did over the Catholic Church.

• The Byzantine Empire maintained a prominent role in the long-distance trade networks of Eurasia throughout the period, whereas Western Europe's role declined precipitously following the collapse of the Roman Empire in the fifth century, only to reengage with those trade networks after 1000.

• After 1000, Western Europe's influence in the Mediterranean and in Eastern Europe expanded, while the influence of the Byzantine Empire contracted (especially in the Mediterranean basin) after 600 C.E.

2. What accounts for the different historical trajectories of these two expressions of Christendom?

• The survival of a powerful imperial state in the Byzantine Empire resulted in greater state control over the Orthodox Church.

• Cultural differences also played a role. For instance, in the Eastern Orthodox Church, Greek became the language of religious practice instead of the Latin used in the Roman Catholic Church. Moreover, more so than in the West, Byzantine thinkers sought to formulate Christian doctrine in terms of Greek philosophical concepts.

• The Eastern Orthodox faith expanded into Eastern Europe when the Byzantine Empire was at its height, but it was driven from other regions, particularly in North Africa and the Near East, by the expansion of Islam. After 1000, the Roman Catholic tradition became the more expansive of the two expressions, as its influence spread into Islamic Spain, non-Christian northern Europe, and Orthodox Eastern Europe.

3. How did Byzantium and Western Europe interact with each other and with the larger world of the postclassical era?

• Byzantium and Western Europe interacted frequently; for instance, in the 500s C.E., the Byzantine emperor Justinian succeeded in conquering parts of Western Europe in his effort to reconstitute the Roman Empire.

• The two societies were both Christian, which led to frequent interactions, disputes, and ultimately a schism between the two confessions.

• The revival of Western Europe after 1000 C.E. brought it into a closer trade relationship with Byzantium.

• The crusading movement in Western Europe inspired hundreds of thousands of Western Europeans to travel to the eastern Mediterranean and even led to the sack of Constantinople by Crusaders in 1204 C.E.

• In terms of the wider world, Byzantium and Western Europe were both part of the Eurasian long-distance trade network. Byzantium participated actively throughout the period, while Western Europe did so increasingly after 1000 C.E.

• Both interacted with the Islamic world through military conflict, trade, and the exchange of ideas.

• Both had a profound impact on Eastern Europe, especially through their promotion of rival versions of the Christian faith.

4. Was the civilization of the Latin West distinctive and unique, or was it broadly comparable to other third-wave civilizations?

• The book argues strongly that the Latin West shares many of the same features of other third-wave civilizations, especially in its willingness to borrow and then modify and improve upon ideas, business practices, and technological innovations. Therefore, it is broadly comparable to other third-wave civilizations.

• That said, it also makes the point that the Western European experience had distinctive features, including a fragmented political structure, unusually independent towns, and an acceptance of the study of natural philosophy, which ultimately helped to define a distinctive Latin West.

5. How does the history of the Christian world in the postclassical era compare with that of Tang and Song dynasty China?

• The Western Catholic Christian world was less developed in comparison to Tang and Song dynasty China in that the former had smaller cities, weaker political authorities, a fragmented political structure, a less commercialized economy, and inferior technology. It was also a more militarized society, with more privileged cities and a more favorable environment for merchants. By 1500, however, Western Europe had come a long way in catching up and, though it depended more on borrowing than did its Chinese counterpart, deserves comparison to China.

• The Orthodox Christian world was more similar to Tang and Song dynasty China in that it possessed comparable cities, a powerful emperor, a unified government, a professional bureaucracy, a commercialized economy, and a technologically advanced society.

Margin Review Questions

Q. *In what respects did Byzantium continue the patterns of the classical Roman Empire? In what ways did it diverge from those patterns?*

• Continuance can be seen in Byzantium's roads, military structures, centralized administration, imperial court, laws, and Christian organization.

• It can also be seen in Byzantium's pursuit of the long-term Roman struggle with the Persian Empire.

• Byzantium diverged through the development of a reformed administrative system that gave appointed generals civil authority in the empire's provinces and allowed them to raise armies from the landowning

peasants of the region. It also diverged through the new ideas encompassed in caesaropapism that defined the relationship between the state and the Church.

Q. *How did Eastern Orthodox Christianity differ from Roman Catholicism?*

• Unlike Western Europe, where the Catholic Church maintained some degree of independence from political authorities, in Byzantium the emperor assumed something of the role of both "Caesar," as head of state, and the pope, as head of the Church. Thus the Byzantine emperor appointed the patriarch of the Orthodox Church, sometimes made decisions about doctrine, called church councils into session, and generally treated the Church as a government department.

• In the Eastern Orthodox Church, Greek became the language of religious practice instead of the Latin used in the Roman Catholic Church.

• More so than in the West, Byzantine thinkers sought to formulate Christian doctrine in terms of Greek philosophical concepts.

• The Eastern Orthodox and Roman Catholic churches disagreed on a number of doctrinal issues, including the nature of the Trinity, the relative importance of faith and reason, and the veneration of icons.

• Priests in Byzantium allowed their beards to grow long and were permitted to marry, while priests in the West shaved and, after 1050 or so, were supposed to remain celibate.

• Orthodox ritual called for using bread leavened with yeast in the Mass, but Catholics used unleavened bread.

• Eastern Orthodox leaders sharply rejected the growing claims of Roman popes to be the sole and final authority for all Christians everywhere.

Q. *In what ways was the Byzantine Empire linked to a wider world?*

• On a political and military level, Byzantium continued the long-term Roman struggle with the Persian Empire.

• Economically, the Byzantine Empire was a central player in the long-distance trade of Eurasia, with commercial links to Western Europe, Russia, Central Asia, the Islamic world, and China.

• Culturally, Byzantium preserved much of ancient Greek learning and transmitted this classical heritage to both the Islamic world and the Christian West.

• Byzantine religious culture spread widely among Slavic-speaking peoples in the Balkans and Russia.

Q. *How did links to Byzantium transform the new civilization of Kievan Rus?*

• Kievan Rus borrowed Byzantium architectural styles, the Cyrillic alphabet, the extensive use of icons, a monastic tradition stressing prayer and service, and political ideals of imperial control of the Church.

Q. *How did the historical development of the European West differ from that of Byzantium in the postclassical era?*

• Unlike Byzantium, any semblance of large-scale centralized rule vanished in the West, to be replaced by a series of regional kingdoms.

• In addition, urban life diminished sharply, long-distance trade dried up, and literacy lost ground.

• In the West, a social system developed based on reciprocal ties between greater and lesser lords among the warrior elites and between lords and serfs.

• In the West, the Roman Catholic Church was able to maintain greater independence from political authorities than the Orthodox Church did in Byzantium, although, like its Byzantine counterpart, it did actively work with the political authorities.

Q. *What replaced the Roman order in Western Europe?*

• Politically, the Roman imperial order collapsed, to be replaced by a series of regional kingdoms ruled by Germanic warlords.

• But these states maintained some Roman features, including written Roman law and the use of fines and penalties to provide order and justice.

• Some of the larger Germanic kingdoms, including the Carolingian Empire and the empire of Otto I of Saxony, also had aspirations to recreate something of the unity of the Roman Empire, although these kingdoms were short-lived and unsuccessful in reviving anything approaching Roman authority.

• In the West, a social system developed that was based on reciprocal ties between greater and lesser lords among the warrior elites, which replaced the Roman social structure.

• Roman slavery gave way to the practice of serfdom.

• The Roman Catholic Church increased its influence over society.

Q. *In what ways was European civilization changing after 1000?*

• The population grew rapidly.

• New lands were opened for cultivation.

• Long-distance trade was revived and expanded.

• The population of towns grew and attracted new professional groupings that introduced a new and more productive division of labor into European society.

• Women found substantial new opportunities because of economic growth and urbanization, but by the fifteenth century, many of these opportunities were declining.

• Territorial states grew in this period and established more effective institutions of government, commanding the loyalty or at least the obedience of their subjects.

• The Roman Catholic Church expanded the area in which Roman Catholicism was practiced into Eastern Europe and Islamic Spain.

Q. *What was the impact of the Crusades in world history?*

• They marked an expansion of the influence of Western Christendom at the same time that Eastern Christendom and Byzantium were declining.

• They stimulated the demand for Asian luxury goods in Europe.

• They also allowed Europeans to learn techniques for producing sugar on large plantations using slave labor, which had incalculable consequences in later centuries when Europeans transferred the plantation system to the Americas.

• Muslim scholarship, together with the Greek learning that it incorporated, flowed into Europe.

• The Crusades hardened cultural barriers between Eastern Orthodoxy and Roman Catholicism. Moreover, Christian anti-Semitism was exacerbated.

• European empire building, especially in the Americas, continued the crusading notion that "God wills it."

• The Crusades have also on many occasions proved politically or ideologically significant when the worlds of Europe and Islam have collided over the past two centuries.

Q. *In what ways did borrowing from abroad shape European civilization after 1000?*

• Borrowing from abroad played a critical role in establishing a significant tradition of technological innovation that allowed Europe by 1500 to catch up with, and in some areas perhaps to surpass, China and the Islamic world.

• A more efficient horse collar, which probably originated in China or central Asia, contributed to European efforts to plow the heavy soils of northern Europe.

• Gunpowder from China, combined with cannons developed in Western Europe, gave Europeans a military edge over other civilizations.

• Improvements in shipbuilding and navigational techniques, including the magnetic compass and sternpost rudder from China and adaptations of the Arab lateen sail, enabled Europeans to build advanced ships for oceanic voyages.

Q. *Why was Europe unable to achieve the kind of political unity that China experienced? What impact did this have on the subsequent history of Europe?*

• Geographic barriers, ethnic and linguistic diversity, and the shifting balances of power among Europe's many states prevented the emergence of a single European empire like that of China.

Q. *In what different ways did classical Greek philosophy and science have an impact in the West, in Byzantium, and in the Islamic world?*

• In the West after 1000 C.E., a belief in the ability of human reason to penetrate divine mysteries and to grasp the operation of the natural order took shape, and that in turn stimulated a renewed interest in Greek philosophy and science. During this period, European scholars obtained copies of Greek texts from both the Byzantine Empire and the Islamic world. At first this new confidence in human reason was applied primarily to theology, but increasingly it was also applied to the scientific study of nature, known as "natural philosophy," which ultimately became a foundation for the Scientific Revolution.

• In the Byzantine Empire, scholars kept the classical tradition alive, but their primary interest lay in the humanities and theology rather than in the natural sciences or medicine. The Orthodox Church had serious reservations about classical Greek learning, sometimes persecuting scholars who were too enamored with the ancients. Those who studied Greek philosophy and science did so in a conservative spirit, concerned to preserve and transmit the classical heritage rather than using it as a springboard for creating new knowledge.

• The Islamic world undertook a massive translation project in the ninth and tenth centuries that made many Greek texts available in Arabic. This contributed to a flowering of Arab scholarship, especially in the sciences and natural philosophy, between roughly 800 and 1200 C.E. But it also stimulated debate among Muslim thinkers about faith and reason. Unlike church authorities in Western Europe, learned opinion in the Islamic world did not come to regard natural philosophy as a wholly legitimate enterprise. Because of this, the ideas of Plato and Aristotle, while never completely disappearing, receded from Islamic scholarship after the thirteenth century, and natural philosophy did not become a central concern for Islamic higher education as it did in Western Europe.

ADDITIONAL RESOURCES FOR CHAPTER 10

Additional Bedford/St. Martin's Resources

FOR INSTRUCTORS

Computerized Test Bank

This test bank provides over thirty exercises per chapter, including multiple-choice, fill-in-the-blank, short-answer, and full-length essay questions. Instructors can customize quizzes, add or edit both questions and answers, and export questions and answers to a variety of formats, including WebCT and Blackboard. The disc includes correct answers and essay outlines.

Instructor's Resource CD-ROM

This disc provides instructors with ready-made and customizable PowerPoint multimedia presentations built around chapter outlines, maps, figures, and all images from the textbook, plus JPEG versions of all maps, figures, and images.

The following maps and images from Chapter 10 are available in both JPEG and PowerPoint format on the Instructor's Resource CD-ROM:

• Map 10.1: The Byzantine Empire (p. 272)
• Map 10.2: Western Europe in the Ninth Century (p. 280)

- Map 10.3: Europe in the High Middle Ages (p. 286)
- Map 10.4: The Crusades (p. 287)
- Charlemagne (p. 268)
- St. Mark's Basilica (p. 274)
- European Women at Work (p. 284)
- Christians and Muslims (p. 288)
- European Technology (p. 291)
- European University Life in the Middle Ages (p. 294)

FOR STUDENTS

Documents and Essays from *Worlds of History: A Comparative Reader,* Third Edition (Volume 1)

The following documents, essays, and illustrations to accompany Chapter 10 are available in Chapter 10 and Chapter 13 of this reader by Kevin Reilly:

From Chapter 10:

- Fulcher of Chartres, "Pope Urban at Clermont"
- "Chronicle of Solomon bar Simson"
- Anna Comnena, from *The Alexiad*
- Fulcher of Chartres, "The Siege of Antioch"
- Ibn al-Qalanisi, from *The Damascus Chronicle*
- Raymond of St. Giles, Count of Toulouse, "The Capture of Jerusalem by the Crusaders"
- Ibn al-Athir, "The Conquest of Jerusalem"
- "Letter from a Jewish Pilgrim in Egypt"

From Chapter 13:

- Fernand Braudel, *Towns and Cities*
- *Charter of Henry I for London, 1130–1133*
- Gregorio Dati, *Corporation and Community in Florence*

Online Study Guide at bedfordstmartins.com/strayer

The Online Study Guide helps students synthesize the material from the text as well as practice the skills historians use to make sense of the past. Each chapter of the Online Study Guide contains specific testing exercises, including a multiple-choice self-test that focuses on important conceptual ideas; an identification quiz that helps students remember key people, places, and events; a flashcard activity that tests students on their knowledge of key terms; and two interactive map activities intended to strengthen students' geographic skills. Instructors can monitor students' progress through an online Quiz Gradebook or receive email updates.

Further Reading

France, John. *The Crusades and the Expansion of Catholic Christendom, 1000–1714.* London: Routledge, 2005. An interesting and ambitious work by a leading historian of the Crusades.

Halsall, Paul, ed. *Internet Medieval Sourcebook.* http://www.fordham.edu/halsall/sbook.html. A vast array of primary sources available on the Internet. Many of them are short excerpts that are well suited to use in the classroom.

Jordan, William Chester. *Europe in the High Middle Ages.* London: Penguin, 2001. A very readable recent survey.

Keen, Maurice, ed. *Medieval Warfare: A History.* Oxford: Oxford University Press, 1999. A very readable collection of essays that covers just about anything you would want to know about medieval war.

The Labyrinth: Resources for Medieval Studies, http://labyrinth.georgetown.edu/. This site, sponsored by Georgetown University, is a comprehensive resource for material on medieval Europe available on the Internet.

Links Related to Early and Medieval Christianity, http://faculty.fullerton.edu/bstarr/345A.LINKS.htm. An interesting assortment of primary sources, secondary articles, and artworks.

McKitterick, Rosamond, ed. *The Early Middle Ages: Europe, 400–1000.* Oxford: Oxford University Press, 2001. Probably the most balanced among recent studies of the early medieval centuries.

Literature

A vast array of medieval primary sources is available in English translation; the works listed below were selected as particularly suitable for classroom use.

Burgess, Glyn S., trans. *The Song of Roland*. Harmondsworth: Penguin, 1990. Written about the time of the First Crusade, this is widely regarded as the greatest of all medieval epics, telling of the defeat of Charlemagne's rearguard at the Battle of Roncesvalles.

Chrétien de Troyes. *Ywain: The Knight of the Lion.* Trans. Burton Raffel. New Haven: Yale University Press, 1987. A relatively short twelfth-century romance that shows the values of chivalry and courtly love particularly well.

Comnena, Anna. *The Alexiad.* Trans. E. R. A. Sewter. Harmondsworth: Penguin, 1979. A Byzantine princess's account of her father, Emperor Alexius Comnenus. This work is particularly interesting since it includes an account of the First Crusade from a Byzantine perspective.

Einhard and Notker the Stammerer. *Two Lives of Charlemagne.* Harmondsworth: Penguin, 1969. Einhard's classicizing account of his hero Charlemagne provides an inside look at the Carolingian renaissance and how contemporaries regarded the great emperor. Notker's account, written two generations later, shows the development of the Charlemagne legend.

Hamilton, Rita, and Janet Perry, trans. *The Poem of the Cid.* Harmondsworth: Penguin, 1985. A magnificent tale of border warfare in eleventh-century Spain, the hero of this tale is the historic commander Ruy Díaz, better known as "the Cid."

Magnusson, Magnus, and Hermann Pálsson, trans. *The Vinland Sagas: The Norse Discovery of America.* Harmondsworth: Penguin, 1965. Although not written until the thirteenth century, the two short sagas included in this volume provide valuable material about Leif Eriksson's attempt to establish a Scandinavian colony in America.

Procopius. *The Secret History.* Trans. G. A. Williamson and Peter Sarris. Rev. ed. London: Penguin, 2007. A racy, at times downright scurrilous contemporary account of the reign of the Byzantine emperor Justinian and his notorious wife, Theodora.

Film

Byzantium and the Holy Roman Empire: Christianity in the Seventh and Eighth Centuries. Films for the Humanities and Sciences, 1999. 48 minutes. Compares Byzantium to Western Europe during this critical period in which Islam spread across the Near East and North Africa.

Byzantium from Splendor to Ruin. Films for the Humanities and Sciences, 1989. 43 minutes. Traces the rise and decline of Byzantium, from the founding of Constantinople to its conquest by the Ottoman Turks.

Charlemagne and the Holy Roman Empire. Films for the Humanities and Sciences, 1989. 31 minutes. Examines the emergence of the Carolingian Empire in the eighth and ninth centuries.

The Crusades. Discovery Channel, 2003. 50 minutes. Examines the Crusades with an eye toward addressing the myths that surround the phenomenon.

The End of Rome, the Birth of Europe. Films for the Humanities and Sciences, 2002. 52 minutes. Explores the conquest and settlement of Western Europe by Germanic peoples.

The Feudal System. Films for the Humanities and Sciences, 1989. 38 minutes. Explores the economic and social foundations of medieval Europe.

The Luttrell Psalter: Everyday Life in Medieval England. Films for the Humanities and Sciences, 1998. 22 minutes. Uses the evidence in the richly illuminated Luttrell Psalter to reconstruct everyday life on an early fourteenth-century English estate. The film also includes details about how and why the Luttrell Psalter was made.

The Middle Ages. Films for the Humanities and Sciences, 1996. 25 minutes. Provides a brief overview of the Middle Ages.

The Worlds of Islam
Afro-Eurasian Connections, 600–1500

CHAPTER OVERVIEW

Chapter Objectives

- To examine the causes behind the spread of Islam
- To explore the dynamism of the Islamic world as the most influential of the third-wave civilizations
- To consider the religious divisions within Islam and how they affected political development
- To consider Islam as a source of cultural encounters with Christian, African, and Hindu cultures
- To increase student awareness of the accomplishments of the Islamic world in the period 600–1500 C.E.

Chapter Outline

I.   Opening Vignette
  A. By the start of the twenty-first century, Islam had acquired a significant presence in the United States.
    1. more than 1,200 mosques
    2. about 8 million Muslims (some 2 million are African Americans)
  B. The second half of the twentieth century saw the growing international influence of Islam.

  C. Islam had already been prominent in the world between 600 and 1600.
    1. encompassed parts of Africa, Europe, Middle East, and Asia
    2. enormously significant in world history
    3. creation of a new and innovative civilization
    4. was the largest and most influential of the third-wave civilizations
    5. Islam's reach generated major cultural encounters
  D. In the year 2000, there were perhaps 1.2 billion Muslims in the world (22 percent of the world's population).

II.   The Birth of a New Religion
  A. The Homeland of Islam
    1. unlike most religious/cultural traditions, Islam emerged from a marginal region
    2. Arabian Peninsula as home of nomadic Arabs (Bedouins)
      a. fiercely independent clans and tribes
      b. variety of gods
    3. Arabia also had sedentary, agricultural areas
    4. Arabia lay on important East–West trade routes
      a. Mecca became important as a trade center
      b. the Kaaba was the most prominent religious shrine
      c. the Quraysh tribe controlled local trade and pilgrimage

5. Arabia was on the edge of the Byzantine and Sassanid empires
   a. so Arabs knew some practices of these empires
   b. Judaism, Christianity, and Zoroastrianism had spread among Arabs
      i. by 600 C.E., most settled Arabs acknowledged a supreme god (Allah)
      ii. increasingly identified Allah with Yahweh

B. The Messenger and the Message **[see Classroom Activity 1]**
   1. the prophet of Islam was Muhammad Ibn Abdullah (570–632 C.E.)
      a. orphaned at a young age
      b. became a prosperous merchant thanks to marriage to Khadija
      c. took to withdrawal and meditation
   2. beginning of revelations from God in 610 C.E.
      a. revelations recorded in the Quran
      b. when heard in its original Arabic, believed to convey the presence of the divine
   3. radically new teachings
      a. monotheistic
      b. Muhammad as "the seal of the prophets"
      c. return to old, pure religion of Abraham
      d. central tenet: submission to Allah (Muslim = "one who submits")
      e. need to create a new society of social justice, equality, and care for others (the *umma*)
   4. core message summarized in the Five Pillars of Islam
      a. first pillar is simple profession: "There is no god but Allah, and Muhammad is the messenger of God."
      b. prayer five times a day at prescribed times
      c. generous giving to help the community and the needy
      d. fasting during the month of Ramadan
      e. pilgrimage to Mecca (*hajj*)
   5. jihad ("struggle") is sometimes called the "sixth pillar" **[see Discussion Topic 1]**
      a. "greater jihad": personal spiritual striving
      b. "lesser jihad"/"jihad of the sword": armed struggle against unbelief and evil
      c. understanding of the concept has varied widely over time

C. The Transformation of Arabia
   1. Muhammad attracted a small following, aroused opposition from Meccan elites
      a. in 622, emigrated to Yathrib/Medina (the *hijra*)
      b. created Islamic community (umma) in Medina
      c. broke definitively from Judaism
   2. rapid expansion throughout Arabia
      a. military successes led to alliances
      b. large-scale conversion
      c. consolidation of Islamic control throughout Arabia by time of Muhammad's death in 632
   3. fundamental differences between births of Islam and Christianity
      a. Islam did not grow up as persecuted minority religion
      b. Islam didn't separate "church" and state
         i. Muhammad was a religious, political, and military leader
         ii. no separate religious organization
         iii. no professional clergy
         iv. no distinction between religious and civil law; one law (the *sharia*) for everything

III. **The Making of an Arab Empire** [see Lecture Strategy 1]
   A. The Arab state grew to include all or part of Egyptian, Roman/Byzantine, Persian, Mesopotamian, and Indian civilizations.
      1. many both in and out of Arab Empire converted to Islam
      2. Arabic culture and language spread widely
      3. Islam became a new third-wave civilization
   B. War and Conquest
      1. Arabic conquests were a continuation of long-term raiding pattern
      2. new level of political organization allowed greater mobilization
      3. Byzantine and Persian empires were weakened by long wars and internal revolts
      4. limits of Arab expansion:
         a. defeated Sassanid Empire in the 650s, took half of Byzantium

b. in early 700s, conquered most of Spain, attacked France

c. to the east, reached the Indus River

d. in 751, Arabs crushed a Chinese army at the Battle of Talas River

    i. ended Chinese westward expansion

    ii. enabled conversion of Turkic peoples to Islam

5. reasons for expansion:

    a. economic: capture trade routes and agricultural regions

    b. individual Arabs sought wealth and social promotion

    c. communal: conquest helped hold the umma together

    d. religious: bring righteous government to the conquered

        i. did *not* impose Islam

        ii. in early period, Arabs thought Islam was *their* religion

        iii. by mid-eighth century began seeking converts

        iv. still protected "people of the Book"—Christians, Jews, Zoroastrians (*dhimmis*)

        v. non-Muslims paid special tax (the *jizya*) but could practice their own religion

6. conquest was not too destructive

    a. Arab soldiers were restricted to garrison towns

    b. local elites and bureaucracies were incorporated into empire

C. Conversion to Islam

1. initial conversion for many was "social conversion," not deep spiritual change

2. Islam's kinship to Judaism, Christianity, and Zoroastrianism made it attractive

3. Islam was associated from the beginning with a powerful state—suggested that Allah was a good god to have on your side

4. the state provided incentives for conversion

    a. earliest converts included slaves and prisoners of war

    b. converts didn't have to pay the jizya

    c. Islam favored commerce

    d. social climbers were helped by conversion

5. resistance to conversion among Berbers of North Africa, some Spanish Christians, some Persian Zoroastrians

6. around 80 percent of the population of Persia converted between 750 and 900

7. some areas (Egypt, North Africa, Iraq) also converted to Arabic culture and language

D. Divisions in the Islamic World

1. a central problem: who should serve as successor to Muhammad (caliph)?

2. first four caliphs (the Rightly Guided Caliphs, 632–661) were companions of Muhammad

    a. had to put down Arab tribal rebellions and new prophets

    b. Uthman and Ali were both assassinated

    c. civil war by 656

3. result was the Sunni/Shia split of Islam

    a. Sunni Muslims: caliphs were rightful political and military leaders, chosen by the Islamic community

    b. Shia Muslims: leaders should be blood relatives of Muhammad, descended from Ali and his son Husayn

    c. started as a political conflict but became religious

        i. Sunnis: religious authority comes from the community, especially from religious scholars (*ulama*)

        ii. Shias: *imams* have religious authority

    d. Shias identified themselves as opponents of privilege

        i. frequently revolted

        ii. many leaders martyred

        iii. development of idea that defeated leaders are not dead but in hiding—will return as messiah figures

4. over time, caliphs became absolute monarchs

    a. Umayyad dynasty (661–750) was a time of great expansion

        i. caliphs became hereditary rulers

        ii. capital moved to Damascus

        iii. Arab military aristocracy ruled

        iv. decadent rulers and unequal treatment of non-Arab Muslims caused unrest

    b. Abbasid dynasty overthrew Umayyads in 750

    i. founded new capital at Baghdad

    ii. gave much larger role to non-Arabs

    iii. began steep decline in mid-ninth century

    iv. caliph gradually became a figurehead to a number of *de facto* independent states (sultanates)

  5. basic religious issue: what does it mean to be a Muslim?

    a. Islamic law (the sharia) helped answer the question

      i. addressed most aspects of religious and social life

      ii. concern was with correct behavior

      iii. creation of four Sunni schools of law, even more Shia ones

    b. reaction against the distraction of worldly success: *Sufis* [see Lecture Strategy 2]

      i. Sufis were mystics, seeking direct experience of the divine

      ii. renounced the material world

      iii. spiritual union often expressed in terms of drunkenness or sexual experience

      iv. became widely popular by ninth/tenth centuries

      v. Sufis were critical of the sharia and even of reading the Quran

      vi. members of the ulama often thought Sufis were heretics

    c. the ulama and Sufism weren't entirely incompatible—e.g., al-Ghazali (1058–1111)

    d. but there was often tension between the two approaches

 E. Women and Men in Early Islam [see Discussion Topic 2]

  1. what rise of Islam meant for women remains highly controversial

  2. spiritual level: Quran stated explicitly that women and men were equals

  3. social level: Quran viewed women as subordinate, especially in marriage

  4. Quran helped women in some ways (banned female infanticide, gave women control over their own property, granted limited rights of inheritance, required woman's consent to a marriage, recognized a woman's right to sexual satisfaction)

  5. social practices of lands where Islam spread were also important in defining women's roles

    a. early Islam: some women played public roles; prayed in mosques, weren't veiled or secluded

    b. growing restrictions on women (especially in upper classes) under Abbasids

    c. veiling and seclusion became standard among upper, ruling classes

    d. lower-class women didn't have the "luxury" of seclusion

    e. practices were determined by Middle Eastern traditions much more than by Quran

      i. Muslim scholars soon added religious rationale

  6. *hadiths* (traditions about Muhammad) developed more negative images of women

    a. unlike the Quran, hadiths blamed Eve for fall of humankind

  7. Islam gave new religious outlets for women, especially as Sufis

IV. **Islam and Cultural Encounter: A Four-Way Comparison**

 A. The Arab Empire had all but disintegrated politically by the tenth century.

  1. last Abbasid caliph killed when Mongols sacked Baghdad in 1258

  2. but Islamic civilization continued to flourish and expand

 B. The Case of India

  1. Turkic-speaking invaders brought Islam to India

  2. establishment of Turkic and Muslim regimes in India beginning ca. 1000

    a. at first, violent destruction of Hindu and Buddhist temples

    b. Sultanate of Delhi (founded 1206) became more systematic

  3. emergence of Muslim communities in India

    a. Buddhists and low-caste Hindus found Islam attractive

b. newly agrarian people also liked Islam

c. subjects of Muslim rulers converted to lighten tax burden

d. Sufis fit mold of Indian holy men, encouraged conversion

    i. developed a "popular Islam" with Hindu overlap

e. at height, 20–25 percent of Indian population converted to Islam

    i. Muslim communities concentrated in northwest and eastern India

    ii. deep Muslim/Hindu cultural divide

a. monotheism vs. polytheism

b. equality of believers vs. caste system

c. sexual modesty vs. open eroticism

4. interaction of Hindus and Muslims

a. many Hindus served Muslim rulers

b. mystics blurred the line between the two religions

c. Sikhism developed in early sixteenth century; syncretic religion with elements of both Islam and Hinduism

    i. founded by Guru Nanak (1469–1539)

d. Muslims remained as a distinctive minority

C. The Case of Anatolia

1. Turks invaded Anatolia about the same time as India

a. major destruction at early stages in both places

b. Sufi missionaries were important in both places

c. but in Anatolia by 1500, 90 percent of the population was Muslim, and most spoke Turkish

2. reasons for the different results in the two regions

a. Anatolia had a much smaller population (8 million vs. 48 million)

b. far more Turkic speakers settled in Anatolia

c. much deeper destruction of Byzantine society in Anatolia

d. active discrimination against Christians in Anatolia

e. India's decentralized politics and religion could absorb the shock of invasion better

f. Turkish rulers of Anatolia welcomed converts; fewer social barriers to conversion

g. Sufis replaced Christian institutions in Anatolia

3. by 1500, the Ottoman Empire was the most powerful Islamic state

4. Turks of Anatolia retained much of their culture after conversion

a. freer life for women persisted

D. The Case of West Africa

1. Islam came peacefully with traders, not by conquest

2. in West Africa, Islam spread mostly in urban centers

a. provided links to Muslim trading partners

b. provided literate officials and religious legitimacy to state

3. by the sixteenth century, several West African cities were Islamic centers

a. Timbuktu had over 150 Quranic schools and several centers of higher education

b. libraries had tens of thousands of books

c. rulers subsidized building of major mosques

d. Arabic became a language of religion, education, administration, trade

4. did not have significant Arab immigration

5. Sufis played little role until the eighteenth century

6. no significant spread into countryside until nineteenth century

a. rulers made little effort to impose Islam or rule by Islamic law

E. The Case of Spain

1. Arab and Berber forces conquered most of Spain (called al-Andalus by Muslims) in the early eighth century

2. Islam did not overwhelm Christianity there

3. high degree of interaction between Muslims, Christians, and Jews

a. some Christians converted to Islam

b. Christian *Mozarabs* adopted Arabic culture but not religion

4. religious toleration started breaking down by late tenth century

a. increasing war with Christian states of northern Spain

b. more puritanical forms of Islam entered Spain from North Africa

c. in Muslim-ruled regions, increasing limitations placed on Christians

d. many Muslims were forced out of Christian-conquered regions or kept from public practice of their faith

e. completion of Christian reconquest in 1492

i. some 200,000 Jews were expelled from Spain

V. **The World of Islam as a New Civilization** [see Discussion Topic 3 and Classroom Activity 2]

A. By 1500, the Islamic world embraced at least parts of nearly every other Afro-Eurasian civilization.

1. history's first "global civilization"

B. Networks of Faith

1. Islamic civilization was held together by Islamic practices and beliefs

a. beliefs/practices transmitted by the ulama, who served as judges, interpreters, etc.

b. starting in eleventh century: formal colleges (*madrassas*) taught religion, law, and sometimes secular subjects

c. system of education with common texts, sharing of scholarship throughout Islamic world

2. Sufism: branches of Sufism gathered around particular teachers (*shaykhs*) by the tenth century

a. development of great Sufi orders by the twelfth/thirteenth centuries

b. Sufi devotional teachings, practices, writings spread widely

3. many thousands of Muslims made the hajj to Mecca each year

C. Networks of Exchange **[see Lecture Strategy 3]**

1. Islamic world was an immense arena for exchange of goods, technology, and ideas

a. great central location for trade

b. Islamic teaching valued commerce

c. urbanization spurred commerce

2. Muslim merchants were prominent on all the major Afro-Eurasian trade routes

a. aided by banking, partnerships, business contracts, credit instruments

3. exchange of agricultural products and practices between regions

a. Muslim conquest of northwestern India introduced rice, sugarcane, sorghum, hard wheat, cotton, and many fruits and vegetables to Middle East

4. diffusion of technology

a. spread ancient Persian water-drilling techniques

b. improvement of Chinese rockets

c. adoption of papermaking techniques from China in the eighth century

5. exchange of ideas

a. Persian bureaucratic practice, court ritual, poetry

b. ancient Greek, Hellenistic, and Indian texts

c. developments in mathematics, astronomy, optics, medicine, pharmacology

VI. **Reflections: Learning from Outsiders: A Tale of Two Travelers** [see Classroom Activity 3]

A. "Outsider" accounts can be very useful in understanding a culture.

B. Ibn Battuta (1304–1368) traveled nearly 75,000 miles around the Islamic world.

1. often criticized the quality of Muslim observance outside of core lands

2. appalled by freedoms given to women in outlying lands

3. found only China to be completely foreign

C. Marco Polo (1254–1324) traveled from Italy to China, where he served at the court of Khubilai Khan.

1. unlike Ibn Batutta, Polo found himself an outsider everywhere he went

2. did not show as much disapproval of strange behaviors

D. The writings of the two show that Islam was the "central fact" of the Afro-Eurasian world in the thirteenth and fourteenth centuries; Europe was still on the margins.

USING *WAYS OF THE WORLD* IN THE CLASSROOM

Lecture Strategies

Lecture Strategy 1

"The Arab conquests."
This lecture strategy allows you to go into more detail concerning the Arab conquests than was possible in the textbook, exploring the reasons behind the vast expansion of Islamic rule in the seventh and eighth centuries C.E. from a variety of angles. Its objectives are to:

- review and highlight the lessons given in the textbook about the expansion—where, when, and why
- consider conditions in the Persian and Byzantine empires, as well as in the Kingdoms of the Vandals and the Visigoths, that helped the Arabs in their conquests
- consider in greater detail the geographical factors that helped shape the conquests
- explore in greater detail the role of jihad thought in Islam.

A good place to start this lecture is with a physical map of the Islamic world. Discuss the nature of early armies, including Arab reliance on sudden raids moving from desert into settled lands, the need for horses, and the potential of camels in this process. Then encourage the students to consider what the map can tell them about the conquests. Some questions to ask are:

- Did the Arab conquerors reach a "natural" limit to expansion because they moved into geographical zones that no longer favored their fighting style? (consider, for example, the Taurus mountain range of Anatolia, the Hindu Kush, and the Pyrenees on the Spanish/French border)
- What political reasons, drawing on earlier chapters, might also have limited the expansion? (e.g., the defensibility of Constantinople and political consolidation under the early Carolingians in Francia)

Move from there to present the fuller story of the conquests. This can be approached in a variety of ways. Some useful points to include are:

- the massive Byzantine-Persian war of the early decades of the seventh century, including Heraclius's final victory and the devastating impact of the war on both states
- the nature of rule in both the Byzantine and Persian empires and how both systems oppressed large sectors of the population (through taxes, religious repression)
- the unpopularity of Vandal rule in North Africa
- the role of the caliphs in directing the course of the conquest
- the Arab culture of raiding
- the religious propulsion behind the conquests
- Arab moderation toward conquered peoples (I especially recommend using the Pact of Umar, which Caliph Umar made with the Christians of Syria after the initial conquest; there is a translation available at http://www.fordham .edu/halsall/source/pact-umar.html)

Lecture Strategy 2

"Comparative mysticism."
Mysticism played an especially great role in the development of the medieval Islamic world, but of course the individual's quest for direct, personal contact with the divine is common to most religions. From roughly 1100 to around 1500, mysticism flourished, especially in Christianity, Islam, and Judaism. The purpose of this lecture strategy is to explore the common threads of the mystic tradition. Its objectives are to:

- encourage students to recognize how common mysticism is in world history, rather than seeing Islam as novel in this regard
- compare mystic traditions
- consider what makes some periods and regions more mysticism-oriented than others

Enabling this lecture is a wonderful ongoing series of translations of works by mystics from a variety of religious traditions—Paulist Press's Classics of Western Spirituality. If your library has some of these (surprisingly inexpensive) volumes, the lecture can be built around excerpts from the mystics' own writings. For example, you might construct a lecture around two mystics each from Islam, Christianity, and Judaism, using, for example:

for Christianity:

- Gertrude of Helfta, *The Herald of Divine Love*
- Julian of Norwich, *Showings*

for Judaism:

- *Zohar: The Book of Enlightenment*
- *The Early Kabbalah*

for Islam:

- *Early Islamic Mysticism*
- Ibn al-'Arabi, *The Bezels of Wisdom*

Discuss the "mystical path" in the three religions, including:

- who became known as mystics
- whether mystics were loners or part of communities
- biographical details of the mystics you have chosen to highlight
- tensions between mystics and the mainstream religious establishment
- regions where mystics were especially prevalent and possible reasons why
- gender issues and mysticism

Lecture Strategy 3

"The golden age of Islam."
This lecture strategy allows the instructor to delve in greater detail into Islamic culture in the period before the Mongol conquests, as well as providing an opportunity to review Chinese and European material. Its goals are to:

- discuss in detail Snapshot 11-2, "Key Achievements in Islamic Science and Scholarship" (on p. 327)
- compare Islamic scholarly achievements to those of Tang and Song dynasty China
- compare Islamic scholarly achievements to those of Byzantium and Western Europe during the High Middle Ages

A good place to start a lecture like this is with the learning environment in the Islamic world of the eleventh to thirteenth centuries. Discuss literacy levels, the existence of lower schools as well as institutes of higher learning, and

how class issues, gender, and region affected the ability to get a good education. From there, the instructor can take a variety of approaches. Some possibilities:

- Focus the lecture on key inventions and discoveries, talking about the context in which the discovery was made and the use to which it was put (e.g., *why* did al-Khwarazim popularize the use of Arabic numerals and write a book on algebra?). Compare where possible with achievements in Europe and Asia.
- Focus the lecture on the demands imposed by Islamic society—in trade, in supporting a large population in the cities, in interpreting Islamic law, etc.—and how specific needs led to specific solutions from the community of scholars. Compare where possible with similar difficulties and solutions in Europe and Asia.
- Focus the lecture on the major figures named in Snapshot 11-2, discussing the life circumstances that led to their achievements.

Things to Do in the Classroom

Discussion Topics

1. **Misconception/Difficult Topic, large or small group.** "The vexed issue of jihad."
Ask students to discuss the ways in which the term *jihad* is used in modern Islamic culture, compared to its historic meanings. Some possible approaches:

- distribute to the class the passages of the Quran that speak of jihad and ask the students to discuss them
- ask students to outline the points about jihad made in this chapter, and then compare those points to the presentation of the issue in modern media
- ask students to bring to class examples of what can be found on the Internet about jihad, asking for a variety of opinions (popular, journalistic, theological, etc.)

2. **Comparison, large or small group.** "Women in the third-wave civilizations."
Ask students to discuss which of the third-wave civilizations offered the most favorable conditions for women. Be sure to encourage them to consider the difference made by social class.

3. Contextualization, large or small group. "In the year 1200: who's 'winning'?"
Ask students to compare conditions in the Islamic world, China, and Western Europe in the year 1200 C.E. and to answer the question of which society, at that time, seemed the most likely to win a "most dominant society of the world" contest. Encourage them to chart out how they would rank each civilization on a number of points that the members of the class regard as important, such as religious tolerance, economic prosperity, gender equality, population, innovation, and so on.

Classroom Activities

1. Close-reading exercise, large or small group. "Meeting the Quran."
Choose one of the shorter suras of the Quran, such as:

- Number 43: Ornaments of Gold (interesting gender issues)
- Number 46: The Sand Dunes (interesting insight on Muhammad's revelations)
- Number 48: Victory (after the Muslim conquest of Mecca)
- Number 58: She Who Pleaded (on divorce and other social issues)
- Number 77: Those That Are Sent Forth (on the Last Judgment)

(Note: The suras of the Quran are traditionally arranged by length, with the longest at the beginning and the shortest at the end.) Ask students to read the selected sura carefully, listing important points that can be garnered about Islam and/or conditions in Arabia at the time of Muhammad.

2. Role-playing exercise, small group. "An Arabic travelogue."
Choose three groups of students. Ask them to research and present to the class what their impressions would be if they were Arab visitors to Western Europe in the following times and areas:

1. spies for Caliph Umar who go to the papal court in Rome ca. 640 C.E.
2. emissaries of the caliph Harun al-Rashid who have brought an elephant to Charlemagne as a gift ca. 800 C.E.
3. members of the ulama who have heard interesting tales about the University of Paris and have come to investigate the state of learning in Western Europe ca. 1200 C.E.

Note that it is important in each of these cases that the students acquire a reasonable understanding of Islamic society at the time they are presenting, which will of course have an impact on the degree to which they are impressed by or dismissive of the culture they are visiting.

3. Clicker question. Does this chapter help you understand the problems of the modern Islamic world?

Key Terms

Abbasid caliphate: Dynasty of caliphs who ruled an increasingly fragmented Islamic state from 750 to 1258, eventually becoming little more than figureheads. (*pron.* ah-BASS-id)

Andalus, al-: Arabic name for Spain (literally "the land of the Vandals"), most of which was conquered by Arab and Berber forces in the early eighth century C.E. (*pron.* al-AND-ah-loos)

Anatolia: Ancient name of Asia Minor, part of the Byzantine Empire that was gradually overrun by the Turks and that now is the Republic of Turkey. (*pron.* an-ah-TOLE-ee-yah)

Battle of Talas River: Arab victory over the Chinese in 751 C.E. that checked Chinese expansion to the west and enabled the conversion of Central Asia to Islam. (*pron.* tah-las)

Bedouins: Nomadic Arabs. (*pron.* BED-wins)

dhimmis: "Protected subjects" under Islamic rule, non-Muslims who were allowed to practice their faith as "people of the book" in return for their paying special taxes. (*pron.* DIM-ees)

Ghazali, al-: Great Muslim theologian, legal scholar, and Sufi mystic (1058–1111) who was credited with incorporating Sufism into mainstream Islamic thought. (*pron.* al-gha-ZAHL-ee)

hadiths: Traditions passed on about the sayings or actions of Muhammad and his immediate followers; hadiths rank second only to the Quran as a source of Islamic law. (*pron.* hah-DEETHS)

hajj: The pilgrimage to Mecca enjoined on every Muslim who is able to make the journey; one of the Five Pillars of Islam. (*pron.* HAHJ)

hijra: The "flight" of Muhammad and his original seventy followers from Mecca to Yathrib (later Medina) in 622 C.E.; the journey marks the starting point of the Islamic calendar. (*pron.* HIJ-ruh)

House of Wisdom: An academic center for research and translation of foreign texts that was established in Baghdad in 830 C.E. by the Abbasid caliph al-Mamun.

Ibn Battuta: Fourteenth-century Arab traveler (1304–1368) who wrote about his extensive journeys throughout the Islamic world. (*pron.* IB-uhn ba-TOO-tuh)

Ibn Sina: One of the greatest polymaths of the Islamic world (980–1037), a Persian who wrote prolifically on scientific (especially medical) and philosophical issues; he is often known as "Avicenna," the Latinized form of his name. (*pron.* ibn SEE-nah)

imams: In Shia Islam, leaders with high religious authority; the twelve imams of early Shia Islam were Muhammad's nephew Ali and his descendants. (*pron.* EE-mahms)

jihad: Arabic for "struggle," this term describes both the spiritual striving of each Muslim toward a godly life and armed struggle against the forces of unbelief and evil. (*pron.* jee-HAHD)

jizya: Special tax paid by dhimmis in Muslim-ruled territory in return for freedom to practice their own religion. (*pron.* jeez-YAH)

Kaaba: Great stone shrine in Mecca that was a major pilgrimage center for worshippers of many different deities before it was reconsecrated to monotheistic use by Muhammad. (*pron.* KAH-bah)

madrassas: Formal colleges for higher instruction in the teachings of Islam as well as in secular subjects, founded throughout the Islamic world beginning in the eleventh century. (*pron.* MAH-dras-ahs)

Mecca: Key pilgrimage center in Arabia that became the birthplace of Islam.

Mozarabs: "Would-be Arabs" in Muslim-ruled Spain, referring to Christians who adopted much of Arabic culture and observed many Muslim practices without actually converting to Islam. (*pron.* MOH-zah-rabs)

Muhammad Ibn Abdullah: The Prophet of Islam (570–632 C.E.).

Muslim: Literally, "one who submits"; the name was adopted by Muhammad and his followers to describe their submission to God.

Pillars of Islam: The five core practices required of Muslims: a profession of faith, regular prayer, charitable giving, fasting during Ramadan, and a pilgrimage to Mecca (if financially and physically possible).

Polo, Marco: The most famous European traveler of the Middle Ages (1254–1324), whose travel account of his time in China was widely popular in Europe.

Rightly Guided Caliphs: The first four rulers of the Islamic world (632–661) after the death of Muhammad.

Quran: Also transliterated as Qur'án and Koran, this is the most holy text of Islam, recording the revelations given to the prophet Muhammad. (*pron.* kuh-RAHN)

sharia: Islamic law, dealing with all matters of both secular and religious life. (*pron.* sha-REE-ah)

shaykhs: Sufi teachers who attracted a circle of disciples and often founded individual schools of Sufism. (*pron.* SHAKES)

Sikhism: A significant syncretic religion that evolved in India, blending elements of Islam and Hinduism; founded by Guru Nanak (1469–1539). (*pron.* SEEK-ism)

Sufis: Islamic mystics, many of whom were important missionaries of Islam in conquered lands and who were revered as saints. (*pron.* SOO-fees)

Sultanate of Delhi: Major Turkic Muslim state established in northern India in 1206. (*pron.* DEL-ee)

Timbuktu: Great city of West Africa, noted as a center of Islamic scholarship in the fourteenth to sixteenth centuries. (*pron.* tim-buk-TOO)

ulama: Islamic religious scholars. (*pron.* oo-leh-MAH)

Umayyad caliphate: Family of caliphs who ruled the Islamic world from 661 to 750 C.E. (*pron.* oo-MY-ad)

umma: The community of all believers in Islam. (*pron.* UM-mah)

ANSWER GUIDELINES FOR CHAPTER QUESTIONS

The two sets of questions that follow appear in the textbook at the end of the chapter and in the margins of the reading. They are also provided in the Computerized Test Bank with answer guidelines, for your convenience.

The Big Picture Questions

1. What distinguished the first centuries of Islamic history from the early history of Christianity and Buddhism? What similarities and differences characterized their religious outlooks?

- In terms of distinguishing characteristics, Islam differed sharply from Christianity and Buddhism because its founder was not only a religious figure but also a political and military leader.
- Moreover, from the start the Islamic community found itself constituted as a state. Because of this, Islam did not develop as clearly defined a separation between church and state as did both Christianity and Buddhism.
- Concerning the similarities of their religious outlooks, all three religions were founded by single historical figures who had powerful religious experiences;
  - all three provide a clear path to salvation;
  - all three proclaim the equality of all believers.
- Concerning differences in their religious outlooks, Islam's conception of monotheism was stronger than that of Christianity;
  - each religion was shaped in part by the cultural traditions in which it emerged.

2. How might you account for the immense religious and political/military success of Islam in its early centuries?

- In terms of political and military success, for the first time a shared faith in Islam allowed the newly organized state to mobilize the military potential of the entire Arab population.
- The Byzantine and Persian empires were weakened by decades of war with each other and by internal revolts. The two empires also underestimated the Arab threat.
- Merchant leaders of the new Islamic community wanted to capture profitable trade routes and wealthy agricultural regions.
- Individual Arabs found in military expansion a route to wealth and social promotion.
- Expansion provided a common task for the Arab community, which reinforced the fragile unity of the Islamic umma.
- Arabs were motivated by a religious dimension, as many viewed the mission of empire in terms of jihad, bringing righteous government to the peoples they conquered.
- In terms of Islam's success in attracting converts, Muhammad's religious message was attractive to many potential converts.
- Jews, Christians, and Zoroastrians could find familiar elements of their own faiths in Islam.

- Conquests called into question the power of old gods, while the growing prestige of the Arab Empire attracted many to Allah.
- Although forced conversions were rare, living in an Islamic-governed state provided a variety of incentives for claiming Muslim identity.
- Merchants found in Islam a religion friendly to commerce and in the Arab Empire a huge and secure arena for trade.
- People aspiring to official positions found conversion to Islam an aid to social mobility.

3. In what ways can Islamic civilization be described as "cosmopolitan"?

- The Islamic civilization embraced at least parts of virtually every other civilization in the Afro-Eurasian hemisphere.
- The Islamic civilization fostered a network of commerce and exchange that facilitated the spread of crops, technologies, and ideas.
- The common commitment to Islam created an identity that transcended more local political and cultural identities in the Islamic world.

4. "Islam was simultaneously both a single world of shared meaning and interaction and a series of separate and distinct communities, often in conflict with one another." What evidence could you provide to support both sides of this argument?

- In terms of a single world of shared meaning and interaction, at the core of the Islamic world was a common commitment to Islam;
  - the ulama through education and Sufis through their associations served to bind together the Islamic world;
  - the Islamic world also cohered as an immense arena of exchange in which goods, technologies, crops, and ideas circulated widely.
- In terms of separate and distinct communities, Islam was politically fragmented;
  - it included numerous distinct and sometimes hostile religious traditions, including Sunni/Shia and ulama/Sufi splits;
  - it embraced distinctive cultural traditions from sub-Saharan Africa and Southeast Asia that resulted in different attitudes toward social and cultural norms, such as those concerning women.

5. What changes did Islamic expansion generate in those societies that encountered it, and how was Islam itself transformed by those encounters?

• Concerning societies that encountered Islam, the populations of many regions converted wholly or partly to the Islamic faith;

• regions of the Islamic world were tied more closely together through trade and the exchange of technologies, crops, and ideas;

• older religious and political traditions were at times swept away or at least altered.

• Islam was transformed through these encounters, especially when the norms of those societies that converted had an impact on the social and cultural implications of the faith;

• the Islamic world and the understanding of Islam itself was shaped by contact with intellectual and cultural traditions like Greek philosophy.

Margin Review Questions

Q. *In what ways did the early history of Islam reflect its Arabian origins?*

• Islam drew on an older Arab identification of Allah with Yahweh, the Jewish High God, and Arab self-identification as "children of Abraham."

• The Quran denounced the prevailing social practices of an increasingly prosperous Mecca and sought a return to the older values of Arab tribal life.

• The message of the Quran also rejected the Arab tribal and clan structure, which was prone to war, feuding, and violence. Instead, the Quran sought to replace this structure with the *umma*, the community of all believers.

Q. *How does the core message of Islam compare with that of Judaism and Christianity?*

• Islam, like Judaism and Christianity, is monotheistic. Allah is the only God, the all-powerful Creator.

• As "the Messenger of God," Muhammad presented himself in the tradition of earlier prophets like Abraham, Moses, and Jesus.

• Like the Jewish prophets and Jesus, Muhammad demanded social justice and laid out a prescription for its implementation.

Q. *In what ways was the rise of Islam revolutionary, both in theory and in practice?*

• The Islamic community, or umma, broke with the previous tribal structure defined by family and clan in Arabia, replacing it with a system in which membership was a matter of belief rather than birth.

• The early Islamic community found itself constituted as a state at the very beginning of its history.

• Muhammad was not only a religious figure but also a political and military leader able to implement his vision of an ideal Islamic society.

• Islam possessed no separate religious organization, although tension between religious and political goals frequently generated conflict.

• No professional clergy mediating between God and humankind emerged within Islam.

• No distinction between religious law and civil law existed in the Islamic world.

Q. *Why were Arabs able to construct such a huge empire so quickly?*

• For the first time, a shared faith in Islam allowed the newly organized state to mobilize the military potential of the entire Arab population.

• The Byzantine and Persian empires were weakened by decades of war with each other and by internal revolts. They also underestimated the Arab threat.

• Merchant leaders of the new Islamic community wanted to capture profitable trade routes and wealthy agricultural regions.

• Individual Arabs found in military expansion a route to wealth and social promotion.

• Expansion provided a common task for the Arab community, which reinforced the fragile unity of the umma.

• Arabs were motivated by a religious dimension, as many viewed the mission of empire in terms of *jihad*, bringing righteous government to the peoples they conquered.

Q. *What accounts for the widespread conversion to Islam?*

• Jews, Christians, and Zoroastrians could find familiar elements of their own faiths in Islam.

• From the start, Islam was associated with the sponsorship of a powerful state.

• Conquest called into question the power of old gods, while the growing prestige of the Arab Empire attracted many to Allah.

• Although forced conversion was rare, living in an Islamic-governed state provided a variety of incentives for claiming Muslim identity.

• In Islam, merchants found a religion friendly to commerce, and in the Arab Empire they enjoyed a huge and secure arena for trade.

• People aspiring to official positions found conversion to Islam an aid to social mobility.

Q. *What is the difference between Sunni and Shia Islam?*

• Sunnis held that the caliphs were rightful political and military leaders, selected by the Islamic community, while the Shia held that leadership in the Islamic world should derive from the line of Ali and his son Husayn, blood relatives of Muhammad.

• For Sunni Muslims, religious authority in general emerged from the larger community, particularly from the religious scholars known as *ulama*. Meanwhile, the Shia invested their leaders, known as *imams*, with a religious authority that the caliphs lacked, allowing them alone to reveal the true meaning of the Quran and the wishes of Allah.

• The Shia tradition included a messianic element that the Sunni tradition largely lacked.

Q. *In what ways were Sufi Muslims critical of mainstream Islam?*

• Sufism was sharply critical of the more scholarly and legalistic practitioners of the *sharia*; to Sufis, establishment teachings about the law and correct behavior did little to bring the believer into the presence of God.

• Sufis held that many of the ulama of mainstream Islam had been compromised by their association with worldly and corrupt governments.

Q. *How did the rise of Islam change the lives of women?*

• The Quran included a mix of rights, restrictions, and protections for women. It banned female infanticide, gave women the right to own property and granted them rights of inheritance, defined marriage as a contract between consenting parties, granted the right to sue for divorce under certain circumstances, and regulated polygyny. It also allowed men to have sexual relations with consenting female slaves, but only under the condition that any children born of these unions were free, as was the mother once her owner died.

• In practice, as the Arab Empire grew in size, the position of women became more limited. Women started to pray at home instead of in the mosque, and veiling and seclusion of women became standard practice among the upper and ruling classes, with special areas within the home becoming the only place where women could appear unveiled. Such seclusion was less practicable for lower-class women. These new practices derived far more from established traditions of Middle Eastern cultures than from the Quran, but they soon gained a religious rationale in the writings of Muslim thinkers.

• Other signs of tightening patriarchy, such as "honor killing" of women by their male relatives for violating sexual taboos and, in some places, clitorectomy (female circumcision), likewise derived from local cultures, with no sanction in the Quran or Islamic law. But where they were practiced, such customs often came to be seen as Islamic.

• Negative views of women, presenting them variously as weak, deficient, and a sexually charged threat to men and social stability, emerged in the *hadiths*, traditions about the sayings or actions of Muhammad, which became an important source of Islamic law.

• Islam also offered new outlets for women in religious life. The Sufi practice of mystical union with God allowed a greater role for women than did mainstream Islam. Some Sufi orders had parallel groups for women, and a few welcomed women as equal members.

• In Shia Islam, women teachers of the faith were termed *mullahs*, the same as their male counterparts.

• Islamic education, either in the home or in Quranic schools, allowed some women to become literate and a few to achieve higher levels of learning.

• Visits to the tombs of major Islamic figures as well as the ritual of the public bath provided some opportunity for women to interact with other women beyond their own family circle.

Q. *What similarities and differences can you identify in the spread of Islam to India, Anatolia, West Africa, and Spain?*

• Islam spread to India, Anatolia, and Spain in part through force of arms of Islamic armies, while Islam arrived in West Africa with Muslim traders.

• Sufis facilitated conversions by accommodating local traditions, especially in India and Anatolia, but played little role in West Africa until at least the eighteenth century.

• In India, West Africa, and Spain, Islam became one of several faiths within the wider culture, while in Anatolia it became the dominant faith.

Q. *Why was Anatolia so much more thoroughly Islamized than India?*

• The demographic balance made a difference. Unlike India, far more Turkic-speaking peoples settled in Anatolia. This, coupled with the much smaller population of Anatolia and the massacres, enslavement, famine, and flight that occurred during the conquest, gave Turks a much more important position in Anatolia.

• Anatolian society was more centralized than India, and the Christian Church and Byzantine imperial infrastructure in Anatolia were fatally weakened during the Turkic invasion. India's more decentralized civilization was better able to absorb the shock of external invasion.

• The Turkish rulers of Anatolia built a new society that welcomed converts, and the cultural barriers to conversion were arguably less severe there than in India.

Q. *What makes it possible to speak of the Islamic world as a distinct and coherent civilization?*

• At the core of that civilization was a common commitment to Islam.

• No group was more important in the transmission of Islamic beliefs and practices than the ulama, an "international elite" who created a system of education that served to bind together an immense and diverse civilization.

• The Sufi religious orders established an educational network and organized in a variety of larger associations, some of which included chapters throughout the Islamic world.

• The pilgrimage to Mecca (the *hajj*) drew many thousands of Muslims to Mecca each year from all over the Islamic world.

• The Islamic world also cohered as an immense arena of exchange in which goods, technologies, food products, and ideas circulated widely.

Q. *In what ways was the world of Islam a "cosmopolitan civilization"?*

• The Islamic world valued commerce and fostered vibrant networks of exchange. Muslim merchants plied the Silk Roads, Sea Roads, and Sand Roads of the Afro-Eurasian world, and the Islamic world promoted long-distance economic relationships by actively supporting a prosperous, highly developed, "capitalist" economy.

• Islamic civilization also facilitated a substantial exchange of agricultural products and practices. Rice, new strains of sorghum, hard wheat, bananas, lemons, limes, watermelons, coconut palms, spinach, artichokes, sugarcane, and cotton came to the Middle East from India. Sugarcane and cotton also came with knowledge of complex production processes. Some of these Indian crops subsequently found their way to Africa and Europe from the Middle East.

• Technology also diffused widely within the Islamic world. Ancient Persian techniques for obtaining water by drilling into the sides of hills spread to North Africa. Muslim technicians made improvements on rockets developed in China. Techniques for manufacturing paper also arrived in the Middle East from China and later spread from the Middle East to India and Europe.

• Ideas also spread, with Jewish and Christian precedents influencing Islamic thinkers; Persian bureaucratic practice, court ritual, and poetry influencing the elite in particular; and Greek and Indian scientific, medical, and philosophical texts being systematically translated into Arabic and studied throughout the Islamic world.

• Those traditions mixed and blended to generate a distinctive Islamic civilization that made many original contributions to the world of learning—including the development of algebra as a novel mathematical discipline, original work in astronomy and optics, and medicine and pharmacology.

ADDITIONAL RESOURCES FOR CHAPTER 11

Additional Bedford/St. Martin's Resources

FOR INSTRUCTORS

Computerized Test Bank

This test bank provides over thirty exercises per chapter, including multiple-choice, fill-in-the-blank,

short-answer, and full-length essay questions. Instructors can customize quizzes, add or edit both questions and answers, and export questions and answers to a variety of formats, including WebCT and Blackboard. The disc includes correct answers and essay outlines.

Instructor's Resource CD-ROM

This disc provides instructors with ready-made and customizable PowerPoint multimedia presentations built around chapter outlines, maps, figures, and all images from the textbook, plus JPEG versions of all maps, figures, and images.

The following maps and images from Chapter 11 are available in both JPEG and PowerPoint format on the Instructor's Resource CD-ROM:

- Map 11.1: The Arab Empire and the Initial Expansion of Islam (622–900) (p. 309)
- Map 11.2: The Growing World of Islam (900–1500) (p. 317)
- Map 11.3: The Ottoman Empire by the Mid-Fifteenth Century (p. 320)
- Map 11.4: West Africa and the World of Islam (p. 321)
- The Hajj (p. 300)
- Muslims, Jews, and Christians (p. 305)
- The Kaaba (p. 312)
- Men and Women at Worship (p. 315)
- The Great Mosque at Jenne (p. 322)
- A Muslim Astronomical Observatory (p. 326)

FOR STUDENTS

Documents and Essays from *Worlds of History: A Comparative Reader,* Third Edition (Volume 1)

The following documents, essays, and illustrations to accompany Chapter 11 are available in Chapters 7, 8, and 13 of this reader by Kevin Reilly:
From Chapter 7:

- Selections from the *Koran*
- Islamic Expansion, Peace Terms with Jerusalem (636)

From Chapter 8:

- Islam: *Sayings Ascribed to the Prophet*
- Al-Tanukhi, *A Government Job*
- Egyptian Invitation

From Chapter 13:

- S. D. Goitein, *Cairo: An Islamic City in Light of the Geniza*

Online Study Guide at bedfordstmartins.com/strayer

The Online Study Guide helps students synthesize the material from the text as well as practice the skills historians use to make sense of the past. Each chapter of the Online Study Guide contains specific testing exercises, including a multiple-choice self-test that focuses on important conceptual ideas; an identification quiz that helps students remember key people, places, and events; a flashcard activity that tests students on their knowledge of key terms; and two interactive map activities intended to strengthen students' geographic skills. Instructors can monitor students' progress through an online Quiz Gradebook or receive email updates.

Further Reading

Armstrong, Karen. *Islam: A Short History.* New York: Modern Library, 2000. A brief, sensitive, and very readable introduction to the history of Islam as both a religious and a political entity.

Aslan, Reza. *No god but God: The Origins, Evolution, and Future of Islam.* New York: Random House, 2005. A recent best-selling study of Islam.

Chittick, William C. *Sufism: A Short Introduction.* Oxford: Oneworld, 2000. This volume clearly lays out the main Sufi schools and their teachings.

Cornell, Vincent J. *Realm of the Saint: Power and Authority in Moroccan Sufism.* Austin: University of Texas Press, 1998. A detailed and insightful study of Sufism and its influence.

Islam, http://www.aril.org/Islam.html. Links to some of the best Web sites available for both historic and modern Islam.

Islamic Art, Music, and Architecture around the World, http://www.uga.edu/islam/IslArt.html. Interesting images and music clips.

Parrinder, Geoffrey. *Mysticism in the World's Religions.* Oxford: Oneworld, 1995. A short but interesting overview of the mystical tradition.

Selected Internet Resources: Islamic Sites, http://www.library.yale.edu/neareast/islamicsites.html. An excellent list of links to Islamic texts, art, and medicine, created by the Yale University Library.

Literature

Dawood, N. J., trans. *The Koran*. 5th ed. London: Penguin, 1990. The most readily accessible edition of the Quran in English.

Dawood, N. J., trans. *Tales from the Thousand and One Nights*. Hammondsworth: Penguin, 1973. A highly entertaining collection of classic Arabian stories, including the voyages of Sindbad the Sailor and the tale of Aladdin and the lamp.

Halsall, Paul, ed. *Internet Islamic History Sourcebook*. http://www.fordham.edu/halsall/islam/islamsbook.html. Offers an interesting variety of short primary sources, suitable for classroom use.

Ibn al-'Arabi. *The Bezels of Wisdom*. Trans. R. W. J. Austin. New York: Paulist Press, 1980. Ibn al-'Arabi was a Sufi born in Spain in the twelfth century; he is known as "the greatest master," and this work is perhaps the greatest text of medieval Sufism.

Sells, Michael, trans. *Approaching the Qur'án: The Early Revelations*. Ashland, OR: White Cloud Press, 1999. A beautiful translation of the early suras of the Quran, with a useful introduction and commentary. With under fifty pages of Quran (plus commentary), the volume is short enough for effective classroom use. It also includes a CD of Quranic recitations.

Sells, Michael, trans. *Early Islamic Mysticism*. New York: Paulist Press, 1996. An interesting assortment of early Sufi texts.

Film

A wide variety of videos are available on the topic of Islam; here is a selection of particularly useful titles.

The Andalusian Epic: Islamic Spain. Films for the Humanities and Sciences, 1999. 27 minutes. Examines the expansion of Islam into Spain.

The Arabs Make Their Entrance: Islam and Empire. Films for the Humanities and Sciences, 1999. 26 minutes. Charts the rise of Islamic civilization from Muhammad to the Umayyad dynasty.

Essentials of Faith. Films for the Humanities and Sciences, 2006. 24 minutes. Examines the Five Pillars of Islam and the role of cultural and political influences in shaping the practice of Islam.

Hajj: The Pilgrimage. Insight Media, 1999. 53 minutes. Examines the fifth pillar of Islam, the yearly pilgrimage to Mecca.

Islam and Christianity. Films for the Humanities and Sciences, 1993. 30 minutes. Explores the relationship between Christianity and Islam.

Islam and Its Five Pillars. Insight Media, 2004. 28 minutes. Explores the meaning of Islam and its Five Pillars.

Islam: Empire of Faith. Two-part series. PBS Home Video, 2001. 90 minutes each. Examines Islam and Islamic society from their emergence to the twentieth century.

Journeys into Islam. Four-part series. Films for the Humanities and Sciences, 2004. 47–52 minutes each. Examines the spread of Islam into Africa and Asia since the time of Muhammad.

Once upon a Time: Baghdad during the Abbasid Dynasty. Films for the Humanities and Sciences, 1999. 26 minutes. Explores Baghdad at its height, with references to cultural accomplishments and political developments of the Abbasid dynasty.

When the World Spoke Arabic: The Golden Age of Arab Civilization. Seven-part series. Films for the Humanities and Sciences, 1999. 26–27 minutes each. This series explores the most significant cultural, scientific, and technological achievements of the Islamic world.

Pastoral Peoples on the Global Stage
The Mongol Moment, 1200–1500

CHAPTER OVERVIEW

Chapter Objectives

- To make students aware of the significance of pastoral societies in world history
- To examine the conditions of nomadic life
- To investigate the impact of the Mongol Empire on world history
- To consider the implications of the Eurasian trade sponsored by the Mongols

Chapter Outline

I. **Opening Vignette**
   A. Legacy of Chinggis Khan in Mongolia
      1. his spirit banner was destroyed by Communists in 1937
         a. according to Mongol tradition, that means his soul was destroyed
      2. late twentieth-century revival of Chinggis Khan's memory
      3. 2006 was 800th anniversary of foundation of Mongol Empire
   B. The story of the Mongols is an important corrective to historians' focus on agriculturalists.

      1. pastoralists had a lasting impact on development of Afro-Eurasia

II. **Looking Back and Looking Around: The Long History of Pastoral Nomads**
   A. Economies focused on livestock production emerged around 4000 B.C.E.
      1. dependent on horses, camels, goats, sheep, cattle, yaks, reindeer
      2. pastoral societies developed in: **[see Classroom Activity 1]**
         a. grasslands of Eurasia and sub-Saharan Africa
         b. Arabian and Saharan deserts
         c. subarctic regions, Tibetan plateau
         d. not in Americas: lack of large animals for domesticating
   B. The World of Pastoral Societies **[see Lecture Strategy 1]**
      1. standard features of pastoral societies: **[see Classroom Activity 2]**
         a. generally less productive than agricultural societies
         b. needed large grazing areas
         c. populations much smaller than in agricultural societies
         d. lived in encampments of related kinfolk, usually common ancestry in male line
         e. clans sometimes gathered as a tribe; could absorb unrelated people

f. more egalitarian than sedentary societies, but sometimes distinguished between nobles and commoners

g. women usually had higher status than in sedentary societies **[see Discussion Topic 1]**

   i. fewer restrictions

   ii. greater role in public life

   iii. involved in productive labor

h. mobility—nomads

2. pastoralists had deep connections to agricultural neighbors

  a. sought access to foodstuffs, manufactured goods, luxury items

  b. especially in inner Eurasia, longing for civilized products encouraged formation of nomadic states

3. formation of nomadic states was difficult

  a. charismatic leaders like Chinggis Khan could make a series of tribal alliances that became powerful states

  b. when formed, almost the whole male population (and some women) became warriors

4. cultural interaction with agricultural lands

  a. inner Eurasian nomads adopted Judaism, Buddhism, Christianity, Islam, and Manichaeism at various times

5. mastered environments unsuitable for agricultural

  a. brought food-producing revolution and significant human presence to fringe regions

  b. life changed significantly for Inner Asian steppe peoples with introduction of horseback riding ca. 1000 B.C.E.

C. The Xiongnu: An Early Nomadic Empire

1. mounted warfare made nomadic empires possible

2. the Xiongnu (in Mongolian steppes north of China) formed an important early confederacy (from Manchuria to central Asia) in third/second centuries B.C.E.

3. ruler Modun (r. 210–174 B.C.E.) revolutionized nomadic life

  a. created a more centralized, hierarchical political system

  b. divinely sanctioned ruler

c. distinction between "junior" and "senior" clans became more important

d. exacted tribute from other nomads and from China

  i. Han emperor Wen had to acknowledge their equality

4. Xiongnu Empire was a model copied by Turkic and Mongol empires

D. The Arabs and the Turks

1. nomads made their greatest impact on world history between 500 and 1500 C.E.

  a. Arabs, Berbers, Turks, and Mongols created largest empires of that millennium

  b. Islam derived from largely nomadic Arabs, carried by Turks

  c. Byzantium, Persia, India, and China were all controlled at least for a time by formerly nomadic people

2. Bedouin Arabs became effective fighters with development of a good camel saddle (sometime between 500 and 100 B.C.E.)

  a. made control of trade routes through Arabia possible

  b. camel nomads were shock troops of Islamic expansion

3. Turkic-speaking nomads (homeland in Mongolia and southern Siberia)

  a. gradual southward/westward spread

  b. series of short-lived nomadic empires 552–965 C.E.

   i. fragile alliance of tribes, held together by a *kaghan*

  c. spread of Turkic language and culture over much of Inner Asia and beyond

  d. Turkish conversion to Islam between tenth and fourteenth centuries

   i. made them the third major carrier of Islam

   ii. gave Turks a growing role in Islamic heartland

   iii. started as slave soldiers, gradually took power

  e. Seljuk Empire (eleventh–twelfth centuries): Turks began to claim the Muslim title *sultan*; exercised real power

   i. Abbasid caliphs remained as figureheads

  f. carried Islam to India and Anatolia

E. The Masai of East Africa
1. best information on nomad/agrarian relations in Africa comes from after 1500
2. no large states or chiefdoms, pastoral or agricultural, developed in what is now Kenya and Tanzania
3. Masai were nomadic cattle-keepers
   a. linked their people beyond village and clan ties with initiation of adolescent boys, followed by life in an "age-set"
4. Masai had been partly agricultural before eighteenth–nineteenth centuries
   a. several groups returned to agriculture in mid-nineteenth century
5. Masai interaction with settled peoples
   a. Masai would admit outsiders into their society
   b. depended on hunters and farmers
   c. during times of drought or disease, Masai might take refuge with hunters or farmers
   d. farmers adopted elements of Masai culture and military
      i. hairstyles
      ii. cattle terms
      iii. name for High God
      iv. long spear
      v. practice of drinking cow's milk before battle

III. Breakout: The Mongol Empire
A. The Mongols formed the greatest land-based empire in history following their breakout from Mongolia in the thirteenth century.
1. extensive linkage of nomads of inner Eurasian steppes with agricultural civilizations
2. created far greater contact between Europe, China, and Islamic world than ever before
3. total Mongol population was only about 700,000
4. did not have a major cultural impact on the world
   a. did not try to spread their ancestor worship/shamanism to others
   b. mostly interested in exploiting conquered peoples
   c. Mongol culture today largely confined to Mongolia

d. Mongol Empire was the last great nomadic state
B. From Temujin to Chinggis Khan: The Rise of the Mongol Empire [see Discussion Topic 2]
1. Temujin (1162–1227) created the Mongol Empire
2. Mongols before Temujin were unstable collection of feuding tribes and clans
3. Temujin's rise
   a. father was a minor chieftain, but was murdered before Temujin turned ten
   b. Temujin's mother held family together after they were deserted by the clan
   c. when Temujin grew up, he drew together a small following of friends, allied with a more powerful tribal leader
   d. shifting series of alliances, betrayals, military victories
   e. won a reputation as a great leader
4. 1206: Mongol tribal assembly recognized Temujin as Chinggis Khan ("universal ruler")
5. Chinggis Khan then began expansion to hold his followers together
   a. major attack on China in 1209 started 50-year Mongol world war
   b. Chinggis Khan, Ogodei, Mongke, and Khubilai created an empire that included China, Korea, Central Asia, Russia, much of Middle East, and parts of Eastern Europe
   c. setbacks marked outer limits of Mongol Empire
      i. withdrawal from Eastern Europe (1242)
      ii. defeat by Egyptians (1260)
      iii. failed invasions of Japan (1274, 1281)
      iv. difficulty penetrating jungles of Southeast Asia
C. Explaining the Mongol Moment
1. Mongol Empire grew without any grand scheme
2. by the time of his death, Chinggis Khan saw conquests as a mission to unite the whole world
3. Mongols were vastly outnumbered by their enemies

4. Mongol success was due to their well-led, organized, disciplined army
   a. military units of 10, 100, 1,000, and 10,000 warriors
   b. conquered tribes were broken up and scattered among units
   c. tribalism was also weakened by creation of imperial guard
   d. all members of a unit were killed if any deserted in battle
   e. leaders shared the hardships of their men
   f. elaborate tactics: encirclement, retreat, deception
   g. vast numbers of conquered peoples were incorporated into army
      i. nomads joined Mongol cavalry units
      ii. agriculturalists provided infantry and artillery
      iii. conquered subjects also provided labor and cartage
      iv. conquered subjects with skills were moved to where they could be used
5. Mongol reputation for brutality and destructiveness [see **Discussion Topic 3**]
   a. those who resisted were destroyed
   b. kingdom of Khwarizm murdered Mongol envoys
      i. its cities were destroyed
      ii. captured soldiers were executed
      iii. women and skilled craftsmen were enslaved
      iv. unskilled civilians were used as human shields for attacks on the next city or as moat filler
6. ability to mobilize resources
   a. elaborate census taking and systematic taxation
   b. good system of relay stations for communication and trade
   c. centralized bureaucracy began
   d. encouraged commerce
   e. gave lower administrative posts to Chinese and Muslim officials
   f. practiced religious toleration

IV. **Encountering the Mongols: Comparing Three Cases**
   A. China and the Mongols
      1. Mongol conquest of China was difficult, took from 1209 to 1279

2. began in northern China (ruled by dynasties of nomadic origin), was vastly destructive
3. conquest of southern China (ruled by Song dynasty) was far less violent
   a. more interest in accommodation of local populace
   b. landowners were guaranteed their estates in return for support
4. Mongols unified a divided China, made many believe that the Mongols had been granted the Mandate of Heaven
5. Mongols didn't know how to govern an agricultural society, so they used many Chinese practices
   a. gave themselves a Chinese dynastic title, the Yuan ("great beginnings")
   b. built a new capital—Khanbalik ("city of the khan"; now Beijing)
6. Khubilai Khan (r. 1271–1294) had a set of ancestral tablets made
   a. much of his reign was in the model of a benevolent Chinese emperor
7. still, Mongol rule was harsh, exploitative, and foreign
   a. Mongols did not become Chinese
   b. "Forbidden City" in the capital was set up like the steppes
   c. relied heavily on foreigners for administration, rather than the traditional administrative system
   d. few Mongols learned Chinese
   e. Mongol law discriminated against the Chinese
   f. Mongol women were shockingly free by Chinese standards
8. by 1368, rebellions had forced the Mongols out of China
   a. during the succeeding Ming dynasty, memory of brutal Mongol rule stimulated commitment to Confucian values, effort to wipe out all traces of Mongol impact
   B. Persia and the Mongols [see **Lecture Strategy 2**]
      1. conquest of Persia: first invasion led by Chinggis Khan 1219–1221; second assault under his grandson Hulegu 1251–1258

a. Hulegu became first il-khan (subordinate khan) of Persia
2. massive impact of invasion
   a. very destructive
   b. shook faith: how could Muslims be savaged so badly by infidels?
   c. sacking of Baghdad in 1258 ended the Abbasid caliphate
      i. more than 200,000 people massacred
   d. profound damage to Persian/Iraqi agriculture
      i. peasants were driven from land by massive taxation
      ii. much agricultural land was turned to pasture (or desert)
      iii. neglect of fragile irrigation systems
   e. increase in wine and silk production
3. Mongols were transformed far more in Persia than in China
   a. extensive use of Persian bureaucracy
   b. Ghazan (r. 1295–1304) tried to repair some of their earlier damage
   c. Mongols in Persia converted to Islam on a large scale
   d. Mongol elites learned some Persian
   e. some Mongols took up agriculture
4. Mongol dynasty collapsed in 1330s
   a. Mongols were assimilated, not driven out

C. Russia and the Mongols
1. Mongol devastation of Russia 1237–1240
   a. Russia was a number of independent principalities
   b. could not unite against Mongol threat
   c. destruction of cities, widespread slaughter, and deportation of skilled workers
2. Russia was integrated into Mongol Empire as the Kipchak Khanate (Russians called it the "Khanate of the Golden Horde")
   a. but Mongols did not occupy Russia
      i. remained on steppes north of Black and Caspian seas
      ii. collected tribute and heavy taxes; also raided for slaves
3. some Russian princes and the Russian Orthodox Church flourished
4. Moscow became primary tribute-collector for the Mongols
   a. gave Moscow a leading role in the fifteenth century
5. Mongol rulers of Russia were far less assimilated or influenced
   a. were gradually Islamized and assimilated by the Kipchaks of the steppes
6. Russian princes adopted Mongol weapons, diplomatic rituals, court practices, tax system, and military draft
   a. Moscow became the core of a new Russian state
   b. used the Mongol mounted courier service
7. Russians broke free of Mongol rule by the end of the fifteenth century

V. **The Mongol Empire as a Eurasian Network**
A. Toward a World Economy
1. Mongols produced little for distant markets; were not active traders
2. but they promoted international commerce as source of tax revenue
3. made it relatively safe to travel across Central Asia
   a. many Europeans (including Marco Polo) made the journey
4. Mongol trading circuit was central to larger Afro-Eurasian commercial network
B. Diplomacy on a Eurasian Scale
1. Mongol encroachment into Eastern Europe led both the pope and European rulers to dispatch diplomatic missions to the Mongols
   a. had no diplomatic or religious consequences
   b. but brought back valuable information about the East
2. Persian and Chinese courts developed close relationships
C. Cultural Exchange in the Mongol Realm
1. thousands of craftsmen and educated people were forcibly relocated by the Mongols
2. Mongol religious tolerance and support of merchants drew foreigners
3. the Mongol capital of Karakorum was a cosmopolitan center
4. lively exchange of ideas and techniques

a. westward flow of Chinese technology and art (painting, printing, gunpowder weapons, compass navigation, high-temperature furnaces, medical techniques, etc.)

b. Muslim astronomy spread to China

c. circulation of plants and crops

d. Europe benefited particularly from new contact with Asia

    i. *and* Europe wasn't devastated by the Mongols

    ii. some scholars posit that this is the root of Europe's rise to global prominence

D. The Plague: A Eurasian Pandemic **[see Lecture Strategy 3]**

1. the plague (a.k.a. pestilence, Black Death) spread across trade routes of the Mongol Empire in early fourteenth century

    a. probably originated in Central Asia

    b. carried by rodents and transmitted by fleas

2. the plague broke out in northeastern China in 1331

    a. reached Western Europe by 1347

    b. Mongol siege of Caffa (in the Crimea) in 1346: Mongols catapulted plague-infected corpses into city

    c. massive death toll

        i. estimates are that one-third to two-thirds of European population died

    d. periodic returns of the plague for centuries

3. India and sub-Saharan Africa were much less affected

4. best information about the plague's impact comes from Europe

    a. the plague was described in apocalyptic terms

    b. Jews blamed for the plague; many fled to Poland

    c. longer-term changes in European society

        i. led to conflict between scarce workers and the rich

        ii. undermined practice of serfdom

        iii. perhaps encouraged technological innovation

    iv. created more employment opportunities for women

5. the plague was a primary reason for the breakdown of the Mongol Empire in fourteenth–fifteenth centuries

    a. with population contraction, volume of trade was reduced

    b. by 1350, the Mongol Empire was in disarray

    c. within a century, Mongols had lost control of China, Persia, and Russia

    d. the Central Asian trade route largely closed

6. disruption of land routes to the east encouraged Europeans to seek trade routes by sea

    a. European naval technology gave them an advantage

    b. similarity of sixteenth-century Europeans to Mongols: people on the periphery who were economically less developed and forcedly plundered wealthier civilizations

VI. **Reflections: Changing Images of Nomadic Peoples** [see Classroom Activity 3]

A. Nomads have often received "bad press" in history books.

1. only mentioned in regard to their destruction of established civilizations

2. educated sedentary peoples have feared and usually despised nomads

3. nomads were usually illiterate, so we don't have their perspective

4. agricultural societies eventually won out

B. There have been recent efforts to present a more balanced view.

1. emphasize what nomads achieved as well as what they destroyed

2. the total wars and genocides of the twentieth century have made people less judgmental toward the Mongols

3. historians are shaped by their times

USING *WAYS OF THE WORLD* IN THE CLASSROOM

Lecture Strategies

Lecture Strategy 1

"Nomads: A people without history?"
The purpose of this lecture strategy is to explore in greater detail what we know about nomads and how we know it. It is intended to be comparative, rather than focusing on a single nomadic culture. The lecture strategy's main objectives are to:

- explore with students what we can reasonably infer about a culture by means of physical artifacts alone, without the benefit of written accounts
- practice with students how to weigh evidence that comes from prejudiced outsiders
- consider the strengths and limitations of sources written by a culture, but well after the events described or mediated through another culture

Choose three pastoral peoples for which available materials survive that can be used to explore the three lecture objectives. For the "physical artifacts alone" category, we recommend the Scythians—the extremely rich finds from their burial mounds, some of great beauty, make them particularly accessible to students. There is a *little* written evidence about Scythians, too, mostly from Herodotus, which can help confirm theories based on physical remains. Show images of various Scythian finds, encouraging the students to discuss what those artifacts can teach modern scholars. For example:

- The sheer size and structure of royal tombs suggest an ability to organize labor to a high degree.
- The complex tattooing found on several well-preserved bodies suggests that Scythians were marked to identify their clan and perhaps their rank.
- Elaborate felt garments suggest the climate they confronted.
- Elaborate Greek-made wine services, some depicting scenes of Scythian life, show interaction with the Greek world, Scythian

fondness for wine, and at least one way in which members of the elite showed their status.
- Hemp seeds and objects that fit Herodotus's description of small steam tents are also possibilities for discussion.

Go on to a second nomadic culture for which our main source is the accounts of their enemies, such as the Huns or the Xiongnu confederation. Distribute short excerpts of accounts, such as Ammianus Marcellinus's description of the Huns, and go over them in class. Some possible questions you can ask your students are:

- Is everything in the account actually physically possible?
- What is the author's relationship to the subject (e.g., neutral visitor, part of a society actively threatened by nomads, ambassador, etc.)?
- What can the account tell about what the author valued from his own culture?
- What parts of the account can be confirmed by other means?
- Which parts of the account are least plausible? (This is a good point at which to emphasize that one can rarely trust numbers in premodern accounts.)

Finally, consider a written source that comes from a nomadic or formerly nomadic society, such as *The Secret History of the Mongols* or the Turkish *Book of Dede Korkut*. With the students, build a list of questions that ought to be asked of such a source, such as:

- When was it written?
- What were the author's possible sources of information?
- What was the author's intention in writing?

Lecture Strategy 2

"The Middle East in 1200."
This lecture strategy is intended to provide the context for the Mongol eruption into the Middle East in the early thirteenth century. As such, its objectives are to:

- consider the political, economic, and social worlds of Middle Eastern and Central Asian societies around the year 1200
- explore ways in which this situation might have affected the Mongol onslaught

A good place to begin is where the chapter on the Islamic world left off, going into more detail about circumstances in the region. There are many ways to approach this topic; some points to consider for inclusion are:

- the reality of many Muslim-ruled states, rather than the centralized rule of the Abbasid caliph
- what it meant to be an Abbasid caliph in Baghdad ca. 1200
- the rise of the Ayyubid dynasty of Egypt and Syria
- Saladin's conquest of most of the Crusader kingdom of Jerusalem and the Third Crusade
- the cultural divide between the Arabic-, Persian-, and Turkic-speaking parts of the Islamic world
- the conditions of ordinary people in the Islamic world, such as merchants and peasants
- the potential for unified action against the Mongols

Lecture Strategy 3

"Disease in human history."
This lecture strategy provides an opportunity to look back and consider the role of disease in the societies already studied, as well as to look forward to the second half of the course. Its objectives are to:

- help students to consider the role of epidemic disease in history
- help students avoid an overly simplistic understanding of that role
- encourage students to understand the spread of epidemic disease as an inevitable part of interaction between societies

A good place to start is with two modern cases: the AIDS epidemic and fears about the spread of "bird flu." This is a good point at which to educate students about contemporary issues; now that AIDS is to a considerable extent treatable with drugs in affluent societies, it has largely fallen out of U.S. news coverage. It is, of course, still an ongoing, catastrophic human tragedy in much of Africa. Similarly, since bird flu is still confined to Asia, most Americans don't think about it much—but it could prove to be as destructive as the great Spanish Influenza pandemic of 1918. After establishing this context, explore the Black Death in

Eurasia in greater detail than space allowed in the textbook. Some points to consider for inclusion:

- the fear that can be generated when people don't understand how a disease is spread (comparison to the plague pandemic of the sixth century C.E., or to the spread of smallpox among the population of the Americas when Europeans established contact, can be instructive)
- what means the society had to help those suffering from the Black Death (this is a good point at which to emphasize how recently scientists have developed antibiotics and other medications, and the great degree to which care of the sick in the premodern world was simply a matter of nursing)
- the actual effect on a population of *one* epidemic outbreak, as opposed to cyclic reoccurrences (point out that most who die in epidemics are those with weak immune systems—the elderly, who have already finished reproducing, and the young, who in a premodern society had a very good chance of dying of something or other anyway).
- what a catastrophe like the Black Death can mean in terms of spiritual crisis

Things to Do in the Classroom

Discussion Topics

1. **Comparison, large or small group.** "Women in agricultural and pastoral societies."
Ask students whether it was better to be a woman than a man in a nomadic or a farming society, and ask them to explain why. Make sure they consider both elites and commoners.

2. **Contextualization, large or small group.**
"How Temujin became Chinggis Khan."
Distribute to the class the passage of *The Secret History of the Mongols* in which the young Temujin first begins to build up a following from among the Mongol tribes. Ask the students to discuss how he does it. Some supplementary questions to ask are:

- Is money involved?
- What can Temujin offer to his followers?

- What's the glue that makes the confederation hold together?
- What sort of interpersonal relationships are revealed by the text?

3. **Misconception/Difficult Topic, large or small group.** "Nomads, especially the Mongols, were utterly vicious savages who specialized in large-scale massacres."

Ask students to discuss this stereotype of the Mongols and to list points in the text that suggest the need to revise this opinion.

Classroom Activities

1. **Map-analysis exercise, large or small group.** "Where were the nomads?"

Using a physical map of the world, ask students to locate the territory of the following groups of nomads:

- Scythians
- Xiongnu
- Huns
- Magyars
- Turks
- Mongols
- Tibetans
- Lapps
- Bedouin
- Masai

Then ask students to discuss why these regions might have been particularly suitable for nomads.

2. **Role-playing exercise, small group.** "Life among the nomads."

You are a member of a nomadic society (pick whichever one you prefer). How would you spend a typical day if you were a man? If you were a woman?

3. **Clicker question.** Regarded as a whole, was the Mongol impact on world history more positive or negative?

Key Terms

"age-set": Among the Masai, a group of boys united by a common initiation ceremony, who then moved together through the various "age-grades," or ranks, of Masai life.

Black Death: Name later given to the massive plague pandemic that swept through Eurasia beginning in 1331; it is usually regarded as an outbreak of bubonic plague.

Chinggis Khan: Title meaning "universal ruler" that was given to the Mongol leader Temujin in 1206 after he united the Mongols. (*pron.* CHENG-iz KAHN)

"fictive kinship": Common form of tribal bonding in nomadic societies in which allies are designated and treated as blood relatives.

Ghazan Khan: Il-khan (subordinate khan) of Persia who ruled from 1295 to 1304; he is noted for his efforts to repair the Mongol damage to Persia. (*pron.* HAZ-zan KAHN)

Hulegu Khan: Grandson of Chinggis Khan (ca. 1217–1265) who became the first il-khan (subordinate khan) of Persia. (*pron.* hoo-LAY-goo KAHN)

Karakorum: Capital of the Mongol Empire. (*pron.* kah-rah-KOR-um)

khagan: Supreme ruler of a Turkic nomadic confederation. (*pron.* KAH-gahn)

Khanbalik: The "city of the khan," founded as a new capital city for the Mongols after their conquest of China; now the city of Beijing. (*pron.* kahn-BAL-ik)

Khubilai Khan: Grandson of Chinggis Khan who ruled China from 1271 to 1294. (*pron.* KOO-bih-lie KAHN)

Kipchak Khanate: Name given to Russia by the Mongols after they conquered it and incorporated it into the Mongol Empire in the mid-thirteenth century; known to Russians as the "Khanate of the Golden Horde." (*pron.* KIP-chak KAHN-ate)

Masai: Nomadic cattle-keeping people of what is now Kenya and Tanzania. (*pron.* mah-SIGH)

Modun: Great ruler of the Xiongnu Empire (r. 210–174 B.C.E.) who created a centralized and hierarchical political system. (*pron.* moe-DOON)

Mongol world war, the: Term used to describe half a century of military campaigns, massive killing, and empire building pursued by Chinggis Khan and his successors in Eurasia after 1209.

pastoralism: Way of life in which people depend on the herding of domesticated animals for their food.

Temujin: Birth name of the Mongol leader better known as Chinggis Khan (1162–1227). (*pron.* TEM-uh-jin)

Turks: Turkic speakers from Central Asia, originally nomads, who spread westward into the Near East and into India; they created a series of nomadic empires between 552 and 965 C.E. but had a more lasting impact on world history when they became dominant in the Islamic heartland and founded a series of states and empires there.

Xiongnu: People of the Mongolian steppe lands north of China who formed a large-scale nomadic empire in the third and second centuries B.C.E. (*pron.* SHE-OONG-noo)

Yuan dynasty: Mongol dynasty that ruled China from 1271 to 1368; its name means "great beginnings." (*pron.* yu-wen)

ANSWER GUIDELINES FOR CHAPTER QUESTIONS

The two sets of questions that follow appear in the textbook at the end of the chapter and in the margins of the reading. They are also provided in the Computerized Test Bank with answer guidelines, for your convenience.

The Big Picture Questions

1. Prior to the rise of the Mongols, in what ways had pastoral peoples been significant in world history?

• The Xiongnu effected a revolution in nomadic life, transforming earlier fragmented and egalitarian societies into a far more centralized and hierarchical political system in which power was concentrated in a divinely sanctioned ruler and differences in the status of clans were more pronounced. The Xiongnu system became a model for later Turkic and Mongol empires.

• Various nomadic and seminomadic peoples played a role in the collapse of the classical Chinese and Roman empires and the subsequent rebuilding of those civilizations.

• It was within the Arab world that Islam, the largest and most expansive religious tradition of the postclassical period, emerged. Nomadic Bedouin Arabs also provided the shock troops of the Islamic expansion that carved out the Arab Empire.

• The Turks carried Islam to new regions, including northern India and Anatolia; played an increasingly important role in the heartland of an established Islamic civilization, as the Seljuk Turks became the *de*

facto power behind the Abbasid caliphate in the Middle East; and carved important empires out of settled societies, including the Ottoman Empire.

2. What accounts for the often negative attitudes of settled societies toward the pastoral peoples living on their borders? Why have historians often neglected pastoral peoples' role in world history?

• Settled societies feared pastoral peoples, seeing them as bloodthirsty savages or barbarians who brought only chaos and destruction in their wake.

• Settled societies often despised the lifestyle of pastoral peoples, who lacked proper houses and had a diet that was very different from that of settled societies.

• Settled societies on occasion competed for resources with their pastoral counterparts.

• In terms of the neglect of historians, nomadic peoples generally did not have written languages, and thus the sources available to historians came from adjacent agricultural civilizations;

• agricultural civilizations ultimately triumphed in their long-running conflict with nomadic peoples.

3. In what ways did the Mongol Empire resemble other empires, and in what ways did it differ from them? Why did it last a relatively short time?

• It resembled other empires in that it relied on the military capabilities of pastoral peoples;

• it brought together numerous pastoral clans under a single leader;

• and it relied on the extraction of resources from settled societies to hold its confederation together.

• The Mongol Empire lasted a relatively short period of time for a number of reasons:

• intense factionalism among the Mongols, rapidly rising prices, furious epidemics of the plague, and growing peasant revolts forced the Mongols out of China by 1368, less than a century after they had finally conquered the Chinese;

• a succession crisis in the Mongol regime in Persia resulted in the collapse of their rule in the 1330s and the subsequent assimilation of many Mongols into Persian society;

• divisions among the Mongols and the growing strength of the Russian state enabled the Russians to break the Mongols' hold by the end of the fifteenth century.

• On a broader level, the rapid spread of the Black Death in the 1330s and 1340s destabilized the Mongol

Empire, decimated the pastoral populations of steppe lands, and damaged long-distance commerce.

4. In what different ways did Mongol rule affect the Islamic world, Russia, China, and Europe?

• In the Islamic world, the Mongol conquest of Persia resulted in the conversion of large numbers of Mongols to the Muslim faith. While Mongol domination of Persia did damage Persian agriculture, the Mongols had less of an impact on Persian government, as Mongol rulers made extensive use of the sophisticated Persian bureaucracy. Ultimately, a number of Mongols turned to farming, married local people, and were assimilated into Persian society.

• The Mongols conquered but did not occupy Russia. Instead, Russian princes received appointment from the khan in return for sending substantial tribute. The impact of the conquest was uneven, but in general the absence of direct Mongol rule meant that the Mongols were far less influenced by or assimilated within Russian cultures than their counterparts in China and Persia had been. Russians, on the other hand, were profoundly affected by Mongol domination. Russian princes found it useful to adopt the Mongols' weapons, diplomatic rituals, court practices, taxation system, and military draft.

• The Mongols united a divided China. However, in terms of governing techniques and the position of the emperor, the Mongols adopted many preexisting Chinese systems and ideas.

• Europe was stimulated by a flow of ideas and technologies through Mongol-facilitated networks of exchange, by the opportunity for Europeans to travel the length of the Mongol Empire (expanding the mental horizon of Europe), and by the collapse of the Mongol Empire (which provided an incentive for Europeans to take to the sea in their continuing efforts to reach the riches of Asia). Europe was also affected adversely by the spread of the Black Death along these same networks of exchange.

5. How would you define both the immediate and the long-term significance of the Mongols in world history?

• In the short term, the Mongols constructed the largest Eurasian empire to date.

• In the process, they destroyed a series of well-established empires.

• They wreaked extensive destruction on settled populations.

• They encouraged trade and exchange across the Eurasian network.

• They fostered the spread of the Black Death across Eurasia.

• In the long term, the Mongol-enforced movement of conquered peoples from their homelands to distant parts of the empire facilitated the exchange of ideas and techniques, as exemplified by the flow of Chinese technology and artistic conventions westward to the Middle East and Europe;

• the disruption of Mongol-based land routes to the east following the collapse of the Mongol Empire provided an important incentive for Europeans to take to the sea in their continuing efforts to reach the riches of Asia.

6. How would you assess the perspective of this chapter toward the Mongols? Does it strike you as negative and critical of the Mongols, as "bending over backwards" to portray them in a positive light, or as a balanced presentation?

• The chapter does examine the often brutal methods of conquest used by the Mongols;

• and it discusses their harsh, often exploitative regimes, especially in China.

• However, it also highlights the importance of the Mongol Empire as a facilitator of trade and the importance of the exchange of ideas and technologies;

• it gives credit to the Mongols' skills in mobilization and organization that in part explain their military success;

• and it notes the Mongols' tolerance of the religions of conquered peoples.

Margin Review Questions

Q. *In what ways did pastoral societies differ from their agricultural counterparts?*

• Pastoral societies supported far smaller populations.

• Pastoral societies generally lived in small and widely scattered encampments of related kinfolk.

• Pastoral societies generally offered women a higher status, fewer restrictions, and a greater role in public life.

• Pastoral societies were far more mobile.

Q. *In what ways did pastoral societies interact with their agricultural neighbors?*

• Economically, nomads sought access to the foodstuffs, manufactured goods, and luxury items available only from their agricultural neighbors.

• Politically and militarily, pastoral peoples at times came together to extract wealth from agricultural societies through trading, raiding, or extortion.

• Culturally, members of some pastoral societies adopted the religions of their agricultural neighbors, including Judaism, Buddhism, Christianity, Islam, and Manichaeism.

Q. *In what ways did the Xiongnu, Arabs, and Turks make an impact on world history?*

• The Xiongnu effected a revolution in nomadic life, transforming earlier fragmented and egalitarian societies into a far more centralized and hierarchical political system in which power was concentrated in a divinely sanctioned ruler and differences in the status of clans were more pronounced. The Xiongnu system created a model that later Turkic and Mongol empires emulated.

• It was within the Arab world that Islam, the largest and most expansive religious tradition of the postclassical period, emerged. Pastoral Arabs also provided the shock troops of the Islamic expansion that carved out the Arab Empire.

• The Turks carried Islam to new regions, including northern India and Anatolia; played an increasingly important role in the heartland of an established Islamic civilization, as the Seljuk Turks became the *de facto* power behind the Abbasid caliphate in the Middle East; and carved important empires out of settled societies, including the Ottoman Empire.

Q. *Did the history and society of the East African Masai people parallel that of Asian nomads?*

• Unlike Inner Asia, no large states or chiefdoms developed among pastoral or agricultural peoples in East Africa. Instead, the nomadic cattle-keeping Masai and their settled agricultural neighbors were bound together by the ties of village and clan as well as through an initiation ritual that created a profound and lasting bond among the adolescent boys of various villages and lineages.

• The Masai did not fully abandon cultivation until the eighteenth and nineteenth centuries C.E.

• However, the Masai experience did parallel that of Asian nomads in that they regularly traded with or raided agricultural peoples.

Q. *Identify the major steps in the rise of the Mongol Empire.*

• Temujin, later dubbed Chinggis Khan, succeeded in bringing the Mongols together, unifying them in the Great Mongol Nation by 1206.

• In order to hold his alliance together, Chinggis Khan launched a series of military campaigns against the settled agricultural societies of Eurasia over the half century after 1209.

• Through this Mongol world war, Chinggis Khan and his successors constructed an empire that included China, Korea, Central Asia, Russia, much of the Islamic Middle East, and parts of Eastern Europe.

Q. *What accounts for the political and military success of the Mongols?*

• By the end of Chinggis Khan's reign, the Mongol Empire had developed an ideology centered on a mission to unite the whole world in one empire.

• The Mongol army was better organized, better led, and better disciplined than the armies of its opponents.

• The Mongol army was organized to diminish the divisive tribalism of the pastoral clan structure, partly by spreading members of tribes among different units of the army.

• The Mongols made up for their small numbers by incorporating huge numbers of conquered peoples into their military forces.

• The Mongols quickly acquired Chinese techniques and technology of siege warfare, which allowed them to overcome the elaborate fortifications of walled cities.

• Mongol forces were effective in part because of their growing reputation for a ruthless brutality and utter destructiveness. Their reputation served as a form of psychological warfare, a practical inducement to surrender.

• The Mongols displayed an impressive ability to mobilize both the human and material resources of their growing empire through census taking, an effective system of relay stations for rapid communication, and the beginnings of a centralized bureaucracy in the capital of Karakorum.

• The Mongols fostered commerce.

• The Mongols drew on conquered peoples to fill advisory and lower-level administrative positions.

• The Mongols welcomed and supported many religious traditions as long as they did not become the focus of political opposition.

Q. *How did Mongol rule change China? In what ways were the Mongols changed by China?*

• The Mongols united a divided China.
• The Mongols took a Chinese dynastic title, the Yuan, and moved their capital to a new capital city known as Khanbalik, the "city of the khan" (present-day Beijing).
• The Mongols made use of Chinese administrative practices and techniques of taxation and their postal system.
• Mongol khans made use of traditional Confucian rituals, supported the building of some Daoist temples, and were particularly attracted to a Tibetan form of Buddhism, which returned the favor with strong political support for the invaders.

Q. *How was Mongol rule in Persia different from that in China?*

• Heavy taxation pushed Persian peasants off their land, while Mongol herds of sheep and goats and Mongol neglect of fragile underground water channels did extensive damage to Persian agricultural land.
• The Mongol rulers in Persia were transformed far more than their counterparts in China were, as the Mongols made extensive use of the sophisticated Persian bureaucracy.
• Unlike what occurred in China, the Mongols who conquered Persia converted in large numbers to the local Muslim faith.
• A number of Mongols turned to farming and married local people, so when their rule in Persia collapsed, they were not driven out as they had been from China. Instead, they were assimilated into Persian society.

Q. *How was the Russian experience of Mongol domination different from that of Persia or China?*

• The Mongols conquered Russia but did not occupy it as they had Persia and China. Instead, Russian princes received appointment from the khan and were required to send substantial tribute to the Mongol capital at Sarai.
• Russia was still exploited, but the Mongol impact there was much more uneven than it had been in Persia or China.

• The absence of direct Mongol rule meant that the Mongols were far less influenced by or assimilated within Russian cultures than their counterparts in China and Persia had been.
• On the other hand, Russians were, if anything, more affected by Mongol domination than the Persians and Chinese had been. Russian princes found it useful to adopt the Mongols' weapons, diplomatic rituals, court practices, taxation system, and military draft.

Q. *In what ways did the Mongol Empire contribute to the globalization of the Eurasian world?*

• The Mongols actively promoted international commerce, and the Mongol trading circuit that stretched from China to the Near East was a central element in an even larger commercial network that linked much of the Afro-Eurasian world in the thirteenth century.
• The Mongol Empire also prompted diplomatic relationships from one end of Eurasia to the other, especially between Western Europe and the Mongols and between Persia and China.
• The Mongol Empire also spurred a substantial exchange of peoples and cultures through its policy of forcibly transferring many thousands of skilled craftsmen and educated people from their homelands to distant parts of the empire.
• The Mongol Empire, through its religious tolerance and support of merchants, facilitated the spread of religions.
• The Mongol authorities actively encouraged the exchange of ideas and techniques. A great deal of Chinese technology and artistic conventions flowed westward, including painting, printing, gunpowder weapons, compass navigation, high-temperature furnaces, and medical techniques. Meanwhile, Muslim astronomers brought their skills and knowledge to China.
• Crops were also exchanged.

Q. *Disease changes societies. How might this argument apply to the plague?*

• The loss of population due to the plague created labor shortages that provoked sharp conflict between scarce workers and the rich, which in turn undermined the practice of serfdom in Europe.
• Labor shortages also fostered a greater interest in technological innovation in Europe and created more employment opportunities for women.

• The plague contributed to the downfall of the Mongol Empire.

• The plague caused significant disruption to trade routes to the east, and this trade disruption, along with a desire to avoid Muslim intermediaries, provided an incentive for Europeans to take to the sea in their continuing efforts to reach the riches of Asia.

ADDITIONAL RESOURCES FOR CHAPTER 12

Additional Bedford/St. Martin's Resources

FOR INSTRUCTORS

Computerized Test Bank

This test bank provides over thirty exercises per chapter, including multiple-choice, fill-in-the-blank, short-answer, and full-length essay questions. Instructors can customize quizzes, add or edit both questions and answers, and export questions and answers to a variety of formats, including WebCT and Blackboard. The disc includes correct answers and essay outlines.

Instructor's Resource CD-ROM

This disc provides instructors with ready-made and customizable PowerPoint multimedia presentations built around chapter outlines, maps, figures, and all images from the textbook, plus JPEG versions of all maps, figures, and images.

The following maps and images from Chapter 12 are available in both JPEG and PowerPoint format on the Instructor's Resource CD-ROM:

• Map 12.1: The Mongol Empire (p. 342)
• Map 12.2: Trade and Disease in the Fourteenth Century (p. 355)
• Chinggis Khan at Prayer (p. 332)
• The Scythians (p. 336)
• The Masai (p. 341)
• A Mongol Warrior (p. 346)
• Marco Polo and Khubilai Khan (p. 349)

• Mongol Russia (p. 352)
• The Plague (p. 357)

FOR STUDENTS

Documents and Essays from *Worlds of History: A Comparative Reader,* Third Edition (Volume 1)

The following documents, essays, and illustrations to accompany Chapter 12 are available in Chapters 11 and 13 of this reader by Kevin Reilly:
From Chapter 11:

• From *The Secret History of the Mongols*
• John of Plano Carpini, *History of the Mongols*

From Chapter 13:

• Marco Polo, from *The Travels of Marco Polo*

Online Study Guide at bedfordstmartins.com/strayer

The Online Study Guide helps students synthesize the material from the text as well as practice the skills historians use to make sense of the past. Each chapter of the Online Study Guide contains specific testing exercises, including a multiple-choice self-test that focuses on important conceptual ideas; an identification quiz that helps students remember key people, places, and events; a flashcard activity that tests students on their knowledge of key terms; and two interactive map activities intended to strengthen students' geographic skills. Instructors can monitor students' progress through an online Quiz Gradebook or receive email updates.

Further Reading

Hildinger, Erik. *Warriors of the Steppe: A Military History of Central Asia, 500 B.C. to A.D. 1700.* New York: Sarpedon, 1997. A useful overview of the topic.

Khazanov, Anatoly M. *Nomads and the Outside World.* Trans. Julia Crookenden. 2nd ed. Madison: University of Wisconsin Press, 1992. A very influential study of nomadic society.

The Mongols in World History, http://www.outreachworld.org/resource.asp?Curriculumid=82. An online resource for both teachers and students.

Morgan, David. *The Mongols*. 2nd ed. Oxford: Blackwell, 2007. Perhaps the most balanced study of the Mongols available.

Salzman, Philip. *Pastoralists: Equality, Hierarchy, and the State*. Boulder, CO: Westview Press, 2004. An interesting study of pastoral life.

Web Site of the UN OCHA Pastoralist Communication Initiative, http://www.pastoralists.org/. The focus of this Web site is pastoralism today. It includes nice photos and interesting news from the world of the surviving nomads.

Literature

Bailey, Clinton, trans. *Bedouin Poetry from Sinai and the Negev*. London: Saqi Books, 2002. An interesting collection of modern Bedouin poetry, reflecting both traditional values and response to external pressures.

Dawson, Christopher, ed. *Mission to Asia: Narratives and Letters of the Franciscan Missionaries in Mongolia and China in the Thirteenth and Fourteenth Centuries*. New York: Harper & Row, 1966. This volume includes the accounts of John of Plano Carpini and William of Rubruck.

Herodotus. *The Histories*. Trans. Aubrey de Sélincourt. London: Penguin, 1996. The father of history included an entire book on the Scythians in his *Histories*. It needs to be taken with a grain of salt, but many passages from his writings have been confirmed by archeologists.

Ibn Khaldun. *The Muqaddimah: An Introduction to History*. Trans. Franz Rosenthal, ed. N. J. Dawood. Princeton: Princeton University Press, 2005. This work by one of the greatest historians of the medieval Islamic world includes his views on the Mongols.

Kahn, Paul, trans. *The Secret History of the Mongols*. Boston: Cheng & Tsui, 1998. *The Secret History* is the best source we have for the early history of the Mongol Empire, and this is a beautiful translation.

Lewis, Geoffrey, trans. *The Book of Dede Korkut*. Harmondsworth: Penguin, 1974. A Turkish epic that tells the story of a hero from the nomadic era of Turkish history.

Polo, Marco. *The Travels of Marco Polo*. Trans. Ronald Latham. Harmondsworth: Penguin, 1958. A readable, affordable translation that is full of details about life among the Mongols in China and much else.

Tepilit Ole Saitoti. *The Worlds of a Maasai Warrior: An Autobiography*. Berkeley: University of California Press, 1988. A very interesting modern autobiography of a man born into a traditional Masai society and his efforts to come to grips with Western culture without abandoning his own heritage. At only 170 pages, this book is worth considering as a reading assignment.

Film

China: Under the Mongols—1279–1368. Insight Media, 1977. 18 minutes. Examines Mongol rule in China and its ultimate collapse.

"In Search of Genghis Khan." From *Retracing History*. Films for the Humanities and Sciences, 1994. 54 minutes. Traces the life and legends surrounding Chinggis Khan.

Mongols: Storm from the East. Four-part series. Films for the Humanities and Sciences, 1994. 50 minutes each. Explores the emergence of the Mongol Empire and examines Mongol art, culture, science and technology.

World Conquerors. Films for the Humanities and Sciences, 1993. 50 minutes. Explores the emergence of the Mongol Empire under the rule of Chinggis Khan and his son Ogodei.

The Worlds of the Fifteenth Century

CHAPTER OVERVIEW

Chapter Objectives

- To step back and consider the variety of human experience in the fifteenth century
- To compare conditions in China and Europe on the cusp of the modern world
- To encourage students to consider why Europe came to dominate the world in the modern era, and how well this could have been predicted in 1500
- To examine the Islamic world in the fifteenth century
- To provide a preview of important trends to come in the modern world

Chapter Outline

I. Opening Vignette

A. In 2005, China celebrated the 600th anniversary of the initial launching of the country's great maritime expeditions in 1405.
   1. Admiral Zheng He had commanded a fleet of over 300 ships carrying 27,000 people that sailed as far as the East African coast
   2. Why is Columbus so much more remembered?
B. The fifteenth century was a major turning point in world history.

1. Zheng He's voyages did not have world-historical consequences
2. Columbus's voyages did
C. This chapter's purpose is to review the human story up to the sixteenth century and to establish a baseline against which to measure the transformations of the period 1500–2000.

II. The Shapes of Human Communities

A. In 1500, the world still had all types of societies, from bands of gatherers and hunters to empires, but the balance between them was different than it had been in 500.
B. Paleolithic Persistence
   1. gathering and hunting societies (Paleolithic peoples) still existed throughout all of Australia, much of Siberia, the arctic coastlands, and parts of Africa and the Americas
   2. they had changed over time, interacted with their neighbors
   3. example of Australian gatherers and hunters
      a. some 250 separate groups
      b. had assimilated outside technologies and ideas, e.g., outrigger canoes, fish hooks, netting techniques, artistic styles, rituals, mythological concepts
      c. had not adopted agriculture
      d. manipulated their environment through "firestick farming"
      e. exchanged goods over hundreds of miles
      f. developed sophisticated sculpture and rock painting

4. northwest coast of North America developed very differently
   a. abundant environment allowed development of a complex gathering and hunting culture
   b. had permanent villages, economic specialization, hierarchies, chiefdoms, food storage
5. elsewhere, farming had advanced and absorbed Paleolithic lands

C. Agricultural Village Societies
   1. predominated in much of North America, in Africa south of the equator, in parts of the Amazon River basin and Southeast Asia
   2. their societies mostly avoided oppressive authority, class inequalities, and seclusion of women typical of other civilizations
   3. example of forested region in present-day southern Nigeria, where three different political patterns developed
      a. Yoruba people created city-states, each ruled by a king (*oba*), many of whom were women and who performed both religious and political functions
      b. kingdom of Benin: centralized territorial state ruled by a warrior king named Ewuare
      c. Igbo peoples: dense population and trade, but purposely rejected kingship and state building
         i. relied on other institutions to maintain social cohesion
         ii. system was made famous in Chinua Achebe's novel *Things Fall Apart*
      d. Yoruba, Benin, and Igbo peoples traded among themselves and beyond
      e. the region shared common artistic traditions
      f. all shifted from matrilineal to patrilineal system
   4. in what is now central New York State, agricultural village societies underwent substantial change in the centuries before 1500 **[see Lecture Strategy 1]**
      a. Iroquois speakers had become fully agricultural (maize and beans) by around 1300

   b. population growth, emergence of distinct peoples
   c. rise of warfare as key to male prestige (perhaps since women did the farming, so males were no longer needed for getting food)
   d. warfare triggered the creation of the Iroquois confederation
      i. five Iroquois peoples made an agreement (the Great Law of Peace)
      ii. a confederation council was created to adjudicate disputes
      iii. the Iroquois League of Five Nations ended blood feuds and tribal conflicts; coordinated Iroquois relations with outsiders
   e. some European colonists appreciated Iroquois values of social equality and personal freedom (even for women)
      i. descent was matrilineal
      ii. married couples lived with the wife's family
      iii. women controlled agriculture
      iv. women selected and could depose officeholders

D. Herding Peoples
   1. Turkic warrior Timur (Tamerlane) tried to restore the Mongol Empire ca. 1400
      a. his army devastated Russia, Persia, and India
      b. Timur died in 1405, while preparing invasion of China
      c. his successors kept control of the area between Persia and Afghanistan for a century
      d. Timur's conquest was the last great military success of Central Asian nomads
   2. in the following centuries, the steppe nomads' homeland was swallowed up in expanding Russian and Chinese empires
   3. African pastoralists remained independent from established empires for several centuries longer (until late nineteenth century)
   4. example of the Fulbe (West Africa's largest pastoral society)
      a. gradual eastward migration after 1000 C.E.

b. usually lived in small communities among agriculturalists

c. gradually adopted Islam

d. some moved to towns and became noted religious leaders

e. series of jihads in the eighteenth and nineteenth centuries created new states ruled by the Fulbe

III. **Civilizations of the Fifteenth Century: Comparing China and Europe**

A. By the fifteenth century C.E., a majority of the world's population lived within a major civilization.

B. Ming Dynasty China

1. China had been badly disrupted by Mongol rule and the plague

2. recovery under the Ming dynasty (1368–1644)

   a. effort to eliminate all signs of foreign rule

   b. promotion of Confucian learning

   c. Emperor Yongle (r. 1402–1422) sponsored an 11,000-volume *Encyclopedia* summarizing all the wisdom of the past

3. reestablished the civil service examination system

4. created a highly centralized government

   a. great power was given to court eunuchs

   b. state restored land to cultivation, constructed waterworks, planted perhaps a billion trees

   c. was perhaps the best-governed and most prosperous civilization of the fifteenth century

5. maritime ventures

   a. Chinese sailors and traders had become important in the South China Sea and in Southeast Asian ports in the eleventh century

   b. Emperor Yongle commissioned a massive fleet; launched in 1405

      i. twenty-eight years of maritime expeditions

      ii. Admiral Zheng He tried to enroll distant peoples in the Chinese tribute system

      iii. dozens of rulers took part

iv. no intention of conquering new territories, establishing Chinese settlements, or spreading culture

c. Chinese government abruptly stopped the voyages in 1433

   i. many had regarded them as waste of resources

   ii. and saw voyages as project of hated court eunuchs

d. Chinese merchants and craftsmen continued to settle and trade in Japan, Philippines, Taiwan, and Southeast Asia, but without government support

C. European Comparisons: State Building and Cultural Renewal [see Discussion Topic 1]

1. a similar process of demographic recovery, consolidation, cultural flowering, and European expansion took place in Western Europe

2. European population began to rise again ca. 1450

3. state building, but fragmented, with many independent and competitive states

   a. much of state building was driven by the needs of war, e.g., England and France in the Hundred Years' War (1337–1453)

4. the Renaissance: reclamation of classical Greek traditions

   a. began in the commercial cities of Italy ca. 1350–1500

   b. "returning to the sources" as a cultural standard to imitate

   c. turn to greater naturalism in art (e.g., Leonardo da Vinci, Raphael, Michelangelo)

   d. "humanist" scholars explored secular topics in addition to religious matters

      i. Niccolò Machiavelli's (1469–1527) *The Prince* laid out plans for political success

      ii. greater interest in the individual and in accurate depiction of the world

      iii. challenge to the otherworldliness of Christian culture

D. European Comparisons: Maritime Voyaging

1. Portuguese voyages of discovery began in 1415

2. 1492: Columbus reached the Americas

3. 1497–1498: Vasco da Gama sailed around Africa to India
4. European voyages were very small compared to Chinese ones
5. unlike the Chinese voyages, Europeans were seeking wealth, converts, allies in Crusades against Islam
6. Europeans used violence to carve out empires
7. Chinese voyages ended; European ones kept escalating
   a. no overarching political authority in Europe to end the voyages
   b. rivalry between states encouraged more exploration
   c. much of European elite interested in overseas expansion
   d. China had everything it needed; Europeans wanted the greater riches of the East
   e. China's food production could expand internally; European system expanded by acquiring new lands

IV. **Civilizations of the Fifteenth Century: The Islamic World**
   A. The long-fragmented Islamic world crystallized into four major states or empires.
      1. process of conversion to Islam continued both within and beyond new states
   B. In the Islamic Heartland: The Ottoman and Safavid Empires **[see Lecture Strategy 2]**
      1. Ottoman Empire lasted from fourteenth to early twentieth century
         a. huge territory: Anatolia, eastern Europe, much of Middle East, North African coast, lands around Black Sea
         b. sultans claimed the title "caliph" and the legacy of the Abbasids
         c. effort to bring new unity to the Islamic world
      2. Ottoman aggression toward Christian lands
         a. fall of Constantinople in 1453
         b. 1529 siege of Vienna
         c. Europeans feared Turkish expansion
      3. Safavid Empire emerged in Persia from a Sufi religious order
         a. empire was established shortly after 1500
         b. imposed Shia Islam as the official religion of the state

4. Sunni Ottoman Empire and Shia Safavid Empire fought periodically between 1534 and 1639
   C. On the Frontiers of Islam: The Songhay and Mughal Empires
      1. Songhay Empire rose in West Africa in the second half of the fifteenth century
         a. Islam was limited largely to urban elites
         b. Sonni Ali (r. 1465–1492) followed Muslim practices, but was also regarded as a magician with an invisibility charm
         c. Songhay Empire was a major center of Islamic learning/trade
      2. Mughal Empire in India was created by Turkic group that invaded India in 1526
         a. over the sixteenth century, Mughals gained control of most of India
         b. effort to create a partnership between Hindus and Muslims
         c. Hindu kingdom of Vijayanagara continued to flourish in the south
   D. The age of these four great Muslim empires is sometimes called a "second flowering of Islam."
      1. new age of energy, prosperity, and cultural brilliance
      2. spread of Islam to new areas, such as Southeast Asia
         a. spread by traveling merchants, supported by Sufi holy men
      3. rise of Malacca as a sign of the times— became a major Muslim port city in the fifteenth century
         a. Malaccan Islam blended with Hindu/Buddhist traditions
         b. was a center for Islamic learning

V. **Civilizations of the Fifteenth Century: The Americas** [see Lecture Strategy 3 and Discussion Topic 2]
   A. Both the Aztec and the Inca empires were established by once-marginal peoples who took over and absorbed older cultures.
      1. both empires were destroyed by the Spaniards and their diseases
   B. The Aztec Empire
      1. The Mexica were a seminomadic people who migrated southward from northern Mexico

a. established themselves on an island in Lake Texcoco by 1325

b. built themselves up and established capital city of Tenochtitlán

2. Triple Alliance (1428): Mexica and two other city-states united

a. launched a program of military conquest

b. conquered much of Mesoamerica in under a century

c. Aztec rulers claimed descent from earlier peoples

3. Aztec Empire was a loosely structured, unstable conquest state

a. population of 5–6 million

b. conquered peoples paid regular tribute

c. Tenochtitlán had 150,000–200,000 people

   i. center for large-scale trade

d. local and long-distance trade on a vast scale

   i. professional merchants (*pochteca*) became rich

4. trade included slaves, many intended for sacrifice

a. human sacrifice much more prominent in Aztec Empire than in earlier Mesoamerica

b. Tlacaelel is credited with crystallizing ideology of state giving human sacrifice such importance

   i. the sun needs the life-giving force of human blood to help it fight the ever-encroaching darkness

   ii. gods shed their blood to create humankind, so payback is fair

   iii. Aztec Empire's purpose is to maintain the cosmic order by supplying blood for the gods

5. created an important philosophical/poetic tradition focused on the fragility of human life **[see Classroom Activity 1]**

C. The Inca Empire

1. Quechua speakers established the Inca Empire along the length of the Andes

a. empire was 2,500 miles long

b. around 10 million subjects

2. Inca Empire was more bureaucratic, centralized than the Aztecs

a. emperor was an absolute ruler regarded as divine

b. state theoretically owned all land and resources

c. around 80 provinces, each with an Inca governor

d. subjects grouped into hierarchical units of people (10, 50, 100, 500, etc.), at least in the central regions

e. inspectors checked up on provincial officials

f. population data was recorded on *quipus* (knotted cords)

g. massive resettlement program moved much of the population

3. Incas attempted cultural integration

a. leaders of conquered peoples had to learn Quechua

b. sons were taken to Cuzco (the capital) for acculturation

c. subjects had to acknowledge major Inca deities

   i. but then could carry on their own religious traditions

   ii. human sacrifice, but on much smaller scale than Aztecs

4. almost everyone had to perform labor service (*mita*) for the Inca state

a. work on state farms, herding, mining, military service, state construction

b. also production of goods for the state

   i. most well known were the "chosen women": removed from their homes and trained to make corn beer and cloth

c. state provided elaborate feasts in return

5. the state played a large role in distribution of goods

D. Both the Inca and Aztec civilizations practiced "gender parallelism."

1. women and men operated in "separate but equivalent spheres"

2. parallel religious cults for women and men

3. parallel hierarchies of female and male political officials (especially among Incas)

4. women's household tasks were not regarded as inferior
   i. for Aztecs, sweeping was a powerful, sacred act
5. still, men had top positions in political and religious life
6. glorification of the military probably undermined gender parallelism
7. Inca ruler and his wife governed jointly, were descended from sun and moon, respectively

VI. Webs of Connection

A. Large-scale political systems brought together culturally different people.
   1. efforts to integrate diverse peoples, e.g., in Ottoman, Mughal, and Inca empires
B. Religion both united and divided far-flung peoples.
   1. common religious culture of Christendom, but divided into Roman Catholicism and Eastern Orthodoxy
   2. Buddhism linked people in China, Korea, Tibet, Japan, and parts of Southeast Asia
   3. Islam was particularly good at bringing together its people
      a. the annual hajj
      b. yet conflict within the umma persisted
C. Patterns of trade were very evident in the fifteenth century
   1. trade was going on almost everywhere
   2. the balance of Afro-Eurasian trade was changing
      a. the Silk Road network was contracting
      b. ocean trade in the west Atlantic/Indian Ocean picked up

VII. A Preview of Coming Attractions: Looking Ahead to the Modern Era (1500–2000)
[see Classroom Activity 2]

A. No fifteenth-century connections were truly global.
   1. those came only with European expansion in the sixteenth century
   2. 1500–2000: inextricable linking of the worlds of Afro-Eurasia, the Americas, and Pacific Oceania

B. "Modern" human society emerged first in Europe in the nineteenth century and then throughout the world.
   1. core feature: industrialization
   2. accompanied by massive population increase
   3. societies favored holders of urban wealth over rural landowning elites
   4. states became more powerful and intrusive
   5. opening up of public and political life to more of the population
   6. self-conscious departure from tradition
   7. the modernity revolution was as important as the Agricultural Revolution
      a. introduced new divisions and conflicts, new economic inequalities
      b. destruction of older patterns of human life
C. The prominence of European peoples on the global stage grew over the last 500 years.
   1. after 1500, Western Europe became the most innovative, prosperous, powerful, imitated part of the world
   2. spread of European languages and Christian religion throughout the world
   3. initiated the Scientific Revolution and the Industrial Revolution
   4. origin of modern -*isms*: liberalism, nationalism, feminism, socialism
   5. rest of the world was confronted by powerful, intrusive Europeans

VIII. Reflections: What If? Chance and Contingency in World History [see Discussion Topic 3 and Classroom Activity 3]

A. Might history have been shaped, at least at certain points, by coincidence, chance, or the decisions of a few?
   1. What if Ogodei Khan hadn't died in 1241 and the Mongols had continued their advance into Europe?
   2. What if China had continued maritime exploration after 1433?
   3. What if the Ottomans had taken Vienna in 1529?
B. It's worthwhile to sometimes take a "what if" approach to history.

USING *WAYS OF THE WORLD* IN THE CLASSROOM

Lecture Strategies

Lecture Strategy 1

"North America in 1500."
The average college student knows very little about North America before European encroachment and tends to be curious about the subject. A lecture focusing on the various social/economic systems in North America on the eve of contact will reinforce the chapter's emphasis on the diversity of human social patterns while providing new material to supplement it. The objectives of this lecture strategy are to:

- encourage students to think about the diversity of human life in the year 1500
- encourage students to consider the diversity of life among American Indians before European contact
- reinforce the chapter's (and indeed the first twelve chapters') lessons about the conditions for the development of societies of various complexity.

Probably the easiest way to approach a lecture on this topic is to choose three or four North American peoples who are particularly exemplary of various levels of societal complexity, and to build a comparative narrative of their stories. Some peoples that might be of particular interest to students are:

- Apaches (nomadic)
- Choctaw (chiefdoms)
- Iroquois confederation
- Nez Perce (complex gatherering and hunting society)
- Powhatan confederacy
- Pueblo (village society)

Some points to consider for inclusion are:

- population density and its role in encouraging more complex societies
- suitability of land for agriculture (including availability of water)

- the great number of Indian languages and the role they might have played in discouraging intercommunication
- the fact that Plains Indians did not have horses until the Spaniards arrived
- the potlatch culture of Pacific Northwest Indians
- a comparison of the Iroquois and Powhatan confederations
- domestication of nonfood items (such as tobacco and peyote)

Lecture Strategy 2

"An ascendant society: The Ottoman golden age."
A closer look at the Ottoman Turks—their rise to power, societal structures, and world standing by the time of Suleiman the Magnificent (r. 1520–1566)—will provide an opportunity to explore a basic question: Why was it the Europeans and not the Turks who became the dominant power of the modern world? This lecture strategy has several objectives:

- to help students understand the strengths and weaknesses of the Ottoman Turkic state
- to drive home the lesson that the "rise of Europe" was not inevitable
- to help students understand the long-term tension between Islam and Christianity
- to explore contemporaneous Islamic states by means of comparison to the Ottomans

A good place to begin is with the rise of the Ottoman state in Anatolia in the fourteenth century. A basically chronological, rather than thematic, approach will probably be easiest for students to follow. Some important points to include are:

- jihad as a political tool for expansion of the Ottoman state
- the weakness of the late Byzantine Empire
- Ottoman expansion into the Balkans
- crusades against Ottoman expansion (especially the Crusade of Nicopolis and the Crusade of Varna)
- the *devshirme* system (tribute of boy children from Christian lands)
- the role of the gunpowder revolution in Ottoman success (especially the janissaries)
- Timur's defeat of Bayezid the Thunderbolt

- the conquest of Constantinople
- Ottoman expansion into the Middle East and Egypt
- Ottoman naval efforts (include both sieges of Rhodes)
- the problems of "harem politics" (i.e., the frequent fights between a sultan's sons by different mothers)
- Ottoman support of Muslim education and law
- Ottoman wars with the Safavids as a possible explanation for their failure to prevail against most of Europe

Lecture Strategy 3

"Aztecs and Incas."
A lecture that goes into greater detail about the Aztecs and Incas than is possible in the textbook would be useful, not just because students in general are interested in the topic, but because the Aztecs and Incas provide a good framework with which to review general issues of premodern imperial structures throughout the world. The objectives of this lecture strategy are to:

- help students appreciate the sophistication of these great empires of preconquest America
- compare the American empires to the states of contemporaneous Eurasia in terms of complexity and purpose
- ponder more generally how much a premodern government could intrude on the lives of individuals with the resources available

A good place to start is with a brief review of earlier civilizations of Mesoamerica and the Andes. From there, it is reasonable to follow the textbook's layout by dealing first with the Aztecs and then, when introducing the Incas, to develop comparisons between the two civilizations. Key to making this an effective review lecture besides presenting Aztec and Inca material, though, is the identification of some useful points of comparison. Some comparisons to consider for inclusion are:

- societies other than the Incas that regarded their ruler as a deity (Egypt, Japan)
- the issue of human sacrifice and comparison to other kinds of sacrifice (burial of servants with

their masters among the early Egyptians, early Mesopotamians, Scythians, Vikings; large-scale animal sacrifice in ancient Greece, Rome, and Israel, among others)
- the way societies conceive of the divine
- population displacement by the government (Assyria, Babylonia, and Han China)
- government demands for labor services (ancient Egypt and Mesopotamia)
- exploitation of subjects vs. integration
- communications between the rulers and the ruled (Roman and Persian road systems, courier services, etc.)

Things to Do in the Classroom

Discussion Topics

1. **Misconception/Difficult Topic, large or small group.** "Europe has always been the greatest."
Ask students to list the elements in the fifteenth century that would suggest Europe's eventual rise to world dominance, and the elements that make Europe's rise seem surprising.

2. **Comparison, large or small group.** "Mesoamerica and the world."
By this point, students should have learned about a wide array of governments; thus, this discussion topic provides a useful time for review. Ask groups of students to list the following empires by their degree of government complexity and to be prepared to defend their choices:

- Abbasid caliphate
- Alexander the Great's empire
- Han dynasty China
- Ming dynasty China
- Mongol Empire
- Mughal Empire
- Persian Empire
- Roman Empire
- Songhay Empire
- Xiongnu Empire

Then ask them to add the Aztec and Inca empires to the ordered list they have established, defending their placement.

3. Contextualization, large or small group.

"What if . . . ?"

Ask students to decide on what they regard as a key historical turning point, a "day that the world changed" in world history up to the year 1500 C.E. This could of course be anything from a decisive battle to an invention to the suggestions given in the Reflections section of Chapter 13. It is important to emphasize that the turning point they choose should not be something that was going to happen soon anyway—e.g., if the Ottomans hadn't conquered Constantinople in 1453 they would surely have taken it in a few years, or if Og hadn't discovered that it was possible to make a sharp stone tool, Grawp would probably have done so. After each group has chosen a plausible turning point, ask them to theorize what the consequences would have been if that event had gone differently.

Classroom Activities

1. **Close-reading exercise, small group.** "Encounter with the Aztecs."

Distribute to the class a Mesoamerican poem from the era of Aztec dominance. (Look under "Literature" in the Further Reading section of this chapter for a good source.) Ask them to read it carefully, picking out at least three insights that the poem provides about Mesoamerican society.

2. **Review exercise, large or small group.** "A roadmap of world history."

Most students are unimaginative when it comes to studying, often resorting to rote memorization. For this classroom activity, we suggest that you map out, with the class, two possible ways to study by association rather than by rote: the timeline and the thematic outline.

1. For the timeline, you will need a large chalkboard or equivalent. Draw four very long horizontal lines, labeling them "Asia," "Europe," "Africa," and "The Americas." Mark off centuries with short vertical lines. Then ask the class for items to add to the list. Encourage students to participate—for example, by asking *other* students to provide the time when a particular student has named an event. Ask leading questions to fill in gaps, with an eye toward cultural and religious events as well as political ones. Don't let students ignore the early societies covered in this text.

2. Explain to students the basic concept of memory by association, such as when one makes an outline of points relating to a major theme and then studies the points as a whole. Then, with the class, make a list of the course's major themes to date. Offer suggestions for the sorts of points that might be included under each theme. Then choose a single theme and sketch out a more detailed outline, soliciting as much input as possible from the students.

3. **Clicker question.** Do you think that deeply rooted underlying causes or coincidence and chance play a more important role in shaping the course of world history?

Key Terms

Aztec Empire: Major state that developed in what is now Mexico in the fourteenth and fifteenth centuries; dominated by the seminomadic Mexica, who had migrated into the region from northern Mexico.

Benin: Territorial state that emerged by the fifteenth century in the region that is now southern Nigeria; ruled by a warrior king who consolidated his state through widespread conquest. (*pron.* be-NEEN)

"chosen women": Among the Incas, girls who were removed from their homes at a young age, trained in Inca ideology, and set to producing corn beer and textiles; they later were given as wives to distinguished men or sent to serve as priestesses.

Columbus, Christopher: Genoese mariner (1451–1506) commissioned by Spain to search for a new trading route to Asia; in 1492 he found America instead.

Constantinople, seizure of (1453): Constantinople, the capital and almost the only outpost left of the Byzantine Empire, fell to the army of the Ottoman sultan Mehmed II "the Conqueror" in 1453, an event that marked the end of Christian Byzantium.

"firestick farming": A manipulation of their environment by the Paleolithic peoples of Australia that involved controlled burns to clear underbrush.

Fulbe: West Africa's largest pastoral society, whose members gradually adopted Islam and took on a religious leadership role that led to the creation of a number of new states. (*pron.* FULL-bay)

Gama, Vasco da: Portuguese explorer (ca. 1460–1524) whose 1497–1498 voyage was the first European venture to reach India by circling the tip of South Africa. (*pron.* VAS-coe dah GAHM-ah)

Huitzilopochtli: Patron deity of the Aztec empire, associated with the sun. (*pron.* wheat-zeel-oh-POSHT-lee)

Hundred Years' War: Major conflict between France and England (1337–1453) over rival claims to territory in France; the two states' need to finance the war helped encourage their administrative development.

Igbo: People whose lands were east of the Niger River in what is now southern Nigeria in West Africa; they built a complex society that rejected kingship and centralized statehood and relied on other institutions to provide social coherence. (*pron.* EE-boh)

Inca Empire: The Western Hemisphere's largest imperial state in the fifteenth and early sixteenth centuries; built by a relatively small community of Quechua-speaking people (the Inca), the empire stretched some 2,500 miles along the Andes Mountains, which run nearly the entire length of the west coast of South America, and contained perhaps 10 million subjects.

Iroquois League of Five Nations: Confederation of five Iroquois peoples in what is now New York State; the loose alliance was based on the Great Law of Peace, an agreement to settle disputes peacefully through a council of clan leaders. (*pron.* IR-oh-kwoy)

Malacca: Muslim port city that came to prominence on the waterway between Sumatra and Malaya in the fifteenth century C.E.; it was the springboard for the spread of a syncretic form of Islam throughout the region. (*pron.* mah-LAH-kah)

Mexica: Seminomadic people of northern Mexico who by 1325 had established themselves on a small island in Lake Texcoco, where they built their capital city, Tenochtitlán; the Mexica were the central architects of the Aztec Empire. (*pron.* meh-SHE-ca)

Ming dynasty: Chinese dynasty (1368–1644) that succeeded the Yuan dynasty of the Mongols; noted for its return to traditional Chinese ways and restoration of the land after the destructiveness of the Mongols.

Mughal Empire: One of the most successful empires of India, a state founded by an Islamized Turkic group that invaded India in 1526; the Mughals' rule was noted for their efforts to create partnerships between Hindus and Muslims. (*pron.* MOO-guhl)

Nezahualcoyotl: A poet and king of the city-state of Texcoco, which was part of the Aztec Empire (1402–1472). (*pron.* nes-ah-wahl-koh-YOHT-l)

Ottoman Empire: Major Islamic state centered on Anatolia that came to include the Balkans, the Near East, and much of North Africa.

Paleolithic persistence: The continuance of gathering and hunting societies in substantial areas of the world despite millennia of agricultural advance.

pochteca: Professional merchants in the Aztec Empire whose wealth often elevated them to elite status. (*pron.* poch-TAY-kah)

Renaissance, European: A "rebirth" of classical learning that is most often associated with the cultural blossoming of Italy in the period 1350–1500 and that included not just a rediscovery of Greek learning but also major developments in art, as well as growing secularism in society.

Safavid Empire: Major Turkic empire of Persia founded in the early sixteenth century, notable for it efforts to convert its populace to Shia Islam. (*pron.* SAH-fah-vid)

Songhay Empire: Major Islamic state of West Africa that formed in the second half of the fifteenth century. (*pron.* song-GAH-ee)

Tenochtitlán: The metropolitan capital of the Aztec Empire, with a population of 150,000–200,000 people. (*pron.* the-noch-TIT-lan)

Timbuktu: Great city of West Africa, noted in the fourteenth–sixteenth centuries as a center of Islamic scholarship. (*pron.* tim-buk-TOO)

Timur: Turkic warrior (1336–1405), also known as Tamerlane, whose efforts to restore the Mongol Empire devastated much of Persia, Russia, and India. (*pron.* tem-EER)

Triple Alliance: 1428 agreement between the Mexica and two other nearby city-states that launched the Aztec Empire.

Yongle: Chinese emperor (r. 1402–1422) during the Ming dynasty who was a key figure in the restoration of China to greatness and who commissioned an enormous fleet to spread awareness of Chinese superiority to much of Asia and eastern Africa. (*pron.* yoong-LAW)

Zheng He: Great Chinese admiral (1371–1433) who commanded a fleet of more than 300 ships in a series of voyages of contact and exploration that began in 1405. (*pron.* jung huh)

ANSWER GUIDELINES FOR CHAPTER QUESTIONS

The two sets of questions that follow appear in the textbook at the end of the chapter and in the margins of the reading. They are also provided in the Computerized Test Bank with answer guidelines, for your convenience.

The Big Picture Questions

1. Assume for the moment that the Chinese had *not* ended their maritime voyages in 1433. How might the subsequent development of world history have been different? Is there value in asking this kind of "what if" or counterfactual question? Or is it an irrelevant waste of time?

• If they had continued, Chinese maritime voyages could have had a profound impact on the course of world history. China was the richest, most prosperous, and most technologically advanced civilization in the world at that time, and it would be reasonable to think that, if the Chinese had aggressively competed with their European counterparts, they likely would have prevailed as the preeminent maritime power in the world. This would have had profound implications for the course of world history, most likely limiting the influence of Western Europe and of Christianity on other regions of the globe and increasing Chinese cultural, economic, and political influences beyond East Asia.

• The usefulness of counterfactual questions is debatable. They do allow one both to highlight the role of contingency in the course of human history and to highlight the difficulty of predicting the future because of contingency. Moreover, counterfactual questions go beyond mere speculation, because they encourage students to think of what was *possible* in light of known historical facts. Thus a good "what if" question can help scholars think their way into historical reality and to hone their analytical skills. Still, no one can fully predict what the consequences of a change in events would have been, and in any case, the reality of the situation as it happened is the subject of history.

2. How does this chapter distinguish among the various kinds of societies that comprised the world of the fifteenth century? Are there other ways of categorizing the world's peoples that might work as well or better?

• This chapter organizes societies in two ways. First, it organizes them into Paleolithic peoples, agricultural village societies, herding peoples, and established civilizations and empires. It then organizes those civilizations by region.

• There are other alternatives, including organization by cultural region—Chinese, Indian, Islamic, Mesoamerican, and Christian. Another possibility would have been organization through webs of connections, starting with a single society and radiating out to an exploration of its nearer and more distant contacts.

3. What would surprise a knowledgeable observer from 500 C.E., were he or she to make a global tour in the fifteenth century? What features of that earlier world might still be recognizable?

• Several changes would undoubtedly have surprised a knowledgeable observer, including the emergence of Islam;
• the revival of China and Western Europe;
• the collapse of the Byzantine Empire;
• the emergence of Russia and the spread of Christianity into that region;
• the emergence of states in Southeast Asia;
• the emergence of Japan;
• the emergence of powerful empires in West Africa.
• However, some features would still be recognizable, such as the persistence of Paleolithic, agricultural village, and herding societies;
• the continuance, albeit at a more intense rate, of long-distance commerce and exchange;
• the persistence of broad cultural traditions, especially in the Mesoamerican, Andean, Chinese, European, and Indian civilizations.

4. What predictions about the future might a global traveler of the fifteenth century reasonably have made? Would it depend on precisely when those predictions were made?

• A global traveler of the fifteenth century might have predicted that Islam, Buddhism, and perhaps Christianity would continue to spread;
• that the established cultural regions of China, India, the Islamic world, Christian Europe, the Andes,

and Mesoamerica would continue to develop and expand;

• that long-distance commerce and exchange would continue to have an important impact on the development of civilizations;

• that empires would continue to have a growing influence on world history;

• that the regions occupied by Paleolithic, agricultural village, and herding societies would continue to shrink.

• Precisely when these predictions were made would make a difference. Before 1492, the huge impact of Western European influence on the Americas would have been difficult to predict.

• Before 1433, the relatively modest impact of Chinese overseas exploration would have been difficult to predict.

Margin Review Questions

Q. *In what ways did the gathering and hunting people of Australia differ from those of the northwest coast of North America?*

• The gathering and hunting people of the northwest coast of North America possessed permanent village settlements with large and sturdy houses, considerable economic specialization, ranked societies that sometimes included slavery, chiefdoms dominated by powerful clan leaders, and extensive storage of food; none of those features were part of Australian gathering and hunting societies.

Q. *What kinds of changes were transforming West African agricultural village societies and those of the Iroquois as the fifteenth century dawned?*

• In West Africa, three distinct patterns of political development were taking shape among agricultural village societies, with the Yoruba people creating city-states; the kingdom of Benin taking shape as a small, highly centralized territorial state; and the Igbo peoples relying on other institutions—title societies, women's associations, hereditary ritual experts serving as mediators, a balance of power among kinship groups—to maintain social cohesion beyond the level of the village.

• In addition, the Yoruba, Bini, and Igbo peoples traded actively among themselves as well as with more

distant peoples and changed from a matrilineal to a patrilineal system of tracing their descent.

• In the Americas, in what is now central New York State, an increased level of conflict among Iroquois peoples triggered a remarkable political innovation—a loose alliance or confederation among five Iroquois peoples based on an agreement known as the Great Law of Peace. The Iroquois League of Five Nations kept peace, adjudicated disputes, and operated by consensus. It also gave expression to values of limited government, social equality, and personal freedom.

• The Iroquois developed a system that gave women unusual authority. Descent was matrilineal, married couples lived with the wife's family, and women controlled agriculture. While men were hunters, warriors, and the primary political officeholders, women selected and could depose those leaders.

Q. *What role did Central Asian and West African pastoralists play in their respective regions?*

• In Central Asia, the Turkic warlord Timur constructed a significant empire that retained control of the area between Persia and Afghanistan during the fifteenth century.

• Timur's conquests, however, hid a more long-term change for the pastoral peoples of Central Asia, because his was the last great military success of nomadic peoples from Central Asia; in the centuries that followed, their homelands were swallowed up in the expanding Russian and Chinese empires.

• In West Africa, pastoral peoples retained their independence into the late nineteenth century.

• Groups like the Fulbe, West Africa's largest pastoral society, generally lived in small communities among agricultural peoples;

• as they migrated gradually eastward after 1000 C.E., they maintained their distinctive way of life and a sense of cultural superiority that became more pronounced as they slowly adopted Islam.

• Some Fulbe dropped out of a pastoral life and settled in towns, where they became highly respected religious leaders.

• In the eighteenth and nineteenth centuries, the Fulbe were at the center of a wave of religiously based uprisings (jihads) that greatly expanded the practice of Islam and gave rise to a series of new states ruled by the Fulbe.

Q. *How would you define the major achievements of Ming dynasty China?*

• Under the Ming dynasty, China recovered from the disruption caused by Mongol rule and the ravages of the plague to become perhaps the best-governed and most prosperous of the world's major civilizations;

• it also undertook the largest and most impressive maritime expeditions the world had ever seen.

Q. *What political and cultural differences stand out in the histories of fifteenth-century China and Western Europe? What similarities are apparent?*

• Political consolidation occurred in both China and Western Europe, but in China this meant a unitary and centralized government that encompassed almost the whole of its civilization, while in Europe a decidedly fragmented system of many separate, independent, and competitive states made for a sharply divided Christendom.

• While both experienced cultural flowering, Europe's culture after the Renaissance was rather more different from its own recent past than Ming dynasty China was from its pre-Mongol glory.

• While both sent out ships to explore the wider world, their purposes in doing so were very different.

Q. *In what ways did European maritime voyaging in the fifteenth century differ from that of China? What accounts for these differences?*

• Chinese exploration was undertaken by an enormous fleet composed of several hundred large ships, while European explorations were undertaken by expeditions made up of a handful of small ships.

• European motivations for exploration included the desire for wealth from trade, the search for converts to Christianity, and the recruitment of possible Christian allies against the Muslim powers. China, by contrast, needed no military allies, required little in the way of trade, and had no desire to convert foreigners to Chinese culture or religion.

• The Europeans sought to monopolize by force the commerce of the Indian Ocean and violently carved out empires in the Americas; the Chinese fleet sought neither conquests nor colonies.

• China ended its voyages abruptly after 1433; the European explorations continued and even escalated.

• In terms of why China's explorations were so different from their European counterparts, the fragmentation of political authority in Europe, unlike China's unified empire, ensured that once begun, rivalry alone would drive Europeans to the ends of the earth.

• Much of Europe's elite, including merchants, monarchs, the clergy, and nobles, had an interest in overseas expansion; in China, by contrast, the emperor Yongle was the primary supporter of the Chinese voyages of exploration, and after he passed from the scene, those opposed to the voyages prevailed within the politics of the court.

• The Chinese were very much aware of their own antiquity, believed strongly in the absolute superiority of their culture, and felt that, should they need something from abroad, others would bring it to them. The Europeans also believed themselves unique; however, in material terms, they were seeking out the greater riches of the East, and they were highly conscious that Muslim power blocked easy access to these treasures and posed a military and religious threat to Europe itself.

Q. *What differences can you identify among the four major empires in the Islamic world of the fifteenth and sixteenth centuries?*

• The Ottoman, Safavid, and Mughal empires had Turkic origins, while the Songhay Empire did not.

• The Ottoman and Safavid empires ruled over the heartland of the Muslim world, where a majority of their subjects followed Islam; the Mughal and Songhay empires ruled over regions where Islam was a minority faith.

• The rulers of the Safavid Empire were the only ones to impose a Shia version of Islam as the official religion of the state.

Q. *What distinguished the Aztec and Inca empires from each other?*

• The Inca Empire was much larger than its Aztec counterpart.

• The Aztec Empire controlled only part of the Mesoamerican cultural region, while at its height the Inca state encompassed practically the whole of the Andean civilization.

• In the Aztec realm, the Mexica rulers largely left their conquered people alone, and no elaborate administrative system arose to integrate the conquered territories or to assimilate their people to Aztec culture. The Incas, on the other hand, erected a more bureaucratic empire.

• The Aztec Empire extracted substantial tribute in the form of goods from its subject populations, while the Incas primarily extracted labor services from their subjects.

• The Aztec Empire had a system of commercial exchange that was based on merchants and free markets, whereas the Inca government played a major role in both the production and distribution of goods.

• The authority of the state penetrated and directed the Incas' society and economy far more than did that of the Aztecs.

Q. *How did Aztec religious thinking support the empire?*

• The ideology of state that gave human sacrifice great religious importance shaped the techniques of Aztec warfare, which put a premium on capturing prisoners rather than on killing the enemy.

• Priests and rulers became interdependent, with human sacrifices carried out for political ends.

• Massive sacrificial rituals served to impress enemies, allies, and subjects alike with the immense power of the Aztecs and their gods.

Q. *In what ways did Inca authorities seek to integrate their vast domains?*

• The emperor was an absolute ruler and was regarded as divine.

• In theory, the state owned all land and resources.

• Subjects were organized, at least in the central regions of the empire, into hierarchical units of 10, 50, 100, 500, 1000, and 10,000 people, each headed by local officials, who were supervised by an Inca governor or by the emperor.

• An imperial office of "inspectors" checked on provincial authorities.

• Births, deaths, marriages, and other population data were carefully recorded.

• A resettlement program moved one-quarter or more of the population to new locations.

• Leaders of conquered peoples were required to learn Quechua, and their sons were removed to the capital of Cuzco for instruction in Inca culture and language.

• Subject peoples were required to acknowledge major Inca deities, although once they did so, they were largely free to carry on their own religious traditions.

• The Inca Empire played a major role in the production and distribution of goods.

Q. *In what different ways did the peoples of the fifteenth century interact with one another?*

• They interacted through webs of empire, large-scale political systems that brought together a variety of culturally different people;

• through webs of religion that linked far-flung peoples;

• and through long-established patterns of trade among peoples occupying different environments and producing different goods.

ADDITIONAL RESOURCES FOR CHAPTER 13

Additional Bedford/St. Martin's Resources

FOR INSTRUCTORS

Computerized Test Bank

This test bank provides over thirty exercises per chapter, including multiple-choice, fill-in-the-blank, short-answer, and full-length essay questions. Instructors can customize quizzes, add or edit both questions and answers, and export questions and answers to a variety of formats, including WebCT and Blackboard. The disc includes correct answers and essay outlines.

Instructor's Resource CD-ROM

This disc provides instructors with ready-made and customizable PowerPoint multimedia presentations built around chapter outlines, maps, figures, and all images from the textbook, plus JPEG versions of all maps, figures, and images.

The following maps and images from Chapter 13 are available in both JPEG and PowerPoint format on the Instructor's Resource CD-ROM:

• Map 13.1: Asia in the Fifteenth Century (p. 370)
• Map 13.2: Europe in 1500 (p. 373)
• Map 13.3: Africa in the Fifteenth Century (p. 376)
• Map 13.4: Empires of the Islamic World (p. 379)

- Map 13.5: The Americas in the Fifteenth Century (p. 383)
- Map 13.6: Religion and Commerce in the Afro-Eurasian World (p. 390)
- The Meeting of Two Worlds (p. 362)
- Benin Bronzes (p. 367)
- Comparing Chinese and European Ships (p. 371)
- The Waldseemüller Map of 1507 (p. 377)
- Ottoman Janissaries (p. 380)
- Aztec Women (p. 385)
- Machu Picchu (p. 387)

FOR STUDENTS

Documents and Essays from *Worlds of History: A Comparative Reader,* Third Edition (Volume 2)

The following documents, essays, and illustrations to accompany Chapter 13 are available in Chapters 1, 3, and 4 of Volume 2 of this reader by Kevin Reilly:

From Chapter 1:

- Joseph Kahn, *"China Has an Ancient Mariner to Tell You About"*
- Zheng He, *Inscription to the Goddess*
- Gavin Menzies, from *1421: The Year China Discovered America*
- Christopher Columbus, *Letter to King Ferdinand and Queen Isabella*
- Kirkpatrick Sale, from *The Conquest of Paradise*

From Chapter 3:

- Jonathan Spence, *The Ming Chinese State and Religion*
- Matteo Ricci, *Jesuit Missionaries in Ming China*
- Donald Quataert, *Ottoman Inter-communal Relations*

From Chapter 4:

- *Family Instructions for the Miu Lineage*
- Mao Xiang, *How Dong Xiaowan Became My Concubine*

Online Study Guide at bedfordstmartins.com/strayer

The Online Study Guide helps students synthesize the material from the text as well as practice the skills historians use to make sense of the past. Each chapter of the Online Study Guide contains specific testing exercises, including a multiple-choice self-test that focuses on important conceptual ideas; an identification quiz that helps students remember key people, places, and events; a flashcard activity that tests students on their knowledge of key terms; and two interactive map activities intended to strengthen students' geographic skills. Instructors can monitor students' progress through an online Quiz Gradebook or receive email updates.

Further Reading

Fagan, Brian M. *Ancient North America: The Archaeology of a Continent.* 4th ed. London: Thames and Hudson, 2005. An excellent introduction to the peoples of North America.

Inalcik, Halil. *The Ottoman Empire: The Classical Age, 1300–1600.* 2nd ed. London: Phoenix Press, 2000. A recent, readable introduction to the Ottoman Empire.

The Islamic World to 1600: Rise of the Great Islamic Empires, http://www.ucalgary.ca/applied_history/tutor/islam/empires/. A convenient source for information about the Ottoman, Safavid, and Mughal empires.

Kehoe, Alice Beck. *America before the European Invasions.* London: Longman, 2002. An excellent study that focuses especially on the variety of Indian societies before European contact.

Mann, Charles C. *1491: New Revelations of the Americas before Columbus.* New York: Knopf, 2005. A recent, well-regarded popular history.

Ming China, http://www.wsu.edu/~dee/MING/CONTENTS.HTM. History, an anthology of readings, and references to other Internet resources.

Native American History, http://www2005.lang.osaka-u.ac.jp/~krkvls/history.html. Links to a variety of resources for those studying American Indians, both pre- and post-European contact.

Ottoman Web Site, http://www.osmanli700.gen.tr/english/engindex.html. A rich source of information about Ottoman history and culture, sponsored by the Gilder Lehrman Institute of American History.

Robinson, Francis. *The Mughal Emperors and the Islamic Dynasties of India, Iran, and Central Asia*. London: Thames & Hudson, 2007. A short, very nicely illustrated history of the Mughal Empire.

Savory, Roger. *Iran under the Safavids*. Cambridge: Cambridge University Press, 1980. Probably the best book available on the subject.

Literature

Curl, John, trans. *Ancient American Poets*. Tempe, AZ: Bilingual Press, 2005. An interesting collection of Nahuatl, Maya, and Quechua poems in translation.

Feng Menglong, ed. *Stories Old and New: A Ming Dynasty Collection*. Trans. Shuhui Yang and Yunqin Yang. Honolulu: University of Hawaii Press, 2006.

Halsall, Paul, ed. *Internet Islamic History Sourcebook*. http://www.fordham.edu/halsall/islam/islamsbook .html. An interesting collection of primary sources (especially Ottoman), mostly short excerpts that are a good length for class assignments.

Halsall, Paul, ed. *Internet Medieval Sourcebook: Renaissance*. http://www.fordham.edu/halsall/sbook1x.html. An assortment of classic European Renaissance texts in English translation.

Halsall, Paul, ed. *Internet Modern History Sourcebook: The Early Modern World*. http://www.fordham.edu/halsall/mod/modsbook03.html. A good collection of short primary sources, including letters and diaries of early European explorers.

Machiavelli, Niccolò. *The Prince*. Trans. William J. Connell. Boston: Bedford/St. Martin's, 2004.

Tursun Beg. *The History of Mehmed the Conqueror*. Trans. Halil Inalcik and Rhoads Murphey. Minneapolis: Bibliotheca Islamica, 1978. A contemporary account of the Ottoman sultan who conquered Constantinople.

Film

1421: The Year China Discovered America. PBS Home Videos, 2004. 120 minutes. Recounts the controversial claim that Zheng He led an armada of Chinese ships as far as the western coast of North America.

Africa before the Europeans. Insight Media, 1985. 26 minutes. Includes segments on both the Songhay Empire and the kingdom of Benin.

Akbar the Great, Mogul Emperor of India. Films for the Humanities and Sciences, 2000. 54 minutes. Examines Akbar's successful campaign to forge an empire in India based on political stability and religious tolerance.

The Aztecs. Films for the Humanities and Sciences, 1996. 48 minutes. Explores Aztec history and culture, including the role of human sacrifice in Aztec society.

Discovery of a New World. Films for the Humanities and Sciences, 2004. 30 minutes. Examines European exploration and conquest with particularly good coverage of the late medieval context.

Exploration. Films for the Humanities and Sciences, 1998. 53 minutes. Explores comparatively the motivations for exploration, conquest, and colonization, contrasting the Chinese experience with that of the European powers.

The Great Age of Exploration. Insight Media, 1998. 30 minutes. Recounts the first century and a half of European oceanic exploration and discovery.

Machu Picchu Revealed. Insight Media, 1995. 20 minutes. Explores Incan civilization using Machu Picchu as a focus.

The Ottoman Empire. Films for the Humanities and Sciences, 1996. 47 minutes. Examines the emergence of the Ottoman Empire from 1453 into the sixteenth century, including good coverage of Ottoman interaction with Christian Europe.

The Renaissance. Insight Media, 1999. 48 minutes. Explores aspects of the Renaissance in Europe, including humanism, philosophy, and artistic developments.

Worlds of the Mayas, Aztecs, and Incas. Insight Media, 2003. 24 minutes. An up-to-date video that compares three great pre-Columbian civilizations in the Americas.

Yoruba: Nine Centuries of African Art and Culture. Insight Media, 1992. 15 minutes. Examines Yoruba history and culture through art.

THE EARLY MODERN WORLD
1450–1750

Outline: The Big Picture: Debating the Character of an Era

I. **It is common for historians to give a simple name to particular eras.**
   A. Such simplification is necessary,
   B. but it vastly oversimplifies historical reality.
II. **An Early Modern Era?**
   A. The period covered by Chapters 14–16 is usually labeled as "the early modern era."
      1. term suggests that signs of modernity (globalization, modern societies, and rising European presence in world affairs) are visible
   B. Globalization is visible in European exploration, conquest, and settlement in the Americas.
      1. Atlantic slave trade linked Africa to the Western Hemisphere
      2. New World silver let Europeans buy their way into Asian markets
      3. Columbian exchange created new networks of interaction
      4. Christianity became a truly world religion
      5. Russian, Chinese, and Ottoman expansion also played important parts in an emerging global web
   C. Signs of "modernity" appeared in several regions.
      1. modern population growth, thanks to foods from the Americas
         a. world population more than doubled between 1400 and 1800
      2. more highly commercialized economies developed in parts of Eurasia and the Americas, centered in large cities
      3. emergence of stronger and more cohesive states in various places
         a. promoted trade, manufacturing, and a common culture
         b. great increase in their military power, thanks to the "gunpowder revolution"
      4. Scientific Revolution transformed the worldview of an educated elite in Europe
III. **A Late Agrarian Era?**
   A. These signs of modernity are not the whole story and can be misleading.
      1. the future was still far from clear in 1750
   B. European political and military power was very limited in mainland Asia and Africa.

1. Islam was the most rapidly spreading faith in Asia and Africa
2. in 1750, Europe, India, and China were comparable in manufacturing output

C. There was little sign in 1750 that a modern industrial society was approaching.
   1. almost complete dependency on muscle, wind, and water for power
   2. long-established elites continued to provide leadership and enjoy privilege
      a. "lower class" primarily meant rural peasants, not urban workers
      b. rule was monarchic
      c. male dominance was assumed to be natural
   3. most of the world's peoples lived in long-established ways

D. For the majority of humankind, the period 1450–1750 marked the continuing development of traditional agrarian societies.
   1. the age was as much "late agrarian" as it was "early modern"

IV. **Chapters 14–16 highlight changes in the period, rather than what was traditional.**

Empires and Encounters
1450–1750

CHAPTER OVERVIEW

Chapter Objectives

- To introduce students to the variety of empires of the early modern period
- To emphasize that empire building was not just a Western European phenomenon
- To explore the range of colonial societies that evolved and the reasons for differences between them
- To emphasize the massive social reordering that attended European colonization in the Western Hemisphere

Chapter Outline

I. Opening Vignette
   A. Around the end of the twentieth century, there were many reactions to the empire building of the early modern period.
      1. Uighur attempts to win independence from China
      2. Native American protests against 500th anniversary of Columbus's arrival in America
   B. Early modern European colonies were massively significant.
      1. Russians also constructed a major empire

   2. Qing dynasty China doubled in size
   3. Mughal Empire of India pulled together Hindus and Muslims
   4. Ottoman Empire reestablished some of the older political unity of the Islamic heartland
   C. The empires of the early modern era show a new stage in globalization.

II. European Empires in the Americas
   A. Western European empires were marked by maritime expansion.
      1. Spaniards in Caribbean, then on to Aztec and Inca empires
      2. Portuguese in Brazil
      3. British, French, and Dutch colonies in North America
      4. Europeans controlled most of the Americas by the mid-nineteenth century
   B. The European Advantage
      1. geography: European Atlantic states were well positioned for involvement in the Americas
         a. the Atlantic's fixed winds helped, once they were understood
      2. need: Chinese and Indians had such rich markets in the Indian Ocean that there wasn't much incentive to go beyond
      3. marginality: Europeans were aware of their marginal position in Eurasian commerce and wanted to change it
      4. rivalry: interstate rivalry drove rulers to compete

5. merchants: growing merchant class wanted direct access to Asian wealth
6. wealth and status: colonies were an opportunity for impoverished nobles and commoners
7. religion:
   a. crusading zeal
   b. persecuted minorities looking for more freedom
8. European states and trading companies mobilized resources well
   a. seafaring technology
   b. iron, gunpowder weapons, and horses gave Europeans an initial advantage over people in the Americas
9. Rivalries within the Americas provided allies for European invaders
C. The Great Dying—the demographic collapse of Native American societies **[see Lecture Strategy 1]**
   1. pre-Columbian Western Hemisphere had a population of perhaps 60 million–80 million
   2. no immunity to Old World diseases
   3. Europeans brought European and African diseases
      a. mortality rate of up to 90 percent among Native American populations
      b. native population nearly vanished in the Caribbean
      c. Central Mexico: population dropped from 10 million–20 million to around 1 million by 1650
      d. similar mortality in North America
D. The Columbian Exchange **[see Discussion Topic 1]**
   1. massive native mortality created a labor shortage in the Americas
   2. migrant Europeans and African slaves created entirely new societies
      a. brought plants and animals to the Americas
   3. American food crops (e.g., corn, potatoes, and cassava) spread widely in the Eastern Hemisphere
      a. potatoes especially allowed enormous population growth
      b. corn and sweet potatoes were important in China and Africa
   4. exchange with the Americas reshaped the world economy
      a. importation of millions of African slaves to the Americas
      b. new and lasting link among Africa, Europe, and the Americas
   5. network of communication, migration, trade, transfer of plants and animals (including microbes) is called "the Columbian exchange"
      a. the Atlantic world connected four continents
      b. Europeans got most of the rewards
         i. new information helped lead to the Scientific Revolution
         ii. colonies were an outlet for rapidly expanding European population
         iii. shift in the global balance of power to favor Europe

III. **Comparing Colonial Societies in the Americas** [see Lecture Strategy 2]
A. Europeans did not just conquer and govern established societies: They created wholly new societies.
   1. all were shaped by mercantilism—theory that governments should encourage exports and accumulate bullion to serve their countries
   2. colonies should provide closed markets for the mother country's manufactured goods
   3. but colonies differed widely, depending on native cultures and the sorts of economy that were established
B. In the Lands of the Aztecs and the Incas **[see Lecture Strategy 3]**
   1. Spanish conquest of the Aztec and Inca empires (early sixteenth century)
      a. the most wealthy, urbanized, and populous regions of the Western Hemisphere
      b. within a century, the Spaniards established major cities, universities, and a religious and bureaucratic infrastructure
   2. economic basis of the colonial society was commercial agriculture and mining (gold and silver)
      a. native peoples provided forced labor
   3. rise of a distinctive social order

a. replicated some of the Spanish class hierarchy

b. accommodated Indians, Africans, and racially mixed people

c. Spaniards were at the top, increasingly wanted a large measure of self-government from the Spanish Crown

    i. but the Spaniard minority was also divided

    ii. fights for privilege

    iii. church authorities often fought for better treatment of the native peoples

d. emergence of *mestizo* (mixed-race) population

    i. mestizos became a majority of the Mexican population by the nineteenth century

    ii. Hispanic in culture, but often looked down on

e. gross abuse and exploitation of the Indians

    i. massive death rate

    ii. attacks on their religion

    iii. forced relocations

    iv. many Indians adopted Spanish practices, but much of native tradition survived

f. more racial fluidity than in North America

C. Colonies of Sugar

1. lowland Brazil and the Caribbean developed a different society

    a. regions had not been home to great civilizations and didn't have great mineral wealth until the 1690s

    b. but sugar was in high demand in Europe

    c. these colonies produced almost solely for export

2. Arabs introduced large-scale sugar production to the Mediterranean

    a. Europeans transferred it to Atlantic islands and Americas

    b. Portuguese on Brazilian coast dominated the world sugar market 1570–1670

    c. then British, French, and Dutch in the Caribbean broke the Portuguese monopoly

3. sugar transformed Brazil and the Caribbean

    a. production was very labor intensive, worked best on large scale

    b. can be called the first modern industry

    c. had always been produced with massive use of slave labor

    d. Indians of the area were almost totally wiped out or fled

    e. planters turned to African slaves—80 percent of all Africans enslaved in the Americas ended up in Brazil and the Caribbean

        i. conditions were horrid

4. much more of Brazilian and Caribbean society was of African descent

    a. in Haiti in 1790, 93 percent of the population was entirely or partially of African descent

5. large mixed-race population provided much of urban skilled workforce and supervisors in sugar industry

    a. most were *mulattoes* (mixed Portuguese-African heritage), but Brazil had some 40 separate and named racially mixed groups

6. plantation complex based on African slavery spread to southern parts of North America

    a. but in North America, European women came earlier

    b. result was less racial mixing, less tolerance toward mixed blood

    c. sharply defined racial system evolved

    d. slavery was less harsh

        i. by about 1750, slaves in the United States could keep up their numbers by reproduction

        ii. but manumission and opportunities for free blacks were much greater in Brazil

        iii. in Latin America, color was only one criterion of social class

D. Settler Colonies in North America

1. a different sort of colonial society emerged in British colonies of New England, New York, and Pennsylvania

    a. British got into the game late; got the unpromising lands

    b. but British society was changing more rapidly than Catholic Spain

i. Catholic/Protestant conflict

ii. rise of a merchant capitalist class

iii. major cloth industry

iv. development of Parliament, breakdown of feudalism

2. many British colonists were trying to escape elements of European society

3. British settlers were more numerous; by 1750, they outnumbered Spaniards in New World by five to one

   a. by 1776, 90 percent of population of North American colonies was European

   b. Indians were killed off by disease and military policy

   c. small-scale farming didn't need slaves

4. England was mostly Protestant; didn't proselytize like the Catholics

   a. Protestant Bible-reading led to higher literacy among colonists

5. British colonies developed traditions of local self-government

   a. Britain didn't impose an elaborate bureaucracy like Spain

   b. British civil war (seventeenth century) distracted government from involvement in the colonies

6. North America gradually became dominant, more developed than South America

IV. The Steppes and Siberia: The Making of a Russian Empire [see Discussion Topic 2]

A. A small Russian state centered on Moscow began to emerge ca. 1500.

1. Moscow began to conquer neighboring cities

2. over three centuries grew into a massive empire

3. early expansion into the grasslands to south and east was for security against nomads

4. expansion into Siberia was a matter of opportunity (especially furs), not threat

B. Experiencing the Russian Empire

1. conquest was made possible by modern weapons and organization

   a. defeated peoples swore allegiance to the tsar and paid tribute

2. conquest brought devastating epidemics, especially in remote areas of

Siberia—locals had no immunity to smallpox and measles

3. pressure to convert to Christianity

   a. some tolerance of Islamic subjects (e.g., Catherine the Great)

4. large-scale settlement of Russians in the new lands, where they outnumbered the native population (e.g., in Siberia)

5. discouragement of pastoralism

6. many natives were Russified

C. Russians and Empire

1. with imperial expansion, Russians became a smaller proportion of the overall population

2. rich agricultural lands, furs, and minerals helped make Russia a great power by the eighteenth century

3. became an Asian power as well as a European one

4. long-term Russian identity problem

   a. expansion made Russia a very militarized state

   b. reinforced autocracy

5. colonization experience was different from the Americas

   a. conquest of territories with which Russia had long interacted

   b. conquest took place at the same time as development of the Russian state

   c. the Russian Empire remained intact until 1991

V. Asian Empires [see Classroom Activities 1 and 2]

A. Asian empires were regional, not global.

1. creation of Asian empires did not include massive epidemics

2. did not fundamentally transform their homelands like interaction with the Americas and Siberia did for European powers

B. Making China an Empire

1. Qing dynasty (1644–1912) launched enormous imperial expansion to the north and west

   a. Qing rulers were Manchu nomads who conquered China

2. nomads of the north and west were very familiar to the Chinese

a. 80-year-long Chinese conquest (1680–1760)

b. motivated by security fears; reaction to Zunghar state

3. China evolved into a Central Asian empire

4. conquered territory was ruled separately from the rest of China through the Court of Colonial Affairs

a. considerable use of local elites to govern

b. officials often imitated Chinese ways

c. but government did not try to assimilate conquered peoples

d. little Chinese settlement in the conquered regions

5. Russian and Chinese rule impoverished Central Asia, turned it into a backward region

a. nomadic society was largely destroyed

C. Muslims and Hindus in the Mughal Empire
[see Discussion Topic 3]

1. Mughals united much of India between 1526 and 1707

2. the Mughal Empire's most important divide was religious

a. some 20 percent of the population was Muslim; most of the rest were Hindu

3. Emperor Akbar (r. 1556–1605) attempted serious accommodation of the Hindu majority

a. brought many Hindus into the political-military elite

b. imposed a policy of toleration

c. abolished payment of *jizya* by non-Muslims

d. created a state cult that stressed loyalty to the emperor

e. Akbar and his successors encouraged a hybrid Indian-Persian-Turkic culture

4. Mughal toleration provoked reaction among some Muslims

a. Emperor Aurangzeb (r. 1658–1707) reversed Mughal policy, tried to impose Islamic supremacy

b. Aurangzeb banned *sati* (widow burning), music and dance at court, various vices

c. destruction of some Hindu temples

d. reimposition of jizya

5. Aurangzeb's policy provoked Hindu reaction

a. opposition movements fatally weakened the Mughal Empire after 1707

D. Muslims, Christians, and the Ottoman Empire

1. the Ottoman Empire was the Islamic world's most important empire in the early modern period

2. long conflict (1534–1639) between Sunni Ottomans and Shia Safavids

3. the Ottoman Empire was the site of a significant cross-cultural encounter

a. in Anatolia, most of the conquered Christians converted to Islam

b. in the Balkans, Christian subjects mostly remained Christian

i. few Turkish settlers in the region

ii. Ottomans accommodated the Christian churches

4. in the Balkans, many Christians welcomed Ottoman conquest

a. Ottoman taxed less and were less oppressive

b. Christian churches received considerable autonomy

c. Balkan elites were accepted among the Ottoman elite without conversion

5. Jewish refugees from Spain had more opportunities in the Ottoman Empire

6. *devshirme*: tribute of boys paid by Christian Balkan communities

a. boys were converted to Islam, trained to serve the state

b. the *devshirme* was a means of upward social mobility

7. the Ottoman state threatened Christendom

a. Europeans worried about a Muslim takeover of all Europe

8. some Europeans admired Ottoman rule

a. philosopher Jean Bodin (sixteenth century) praised Ottoman religious tolerance

b. European merchants evaded papal bans on selling firearms to the Turks

c. Ottoman women enjoyed relative freedom

VI. Reflections: Countering Eurocentrism . . . or Reflecting It? [see Classroom Activity 3]

A. The chapter brought together stories of European, Russian, Chinese, Mughal, and Ottoman colonization to counteract a Eurocentric view of the early modern world.

B. Western European empires still got pride of place because they were different and more significant than the others.
   1. they were something wholly new in human history
   2. they had a much greater impact on the people they incorporated

C. Eurocentrism continues to be a controversial issue among world historians.

USING *WAYS OF THE WORLD* IN THE CLASSROOM

Lecture Strategies

Lecture Strategy 1

"The quest for human rights in the Americas."
A useful way to approach the massive exploitation and abuse perpetrated by European colonizers in the Western Hemisphere (against both Native Americans and enslaved Africans) is to examine the people who took a stand for human rights. This can provide a more nuanced picture, not downplaying the human suffering inflicted by Europeans but at least recognizing that the picture was far from black and white. The objectives of this lecture strategy are:

• to examine in greater detail the deep human tragedy of the European invasion of the Americas
• to consider the fate of African slaves brought to the Western Hemisphere
• to consider how such massive enslavement fit into European religious and cultural beliefs in the early modern period
• to investigate the "voices of conscience" who were also products of early modern European beliefs and practices

A good place to begin is with the famous Dominican friar Bartolomé de Las Casas (1484–1566), whose revulsion at the treatment of Indians in the New World led to a lifelong crusade to help them. This is a rich story, including Las Casas's efforts to spread knowledge of the Indians' plight, debates in Spain, and even Emperor Charles V's command to halt all further Spanish expansion while examining the issue of the Indians' human rights. Other useful points to include in such a lecture are:

• how the Spanish *encomienda* system worked and its effects on the native population and slaves
• Aristotle's teaching that some peoples are naturally "slavish" and his influence on medieval and early modern European society
• Biblical support for slavery
• Thomas More's *Utopia* (1516) as a good example of positive valuation of peoples of the Western Hemisphere
• Michel de Montaigne's essay *On Cannibals* (1580) and its role in popularizing the idea of the "noble savage"
• The Law of Burgos (1512) regulating what was owed to Indian laborers
• The arguments of the Spanish legist Francisco de Vitoria (1530s) on Indian rights
• The papal bull *Sublimis Deus* (1537), declaring that Indians are fully human and capable of receiving Christianity
• The role of Spanish and Portuguese missionaries in educating and converting Indians
• Colonists' objections to royal and religious efforts to change things
• The "Black Legend"—Dutch propaganda against the Spaniards for their cruelty in the New World and elsewhere and how much of this propaganda can be accepted without question

Lecture Strategy 2

"A tale of two colonies."
The purpose of this lecture strategy is to present to the students, in greater depth than is possible in the chapter, a comparative study of two American colonies, one British and one Spanish or Portuguese. Its objectives are:

• to review and reinforce the chapter's lessons about the various types of European colonial society and the reasons for the differences between them

- to examine conditions in Britain and on the Iberian peninsula that helped create these differences
- to explore some of the long-term implications of the strong differences between the colonization of North America and that of South America

To make this lecture strategy attractive and accessible to students, it is useful to focus on only two colonies, weaving a narrative that includes the stories of individual colonists as much as possible. Lecturers can probably count on students remembering a bit about North American colonies from high school, but probably not much. Some colonies that are likely to work particularly well are:

North America

- Massachusetts (with dominant themes of flight from religious persecution, the intolerance of the settlers themselves, interaction with the Indians of the region, and trade companies)
- Virginia (especially handy if you wish to explore the differences in slavery between North and South America)
- Maryland (which began as the personal enterprise of Lord Baltimore, who intended the colony as a refuge for Catholics)

South America

- Brazil (with good material about slave rebellions)
- Mexico (in many ways the most important Spanish colony, with much readily available material about cultural accommodation as well as oppression)
- Peru (particularly interesting as an example of colonial resistance to Spanish edicts)

Comparative points to consider include:

- the role of religion (not just the issue of European flight from persecution, but also ecclesiastical authority in the colony and efforts to convert Indians and African slaves)
- governance (how great a role the European king in question played, compared to local or regional self-governance)
- cultural interchange and racial attitudes
- trade relations with Europe
- military preparedness

Lecture Strategy 3

"Spain at the center."

The purpose of this lecture strategy is to examine early modern Spain from three perspectives: as leader of colonization to the Americas; as "defender of Christendom" against the Ottomans in the Mediterranean; and as a developing nation-state within Europe, to explore reasons why it took on the other two roles. The objectives of this lecture strategy are:

- to encourage students to develop a more complex understanding of European states in the age of exploration
- to put the Ottomans into their proper place as key players in sixteenth-century Europe
- to explore the factors that drove Spaniards to such intense engagement in the New World

A good place to begin is with the union of Spain under Ferdinand and Isabella (1479). Some points to consider are:

- the centuries of rivalry between the various Spanish states before the union
- religious tensions with the large Jewish and Muslim populations of Spain
- the conquest of Granada in 1492
- the expulsion of Jews, and later the Muslims, from Spain
- the establishment of the Spanish Inquisition
- the desire to maintain "purity of blood"
- the poverty of much of the Spanish nobility
- the incapacity of the Spanish heiress Juana the Mad and inheritance by her son Charles
- the immensity of Charles V's empire

From there, go on to consider the leading concerns of Charles V (this is an interesting opportunity to get biographical), such as:

- the Reformation in Germany and his difficulties in curbing it
- resentment against his rule in the Netherlands
- the Turkish advance into central Europe and the immediate threat to Charles V's German lands
- difficulties in controlling highly independent *conquistadores* in America
- the role of Christianity and in particular of crusading ideology in shaping the choices of Charles V and others

While it probably would be useful to include brief coverage of the Spanish invasion of America, we recommend a broader view that considers what Charles V and his successors did with their 20-percent share of the profits of conquest. The lion's share of the money went to fight the Turks in the Mediterranean and in central Europe. Some key events to include are:

- the Battle of Mohács (1526) (Turkish defeat of Hungary)
- the Siege of Vienna (1529)
- the formation of "Holy Leagues" to combat the Ottomans
- the Ottoman sieges of Rhodes in 1480 and 1522
- the Ottoman siege of Malta in 1565
- the Battle of Lepanto (1570)

Things to Do in the Classroom

Discussion Topics

1. **Contextualization, large or small group.** "The New World as Europeans saw it."
Select a text by an early European explorer, conqueror, or settler in the Americas, short enough either to be read in class or to distribute beforehand for this discussion. Many texts are readily available. Some good options are:

- Christopher Columbus, *Journal*
- Christopher Columbus, *Letter to the King and Queen of Spain*
- Amerigo Vespucci, *Account of His First Voyage*
- John Cabot, *Voyage to North America*
- Hernan Cortés, *Second Letter to Charles V*
- William Bradford, *History of Plymouth Plantation*

(See under "Literature" in the Further Reading section of this chapter for online selections of all these works.)

Ask students the following questions:

- What can the text teach about the author's home country?
- What is the author's attitude toward Native Americans?

2. **Misconception/Difficult Topic, large or small group.** "Exploration and colonization happened only in the Atlantic world."

The chapter provides much valuable information about Russian colonization, a useful corrective to the tendency to put the Americas at the center of colonial narrative. Ask students to compare the Russian expansion into Siberia with the Western European colonization of the Americas, coming up with at least three points of similarity and three points of difference.

3. **Comparison, large or small group.** "Conquest and religion in the Old World and the New."
Religion is a major sub-theme of colonization and conquest more generally. Ask students to chart out the religious policies of various conquerors (Spaniards, Brazilians, Britons, Russians, Ottomans, and Mughals) and then rate them on scales of interest in religion and religious tolerance. Some supplemental questions to ask are:

- When was religious toleration most likely?
- What conditions made it most likely that the conquerors would try to convert their subjects?
- Do you see a difference in conquerors' reactions depending on whether the subjects' religion is monotheistic or polytheistic?
- In the early modern period, do some religions (or at least the rulers who practiced them) appear to have been more tolerant than others?
- What nonreligious factors might affect how tolerant a state was toward religious diversity?

Classroom Activities

1. **Map-analysis exercise, large or small group.** "Colonial powers, before and after."
Display a map, preferably a physical map of the world. Ask students to identify the core lands of the states that became major imperial powers in the early modern period and then to identify the lands that those states succeeded in claiming. This exercise is particularly effective if your projection equipment allows you to color over or circle parts of the map. Discuss the implications of these expansions.

2. **Role-playing exercise, small group.** "My colony's better than your colony!"
Choose three small groups of students to engage in a debate; the rest of the class will serve as audience and judges. The three debating groups are:

- representatives of the Massachusetts Bay Company in the first generation of the colony

- representatives of the governor of Mexico ca. 1550
- representatives of the tsar of Russia in Siberia ca. 1750

The question for debate is: Which colonial system is best? (Note that, to deal with this question effectively, the students will have to define in some way what "best" means; the assumption is that they will represent the interests of the colonizers, rather than those of the subject peoples.)

3. **Clicker question.** Is this chapter too Eurocentric?

Key Terms

Akbar: The most famous emperor of India's Mughal Empire (r. 1556–1605); his policies are noted for their efforts at religious tolerance and inclusion. (*pron.* AHK-bar)

Aurangzeb: Mughal emperor (r. 1658–1707) who reversed his predecessors' policies of religious tolerance and attempted to impose Islamic supremacy. (*pron.* ow-rang-ZEB)

Columbian exchange: The massive transatlantic interaction and exchange between the Americas and Afro-Eurasia that began in the period of European exploration and colonization.

conquistadores: Spanish conquerors of the Native American lands, most notably the Aztec and Inca empires. (*pron.* kon-KEY-stuh-dor-ays)

Constantinople, 1453: Constantinople, the capital and almost the only outpost left of the Byzantine Empire, fell to the army of the Ottoman sultan Mehmed II "the Conqueror" in 1453, an event that marked the end of Christian Byzantium.

creoles: Spaniards born in the Americas.

devshirme: The tribute of boy children that the Ottoman Turks levied from their Christian subjects in the Balkans; the Ottomans raised the boys for service in the civil administration or in the elite Janissary infantry corps. (*pron.* dev-sheer-MEH)

fixed winds: The prevailing winds of the Atlantic, which blow steadily in the same direction; an understanding of these winds made European exploration and colonization of the Americas possible.

"great dying," the: Term used to describe the devastating demographic impact of European-borne epidemic diseases on the Americas.

jizya: Special tax levied on non-Muslims in Islamic states; the Mughal Empire was notable for abolishing the jizya for a time. (*pron.* JIZ-yah)

mercantilism: An economic theory that argues that governments best serve their states' economic interests by encouraging exports and accumulating bullion.

mestizo: Literally, "mixed"; a term used to describe the mixed-race population of Spanish colonial societies in the Americas. (*pron.* mess-TEE-zoh)

Mughal Empire: One of the most successful empires of India, a state founded by Muslim Turks who invaded India in 1526; their rule was noted for efforts to create partnerships between Hindus and Muslims. (*pron.* MOO-guhl)

mulattoes: Term commonly used for people of mixed African and European blood.

Ottoman Empire: Major Islamic state centered on Anatolia that came to include the Balkans, the Near East, and much of North Africa.

peninsulares: In the Spanish colonies of Latin America, the term used to refer to people who had been born in Spain; they claimed superiority over Spaniards born in the Americas. (*pron.* pen-in-soo-LAHR-es)

plantation complex: Agricultural system based on African slavery that was used in Brazil, the Caribbean, and the southern colonies of North America.

Qing dynasty: Ruling dynasty of China from 1644 to 1912; the Qing rulers were originally from Manchuria, which had conquered China. (*pron.* ching)

settler colonies: Colonies in which the colonizing people settled in large numbers, rather than simply spending relatively small numbers to exploit the region; particularly noteworthy in the case of the British colonies in North America.

Siberia: Russia's great frontier region, a vast territory of what is now central and eastern Russia, most of it unsuited to agriculture but rich in mineral resources and fur-bearing animals.

yasak: Tribute that Russian rulers demanded from the native peoples of Siberia, most often in the form of furs. (*pron.* YAH-sahk)

Zunghars: Western Mongol group that created a substantial state (1671–1760); the Zunghar threat provoked Qing expansion into Central Asia. (*pron.* ZOON-gars)

ANSWER GUIDELINES FOR CHAPTER QUESTIONS

The two sets of questions that follow appear in the textbook at the end of the chapter and in the margins of the reading. They are also provided in the Computerized Test Bank with answer guidelines, for your convenience.

The Big Picture Questions

1. In comparing the European empires in the Americas with the Russian, Chinese, Mughal, and Ottoman empires, should world historians emphasize the similarities or the differences? What are the implications of each approach?

• In terms of similarities, one could emphasize that Europe was not the only center of vitality and expansion during the early modern period and that the interaction of culturally different peoples occurred in the European, Russian, Chinese, Mughal, and Ottoman empires.

• However, there were important differences between these empires: the European empires represented something wholly new in human history through their creation of an interacting Atlantic world;

• they had a far more significant impact on the people that they incorporated than did the other empires;

• and they had a far wider impact on the world as a whole.

• By emphasizing similarities, one counteracts Eurocentrism but runs the risk of downplaying the significant and unique developments that the Western European empires contributed to the course of world history.

• By emphasizing differences, one gives weight to the significant and unique developments that the European empires contributed to the course of world history but runs the risk of overemphasizing the importance of Western Europe to the point of downplaying or neglecting the other sources of vitality, expansion, and cross-cultural interaction that shaped the period.

2. In what different ways was European colonial rule expressed and experienced in the Americas?

• European colonial rule in the Americas varied with the cultures and policies of the colonizing power, the character of the Native American cultures, and the kind of economy established in a particular region.

• In the lands of the Aztecs and the Incas, the Spanish empire ruled over the most densely settled of the indigenous populations in the Americas and developed an economic system based on commercial agriculture and mining. Under such circumstances, colonial rule replicated something of the Spanish class hierarchy while accommodating the racially and culturally different Indians and Africans.

• In the plantation colonies of Brazil and the Caribbean, colonial powers ruled over regions where no earlier civilization existed and where the production of sugar for export defined the economy. In these regions, large numbers of Africans were imported as slave labor, and a considerable amount of racial mixing took place. From the mixed-race population were drawn much of the urban skilled workforce and supervisors in the sugar industry, as well as some prominent members of the community. A variation on the colonial rule of a plantation-based economy occurred in British North America, where the raising of different crops (including tobacco, cotton, rice, and indigo), less racial mixing, and a self-reproducing slave workforce shaped a different society.

• A third distinctive type of colonial society emerged in the northern British colonies of New England, New York, and Pennsylvania. Upon the arrival of British settlers, these regions were not heavily settled with Native Americans, in part because of the ravages of European-borne epidemic diseases. Because of the availability of land, the climate and geography of North America, and the "outsider" status of many British settlers, they set up an economic and social system of small independent farmers without sharp class hierarchy, large rural estates, or dependent laborers. Because of weak British rule, the largely literate population of the region developed traditions of local self-government, elected colonial assemblies, and vigorously contested the prerogatives of royal governors sent to administer their affairs.

3. Why did the European empires in the Americas have such an enormously greater impact on the

conquered people than did the Chinese, Mughal, and Ottoman empires?

• Unlike in the Eurasian empires, European ironworking technology, gunpowder weapons, and horses initially had no parallel in the Americas.

• European germs and diseases to which Native Americans had no immunities decimated indigenous populations, sometimes in advance of the Europeans' actual arrival.

4. In what ways did the empires of the early modern era continue patterns of earlier empires? In what ways did they depart from those patterns?

• Early modern empires continued many patterns of earlier empires, including rule over multiple cultural regions;

• use of coercion in their creation and maintenance;

• and the use of older imperial traditions of government, taxation, and law to administer the newer empires.

• However, those empires created by Western Europeans departed from previous patterns because they were initiated by maritime expansion;

• they conquered territories an ocean away from their imperial heartlands, rather than adjacent to them;

• the empires lay at the heart of patterns of global exchange that did not exist before their creation.

Margin Review Questions

Q. *What enabled Europeans to carve out huge empires an ocean away from their homelands?*

• Europeans were much closer to the Americas than were their potential Asian competitors.

• Europeans were powerfully motivated after 1200 to gain access to the world of Eurasian commerce.

• Groups within European society—including competing monarchs, merchants, impoverished nobles and commoners, Christian missionaries, and persecuted minorities—all had strong, if different, motivations for participating in empire building.

• European states and trading companies enabled the effective mobilization of both human and material resources.

• European seafaring technology, built on Chinese and Islamic precedents, allowed Europeans to cross the Atlantic with growing ease.

• European ironworking technology, gunpowder weapons, and horses initially had no parallel in the Americas.

• Divisions within and between local societies provided allies for European invaders.

• European germs and diseases to which Native Americans had no immunities decimated society after society, sometimes in advance of the Europeans' actual arrival.

Q. *What large-scale transformations did European empires generate?*

• European empire building caused the demographic collapse of Native American societies.

• Combinations of indigenous, European, and African peoples created entirely new societies in the Americas.

• Large-scale exchanges of plants and animals transformed the crops and animals raised both in the Americas and in the Eastern Hemisphere. This was the largest and most consequential exchange of plants and animals to this point in human history, and it remade the biological environment of the planet.

• The silver mines of Mexico and Peru fueled both transatlantic and transpacific commerce.

• The need for plantation workers and the sugar and cotton trade created a lasting link among Africa, Europe, and the Americas, while scattering peoples of African origins throughout the Western Hemisphere.

• The "Columbian exchange" produced an interacting Atlantic world connecting four continents.

• New information flooded into Europe, shaking up conventional understandings of the world and contributing to a revolutionary new way of thinking known as the Scientific Revolution.

• Profits from the colonial trade provided one of the foundations on which Europe's Industrial Revolution was built.

• Colonial empires provided outlets for the rapidly growing population of European societies and represented an enormous extension of European civilization.

• Colonial empires of the Americas facilitated a changing global balance of power, which now thrust the previously marginal Western Europeans into an increasingly central and commanding role on the world stage.

Q. *What was the economic foundation of colonial rule in Mexico and Peru? How did it shape the kinds of societies that arose there?*

• The economic foundation of colonial rule lay in commercial agriculture and in silver and gold mining based on forced labor and wage labor by indigenous populations.

• On this economic base, a distinctive social order grew up, replicating something of the Spanish class hierarchy while accommodating the racially and culturally different Indians and Africans as well as growing numbers of racially mixed people. Spaniards, *mestizos,* and Indians represented the major social groups in the colonial lands of what had been the Inca and Aztec empires, while African slaves and freemen were far less numerous than elsewhere in the Americas. The society was dominated by Europeans, but with a rather more fluid and culturally blended society than in the racially rigid colonies of North America. *Mestizos* in particular found some social movement possible.

Q. *How did the plantation societies of Brazil and the Caribbean differ from those of southern colonies in British North America?*

• The social outcomes of these plantation colonies were quite different. In North America, there was less racial mixing and less willingness to recognize the offspring of such unions and accord them a place in society.

• Slavery in North America was different, being perhaps less harsh there than in the sugar colonies. By 1750, slaves in the United States had become self-reproducing, and a century later almost all North American slaves had been born in the New World. That was never the case in Brazil and the Caribbean.

• Many more slaves were voluntarily set free by their owners in Brazil than was ever the case in North America, and free blacks and mulattoes in Brazil had far greater opportunities than did their counterparts in North America.

• Ideas about race differed. In North America, any African ancestry, no matter how small or distant, made a person "black"; in Brazil, an individual of African and non-African ancestry was considered, not black, but some other mixed-race category. Moreover, color was only one criterion of class status in Brazil, and the perception of color changed with the educational or economic standing of individuals.

Q. *What distinguished the British settler colonies of North America from their counterparts in Latin America?*

• Many of the British settlers sought to escape aspects of an old European society rather than to recreate it, as was the case for most Spanish and Portuguese colonists.

• The easy availability of land, the climate and geography of North America, and the "outsider" status of many British settlers made it even more difficult to follow the Spanish or Portuguese colonial pattern of sharp class hierarchy, large rural estates, and dependent laborers.

• British settlers in North America were much more numerous than Spanish or Portuguese settlers in Latin America, making up some 90 percent or more of the population of the New England and middle Atlantic colonies by the time of the American Revolution.

• The British colonies were almost pure settler colonies, without the racial mixing that was so prominent in Spanish and Portuguese territories.

• A largely Protestant England was far less interested in spreading Christianity among the remaining native peoples than were the large and well-funded missionary societies of Catholic Spain. Moreover, church and state were not so closely connected in the British colonies as they were in Latin America.

• British colonies developed greater mass literacy and traditions of local self-government and vigorously contested the prerogatives of royal governors sent to administer their affairs.

• Britain had nothing resembling the elaborate bureaucracy that governed Spanish colonies.

Q. *What motivated Russian empire building?*

• Russian expansion into the grasslands south and east of the Russian heartland was driven by the problem of security. The pastoral peoples of this region frequently raided Russian territory, selling many captives into slavery.

• Russian expansion into Siberia was driven by demand on the world market for the pelts of fur-bearing animals, although later some agricultural settlement took place. The motivations of defending Russian frontiers, enhancing the power of the Russian state, and bringing Christianity, civilization, and enlightenment to the indigenous peoples were also cited by political leaders and educated Russians generally.

Q. *How did the Russian Empire transform the life of its conquered people and of the Russian homeland itself?*

- In terms of its conquered people, conquest meant the taking of an oath of loyalty to the Russian ruler;
  - the payment of tribute;
  - devastating epidemics, particularly in the more remote regions of Siberia where local people had little immunity to smallpox or measles;
    - intermittent pressure to convert to Christianity;
    - the influx of Russian settlers;
    - the loss of hunting grounds and pasturelands to Russian agricultural settlers, which disrupted the local economy and left local populations dependent on Russian markets.
- In terms of the impact of the empire on the Russian homeland, it diminished the proportion of Russians in the overall population of the empire;
    - the wealth of empire played a major role in making Russia one of the great powers of Europe by the eighteenth century;
      - it created problems of identity;
      - it made Russia a highly militarized state and reinforced the highly autocratic character of the Russian state.

Q. *What were the major features of Chinese empire building in the early modern era?*

- Chinese empire building vastly enlarged the territorial size of China and brought a number of non-Chinese people into the kingdom.
- It was driven largely by security concerns.
- Conquered regions in central Eurasia were administered separately from the rest of China.
- The empire made active use of local notables.
- Chinese officials generally did not seek to assimilate local people into Chinese culture and showed considerable respect for the Mongolian, Tibetan, and Muslim cultures of the region.

Q. *How did Mughal attitudes and policies toward Hindus change from the time of Akbar to that of Aurangzeb?*

- Akbar recognized the fundamental reality that Hindus made up a majority of the population of the Mughal Empire and acted deliberately to accommodate the Hindu majority through actions that included allowing the Hindu princesses that he married to keep their Hindu faith;

- incorporating a substantial number of Hindus into the political-military elite of the empire;
  - supporting the building of Hindu temples;
  - imposing a policy of toleration;
  - deliberately restraining the more militantly Islamic ulama;
  - removing the special tax on non-Muslims;
  - promoting a state cult that drew on Islam, Hinduism, and Zoroastrianism.
- Aurangzeb, on the other hand, reversed Akbar's policy of accommodation by taking actions that included the forbidding of the Hindu practice of *sati*;
  - banning music and dance at court;
  - banning gambling, drinking, prostitution, and narcotics;
  - destroying some Hindu temples;
  - reimposing the special tax on non-Muslims;
  - posting "censors of public morals" to large cities to enforce Islamic law.

Q. *In what ways was the Ottoman Empire important for Europe in the early modern era?*

- The Ottoman Empire represented a military threat to Europe;
  - impressed some European intellectuals because of its religious tolerance;
  - occasionally allied with France against their common enemy of Habsburg Austria;
  - was an important trading partner.

ADDITIONAL RESOURCES FOR CHAPTER 14

Additional Bedford/St. Martin's Resources

FOR INSTRUCTORS

Computerized Test Bank

This test bank provides over thirty exercises per chapter, including multiple-choice, fill-in-the-blank, short-answer, and full-length essay questions. Instructors can customize quizzes, add or edit both questions and answers, and export questions and answers to a variety of formats, including WebCT and Blackboard. The disc includes correct answers and essay outlines.

Instructor's Resource CD-ROM

This disc provides instructors with ready-made and customizable PowerPoint multimedia presentations built around chapter outlines, maps, figures, and all images from the textbook, plus JPEG versions of all maps, figures, and images.

The following maps and images from Chapter 14 are available in both JPEG and PowerPoint format on the Instructor's Resource CD-ROM:

- Map 14.1: European Colonial Empires in the Americas (p. 405)
- Map 14.2: The Russian Empire (p. 418)
- Map 14.3: The Ottoman Empire (p. 426)
- The Mughal Empire (p. 402)
- Plants and Animals of the Columbian Exchange (p. 408)
- Mestizos (p. 411)
- Plantation Life in the Caribbean (p. 413)
- A Cossack Jail (p. 419)
- The Ottoman Siege of Vienna, 1683 (p. 428)

FOR STUDENTS

Documents and Essays from *Worlds of History: A Comparative Reader,* Third Edition (Volume 2)

The following documents, essays, and illustrations to accompany Chapter 14 are available in Chapter 2 of Volume 2 of this reader by Kevin Reilly:

- Bernal Díaz, from *The Conquest of New Spain*
- From *The Broken Spears: The Aztec Account of the Conquest of Mexico*
- Bartolomeo de Las Casas, from *The Devastation of the Indies*
- *Two European Views of Native Americans* (De Bry's engraving of cannibals and Albert Eckhout's Tapuya native)
- David Pieterzen deVries, *A Dutch Massacre of the Algonquins*
- Nzinga Mbemba, *Appeal to the King of Portugal*
- William Bosman, *Slave Trader*
- Olaudah Equiano, *Enslaved Captive*

Online Study Guide at bedfordstmartins.com/strayer

The Online Study Guide helps students synthesize the material from the text as well as practice the skills historians use to make sense of the past. Each chapter of the Online Study Guide contains specific testing exercises, including a multiple-choice self-test that focuses on important conceptual ideas; an identification quiz that helps students remember key people, places, and events; a flashcard activity that tests students on their knowledge of key terms; and two interactive map activities intended to strengthen students' geographic skills. Instructors can monitor students' progress through an online Quiz Gradebook or receive email updates.

Further Reading

Cook, Noble. *Born to Die: Disease and the New World Conquest, 1492–1650.* Cambridge: Cambridge University Press, 1998. A chilling look at the impact of epidemic disease on the peoples of the Americas.

Crosby, Alfred. *The Columbian Exchange.* Westport, CT: Greenwood, 1972. The classic study of the Columbian exchange.

Crosby, Alfred. *Ecological Imperialism.* Cambridge: Cambridge University Press, 1986. A more up-to-date discussion of the impact of biological exchange by a leading scholar in the field.

Discoverers Web, http://www.win.tue.nl/cs/fm/engels/discovery/. A great collection of Internet resources on exploration and discovery, ranging from ancient explorers to visits to the North and South poles.

Elliott, John H. *Empires of the Atlantic World.* New Haven: Yale University Press, 2007. A magisterial study of the British and Spanish empires in the Americas.

The History Guide: Resources for the Study of the Age of Exploration, http://www.historyguide.org/earlymod/exploration.html. An excellent selection of links to Internet sources on the topic, as well as a substantial bibliography (though some of the works listed there are badly dated).

Russia and the Former U.S.S.R., http://www.teacheroz.com/russia.htm. An excellent guide to Russian history on the Internet.

Stevens, Carol Belkin. *Russia's Wars of Emergence, 1460–1730*. London: Longman, 2007. An interesting study of the early Russian expansion.

Waley-Cohen, Joanna. *The Culture of War in China: Empire and the Military under the Qing Dynasty*. London: I. B. Tauris, 2006. A useful study of how China's expansion into Central Asia affected societal attitudes.

Literature

Babur. *The Baburnama*. Trans. W. M. Thackston. New York: Modern Library, 2002. A fascinating memoir by the founder of the Mughal Empire.

Columbus, Christopher. *The Four Voyages*. Trans. J. M. Cohen. London: Penguin, 1992. A readable translation of Columbus's journals.

Cortés, Hernan. *Letters from Mexico*. Trans. Anthony Pagden. 2nd ed. New Haven: Yale University Press, 2001. Letters written to Emperor Charles V, masterpieces of self-justification and glorification.

Díaz del Castillo, Bernal. *The Conquest of New Spain*. Trans. John M. Cohen. London: Penguin, 1963. A contemporary account of the Spanish conquest of the Aztec Empire.

Halsall, Paul, ed. *Internet Medieval Sourcebook* (Exploration). http://www.fordham.edu/halsall/sbook.html. A collection of texts by early explorers, including excerpts from Christopher Columbus's journals, accounts of John Cabot's voyages, and Sir Walter Raleigh's *Discovery of Guiana*.

Halsall, Paul, ed. *Internet Modern History Sourcebook* (Colonial North America and Colonial South America). http://www.fordham.edu/halsall/mod/modsbook.html. A good collection of readings short enough for classroom use, including, among others, William Bradford's *History of Plymouth Plantation* and Hernan Cortés's accounts of his invasion of Mexico.

Las Casas, Bartolomé de. *A Short Account of the Destruction of the Indies*. Trans. Nigel Griffin. London: Penguin, 1992. Short enough to assign to a class, this is an account of Spanish atrocities in the New World written by the greatest spokesman for Native American rights of the colonial period.

Leon-Portilla, Miguel, ed. *The Broken Spears: The Aztec Account of the Conquest of Mexico*. 2nd ed. Boston: Beacon Press, 1992. Leon-Portilla has assembled Aztec accounts from several centuries to produce a narrative of the Spanish invasion from the Aztec perspective.

More, Thomas. *Utopia*. Trans. Paul Turner. London: Penguin, 2003. This classic by Thomas More, the greatest humanist of sixteenth-century England, is a revealing look at European philosophy and attitudes toward the New World.

Film

Akbar the Great, Mogul Emperor of India. Films for the Humanities and Sciences, 2000. 54 minutes. Examines Akbar's successful campaign to forge an empire in India based on political stability and religious tolerance.

Black Sugar. Films for the Humanities and Sciences, 1989. 26 minutes. Presents the African slave trade from a West African perspective.

The Conquest of Mexico. Films for the Humanities and Sciences. 35 minutes. Provides portraits of both Hernan Cortés and the Aztec civilization that he conquered, along with an examination of the military campaign masterminded by Cortés.

Conquistadores. Four-part series. PBS Home Video, 2001. 60 minutes each. Examines the Spanish leaders who conquered the Aztec and Inca empires, laying the foundation for the Spanish Empire in the Americas.

The Ottoman Empire. Films for the Humanities and Sciences, 1996. 47 minutes. Examines the emergence of the Ottoman Empire from 1453 to the sixteenth century, including good coverage of Ottoman interaction with Christian Europe.

Global Commerce
1450–1750

CHAPTER OVERVIEW

Chapter Objectives

- To explore the creation of the first true global economy in the period 1450–1750
- To examine Western European commercial expansion in a context that gives due weight to the contributions of other societies
- To encourage appreciation of China as the world's largest economy in the early modern period
- To increase student awareness of the high costs of the commercial boom of the early modern period in ecological and human terms
- To investigate the various models of trading post empires that were created in this period

Chapter Outline

I. **Opening Vignette**
    A. The Atlantic slave trade was and is enormously significant.
    B. The slave trade was only one part of the international trading networks that shaped the world between 1450 and 1750.
       1. Europeans broke into the Indian Ocean spice trade
       2. American silver allowed greater European participation in the commerce of East Asia

   3. fur trapping and trading changed commerce and the natural environment
    C. Europeans were increasingly prominent in long-distance trade, but other peoples were also important.
    D. Commerce and empire were the two forces that drove globalization between 1450 and 1750.
       1. gradual creation of a single "new world" from the many premodern "old worlds"

II. **Europeans and Asian Commerce** [see Classroom Activity 1]
    A. Europeans wanted commercial connections with Asia.
       1. Columbus and Vasco da Gama both sought a route to Asia
       2. motivation above all was the desire for spices (though other Eastern products were also sought) **[see Discussion Topic 1]**
       3. European civilization had recovered from the Black Death
       4. national monarchies were learning to govern more effectively
          a. substantial military buildup (with gunpowder weapons)
       5. some cities were becoming international trade centers
          a. development of a more capitalist economy
       6. the problems of old trade systems from the Indian Ocean network
          a. Muslims controlled supply

b. Venice was chief middleman for trade with Alexandria; other states resented it

c. desire to find Prester John and enlist his support in the Crusades

d. constant trade deficit with Asia

    i. Europeans longed for sources of precious metals

B. A Portuguese Empire of Commerce

  1. Indian Ocean commerce was highly rich and diverse

  2. Portuguese did not have goods of a quality for effective competition

  3. Portuguese took to piracy on the sea lanes **[see Lecture Strategy 1]**

    a. Portuguese ships were more maneuverable, carried cannons

    b. established fortified bases at key locations (Mombasa, Hormuz, Goa, Malacca, Macao)

      i. all but Macao were taken by force

  4. Portuguese created a "trading post empire"

    a. goal was to control commerce, not territories or populations

    b. operated by force of arms, not economic competition

    c. at height, controlled about half of the spice trade to Europe

  5. Portuguese gradually assimilated to Indian Ocean trade patterns

    a. carried Asian goods to Asian ports

    b. many Portuguese settled in Asian or African ports

    c. their trading post empire was in steep decline by 1600

C. Spain and the Philippines

  1. Spain was the first to challenge Portugal's control of Asian trade

  2. establishment of a Spanish base in the Philippines

    a. first encountered when Ferdinand Magellan circumnavigated the globe (1519–1521)

    b. Philippines were organized in small, competitive chiefdoms

    c. Spaniards established full colonial rule there (takeover occurred 1565–1650)

    d. the Philippines remained a Spanish colonial territory until 1898, when U.S. assumed control

  3. major missionary campaign made Filipino society the only major Christian outpost in Asia

    a. competition with Islam on the island of Mindanao

  4. Spaniards introduced forced relocation, tribute, taxes, unpaid labor

    a. large estates for Spanish settlers, religious orders, and Filipino elite

    b. women's ritual and healing roles were attacked

  5. Manila became a major center with a diverse population

  6. periodic revolts by the Chinese population; Spaniards expelled or massacred them several times

D. The East India Companies **[see Lecture Strategy 2]**

  1. Dutch and English both entered Indian Ocean commerce in the early seventeenth century

    a. soon displaced the Portuguese

    b. competed with each other

  2. ca. 1600: both the Dutch and the English organized private trading companies to handle Indian Ocean trade

    a. merchants invested, shared the risks

    b. Dutch and British East India companies were chartered by their respective governments

    c. had power to make war and govern conquered peoples

  3. established their own trading post empires

    a. Dutch empire was focused on Indonesia

    b. English empire was focused on India

    c. French company was also established

  4. Dutch East India Company

    a. controlled both shipping and production of cloves, cinnamon, nutmeg, and mace

    b. seized small spice-producing islands and forced people to sell only to the Dutch

      i. case of Banda Islands: Dutch killed or enslaved almost the entire population (15,000 people); replaced them with Dutch planters and slaves

    c. destroyed the local economy of the Spice Islands; made the Dutch rich

5. British East India Company
   a. was not as well financed or as commer-cially sophisticated as the Dutch; couldn't break into the Spice Islands
   b. established three major trade settlements in India (seventeenth century)
      i. Bombay
      ii. Calcutta
      iii. Madras
   c. British navy gained control of Arabian Sea and Persian Gulf
   d. could not compete with the Mughal Empire on land
   e. negotiated with local rulers for peaceful establishment of trade bases
   f. Britons traded pepper and other spices, but cotton textiles became more important
6. Dutch and English also became involved in "carrying trade" within Asia
7. both gradually evolved into typical colonial domination

E. Asian Commerce
1. European presence was much less significant in Asia than in Americas or Africa
2. Europeans were no real military threat to Asia
3. the case of Japan **[see Lecture Strategy 3]**
   a. Portuguese reached Japan in the mid-sixteenth century
   b. Japan at the time was divided by constant conflict among feudal lords (*daimyo*) supported by *samurai*
   c. at first, Europeans were welcome
      i. around 300,000 Japanese converted to Christianity
   d. but Japan unified politically under the Tokugawa *shogun* in the early seven-teenth century
      i. increasingly regarded Europeans as a threat to unity
      ii. expulsion of missionaries, massive persecution of Christians
      iii. Japanese were barred from travel abroad
      iv. Europeans were banned, except the Dutch at a single site

   e. Japan was closed off from Europe from 1650 to 1850
4. Asian merchants continued to operate, despite European presence
   a. overland trade within Asia remained in Asian hands
   b. tens of thousands of Indian merchants lived throughout Central Asia, Persia, and Russia

III. **Silver and Global Commerce**
A. The silver trade was even more important than the spice trade in creating a global exchange network.
1. enormous silver deposits were discovered in Bolivia and Japan in the mid-sixteenth century
2. in the early modern period, Spanish America produced around 85 percent of the world's silver
   a. the Philippines were the critical link between Spanish America and Asian markets
B. China's economy was huge and had a growing demand for silver.
1. 1570s: the Chinese government consolidated taxes into a single tax to be paid in silver
   a. value of silver skyrocketed
   b. foreigners with silver could purchase more Chinese products than before
C. Silver was central to world trade.
1. "silver drain" to Asia: bulk of the world's silver supply ended up in China (most of the rest reached other parts of Asia)
2. Spanish silver brought to Europe was used to buy Asian goods
3. silver bought African slaves and Asian spices
4. the Spanish "piece of eight" was widely used for international exchange
5. Potosí, Bolivia, became the largest city in the Americas (population: 160,000) because it was at the world's largest silver mine
   a. the city's wealthy European elite lived in luxury
   b. Native American miners lived in horrid conditions
D. Silver vastly enriched the Spanish monarchy.

   1. caused inflation, not real economic growth in Spain
      a. Spanish economy was too rigid
      b. Spanish aristocrats were against economic enterprise
   2. Spain lost its dominance when the value of silver fell ca. 1600
   E. Japanese government profited more from silver production than did Spain.
      1. Tokugawa shoguns used silver revenues to defeat rivals and unify the country
      2. worked with the merchant class to develop a market-based economy
      3. heavy investment in agriculture and industry
      4. averted ecological crisis, limited population growth
   F. In China, silver further commercialized the country's economy.
      1. people needed to sell something to obtain silver to pay their taxes
      2. economy became more regionally specialized
      3. deforestation was a growing problem; wasn't addressed as it was in Japan
   G. Europeans were essentially middlemen in world trade.
      1. funneled American silver to Asia
      2. Asian commodities took market share from European products

IV. The "World Hunt": Fur in Global Commerce [see Discussion Topic 2]
   A. Europe's supply of fur-bearing animals was sharply diminished by 1500.
      1. the Little Ice Age may have increased demand for furs
   B. There was intense competition for the furs of North America.
      1. French were prominent in St. Lawrence valley, Great Lakes, and along the Mississippi
      2. British traders moved into Hudson Bay region
      3. Dutch moved into what is now New York
   C. North American fur trade
      1. Europeans usually traded with Indians for furs or skins, rather than hunting or trapping animals themselves

   2. beaver and other furry animals were driven to near extinction
   3. by the 1760s, hunters in the southeastern British colonies took around 500,000 deer every year
   4. trade was profitable for the Indians
      a. received many goods of real value
      b. Huron chiefs enhanced their authority with control of European goods
      c. but Indians fell prey to European diseases
      d. fur trade generated much higher levels of inter-Indian warfare
         i. competition
         ii. "mourning wars" to get captives to replenish societies devastated by disease
         iii. Indians had to take sides in century-long (1664–1763) French-British rivalry for North America
   5. Native Americans became dependent on European trade goods.
      a. iron tools and cooking pots
      b. gunpowder weapons
      c. European textiles
      d. as a result, many traditional crafts were lost
      e. many animal species were depleted through overhunting
      f. deeply destructive power of alcohol on Indian societies
   D. Russian fur trade
      1. profits of fur trade were the chief incentive for Russian expansion
      2. had a similar toll on native Siberians as it had on Indians
         a. dependence on Russian goods
         b. depletion of fur-bearing animal populations
      3. Russians didn't have competition, so they forced Siberians to provide furs instead of negotiating commercial agreements
      4. private Russian hunters and trappers competed directly with Siberians

V. Commerce in People: The Atlantic Slave Trade [see Classroom Activity 2]
   A. Between the mid-fifteenth and mid-nineteenth centuries, the Atlantic slave trade

took an estimated 11 million people from Africa to the Americas.

1. millions more died in the process
2. vast human tragedy
3. African slave trade transformed the societies of all participants
   a. the African diaspora created racially mixed societies in the Americas
   b. slave trade and slavery enriched many
   c. slavery became a metaphor for many types of social oppression

B. The Slave Trade in Context **[see Discussion Topic 3]**
   1. most human societies have had slaves
   2. Africans had practiced slavery and sold slaves for centuries
      a. trans-Saharan trade took slaves to the Mediterranean world
      b. East African slave trade
   3. slavery took many forms, depending on the region and time period
      a. slaves were often assimilated into their owners' households
      b. children of slaves were sometimes free, sometimes slaves
      c. Islamic world preferred female slaves; Atlantic slave trade favored males
      d. not all slaves had lowly positions (in Islamic world, many slaves had military or political status)
      e. most premodern slaves worked in households, farms, or shops
   4. distinctiveness of slavery in the Americas
      a. the scale and importance of the slave trade in the Americas was enormous
      b. largely based on plantation agriculture, with slaves denied any rights at all
      c. slave status was inherited
      d. little hope of manumission
      e. widespread slavery in society that valued human freedom and equality—unlike anywhere else except maybe ancient Greece
      f. slavery was wholly identified with Africa and with "blackness"
   5. origins of Atlantic slavery lay in the Mediterranean and with sugar production

   a. sugar production was the first "modern" industry (major capital investment, technology, disciplined workers, mass market)
   b. the work was very difficult and dangerous—slaves were ideal
   c. at first, Slavs from the Black Sea region provided most slaves for Mediterranean sugar plantations
      i. Ottoman conquest of Constantinople (1453) cut off supply
   d. Portuguese found an alternative slave source in West Africa
   6. Africans became the primary source of slave labor for the Americas
      a. Slavs weren't available
      b. Indians died of European diseases
      c. Europeans were a bad alternative: Christians from marginal lands couldn't be enslaved; indentured servants were expensive
      d. Africans were farmers, had some immunity to diseases, were not Christian, and were readily available
      e. long debate on how much racism was involved
         i. Muslims had some racism in regard to sub-Saharan Africans
         ii. English had developed anti-Irish racism, may have transferred it to Africans
         iii. made exploitation of Africans palatable by dehumanizing them

C. The Slave Trade in Practice
   1. slave trade was driven by European demand
   2. but Europeans didn't raid Africa for slaves; they traded freely with African merchants and elites
      a. from capture to sale on the coast, trade was in African hands
      b. Africans received trade goods in return, often bought with American silver
   3. destabilization of African societies
      a. many smaller societies were completely disrupted by slave raids from their neighbors
      b. even larger states were affected (e.g., kingdom of Kongo)

c. some African slave traders were themselves enslaved by unscrupulous Europeans

4. increasing pace of Atlantic slave trade
    a. between 1450 and 1600, fewer than 4,000 slaves were shipped annually
        i. Portuguese wanted African gold, spices, and textiles, too
        ii. were often involved in transporting goods within Africa
    b. in the seventeenth century, average of 10,000 slaves per year taken to the Americas
        i. high point of the slave trade: by the 1750s, more than 60,000 slaves brought to the Americas each year

5. Who was enslaved?
    a. people from West Africa (present-day Mauritania to Angola)
    b. mostly people from marginal groups (prisoners of war, debtors, criminals)
    c. Africans generally did not sell their own peoples
        i. no sense of a common "African" identity

6. 80 percent of slaves ended up in Brazil and the Caribbean
    a. 5–6 percent in North America
    b. the rest in mainland Spanish America or in Europe
    c. about 15 percent of those enslaved died during the Middle Passage

D. Comparing Consequences: The Impact of the Slave Trade in Africa
1. created new transregional linkages
    a. Africa became a permanent part of the Atlantic world
2. slowed Africa's growth, while Europe and China expanded in population
    a. sub-Saharan Africa had about 18 percent of the world's population in 1600 but only 6 percent in 1900
    b. slave trade generated economic stagnation and political disruption in Africa
        i. those who profited in the trade did not invest in production
        ii. did not generate breakthroughs in agriculture or industry—since

Europeans didn't increase demand for Africa's products, just for its people

3. political effects
    a. some kingdoms (Kongo, Oyo) gradually disintegrated
    b. some took advantage of the slave trade
    c. Benin was one of the most developed states of the coastal hinterland
        i. state dates back to about the eleventh century C.E.
        ii. monarch (oba) controlled trade
        iii. largely avoided involvement in the slave trade
        iv. diversified its exports
    d. Aja-speaking peoples to the west of Benin
        i. slave trade disrupted several small, weak states
        ii. inland kingdom of Dahomey rose in the early eighteenth century
        iii. was a highly authoritarian state
        iv. turned to deep involvement in the slave trade, but under royal control
        v. annual slave raids by the army
        vi. government depended on slave trade for revenue

VI. **Reflections: Economic Globalization—Then and Now** [see Classroom Activity 3]
A. A study of global commerce in the early modern period shows both how different from and how similar we are to people of the past.
B. Globalization isn't just a twentieth-century phenomenon.
1. but early modern globalization was much slower and on a smaller scale
    a. communications between England and India took 18 months in the eighteenth century
2. early modern globalization was not yet centered on Western civilizations
3. early modern economic life was mostly preindustrial
4. early modern globalization was tied to empire building and slavery

USING *WAYS OF THE WORLD* IN THE CLASSROOM

Lecture Strategies

Lecture Strategy 1

"Of ships and the sea: The mechanics of a new world order."

We tend to ignore ships and shipping, at most mentioning in accounts of exploration and increasing globalization that the Europeans had good ships. This lecture strategy proposes to explore ships, shipping, winds, oceanic travel, and ports in the early modern period. Its objectives are:

- to examine European maritime technology comparatively with that of other parts of the world in an effort to understand how Europe could come to dominate the seas
- to examine the conditions on European ships—how they got from place to place, the amount of manpower required, etc.
- to explore in greater detail what conditions were like in the great international ports of the period 1450–1750

A good place to start is with a discussion of the *Mary Rose*, a warship constructed by order of Henry VIII of England that sank on its maiden voyage. The ship has now been raised from the sea and has been thoroughly studied, thus providing a readily available source of information about sixteenth-century ships. Some important points to note are:

- the problem of what to do with cannons on ships (open gunports caused the ship to sink)
- the ship's ability to sail in different winds
- the ship's capacity
- the ship's construction (note especially the keel, which makes a strong contrast to Chinese vessels of the period)

From there, explore the development of naval seapower. Some important points to consider are:

- the contributions of Arabic and Chinese technology
- the development of the galleon

- progressive developments in rigging, which made it possible to tack against the wind
- how many tons of goods a ship could hold
- the European "arms race" in maritime technology, both because of encounters between Christian and Muslim fleets in the Mediterranean and because of England's rivalry with the French, Spaniards, and Dutch
- the Spanish Armada
- the growing importance and usefulness of shipboard cannons over time
- the relatively static nature of Chinese, Arabic, and Indian shipping in the same period

Some more general issues to include are:

- the need for ships of advanced design in order to brave the inhospitable coast of West Africa
- what European ships could offer by way of maneuverability compared to their Asian competitors
- the horrid conditions usually encountered by ships sailing south of either South America or Africa

Lecture Strategy 2

"The companies."

One of the most fascinating stories of the age of commercial globalization is the role played by the Dutch and British East India companies. A lecture exploring and comparing these two great enterprises can provide a useful platform from which to examine two significant regions of Europe as well as the issue of trade with Asia. The objectives of this lecture strategy are:

- to develop an understanding of European mercantilism
- to investigate Dutch and British political and social development in the early modern period
- to consider European interactions with Asian societies in greater detail than the chapter allows
- to explore how trade companies functioned

A good place to start is with the foundation of the "Honorable East India Company" by Elizabeth I of England on December 31, 1600, and the establishment of the Dutch East India Company by the States-General of the Netherlands in 1602. Some points to include are:

- the dominance of merchant interests in both countries
- the practice of granting state monopolies
- the Dutch wars of independence from Spain and their implications for mercantile history
- the Dutch East India Company's role as the first company ever to issue public stock
- how the two companies actually functioned in terms of investment and dividends

Go on from there to consider the work of the two companies, focusing on the early modern period (the Dutch East India Company dissolved in 1800; the British East India Company still exists). Some points to include are:

- development of the story already related in this chapter of the Dutch takeover of the Spice Islands
- exploration of how British traders established ascendancy in Indian trade
- the relationship between company shipping and the navies of their respective countries
- other ways in which the Netherlands and England (later Great Britain) supported their respective trade companies
- how many Dutch and English merchants actually went to Asia and what they did while there
- how much profit there was in the business
- impressions that European traders brought home of the peoples they encountered
- damage done to the peoples or states encountered by the Europeans

Lecture Strategy 3

"The Tokugawa shogunate."
A thread of Japanese history runs through this chapter, and it is well worth exploring both as an example of early modern responses to globalization and as a foreshadowing of Japan's massive world significance in later centuries. The objectives of this lecture strategy are:

- to explore the history of Japan in the early modern period
- to use Japan as a model that can help students understand the attractions and dangers of the European presence in Asia

It is useful to begin this lecture from a long historical perspective, by examining feudal Japan during the Kamakura (1185–1333) and Muromachi (1336–1573) periods. Important points to include are:

- the figurehead status of Japanese emperors and the role of shoguns
- the fragmentation of Japanese political life
- the centrality of military rule, including the role of the samurai

From there, examine the arrival of the Europeans, including such points as:

- the Battle of Nagashino (1575), at which European firearms massacred enemy samurai
- the evangelization of St. Francis Xavier and other missionaries
- the establishment of Christian communities in Japan

Weave that narrative in with the parallel series of events that led to the creation of the Tokugawa shogunate in 1600, including such points as:

- Tokugawa Ieyasu's rise to power
- exploitation of Japanese silver deposits
- the nature of Japanese society in the period

The lecture should conclude with the events that led the Tokugawa shogun to decide to close Japan to Western influence, how this decision was carried out, and the persecution of the Christian communities in Japan.

Things to Do in the Classroom

Discussion Topics

1. **Misconception/Difficult Topic, large or small group.** "Why Europeans wanted spices."
Ask your students to list the reasons why they think Europeans craved Asian spices so badly. In an average class, reasons will include the strange myth that Europeans wanted spices to cover the taste of rotting meat. Students are far less likely to consider the role of spices as an important status symbol (rather like furs). After the initial student list is established, lead a discussion that works in such points as:

- the fact that microbes will make you just as sick, whether you mask the taste with spices or not
- medicinal use of spices

- the much wider range of foods to which spices were added, compared to typical American cuisine today
- the high price of spices
- how people in early modern Europe displayed their status more generally

2. **Contextualization, large or small group.** "In pursuit of 'soft gold.'"

Ask students to discuss the *human* cost of the fur trade in both Siberia and North America compared to other forms of large-scale trade that developed in the early modern period.

3. **Comparison, large or small group.** "Slavery, old and new."

This discussion question allows a review of material included in the chapter, as well as the possibility of drawing material from other chapters. Ask students to come up with at least five examples of slavery in various world societies before the beginning of the Columbian exchange. The students should rank their five examples by (1) the degree of impact slavery had on each society and (2) the societies' relative harshness toward the slaves themselves, and they should be able to explain their ranking. Next, ask students to add two forms of African slavery in the Americas to their list, considering where they should be placed in relation to the premodern examples.

Classroom Activities

1. **Analysis exercise, large or small group.** "Find the ports."

Ask students to pick out the major ports mentioned in Chapter 15. Then, using a world map, ask students to find the major ports used by Spanish, Portuguese, Dutch, and British traders in the early modern period. Color-coding the ports of various countries will make it possible to see concentrations of mercantile interests.

2. **Role-playing exercise, small group.** "Justifying slavery."

Choose three groups to represent slaveholders (1) in West Africa, (2) in the Caribbean, and (3) in the British colonies of North America. Ask each group to do some research and then to present to the rest of the class a five-minute defense of slavery as they practice it. After all three groups have presented, the role of the rest of the class will be to debate *against* the presenters.

The greatest challenge to all the students engaged will be to remain true to cultural mores of the early modern period—make it clear in the assignment that you are the representative of the anachronism police and will not allow anachronism to drift in.

3. **Clicker question.** Was the world better or worse off for the globalization of the early modern period?

Key Terms

African diaspora: Name given to the spread of African peoples across the Atlantic via the slave trade.

Banda Islands: Infamous case of the Dutch forcibly taking control of the spice trade; nearly the entire population of these nutmeg-producing islands was killed or enslaved and then replaced with Dutch planters. (*pron.* BAHN-dah)

Benin: West African kingdom (in what is now Nigeria) whose strong kings sharply limited engagement with the slave trade. (*pron.* be-NEEN)

British/Dutch East India companies: Private trading companies chartered by the governments of England and the Netherlands around 1600; they were given monopolies on Indian Ocean trade, including the right to make war and to rule conquered peoples.

cartaz: A pass that the Portuguese required of all merchant vessels attempting to trade in the Indian Ocean. (*pron.* car-TAHZ)

Dahomey: West African kingdom that became strong through its rulers' exploitation of the slave trade. (*pron.* dah-HOH-mee)

daimyo: Feudal lords of Japan who ruled with virtual independence thanks to their bands of *samurai* warriors. (*pron.* DIME-yoh)

Hurons: Native American people of northeastern North America who were heavily involved in the fur trade. (*pron.* HYOOR-ons)

Indian Ocean commercial network: The massive, interconnected web of commerce in premodern times between the lands that bordered on the Indian Ocean (including East Africa, India, and Southeast Asia); the network was badly disrupted by Portuguese intrusion beginning around 1500.

Little Ice Age: A period of cooling temperatures and harsh winters that lasted for much of the early modern era.

Magellan, Ferdinand: Portuguese mariner who commanded the first European (Spanish) fleet to circumnavigate the globe (1519–1521). (*pron.* mah-GELL-an)

Manila: Capital of the Spanish Philippines and a major multicultural trade city that already had a population of more than 40,000 by 1600.

Middle Passage: Name commonly given to the journey across the Atlantic undertaken by African slaves being shipped to the Americas.

piece of eight: Standard Spanish coin that became a medium of exchange in North America, Europe, India, Russia, and West Africa as well as in the Spanish Empire; so called because it was worth 8 *reales*.

Potosí: City that developed high in the Andes (in present-day Bolivia) at the site of the world's largest silver mine and that became the largest city in the Americas, with a population of some 160,000 in the 1570s. (*pron.* poh-toh-SEE)

samurai: The warrior elite of medieval Japan. (*pron.* SAH-moo-rie)

shogun: In Japan, a supreme military commander. (*pron.* SHOW-gun)

"silver drain": Term often used, along with "specie drain," to describe the siphoning of money from Europe to pay for the luxury products of the East, a process exacerbated by the fact that Europe had few trade goods that were desirable in Eastern markets; eventually, the bulk of the world's silver supply made its way to China.

"soft gold": Nickname used in the early modern period for animal furs, highly valued for their warmth and as symbols of elite status; in several regions, the fur trade generated massive wealth for those engaged in it.

Spanish Philippines: An archipelago of Pacific islands colonized by Spain in a relatively bloodless process that extended for the century or so after 1565, a process accompanied by a major effort at evangelization; the Spanish named them the Philippine Islands in honor of King Philip II of Spain.

Tokugawa shogunate: Military rulers of Japan who successfully unified Japan politically by the early seventeenth century and established a "closed door" policy toward European encroachments. (*pron.* toe-koo-GOW-ah SHOW-gun-at)

trading post empire: Form of imperial dominance based on control of trade rather than on control of subject peoples.

ANSWER GUIDELINES FOR CHAPTER QUESTIONS

The two sets of questions that follow appear in the textbook at the end of the chapter and in the margins of the reading. They are also provided in the Computerized Test Bank with answer guidelines, for your convenience.

The Big Picture Questions

1. In what specific ways did trade foster change in the world of the early modern era?

• It created completely new trade networks across the Atlantic and Pacific oceans.

• The slave trade brought large numbers of Africans to the Americas.

• It drew the remote peoples of Siberia and North America into global trade networks through the fur trade.

• It slowed population growth, disrupted the economy, and sometimes shaped the political system in West Africa.

• It was the driving force behind the large-scale slave economy that emerged in the Americas.

• It further commercialized the economies of the world, especially that of China, through inflows of silver from South America and Japan.

2. To what extent did Europeans transform earlier patterns of commerce, and in what ways did they assimilate into those older patterns?

• Europeans for the first time operated on a global scale, forging new trade networks across the Atlantic and Pacific oceans;

• they also facilitated the full integration of fur-supplying regions into wider trade networks.

• But in other ways, the Europeans assimilated older patterns, as in the Indian Ocean, where they sought to dominate previously established trade routes;

• and they continued to trade many of the same products.

3. Describe and account for the differing outcomes of European expansion in the Americas, Africa, and Asia.

• In the Americas, Europeans conquered the region politically and dominated it economically. The primary reasons for this were the devastation caused to Native American populations by European diseases and the technological advantages that Europeans possessed when they arrived.

• In Africa, Europeans established much stronger trade relationships and set up several trading posts on the east coast of Africa. However, they made no effort to conquer large territories, in large part because the most attractive regions for European conquest, such as West Africa, possessed too many deadly tropical diseases against which Europeans had little immunity.

• In Asia, Europeans (aside from the Spanish, who succeeded in establishing a colonial state in the Philippines) sought to found trading post empires, with mixed success. The Dutch were able to dominate several Spice Islands, and both the British and the Portuguese were able to set up fortified trading posts along the Indian Ocean coast. But none of these powers ever tried to conquer large territories, and in some cases, such as in Japan, the Europeans were only able to trade under conditions set by the local authorities. These developments show that, while the Spanish and Dutch were able to dominate relatively small regions, the larger established civilizations of Asia were too powerful for the Europeans to hope to rule, and in any case the great distances between Asia and Europe made such a colonial empire impractical.

4. How should we distribute the moral responsibility or blame for the Atlantic slave trade? Is this a task appropriate for historians?

• This is obviously a question intended to encourage student thought, without a simple or clear-cut answer.

• It is evident that Europeans played an important role both in stimulating the slave trade and in developing a slave system that was unusually dehumanizing, degrading, and dangerous for those forced to participate as slaves.

• It is also clear that some Africans willingly participated in the trade, capturing and selling slaves to the Europeans.

• Whether assessing moral responsibility or blame is a task appropriate for historians is debatable. One could reasonably make a case for or against this idea.

• Students should be encouraged to think about historical *context*, rather than judging by the standards of our own era.

• Students should be encouraged not to think in all-or-nothing terms, such as assertions that all Europeans were (and are) morally guilty for the slave trade, when the vast majority of Europeans had nothing to do with it.

• Similarly, students should be encouraged to recognize that the fact that some African rulers and individuals participated in the slave trade does not imply moral guilt for all.

5. What lasting legacies of early modern globalization are evident in the early twenty-first century? Pay particular attention to the legacies of the slave trade.

• There are numerous lasting legacies, including the Atlantic trading network;

• the Pacific trading network between the Americas and East Asia;

• the influence of European civilizations, especially in the Americas and the Philippines;

• the engagement of even remote peoples, such as those of Siberia, in world trade networks;

• the large populations in the Americas of peoples of African and European origins;

• African cultural influences in the Americas;

• ideas of race, particularly of "blackness";

• the demographic and economic legacy of the slave trade in West Africa.

Margin Review Questions

Q. *What drove European involvement in the world of Asian commerce?*

• European involvement in Asian commerce was motivated by a number of factors, including the desire for tropical spices, Chinese silk, Indian cottons, rhubarb, emeralds, rubies, and sapphires;

• the general recovery of European civilization following the disaster of the Black Death;

• a resentment of the Muslim monopoly on the flow of Indian Ocean products to Europe, and the dislike that many European powers had for Venice's role as intermediary in the trade;

• the hope of discovering and allying with the mythical Christian kingdom of Prester John to continue the Crusades and combat a common Islamic enemy;

• the need to secure gold and silver to pay for Asian spices and textiles.

Q. *To what extent did the Portuguese realize their own goals in the Indian Ocean?*

• Their original goal of creating a trading post empire that controlled the commerce of the Indian Ocean was at best only partially realized. They never succeeded in controlling much more than half the spice trade to Europe, and by 1600, their trading post empire was in steep decline.

Q. *How did the Portuguese, Spanish, Dutch, and British initiatives in Asia differ from one another?*

• The Portuguese sought to set up a trading post empire that controlled the trade routes of the Indian Ocean.

• The Spanish established colonial rule over the Philippine Islands. In doing so, they drew on their experience in the Americas, converting most of the population to Christianity, ruling over the islands directly, and setting up large landed estates owned by Spanish settlers.

• The Dutch and British organized their Indian Ocean ventures through private trading companies, which were able to raise money and share risks among a substantial number of merchant investors. These trading companies obtained government charters granting them trading monopolies, the power to make war, and the right to govern conquered peoples. They established their own parallel and competing trading post empires; the Dutch seized control of some of the Spice Islands, while the British set up trading centers in India by securing the support of the Mughal Empire or of local authorities.

Q. *To what extent did the British and Dutch trading companies change the societies they encountered in Asia?*

• The Dutch acted to control not only the shipping but also the production of cloves, cinnamon, nutmeg, and mace. With much bloodshed, the Dutch seized control of a number of small spice-producing islands, forcing their people to sell only to the Dutch.

• On the Banda Islands, the Dutch killed, enslaved, or left to starve virtually the entire population and then replaced them with Dutch planters, using a slave labor force to produce the nutmeg crop.

• Ultimately, the local economy of the Spice Islands was shattered by Dutch policies, and the people there were impoverished.

• The British established three major trading settlements in India during the seventeenth century: Bombay, Calcutta, and Madras. They secured their trading bases with the permission of Mughal authorities or local rulers.

• British traders came to specialize in Indian cotton textiles, and hundreds of villages in the interior of southern India became specialized producers for the British market.

Q. *What was the world historical importance of the silver trade?*

• The silver trade was the first direct and sustained link between the Americas and Asia, and it initiated a web of Pacific commerce that grew steadily over the centuries.

• It transformed Spain and Japan, the two states that controlled the principal new sources of silver.

• It deepened the already substantial commercialization of China's economy, which fueled global commerce.

• It became a key commodity driving long-distance trade and offered the Europeans a product that they could produce that was also in demand elsewhere in the world.

Q. *Describe the impact of the fur trade on North American native societies.*

• The fur trade did bring some benefits, including the trade of pelts for goods of real value;

• enhanced influence and authority for some Native American leaders;

• the protection of Native Americans involved in the fur trade, at least for a time, from the kind of extermination, enslavement, or displacement that was the fate of some native peoples elsewhere in the Americas.

• But the fur trade also had a negative impact, such as in exposing Native Americans to European diseases;

• generating warfare beyond anything previously known;

• leaving Native Americans dependent on European goods without a corresponding ability to manufacture the goods themselves;

• bringing alcohol into Indian societies, often with deeply destructive effects.

Q. *How did the North American and Siberian fur trades differ from each other? What did they have in common?*

• Both trades were driven by the demands of the world market.

• Both had similar consequences for the native populations that participated in them, as both native Siberians and Native Americans suffered from new diseases and became dependent on the goods for which they traded furs.

• However, the trades also differed in that Native Americans dealt with several competing European nations who generally obtained their furs through commercial negotiations. No such competition existed in Siberia, where Russian authorities imposed a tax or tribute, payable in furs, on every able-bodied Siberian male between eighteen and fifty years of age.

• A further difference lay in the large-scale presence of private Russian hunters and trappers, who competed directly with their Siberian counterparts.

Q. *What was distinctive about the Atlantic slave trade? What did it share with other patterns of slave owning and slave trading?*

• The Atlantic slave trade had many distinctive features, including the immense size of the traffic in slaves;

• a distinctive racial dimension, as Atlantic slavery came to be identified wholly with Africa and with "blackness";

• the centrality of slavery to the economies of colonial America;

• the prominence of slave labor in plantation agriculture;

• the treatment of slaves as a form of dehumanized property, lacking any rights in the society of their owners;

• the practice of slave status being inherited across the generations, with little hope of eventual freedom for the vast majority;

• the fact that American slaveholding took place in the only society, with the possible exception of ancient Greece, that affirmed values of human freedom and equality while permitting widespread slavery.

• But the Atlantic slave trade did possess some similarities with other patterns of slave owning, including the acquisition of slaves from Africa;

• the enslavement of outsiders and other vulnerable people;

• and the fact that slavery was a common practice since the earliest civilizations.

Q. *What explains the rise of the Atlantic slave trade?*

• The immense difficulty and danger of the work, the limitations attached to serf labor, and the general absence of wage workers all pointed to slavery as the only source of labor for sugar-producing plantations.

• The cutting off of the supply of Slavic slaves, the demographic collapse of Native American populations, and the Christian faith of marginal Europeans left Africans as the only viable source of slaves for the plantation economies of the Americas.

Q. *What roles did Europeans and Africans play in the unfolding of the Atlantic slave trade?*

• European demand for slaves was clearly the chief cause of the trade.

• From the point of sale on the African coast to the massive use of slave labor on American plantations, the entire enterprise was in European hands.

• Europeans tried to exploit African rivalries to obtain slaves at the lowest possible cost, and the firearms that they funneled into West Africa may well have increased the warfare from which so many slaves were derived.

• From the point of initial capture to sale on the coast, the slave trade was normally in African hands. African elites and merchants secured slaves and brought them to the coast for sale to Europeans waiting on ships or in fortified settlements.

• Africans who were transported as slaves also played a critical, if unwilling and tragic, role in the trade.

Q. *In what different ways did the Atlantic slave trade transform African societies?*

• Africa became a permanent part of an interacting Atlantic world, both commercially and demographically.

• The Atlantic slave trade slowed Africa's population growth at a time when the populations of Europe, China, and other regions were expanding.

• The slave trade in general stimulated little positive economic change in Africa and led to economic stagnation.

• It also led to considerable political disruption, particularly for small-scale societies with little central authority that were frequently subject to slave raids.

• Some larger kingdoms such as Kongo and Oyo also slowly disintegrated because of the slave trade.

• But in other regions, like Benin and Dahomey, African authorities sought to take advantage of the new commercial opportunities to manage the slave trade in their own interests.

ADDITIONAL RESOURCES FOR CHAPTER 15

Additional Bedford/St. Martin's Resources

FOR INSTRUCTORS

Computerized Test Bank

This test bank provides over thirty exercises per chapter, including multiple-choice, fill-in-the-blank, short-answer, and full-length essay questions. Instructors can customize quizzes, add or edit both questions and answers, and export questions and answers to a variety of formats, including WebCT and Blackboard. The disc includes correct answers and essay outlines.

Instructor's Resource CD-ROM

This disc provides instructors with ready-made and customizable PowerPoint multimedia presentations built around chapter outlines, maps, figures, and all images from the textbook, plus JPEG versions of all maps, figures, and images.

The following maps and images from Chapter 15 are available in both JPEG and PowerPoint format on the Instructor's Resource CD-ROM:

- Map 15.1: Europeans in Asia in the Early Modern Era (p. 436)
- Map 15.2: The Global Silver Trade (p. 442)
- Map 15.3: The North American Fur Trade (p. 446)
- Map 15.4: The Atlantic Slave Trade (p. 449)
- The Atlantic Slave Trade (p. 432)
- The Spice Trade (p. 437)

- A European View of Asian Commerce (p. 440)
- Potosí (p. 443)
- Fur and the Russians (p. 448)
- The Middle Passage (p. 451)

FOR STUDENTS

Documents and Essays from *Worlds of History: A Comparative Reader,* Third Edition (Volume 2)

The following documents, essays, and illustrations to accompany Chapter 15 are available in Chapter 2 of Volume 2 of this reader by Kevin Reilly:

- Bartolomeo de Las Casas, from *The Devastation of the Indies*
- *Two European Views of Native Americans* (De Bry's engraving of cannibals and Albert Eckhout's Tapuya native)
- David Pieterzen deVries, *A Dutch Massacre of the Algonquins*
- Nzinga Mbemba, *Appeal to the King of Portugal*
- William Bosman, *Slave Trader*
- Olaudah Equiano, *Enslaved Captive*

Online Study Guide at bedfordstmartins.com/strayer

The Online Study Guide helps students synthesize the material from the text as well as practice the skills historians use to make sense of the past. Each chapter of the Online Study Guide contains specific testing exercises, including a multiple-choice self-test that focuses on important conceptual ideas; an identification quiz that helps students remember key people, places, and events; a flashcard activity that tests students on their knowledge of key terms; and two interactive map activities intended to strengthen students' geographic skills. Instructors can monitor students' progress through an online Quiz Gradebook or receive email updates.

Further Reading

East & Southeast Asia: An Annotated Directory of Internet Resources: History of Japan, http://newton.uor.edu/Departments&Programs/AsianStudiesDept/japan-history.html. An excellent guide to works available online.

Glete, Jan. *Warfare at Sea, 1500–1650: Maritime Conflicts and the Transformation of Europe.* London: Routledge, 2002. An interesting account that includes considerable information about ship design and capabilities.

The History Page: The East India Trade, http://www .scholiast.org/history/hi-eitr.html. A useful collection of links to the history of the British and Dutch East India companies in the period 1500–1800.

Keay, John. *The Honourable Company: A History of the English East India Company.* 2nd ed. New York: HarperCollins, 1993. Probably the most accessible history of the British East India Company.

Parry, J. H. *The Spanish Seaborne Empire.* Berkeley: University of California Press, 1990. A long but readable history of the Spanish Empire.

Pastor, Xavier. *The Ships of Christopher Columbus.* London: Conway Maritime Press, 1992. A detailed examination of European ships and shipbuilding around 1500.

Russell-Wood, A. J. *Slavery and Freedom in Colonial Brazil.* 2nd ed. Oxford: Oneworld, 2002. An interesting and readable exploration of the subject.

Stein, Stanley J., and Barbara H. Stein. *Silver, Trade, and War: Spain and America in the Making of Early Modern Europe.* 2nd ed. Baltimore: Johns Hopkins University Press, 2003. A thought-provoking account of the intersection of trade and war in the early modern era.

Tracy, James D., ed. *The Rise of Merchant Empires: Long-Distance Trade in the Early Modern World, 1350–1750.* Cambridge: Cambridge University Press, 1993. An interesting collection of essays on the topic.

Camoes, Luis Vaz de. *The Lusiads.* Trans. Landeg White. 2nd ed. Oxford: Oxford World Classics, 2002. One of the greatest Renaissance epics, this poem (first published in 1572) tells of Portugal's voyages of discovery.

Equiano, Olaudah. *The Interesting Narrative of the Life of Olaudah Equiano.* Ed. Robert Allison. Boston: Bedford/St. Martins, 1995. Account of the Atlantic slave trade through the eyes of an African slave.

Halsall, Paul, ed. *Indian History Sourcebook: England, India, and the East Indies, 1617 C.E.* http://www .fordham.edu/halsall/india/1617englandindies.html. A collection of short documents, including the Mughal emperor Jahangir's letter to James I of England.

Halsall, Paul, ed. *Internet Modern History Sourcebook: The Early Modern World.* http://www.fordham.edu/halsall/mod/modsbook03.html. An interesting collection of accounts by world travelers, including accounts of Francis Drake's and Ferdinand Magellan's circumnavigations, letters from St. Francis Xavier, and more.

Pepys, Samuel. *A Pepys Anthology.* Berkeley: University of California Press, 2000. A nice selection from Pepys's voluminous diaries. Pepys was an English official who worked for the navy in the late seventeenth century.

Pinto, Fernão Mendes. *The Travels of Mendes Pinto.* Ed. and trans. Rebecca D. Catz. Chicago: University of Chicago Press, 1989. Fascinating account of this merchant adventurer's travels along the sea routes of the Indian Ocean and East Asia as the Portuguese trading post empire was taking shape.

Literature

Barbot, Jean. *Barbot on Guinea: The Writings of Jean Barbot on West Africa, 1678–1712.* Ed. P. E. H. Hair, Adam Jones, and Robin Law. 2 vols. London: Hakluyt Society, 1992. A description of the West African coast through the eyes of a European merchant.

Behn, Aphra. *Oroonoko.* 2nd ed. London: Penguin, 2004. An extraordinary novel, written in 1678, about an African prince captured and enslaved in the Caribbean.

Film

Black Sugar. Films for the Humanities and Sciences, 1989. 26 minutes. Presents the African slave trade from a West African perspective.

The Blue Highway: Trade Routes across the Sea. Films for the Humanities and Sciences, 1990. 26 minutes. Traces the history of seaborne commerce in the Orient, including segments on the Portuguese and on the Dutch East India Company.

Exploration. Films for the Humanities and Sciences, 1998. 53 minutes. Explores comparatively the motivations for exploration, conquest, and colonization, contrasting the Chinese experience with that of the European powers.

Gorée: Door of No Return. Films for the Humanities and Sciences, 1992. 30 minutes. Documentary on the history of the slave trade, focusing on Gorée Island off the coast of West Africa, where slaves were held before making the dangerous Middle Passage.

The Great Age of Exploration. Insight Media, 1998. 30 minutes. Recounts the first century and a half of European oceanic exploration and discovery.

History of Trade in China. Insight Media, 2000. 26 minutes. Offers an overview of Chinese trade from antiquity to the twentieth century, with segments on the early modern period.

Slave Ship. Discovery Channel, 1997. 52 minutes. Takes an in-depth look at the Atlantic slave trade, with segments on the preexisting trade in Africa before European demand transformed it.

Religion and Science
1450–1750

CHAPTER OVERVIEW

Chapter Objectives

- To explore the early modern roots of modern tension between religion and science
- To examine the Reformation movements in Europe and their significance
- To investigate the global spread of Christianity and the extent to which it syncretized with native traditions
- To expand the discussion of religious change to include religious movements in China, India, and the Islamic world
- To explore the reasons behind the Scientific Revolution in Europe, and why that movement was limited in other parts of the world
- To explore the implications of the Scientific Revolution for world societies

Chapter Outline

I. Opening Vignette

A. The current evolution vs. "intelligent design" debate has its roots in the early modern period.
   1. Christianity achieved a global presence for the first time
   2. the Scientific Revolution fostered a different approach to the world

3. there is continuing tension between religion and science in the Western world

B. The early modern period was a time of cultural transformation.
   1. both Christianity and scientific thought connected distant peoples
   2. Scientific Revolution also caused new cultural encounter, between science and religion
      a. science was a new worldview, almost a new religion for some
   3. science became part of the definition of global modernity

C. Europeans were central players, but they did not act alone.

II. The Globalization of Christianity

A. In 1500, Christianity was mostly limited to Europe.
   1. small communities in Egypt, Ethiopia, southern India, and Central Asia
   2. serious divisions within Christianity (Roman Catholic vs. Eastern Orthodox)
   3. on the defensive against Islam
      a. loss of the Holy Land by 1300
      b. fall of Constantinople to the Ottomans in 1453
      c. Ottoman siege of Vienna in 1529

B. Western Christendom Fragmented: The Protestant Reformation **[see Lecture Strategy 1 and Discussion Topic 1]**
   1. Protestant Reformation began in 1517

a. Martin Luther posted the Ninety-five Theses, asking for debate about ecclesiastical abuses

b. Luther's was one of many criticisms of the Roman Church

c. Luther's protest was more deeply grounded in theological difference

  i. argued a new understanding of salvation—through faith alone rather than through good works

  ii. the Bible, not Church teaching, is the ultimate authority

  iii. gave large role to individual conscience

d. questioned the special role of the clerical hierarchy (including the pope)

2. Luther's ideas provoked a massive schism in Catholic Christendom

a. fed on political, economic, and social tension, not just religious differences

b. some monarchs used Luther to justify independence from the papacy

c. gave a new religious legitimacy to the middle class

d. commoners were attracted to the new religious ideas as a tool for protest against the whole social order

  i. German peasant revolts in the 1520s

3. many women were attracted to Protestantism, but the Reformation didn't give them a greater role in church or society

a. Protestants ended veneration of Mary and other female saints

  i. male Christ figure was left as sole object of worship

b. Protestants closed convents, which had given some women an alternative to marriage

c. only Quakers among the Protestants gave women an official role in their churches

d. some increase in the education of women, because of emphasis on Bible reading

  i. but there was little use for education beyond the family

4. the recently invented printing press helped Reformation thought spread rapidly

a. Luther issued many pamphlets and a German translation of the New Testament

5. as the Reformation spread, it splintered into an array of competing Protestant churches

6. religious difference made Europe's fractured political system even more volatile

a. 1562–1598: French Wars of Religion (Catholics vs. Huguenots)

  i. August 24, 1572: massacre of thousands of Huguenots

  ii. Edict of Nantes issued by Henry IV in 1598: granted considerable religious toleration to Protestants

b. 1618–1648: the Thirty Years' War

  i. Catholic-Protestant fight started in the Holy Roman Empire

  ii. spread to most of Europe

  iii. killed off 15–30 percent of the German population

  iv. Peace of Westphalia (1648): each state is sovereign and can decide its own religious affairs

7. Protestant Reformation provoked a Catholic Counter-Reformation

a. Council of Trent (1545–1563) clarified Catholic doctrines and practices

b. corrected the abuses and corruption that the Protestants had protested

c. new emphasis on education and supervision of priests

d. crackdown on dissidents

e. new attention given to individual spirituality and piety

f. new religious orders (e.g., the Society of Jesus [Jesuits]) were committed to renewal and expansion

8. the Reformation encouraged skepticism toward authority and tradition

a. fostered religious individualism

b. in the following centuries, the Protestant habit of independent thinking led to skepticism about all revealed religion

C. Christianity Outward Bound

1. Christianity motivated and benefited from European expansion

a. Spaniards and Portuguese saw overseas expansion as a continuation of the crusading tradition

b. explorers combined religious and material interests

2. imperialism made the globalization of Christianity possible

a. settlers and traders brought their religion with them

b. missionaries, mostly Catholic, actively spread Christianity

i. missionary orders: Dominicans, Franciscans, Jesuits

ii. Portuguese missionaries led in Africa and Asia

iii. Spanish and French were prominent in the Americas

iv. Russian Orthodox missionaries worked in Siberia

c. missionaries were most successful in Spanish America and the Philippines

i. European success encouraged belief that the old gods had been defeated

ii. Christians didn't confront a literate world religion there

iii. Confucians, Buddhists, Hindus, and Muslims resisted Christianity much more

D. Conversion and Adaptation in Spanish America **[see Discussion Topic 2]**

1. process of population collapse, conquest, and resettlement made Native Americans receptive to the conquering religion

a. vast majority were baptized by 1700

2. Europeans claimed exclusive religious truth, tried to destroy traditional religions instead of accommodating them

a. occasional campaigns of destruction against the old religions

b. some overt resistance movements

i. e.g., Taki Onqoy ("dancing sickness") in central Peru (1560s)

3. blending of two religious traditions was more common

a. local gods (*huacas*) remained influential

b. immigrant Christianity took on patterns of pre-Christian life

c. Christian saints took on functions of precolonial gods

d. leader of the church staff (*fiscal*) was a prestigious native who carried on the role of earlier religious specialists

e. many rituals survived, often with some Christian influence

E. An Asian Comparison: China and the Jesuits **[see Classroom Activity 1]**

1. Christianity reached China in the powerful, prosperous Ming and Qing dynasties

a. called for a very different missionary strategy; needed government permission for operation

b. Jesuits especially targeted the official Chinese elite

i. like Matteo Ricci (in China 1582–1610), they dressed like Chinese scholars, emphasized exchange of ideas

ii. were respectful of Chinese culture, tried to accommodate it

2. no mass conversion in China

a. some scholars and officials converted

b. Jesuits were appreciated for mathematical, astronomical, technological, and cartographical skills

c. missionary efforts gained 200,000–300,000 converts in 250 years

3. missionaries didn't offer much that the Chinese needed

a. Christianity was unappealing as an "all or nothing" religion that would call for rejection of much Chinese culture

b. early eighteenth century: papacy and other missionary orders opposed Jesuit accommodation policy

i. was regarded as an affront to Chinese culture and the emperor's authority

III. **Persistence and Change in Afro-Asian Cultural Traditions**

A. African religious elements accompanied slaves to the Americas

1. development of Africanized forms of Christianity in the Americas, with divination, dream interpretation, visions, spirit possession

2. Europeans often tried to suppress African elements as sorcery

3. persistence of syncretic religions (Vodou, Santeria, Candomble, Macumba)

B. Expansion and Renewal in the Islamic World
   1. continued spread of Islam depended not on conquest but on wandering holy men, scholars, and traders
      a. offered connections to the wider, prosperous world of Islam
   2. the syncretism of Islamization was increasingly offensive to orthodox Muslims
      a. helped provoke movements of religious renewal in the eighteenth century
      b. series of jihads in West Africa (eighteenth/early nineteenth centuries) attacked corrupt Islamic practices
      c. growing tension between localized and "pure" Islam
   3. the most well-known Islamic renewal movement of the period was Wahhabism
      a. developed in the Arabian Peninsula in mid-eighteenth century
      b. founder Abd al-Wahhab (1703–1792) was a theologian
      c. aimed to restore absolute monotheism, end veneration of saints
      d. aimed to restore strict adherence to the sharia (Islamic law)
      e. movement developed a political element when Abd al-Wahhab allied with Muhammad Ibn Saud; led to creation of a state
      f. the state was "purified"
         i. women were expected to subject themselves to husbands
         ii. "idols" were destroyed
         iii. tobacco, hashish, and musical instruments were banned
         iv. certain taxes were abolished
      g. the political power of the Wahhabis was broken in 1818, but the movement remained influential in Islamic world
      h. reform movements persisted and became associated with resisting Western cultural intrusion

C. China: New Directions in an Old Tradition
   1. Chinese and Indian cultural/religious change wasn't as dramatic as what occurred in Europe
      a. Confucian and Hindu cultures didn't spread widely in early modern period
      b. but neither remained static
   2. Ming and Qing dynasty China still operated within a Confucian framework
      a. addition of Buddhist and Daoist thought led to creation of Neo-Confucianism
      b. both dynasties embraced the Confucian tradition
   3. considerable amount of debate and new thinking in China **[see Lecture Strategy 2]**
      a. Wang Yangmin (1472–1529): anyone can achieve a virtuous life by introspection, with Confucian education
         i. critics later argued that this individualism contributed to the Manchu conquest of China
      b. Chinese Buddhists also tried to make religion more accessible to commoners—withdrawal from the world not necessary for enlightenment
      c. similarity to Martin Luther's argument that individuals could seek salvation without help from a priestly hierarchy
      d. *kaozheng* ("research based on evidence") was a new direction in Chinese elite culture
         i. emphasized need for analysis, instead of unsupported speculation
         ii. led to new works on agriculture, medicine, etc.
         iii. included critical analysis of ancient historical documents
         iv. scientific approach to knowledge (applied more to the past than to the natural world)
   4. lively popular culture among the less well educated
      a. production of plays, paintings, and literature
      b. great age of novels, such as Cao Xueqin's *The Dream of the Red Chamber* (mid-eighteenth century)

D. India: Bridging the Hindu/Muslim Divide
   1. several movements brought Hindus and Muslims together in new forms of religious expression
   2. *bhakti* movement was especially important

a. devotional Hinduism

b. effort to achieve union with the divine through songs, prayers, dances, poetry, and rituals

c. appealed especially to women

d. often set aside caste distinctions

e. much common ground with Sufism, helped to blur the line between Islam and Hinduism in India

f. Mirabai (1498–1547) is one of the best-loved bhakti poets

   i. high-caste woman who refused to commit *sati* when her husband died

   ii. took an untouchable as her guru

   iii. poetry of yearning for union with Krishna

3. growth of Sikhism, a religion that blended Islam and Hinduism

a. founder Guru Nanak (1469–1539) had been part of the bhakti movement; came to believe that Islam and Hinduism were one

b. Nanak and his successors set aside caste distinctions and proclaimed essential equality of men and women

c. gradually developed as a new religion of the Punjab

   i. developed a Sikh holy book, the Guru Granth (teacher book)

   ii. created a central shrine, the Golden Temple of Amritsar

   iii. mandated distinctive dress for men

d. evolved into a militant community in response to hostility

IV. A New Way of Thinking: The Birth of Modern Science [see Discussion Topic 3]

A. The Scientific Revolution was an intellectual and cultural transformation that occurred between the mid-sixteenth century and the early eighteenth century.

1. was based on careful observations, controlled experiments, and formulation of general laws to explain the world

2. creators of the movement saw themselves as making a radical departure

a. sense that they were "moderns" combating "ancients"

3. Scientific Revolution was vastly significant

a. fundamentally altered ideas about the place of humankind within the cosmos

b. challenged the teachings and authority of the Church

c. challenged ancient social hierarchies and political systems

d. also used to legitimize racial and gender inequality

e. by the twentieth century, science had become the chief symbol of modernity around the world

B. The Question of Origins: Why Europe?

1. the Islamic world was the most scientifically advanced realm in period 800–1400

2. China's technological accomplishments and economic growth were unmatched for several centuries after the millennium

3. but European conditions were uniquely favorable to rise of science

a. evolution of a legal system that guaranteed some independence for a variety of institutions by twelfth/thirteenth centuries

b. idea of the "corporation"—collective group treated as a legal unit with certain rights

c. autonomy of emerging universities

   i. University of Paris recognized as a corporation by 1215

   ii. universities became zones of intellectual autonomy

   iii. study of natural order began to separate from philosophy and theology

4. in the Islamic world, science remained mostly outside of the system of higher education

a. in madrassas (colleges), growing disdain for scientific and philosophical inquiry

5. Chinese authorities did not permit independent institutions of higher learning

a. Chinese education focused on preparing for civil service exams

b. emphasis was on classical Confucian texts

6. Western Europe could draw on the knowledge of other cultures **[see Lecture Strategy 3]**

a. Arab texts were very important in the development of European science between 1000 and 1500

7. sixteenth–eighteenth centuries: Europeans were at the center of a massive new information exchange
   a. tidal wave of knowledge shook up old ways of thinking
   b. explosion of uncertainty and skepticism allowed modern science to emerge

C. Science as Cultural Revolution
   1. dominant educated-European view of the world before the Scientific Revolution:
      a. derived from Aristotle and Ptolemy
      b. earth is stationary, at the center of the universe
      c. a universe of divine purpose
   2. initial breakthrough was by Nicolaus Copernicus
      a. *On the Revolutions of the Heavenly Spheres* (1543)
      b. promoted a heliocentric view of the universe
   3. other scientists built on Copernicus's insight
      a. some argued that there were other inhabited worlds
      b. Johannes Kepler demonstrated elliptical orbits of the planets
      c. Galileo Galilei (1564–1642) developed an improved telescope
         i. questioned the perfection of heavenly bodies
         ii. discovered the moons of Jupiter and new stars
         iii. provoked ideas of an infinite universe
   4. Sir Isaac Newton was the apogee of the Scientific Revolution
      a. formulated laws of motion and mechanics
      b. central concept: universal gravitation
      c. natural laws govern both the micro- and the macrocosm
   5. by Newton's death, educated Europeans had a fundamentally different view of the physical universe
      a. not propelled by angels and spirits but functioned according to mathematical principles

b. the "machine of the universe" is self-regulating
c. knowledge of the universe can be obtained through reason

6. the human body also became less mysterious
   a. the heart as a pump rather than as mysterious center of the body's passions, etc.

7. Catholic Church strenuously opposed much of this thinking
   a. burning of Giordano Bruno in 1600 for proclaiming an infinite universe
   b. Galileo was forced to renounce his belief that the earth moved around an orbit and rotated on its axis
   c. but no early scientists rejected Christianity

D. Science and Enlightenment **[see Classroom Activity 2]**
   1. the Scientific Revolution gradually reached a wider European audience
      a. development of a popular press and scientific societies
   2. scientific approach to knowledge was applied to human affairs
      a. Adam Smith (1723–1790) formulated economic laws
      b. people believed that scientific development would bring "enlightenment" to humankind
   3. Immanuel Kant (1724–1804) defined Enlightenment as a "daring to know"
   4. Enlightenment thinkers believed that knowledge could transform human society
      a. tended to be satirical, critical, and hostile to established authorities
      b. attacked arbitrary government, divine right, and aristocratic privilege
      c. John Locke (1632–1704) articulated ideas of constitutional government
      d. many writers advocated education for women
   5. much Enlightenment thought attacked established religion
      a. in his *Treatise on Toleration,* Voltaire (1694–1778) attacked the narrow particularism of organized religion

b. many thinkers were deists—belief in a remote deity who created the world but doesn't intervene

c. some were pantheists—equated God and nature

d. some even regarded religion as a fraud

6. Enlightenment thought was influenced by growing global awareness

7. central theme of Enlightenment: the idea of progress

8. some thinkers reacted against too much reliance on human reason

a. Jean-Jacques Rousseau (1712–1778) argued for immersion in nature rather than book learning

b. the Romantic movement appealed to emotion and imagination

c. religious awakenings made an immense emotional appeal

E. Looking Ahead: Science in the Nineteenth Century

1. modern science was cumulative and self-critical

2. in the nineteenth century, science was applied to new sorts of inquiry; in some ways, it undermined Enlightenment assumptions

3. Charles Darwin (1809–1882) argued that all of life was in flux

a. *The Origin of Species* (1859) and *The Descent of Man* (1871) were shattering to traditional religious views

4. Karl Marx (1818–1883) presented human history as a process of change and struggle

a. individualism lost ground to view of all species caught in systems of conflict

5. Sigmund Freud (1856–1939) cast doubt on human rationality

F. European Science beyond the West

1. science became the most widely desired product of European culture

a. but early modern Asia was only modestly interested

2. Chinese had selective interest in Jesuits' teaching

a. most interested in astronomy and mathematics

b. European science had substantial impact on the Chinese kaozheng movement

3. Japan kept up some European contact via trade with the Dutch

a. import of Western books allowed, starting in 1720

b. a small group of Japanese scholars was interested in Western texts, anatomical studies in particular

4. Ottoman Empire chose not to translate major European scientific works

a. Ottoman scholars were only interested in ideas of practical utility (e.g., maps, calendars)

b. Islamic educational system was conservative, made it hard for theoretical science to do well

V. **Reflections: Cultural Borrowing and Its Hazards** [see Classroom Activity 3]

A. Ideas shape peoples' mental or cultural worlds and influence behavior.

1. many early modern ideas are still highly significant

B. The development of early modern ideas took place in an environment of great cultural borrowing.

1. borrowing was selective

2. borrowing sometimes caused serious conflict

a. efforts to stop cultural influence

b. efforts to suppress the original culture

3. foreign ideas and practices were often "domesticated"

USING *WAYS OF THE WORLD* IN THE CLASSROOM

Lecture Strategies

Lecture Strategy 1

"The Reformations and their global significance."
The religious upheavals of the sixteenth century make the period one of the most influential in European history. The objectives of this lecture strategy are:

- to explore how the Reformations, both Protestant and Catholic, came about

- to examine the factors that made the Reformations happen in the sixteenth century
- to discuss the implications of the Reformations for European society and politics
- to consider the implications of the Reformations in the globalization of Christianity

A good place to start is with late medieval Christianity. It simply isn't good enough just to say something along the line of "Christianity was corrupt and needed fixing." A much more nuanced and truthful account will include:

- the influence of the printing press on European society
- the particular ecclesiastical abuses that developed in fragmented Germany
- the role of Renaissance humanism in rethinking the *purpose* of religion (a shift from ritual participation toward cerebral comprehension)
- the communal and individual satisfactions of a highly ritual religious structure

Go on from there to tell the basic story of the three main branches of the Protestant Reformation (Lutheran/Calvinist, Anabaptist, and Anglican) and of the Catholic Counter-Reformation. Some important points to include:

- the Martin Luther story (already outlined in the text)
- the Calvinist development of Lutheranism
- England's break from the papacy, but its only partial acceptance of Lutheran/Calvinist theology (Henry VIII's divorce)
- the German Peasants' War
- the Anabaptist threat, including the Anabaptist takeover of Münster
- the cleaning up of the Renaissance papacy
- the 1527 sack of Rome
- the Council of Trent
- the large number of religious persecutions
- the new religious justification for assassinating rulers
- the European wars of religion

And, looking more broadly, consider the impact of the European religious divide on colonial expansion and missionary work, including:

- the foundation of the Society of Jesus (Jesuits) to support Catholic renewal in Europe, and its

evolution shortly after into a major missionary force beyond Europe's borders
- reasons for the much smaller interest in evangelization among Protestant colonists
- the religious edge to European states' competition for New World resources

Lecture Strategy 2

"Asia and the individual."

The purpose of this lecture strategy is to explore movements that promoted individualism in the East and the West in the early modern period. Its objectives are:

- to reinforce the chapter's lessons about individualist movements of the period
- to examine in greater detail the scope of Chinese and Indian individualist movements
- to explore who was affected by Chinese and Indian individualist movements
- to consider the limitations of individualism in Europe
- to attempt to examine conditions for the often neglected 90 percent of the population—the poor and most women
- to try to reach a more balanced understanding of individualism in both hemispheres

A good place to begin is with a frank discussion, with as much student participation as possible, of Jean-Jacques Rousseau's statement that "man is born free, yet everywhere he is in chains." Discuss the limits on individualism in modern America—how family ties, socioeconomic circumstances, gender, age, education, etc. can affect the degree to which a person can be regarded as a fully self-standing "individual." You might include the question of whether religion fosters or discourages individualism.

Go on from there to consider some of the following questions:

- Can a subsistence-level peasant ever be regarded fully as an individual in the early modern era, no matter which part of the world s/he lives in?
- Did European society have movements of individual religious exploration comparable to the Indian bhakti movement?
- What effects did the European Reformation movements have on the role of the individual? Were all socioeconomic classes involved?

- Who in European society was affected by the Scientific Revolution?
- Who in European society was affected by the Enlightenment?
- How did literacy rates compare in Europe, China, and India?
- Where was there a popular press that could feed the imaginations of a wide audience?
- How much was behavior dictated by a religious establishment in different regions of the East and West?
- Did some political systems of the early modern period make individualism more difficult than did others?

Lecture Strategy 3

"Science and the world."
The text briefly mentions how much the development of the scientific method in Europe was influenced by world exploration. The purpose of this lecture strategy is to develop that idea, showing specific discoveries and some of their ramifications in the intellectual world of the early modern era. Its objectives are:

- to emphasize the lesson of the important role of global interaction in the Scientific Revolution
- to drive home the lesson with specific examples that will add color and reality for students
- to review and reemphasize the basic practices of the scientific method

A good place to begin is the accounts of the cultures of Native America that European explorers brought back to Europe. It can be useful to read short descriptions, for example, from Columbus's journals, or the works of Bartolomé de Las Casas, Bernal Díaz, or William Bradford. From there, go on to examine how the image of the "Indian" was popularized—European artwork depicting natives is readily available. Some points to consider while discussing these European impressions of Americans are:

- the notion of the "noble savage" and how it fit into European literary and philosophical traditions
- Michel de Montaigne's essay *On Cannibals*, with its clever use of Native Americans to form a devastating critique of European society
- William Shakespeare's *The Tempest*, with its suggestions of the dark side of unreformed savages in the character Caliban

- Thomas More's *Utopia* and its critique of European society

Go on from there to consider several other cases of European intellectual interaction with the Western Hemisphere or Asia. Some avenues of inquiry that you might find particularly satisfying are:

- the implications of the fact that the world was much bigger than Europeans had thought, and that millions of people had never had access to what most Europeans regarded as the only true religion
- the discovery of marsupials in Australia
- James Cook's voyages of exploration and surveying in the Pacific and Indian oceans
- the development of accurate maps
- Carl Linnaeus's development of a system of nomenclature for plants and animals
- the effect that the import of coffee and tea had on the intellectual climate of Europe

Things to Do in the Classroom

Discussion Topics

1. **Comparison, large or small group.** "The effects of the Reformations."
Ask students to *outline* the effects of the Reformation movements on European society. Besides reviewing the chapter material, this provides students with an opportunity to practice making outlines.

2. **Misconception/Difficult Topic, large or small group.** "Conversion is an all-or-nothing experience." This chapter gives a thoughtful presentation of the processes of syncretism and accommodation that accompany the conversion of people from one religion to another. Yet this is a difficult topic for many students, especially if they are asked to regard Christianity with non-Christian elements as a valid religion.

A broad discussion that encourages students to pull in material from earlier chapters would probably serve you best when addressing this topic. Encourage discussion of the following questions:

- What are the major types of religious syncretism discussed in the chapter? (Be sure to encourage a discussion of Islam, Confucianism, and Hinduism, not just Christianity.)

- Where's the dividing line between cultural practices and religious practices?
- Is there a religious practice anywhere in the world today that is not in some way syncretic?

3. Contextualization, large or small group.
"What did we get from the Scientific Revolution?"
Ask students to discuss and list both objects and attitudes of the present day that we would not have if it had not been for the Scientific Revolution. Encourage students not to itemize hundreds of individual inventions but to focus on the big picture. Lead them to include less tangible things, such as the notion that democracy is the ideal form of human society, or watching football on Sundays instead of going to church.

Classroom Activities

1. Role-playing exercise, small group. "Matteo Ricci in China."
Your students are the Jesuit missionary Matteo Ricci and a group of his assistants. Ask them to consider carefully the following: You badly want to convert the Chinese—what should you do to be as effective at the job as possible?

2. Close-reading exercise, large or small group. "The social contract."
Distribute a selection from Jean-Jacques Rousseau's *The Social Contract* that you think demonstrates "enlightened" thought particularly well. Ask students to analyze it, looking especially for points at which they can see the impact of the Scientific Revolution and the Enlightenment.

3. Clicker question. Taken as a whole, was the Scientific Revolution beneficial or not for humankind?

Key Terms

bhakti: Hindu devotional movement that flourished in the early modern era, emphasizing music, dance, poetry, and rituals as means by which to achieve direct union with the divine. (*pron.* BAHK-tee)

Catholic Counter-Reformation: An internal reform of the Catholic Church in the sixteenth century; thanks especially to the work of the Council of Trent (1545–1563), Catholic leaders clarified doctrine, corrected abuses and corruption, and put a new emphasis on education and accountability.

Condorcet and the idea of progress: The Marquis de Condorcet (1743–1794) was a French philosopher and political scientist who argued that human affairs were moving into an era of near-infinite improvability, with slavery, racism, tyranny, and other human trials swept away by the triumph of reason. (*pron.* kahn-dor-SAY)

Copernicus, Nicolaus: Polish mathematician and astronomer (1473–1543) who was the first to argue for the existence of a heliocentric cosmos.

Council of Trent: The main instrument of the Catholic Counter-Reformation (1545–1563), at which the Catholic Church clarified doctrine and corrected abuses.

Darwin, Charles: Highly influential English biologist (1809–1882) whose theory of natural selection continues to be seen by many as a threat to revealed religious truth.

deism: Belief in a divine being who created the cosmos but who does not intervene directly in human affairs.

Edict of Nantes: 1598 edict issued by French king Henry IV that granted considerable religious toleration to French Protestants and ended the French Wars of Religion. (*pron.* nahnt)

European Enlightenment: European intellectual movement of the eighteenth century that applied the lessons of the Scientific Revolution to human affairs and was noted for its commitment to open-mindedness and inquiry and the belief that knowledge could transform human society.

Freud, Sigmund: Austrian doctor and the father of modern psychoanalysis (1856–1939); his theories about the operation of the human mind and emotions remain influential today.

Galilei, Galileo: Italian astronomer (1564–1642) who further developed the ideas of Copernicus and whose work was eventually suppressed by the Catholic Church.

huacas: Local gods of the Andes. (*pron.* HWA-kaws)

Huguenots: The Protestant minority in France. (*pron.* HUGH-ghe-noes)

Jesuits in China: Series of Jesuit missionaries in the late sixteenth and seventeenth centuries who, inspired by the work of Matteo Ricci, made extraordinary efforts to understand and become a part of Chinese culture in their efforts to convert the Chinese elite, although with limited success.

kaozheng: Literally, "research based on evidence"; Chinese intellectual movement whose practitioners emphasized the importance of evidence and analysis, applied especially to historical documents. (*pron.* kow-jung)

Luther, Martin: German priest and theologian (1483–1546) who inaugurated the Protestant Reformation movement in Europe.

Marx, Karl: German philosopher (1818–1883) whose view of human history as a class struggle formed the basis of socialism.

Mirabai: One of India's most beloved bhakti poets (1498–1547), she helped break down the barriers of caste and tradition. (*pron.* MIR-ah-bye)

Nanak, Guru: The founder of Sikhism (1469–1539). (*pron.* NAH-nahk)

Newton, Isaac: English natural scientist (1643–1727) whose formulation of the laws of motion and mechanics is regarded as the culmination of the Scientific Revolution.

Ninety-five Theses: List of ninety-five debating points about the abuses of the Church, posted by Martin Luther on the door of a church in Wittenberg in 1517; the Church's strong reaction eventually drove Luther to separate from Catholic Christianity.

Protestant Reformation: Massive schism within Christianity that had its formal beginning in 1517 with the German priest Martin Luther; while the leaders of the movement claimed that they sought to "reform" a Church that had fallen from biblical practice, in reality the movement was radically innovative in its challenge to Church authority and its endorsement of salvation "by faith alone."

Ricci, Matteo: The most famous Jesuit missionary in China in the early modern period; active in China from 1582 to 1610. (*pron.* maht-TAY-oh REE-chee)

Scientific Revolution: Great European intellectual and cultural transformation that was based on the principles of the scientific method.

Sikhism: Religious tradition of northern India founded by Guru Nanak ca. 1500; combines elements of Hinduism and Islam and proclaims the brotherhood of all humans and the equality of men and women. (*pron.* SEEK-ism)

Society of Jesus: Also called "Jesuits," this Catholic religious society was founded to encourage the renewal of Catholicism through education and preaching; it soon became a leading Catholic missionary order beyond the borders of Europe.

Taki Onqoy: Literally, "dancing sickness"; a religious revival movement in central Peru in the 1560s whose members preached the imminent destruction of Christianity and of the Europeans in favor of a renewed Andean golden age. (*pron.* TAH-kee OHN-koy)

Thirty Years' War: Highly destructive war (1618–1648) that eventually included most of Europe; fought for the most part between Protestants and Catholics, the conflict ended with the Peace of Westphalia (1648).

Voltaire: Pen name of the French philosopher François-Marie Arouet (1694–1778), whose work is often taken as a model of Enlightenment questioning of traditional values and attitudes; noted for his deism and his criticism of traditional religion. (*pron.* vol-TARE)

Wahhabi Islam: Major Islamic movement led by the Muslim theologian Abd al-Wahhab (1703–1792) that advocated an austere lifestyle and strict adherence to the sharia (Islamic law). (*pron.* wah-HAB-ee)

Wang Yangmin: Prominent Chinese philosopher (1472–1529) who argued that it was possible to achieve a virtuous life by introspection, without the extensive education of traditional Confucianism. (*pron.* wahng yahng-min)

ANSWER GUIDELINES FOR CHAPTER QUESTIONS

The two sets of questions that follow appear in the textbook at the end of the chapter and in the margins of the reading. They are also provided in the Computerized Test Bank with answer guidelines, for your convenience.

The Big Picture Questions

1. Why did Christianity take hold in some places more than in others?

• Christianity integrated most fully into regions where European colonial powers ruled, where there was an overwhelming European presence, where the established society had been defeated and disrupted, and where no literate world religion was already established.

• It had the least impact when it had to operate with the permission of non-Christian rulers, when it sought to convert in a society that was stable and well established, and when it sought to convert in a region where a literate world religion already existed.

2. In what ways was the missionary message of Christianity shaped by the cultures of Asian and American peoples?

• In China, Christian missionaries downplayed their mission to convert and were at pains to be respectful of Chinese culture, pointing out parallels between Confucianism and Christianity rather than portraying Christianity as something new and foreign. Chinese conversions occurred primarily among those elite scholars who were interested in Western science and who were attracted by the personal lives of the missionaries and by the moral certainty that Christianity offered. While their primary goal was elite conversions, missionaries also attracted a small following among members of the general population who were attracted by tales of miracles attributed to the Christian God. However, there was only limited acceptance of Christianity in China after it became apparent that conversion to Christianity required abandonment of many Chinese practices.

• In the Americas, especially in the Spanish possessions explored in this chapter, the Christian missionary message was more strident and less accommodating, which reflected the reality of European political dominance. Missionaries sought to convert the whole population to the Christian faith, drawing on the political authority of Christian rulers and the disruption in Native American society occasioned by conquest. They were only partially successful, as local populations occasionally resisted their conversion efforts openly but more often worked to blend Christian and indigenous religious traditions and assimilate Christianity into patterns of local culture. Elsewhere in the Americas, African and Christian traditions were blended in religions such as Vodou in Haiti, Santeria in Cuba, and Candomble and Macumba in Brazil.

3. Compare the processes by which Christianity and Islam became world religions.

• Christianity began the early modern period as a faith largely limited to Europe.
• But by riding the currents of European empire building and commercial expansion, Christianity was

solidly established in the Americas and the Philippines and, to a far more modest degree, in Siberia, China, Japan, and India.

• Islam became more than a regional religion much earlier than did Christianity, spreading with the rapidly expanding Arab empire in the seventh and eighth centuries and then through the conversion of some pastoral peoples of Central Asia.

• Later, the Mughal and Songhay empires helped to establish Islam more firmly in India and West Africa, respectively. Meanwhile, the conversion of Swahili city-states along the east coast of Africa expanded the presence of Islam in this region.

• From early in Islam's history, Muslim traders and missionaries also brought the faith to regions beyond the control of Islamic states.

• In sub-Saharan Africa, in the eastern and western wings of India, and in Central and Southeast Asia, the expansion of the Islamic frontier continued throughout the early modern era. This expansion depended on wandering Muslim holy men, Islamic scholars, and itinerant traders.

• During the early modern period, Islam also extended modestly to the Americas, where enslaved African Muslims planted their faith, particularly in Brazil.

4. In what ways did the spread of Christianity, Islam, and modern science give rise to culturally based conflicts?

• Christianity is a strongly monotheistic religion, and missionaries seeking to spread it to the Americas frequently opposed the efforts of local populations who worked to blend Christian and indigenous religious traditions and assimilate Christianity into patterns of local culture.

• The spread of Islam through the work of wandering holy men, Islamic scholars, and itinerant traders allowed communities to adopt elements of Islam while retaining many local religious traditions and ideas. To some more orthodox Muslims, this religious blending became increasingly offensive, even heretical, and such sentiments led to movements of religious renewal and reform that emerged throughout the vast Islamic world during the eighteenth century.

• The emergence of modern science during the Scientific Revolution challenged the beliefs and ideas on which European political and religious authorities relied, leading to conflicts. In the nineteenth century, scientific thinkers like Darwin, Marx, and Freud defined the very basis of human life around struggle and conflict.

5.   Based on Chapters 13 through 16, how does the history of Islam in the early modern era challenge a Eurocentric understanding of those centuries?

• Throughout the early modern era, the Islamic world maintained a central role in world history.

• The Islamic faith continued to expand, mostly through voluntary conversion.

• It also remained vibrant, with a series of reform movements and new traditions taking shape.

• The Islamic world supported several powerful empires and maintained a central place in long-distance commerce.

• The expansion of European influence had little impact on the Islamic world.

• Meanwhile, the Ottoman Empire expanded its influence in the Christian world, especially in the Balkans.

• These developments challenge a Eurocentric understanding of the early modern era, in that the Islamic world's history was to a large extent independent of the Western European experience. Thus, to focus on Europe would result in the neglect of the Islamic world.

Margin Review Questions

Q.   *In what ways did the Protestant Reformation transform European society, culture, and politics?*

• It created a permanent schism within Catholic Christendom.

• It gave some kings and princes a justification for their own independence from the Church and an opportunity to gain the lands and taxes previously held by the Church.

• It provided the urban middle classes a new religious legitimacy for their growing role in society.

• It was used by common people to express their opposition to the whole social order.

• It had a less profound impact on the lives of women, although it did stimulate female education and literacy, even if there was little space for women to make use of that education outside the family.

• Religious difference led to sectarian violence, to war, and ultimately to religious coexistence.

• Its successful challenge to the immense prestige and power of the pope and the established Church encouraged a skeptical attitude toward authority and tradition.

• It fostered religious individualism as people were encouraged to read and interpret the scriptures themselves and to seek salvation without the mediation of the Church.

Q.   *How was European imperial expansion related to the spread of Christianity?*

• Christianity motivated European imperial expansion and also benefited from it.

• The Portuguese and Spanish both saw their movement overseas as a continuation of a long crusading tradition, which only recently had completed the liberation of their countries from Muslim control.

• Colonial settlers and traders brought their faith with them and sought to replicate it in their newly conquered homelands.

• Missionaries, mostly Catholic, actively spread the Christian message beyond European communities in the Americas, Africa, and Asia. In Siberia, missionaries of the Russian Orthodox Church did likewise.

• But missionaries had their greatest successes in Spanish America and the Philippines, where their efforts were strengthened by an overwhelming European presence, experienced variously as military conquest, colonial settlement, missionary activity, forced labor, social disruption, and disease.

Q.   *In what ways was European Christianity assimilated into the Native American cultures of Spanish America?*

• Native Americans frequently sought to reinterpret Christian practices while incorporating local elements, as in the Andes, where dancers in the Taki Onqoy movement sometimes took the names of Christian saints;

• where people might offer the blood of a llama to strengthen a village church;

• where believers might make a cloth covering for the Virgin Mary and a shirt for an image of a native huaca with the same material.

• In Mexico, an immigrant Christianity was assimilated into patterns of local culture: parishes were organized largely around precolonial towns or regions;

• churches were built on or near the sites of old temples;

- *cofradias*, church-based associations of laypeople, organized community processions and festivals and made provision for a proper funeral and burial for their members;
- Christian saints closely paralleled the functions of precolonial gods;
- the *fiscal*, or leader of the church staff, was a native Christian of great local prestige, who carried on the traditions and role of earlier religious specialists.
- Throughout the colonial period and beyond, many Mexican Christians also took part in rituals derived from the past, with little sense that this was incompatible with Christian practices. These practices sought spiritual assistance in those areas of everyday life not directly addressed by Christian rites, but they also showed signs of Christian influence.

Q. *Why were missionary efforts to spread Christianity so much less successful in China than in Spanish America?*

- The political context was very different, with missionaries to China working within the context of the powerful and prosperous Ming and Qing dynasties, while missionaries to Spanish America worked among a defeated population whose societies had been thoroughly disrupted and whose cultural confidence was shaken.
- European missionaries required the permission of Chinese authorities to operate in China, while Spanish missionaries working in a colonial setting were less constrained. Ultimately, missionaries in China lost favor at the Chinese imperial court.
- Missionaries to China deliberately sought to convert the official Chinese elite, while missionaries to Spanish America sought to convert the masses.
- Missionary efforts in China were less successful because the missionaries offered little that the Chinese really needed, since traditional Chinese philosophies and religions provided for the spiritual needs of most Chinese. Moreover, Christianity required the converts to abandon much of traditional Chinese culture. In the Americas, local gods had in part been discredited by the Spanish conquest, and in any case, Christianity was a literate world religion, something different from what had been practiced in the region before.

Q. *What accounts for the continued spread of Islam in the early modern era and for the emergence of reform or renewal movements within the Islamic world?*

- Islam continued to spread because conversion to Islam generally did not mean a sudden abandonment of old religious practices, but rather more often the assimilation of "Islamic rituals, cosmologies, and literatures into . . . local religious systems."
- Continued Islamization depended on wandering Muslim holy men, Islamic scholars, and itinerant traders, who posed no threat and often proved useful to local rulers and communities.
- In part, the emergence of reform or renewal movements was a reaction to the blending or syncretism that accompanied Islamization almost everywhere and that came to be seen as increasingly offensive, even heretical, by more orthodox Muslims.

Q. *In what ways did Asian cultural changes in the early modern era parallel those of Europe, and in what ways were they different?*

- In terms of parallel developments, both Confucianism and Buddhism developed traditions during the early modern period that bore some similarity to the thinking of Martin Luther in Europe in that they promoted a moral or religious individualism that encouraged individuals to seek enlightenment on their own.
- As in Christian Europe, challenges to established orthodoxies emerged as commercial and urban life, as well as political change, fostered new thinking.
- In Chinese elite culture, there emerged a movement known as *kaozheng*, or "research based on evidence," which bears some comparison to the genuinely scientific approach to knowledge sponsored by Western Europe.
- In terms of differences, despite the similarity of kaozheng to the Western scientific approach, in China it was applied more to the study of the past than to the natural world, as occurred in Western Europe.
- Cultural change in China was less dramatic than in Europe.
- Confucian culture did not spread as widely as Christianity.

Q. *Why did the Scientific Revolution occur in Europe rather than in China or the Islamic world?*

- Europe's historical development as a reinvigorated and fragmented civilization arguably gave rise to conditions uniquely favorable to the Scientific Revolution, including a legal system that guaranteed a measure of independence for a variety of institutions and unusually autonomous universities in which scholars could pursue their studies in relative freedom from the dictates of church or state authorities.

• Western Europe was in a position to draw extensively upon the knowledge of other cultures, especially that of the Islamic world.

• In the sixteenth through the eighteenth century, Europeans found themselves at the center of a massive new exchange of information as they became aware of lands, peoples, plants, animals, societies, and religions from around the world. This wave of new knowledge, uniquely available to Europeans, clearly shook up older ways of thinking and opened the way to new conceptions of the world.

• In the Islamic world, science was patronized by a variety of local authorities, but it occurred largely outside the formal system of higher education, where philosophy and natural science were viewed with great suspicion.

• In China, education focused on preparing for a rigidly defined set of civil service examinations and emphasized the humanistic and moral texts of classical Confucianism. The pursuit of scientific knowledge was relegated to the margins of the Chinese educational system.

Q. *What was revolutionary about the Scientific Revolution?*

• The Scientific Revolution was revolutionary because it put an end to the idea that the earth was stationary and at the center of the universe, which had been the dominant view of the world in Western Europe.

• It was also revolutionary because the laws formulated by Isaac Newton showed that the universe was not propelled by angels and spirits but functioned on its own according to timeless principles that could be described mathematically. A corollary of this view was the idea that knowledge of the universe could be obtained through human reason alone, without the aid of ancient authorities or divine revelation.

• Above all, it was revolutionary because it challenged educated people to question traditional views of the world and humankind's place in it.

Q. *In what ways did the Enlightenment challenge older patterns of European thinking?*

• It applied a new approach to the conduct of human affairs, one that was rooted in human reason,

skeptical of authority, and expressed in natural laws. This challenged the aristocratic privileges of European society and the claims to authority of arbitrary governments who relied on the "divine right of kings" for legitimacy.

• The Enlightenment challenged the authority of established religion, accusing the Church of fostering superstition, ignorance, and corruption.

• It also challenged older patterns of thinking through its promotion of the idea of progress. Human society, according to Enlightenment thinkers, was not fixed by tradition or divine command but could be changed, and improved, by human action guided by reason. These ideas ultimately underpinned revolutionary movements in America, France, Haiti, and Latin America.

Q. *How did nineteenth-century developments in the sciences challenge the faith of the Enlightenment?*

• Nineteenth-century intellectuals such as Darwin and Marx still believed in progress, but they emphasized conflict and struggle rather than reason and education as the motors of progress.

• Freudian psychology cast doubt on Enlightenment conceptions of human rationality, emphasizing instead that at the core of each person lay primal impulses toward sexuality and aggression, which were only barely held in check by the thin veneer of social conscience derived from civilization.

Q. *In what ways was European science received in the major civilizations of Asia in the early modern era?*

• In China, European scientific knowledge was sought after selectively. Qing dynasty emperors and scholars were most interested in European astronomy and mathematics. However, they had little interest in European medicine.

• Japanese authorities after 1720 allowed for the importation and translation of European texts in medicine, astronomy, geography, mathematics, and other disciplines. These texts were studied by a small group of Japanese scholars who were especially impressed with Western anatomical studies. But this small center of learning remained isolated, and it was not until the second half of the nineteenth century that European science assumed a prominent place in Japanese culture.

• Scholars in the Ottoman Empire were broadly aware of European scientific achievements by 1650, but they took an interest only in those developments that offered practical utility, such as in making maps and calendars.

ADDITIONAL RESOURCES FOR CHAPTER 16

Additional Bedford/St. Martin's Resources

FOR INSTRUCTORS

Computerized Test Bank

This test bank provides over thirty exercises per chapter, including multiple-choice, fill-in-the-blank, short-answer, and full-length essay questions. Instructors can customize quizzes, add or edit both questions and answers, and export questions and answers to a variety of formats, including WebCT and Blackboard. The disc includes correct answers and essay outlines.

Instructor's Resource CD-ROM

This disc provides instructors with ready-made and customizable PowerPoint multimedia presentations built around chapter outlines, maps, figures, and all images from the textbook, plus JPEG versions of all maps, figures, and images.

The following maps and images from Chapter 16 are available in both JPEG and PowerPoint format on the Instructor's Resource CD-ROM:

- Map 16.1: Reformation Europe in the Sixteenth Century (p. 466)
- The Virgin of Guadalupe (p. 460)
- The Protestant Reformation (p. 463)
- Japanese Christian Martyrs (p. 468)
- Jesuits in China (p. 471)
- Guru Nanak (p. 476)
- Muslim Astronomy and the Scientific Revolution (p. 479)
- Uncovering the Human Skeleton (p. 483)

FOR STUDENTS

Documents and Essays from *Worlds of History: A Comparative Reader*, Third Edition (Volume 2)

The following documents, essays, and illustrations to accompany Chapter 16 are available in Chapters 3 and 5 of Volume 2 of this reader by Kevin Reilly:

From Chapter 3:

- Jonathan Spence, *The Ming Chinese State and Religion*
- Matteo Ricci, *Jesuit Missionaries in Ming China*
- Martin Luther, *Law and the Gospel: Princes and Turks*
- Roger Williams, *The Bloody Tenet of Persecution for Cause of Conscience*

From Chapter 5:

- Thinking Historically: Distinguishing Change from Revolution
- Franklin Le Van Baumer, *The Scientific Revolution in the West*
- Galileo Galilei, *Letter to the Grand Duchess Christina*
- Natalie Zemon Davis, *Metamorphoses: Maria Sibylla Merian*
- Lady Mary Wortley Montague, *Letter on Turkish Smallpox Inoculation*
- Lynda Norene Shaffer, *China, Technology, and Change*
- Sugita Gempaku, *A Dutch Anatomy Lesson in Japan*
- Benjamin Franklin, *Letter on a Balloon Experiment in 1783*

Online Study Guide at bedfordstmartins.com/strayer

The Online Study Guide helps students synthesize the material from the text as well as practice the skills historians use to make sense of the past. Each chapter of the Online Study Guide contains specific testing exercises, including a multiple-choice self-test that focuses on important conceptual ideas; an identification quiz that helps students remember key people, places, and events; a flashcard activity that tests students on their knowledge of key terms; and two interactive map activities intended to strengthen students' geographic skills. Instructors can monitor students' progress through an online Quiz Gradebook or receive email updates.

Further Reading

Early Modern Resources, http://earlymodernweb.org.uk/emr/. A definitive collection, compiled by Sharon Howard, of materials available on the Internet, including resources on Asia, Africa, and the Americas as well as Europe.

Explorers of the Millennium, http://library.thinkquest.org/4034/. A major Web resource for explorers in world history.

Henry, John. *The Scientific Revolution and the Origins of Modern Science*. 2nd ed. New York: Palgrave Macmillan, 2002. An accessible history of the topic.

Jacob, Margaret C. *The Enlightenment: A Brief History with Documents*. Boston: Bedford/St. Martin's, 2001. Clearly written, with an interesting variety of primary sources.

Martin Luther: The Reluctant Revolutionary, http://www.pbs.org/empires/martinluther/. An interesting and interactive PBS Web site on the great reformer.

Rublack, Ulinka. *Reformation Europe*. Cambridge: Cambridge University Press, 2005. A recent overview of the Reformation movements, short enough to be useful when preparing world civ. lectures.

The Scientific Revolution, http://web.clas.ufl.edu/users/rhatch/pages/03-Sci-Rev/SCI-REV-Home/. A very rich resource (part of the Web page of Robert A. Hatch) that lists both primary and secondary sources.

Spence, Jonathan D. *The Memory Palace of Matteo Ricci*. London: Penguin, 1985. Drawing heavily on Ricci's own journals, this work paints a brilliant picture of Matteo Ricci and the Jesuit mission to China.

Literature

Cao Xueqin. *The Golden Days (The Story of the Stone, or The Dream of the Red Chamber*, vol. 1). Trans. Hsueh-Chin Tsao et al. London: Penguin, 1974. The first volume of Penguin's five-volume translation of this great early modern Chinese classic.

Galilei, Galileo. *Sidereus Nuncius,* or *The Sidereal Messenger*. Trans. Albert van Helden. 2nd ed. Chicago: University of Chicago Press, 1989. A good translation of Galileo's most important work.

Hawley, John Stratton, ed. *Songs of the Saints of India*. 2nd ed. Oxford: Oxford University Press, 2004. An interesting selection of bhakti poetry in translation.

Janz, Denis, ed. *A Reformation Reader*. Minneapolis: Fortress Press, 1999.

Mirabai. *Ecstatic Poems*. Trans. Robert Bly. Boston: Beacon Press, 2004. Deeply sensual and moving poetry by one of the greatest bhakti saints.

Reformation Ink, http://homepage.mac.com/shanerosenthal/reformationink/classic.htm. Links to Reformation classics available on the Internet.

Rousseau, Jean-Jacques. *The Social Contract*. Trans. Maurice Cranston. London: Penguin, 1968. Perhaps the most influential work of the Enlightenment.

Voltaire. *Candide, or Optimism*. Trans John Butt. Harmondsworth: Penguin, 1950. A wonderful satire of life and attitudes in Enlightenment Europe, short enough for classroom use.

Voltaire. *A Treatise on Toleration and Other Essays*. Trans. Joseph McCabe. Buffalo, NY: Prometheus Books, 1994. A scathing critique of Christianity as it was practiced in Voltaire's day.

Film

The Age of Reason. Insight Media, 1995. 23 minutes. A survey of intellectual history in the seventeenth and eighteenth centuries, with special emphasis on scientific discoveries.

The Enlightenment. Insight Media, 1992. 42 minutes. Provides an overview of developments in thought, art, and politics in eighteenth-century Western Europe.

Food for the Ancestors. PBS Home Video, 1999. 52 minutes. Using the history of food as its focus, this entertaining video explores the Mexican religious festival known as the Days of the Dead, in which Christian and older indigenous religious traditions mingle.

Renaissance, Reformation, and Enlightenment. Insight Media, 2006. 31 minutes. A short video that looks at three transformative intellectual movements in late medieval and early modern Europe.

Revolution of Conscience: The Life, Convictions, and Legacy of Martin Luther. Films for the Sciences and Humanities, 2003. 56 minutes. Up-to-date documentary that chronicles Luther's life and his impact on European religion and society.

PART FIVE

THE EUROPEAN MOMENT IN WORLD HISTORY
1750–1914

Outline: The Big Picture: European Centrality and the Problem of Eurocentrism

I. **Two major phenomena mark the "long nineteenth century" (1750–1914):**
   A. the creation of "modern" human societies, an outgrowth of the Scientific, French, and Industrial revolutions (Chapters 17–18);
   B. and the ability of these modern societies to exercise enormous power and influence over the rest of the world.
      1. colonial empires founded in some places
      2. informal control (economic, military, diplomatic, and missionary) established in others

C. The two phenomena gave Western Europe (and to some extent North America) more prominence in world history than ever before.
      1. achieved something approaching global dominance by early 1900s

II. **Eurocentric Geography and History**
   A. Europe's new power included the ability to center human history and geography on Europe.
      1. Europe was placed at the center of the world on maps
      2. Europe was regarded as a continent in its own right
      3. the rest of the world was defined in terms of distance from Europe (e.g., the Far East)
      4. longitude was measured from the "prime meridian," running through Greenwich, England
   B. History textbooks were Eurocentric.
      1. non-European peoples were regarded as static and unchanging
      2. general view that "backward" peoples must either Europeanize or go extinct
      3. Eurocentrism wasn't really challenged until around 1950

C. The discipline of world history emerged after World War II with a goal of counteracting Eurocentrism.

1. but in recent centuries, Europeans *have* been central

III. **Countering Eurocentrism—five answers to the problem of European centrality**

A. We need to remind ourselves how recent the European moment in world history has been.

1. other peoples have had times of "cultural flowering"

B. Europe rose to dominance within an international context.

1. only the withdrawal of the Chinese fleet allowed European domination of the Indian Ocean (sixteenth century)

2. disease and internal divisions of Native Americans made the European takeover of the Americas possible

3. the Scientific Revolution drew on Islamic science and information from around the world

4. the Industrial Revolution benefited from New World resources and markets

5. local elites cooperated in European domination

C. Europe's rise to global dominance was not easy or automatic.

1. many cases of fierce resistance

D. Peoples of the world used Europeans and their ideas for their own purposes.

1. adaptation of borrowings to local circumstances

2. encounters between culturally different peoples are the most interesting stories of modern world history

E. Europeans were not the only game in town—Asians, Africans, and Middle Easterners had other concerns, too.

IV. **Yes, the European moment in world history is significant, but it's best understood in a larger context of interaction and exchange**

Atlantic Revolutions and Their Echoes
1750–1914

CHAPTER OVERVIEW

Chapter Objectives

- To make students aware of the number and diversity of Atlantic revolutions in the eighteenth and nineteenth centuries
- To explore the cross-pollination between revolutionary movements
- To investigate the real impact of the Atlantic revolutions
- To consider the broader long-term implications of the revolutionary movements for sweeping social change

Chapter Outline

I. **Opening Vignette**
   A. In 1989, celebration of the bicentennial of the French Revolution coincided with the Chinese government's crackdown on demonstrators in Tiananmen Square.
      1. The French Revolution was the centerpiece of a revolutionary process all around the Atlantic world between 1775 and 1875

   2. Atlantic revolutions had an impact far beyond the Atlantic world
      a. French invasions of Egypt, Poland, and Russia
      b. inspired efforts to abolish slavery, give women greater rights, and extend the franchise in many countries
      c. nationalism was shaped by revolutions
      d. principles of equality eventually gave birth to socialism and communism

II. **Comparing Atlantic Revolutions** [see Lecture Strategy 1 and Classroom Activity 1]
   A. The revolutions of North America, Europe, Haiti, and Latin America influenced each other.
      1. they also shared a set of common ideas
      2. grew out of the European Enlightenment
         a. notion that it is possible to engineer, and improve, political and social life
         b. traditional ways of thinking were no longer sacrosanct
      3. the core political idea was "popular sovereignty"—that the authority to govern comes from *the people*, not from God or tradition
         a. John Locke (1632–1704) argued that the "social contract" between ruler and

ruled should last only as long as it served the people well

4. except in Haiti, the main beneficiaries of revolution were middle-class white males
   a. but in the long term, the revolution gave ammunition to groups without political rights
   b. goal was to extend political rights further than ever before, so can be called "democratic revolutions"

5. considerable differences between the Atlantic revolutions

B. The North American Revolution, 1775–1787 **[see Discussion Topic 1]**
   1. basic facts of the American Revolution are well known
   2. a bigger question is what it changed
   3. American Revolution was a conservative political movement
      a. aimed to preserve colonial liberties, rather than gain new ones
      b. for most of seventeenth and eighteenth centuries, the British North American colonies had much local autonomy
      c. colonists regarded autonomy as their birthright
      d. few thought of breaking away from Britain before 1750
   4. colonial society
      a. was far more egalitarian than in Europe
      b. in manners, they were republican well before the revolution
   5. Britain made a new drive to control the colonies and get more revenue from them in the 1760s
      a. Britain needed money for its global war with France
      b. imposed a number of new taxes and tariffs on the colonies
      c. colonists were not represented in the British parliament
      d. appeared to deny the colonists' identity as true Englishmen
      e. challenged colonial economic interests
      f. attacked established traditions of local autonomy
   6. British North America was revolutionary for the society that had already emerged, not for the revolution itself

   a. no significant social transformation came with independence from Britain
   b. accelerated democratic tendencies that were already established
   c. political power remained in the hands of existing elites
      i. property requirements for voting were lowered
      ii. property rights remained intact
   7. Many Americans *thought* they were creating a new world order
      a. some acclaimed the United States as "the hope and model of the human race"
      b. declaration of the "right to revolution" inspired other colonies around the world
      c. the U.S. Constitution was one of the first lasting efforts to put Enlightenment political ideas into practice

C. The French Revolution, 1789–1815 **[see Classroom Activity 2]**
   1. thousands of French soldiers had fought for the American revolutionaries
   2. French government was facing bankruptcy
      a. had long attempted to modernize the tax system and make it fairer, but was opposed by the privileged classes
      b. King Louis XVI called the Estates General into session in a new effort to raise taxes
         i. first two estates (clergy and nobility) were around 2 percent of the population
         ii. Third Estate was everyone else
   3. when the Estates General convened in 1789, Third Estate representatives broke loose and declared themselves the National Assembly
      a. drew up the Declaration of the Rights of Man and Citizen
      b. launched the French Revolution
   4. unlike the American Revolution, the French rising was driven by pronounced social conflicts
      a. titled nobility resisted monarchic efforts to tax them
      b. middle class resented aristocratic privileges

c. urban poor suffered from inflation and unemployment

d. the peasants were oppressed

5. Enlightenment ideas gave people a language to articulate grievances

6. French Revolution was violent, far-reaching, and radical

   a. ended hereditary privilege

   b. even abolished slavery (for a time)

   c. the Church was subjected to government authority

   d. king and queen were executed (1793)

   e. the Terror (1793–1794) killed tens of thousands of people regarded as enemies of the revolution

7. effort to create a wholly new society

   a. 1792 became Year I of a new calendar

   b. briefly passed a law for universal male suffrage

   c. France was divided into 83 territorial departments

   d. created a massive army (some 800,000 men) to fight threatening neighbors

      i. all adult males were required to serve

      ii. officers came from middle and lower classes

   e. spurt of nationalism, with revolutionary state at the center

   f. radicals especially pushed the idea of new beginnings

8. influence of French Revolution spread through conquest

   a. Napoleon Bonaparte (r. 1799–1814) seized power in 1799

   b. preserved many moderate elements of the revolution

   c. kept social equality, but got rid of liberty

   d. subdued most of Europe

   e. imposed revolutionary practices on conquered regions

   f. resentment of French domination stimulated national consciousness throughout Europe

      i. national resistance brought down Napoleon's empire by 1815

D. The Haitian Revolution, 1791–1804

1. Saint Domingue (later called Haiti) was a French Caribbean colony

   a. regarded as the richest colony in the world

   b. vast majority of population were slaves

      i. around 500,000 slaves, 40,000 whites, 30,000 "free people of color"

2. example of the French Revolution sparked a spiral of violence

   a. but revolution meant different things to different people

   b. massive slave revolt began in 1791

   c. became a war between a number of factions

   d. power gradually shifted to the slaves, who were led by former slave Toussaint Louverture

3. the result was a unique revolution—the only completely successful slave revolt in world history

   a. renamed the country Haiti ("mountainous" in Taino)

   b. identified themselves with the original native inhabitants

   c. declared equality for all races

   d. divided up plantations among small farmers

4. Haiti's success generated great hope and great fear

   a. created new "insolence" among slaves elsewhere, inspired other slave rebellions

   b. caused horror among whites, led to social conservatism

   c. increased slavery elsewhere, as plantations claimed Haiti's market share

   d. Napoleon's defeat in Haiti convinced him to sell Louisiana Territory to the U.S.

E. Spanish American Revolutions, 1810–1825

1. Latin American revolutions were inspired by earlier revolutionary movements

2. native-born elites (*creoles*) in Spanish colonies of Latin America were offended at the Spanish monarchy's efforts to control them in the eighteenth century

   a. but there were only scattered and uncoordinated protests initially

3. reasons why Latin American independence movements were limited at first

   a. little tradition of local self-government

b. society was more authoritarian, with stricter class divisions

c. whites were vastly outnumbered

4. creole elites had revolution thrust upon them by events in Europe

    a. 1808: Napoleon invaded Spain and Portugal, put royal authority in disarray

    b. Latin Americans were forced to take action

    c. most of Latin America was independent by 1826

5. longer process than in North America

    a. Latin American societies were torn by class, race, and regional divisions

        i. e.g., in Mexico, move toward independence began with a peasant revolt (1810) led by priests Miguel Hidalgo and José Morelos

        ii. creole elites and clergy raised an army, crushed revolt

        iii. such class violence was common elsewhere

    b. fear of social rebellion from below shaped the whole independence movement

        i. Peruvian revolt (1780s) in the name of Tupac Amaru, the last Inca emperor

        ii. most people in society were exploited and oppressed

6. leaders of independence movements appealed to the lower classes in terms of nativism: all free people born in the Americas were *Americanos*

    a. many whites and mestizos regarded themselves as Spanish

    b. but many leaders were liberals, influenced by the ideals of the Enlightenment and the French Revolution

    c. in reality, lower classes, Native Americans, and slaves got little benefit from independence

7. it proved impossible to unite the various Spanish colonies, unlike the United States

    a. distances were greater

    b. colonial experiences were different

    c. stronger regional identities

8. after Latin America gained independence, its traditional relationship with North America was gradually reversed

    a. the U.S. grew wealthier and more democratic, became stable

    b. Latin American countries became increasingly underdeveloped, impoverished, undemocratic, and unstable

III. **Echoes of Revolution** [see Classroom Activity 3]

A. Smaller European revolutions occurred in 1830, 1848, and 1870.

    1. led to greater social equality and liberation from foreign rule

    2. enlarged voting rights: by 1914, major states of Western Europe, the U.S., and Argentina had universal male suffrage

    3. even in Russia, there was a constitutional movement in 1825

    4. abolitionist, nationalist, and feminist movements arose to question other patterns of exclusion and oppression

B. The Abolition of Slavery **[see Discussion Topic 2]**

    1. slavery was largely ended around the world between 1780 and 1890

    2. Enlightenment thinkers were increasingly critical of slavery

        a. American and French revolutions focused attention on slaves' lack of liberty and equality

        b. religious groups, especially Quakers and Protestant evangelicals, became increasingly vocal in opposition to slavery

        c. growing belief that slavery wasn't necessary for economic progress

            i. notion that slavery was out of date

    3. three major slave rebellions in the British West Indies showed that slaves were discontent; brutality of suppression appalled people

    4. abolitionist movements were most powerful in Britain

        a. 1807: Britain forbade the sale of slaves within its empire

        b. 1834: Britain emancipated all slaves

        c. other nations followed suit, under growing international pressure

        d. most Latin American countries abolished slavery by 1850s

            i. Brazil was the last (1888)

        e. emancipation of the Russian serfs (1861)

5. resistance to abolition was vehement among interested parties
   a. in the U.S., it took a major civil war to end slavery (1861–1865)
6. abolition often didn't lead to the expected results
   a. usually there was little improvement in the economic lives of former slaves
      i. highly dependent forms of labor emerged
   b. unwillingness of former slaves to work on plantations led to a new wave of global migration, especially from India and China
   c. few of the newly freed gained anything like political equality
      i. in southern U.S., a period of political rights was followed by segregationist, racist reaction
   d. most former Russian serfs remained impoverished
   e. more slaves were used within Africa to produce export crops
      i. Europeans used this to justify colonial rule in Africa in the late nineteenth century

C. Nations and Nationalism **[see Lecture Strategy 2 and Discussion Topic 3]**
   1. revolutionary movements gave new prominence to more recent kind of human community—the nation
      a. idea that humans are divided into separate nations, each with a distinct culture and territory and deserving an independent political life
      b. before the nineteenth century, foreign rule in itself wasn't regarded as heinous
      c. most important loyalties were to clan, village, or region
   2. independence movements acted in the name of new nations
      a. Napoleon's conquests stimulated national resistance
   3. erosion of older identities and loyalties
      a. science weakened the hold of religion
      b. migration to cities or abroad weakened local allegiances
      c. printing standardized languages
   4. nationalism was often presented as a reawakening of older cultural identities

5. nationalism was enormously powerful in the nineteenth century
   a. inspired political unification of Germany and Italy
   b. inspired separatist movements by Greeks, Serbs, Czechs, Hungarians, Poles, Ukrainians, the Irish, and Jews
   c. fueled preexisting rivalry among European states
      i. drive for colonies in Asia and Africa
      ii. can see its height in the suffering of World War I
   d. efforts to instill national loyalty in citizens
6. nationalism took on a variety of political ideologies
   a. "civic nationalism" identified the "nation" with a particular territory, encouraged assimilation
   b. some defined the nation in racial terms (e.g., Germany)
7. nationalism was not limited to Europe

D. Feminist Beginnings **[see Lecture Strategy 3]**
   1. a feminist movement developed in the nineteenth century, especially in Europe and North America
      a. transformed the interaction of women and men in the twentieth century
   2. European Enlightenment thinkers sometimes challenged the idea that women were innately inferior
      a. during the French Revolution, some women argued that liberty and equality must include women
      b. more educational opportunities and less household drudgery for middle-class women
      c. women increasingly joined temperance movements, charities, abolitionist movements, missionary work, etc.
      d. maternal feminism: argued women's distinctive role as mothers
   3. first organized expression of feminism: women's rights conference in Seneca Falls, New York, in 1848
   4. feminist movement was transatlantic from the beginning
      a. argued for a radical transformation of the position of women

5. by the 1870s, movements focused above all on suffrage
   a. became a middle-class, not just elite, movement
   b. most worked through peaceful protest and persuasion
      i. one British group had a campaign of violence
   c. became a mass movement in the most industrialized countries by turn of century
6. by 1900:
   a. some women had been admitted to universities
   b. women's literacy rates were rising
   c. some U.S. states passed laws allowing women to control their property and wages
   d. some areas liberalized divorce laws
   e. some women made their way into new professions
      i. teaching
      ii. nursing (professionalized by Florence Nightingale)
      iii. social work (Jane Addams)
   f. 1893: New Zealand was the first to grant universal female suffrage
      i. Finland followed in 1906
7. the movement led to discussion of the role of women in modern society
   a. taboo sexual topics were aired
   b. deep debates over women's proper roles
8. bitter opposition
   a. some argued that strains of education and life beyond the home would cause reproductive damage
   b. some saw suffragists, Jews, and socialists as "a foreign body" in national life
9. feminism spread beyond Europe and the U.S., but less widely than nationalism

IV. **Reflections: Revolutions Pro and Con**
   A. The legacies of the Atlantic revolutions are still controversial.
      1. to some people, they opened new worlds of human potential
      2. but the revolutions also had many victims, critics, and opponents
         a. conservatives believed that societies were organisms that should evolve slowly; radical change invited disaster
         b. argued that revolutions were largely unnecessary
   B. Historians also struggle with the pros and cons of revolutionary movements.

USING *WAYS OF THE WORLD* IN THE CLASSROOM

Lecture Strategies

Lecture Strategy 1

"What makes a successful colonial revolution? Looking at the Americas—and Ireland."

This chapter rightly focuses on successful revolutions, the ones that changed the world in significant ways. To understand the revolutionary processes themselves, however, it is useful to examine a failed revolution—in this case, the 1798 Rising against British rule in Ireland—so that students have a better sense of the forces that confronted revolutionaries. The objectives of this lecture strategy are:

- to introduce students to the topic of Ireland as a British colony and the long struggle for Irish independence
- to use the case of "the '98" as a springboard from which to review and compare the course of revolution in the Americas
- to employ the case of Ireland's failed rebellion to explore in greater depth the issues that lay behind oppression by colonial powers

A good place to start is with England's successful conquest of Ireland, beginning with the loose overlordship established by Henry II in the 1170s and going on to consider the Nine Years' War (1594–1603), English/Scottish plantations in Ireland, Cromwell's devastation of the island, and the success of William of Orange there. From that point, some important points to include are:

- anti-Catholic legislation
- efforts to abolish the Irish language
- the Penal Laws
- Catholic resettlement in Connacht
- massive Catholic emigration to the continent, especially as soldiers

- the role of the United Irishmen
- the influence of American and French revolutionary ideas
- Irish hope for help from the French revolutionary government
- atrocities on both sides in the conflict

As you work your way through the course of the Irish rising, make comparisons as appropriate to the colonial risings in North and South America.

Lecture Strategy 2

"One nation under God: Revolutions and nationalist movements."

The purpose of this lecture strategy is to review and expand on the textbook's coverage of nascent nationalism in the eighteenth and nineteenth centuries, exploring in particular the relationship between revolutionary movements and nationalism. Its objectives are:

- to make students conscious of the ways in which nationalist movements reimagine and romanticize the past
- to increase student awareness of the power of historical consciousness in nationalist movements
- to explore the ways in which both resistance groups and government authorities can lead people to a sense of nationalism

A good place to start this lecture strategy is with Napoleon Bonaparte—not a refighting of his campaigns, but a consideration of how he encouraged nationalism among the French and in other countries.

For French nationalism, some important points to consider are:

- the military draft
- the creation of the Napoleonic Code
- the ways in which national triumphs were celebrated (e.g., the Arc de Triomphe)
- Napoleon's appropriation of the past (everything ranging from his use of the symbolism from a sixth-century Frankish royal tomb to stealing columns from Charlemagne's Palatine Chapel in Aachen)

For the ways in which resistance to Napoleon encouraged nationalism elsewhere, consider:

- the English hero-worship of Horatio Nelson
- the ways in which England celebrated victories over Napoleonic armies

- German anti-Napoleon movements
- Spanish resistance to French occupation

Go on from the case of Napoleon to the ways in which the idea of "nation" gradually won the hearts and minds of citizens of Western Europe, the United States, Japan, India, and Turkey. Depending on which regions you choose to emphasize, this topic could be approached in a variety of ways. Some basic issues that it would be useful to address are:

- the ways in which the popular press and popular art interpreted great "national" heroes of the past and the present
- what the most important symbols of nationalism were—flags, coinage, public art, rousing speeches advocating a return to an earlier age, public buildings, the ruler, a particular form of religious expression, etc.
- the ways in which nationalists rewrote the past to establish the "natural right" of a particular population or ideal
- who advocated nationalism, and how nationalist thought could be used either by a government or against it
- issues that emerged as truly "national"
- language reforms and standardization

Lecture Strategy 3

"At last—a woman's voice."

The intent of this lecture strategy is to take a long look at women's lives in nonindustrial societies (industrialism comes later) and to consider the factors that led small women's movements to emerge in some of these societies. Its objectives are:

- to encourage student awareness of the role women have played in social, economic, and cultural history, even when they were not very visible in the world of politics
- to explore the factors that began to give nonroyal women a public voice in parts of the world

A good place to begin is with a conscious look at the everyday life of most of the population of most parts of the world—agriculture. It is tempting to treat women's history as a "history of oppression," but it can be much more useful to include women among the "voiceless" people of world history more generally, those with no say in politics, who usually lived close to the subsistence level, and who had little in the way of personal freedoms. Points to include are:

- whether life at the subsistence level on a farm has room for anything but a "partnership marriage" in which the labor of both wife and husband are essential for survival
- what women's work was in a typical farming economy, and how very much work there was before the invention of modern labor-saving devices
- the odd circumstance that leisure-class females in world history have usually suffered much more restraint than have their poorer sisters (Did Chinese peasants bind their daughters' feet? Were impoverished Athenian women socially secluded?)
- the frustrations of urban life and women's exclusion from the public sphere there
- the question of what a woman who has servants to take care of all the work does with her time

Go on from there to discuss the role of women in Enlightenment and revolutionary movements, along with the role of men who accepted the premise that liberty should extend to the female of the species.

Things to Do in the Classroom

Discussion Topics

1. **Misconception/Difficult Topic, large or small group.** "The American Revolution was 'revolutionary.'"
Ask students to discuss the chapter's argument that there was very little about the American Revolution that was actually revolutionary and to compile a list of the main reasons the text gives to support that contention. Then, ask them to list any arguments that they can come up with for why it *was* revolutionary.

2. **Contextualization, large or small group.** "Why abolish slavery?"
Ask students to draw up a list of reasons why people were increasingly willing to abolish slavery in the eighteenth and nineteenth centuries, organizing them under the following headings:

- economic reasons
- political reasons
- cultural/religious reasons

When the students have finished, ask them to consider which of these reasons were new or had become noticeably more central in the abolitionist era.

3. **Comparison, large or small group.**
"Nationalist expressions of the nineteenth century."
Display several nationalist images of the nineteenth century. Some readily available examples are:

- the statue of Vercingetorix at Alesia
- the statue of Alfred the Great at Winchester
- the statue of Hermann the German in the Thuringian Forest

Encourage students to discuss the following questions:

- When did the figure depicted actually live?
- What did he do?
- Why would he have become a nationalist rallying point in the nineteenth century?

Classroom Activities

1. **Timeline exercise, large or small group.** "Revolutions and ideas."
With your students, make a timeline of the major revolutionary movements covered in this chapter. Add to it important events in the history of the Enlightenment, as presented in Chapter 16. Then lead a discussion of what significance the chronological intersection of events might have.

2. **Role-playing exercise, small group.** "What to do with Louis XVI."
The class is the French National Assembly, convened to consider what to do with the deposed French king Louis XVI (and with his wife, Marie Antoinette). Choose three groups of advocates to argue the case for (1) execution, (2) exile, or (3) acquittal, and then have the Assembly as a whole vote on the appropriate sentence.

3. **Clicker question.** Revolutions did more harm than good. Agree or disagree.

Key Terms

abolitionist movement: An international movement that between approximately 1780 and 1890 succeeded in condemning slavery as morally repugnant and abolishing it in much of the world; the movement was especially prominent in Britain and the United States.

creoles: Native-born elites in the Spanish colonies. (*pron.* KREE-ohls)

Declaration of the Rights of Man and Citizen: Document drawn up by the French National Assembly in 1789 that proclaimed the equal rights of all men; the declaration ideologically launched the French Revolution.

Declaration of the Rights of Woman: Short work written by the French feminist Olympe de Gouges in 1791 that was modeled on the Declaration of the Rights of Man and Citizen and that made the argument that the equality proclaimed by the French revolutionaries must also include women.

Estates General: French representative assembly called into session by Louis XVI to address pressing problems and out of which the French Revolution emerged; the three estates were the clergy, the nobility, and the commoners.

Freetown: West African settlement in what is now Sierra Leone at which British naval commanders freed Africans they rescued from illegal slave ships.

French Revolution: Massive dislocation of French society (1789–1815) that overthrew the monarchy, destroyed most of the French aristocracy, and launched radical reforms of society that were lost again, though only in part, under Napoleon's imperial rule and after the restoration of the monarchy.

gens de couleur libres: Literally, "free people of color"; term used to describe freed slaves and people of mixed racial background in Saint Domingue on the eve of the Haitian Revolution. (*pron.* zhahn deh koo-LUHR LEE-bruh)

Haiti: Name that revolutionaries gave to the former French colony of Saint Domingue; the term means "mountainous" or "rugged" in the Taino language.

Haitian Revolution: The only fully successful slave rebellion in world history; the uprising in the French Caribbean colony of Saint Domingue (later renamed Haiti) was sparked by the French Revolution and led to the establishment of an independent state after a long and bloody war (1791–1804).

Hidalgo-Morelos rebellion: Socially radical peasant insurrection that began in Mexico in 1810 and that was led by the priests Miguel Hidalgo and José Morelos. (*pron.* ee-DAHL-goe moh-RAY-lohs)

Latin American revolutions: Series of risings in the Spanish colonies of Latin America (1810–1826) that established the independence of new states from Spanish rule but that for the most part retained the privileges of the elites despite efforts at more radical social rebellion by the lower classes.

Louverture, Toussaint: First leader of the Haitian Revolution, a former slave (1743–1803) who wrote the first constitution of Haiti and served as the first governor of the newly independent state. (*pron.* too-SAN loo-ver-TOUR)

maternal feminism: Movement that claimed that women have value in society not because of an abstract notion of equality but because women have a distinctive and vital role as mothers; its exponents argued that women have the right to intervene in civil and political life because of their duty to watch over the future of their children.

Napoleon Bonaparte: French head of state from 1799 until his abdication in 1814 (and again briefly in 1815); Napoleon preserved much of the French Revolution under an autocratic system and was responsible for the spread of revolutionary ideals through his conquest of much of Europe.

nation: A clearly defined territory whose people have a sense of common identity and destiny, thanks to ties of blood, culture, language, or common experience.

nationalism: The focusing of citizens' loyalty on the notion that they are part of a "nation" with a unique culture, territory, and destiny; first became a prominent element of political culture in the nineteenth century.

North American Revolution: Successful rebellion conducted by the colonists of parts of North America (not Canada) against British rule (1775–1787); a conservative revolution whose success assured property rights but established republican government in place of monarchy.

petit blancs: The "little" (or poor) white population of Saint Domingue, which played a significant role in the Haitian Revolution. (*pron.* pay-TEE blawnk)

Seneca Falls Conference: The first organized women's rights conference, which took place at Seneca Falls, New York, in 1848.

Stanton, Elizabeth Cady: Leading figure of the early women's rights movement in the United States (1815–1902).

Terror, the: Term used to describe the revolutionary violence in France in 1793–1794, when radicals under the leadership of Maximilien Robespierre executed tens of thousands of people deemed enemies of the revolution.

Third Estate: In prerevolutionary France, the term used for the 98 percent of the population that was neither clerical nor noble, and for their representatives at the Estates General; in 1789, the Third Estate declared itself a National Assembly and launched the French Revolution.

Tupac Amaru: The last Inca emperor; in the 1780s, a Native American rebellion against Spanish control of Peru took place in his name. (*pron.* TOO-pahk ah-MAH-roo)

ANSWER GUIDELINES FOR CHAPTER QUESTIONS

The two sets of questions that follow appear in the textbook at the end of the chapter and in the margins of the reading. They are also provided in the Computerized Test Bank with answer guidelines, for your convenience.

The Big Picture Questions

1. Make a chart comparing the North American, French, Haitian, and Spanish American revolutions. What categories of comparison would be most appropriate to include?

- A number of different categories could be successfully used to construct a chart, including:
  - grievances
  - racial factors
  - religious factors
  - political outcomes
  - social outcomes
  - cultural outcomes
  - influence on other revolutions

2. Do revolutions originate in oppression and injustice, in the weakening of political authorities, in new ideas, or in the activities of small groups of determined activists?

- Revolutions originate for all of these reasons—for instance:
- oppression and injustice lay at the heart of the Haitian Revolution in particular;

- the weakening of political authorities especially played a role in the Latin American and French revolutions;
- the new ideas of the Enlightenment influenced the American, French, Haitian, and Latin American revolutions;
- the activities of small groups of determined people were especially central to the feminist revolution.

3. "The influence of revolutions endured long after they ended." To what extent does this chapter support or undermine this idea?

- This chapter strongly supports this assertion—the opening pages reflect upon the impact of the French Revolution on the Tiananmen Square demonstration in China in 1989.
- The Reflections section at the conclusion of the chapter also emphasizes the long-term implications of the French Revolution when it opens with a comment by the Chinese revolutionary leader Zhou Enlai, who in 1976 famously said that it was still "too early to say" what he thought about the French Revolution.
- Within the chapter, the Echoes of Revolution section focuses on long-term repercussions of the Atlantic revolutions in the abolition of slavery, the rise of nations and nationalism, and the emergence of the feminist movement.

4. In what ways did the Atlantic revolutions and their echoes give a new and distinctive shape to the emerging societies of nineteenth-century Europe and the Americas?

- In regions like France, the United States, and Latin America, governments based on popular sovereignty emerged, although in the case of France the government did revert to monarchy at times.
- The ideas of the revolutions, along with social pressures, pushed major states to enlarge their voting publics.
- The concept of the nation-state and nationalism strengthened, shaping popular identities.
- The Atlantic revolutions provided some of the ideological and intellectual underpinnings for the abolitionist and feminist movements.

Margin Review Questions

Q. *In what ways did the ideas of the Enlightenment contribute to the Atlantic revolutions?*

• The Enlightenment promoted the idea that human political and social arrangements could be engineered, and improved, by human action.

• New ideas of liberty, equality, free trade, religious tolerance, republicanism, human rationality, popular sovereignty, natural rights, the consent of the governed, and social contracts developed during the Enlightenment, providing the intellectual underpinnings of the Atlantic revolutions.

Q. *What was revolutionary about the American Revolution, and what was not?*

• It was revolutionary in that it marked a decisive political change.

• It was not revolutionary in that it sought to preserve the existing liberties of the colonies rather than to create new ones.

Q. *How did the French Revolution differ from the American Revolution?*

• While the American Revolution expressed the tensions of a colonial relationship with a distant imperial power, the French insurrection was driven by sharp conflicts within French society.

• The French Revolution, especially during its first five years, was a much more violent, far-reaching, and radical movement than its American counterpart.

• The French revolutionaries perceived themselves as starting from scratch in recreating the social order, while the Americans sought to restore or build upon earlier freedoms.

• Unlike the American Revolution, the French Revolution led to efforts to create a wholly new society, symbolized by such things as a new calendar, a new administrative system, and new street names.

• The French Revolution also differed from the American Revolution in the way that its influence spread. At least until the United States became a world power at the end of the nineteenth century, what inspired others was primarily the example of its revolution and its constitution. French influence, by contrast, spread primarily through conquest.

Q. *What was distinctive about the Haitian Revolution, both in world history generally and in the history of Atlantic revolutions?*

• Its key distinctive feature in both world history and the history of Atlantic revolutions was that it was the only completely successful slave revolt.

Q. *How were the Spanish American revolutions shaped by the American, French, and Haitian revolutions that happened earlier?*

• Napoleon conquered Spain and Portugal, deposing the monarchs who ruled over Latin America and forcing Latin Americans to take action.

• Enlightenment ideas that had inspired earlier revolutions also inspired the revolutions in Latin America.

• The violence of the French and Haitian revolutions was a lesson to Latin American elites that political change could easily get out of hand and was fraught with danger to themselves.

Q. *What accounts for the end of Atlantic slavery during the nineteenth century?*

• Enlightenment thinkers in eighteenth-century Europe had become increasingly critical of slavery as a violation of the natural rights of every person, and the public pronouncements of the American and French revolutions about liberty and equality likewise focused attention on this obvious breach of those principles.

• Some Christians in Britain and the United States felt that slavery was incompatible with their religious beliefs.

• There was a growing belief that slavery was not essential for economic progress.

• The actions of slaves, including the successful slave rebellion in Haiti and unsuccessful rebellions elsewhere, hastened the end of slavery by making slavery appear politically unwise.

• Abolitionist movements brought growing pressure on governments to close down the trade in slaves and then to ban slavery itself.

Q. *How did the end of slavery affect the lives of the former slaves?*

• In most cases, the economic lives of the former slaves did not improve dramatically.

• Outside of Haiti, newly freed people did not achieve anything close to political equality.

• The greatest change was that former slaves were now legally free.

Q. *What accounts for the growth of nationalism as a powerful political and personal identity in the nineteenth century?*

• The Atlantic revolutions declared that sovereignty lay with the people.

• Increasingly, populations saw themselves as citizens of a nation, deeply bound to their fellows by ties of blood, culture, or common experience.

• Other bonds weakened during the nineteenth century as science weakened the hold of religion on some, and migration to industrial cities or abroad diminished allegiance to local communities. At the same time, printing and the publishing industry standardized a variety of dialects into a smaller number of European languages, which allowed a growing reading public to think of themselves as members of a common linguistic group or nation.

• Nationalism was often presented as a reawakening of older linguistic or cultural identities and certainly drew upon songs, dances, folktales, historical experiences, and collective memories of earlier cultures.

• Governments throughout the Western world claimed to act on behalf of their nations and deliberately sought to instill national loyalties in their citizens through schools, public rituals, the mass media, and military service.

• Nationalism took on a variety of political ideologies as groups across the political spectrum tried to channel nationalism for their own purposes.

Q. *What were the achievements and limitations of nineteenth-century feminism?*

• The achievements of the women's movement include the admission of small numbers of women to universities and growing literacy rates among women more generally;

• in the United States, a number of states passed legislation allowing women to manage and control their own property and wages, separate from their husbands;

• divorce laws were liberalized in some places;

• professions such as medicine opened to a few, while teaching beckoned to many more;

• nursing was professionalized in Britain and attracted thousands of women into it, and social work, soon to be another female-dominated profession, took shape in the United States;

• the movement prompted an unprecedented discussion about the role of women in modern society.

• As far as limitations, aside from New Zealand, women failed to secure the right to vote in the nineteenth century.

• Nowhere did nineteenth-century feminism have really revolutionary consequences.

ADDITIONAL RESOURCES FOR CHAPTER 17

Additional Bedford/St. Martin's Resources

FOR INSTRUCTORS

Computerized Test Bank

This test bank provides over thirty exercises per chapter, including multiple-choice, fill-in-the-blank, short-answer, and full-length essay questions. Instructors can customize quizzes, add or edit both questions and answers, and export questions and answers to a variety of formats, including WebCT and Blackboard. The disc includes correct answers and essay outlines.

Instructor's Resource CD-ROM

This disc provides instructors with ready-made and customizable PowerPoint multimedia presentations built around chapter outlines, maps, figures, and all images from the textbook, plus JPEG versions of all maps, figures, and images.

The following maps and images from Chapter 17 are available in both JPEG and PowerPoint format on the Instructor's Resource CD-ROM:

• Map 17.1: The Expansion of the United States (p. 502)
• Map 17.2: Napoleon's European Empire (p. 508)
• Map 17.3: Latin American Independence (p. 511)
• Map 17.4: The Nations and Empires of Europe, ca. 1880 (p. 518)
• The Three Estates of *Old-Regime* France (p. 498)
• The Execution of Robespierre (p. 506)
• The Haitian Revolution (p. 509)
• Simón Bolívar (p. 512)
• Abolitionism (p. 514)
• Nationalism in Poland (p. 519)
• Women's Suffrage (p. 522)

FOR STUDENTS

Documents and Essays from *Worlds of History: A Comparative Reader*, Third Edition (Volume 2)

The following documents, essays, and illustrations to accompany Chapter 17 are available in Chapter 6 of Volume 2 of this reader by Kevin Reilly:

- David Hume, *On Miracles*
- Denis Diderot, *Supplement to the Voyage of Bougainville*
- The American Declaration of Independence
- The French Declaration of the Rights of Man and Citizen
- Mary Wollstonecraft, *A Vindication of the Rights of Woman*
- Toussaint Louverture, *Letter to the Directory*
- Simón Bolívar, *A Constitution for Venezuela*

Online Study Guide at bedfordstmartins.com/strayer

The Online Study Guide helps students synthesize the material from the text as well as practice the skills historians use to make sense of the past. Each chapter of the Online Study Guide contains specific testing exercises, including a multiple-choice self-test that focuses on important conceptual ideas; an identification quiz that helps students remember key people, places, and events; a flashcard activity that tests students on their knowledge of key terms; and two interactive map activities intended to strengthen students' geographic skills. Instructors can monitor students' progress through an online Quiz Gradebook or receive email updates.

Further Reading

The American Revolution, http://theamerican revolution.org/. A useful site for teachers, with documents, short biographies of important figures, and recommendations for further reading.

Bushnell, David, and Neill Macaulay. *The Emergence of Latin America in the Nineteenth Century*. 2nd ed. Oxford: Oxford University Press, 1994. This handy survey covers a great deal of material in a single volume.

Davis, David Brion. *Inhuman Bondage: The Rise and Fall of Slavery in the New World*. Oxford: Oxford University Press, 2006.

Hobsbawm, Eric. *The Age of Revolution: 1789–1848*. New York: Vintage, 1996. An interesting and readable one-volume survey, part of a larger survey of modern history.

Hobsbawm, Eric. *Nations and Nationalism since 1780: Programme, Myth, Reality*. 2nd ed. Cambridge: Cambridge University Press, 1992.

Links: Latin American History, http://www.csuohio. edu/history/courses/Josehis165/LINKS.htm. An interesting collection of resources on all periods of Latin American history.

McCullough, David. *1776*. New York: Simon & Schuster, 2005. A very popular recent study of the American Revolution.

The Nationalism Project: Nationalism Links, http:// www.nationalismproject.org/nationalism.htm. This site provides links, broken down by country, to both primary and secondary sources about nationalism.

National 1798 Visitor Centre, Enniscorthy, http:// www.iol.ie/~98com/. The official Web site of an Irish museum dedicated to the 1798 rebellion.

Toussaint Louverture, http://www.archivex-ht.com/ links/Toussaint_Louverture.html. A fine listing of English and French Internet resources on the Haitian Revolution.

Literature

Bolívar, Simón. *El Libertador: Writings of Simón Bolívar*. Ed. David Bushnell. Trans. Frederick Fornoff. Oxford: Oxford University Press, 2003. An interesting collection of essays, proclamations, and letters from Latin America's most charismatic nineteenth-century revolutionary.

Burke, Edmund. *Reflections on the Revolution in France*. London: Penguin, 1982. A scathing indictment (from a British perspective) of the revolutionaries in France, written soon after the beginning of the French Revolution.

Dickens, Charles. *A Tale of Two Cities*. London: Penguin, 2003. Dickens's classic tale of love and death during the Terror.

Franklin, Benjamin. *The Autobiography and Other Writings*. New York: Penguin, 2003. A fascinating look at colonial and revolutionary America as seen through the eyes of America's least conventional rebel.

Ibsen, Henrik. *A Doll's House and Other Plays*. Trans. Peter Watts. London: Penguin, 1965. *A Doll's House*, first published in 1879, explores the stifling emptiness of life as a middle-class woman.

Paine, Thomas. *Common Sense*. London: Penguin, 1982. This work was the most important text to directly influence the American Revolution; at 128 pages, it's short enough to assign to classes.

Sarmiento, Domingo F. *Facundo; or, Civilization and Barbarism*. Trans. Mary Mann. London: Penguin, 1998. This work, penned by an Argentinian in 1845, is a romantic, sociological essay on the course of revolution in the author's homeland and the reasons for the revolution's ultimate failure.

Stendhal. *The Red and the Black*. Trans. Roger Gard. London: Penguin, 2002. This classic, first published in 1830, paints a chilling picture of greed and corruption in postrevolutionary France.

Stowe, Harriet Beecher. *Uncle Tom's Cabin*. Ware: Wordsworth Editions, 1999. The most famous work in all abolitionist literature, this is the classic tale of a good man sold "down river," a woman who fled her master to save her son, and the human dignity even of the enslaved.

Film

An Age of Revolutions. Films for the Humanities and Sciences. 1996. 23 minutes. Examines the impact of the French and Industrial revolutions on European society.

The Age of Revolutions: 1776–1848. Insight Media, 1985. 26 minutes. Provides an overview of the North American, French, and South American revolutions.

Breaking the Trade: The Abolition of Slavery in the British Empire. Films for the Humanities and Sciences, 2001. 30 minutes. Examines the abolitionist campaign in Britain, one of the most influential in Europe.

Jean-Jacques Rousseau. Films for the Humanities and Sciences, 1995. 15 minutes. A short film that explores the life and works of this key Enlightenment figure, whose writings on the social contract influenced both American and French revolutionaries.

Napoleon Bonaparte. Two-part series. Films for the Humanities and Sciences, 1999. 53 minutes and 57 minutes. Examines Napoleon Bonaparte and the impact of his empire on Europe.

The Nationalists. Films for the Humanities and Sciences, 1996. 25 minutes. Explores how the ideas of the French Revolution influenced the rise of nationalism in Europe.

Simón Bolívar: The Liberator. Films for the Humanities and Sciences, 2000. 30 minutes. Examines the Latin American revolutions through a focus on their principal leader, Simón Bolívar.

Women and Revolutions. Insight Media, 1997. 27 minutes. A wide-ranging video that examines theocracy, church and state, natural rights, and the influence of the Enlightenment on women's rights.

Revolutions of Industrialization
1750–1914

CHAPTER OVERVIEW

Chapter Objectives

- To explore the causes and consequences of the Industrial Revolution
- To root Europe's Industrial Revolution in a global context
- To examine the question of why industrialization first "took off" in Great Britain
- To heighten student awareness of both the positive and the negative effects of the Industrial Revolution
- To examine some of the ways in which nineteenth-century industrial powers exerted an economic imperialism over their nonindustrialized neighbors

Chapter Outline

I. **Opening Vignette**
    A. Mahatma Gandhi criticized industrialization as economic exploitation.
       1. few people have agreed with him
       2. every kind of society has embraced at least the *idea* of industrialization since it started in Great Britain in the late eighteenth century

B. The Industrial Revolution was one of the most significant elements of Europe's modern transformation.
   1. initial industrialization period was 1750–1900
   2. drew on the Scientific Revolution
   3. utterly transformed European society
   4. pushed Europe into a position of global dominance
   5. was more fundamental than any breakthrough since the Agricultural Revolution
C. We don't know where we are in the industrial era—at the beginning, in the middle, or at the end.

II. **Explaining the Industrial Revolution**
    A. At the heart of the Industrial Revolution lay a great acceleration in the rate of technological innovation, leading to enormous increases in the output of goods and services.
       1. use of new energy sources (steam engines, petroleum engines)
       2. in Britain, output increased some fiftyfold in the period 1750–1900
       3. based on a "culture of innovation"
       4. before 1750/1800, the major Eurasian civilizations were about equal technologically

5. greatest breakthrough was the steam engine
   a. soon spread from the textile industry to many other types of production
   b. agriculture was transformed
6. spread from Britain to Western Europe, then to the U.S., Russia, and Japan
   a. became global in the twentieth century

B. Why Europe?
1. many scholars have debated why industrialization appeared first in Great Britain, and why it started in the late nineteenth century
   a. older views: there's something unique about European society
2. that view has been challenged by:
   a. the fact that other parts of the world have had times of great technological and scientific flourishing
      i. Islamic world 750–1100 C.E.
      ii. India was the center of cotton textile production and source of many agricultural innovations
      iii. China led the world in technological innovation between 700 and 1400 C.E.
      iv. all had slowed or stagnated by the early modern era
   b. the fact that Europe did not enjoy any overall economic advantage as late as 1750
      i. across Eurasia, life expectancy, consumption and nutrition patterns, wage levels, living standards, etc., were broadly similar in the eighteenth century
   c. the rapid spread of industrial techniques to much of the world in the past 250 years
3. contemporary historians tend to see the Industrial Revolution as a rather quick and unexpected eruption in the period 1750–1850
4. why it might have occurred in Europe
   a. some patterns of European internal development favored innovation
      i. small, highly competitive states
   b. European rulers had an unusual alliance with merchant classes

   i. groups of merchant capitalists were often granted special privileges
   ii. it was in governments' interest to encourage commerce and innovation
   iii. in Venice and Holland, merchants controlled the state
5. other societies developed market-based economies by the eighteenth century (e.g., Japan, India, and China)
   a. but Europe was at the center of the most varied exchange network
   b. contact with culturally different peoples encouraged change and innovation
      i. quest for the products and ideas of Asia
      ii. competition with Indian cotton cloth manufacture
      iii. popularity of other Asian goods prompted imitation
   c. the Americas provided silver, raw materials, and foods

C. Why Britain?
1. Britain was the most commercialized of Europe's larger countries
   a. small farmers had been pushed out (enclosure movement)
   b. market production fueled by a number of agricultural innovations
   c. guilds had largely disappeared
2. ready supply of industrial workers with few options
3. British aristocrats were interested in commerce
4. British commerce was worldwide
   a. Royal Navy protected a large merchant fleet
5. British political life encouraged commercialization and economic innovation
   a. policy of religious toleration (established 1688) welcomed people with technical skills regardless of faith
   b. British government imposed tariffs to protect its businessmen
   c. it was easy to form companies and forbid workers' unions
   d. unified internal market, thanks to road and canal system
   e. patent laws protected inventors' interests

  f. checks on royal authority gave more room for private enterprise

 6. emphasis of the Scientific Revolution was different in Great Britain

  a. on the continent: logic, deduction, mathematical reasoning

  b. in Britain: observation and experiment, measurement, mechanical devices, practical applications

  c. in Britain, artisan/craftsman inventors were in close contact with scientists and entrepreneurs

  d. the British Royal Society (founded 1660) took the role of promoting "useful knowledge"

   i. publicized information on recent scientific advances

 7. Britain had plenty of coal and iron ore, often conveniently located

 8. Britain was not devastated by the Napoleonic wars

 9. social change was possible without revolution

III. The First Industrial Society [see Lecture Strategy 1 and Classroom Activity 1]

 A. There was a massive increase in output as industrialization took hold in Britain.

  1. rapid development of railroad systems

  2. much of the dramatic increase was in mining, manufacturing, and services

  3. agriculture became less important by comparison (in 1891, agriculture generated only 8 percent of British national income)

  4. vast transformation of daily life

   a. it was a traumatic process for many

   b. different people were affected in different ways

 B. The British Aristocracy **[see Discussion Topic 1]**

  1. landowning aristocrats had little material loss in the Industrial Revolution

  2. but the aristocracy declined, because urban wealth became more important

   a. many businessmen, manufacturers, and bankers were enriched

   b. aristocrats had declining political clout

    i. e.g., high tariffs on agricultural imports were abolished in 1840s

   c. by 1900, businessmen led the major political parties

  3. titled nobles retained great social prestige and personal wealth

   a. many found an outlet in Britain's colonial possessions

 C. The Middle Classes

  1. the middle classes had the most obvious gains from industrialization

  2. upper middle class: some became extremely wealthy, bought into aristocratic life

  3. middle class: large numbers of smaller businessmen and professionals

   a. politically liberal

   b. stood for thrift, hard work, rigid morals, and cleanliness

   c. Samuel Smiles, *Self-Help* (1859): individuals are responsible for their own destiny

   d. middle-class women were more frequently cast as homemakers, wives, and mothers

    i. moral centers of society

    ii. managers of consumption (rise of "shopping")

    iii. rising "ideology of domesticity"

  4. lower middle class: service sector workers (clerks, secretaries, etc.)

   a. by 1900, they were around 20 percent of Britain's population

   b. employment opportunities for women as well as men

    i. almost all were single and expected to marry and give up jobs

 D. The Laboring Classes

  1. in the nineteenth century, about 70 percent of Britons were workers

  2. laboring classes suffered most/benefited least from industrialization

  3. rapid urbanization

   a. by 1851, a majority of Britain's population was urban

   b. by 1900, London was the largest city in the world (6 million)

  4. horrible urban conditions

   a. vast overcrowding

   b. inadequate sanitation and water supplies

   c. epidemics

d. few public services or open spaces

e. little contact between the rich and the poor

5. industrial factories offered a very different work environment

   a. long hours, low wages, and child labor were typical for the poor

   b. what was new was the routine and monotony of work, direct supervision, discipline

   c. industrial work was insecure

   d. many girls and young women worked

      i. usually left outside paid employment when they married

      ii. but often continued to earn money within the home

E. Social Protest among the Laboring Classes **[see Lecture Strategy 2]**

   1. "friendly societies," especially of artisans, for self-help were common

   2. other skilled artisans sometimes wrecked machinery and burned mills

   3. some joined political movements, aimed to enfranchise working-class men

   4. trade unions were legalized in 1824

      a. growing numbers of factory workers joined them

      b. fought for better wages and working conditions

      c. at first, upper classes feared them

   5. socialist ideas spread gradually **[see Classroom Activity 2]**

      a. Karl Marx (1818–1883) laid out a full ideology of socialism

         i. human history is a history of class struggle

         ii. in his own time, saw a growing hostility between the *bourgeoisie* and the *proletariat*

         iii. argued that capitalism can never end poverty

         iv. foretold a future (communist) golden age when industrial technology would serve the whole community

      b. socialist ideas were attractive among more radical trade unionists and some middle-class intellectuals in the late nineteenth century

         i. even more attractive in Germany

      ii. but the British working class was not overtly revolutionary by then

   6. British working-class movement remained moderate

      a. material conditions for workers improved in second half of the century

      b. capitalists and impoverished working class didn't polarize because of the large middle and lower middle class

      c. workers bettered their standard of living

         i. wages improved

         ii. cheap imported food improved diets

         iii. infant death rates fell

         iv. male workers gradually got the vote

         v. sanitary reform cleaned up cities

         vi. even some urban parks were established

   7. but immense inequalities remained

   8. by 1900, Britain was in economic decline relative to newly industrialized states like Germany and the U.S.

IV. **Variations on a Theme: Comparing Industrialization in the United States and Russia**

A. The Industrial Revolution soon spread to continental Western Europe.

   1. by 1900, it was established in the U.S., Russia, and Japan

   2. industrialization had broadly similar outcomes wherever it was established

      a. aristocratic, artisanal, and peasant classes declined

      b. middle-class women withdrew from paid labor altogether

         i. working-class women tried to leave paid labor after marriage

         ii. women received lower wages than men, were accused of taking jobs from men

      c. establishment of trade unions and socialist movements

   3. but the spread of industrialization was affected by the cultures of the lands where it was established, pace and timing of **industrialization**, nature of major **industries**, role of the state, political **expression** of social conflict, etc.

      a. **French** industrialization was slower, **perhaps** less disruptive

  b. Germany focused at first on heavy industry
    i. was far more concentrated in huge companies
    ii. generated a more militant and Marxist-oriented labor movement
  4. variations are most apparent in the cases of the U.S. and Russia
B. The United States: Industrialization without Socialism
  1. American industrialization began with New England textiles (1820s)
  2. explosive growth after the Civil War
    a. by 1914, the U.S. was the world's leading industrial power
    b. closely linked to European industrialization
      i. Europeans provided around one-third of the capital investment
  3. the U.S. government played an important role through tax breaks, land grants to railroads, laws making formation of corporations easy, absence of overt regulation
    a. encouraged development of very large enterprises
  4. pioneering of mass production techniques
  5. creation of a "culture of consumption" through advertising, catalogs, and department stores
  6. self-made industrialists became cultural heroes (Ford, Carnegie, Rockefeller)
  7. serious social divisions rose
    a. growing gap between rich and poor
    b. constant labor of the working class
    c. creation of vast slums
    d. growing labor protest
      i. sometimes erupted in violence
      ii. but no major political party emerged to represent the working class
      iii. socialism (especially Marxism) didn't have great appeal for Americans
      iv. even in the Great Depression (1930s), no major socialist movement emerged
    e. Why didn't socialism appeal to American workers?
      i. U.S. union organizations were relatively conservative
      ii. American Federation of Labor focused on skilled workers
      iii. American population was extremely heterogeneous
      iv. American workers had a higher standard of living than did their European counterparts
      v. middle-class aspirations of white-collar workers
    f. "Populists" denounced corporate interests
      i. but populism had little appeal in growing industrial areas
    g. "Progressives" were more successful, especially after 1900
      i. aimed to remedy the ills of industrialization
    h. socialism was labeled as fundamentally "un-American"
C. Russia: Industrialization and Revolution
[see Classroom Activity 3]
  1. Russia was an absolute monarchy, with the greatest state control of anywhere in the Western world
    a. in 1900: no national parliament, no legal political parties, no nationwide elections
    b. dominated by a titled nobility (many highly Westernized)
    c. until 1861, most Russians were serfs
  2. in Russia, the state, not society, usually initiated change
    a. Peter the Great (r. 1689–1725) was an early example of "transformation from above"
    b. Catherine the Great (r. 1762–1796) also worked to Europeanize Russian culture and intellectual life
    c. the state directed freeing of the serfs in 1861
      i. stimulated by Russia's defeat in the Crimean War
    d. the state set out to improve Russia's economic and industrial backwardness
  3. Russian Industrial Revolution was launched by the 1890s
    a. focused on railroads and heavy industry
    b. substantial foreign investment
    c. industry was concentrated in a few major cities

d. fewer but larger factories than was typical in Western Europe

4. growing middle class disliked Russia's deep conservatism, sought a greater role in political life
   a. but they were dependent on the state for contracts and jobs
   b. also relied on the state to suppress worker radicalism

5. Russian working class (only about 5 percent of the population) rapidly radicalized
   a. harsh conditions
   b. no legal outlet for grievances
   c. large-scale strikes

6. Marxist socialism appealed to some educated Russians, gave them hope for the future
   a. founded the Russian Social-Democratic Labor Party (1898)
   b. got involved in workers' education, union organizing, and revolutionary action

7. major insurrection broke out in 1905, after defeat in war by Japan
   a. in Moscow and St. Petersburg, workers went on strike, created their own representative councils ("soviets")
   b. peasant uprisings, student demonstrations
   c. non-Russian nationalities revolted
   d. military mutiny
   e. brutally suppressed, but forced the tsar's regime to make reforms
      i. granted a constitution
      ii. legalized trade unions and political parties
      iii. created a national assembly (the Duma)

8. limited political reforms failed to pacify the radicals or bring stability
   a. growing belief that only a revolution would help
   b. World War I provided the revolutionary moment

9. Russian Revolution broke out in 1917
   a. brought the most radical of the socialist groups to power—the Bolsheviks, led by Vladimir Ulyanov (Lenin)
   b. only in Russia did industrialization lead to violent social revolution

V. **The Industrial Revolution and Latin America in the Nineteenth Century** [see Lecture Strategy 3 and Discussion Topic 2]
A. Beyond Europe and North America
   1. only Japan underwent major industrialization in the nineteenth century
   2. elsewhere, only modest experiments in industry
   3. did not transform societies
   4. nonindustrialized societies still felt the impact of European and North American developments

B. After Independence in Latin America
   1. the struggle for independence in Latin America took a long time and was very destructive
   2. the four vice-royalties of Spanish America became eighteen separate countries
   3. international wars hindered development of the new nations
      a. Mexico lost vast territories to the U.S. (1846–1848)
      b. Paraguay was devastated by war (1864–1870)
   4. political life was highly unstable
      a. conservatives tried to maintain the old status quo
      b. liberals attacked the Church, sought some social reforms, preferred federalism to a centralized government system
      c. often, military strongmen (*caudillos*) gained power
         i. they were unstable, too
      d. states ran through multiple constitutions
   5. independence brought little fundamental change to social life
      a. slavery was abolished (though not until late 1880s in Brazil and Cuba)
      b. most legal distinctions between racial categories were abolished
      c. but creole whites remained overwhelmingly in control of productive economic resources
      d. small middle class allowed social mobility for a few
      e. the vast majority were impoverished
         i. Caste War of Yucatán (1847–1901) was one of the few rebellions of the poor

C. Facing the World Economy
1. second half of the nineteenth century: greater stability, integration into world economy
2. rapid growth of Latin American exports to industrializing countries
   a. exported food products and raw materials
   b. imported textiles, machinery, tools, weapons, luxury goods
3. major investment of European and U.S. capital in Latin America
D. Becoming like Europe?
1. rapid population increase
2. rapid urbanization
3. actively sought European immigrants
4. few people benefited from the export boom
   a. upper-class landowners did very well
   b. middle class grew some
   c. but over 90 percent of the population was still lower-class
5. industrial workers made up a modest segment of the lower class
   a. attempted unions and strikes
   b. harshly repressed
6. most of the poor remained rural
   a. many farmers were forced off their land, became dependent laborers
7. only in Mexico did conditions provoke a nationwide revolution
   a. overthrow of the dictator Porfirio Díaz (1876–1911)
   b. major, bloody conflict (1910–1920)
   c. huge peasant armies
   d. transformed Mexico
      i. new constitution (1917) proclaimed universal suffrage, land redistribution, disestablishment of the Catholic Church, minimum wage, eight-hour workday, etc.
8. the export boom did *not* cause a thorough Industrial Revolution
   a. there was little internal market for manufactured goods
   b. rich landowners and cattlemen had little incentive to invest in manufacturing
   c. governments supported free trade, so cheaper and higher-quality foreign

goods were available than could be made at home
   d. instead, economic growth was dependent on Europe and North America
      i. some have regarded it as a new form of colonialism
      ii. the case of the "banana republics" under pressure from the U.S.
      iii. repeated U.S. military intervention
VI. **Reflections: History and Horse Races** [see Discussion Topic 3]
A. Historians are fascinated by historic "firsts."
B. But a focus on "firsts" can be misleading.
1. most "first achievements" in history were not intentional
2. the Industrial Revolution was certainly an "unexpected outcome of converging circumstances"
C. Europeans have used their development of industrialization to claim an innate superiority.
1. it's important to emphasize the unexpectedness of the Industrial Revolution
2. spread of industrialization around the world diminishes the importance of the "why Europe?" question
3. industrialization will increasingly be seen as a global process

USING *WAYS OF THE WORLD* IN THE CLASSROOM

Lecture Strategies

Lecture Strategy 1

"Imagining the Industrial Revolution."
It is often difficult for students to imagine the physical reality of the early Industrial Revolution, so this lecture strategy is intended to help students conceptualize and visualize the new world of machines. It is possible to approach this lecture strategy using images or literature, or a combination of the two. Its objectives are:

• to help students picture the course of the Industrial Revolution—its major inventions and how they were employed

- to encourage students to consider the physical and emotional costs and benefits of industrialization

A good place to start is with a literary figure who will probably be familiar to most students—Bob Cratchit, the lowly clerk in Charles Dickens's *A Christmas Carol* (you might care to show a clip from one of the movie versions of the novel). Explore with students this depiction of a member of the lower middle class in the 1840s—the difficult conditions of his life, his utter dependence on a skinflint tyrant, and the novelty of jobs like Cratchit's in the early Industrial Revolution. Go on to consider what had changed in British life by the 1840s, at the time Dickens wrote his novel. From there, one could take a variety of approaches. Here are a few possibilities.

Consider the physical presence of machines, a handy point at which to introduce students to important early industrial inventions and how they affected patterns of work. Some machines to include are:

- the Watt steam engine (How big was it? How loud was it? How hot was it?)
- Arkwright's water frame
- Hargreaves's spinning jenny
- the power loom
- the reverberatory furnace
- the railroad

Discuss working conditions, taking care to consider the context of the time (e.g., child labor was perfectly normal among the poor). Particular points to include are:

- how physically demanding different sorts of work were
- the danger of death or maiming
- whether wages were sufficient for a family to live decently

Help your students to imagine living conditions in an early industrial city, such as Manchester, England, dubbed "Cottonopolis" in the nineteenth century. Particular points to consider are:

- types of housing available to workers
- means of heating or cooling
- the availability of reasonably nutritious food in adequate quantities
- what the city might have smelled like
- the fears of epidemic disease

Consider other social classes, including such points as:

- how enviable Bob Cratchit's position was compared to that of a factory worker
- the strains that attended life in the middle class
- the satisfactions of a new culture of consumption

Include literary, film, or photographic examples to emphasize your points (see the Further Reading section of this chapter).

Lecture Strategy 2

"Socialism."

The topic of this lecture is socialism—where it came from, its principles, where it flourished, and why it was feared. The lecture strategy's objectives are:

- to help students understand that socialism is a phenomenon with a long history
- to explore the thought of Marx and Engels and their influence in world history
- to examine what it was that socialists wanted
- to investigate whether the fear and hatred that the upper classes and governments felt toward socialism was justified in the nineteenth century

A good place to begin is by reading a short excerpt from Plato's *Republic*, in which he outlines the ideal society. Ask students what they think the source is (leave out any specific reference to ancient Greece that could give the game away). With any luck, somebody will think it is Marx's *Communist Manifesto*. This can lead to a presentation on the early socialists. Some points to include are:

- a careful definition of socialism
- precursors of socialism (such as Plato, or Thomas More's *Utopia*)
- the radicalizing effect of the Peterloo Massacre (1819)
- the Chartist movement
- the writings of intellectuals such as Robert Owen, Charles Fourier, and Louis Blanc

Go on from there to examine Karl Marx and his legacy. Some important points are:

- Marx's biography
- his collaboration with Friedrich Engels

- his historical approach to the problem of industrialization
- *The Communist Manifesto*: what it says, why it says it, and what impact it had

In the remaining time, one could take several approaches. Some points to consider are:

- what socialism had to offer women
- whether socialism had anything to offer peasants
- what means socialists advocated to realize their goals for society
- whether all socialists were violent
- whether Marx would have recognized the form of socialism that initiated the Russian Revolution of 1917

Lecture Strategy 3

"Economic imperialism."
Americans are often indignant at the suggestion that *we* could be regarded as imperialists, yet this chapter presents a form of economic imperialism in Latin America in which the United States was deeply involved. The purpose of this lecture strategy is to examine U.S. relations with Latin America in the nineteenth century in greater detail, considering economic imperialism as a factor. For the sake of comparison, it is suggested that the lecturer weave in a discussion of the more overt economic imperialism that Great Britain exercised over India. The purposes of this lecture strategy are:

- to explore in greater detail the history of Latin America after independence
- to examine the relationship between Latin America and its big sister the United States in the nineteenth century
- to discuss the ways in which foreign economic manipulation could shape states that were only marginally industrialized
- to compare Britain's economic sway over India to that of the United States over Latin America

A good place to begin is with a clip from the glorious 1982 film *Gandhi*, specifically the scene in which a desperate villager enlists Gandhi's help after the British stop buying the products they had ordered the Indians

to produce. This can proceed naturally to a wider presentation of industrial nations' unrelenting quest for raw materials and for markets for their finished products. From there, tell the tale of industrial nations' involvement in Latin America and India. Some issues to consider are:

- how local elites were made to participate in the system in the two regions
- the type of foreign involvement (investment, direct ownership, etc.)
- how each region increased its exports to satisfy foreign need
- internal movements that resisted the process
- the effects on Latin America and India
- the role of warfare in both cases

Things to Do in the Classroom

Discussion Topics

1. **Contextualization, large or small group.** "Jane Austen's England meets the Industrial Revolution."
Show the class a clip from a Jane Austen movie such as *Emma*, *Pride and Prejudice*, or *Sense and Sensibility*. Then divide the class into groups and ask them to discuss what relationship Jane Austen's world might have to the early Industrial Revolution.

2. **Comparison, large or small group.** "Industrial Revolution and global divide."
Direct your students' attention to the Snapshot on page 548 entitled "The Industrial Revolution and the Global Divide." Encourage them to make a list of the patterns they see in the table and to discuss the implications of those patterns.

3. **Misconception/Difficult Topic, large or small group.** "Europe must be special, since it came up with the Industrial Revolution."
The main thrust of this chapter is to argue against this common misconception. Ask students to take a few minutes to reread the Reflections section at the end of the chapter. Then ask them to discuss whether they are convinced by the author's argument that the Industrial Revolution's development in Great Britain in the decades around 1800 was more an accident than anything else.

Classroom Activities

1. **Analysis exercise, large or small group.** "Life in an industrial city, ca. 1850."

We tend to take the organization of urban space for granted—on payment of a small fee, our garbage is collected, water miraculously appears in our houses, we're hooked up to an electrical system, and mail even turns up on our doorsteps. The purpose of this exercise is to help students consider how hard it really is to make a modern city functional, thus encouraging them to consider how intractable some of the problems of industrialization really were. This exercise has several parts:

a. encourage the class as a whole to come up with several end results that they consider necessary to reasonably healthy and bearable life in a city of 100,000 people (such as a municipal water system that pumps clean water to somewhere reasonably close to most people's homes);

b. divide the class into groups, assigning one end result to each group;

c. ask the students in each group to discuss and make a list of the conditions that would have to be satisfied to reach their end result (e.g., in the case of water supply, the need to dig wells or divert other water sources, some sort of water treatment facility, miles and miles of pipes laid, the creation of pumping stations, etc.);

d. bring the groups back together to discuss their findings.

2. **Clicker question.** Do you find socialism appealing?

3. **Role-playing exercise, small group.** "Where to invest?"

The members of the class are the board of directors of a major bank based in London; the year is 1880. They wish to invest a large amount of capital in heavy industry and are hearing reports from their agents to help them decide the best place for their capital investment. Choose three groups of students to make the case for Mexico, Russia, or Great Britain itself as the best place to invest. After the groups have made their arguments, let the board of directors vote. Finish the class by discussing what really was the most likely to happen historically to each of the three investment possibilities, and why.

Key Terms

bourgeoisie: Term that Karl Marx used to describe the owners of industrial capital; originally meant "townspeople." (*pron.* boor-zwah-ZEE)

British Royal Society: Association of scientists established in England in 1660 that was dedicated to the promotion of "useful knowledge."

Caste War of Yucatán: Long revolutionary struggle (1847–1901) of the Maya people of Mexico against European and mestizo intruders.

caudillo: A military strongman who seized control of a government in nineteenth-century Latin America. (*pron.* kow-DEE-yohs)

Crimean War: Major international conflict (1854–1856) in which British and French forces defeated Russia; the defeat prompted reforms within Russia.

dependent development: Term used to describe Latin America's economic growth in the nineteenth century, which was largely financed by foreign capital and dependent on European and North American prosperity and decisions.

Díaz, Porfirio: Mexican dictator from 1876 to 1911 who was eventually overthrown in a long and bloody revolution. (*pron.* por-FEAR-ee-oh DEE-ahz)

Duma, the: The elected representative assembly grudgingly created in Russia by Tsar Nicholas II in response to the 1905 revolution. (*pron.* DOO-mah)

Indian cotton textiles: For much of the eighteenth century, well-made and inexpensive cotton textiles from India flooded Western markets; the competition stimulated the British textile industry to industrialize, which led to the eventual destruction of the Indian textile market both in Europe and in India.

Labour Party: British working-class political party established in the 1890s and dedicated to reforms and a peaceful transition to socialism, in time providing a viable alternative to the revolutionary emphasis of Marxism.

Latin American export boom: Large-scale increase in Latin American exports (mostly raw materials and foodstuffs) to industrializing countries in the second half of the nineteenth century, made possible by major improvements in shipping; the boom mostly benefited the upper and middle classes.

Lenin: Pen name of Russian Bolshevik Vladimir Ulyanov (1870–1924), who was the main leader of the Russian Revolution of 1917. (*pron.* vlad-EE-mir ool-YAHN-off)

lower middle class: Social stratum that developed in Britain in the nineteenth century and that consisted of people employed in the service sector as clerks, salespeople, secretaries, police officers, and the like; by 1900, this group comprised about 20 percent of Britain's population.

Marx, Karl: The most influential proponent of socialism, Marx (1818–1883) was a German expatriate in England who advocated working-class revolution as the key to creating an ideal communist future.

Mexican Revolution: Long and bloody war (1911–1920) in which Mexican reformers from the middle class joined with workers and peasants to overthrow the dictator Porfirio Díaz and create a new, much more democratic political order.

middle-class values: Belief system typical of the middle class that developed in Britain in the nineteenth century; it emphasized thrift, hard work, rigid moral behavior, cleanliness, and "respectability."

Model T: The first automobile affordable enough for a mass market; produced by American industrialist Henry Ford.

Owens, Robert: Socialist thinker and wealthy mill owner (1771–1858) who created an ideal industrial community at New Lanark, Scotland.

Peter the Great: Tsar of Russia (r. 1689–1725) who attempted a massive reform of Russian society in an effort to catch up with the states of Western Europe.

populism: Late-nineteenth-century American political movement that denounced corporate interests of all kinds.

progressivism: American political movement in the period around 1900 that advocated reform measures to correct the ills of industrialization.

proletariat: Term that Karl Marx used to describe the industrial working class; originally used in ancient Rome to describe the poorest part of the urban population. (*pron.* proh-li-TARE-ee-at)

Russian Revolution of 1905: Spontaneous rebellion that erupted in Russia after the country's defeat at the hands of Japan in 1905; the revolution was suppressed, but it forced the government to make substantial reforms.

socialism in the United States: Fairly minor political movement in the United States, at its height in 1912 gaining 6 percent of the vote for its presidential candidate.

steam engine: Mechanical device in which the steam from heated water builds up pressure to drive a piston, rather than relying on human or animal muscle power; the introduction of the steam engine allowed a hitherto unimagined increase in productivity and made the Industrial Revolution possible.

ANSWER GUIDELINES FOR CHAPTER QUESTIONS

The two sets of questions that follow appear in the textbook at the end of the chapter and in the margins of the reading. They are also provided in the Computerized Test Bank with answer guidelines, for your convenience.

The Big Picture Questions

1. What was revolutionary about the Industrial Revolution?

• Not since the Agricultural Revolution had human ways of life been so fundamentally altered.

• The Industrial Revolution created new classes of people in society.

• It created new work patterns.

• It enormously increased the output of goods and services because of a wholly unprecedented jump in the capacities of human societies to produce wealth.

• It was underpinned by a culture of innovation, a widespread and almost obsessive belief that things could be improved endlessly.

2. What was common to the process of industrialization everywhere, and in what ways did it vary from place to place?

• In terms of common features, new technologies and sources of energy generated vast increases in production;

- unprecedented urbanization took place;
- class structures changed as aristocrats, artisans, and peasants declined as classes, while the middle classes and a factory working class grew in numbers and social prominence;
- middle-class women generally withdrew from paid labor altogether, while working-class women sought to do so after marriage;
- working women usually received lower wages than their male counterparts, had difficulty joining unions, and were subject to charges that they were taking jobs from men;
- working-class frustration and anger gave rise to trade unions and socialist movements.
- In terms of differences, the pace and timing of the Industrial Revolution varied by country;
    - the size and shape of major industries varied;
    - the role of the state varied;
    - the political expression of social conflict varied;
    - the relative influence of Marxism varied.

3. What did humankind gain from the Industrial Revolution, and what did it lose?

- Among the gains were an enormous increase in the output of goods and services because of a wholly unprecedented jump in the capacities of human societies to produce wealth;
    - unprecedented technological innovation;
    - new sources of power;
    - new employment opportunities for participants.
- The losses included the destruction of some older ways of life;
- the demise of some older methods of production;
- miserable working and living conditions for many in the laboring classes;
- new and sometimes bitter social- and class-based conflicts;
- environmental degradation.

4. In what ways might the Industrial Revolution be understood as a global rather than simply a European phenomenon?

- The Industrial Revolution rapidly spread beyond the confines of Europe and was easily adopted across cultures.
- Europe's initial industrialization was influenced by its new position as a hub of the most extensive network of exchange in the world, by its extraction of wealth from the Americas, and by its dominance of the growing market for goods in the Americas.
- Even areas that did not industrialize were affected by the Industrial Revolution, such as Latin America, where the economy was defined by exports of raw materials to supply the factories and the workforces of industrial countries in Europe and the United States.

Margin Review Questions

Q. *In what respects did the roots of the Industrial Revolution lie within Europe? In what ways did that transformation have global roots?*

- In terms of European roots, the political system of Europe, which was composed of many small and highly competitive states, favored innovation;
- the relative newness of European states and their monarchs' desperate need for revenue in the absence of an effective tax-collecting bureaucracy pushed European royals into an unusual alliance with their merchant classes, resulting in an unusual degree of freedom from state control and a higher social status for merchants than in more established civilizations.
- In terms of global roots, Europe after 1500 became the hub of the largest and most varied network of exchange in the world, which generated extensive change and innovation and stimulated European commerce;
- the conquest of the Americas allowed Europeans to draw disproportionately on world resources and provided a growing market for European machine-produced goods.

Q. *What was distinctive about Britain that may help to explain its status as the breakthrough point of the Industrial Revolution?*

- Britain was the most highly commercialized of Europe's larger countries;
- Britain had a rapidly growing population that provided a ready supply of industrial workers with few alternatives available to them;
- British aristocrats, unlike their counterparts elsewhere in Europe, had long been interested in commerce;
- British commerce extended around the world, its large merchant fleet protected by the Royal Navy;

- British political life promoted commercialization and economic innovation in part through a policy of religious toleration, which removed barriers against religious dissenters with technical skills;

- British government favored men of business with tariffs, laws that made it easy to form companies and to forbid workers' unions, infrastructure investment, and patent laws;

- checks on royal authority provided a freer arena for private enterprise.

- Europe's Scientific Revolution also took a distinctive form in Great Britain in ways that fostered technological innovation, focusing on observation and experiment, precise measurements, mechanical devices, and practical commercial applications rather than logic, deduction, and mathematical reasoning.

- Britain possessed a ready supply of coal and iron ore, often located close to each other and within easy reach of major industrial centers;

- Britain's island location protected it from the kind of invasions that so many continental European states experienced during the era of the French Revolution;

- Britain's relatively fluid society allowed for adjustments in the face of social changes without widespread revolution.

Q. *How did the Industrial Revolution transform British society?*

- While landowning aristocrats suffered little in material terms, they declined as a class as elite urban groups grew in wealth and ultimately eclipsed the landowning aristocracy as a political force in the country. Titled nobles retained their social status and found opportunities in the empire.

- The upper middle class, composed of extremely wealthy factory and mine owners, bankers, and merchants, benefited most from the Industrial Revolution, and many readily assimilated into aristocratic life at the top of British society.

- Smaller businessmen, doctors, lawyers, engineers, teachers, journalists, scientists, and other professionals became more prominent as a social group and developed their own values and outlooks that emphasized ideas of thrift and hard work, a rigid morality, and cleanliness. The central value of the culture was "respectability," a term that combines notions of social status and virtuous behavior.

- As Britain's industrial economy matured, it gave rise to a sizeable "lower middle class"—people

employed in the growing service sector as clerks, salespeople, bank tellers, hotel staff, secretaries, telephone operators, police officers, and the like. This group distinguished itself from the working class because they did not undertake manual labor.

- The laboring classes lived in new, overcrowded, and poorly serviced urban environments; they labored in industrial factories where new and monotonous work, performed under constant supervision designed to enforce work discipline, replaced the more varied drudgery of earlier periods. Ultimately, members of the laboring classes developed new forms of sociability, including "friendly societies" that provided some insurance against sickness, a decent funeral, and an opportunity for social life in an otherwise bleak environment. Over time, laboring classes also sought greater political participation, organized after 1824 into trade unions to improve their conditions, and developed socialist ideas that challenged the assumptions of capitalist society.

- Artisans and those who labored in agriculture declined in prominence.

Q. *How did Britain's middle classes change during the nineteenth century?*

- Middle-class society was composed of political liberals who favored constitutional government, private property, free trade, and social reform within limits.

- Ideas of thrift and hard work, a rigid morality, and cleanliness characterized middle-class culture.

- The central value of the culture was "respectability," a term that combines notions of social status and virtuous behavior.

- Women were cast as homemakers, wives, and mothers and charged with creating an emotional haven for their men. They were also the moral center of family life and the educators of "respectability" as well as the managers of consumption in a setting in which "shopping" became a central activity. An "ideology of domesticity" defined the home and charitable activities as the proper sphere for women.

- A sizeable lower middle class took shape that included people employed as clerks, salespeople, bank tellers, secretaries, police officers, and the like. They distinguished themselves from the laboring classes by their work in the growing service sector, which did not require manual labor.

Q. *How did Karl Marx understand the Industrial Revolution? In what ways did his ideas have an impact in the industrializing world of the nineteenth century?*

• In terms of Marx's understanding, he saw the Industrial Revolution as the story of class struggle between the oppressor (the *bourgeoisie*, or the owners of industrial capital) and the oppressed (the *proletariat*, or the industrial working class).

• For Marx, the Industrial Revolution bore great promise as a phase in human history, for it made humankind far more productive, thus bringing the end of poverty in sight.

• However, according to Marx, capitalist societies could never eliminate poverty, because private property, competition, and class hostility prevented those societies from distributing the abundance of industrial economies to the workers whose labor had created that abundance.

• Marx predicted the eventual collapse of capitalism amid a working-class revolution as society polarized into rich and poor. After that revolution, Marx looked forward to a communist future in which the great productive potential of industrial technology would be placed in the service of the entire community.

• In terms of its impact in the industrializing world of the nineteenth century, Marx's ideas were echoed in the later decades of the nineteenth century among more radical trade unionists and some middle-class intellectuals in Britain, and even more so in a rapidly industrializing Germany.

• But the British working-class movement by then was not overtly revolutionary, and when the working-class political party known as the Labour Party was established in the 1890s, it advocated a reformist program and a peaceful democratic transition to socialism, largely rejecting the class struggle and revolutionary emphasis of Marxism.

Q. *What were the differences between industrialization in the United States and that in Russia?*

• Industrialization in the United States took place in one of the Western world's most exuberant democracies, while Russia's took place in the last outpost of absolute monarchy, in which the state exercised far greater control over individuals and society than anywhere in the Western world.

• In the United States, social and economic change bubbled up from society as free farmers, workers, and businessmen sought new opportunities and operated in a political system that gave them varying degrees of expression. In autocratic Russia, change was far more often initiated by the state itself, in its continuing efforts to catch up with the more powerful and innovative states of Europe.

• In the United States, working-class consciousness among factory laborers did not develop as quickly and did not become as radical, in part because workers were treated better and had more outlets for grievances in the United States than in Russia.

• Unlike industrialization in the United States, Russian industrialization was associated with a violent social revolution through which a socialist political party, inspired by the teachings of Karl Marx, was able to seize power.

Q. *Why did Marxist socialism not take root in the United States?*

• A number of factors underlie the failure of Marxist socialism to take root in the United States, including the relative conservatism of major American union organizations;

• the immense religious, ethnic, and racial divisions of American society, which undermined the class solidarity of American workers and made it far more difficult to sustain class-oriented political parties and a socialist labor movement;

• the country's remarkable economic growth, which generated on average a higher standard of living for American workers than their European counterparts experienced;

• a higher level of home ownership among workers.

• By 1910, a particularly large group of white-collar workers in sales, services, and offices outnumbered factory laborers.

Q. *What factors contributed to the making of a revolutionary situation in Russia by the beginning of the twentieth century?*

• Rapid state-directed industrialization concentrated in a few major cities led to explosive social outcomes, including the emergence of a modern and educated middle class of businessmen and professionals, many of whom objected strongly to the deep conservatism of tsarist Russia and sought a greater role in political life;

• Russian factory workers quickly developed an unusually radical class consciousness, based on harsh conditions and the absence of any legal outlet for their grievances;

• a small but growing number of educated Russians found in Marxist socialism a way of understanding the changes they witnessed daily and hope for the future in a revolutionary upheaval of workers;

• the tsar's reforms after the failed 1905 revolution failed to tame working-class radicalism or to bring social stability to Russia.

• Revolutionary groups published pamphlets and newspapers, organized trade unions, and spread their messages among workers and peasants. Particularly in the cities, these revolutionary parties had an impact in that they provided the language through which workers could express their grievances, created links among workers from different factories, and furnished leaders able to act when the revolutionary moment arrived.

• World War I caused enormous hardships that, when coupled with the immense social tensions of industrialization within a still autocratic political system, sparked the Russian Revolution of 1917.

Q. *In what ways and with what impact was Latin America linked to the global economy of the nineteenth century?*

• Latin America exported food products and raw materials to industrializing nations, increasing exports by a factor of ten in the sixty years or so after 1850.

• In return for these exports, Latin America imported the textiles, machinery, tools, weapons, and luxury goods of Europe and the United States.

• Both Europeans and Americans invested in Latin America, buying up food and raw material-producing assets and building railroads, largely to funnel Latin American products to the coast for export.

• Upper-class landowners benefited from the trade as exports flourished and the value of their land soared.

• Middle-class urban dwellers also grew in number and prosperity.

• But the vast majority of the population lived in rural areas, where they suffered the most and benefited the least from exports to the global economy; many lower-class farmers were pushed off their land, ending up either in remote and poor areas or working as dependent laborers for poor wages on the plantations of the wealthy.

• In Mexico, inequalities exacerbated by the global economy sparked a nationwide revolution in which middle-class reformers, workers, and peasants overthrew the government and instituted some reforms that benefited the lower classes.

• Participation in the global economy did not jump-start a thorough Industrial Revolution anywhere in Latin America.

• The Latin American economy became dependent upon Europe and America, with its development dependent on investment from and access to the economies of Europe and the United States.

Q. *Did Latin America follow or diverge from the historical path of Europe during the nineteenth century?*

• The population of Latin America increased rapidly, as did urbanization, similar to what was occurring in Europe.

• Many Europeans immigrated to Latin America.

• A middle class formed, although it was much smaller than that of Europe.

• However, Latin America did in other ways diverge from the historical path of Europe; central to this divergence was the lack of a thorough Industrial Revolution anywhere in Latin America and the development instead of an economy dependent on financial capital from and exports to the industrial economies of Europe.

ADDITIONAL RESOURCES FOR CHAPTER 18

Additional Bedford/St. Martin's Resources

FOR INSTRUCTORS

Computerized Test Bank

This test bank provides over thirty exercises per chapter, including multiple-choice, fill-in-the-blank, short-answer, and full-length essay questions. Instructors can customize quizzes, add or edit both questions and answers, and export questions and answers to a variety of formats, including WebCT and Blackboard. The disc includes correct answers and essay outlines.

Instructor's Resource CD-ROM

This disc provides instructors with ready-made and customizable PowerPoint multimedia presentations built around chapter outlines, maps, figures, and all images from the textbook, plus JPEG versions of all maps, figures, and images.

The following maps and images from Chapter 18 are available in both JPEG and PowerPoint format on the Instructor's Resource CD-ROM:

- Map 18.1: The Early Phase of Europe's Industrial Revolution (p. 531)
- Map 18.2: The Industrial United States in 1900 (p. 543)
- Map 18.3: Latin America and the World, 1825–1935 (p. 551)
- Industrial Britain (p. 526)
- Railroads (p. 534)
- The Industrial Middle Class (p. 536)
- The Urban Poor of Industrial Britain (p. 538)
- Socialist Protest (p. 540)
- Russian Serfdom (p. 545)
- The Mexican Revolution (p. 553)

FOR STUDENTS

Documents and Essays from *Worlds of History: A Comparative Reader*, Third Edition (Volume 2)

The following documents, essays, and illustrations to accompany Chapter 18 are available in Chapter 7 of Volume 2 of this reader by Kevin Reilly:

- Arnold Pacey, *Asia and the Industrial Revolution*
- Adam Smith, from *The Wealth of Nations*
- From *The Sadler Report of the House of Commons*
- Karl Marx and Friedrich Engels, from *The Communist Manifesto*
- Peter N. Stearns, *The Industrial Revolution Outside the West*
- John H. Coatsworth, *Economic Trajectories in Latin America*
- Iwasaki Yataro, *Mitsubishi Letter to Employees*

Online Study Guide at bedfordstmartins.com/strayer

The Online Study Guide helps students synthesize the material from the text as well as practice the skills historians use to make sense of the past. Each chapter of the Online Study Guide contains specific testing exercises, including a multiple-choice self-test that focuses on important conceptual ideas; an identification quiz that helps students remember key people, places, and events; a flashcard activity that tests students on their knowledge of key terms; and two interactive map activities intended to strengthen students' geographic skills. Instructors can monitor students' progress through an online Quiz Gradebook or receive email updates.

Further Reading

Acker, Alison. *Honduras: The Making of a Banana Republic*. Boston: South End Press, 1989. An interesting study of U.S.-Honduran relations.

Deane, Phyllis. *The First Industrial Revolution*. 2nd ed. Cambridge: Cambridge University Press, 1980. A clearly written and useful survey of the Industrial Revolution in the period 1750–1850.

Frader, Laura L. *The Industrial Revolution: A History in Documents*. Oxford: Oxford University Press, 2006. A slim volume that weaves together narrative and documents, suitable for classroom use.

The History Guide: Industrial Revolution Resources, http://www.historyguide.org/intellect/ind_rev.html. This site supplies both Internet links and a useful bibliography of books on the subject.

Marxism Page, http://www.anu.edu.au/polsci/marx/marx.html. This site includes Marxist classics, graphics, and even a recording of "The Internationale."

Newman, Michael. *Socialism: A Very Short Introduction*. New York: Oxford University Press, 2005. Very short indeed at 144 pages, this is an excellent introduction to the subject.

Stearns, Peter N. *The Industrial Revolution in World History*. 3rd ed. Boulder, CO: Westview Press, 2007. An examination of the impact of industrialization on several major societies.

Victorian England: Directory of Online Resources, http://www.academicinfo.net/histukvictorian.html. An excellent collection.

Web sites for the Gilded Age and Progressive Era, http://bss.sfsu.edu/cherny/gapesites.htm. A nice selection of both primary and secondary materials on U.S. history between 1865 and 1920.

Literature

Alger, Horatio. *Ragged Dick; and, Struggling Upward.* London: Penguin, 1985. Two terrific "rags to riches" stories, originally sold as dime novels, by a great nineteenth-century American advocate of success through hard work.

Crane, Stephen. *Maggie: A Girl of the Streets, and Other Tales of New York.* 2nd ed. London: Penguin, 2000. First published in 1893, the title story gives a chilling picture of life in New York City.

Dickens, Charles. *A Christmas Carol and Other Christmas Writings.* 2nd ed. London: Penguin, 2003. The famous tale of a capitalist and his reclamation.

Dickens, Charles. *Hard Times.* 3rd ed. New York: Norton, 2000. A hard look at capitalist exploitation and what comes of trying to make humans into machines.

Engels, Friedrich. *The Condition of the Working-Class in England.* London: Penguin, 1987. A scathing indictment of nineteenth-century capitalism.

Halsall, Paul, ed. *Internet Modern History Sourcebook.* http://www.fordham.edu/halsall/mod/modsbook.html. A large number of primary sources that address a range of issues of the nineteenth-century world.

Howells, William Dean. *The Rise of Silas Lapham.* New York: Barnes & Noble Classics, 2007. The tale of a *nouveau riche* American industrialist and his efforts to be accepted into the social elite.

Marx, Karl, and Friedrich Engels. *The Communist Manifesto.* Trans. Samuel Moore. 2nd ed. London: Penguin, 2002. A political classic that everyone should read.

Sinclair, Upton. *The Jungle.* London: Penguin, 1985. One of the great masterpieces of the Industrial Revolution, *The Jungle* is a penetrating look at the meatpacking industry and worker movements from the perspective of an immigrant family in America.

Smiles, Samuel. *Self-Help.* 2nd ed. Oxford: Oxford World's Classics, 2002. First published in 1859, this vastly popular book advocates social advancement through hard work.

Film

An Age of Revolutions. Films for the Humanities and Sciences, 1996. 23 minutes. Examines the impact of the French and Industrial revolutions on European society.

The Age of Revolutions: 1776–1848. Insight Media, 1985. 26 minutes. Surveys the Atlantic revolutions in America, Latin America, and France before examining the influence of Marx in this wider context.

The Growth of Towns and Cities. Films for the Humanities and Sciences, 1990. 19 minutes. Explores the rapid urbanization of cities during the Industrial Revolution.

The Industrial Revolution. Five-part series. Films for the Humanities and Sciences. 19–20 minutes each. A series of short programs, each focused on one of the following themes: "Working Lives"; "Evolving Transportation Systems"; "The Railway Age"; "Harnessing Steam"; "The Growth of Towns and Cities."

Karl Marx. Insight Media, 2006. 22 minutes. Examines the life and ideas of Karl Marx in the context of the Industrial Revolution.

Organizing America: The History of Trade Unions. Films for the Humanities and Sciences, 1994. 38 minutes. Traces the history of American trade unions from the formation of "friendly societies" in the eighteenth century to the 1990s.

Working Lives. Films for the Humanities and Sciences, 1992. 20 minutes. Examines the changes to working lives caused by the Industrial Revolution.

Internal Troubles, External Threats: China, the Ottoman Empire, and Japan
1800–1914

CHAPTER OVERVIEW

Chapter Objectives

- To make students aware of the refocusing of racism in the nineteenth-century West
- To examine the effects of Western dominance on the empires of Asia
- To explore the reasons behind the collapse of the Chinese and Ottoman empires
- To investigate the reasons for Japan's rise to its position as an industrial superpower and to compare Japan's experience with that of China

Chapter Outline

I. **Opening Vignette**
   A. Japanese history textbooks became controversial around 2000, with the Chinese expressing outrage over what they regarded as a whitewashing of Japanese offenses against China.
      1. the controversy reflects Japan's surprising rise to world importance, which started in the mid-nineteenth century

   2. both Japan and China had to face the threat of European dominance
   B. Most peoples of Asia, Middle East, Africa, and Latin America had to deal in some way with European imperialism.
      1. they also had to deal with internal problems and challenges
   C. This chapter focuses on societies that faced internal crises while maintaining formal independence.
   D. Four main dimensions of European imperialism confronted these societies:
      1. military might and political ambitions of rival European states
      2. involvement in a new world economy that radiated from Europe
      3. influence of aspects of traditional European culture (e.g., language, religion, literature)
      4. engagement with the culture of modernity

II. **The External Challenge: European Industry and Empire**
   A. The nineteenth century was Europe's greatest age of global expansion.
      1. became the center of the world economy
      2. millions of Europeans moved to regions beyond Europe

3. explorers and missionaries reached nearly everywhere
4. much of the world became part of European colonies

B. New Motives, New Means
1. the Industrial Revolution fueled much of Europe's expansion
   a. demand for raw materials and agricultural products
   b. need for markets to sell European products
   c. European capitalists often invested money abroad
   d. foreign markets kept workers within Europe employed
2. growth of mass nationalism in Europe made imperialism broadly popular
   a. Italy and Germany unified by 1871
   b. colonies were a status symbol
3. industrial-age developments made overseas expansion possible
   a. steamships
   b. underwater telegraph
   c. quinine
   d. breech-loading rifles and machine guns

C. New Perceptions of the "Other" **[see Lecture Strategy 1]**
1. in the past, Europeans had largely defined others in religious terms
   a. but had also adopted many foreign ideas and techniques
   b. mingled more freely with Asian and African elites
   c. had even seen technologically simple peoples at times as "noble savages"
2. the industrial age promoted a secular arrogance among Europeans
   a. was sometimes combined with a sense of religious superiority
   b. Europeans increasingly despised other cultures
   c. African societies lost status
      i. earlier: were regarded as nations, their leaders as kings
      ii. nineteenth century: became tribes led by chiefs in European eyes
   d. new kind of racism, expressed in terms of modern science
      i. scientific "proof" of some peoples' inferiority
      ii. creation of a hierarchy of races
      iii. view of race as determining intelligence, moral development, and destiny
      iv. view that inferior peoples threatened Europeans with their diseases
3. sense of responsibility to the "weaker races"
   a. duty to civilize them
   b. bringing them education, health care, Christianity, good government, etc., was regarded as "progress" and "civilization"
4. social Darwinism: an effort to apply Darwin's evolutionary theory to human history
   a. regarded as inevitable that the "unfit" races should be displaced or destroyed

III. **Reversal of Fortune: China's Century of Crisis** [see Discussion Topic 1, Classroom Activity 1, and Classroom Activity 2]
A. In 1793, the Chinese emperor Qianlong rebuffed Britain's request that China rescind or loosen restrictions on trade.
1. Chinese authorities had controlled and limited European activities for centuries
2. by 1912, Chinese empire had collapsed, became a weak junior member in European-dominated world

B. The Crisis Within
1. China was, to a large degree, the victim of its own success
   a. population had grown from about 100 million in 1685 to some 430 million in 1853
   b. but China didn't have an accompanying Industrial Revolution
   c. growing pressure on the land, impoverishment, starvation
2. Chinese bureaucracy did not keep pace with growing population
   a. by 1800, county magistrates had to deal with four times as many people as in 1400
   b. central state gradually lost control of provincial officials and gentry
      i. corruption became endemic
      ii. harsh treatment of peasants

3. bandit gangs and peasant rebellions became common
   a. charismatic figures preached a millenarian message
4. culmination of China's internal crisis: the Taiping Uprising [see Lecture Strategy 2]
   a. affected much of China 1850–1864
   b. leader Hong Xiuquan (1814–1864) proclaimed himself the younger brother of Jesus, sent to establish a "heavenly kingdom of great peace"
   c. called for radical equality
   d. even planned to industrialize China
   e. Taiping forces established their capital at Nanjing (1853)
   f. rebellion was crushed by 1864
      i. rebellion was *not* suppressed by imperial military forces
      ii. provincial landowners mobilized their own armies
5. resolution of the Taiping rebellion consolidated the power of the provincial gentry even more
   a. intense conservatism, so China's problems weren't resolved
   b. the massive civil war had seriously weakened the Chinese economy
   c. 20 million–30 million people died in the rebellion
C. Western Pressures
1. the Opium Wars show the transformation of China's relationship with Europe
   a. opium had been used on a small scale in China for centuries
   b. British began to sell large quantities of Indian opium in China
   c. Chinese authorities recognized the dangers of opium addiction, tried to stop the trade
   d. European merchants bribed officials to smuggle opium in
   e. China suffered a specie drain from large quantities of silver spent on opium
   f. 1836: the emperor decided to suppress the trade
      i. Commissioner Lin Zexu campaigned against opium use

      ii. seized and destroyed over three million pounds of opium from Western traders, expelled them from China
2. the British responded with the first Opium War (1839–1842)
   a. forced Chinese to accept free trade and "proper" relations among countries
   b. Treaty of Nanjing (1842):
      i. China agreed to pay a $21 million indemnity
      ii. China ceded Hong Kong
      iii. five ports were opened to trade
      iv. tariffs fixed at a low rate
      v. foreigners received the right to live in China under their own laws
3. second Opium War (1856–1858)
   a. Europeans vandalized the imperial Summer Palace
   b. more treaty ports were opened to foreigners
   c. China was opened to foreign missionaries
   d. Western powers were given the right to patrol some of China's interior waterways
4. China was also defeated by the French (1885) and Japanese (1895)
5. Qing dynasty was deeply weakened at a time when China needed a strong government to deal with modernization
6. "unequal treaties" inhibited China's industrialization
D. The Failure of Conservative Modernization
1. the Chinese government tried to act against problems
   a. policy of "self-strengthening" in 1860s and 1870s
   b. application of traditional Confucian principles, along with very limited borrowing from the West
   c. efforts to improve examination system
   d. restoration of rural social and economic order
   e. establishment of some modern arsenals and shipyards, some study of other languages and sciences
   f. foundation of a few industrial factories

2. conservative leaders feared that development would harm the landlord class
3. Boxer Rebellion (1900): militia organizations killed many Europeans and Chinese Christians, besieged foreign embassies in Beijing
   a. Western powers and Japan occupied Beijing to crush the revolt
   b. imposed massive reparation payments on China
4. growing number of educated Chinese became disillusioned with the Qing dynasty
   a. organizations to examine the situation and propose reforms
   b. growing drive for a truly unified nation in which more people took part in public life
   c. Chinese nationalism was against both foreign imperialists and the foreign Qing dynasty
5. the government agreed to some reforms in the early twentieth century, but not enough—the imperial order collapsed in 1911

IV. **The Ottoman Empire and the West in the Nineteenth Century** [see Discussion Topic 2 and Classroom Activity 3]
   A. Both China and the Ottoman Empire:
      1. had felt that they did not need to learn from the West
      2. avoided direct colonial rule, but were diminished
      3. attempted "defensive modernization"
      4. suffered a split in society between modernists and those holding traditional values
   B. "The Sick Man of Europe"
      1. 1750: the Ottoman Empire was still strong, at center of the Islamic world; by 1900, was known as "the sick man of Europe"
      2. region by region, Islamic world fell under Christian rule, and the Ottomans couldn't prevent it
         a. Ottomans lost territory to Russia, Britain, Austria, and France
         b. Napoleon's 1798 invasion of Egypt was especially devastating

   c. Greece, Serbia, Bulgaria, and Rumania attained independence
      3. central Ottoman state had weakened
         a. provincial authorities and local warlords gained more power, limited the government's ability to raise money
         b. the Janissaries had become militarily ineffective
      4. the economy was hit hard by Western developments
         a. Europeans achieved direct access to Asia
         b. cheap European manufactured goods harmed Ottoman artisans
         c. foreign merchants won immunity from Ottoman laws and taxes
            i. foreign consuls granted the same privileges to hundreds of thousands of Ottoman citizens (especially Jews, Greeks, and Armenians)
         d. government came to rely on foreign loans to finance economic development efforts
            i. by 1882, much of the Ottoman revenue system was controlled by foreigners
            ii. British occupied Egypt
      5. had reached a state of dependency on Europe
   C. Reform
      1. Ottomans attempted ambitious reforms, going considerably further than the Chinese
         a. didn't have an internal crisis on the scale of China
         b. did not have to deal with explosive population growth
         c. rulers were Turkic and Muslim, not like foreign Qing
      2. late eighteenth century: Selim III tried to establish new military and administrative structures
         a. sent ambassadors to study European methods
         b. imported European advisers
         c. established technical schools
      3. after 1839: more far-reaching measures (*Tanzimat*, or "reorganization") emerged
         a. beginning of an extensive process of industrialization and modernization

b. acceptance of the principle that all citizens are equal before the law
  i. challenged the Islamic character of the state
  ii. more Christians attained high office
c. tide of secular legislation and secular schools

D. Identity

1. Selim III's modest reforms stirred up so much hostility among the ulama and Janissaries that he was deposed in 1807
2. movements of Islamic renewal outside of the Ottoman Empire presented another model for dealing with Europe
  a. Sumatra: Islamic renewal became a war of resistance against the Dutch (early nineteenth century)
  b. Muslim leaders in Chechnya and Dagestan organized jihads against Russian intrusion
  c. Muslim-based resistance movement against the French invasion of Algeria (1830)
  d. such movements had little impact within the Ottoman Empire
3. supporters of reform saw the Ottoman Empire as a secular state
  a. reform created a new class of writers, etc.—the "Young Ottomans"
  b. urged creation of a constitutional regime
  c. Islamic modernism: accepted Western technology and science but not its materialism
4. Sultan Abd al-Hamid II (r. 1876–1909) accepted a new constitution in 1876 that limited the sultan's authority
  a. almost immediately suspended it
  b. turned to decisive autocracy in the face of a Russian invasion
    i. continued many educational, economic, and technical reforms
    ii. reactivated claim that the Ottoman sultans were also caliphs and spoke for the whole Islamic world
    iii. restored the prestige of the ulama
    iv. reintroduced distinction between Muslim and non-Muslim subjects

5. opposition coalesced around the "Young Turks" (military and civilian elites) **[see Lecture Strategy 3]**
  a. advocated a militantly secular public life
  b. shift to thinking in terms of a Turkish national state
6. after 1900, growing efforts to define a Turkish national character
7. military coup (1908) gave the Young Turks real power
  a. antagonized non-Turkic peoples in the Ottoman Empire
  b. stimulated Arab and other nationalisms
  c. the Ottoman Empire completely disintegrated after WWI

E. Outcomes: Comparing China and the Ottoman Empire

1. by 1900, both China and the Ottoman Empire were "semicolonies"
2. both gave rise to a new nationalist conception of society
3. China: the imperial system collapsed in 1911
  a. followed by a vast revolution
  b. creation of a Communist regime by 1949, within the same territory
4. Ottoman Empire: the empire collapsed following WWI
  a. a new, much smaller nation-state was created in the Turkish heartland
5. Chinese revolutionaries rejected Confucian culture much more than Turkish leaders rejected Islam

V. **The Japanese Difference: The Rise of a New East Asian Power** [Discussion Topic 3]

A. Japan was forced to open up to more "normal" relations with the world by U.S. commodore Matthew Perry in 1853.
  1. 1853–1900: radical transformation of Japanese society
  2. Japan became powerful, modern, united, industrialized
  3. Japan created its own East Asian empire

B. The Tokugawa Background
  1. Tokugawa shoguns had ruled since about 1600
    a. main task was preventing civil war among rival feudal lords (the daimyo)

b. Japan enjoyed internal peace from 1600 to 1850

c. daimyo were strictly regulated but retained considerable autonomy

d. Japan wasn't unified by a single law, currency, or central authority that reached to the local level

e. hierarchical society: samurai at the top, then peasants, artisans, and merchants at the bottom

2. considerable change in Japan in the Tokugawa period

   a. samurai evolved into a bureaucratic/administrative class

   b. great economic growth, commercialization, and urban development

   c. by 1750, Japan was perhaps the most urbanized country

     i. 10 percent of population lived in cities or towns

     ii. Edo (Tokyo) had a million residents

   d. high literacy rates (40 percent of males, 15 percent of females)

   e. change made it impossible for the shogunate to freeze society

     i. some samurai turned to commerce

     ii. many merchants prospered

     iii. many peasants moved to cities, despite edicts

3. corruption was widespread

   a. uprisings of the poor, both rural and urban

C. American Intrusion and the Meiji Restoration

1. U.S. sent Commodore Perry in 1853 to demand better treatment for castaways, right to refuel and buy provisions, and the opening of trade ports

   a. the shogun gave in to Perry's demands

2. the shogun's spinelessness triggered a civil war

3. in 1868, a group of young samurai from the south took over

   a. they claimed to be restoring the 15-year-old emperor Meiji to power

   b. aimed to save Japan from the foreigners by transformation of Japanese society rather than by resistance

4. the West wasn't as interested in Japan as it was in China

D. Modernization Japanese Style

1. first task was creating national unity

   a. attacked power and privileges of the daimyo and the samurai

   b. dismantled the Confucian-based social order

   c. almost all Japanese became legally equal

2. widespread interest in many aspects of the West, from science to hairstyles

   a. official missions were sent to the West

   b. hundreds of students studied abroad

   c. translation of Western books into Japanese

3. eventually settled down to more selective borrowing from the West

   a. combined foreign and Japanese elements, e.g., in the 1889 constitution

4. feminism and Christianity made little progress

5. Shinto was raised to the level of a state cult

6. state-guided industrialization program

   a. established model factories, opened mines, built railroads, created postal, telegraph, and banking systems

   b. many state enterprises were then sold to private investors

   c. accomplished modernization without acquiring foreign debt

7. society paid a heavy price

   a. many peasant families were impoverished

   b. countryside suffered infanticide, sale of daughters, and famine

   c. early urban workers received harsh treatment

   d. efforts to organize unions were repressed

     i. nascent labor movement was crushed by end of 1901

     ii. authorities emphasized theme of service to the state and ideas of the enterprise as a family

E. Japan and the World

1. by the early twentieth century, Western powers readjusted treaties in Japan's favor

   a. Anglo-Japanese Treaty of 1902 recognized Japan as an equal

2. Japanese empire building

   a. wars against China (1894–1895) and Russia (1904–1905)

      b. gained colonial control of Taiwan and Korea, won a foothold in Manchuria

   3. Japan's rise was widely admired

   4. Japan's colonial policies were at least as brutal as European ones

VI. Reflections: Success and Failure in History

  A. We must be very careful in applying ideas of "success" and "failure" to historical complexities.

    1. much depends on the criteria we apply

    2. need to consider the issue of "success for whom?"

    3. historical actors are never completely free in making decisions and lack the benefit of hindsight

USING *WAYS OF THE WORLD* IN THE CLASSROOM

Lecture Strategies

Lecture Strategy 1

"Confronting racism."

As outlined in the text, the nineteenth century gave birth to a new sort of racism, one based on smug European assumptions of superiority. For this lecture strategy, we propose focusing on the issue of racism in the nineteenth century but placing it in a broader context of racism through world history. The objectives are:

- to make students aware of the many sorts of racism and prejudice that exist and have existed in world history
- to evaluate the factors that made racism more pervasive than ever before in the nineteenth century
- to consider the legacies of nineteenth-century racism in our own society

A good place to start is by encouraging students to name points at which they saw racism in earlier world civ. lectures and readings. Some points they might come up with are:

- Greek antipathy toward the Persians at the time of the Persian Wars

- Chinese hatred of the Xiongnu nomads
- everyone's hatred of the Mongols
- persecution of the Jews in medieval Europe
- European hatred of the Turks in the early modern period
- Arabic hatred of Europeans, and vice versa, during the Crusades
- European contempt for Native Americans

Such cases should lead easily into a discussion of when the term "racism" should properly be employed and of other factors that might be involved, such as religious disagreement or fear of a dangerous neighbor.

Go on from there to discuss the history of racism. Some important points to include are:

- Aristotle's theory of naturally inferior races
- whether Muslims like Ibn Battuta were racist (his descriptions of sub-Saharan Africa are often very negative)
- anti-Judaism vs. anti-Semitism in the European Middle Ages
- early modern attitudes toward "noble savages" and dangerous Turks

And of course, a discussion of the history of racism should address the factors that can make people of one society feel contempt for those of another and the ways in which many of those factors came together. For example, you might include:

- prosperity
- cleanliness
- ability to control disease
- complexity of government
- overwhelming defeats in war (it's much easier to respect a valiant enemy than an abject one)
- other factors that the Industrial Revolution contributed to European self-esteem

The poetry of Rudyard Kipling is particularly useful for this lecture.

Lecture Strategy 2

"The nineteenth century and the millennium."
This lecture strategy focuses especially on China's Taiping Uprising but places it in the context of the extraordinary number of millenarian movements that

shook much of the world in response to modernization. Its objectives are:

- to encourage students to understand apocalyptic thought as a product of particular social circumstances
- to drive home the message of how painfully stressful modernization was for many people and societies
- to point to the international and interreligious nature of millenarianism

A handy place to start this lecture is with the Millerites of the United States, a particularly notable millenarian sect whose members believed that Christ would come again in 1843. The Millerites provide a useful platform from which to discuss (1) the meaning of "millenarianism" and (2) the relationship between the phenomenon and mainstream religion. The Millerites are also useful because they were contemporaneous to Hong Xiuquan, Christ's younger brother and the moving spirit of the Taiping rebellion.

From there, craft a lecture on the theme of apocalypticism as a response to crisis in society, using the Taiping Uprising as a central example. Some other good millenarian leaders and movements to include are:

- the Taborites of Bohemia (fifteenth century)
- the Anabaptists of Münster (1530s)
- Sabbatai Zvi, the most important Jewish messiah claimant (1660s)
- Joanna Southcott (1750–1814) of England
- the millenarian culture of the "Great Awakening" in England and America (1760–1850)
- the Mahdi of the Sudan (1881–1885)
- the Native American Ghost Dance (1870 and 1890)
- the "Vailala Madness," an early Cargo Cult of Melanesia (1919–1923)
- Russian Old Believers' attack on Lenin as the Antichrist
- the Branch Davidian sect of Waco, Texas (crisis in 1993)
- the Aum Shinri Kyo "doomsday cult" in Japan (subway attacks, 1995)

Lecture Strategy 3

"The Meiji restoration and the Young Turks."
This lecture strategy proposes a more detailed analytical comparison of the transformation of Japan and the partial reforms of the Ottoman Empire in the nineteenth century. Its objectives are:

- to encourage discussion about what factors made the two societies react differently to the pressures of industrialization and modernization
- to explore in greater detail the reform efforts in the nineteenth-century Ottoman Empire
- to examine in greater detail the successes and problems of the Meiji restoration in Japan

A good place to start is with two maps (preferably physical maps) of the Ottoman Empire and Japan. Encourage students to discuss the following issues:

- physical factors that encouraged or inhibited a centralized state
- the ethnic and religious issues of the Ottoman Empire
- how exposed the two states were to outside influences, and from which direction

From there, choose either Japan or the Ottoman Empire as your major example, inserting comparisons to the other as is appropriate. Some Meiji points to include:

- the threat of Commodore Perry
- why Tokugawa Yoshinobu (the shogun) resigned, and what that resignation meant
- the Boshin War
- the attempt to create a breakaway Republic of Ezo
- what happened to the daimyo when their domains were returned to imperial control
- the steps taken to abolish the samurai class and the samurai riots
- how the process of industrialization worked

Some Young Turk points to include:

- the specific reforms of the Tanzimat period
- the problem of foreign invasions and public debt to foreign banks
- the role of the Committee of Union and Progress
- the coup of 1913
- the role of Turkish nationalism (and its effects on Jewish, Greek, and Armenian minority populations)

Things to Do in the Classroom

Discussion Topics

1. **Contextualization, large or small group.** "China's turning point."

This chapter portrays an abrupt shift from China as international superpower to an enfeebled China breaking apart under the force of foreign dominance and internal rebellion. Ask your students to discuss: What was the turning point in China's history? Is it possible to isolate a single factor or group of factors that made the fall of the Qing dynasty inevitable? When was the last point at which China's decline could have been reversed?

2. **Misconception/Difficult Topic, large or small group.** "The Ottoman Empire was a 'sick old man' that just collapsed."

The textbook provides a much more nuanced picture of the late Ottoman Empire, stressing efforts at governmental reform and the problems, both internal and foreign, that led to the empire's breakup. Ask students to discuss this issue, and to make two lists, one of positive features of the nineteenth-century Ottoman Empire and one of negative features. After small groups have completed their lists, bring discussion back to the larger group, first sharing what the various groups came up with and then encouraging a discussion of how much of what they have listed is biased by a "Western" perspective and how much of it is either good or bad by any standards.

3. **Comparison, large or small group.** "Why was Japan so different?"

It would seem logical that Japan would have reacted very negatively to Western encroachment—after all, Commodore Perry rammed a new policy of openness down Japanese throats, and Japan had turned definitively against Western influences in the early seventeenth century. Yet among the Asian nations, it was only Japan that embraced Western ideas and technology. Ask your students to discuss this apparently unexpected historic development, trying to answer the question of why Japan's encounter with industrialization and modernization was so different from that of the other states of Asia.

Classroom Activities

1. **Clicker question.** With stronger leadership, could the Chinese Empire have been saved?

2. **Role-playing exercise, small group.** "The dowager empress."

You, the instructor, are Cixi, the dowager empress of China (*de facto* ruler from 1861 to 1908). Selected groups of students are your advisers. The year is 1899, and the great question is what to do with the imperialist foreign devils who are overrunning your country. Warn your students that they must make their arguments in ways that will not outrage traditional Chinese beliefs, and then ask different groups to argue the following proposals:

- that the government hire 1,000 foreign advisers and make serious efforts to industrialize, following the Japanese model
- that the government permit the foreigners to visit China, but that it order the Chinese population to have nothing to do with them
- that the government encourage the Chinese to kill all foreigners in the country

3. **Map-analysis exercise, large or small group.** "The Ottoman Empire and its enemies."

Display a good map of the Middle East—ideally it would be one that clearly defines the Ottoman Empire in the nineteenth century, but a map with modern political borders would also do. Go over the map with your students, discussing the ethnic and religious makeup of each region and reminding students when each region became a part of the Ottoman Empire. Also identify clearly the direction from which foreign threats to the Ottomans came.

Key Terms

Abd al-Hamid II: Ottoman sultan (r. 1876–1909) who accepted a reform constitution but then quickly suppressed it, ruling as a reactionary autocrat for the rest of his long reign. (*pron.* AHB-dahl-hahm-EED)

Boxer Rebellion: Rising of Chinese militia organizations in 1900 in which large numbers of Europeans and Chinese Christians were killed.

China, 1911: The collapse of China's imperial order, officially at the hands of organized revolutionaries but for the most part under the weight of the troubles that had overwhelmed the government for the previous half-century.

daimyo: Feudal lords of Japan who retained substantial autonomy under the Tokugawa shogunate and only lost their social preeminence in the Meiji restoration. (*pron.* DIME-yoh)

Hong Xiuquan: Chinese religious leader (1814–1864) who sparked the Taiping Uprising and won millions to his unique form of Christianity, according to which he himself was the younger brother of Jesus, sent to establish a "heavenly kingdom of great peace" on earth. (*pron.* hong shee-OH-chew-an)

informal empire: Term commonly used to describe areas that were dominated by Western powers in the nineteenth century but that retained their own governments and a measure of independence, e.g., Latin America and China.

Meiji restoration: The overthrow of the Tokugawa shogunate of Japan in 1868, restoring power at long last to the emperor Meiji. (*pron.* MAY-gee)

Perry, Matthew: U.S. navy commodore who in 1853 presented the ultimatum that led Japan to open itself to more normal relations with the outside world.

Opium Wars: Two wars fought between Western powers and China (1839–1842 and 1856–1858) after China tried to restrict the importation of foreign goods, especially opium; China lost both wars and was forced to make major concessions.

Russo-Japanese War, 1904–1905: Ending in a Japanese victory, this war established Japan as a formidable military competitor in East Asia and precipitated the Russian Revolution of 1905.

samurai: Armed retainers of the Japanese feudal lords, famed for their martial skills and loyalty; in the Tokugawa shogunate, the samurai gradually became an administrative elite, but they did not lose their special privileges until the Meiji restoration. (*pron.* SAH-moo-rie)

self-strengthening movement: China's program of internal reform in the 1860s and 1870s, based on vigorous application of Confucian principles and limited borrowing from the West.

Selim III: Ottoman sultan (r. 1789–1807) who attempted significant reforms of his empire, including the implementation of new military and administrative structures. (*pron.* seh-LEEM)

"sick man of Europe, the": Western Europe's unkind nickname for the Ottoman Empire in the nineteenth and early twentieth centuries, a name based on the sultans' inability to prevent Western takeover of many regions and to deal with internal problems; it fails to recognize serious reform efforts in the Ottoman state during this period.

social Darwinism: An application of the concept of "survival of the fittest" to human history in the nineteenth century.

Taiping Uprising: Massive Chinese rebellion that devastated much of the country between 1850 and 1864; it was based on the millenarian teachings of Hong Xiuquan. (*pron.* tie-PING)

Tanzimat reforms: Important reform measures undertaken in the Ottoman Empire beginning in 1839; the term "Tanzimat" means "reorganization." (*pron.* TAHNZ-ee-MAT)

Tokugawa shogunate: Rulers of Japan from 1600 to 1868. (*pron.* toe-koo-GAH-wah SHOW-gun-at)

unequal treaties: Series of nineteenth-century treaties in which China made major concessions to Western powers.

Young Ottomans: Group of would-be reformers in the mid-nineteenth-century Ottoman Empire that included lower-level officials, military officers, and writers; they urged the extension of Westernizing reforms to the political system.

Young Turks: Movement of Turkish military and civilian elites that developed ca. 1900, eventually bringing down the Ottoman Empire.

ANSWER GUIDELINES FOR CHAPTER QUESTIONS

The two sets of questions that follow appear in the textbook at the end of the chapter and in the margins of the reading. They are also provided in the Computerized Test Bank with answer guidelines, for your convenience.

The Big Picture Questions

1. How did European expansion in the nineteenth century differ from that of the early modern era?

• Europe in the nineteenth century drew on immense new resources created by the Industrial Revolution to underpin its expansion.

• European states were more powerful in the nineteenth century and were able to field more military resources in their imperialist competition with each other.

• To a greater extent than before, in the nineteenth century Europe enmeshed other parts of the world in networks of trade, investment, and sometimes migration. This ultimately generated a new world economy.

• Unlike the early modern period, in the nineteenth century European expansion brought with it a new culture of modernity—its scientific rationalism and technological achievements, its belief in a better future, and its ideas of nationalism, socialism, feminism, and individualism.

2. What differences can you identify in how China, the Ottoman Empire, and Japan experienced Western imperialism and confronted it? How might you account for those differences?

• Both China and the Ottoman Empire became more reliant on Western finance than Japan.

• Both China and the Ottoman Empire experienced occupation of some of their territory by Western military forces; Japan did not.

• China, the Ottoman Empire, and Japan all were forced by Western powers to sign "unequal treaties" or "capitulations," but Japan eventually was able to renegotiate its treaties in its favor.

• All three launched modernization programs, but Japan's was more thorough and more successful than those of China and the Ottoman Empire, turning Japan into a modern, united, industrial nation.

• A number of factors can explain the differences in how they experienced Western imperialism, including the amount of internal strife within each state, the strategic and economic importance to European powers of the Ottoman Empire and China as compared to Japan, and the relatively late and fortuitous timing of Japan's interactions with Western powers.

3. "The response of each society to European imperialism grew out of its larger historical development and its internal problems." What evidence might support this statement?

• Certainly the growing military and political power of Western states after the Industrial Revolution and their determination to gain influence in each society provided a larger historical development that shaped responses.

• However, internal problems shaped individual responses.

• For instance, the weakened imperial state in China and the social problems that led to serious peasant revolts like the Taiping Uprising speak to the internal problems that shaped the response of China.

• The loss of territories, the weakening of the central state, the increasing obsolescence of the army, the increasing indebtedness of the state, the decline of its centrality in Eurasian trade, and commercial competition from industrial Europe were internal problems that shaped the Ottoman Empire's response.

• Corruption within the Tokugawa regime, social change, and a mounting wave of local peasant uprisings and urban riots all shaped Japan's response to demands by the West.

4. What kind of debates, controversies, and conflicts were generated by European intrusion within each of the societies examined in this chapter?

• While there are numerous individual examples, all of the societies explored in the chapter reacted to growing European intrusions through modernization programs, although Japan's modernization program was more radical and far-reaching than the programs of China and the Ottoman Empire.

• All of the societies also dealt with issues of identity, as they sought new ways to define themselves. This is especially notable in the Ottoman Empire, where a new nationalist Turkish identity took shape.

• All of the societies debated the extent to which Western models should be followed.

• All of the societies dealt with conflicts between modernizers and more conservative elements in their societies.

Margin Review Questions

Q. *In what ways did the Industrial Revolution shape the character of nineteenth-century European imperialism?*

• The enormous productivity of industrial technology and Europe's growing affluence created the need for extensive raw materials and agricultural products found in other parts of the world.

• Europe needed to sell its own products, and foreign regions proved to be important markets.

• European capital sought investments abroad both for the profits that they promised and to stimulate demand for European products—in part to keep the laboring classes fully employed and thus less inclined to class conflict.

• The Industrial Revolution produced technological innovations such as the steamship, the breech-loading rifle, and the telegraph that facilitated imperialism.

Q. *What contributed to changing European views of Asians and Africans in the nineteenth century?*

• The accomplishments of the Industrial Revolution, including the unlocking of the secrets of nature and the creation of a society that enjoyed unprecedented wealth, led Europeans to develop a secular arrogance that fused with or in some cases replaced their long-standing notions of religious superiority.

• Increasingly, Europeans viewed the culture and achievements of Asian and African peoples through the prism of a new kind of racism, expressed now in terms of modern science. Europeans used allegedly scientific methods to classify humans, concluding that whites were more advanced. Collectively, these studies created a hierarchy of race, with whites on top and less developed "child races" beneath them.

• The belief among Europeans that they were the superior race led to a further set of ideas that European expansion was inevitable and that Europeans were fated to dominate the "weaker races." They saw it as their duty to undertake a "civilizing mission" that included bringing Christianity to the heathen, good government to disordered lands, work discipline and production for the market to "lazy natives," a measure of education to the ignorant and illiterate, clothing to the naked, and health care to the sick, while suppressing "native customs" that ran counter to Western ways of living.

• The idea of "social Darwinism" made imperialism, war, and aggression in Africa and Asia seem both natural and progressive, for they served to weed out the weaker peoples of the world, allowing the stronger to flourish.

Q. *What accounts for the massive peasant rebellions of nineteenth-century China?*

• China's population grew rapidly between 1685 and 1853, but agricultural production was unable to keep up; this led to growing pressure on the land, smaller farms for China's huge peasant population, and, in all too many cases, unemployment, impoverishment, misery, and starvation.

• China's centralized bureaucratic state did not enlarge itself to keep pace with the growing population and lost influence at the local level to provincial officials and local gentry, who tended to be more corrupt and harsh.

• Peasants frequently embraced rebellion, finding leadership in charismatic figures who proclaimed a millenarian religious message.

• Peasants also increasingly articulated their opposition to the Qing dynasty on account of its foreign Manchurian origins.

• The Taiping Uprising between 1850 and 1864 found its inspiration in a unique form of Christianity.

Q. *What was the impact of Western pressures on China during the nineteenth century?*

• China was forced to continue to import opium;

• cede Hong Kong to Britain and open a number of other ports to European merchants;

• set import tariffs into China at the low rate of 5 percent.

• Foreigners were given the right to live in China under their own laws;

• foreigners received the right to buy land in China;

• China was opened to Christian missionaries;

• Western powers were permitted to patrol some of the interior waterways of China;

• China lost control of Vietnam, Korea, and Taiwan.

• By the end of the nineteenth century, the Western nations plus Japan and Russia all had carved out spheres of influence within China, granting them special privileges to establish military bases, extract raw materials, and build railroads.

• Ultimately, Western pressure enfeebled the Chinese state at precisely the time when China required a strong government to manage its entry into the modern world, and restrictions imposed by the "unequal treaties" also inhibited China's industrialization.

Q. *Why was China unable to respond effectively to mounting pressures from the West in the nineteenth century?*

• The "self-strengthening" program was inhibited by the fears of conservative leaders that urban, industrial, or commercial development would erode the power and privileges of the landlord class.

• New industries remained largely dependent on foreigners for machinery, materials, and expertise.

• Regional officials, rather than the central government, largely controlled industrial enterprises and used them to strengthen their own position rather than that of the nation as a whole.

- The Boxer Rebellion failed.
- Growing numbers of educated Chinese, including many in official elite positions, became highly disillusioned with the Qing dynasty.

Q. *What lay behind the decline of the Ottoman Empire in the nineteenth century?*

- The empire shrank in size both because of European aggression in places like Egypt and because of successful nationalist independence movements in the Balkans.
- The Ottoman state had weakened, particularly in its ability to raise revenue, as provincial authorities and local warlords gained greater power.
- It had also weakened militarily, as the Janissaries (the elite military corps of the Ottoman state) had become reactionary defenders of the status quo whose military ineffectiveness was increasingly obvious.
- The technological gap with the West was clearly growing.
- The earlier centrality of the Ottoman and Arab lands in Afro-Eurasian commerce diminished as Europeans achieved direct oceanic access to the treasures of Asia.
- Competition from cheap European manufactured goods hit Ottoman artisans hard and led to urban riots protesting foreign imports.
- A lengthening set of capitulations gave foreign merchants immunity from Ottoman laws and legal procedures, exempted them from internal taxes, and limited import and export duties on their products. Moreover, foreign consuls could grant these privileges to Ottoman citizens.
- The Ottoman Empire grew increasingly indebted and became reliant on foreign loans. Its inability to pay the interest on those loans led to foreign control of much of its revenue-generating system and the outright occupation of Egypt by the British.

Q. *In what ways did the Ottoman state respond to its problems?*

- It launched a program of "defensive modernization" that included the establishment of new military and administrative structures alongside traditional institutions as a means of enhancing and centralizing state power.
- Ambassadors were sent to the courts of Europe to study administrative methods, and European advisers were imported.

- Technical schools to train future officials were established.
- The *Tanzimat*, or "reorganization," emerged in the several decades after 1839 as the Ottoman leadership sought to provide the economic, social, and legal underpinnings for a strong and newly recentralized state. Manifestations of this process included the establishment of factories producing cloth, paper, and armaments; modern mining operations; reclamation and resettlement of agricultural land; telegraphs, steamships, railroads, and a modern postal service; Western-style law codes and courts; and new elementary and secondary schools.
- The legal status of the empire's diverse communities was changed in an effort to integrate non-Muslim subjects more effectively into the state. As part of this process, the principle of equality of all citizens before the law was accepted.

Q. *In what different ways did various groups define the Ottoman Empire during the nineteenth century?*

- The "Young Ottomans" defined the empire as a secular state whose people were loyal to the dynasty that ruled it, rather than a primarily Muslim state based on religious principles. In the middle decades of the nineteenth century, this group argued that the empire needed to embrace Western technical and scientific knowledge, while rejecting its materialism. In pursuit of these goals, the group argued that it was possible to find in Islam itself the basis for freedom, progress, rationality, and patriotism.
- During the reactionary reign of Sultan Abd al-Hamid II, a second identity took shape, in which the empire was defined as a despotic state with a pan-Islamic identity.
- Opposition to Abd al-Hamid II coalesced around another identity associated with the "Young Turks," who were led by both military and civilian elites. They largely abandoned any reference to Islam and advocated instead a militantly secular public life. Some among them began to think of the empire as neither a dynastic state nor a pan-Islamic empire, but rather as a Turkish national state.

Q. *How did Japan's historical development differ from that of China and the Ottoman Empire during the nineteenth century?*

- Japan enjoyed internal peace between 1600 and 1850.

• Japan agreed to a series of unequal treaties with various Western powers in order to avoid the problems of China, which initially resisted such treaties.

• Japan, unlike China or the Ottoman Empire, sought in the aftermath of the Meiji restoration to save Japan from foreign domination by a thorough transformation of Japanese society, drawing upon all that the modern West had to offer.

• The Meiji restoration was less destructive than the Taiping Uprising, which left Japan in a better position to reform.

• Japan was of less interest to Western powers than either China or the Ottoman Empire, allowing it to reform while under less pressure.

• The reforms instituted following the Meiji restoration transformed Japan far more thoroughly than even the most radical of the Ottoman or Chinese efforts.

• Japan industrialized more thoroughly than either China or the Ottoman Empire.

• Japan did not become as dependent on foreign capital as the Ottoman Empire.

Q. *In what ways was Japan changing during the Tokugawa era?*

• The samurai, in the absence of wars to fight, evolved into a salaried bureaucratic or administrative class.

• Centuries of peace contributed to a remarkable burst of economic growth, commercialization, and urban development.

• Japan became perhaps the world's most urbanized country.

• Education led to high rates of literacy.

• Merchants prospered but enjoyed little rise in social status. This, coupled with samurai who enjoyed high social status but were often indebted to inferior merchants, led to social tension.

• Peasants often moved to the cities to take on new trades.

• Corruption undermined the Tokugawa regime.

• A mounting wave of local peasant uprisings and urban riots expressed the grievances of the poor.

Q. *Does Japan's nineteenth-century transformation deserve to be considered revolutionary?*

• Its cumulative effect could be considered revolutionary as it included an attack on the power and privileges of both the diamyo and the samurai and

their replacement with governors responsible to the central government;

• a dismantling of the old Confucian-based social order through the abolition of class restrictions on occupation, residence, marriage, and clothing;

• the dismantling of limitations on travel and trade;

• the study of the science and technology of the West and of its various political and constitutional arrangements, its legal and educational systems, and its dances, clothing, hairstyles, and literature;

• selective borrowing of Western ideas, combining foreign and Japanese elements in distinctive ways;

• a state-guided industrialization program.

• And, of course, industrialization was as revolutionary in Japan as it was in any other agricultural society of the world.

Q. *How did Japan's relationship to the larger world change during its modernization process?*

• The unequal treaties were rewritten in Japan's favor;

• Japan launched its own empire-building enterprise, leaving it with colonial control of Taiwan, Korea, and parts of Manchuria;

• Japan fought successful wars with China and Russia in the process;

• in sum, Japan became an economic, political, and military competitor for Western powers.

• Japan also became an inspiration for other subject peoples, who saw in Japan a model for their own modern development and perhaps an ally in the struggle against imperialism.

ADDITIONAL RESOURCES FOR CHAPTER 19

Additional Bedford/St. Martin's Resources

FOR INSTRUCTORS

Computerized Test Bank

This test bank provides over thirty exercises per chapter, including multiple-choice, fill-in-the-blank,

short-answer, and full-length essay questions. Instructors can customize quizzes, add or edit both questions and answers, and export questions and answers to a variety of formats, including WebCT and Blackboard. The disc includes correct answers and essay outlines.

Instructor's Resource CD-ROM

This disc provides instructors with ready-made and customizable PowerPoint multimedia presentations built around chapter outlines, maps, figures, and all images from the textbook, plus JPEG versions of all maps, figures, and images.

The following maps and images from Chapter 19 are available in both JPEG and PowerPoint format on the Instructor's Resource CD-ROM:

- Map 19.1: China and the World in the Nineteenth Century (p. 569)
- Map 19.2: The Contraction of the Ottoman Empire (p. 572)
- Map 19.3: The Rise of Japan (p. 585)
- Carving Up the Pie of China (p. 558)
- The Gatling Gun (p. 562)
- European Racial Images (p. 564)
- Addiction to Opium (p. 568)
- The Ottoman Empire and the West (p. 574)
- The "Opening" of Japan (p. 580)
- Japan's Modernization (p. 583)

FOR STUDENTS

Documents and Essays from *Worlds of History: A Comparative Reader*, Third Edition (Volume 2)

The following documents, essays, and illustrations to accompany Chapter 19 are available in Chapter 8 of Volume 2 of this reader by Kevin Reilly:

- Jurgen Osterhammel, from *Colonialism*
- George Orwell, from *Burmese Days*
- David Cannadine, from *Ornamentalism*
- Joseph Conrad, from *Heart of Darkness*
- Chinua Achebe, *An Image of Africa: Racism in Conrad's* Heart of Darkness
- Rudyard Kipling, *The White Man's Burden*

Online Study Guide at bedfordstmartins.com/strayer

The Online Study Guide helps students synthesize the material from the text as well as practice the skills historians use to make sense of the past. Each chapter of the Online Study Guide contains specific testing exercises, including a multiple-choice self-test that focuses on important conceptual ideas; an identification quiz that helps students remember key people, places, and events; a flashcard activity that tests students on their knowledge of key terms; and two interactive map activities intended to strengthen students' geographic skills. Instructors can monitor students' progress through an online Quiz Gradebook or receive email updates.

Further Reading

Barkun, Michael. *Disaster and the Millennium.* New Haven: Yale University Press, 1974. A fine study of how people turn to millenarian ideas when disaster strikes the world they know.

Fredrickson, George M. *Racism: A Short History.* 2nd ed. Princeton, NJ: Princeton University Press, 2003. An insightful book that focuses on views of Africans and Jews.

Gordon, Andrew. *A Modern History of Japan: From Tokugawa Times to the Present.* Oxford: Oxford University Press, 2003. A very readable history of modern Japan.

Hanioglu, M. Sukru. *A Brief History of the Late Ottoman Empire.* Princeton, NJ: Princeton University Press, 2008. A promising new history of the subject.

Japan, http://asnic.utexas.edu/asnic/countries/japan/index.html. A major collection of online resources, divided by topic.

Ravina, Mark. *The Last Samurai: The Life and Battles of Saigo Takamori.* Hoboken, NJ: Wiley, 2004. The tale of Saigo Takamori, leader of the great samurai rebellion against the Meiji restoration in 1877.

Spence, Jonathan D. *God's Chinese Son: The Taiping Heavenly Kingdom of Hong Xiuquan.* New York: W. W. Norton & Co., 1996. A brilliant study of the Taiping Uprising.

Literature

Fukuzawa Yukichi. *The Autobiography of Yukichi Fukuzawa.* Trans. Eiichi Kiyooka. Rev. ed. New York: Columbia University Press, 2007. The life of a leading intellectual of the Meiji restoration.

Halsall, Paul, ed. *Internet Modern History Sourcebook: Imperialism.* http://www.fordham.edu/halsall/mod/modsbook34.html. Short primary sources that deal with the relationship between Europe and several countries (including China, Japan, and the Ottoman Empire) in the nineteenth century.

Kipling, Rudyard. *Complete Verse.* New York: Anchor Press, 1989. The works of Kipling, the greatest of the "poets of empire," are a treasure trove of benevolent European attitudes toward "inferior" races.

Li Boyuan. *Officialdom Unmasked.* Trans. T. L. Yang. Hong Kong: Hong Kong University Press, 2001. A meaty novel by a leading writer of the late Qing dynasty.

Liu E. *The Travels of Lao Ts'an.* Trans. Harold Shadick. New York: Columbia University Press, 1990. Liu E (1857–1909) was one of the most forward-looking authors of the late Qing dynasty.

Nakae Chomin. *A Discourse by Three Drunkards on Government.* Trans. Nobuko Tsukui. New York: Weatherhill, 1992. A debate from the late nineteenth century between Western ideals and traditional samurai values, short enough to be used in the classroom.

Natsume Soseki. *I Am a Cat.* Trans. Aiko Ito and Graeme Wilson. Boston: Tuttle, 2002. An entertaining satire of life in Japan under Emperor Meiji, written in 1905–1906.

Satow, Ernest. *A Diplomat in Japan.* Berkeley: Stone Bridge Press, 2006. The most important account of Japan's transformation in the Meiji restoration.

Film

Japan Past and Present: The Age of the Shoguns (1600–1868). Films for the Humanities and Sciences, 1989. 50 minutes. Offers a good overview of Japan's social, political, and cultural history during its period of isolation from the outside world.

Japan Past and Present: The Meiji Period (1868–1912). Films for the Humanities and Sciences, 1989. 50 minutes. Examines the rapid modernization of Japan and the establishment of the Japanese empire.

The Meiji Transformation. Films for the Humanities and Sciences, 1978. 29 minutes. Explores the transformation of Japanese culture, social structure, political system, and economy from the late 1860s to the opening of the twentieth century.

The Ottoman Empire. Films for the Humanities and Sciences, 1996. 47 minutes. Examines the origins and evolution of the Ottoman Empire.

Colonial Encounters
1750–1914

CHAPTER OVERVIEW

Chapter Objectives

- To examine the ways in which Europeans created their nineteenth-century empires
- To consider the nineteenth-century development of racism as an outcrop of European feelings of superiority and to investigate the ways in which subject peoples were themselves affected by European racial categorization
- To consider the extent to which the colonial experience transformed the lives of Asians and Africans
- To define some of the distinctive qualities of modern European empires in relationship to earlier examples of empire

Chapter Outline

I.   **Opening Vignette**
   A. The author describes his experience in postcolonial Kenya.
      1. discovery of reluctance to teach Africans English
      2. colonial concern to maintain distance between whites and blacks
         a. was a central feature of many colonial societies in the nineteenth and early twentieth centuries

   B. The British, French, Germans, Italians, Belgians, Portuguese, Russians, and Americans all had colonies.
      1. colonial policy varied depending on time and country involved
      2. the actions and reactions of the colonized people also shaped the colonial experience

II. **A Second Wave of European Conquests**
   A. The period 1750–1900 saw a second, distinct phase of European colonial conquest.
      1. focused on Asia and Africa
      2. several new players (Germany, Italy, Belgium, U.S., Japan)
      3. was not demographically catastrophic like the first phase
      4. was affected by the Industrial Revolution **[see Lecture Strategy 1]**
      5. in general, Europeans preferred informal control (e.g., Latin America, China, the Ottoman Empire)
   B. The establishment of the second-wave European empires was based on military force or the threat of using it.
      1. original European military advantage lay in organization, drill, and command structure
      2. over the nineteenth century, Europeans developed an enormous firepower advantage (repeating rifles and machine guns)
      3. numerous wars of conquest: the Westerners almost always won

C. Becoming a colony happened in a variety of ways. **[see Discussion Topic 1]**

1. India and Indonesia: grew from interaction with European trading firms.
   a. assisted by existence of many small and rival states
2. most of Africa, Southeast Asia, and the Pacific islands: deliberate conquest **[see Lecture Strategy 2 and Classroom Activity 1]**
   a. "the scramble for Africa" was based on inter-European rivalry over only about 25 years (1875–1900)
3. decentralized societies without a formal state structure were the hardest to conquer
4. Australia and New Zealand: more like the colonization of North America (with massive European settlement and diseases killing off most of the native population)
5. Taiwan and Korea: Japanese takeover was done European-style
6. U.S. and Russia continued to expand
7. Liberia: settled by freed U.S. slaves
8. Ethiopia and Siam (Thailand) avoided colonization skillfully

D. Asian and African societies generated a wide range of responses to the European threat.

III. **Under European Rule** [see Lecture Strategy 3]

A. European takeover was often traumatic for the colonized peoples; the loss of life and property could be devastating.
   1. disruption of natural harmonies of life

B. Cooperation and Rebellion
   1. some groups and individuals cooperated willingly with their new masters
      a. employment in the armed forces
      b. elite often kept much of their status and privileges
         i. shortage of European administrators made it necessary to rely on them
   2. governments and missionaries promoted European education
      a. growth of a small class with Western education
      b. governments relied on them increasingly over time
   3. periodic rebellions **[see Discussion Topic 2]**
      a. e.g., the Indian Rebellion (1857–1858), based on a series of grievances
      b. Indian Rebellion began as a mutiny among Indian troops
      c. rebel leaders advocated revival of the Mughal Empire
      d. widened India's racial divide; the British were less tolerant of natives
      e. led the British government to assume direct control over India

C. Colonial Empires with a Difference **[see Classroom Activity 2]**
   1. in the new colonial empires, race was a prominent point distinguishing rulers from the ruled
      a. education for colonial subjects was limited and emphasized practical matters, suitable for "primitive minds"
      b. even the best-educated natives rarely made it into the upper ranks of the civil service
   2. racism was especially pronounced in areas with a large number of European settlers (e.g., South Africa)
      a. in South Africa, whites attempted to industrialize based on cheap African labor, but without social and political integration
   3. colonial states imposed deep changes in people's daily lives
   4. colonizers were fascinated with counting and classifying their new subjects
      a. in India, appropriated an idealized caste system
      b. in Africa, identified or invented distinct "tribes"
   5. colonial policies contradicted European core values and practices at home
      a. colonies were essentially dictatorships
      b. colonies were the antithesis of "national independence"
      c. racial classifications were against Christian and Enlightenment ideas of human equality
      d. many colonizers were against spreading "modernization" to the colonies
      e. in time, the visible contradictions in European behavior helped undermine the foundations of colonial rule

IV. **Ways of Working: Comparing Colonial Economies**

A. Colonial rule had a deep impact on people's ways of working.
   1. world economy increasingly demanded Asian and African raw materials
   2. subsistence farming diminished
      a. need to sell goods for money to pay taxes
      b. desire to buy new products
   3. artisans were largely displaced by manufactured goods
   4. Asian and African merchants were squeezed out by Europeans

B. Economies of Coercion: Forced Labor and the Power of the State
   1. many colonial states demanded unpaid labor on public projects
   2. worst abuses were in the Congo Free State
      [see Discussion Topic 3]
      a. personally governed by Leopold II of Belgium
      b. reign of terror killed millions with labor demands
      c. forced labor caused widespread starvation, as people couldn't grow their own crops
      d. Belgium finally stepped in and took control of the Congo (1908) to stop abuses
   3. "cultivation system" of the Netherlands East Indies (Indonesia)
      a. peasants had to devote at least 20 percent of their land to cash crops to pay as taxes
      b. the proceeds were sold for high profits, financed the Dutch economy
      c. enriched the traditional authorities who enforced the system
   4. many areas resisted the forced cultivation of cash crops
      a. German East Africa: major rebellion in 1905 against forced cotton cultivation
      b. Mozambique: peasant sabotage and smuggling kept the Portuguese from achieving their goals there

C. Economies of Cash-Crop Agriculture: The Pull of the Market
   1. many people were happy to increase production for world markets
   2. considerable profit to small farmers in areas like the Irrawaddy Delta
   3. in the southern Gold Coast (Ghana), African farmers took the initiative to develop export agriculture
      a. leading supplier of cocoa by 1911
      b. created a hybrid peasant-capitalist society
      c. but labor shortages led to exploitation of former slaves, men marrying women for their labor power, influx of migrants
   4. many colonies specialized in one or two cash crops, creating dependence

D. Economies of Wage Labor: Working for Europeans
   1. wage labor in European enterprises was common
   2. hundreds of thousands of workers came to work on Southeast Asian plantations
      a. low pay, bad conditions, high death rate
   3. millions of Indians migrated to work elsewhere in the British Empire
   4. especially in Africa, people moved to European farms/plantations because they had lost their own land
      a. European communities obtained vast amounts of land
      b. South Africa in 1913: 88 percent of the land belonged to whites
      c. much of highland Kenya was taken over by 4,000 white farmers
      d. many former farmers were sent to "native reserves"
   5. mines employed many
      a. Malaysian tin mines attracted millions of Chinese workers
         i. appallingly high death rates
      b. South African diamond mines created a huge pattern of worker migration
         i. African miners were exploited, kept on short-term contracts
   6. colonial cities attracted many workers
      a. were seen as centers of opportunity
      b. segregated, unsanitary, overcrowded
      c. **created** a place for a native, **Western**-educated middle class
      d. **created** an enormous class of urban poor **that could** barely live and couldn't raise **families**

E. Women and the Colonial Economy: An African Case Study
  1. in precolonial Africa, women were usually active farmers, had some economic autonomy
  2. in the colonial economy, women's lives diverged even more from men
    a. men tended to dominate the lucrative export crops
    b. women were left with almost all of the subsistence work
    c. large numbers of men (sometimes a majority of the population) migrated to work elsewhere
    d. women were left home to cope, including supplying food to men in the cities
  3. women coped in a variety of ways
  4. the colonial economy also provided some opportunities to women
    a. especially small trade and marketing
    b. sometimes women's crops came to have greater cash value
    c. some women escaped the patriarchy of husbands or fathers
    d. led to greater fear of witchcraft and efforts to restrict female travel and sexuality

F. Assessing Colonial Development
  1. What was the overall economic impact of colonial rule?
    a. defenders: it jump-started modern growth
    b. critics: long record of exploitation and limited, uneven growth
  2. colonial rule *did* help integrate Asian and African economies into a global exchange network
    a. though in many cases, that process had already been underway in precolonial times
  3. colonial rule *did* introduce some modernizing elements
    a. administrative and bureaucratic structures
    b. communication and transportation infrastructure
    c. schools
    d. health care

  4. colonial rule did *not* lead to breakthroughs to modern industrial societies
    a. when India won independence, it was one of the poorest developing countries
      i. British rule certainly did not help overcome poverty

V. **Believing and Belonging: Identity and Cultural Change in the Colonial Era**
A. Education
  1. getting a Western education created a new identity for many
    a. the almost magical power of literacy
    b. escape from obligations like forced labor
    c. access to better jobs
    d. social mobility and elite status
  2. many people embraced European culture
    a. created a cultural divide between them and the vast majority of the population
  3. many of the Western-educated elite saw colonial rule as the path to a better future, at least at first
    a. in India, they organized reform societies to renew Indian culture
      i. combined Western ideas and classic Hindu texts
      ii. European education as a tool to win freedom from oppressive tradition
    b. hopes for renewal through colonial rule were disappointed
      i. Europeans did not treat their Asian and African subjects as equal partners
      ii. denigrated the colonized cultures

B. Religion
  1. widespread conversion to Christianity in New Zealand, the Pacific islands, and non-Muslim Africa
    a. around 10,000 missionaries had gone to Africa by 1910
    b. by the 1960s, some 50 million Africans were Christian
  2. Christianity was attractive to many in Africa
    a. military defeat shook belief in the old gods
    b. Christianity was associated with modern education
    c. Christianity gave opportunities to the young, the poor, and many women

    d. Christianity spread mostly through native Africans

  3. Christianity was Africanized

    a. continuing use of charms, medicine men

    b. some simply demonized their old gods

    c. wide array of "independent churches" was established

  4. Christianity did not spread widely in India

    a. but it led intellectuals and reformers to define Hinduism

    b. Hindu leaders looked to offer spiritual support to the spiritually sick Western world

      i. First World Parliament of Religions, Chicago, 1893

    c. new definition of Hinduism helped a clearer sense of Muslims as a distinct community to emerge

      i. so did British laws

      ii. beginning of a profound religious/political divide

C. "Race" and "Tribe"

  1. notions of race and ethnicity were central to new ways of belonging

  2. by 1900, some African thinkers began to define an "African identity"

    a. united for the first time by the experience of colonial oppression

    b. some argued that African culture and history had the characteristics valued by Europeans (complex political systems, etc.)

      i. C. A. Diop of Senegal argued that black Africans produced ancient Egyptian civilization and that European civilization was derived from it and thus from Africa

    c. some praised the differences between Africa and Europe

      i. Edward Blyden argued that each race had a distinctive contribution to make to the world

      ii. Africa's contribution was communal, cooperative, and egalitarian societies

  3. in the twentieth century, such ideas reached a broader public

    a. hundreds of thousands of Africans took part in WWI

    b. some Africans traveled widely

  4. for most Africans, the most important new sense of belonging was the idea of "tribe" or ethnic identity

    a. ethnic groups were defined much more clearly, thanks to Europeans

    b. Africans found ethnic identity useful

      i. migrants categorized themselves ethnically

      ii. organized mutual assistance based on ethnicity

      iii. e.g., organization of the Igbos in Nigeria by the 1940s

VI. Reflections: Who Makes History? [see Classroom Activity 3]

A. Winners don't make history, at least not alone.

  1. dominant groups are limited by the presence of subordinated peoples

B. A recent trend in historical study examines how subordinated peoples, even when oppressed, have been able to work for their own interests.

USING *WAYS OF THE WORLD* IN THE CLASSROOM

Lecture Strategies

Lecture Strategy 1

"Creating a communication and transportation infrastructure."

The intent of this lecture strategy is to explore the "sinews" of empire—how the Industrial Revolution and imperial dreams worked together to enable Europeans to control such an enormous proportion of the world. In particular, we recommend a lecture that focuses on the way the application of three inventions transformed the world: the steamship, the railroad, and the telegraph. Thus the objectives of this lecture strategy are straightforward:

• to consider the implications in world history of the invention of the steamship, the railroad, and the telegraph

- to help students to understand these inventions as products of the Industrial Revolution
- to investigate the process by which these new technologies were spread throughout the Western world and its colonies
- to examine what difference these inventions made in people's lives

A good place to begin is with the famous 1869 photograph that shows the driving in of the Golden Spike, symbolizing the completion of the United States' first transcontinental railroad. The photo shows clearly what a great event this was in U.S. history and can serve as a good starting point for a discussion of (1) the invention of the railroad, (2) what was actually involved in laying long distances of track, and (3) how the transcontinental railroad "opened up" the western United States to a hitherto unheard-of degree. From there, it is a simple step to consider the spread of railroad technology more generally, using examples from several parts of the world to consider what this new technology of access meant especially for inland regions.

Move from there to a consideration of ships and the sea, and what a difference steam power made as steamships ended the age of sail. Again, students will probably be interested in hearing about early experiments with steamships and can easily be drawn into a discussion of the advantages of steam over sail. Any discussion should include some consideration of what real differences came about thanks to the greater speed and dependability of steamships.

Last, consider the case of the telegraph. The first message ever sent in a public demonstration of the telegraph was "What hath God wrought?"—a question that may well be asked when one considers the telegraph's importance in world history. As with the other two great inventions in this lecture, it is useful to consider who invented the telegraph and why it was considered useful, as well as the challenges that had to be overcome to allow widespread use of the new means of communication. It is worth emphasizing that the telegraph, more than any other invention, allowed for a degree of centralization never before imagined. In accordance with the focus of this chapter, the emphasis should be on Europe's colonial empires, but it is also useful to consider other centralizations enabled by the telegraph, including that of the nineteenth-century Roman Catholic Church under a series of ultramontane popes who understood the potential of the new technology.

Lecture Strategy 2

"The scramble for Africa."
The European imperialist takeover of Africa is one of the most exciting—and chilling—tales in world history. The purpose of this lecture strategy is to examine what happened when and why, thus providing a framework for the more thematic information contained in the chapter. Its objectives are:

- to consider the motivations and means of colonial powers
- to examine how they gained control of almost the entire continent of Africa in an astonishingly short time
- to investigate the effects of imperialism on the rulers as well as on their subjects

A good place to begin is by considering what you would like to be the main emphasis of this lecture, to keep from relying simply on narrative with little analysis. Some possible lecture foci are:

- the high human cost of the scramble for Africa
- the scramble for Africa as an expression of European competition for power in the period preceding World War I
- the outpouring of European exuberance and talent that went into the scramble for Africa
- the scramble for Africa as a dark page in the history of racism
- the benefits of imperialism for the African people themselves
- the scramble for Africa as an interesting page in the history of warfare

Whatever your main focus, you will find a great deal of material within this large topic. Some issues to be sure to include are:

- the great explorers (such as David Livingstone, Serpa Pinto, and Richard Burton)
- the African products desired by the Europeans
- the amazing story of Cecil Rhodes and Rhodesia
- some of the specifics of European technological (especially military) superiority
- the digging of the Suez Canal
- Otto von Bismarck's "World Politics" after German unification

- the American colony of Liberia
- the Berlin Conference of 1884–1885
- the Boer Wars
- British occupation of Egypt
- the rise of West African Muslim holy men to prominence
- the "Mad Mahdi" of the Sudan and the "gallant Gordon"
- the sack of Benin
- the Herero and Namaka genocide
- "ethnological spectacles" at which caged Africans were shown to European and American audience under zoolike conditions

Lecture Strategy 3

"The Raj."

"Raj" is the Sanskrit word for "rule" and is a term commonly used for British rule of India from 1858 to 1947. This lecture strategy is intended to investigate how that rule worked, with an emphasis on administrative structures and the Britons who went to India to govern this important part of the British Empire. Its objectives are:

- to help students imagine how colonial rule actually worked
- to investigate what it meant to Great Britain to rule India
- to consider what it meant to Indians to be ruled by Great Britain
- to explore the effects, both good and ill, of the colonial period

A good place to start is with a consideration of India in the 1850s, before direct British rule began. Discuss the rule of the British East India Company and how it established ascendancy over the princely states of India. Also be sure to point out the lack of internal unity (political, religious, or linguistic) within the subcontinent.

From there, go on to a discussion of the Indian Rebellion of 1857–1858—why it happened, what the rebels did, and what the results were in British policy-making. After the establishment of the Raj, there are many ways to approach a lecture. Some points you should consider including in any lecture are:

- British efforts at social reform (such as bans on suttee) and evangelization and how these interventions were limited after 1857

- the powers vested in the British viceroy of India
- how many Britons in an average year were actually present in India in administrative or other positions
- the extent to which the British applied economic force in the matter of imports and exports
- British playing off of Muslim/Hindu rivalries, and whether it was done intentionally or unintentionally
- how many Indians were employed in skilled positions
- the use of Indians as the rank and file in police departments and armies
- British steps toward self-government (the appointment of Indian councilors for the viceroy, the creation of municipal corporations, etc.)
- possible benefits for India of the Raj

Things to Do in the Classroom

Discussion Topics

1. **Comparison, large or small group.** "Asia or Africa—which suffered the most?"

For this exercise, ask students to cull material from the textbook about the conditions of colonial subjects in both Asia and Africa, sorting the material into two columns. It might also be useful to encourage brief Internet searches for more information about European colonialism on the two continents (focusing on direct colonies, rather than regions that retained their own government). Then encourage students to compare the colonial experience in the two regions. Taken as a whole, was the experience of one continent worse than that of the other? If the answer is yes, why?

2. **Contextualization, large or small group.** "A Passage to India."

To help students imagine the conditions of life in colonial India, show a clip from the 1984 movie *A Passage to India*, which is set in British India in 1928. The scene at the Caves, when *something* happens to destroy the Hindu/English friendship that had developed, is particularly spectacular. Then ask students to discuss the following questions:

- How much can or should we trust Hollywood to be true to history?

- How can we test the accuracy of scenes like the one we have just seen?
- Does the film's presentation of colonial life in India agree or disagree with the textbook's presentation of colonial societies?
- What is the most striking thing that this clip can teach us about life under the Raj?

3. **Misconception/Difficult Topic, large or small group.** "The deep corruption of colonial rule." This discussion topic is not a misconception but rather something difficult for many students to fathom: how could Europeans, many of them from the middle or upper classes and nearly all of them professing Christianity, have perpetrated horrors like King Leopold's genocidal control of the Congo? Ask students to discuss this issue, encouraging them to draw information from other courses (such as psychology, sociology, and economics) to help them come up with a list of possible reasons for large-scale colonial atrocities. Be sure to remind them that there is rarely *one* right answer to big questions—and also remind them that a simple response that "they were evil" isn't a very satisfying historical explanation.

Classroom Activities

1. **Map-analysis exercise, large or small group.** "Scrambling for Africa."
Display a map of Africa. If you have a Promethean Board available (or similar technology that will allow you to draw over an image), a map of modern Africa or a physical map would be interesting; otherwise, try to find a map of Africa ca. 1900.

Begin by identifying which regions came under the control of which European power. From there, discuss the reasons *why* each European nation came to control the region it did, emphasizing as much as possible geographical reasoning in which your students can take part (e.g., Britain's takeover of South Africa from the Boers makes sense in light of the vast quantity of British shipping to India that had to round the Cape).

2. **Close-reading exercise, small group.** "The White Man's Burden."
Distribute to the class copies of Rudyard Kipling's 1899 poem "The White Man's Burden" (a copy is available online at http://www.fordham.edu/halsall/mod/Kipling.html). Ask the students to read it carefully and then to list the important assumptions the

author makes about Europe and Europeans on the one hand and about colonial subjects on the other. Then encourage a discussion of the themes the students have identified.

3. **Clicker question.** Which was worse, the first or the second wave of European colonialism?

Key Terms

Africanization of Christianity: Process that occurred in non-Muslim Africa, where millions who were converted to Christianity sought to maintain older traditions alongside new Christian ideas; many converts continued using protective charms and medicines and consulting local medicine men, and many continued to believe in their old gods and spirits.

apartheid: Afrikaans term literally meaning "aparthood"; system that developed in South Africa of strictly limiting the social and political integration of whites and blacks. (*pron.* uh-PART-hite)

Blyden, Edward: Prominent West African scholar and political leader (1832–1912) who argued that each civilization, including that of Africa, has its own unique contribution to make to the world.

cash-crop agriculture: Agricultural production, often on a large scale, of crops for sale in the market, rather than for consumption by the farmers themselves.

colonial racism: A pattern of European racism in their Asian and African colonies that created a great racial divide between themselves and the natives and limited native access to education and the civil service, based especially on pseudo-scientific notions of naturally superior and inferior races.

colonial tribalism: A European tendency, especially in African colonies, to identify and sometimes invent distinct "tribes" that had often not existed before, reinforcing European notions that African societies were primitive.

Congo Free State/Leopold II: Leopold II was king of Belgium from 1865 to 1909; his rule as private owner of the Congo Free State during much of that time is typically held up as the worst abuse of Europe's second wave of colonization, resulting as it did in millions of deaths.

cultivation system: System of forced labor used in the Netherlands East Indies in the nineteenth century; peasants were required to cultivate at least 20 percent of their land in cash crops such as sugar or coffee for sale at low and fixed prices to government contractors, who then earned enormous profits from further sale of the crops.

Indian Rebellion, 1857–1858: Massive uprising of much of India against British rule; also called the Indian Mutiny or the Sepoy Mutiny from the fact that the rebellion first broke out among Indian troops in British employ.

informal empires: Term commonly used to describe areas such as Latin America and China that were dominated by Western powers in the nineteenth century but that retained their own governments and a measure of independence.

invention of tradition: In many colonial states, a process of forging new ways of belonging and self-identification that defined and to some extent mythologized the region's past, especially to create broader terms of belonging than had existed before.

scramble for Africa: Name used for the process of the European countries' partition of the continent of Africa between themselves in the period 1875–1900.

Vivekananda, Swami: Leading religious figure of nineteenth-century India (1863–1902); advocate of a revived Hinduism and its mission to reach out to the spiritually impoverished West. (*pron.* vee-vi-kah-NAHN-dah)

Western-educated elite: The main beneficiaries in Asian and African lands colonized by Western powers; schooled in the imperial power's language and practices, they moved into their country's professional classes but ultimately led anticolonial movements as they grew discouraged by their inability to win equal status to the colonizers.

ANSWER GUIDELINES FOR CHAPTER QUESTIONS

The two sets of questions that follow appear in the textbook at the end of the chapter and in the margins of the reading. They are also provided in the Computerized Test Bank with answer guidelines, for your convenience.

The Big Picture Questions

1. Why were Asian and African societies incorporated into European colonial empires later than those of the Americas? How would you compare their colonial experiences?

• Europeans incorporated Asian and African societies into their empires later than those of the Americas for a number of reasons, including their lack of a disease advantage over indigenous populations and, indeed, in the case of tropical regions the distinct disease disadvantage of Europeans compared to indigenous populations;

• their reliance on military advantages gained from the Industrial Revolution;

• internal competition between European states that drove the accumulation of colonial territories in the nineteenth century despite the inherent risks and expenses involved in ruling directly.

• In terms of comparing their colonial experiences, the colonial period in Asia and Africa had nothing like the devastating demographic consequences for indigenous peoples in the Americas;

• slavery on plantations was a critical feature of the colonial experience in the Americas but not in Asia and Africa;

• Spain and Portugal played a much smaller role in the creation of European colonial empires in Asia and Africa as compared to the Americas;

• while European colonizers did have an impact on some regions of Africa, they had a greater impact on the Americas.

2. In what ways did colonial rule rest upon violence and coercion, and in what ways did it elicit voluntary cooperation or generate benefits for some people?

• It rested upon violence and coercion in that many colonies were seized with military force;

• rebellions were regularly suppressed using violence;

• forced labor was regularly extracted from the populations of colonies.

• However, the colonial system also relied on voluntary cooperation in that local leaders were often used as intermediary rulers between the colonial administrators and the populations, thus those local leaders were able to maintain much of their social prestige and often gained in wealth;

• a small group of Western-educated members of colonial societies benefited from better-paying jobs, elite status within their own societies, and escape from the most onerous obligations of living under European control, such as forced labor;

• some common people benefited by gaining access to foreign markets for their cash crops or by securing relatively good employment, working as soldiers, on railways, at ports, or for other parts of the colonial regime.

3. In what respects were colonized people more than victims of colonial conquest and rule? To what extent could they act in their own interests within the colonial situation?

• Although clearly many colonial people suffered under colonial rule, this chapter includes numerous examples of colonized peoples working within the new colonial system to their own benefit, including cash-crop farmers in Burma and Ghana who benefited from colonial trade;

• some African women who became small-scale traders within the colonial system or were able to alter traditional parts of the patriarchal system;

• those colonial people who secured Western educations and then used them to secure a higher social status and better jobs;

• those local rulers who became intermediaries between local populations and colonial powers and benefited from their positions.

4. Was colonial rule a transforming, even a revolutionary, experience, or did it serve to freeze or preserve existing social and economic patterns? What evidence can you find to support both sides of this argument?

• Colonial rule varied from place to place, and so evidence for both of these scenarios can be found.

• In terms of colonial rule being a transforming, even a revolutionary, experience, one might point toward the experience of African women, some of whom found greater autonomy over their day-to-day lives than before because of changed living patterns that removed men to the cities;

• African women also found new economic autonomy as they took advantage of opportunities in trade.

• One could also point to the new opportunities offered to some farmers of cash crops, like those in Burma or Ghana, who were able to tap into the colonial trade networks for their own benefit.

• Large-scale conversion of some populations to Christianity was also a transformative experience for those who converted.

• Finally, one might point to the minority who secured Western educations, which transformed both their lives and often their vision of their own society.

• As far as freezing or preserving existing social and economic patterns, one could point to the detrimental aspects of the colonial economy, which meant that no colonial society underwent industrialization in anything like the manner of Japan;

• this effectively meant that the economies of colonized countries remained based in agriculture and the production of raw materials and cash crops;

• it also stunted the growth of the middle class in those countries;

• moreover, the tendency of colonial states to rule through local elites had the effect of maintaining the social status quo.

Margin Review Questions

Q. *In what different ways did the colonial takeover of Asia and Africa occur?*

• In many regions, European colonial takeovers occurred through the use (or threatened use) of military force.

• Particularly in India, the British East India Company, rather than the British government directly, played the leading role in the colonial takeover of South Asia.

• The British in South Asia and the Dutch in Indonesia were able to assert themselves in part because the regions were politically fragmented.

• In Africa, the colonial takeover coincided with intense competition between European powers to establish colonial holdings, followed by slower efforts to enforce their claims.

Q. *Why might subject peoples choose to cooperate with the colonial regime? What might prompt them to rebel or resist?*

• Subject peoples might choose to cooperate for a number of reasons, including the employment, status, and security that they found in European-led armed forces;

• or the opportunity for some local elites to maintain much of their earlier status and privileges while gaining considerable wealth by working as local intermediaries for the colonial powers and exercising authority, both legally and otherwise, at the local level.

• European education created a small Western-educated class, whose members served the colonial state.

• Many chose to resist colonial rule, including local rulers who had lost power;

• landlords deprived of their estates or their rent;

• peasants overtaxed by moneylenders and landlords alike;

• unemployed weavers displaced by machine-manufactured European goods;

• local religious leaders threatened by the missionary activities that accompanied colonial expansion.

Q. *What was distinctive about European colonial empires of the nineteenth century?*

• The nineteenth-century European colonial empires differed from earlier empires in several important ways, including the prominence of race in distinguishing between rulers and ruled;

• the extent to which colonial states were able to penetrate the societies they governed;

• their penchant for counting and classifying their subject peoples;

• their policies for administrating their colonies, which contradicted their core values and their practices at home to an unusual degree.

Q. *How did the power of colonial states transform the economic lives of colonial subjects?*

• Some groups found ways of working within and profiting from the colonial system, including some farmers who produced cash crops for export, as was the case of rice cultivation for export in Burma and the raising of cacao in Ghana.

• Others learned to find a place within the system, like those African women who became small-scale traders.

• Wage labor on plantations and in mines became a far more common way to sustain oneself.

Q. *How did cash-crop agriculture transform the lives of colonized peoples?*

• In some regions, like Burma and the Gold Coast, colonial promotion of cash crops for trade benefited the farmers who participated in the system.

• In other regions, like the Netherlands East Indies, cash-crop agriculture was forced on the local population by the colonial power, burdening the people and contributing to a wave of famines.

• Cash-crop agriculture did lead to some social changes, as the cultivation of crops for markets and wage labor on plantations that were set up to grow cash crops shifted normal labor patterns.

Q. *What kinds of wage labor were available in the colonies? Why might people take part in it? How did doing so change their lives?*

• Members of colonial societies could find paid work in European-owned plantations and mines, on construction projects, or as household servants.

• Their participation was driven by the need for money, by the loss of land adequate to support their families, or sometimes by the orders of colonial authorities.

• Their lives became dependent on wages that were low and earned through hard and often dangerous labor. Many colonial workers settled in over-crowded cities where, because of the cost of living, normal family life was virtually impossible for many wage laborers.

Q. *How were the lives of women altered by colonial economies?*

• The text uses Africa as a case study.

• Before colonization, African women were almost everywhere active farmers, with responsibility for planting, weeding, and harvesting in addition to food preparation and child care. Women were expected to feed their own families and often were allocated their own fields for that purpose, and many were also involved in local trading activity. Though clearly subordinate to men, African women nevertheless had a measure of economic autonomy.

• Following colonization, women's lives diverged more and more from those of men. Women dominated subsistence production, while men took a dominant role in cash-crop agriculture.

• Men migrated to the cities, leaving women to manage the domestic economy almost alone. Women were forced to take on traditionally male tasks in addition to their normal responsibilities.

• The lives and cultures of men and women increasingly diverged, with one focused on the cities and working for wages and the other on village life and subsistence agriculture.

• In response to the situation, women sought closer relations with their birth families, introduced laborsaving crops, adopted new farm implements, and earned some money as traders. In the cities, they established a variety of self-help associations.

• The colonial economy sometimes offered women a measure of opportunity, particularly in small-scale trade and marketing, that could on occasion give them considerable economic autonomy.

• Women of impoverished rural families often became virtually independent heads of household in the absence of their husbands, while others took advantage of new opportunities in mission schools, towns, and mines to flee the restrictions of rural patriarchy.

Q. *Did colonial rule bring "progress" in its wake?*

• This question is debatable, especially since definitions of "progress" vary widely, but however one views the impact of colonial rule, it is clear that several important developments took place during the period.

• Colonial rule served, for better or worse, to further the integration of Asian and African economies into a global network of exchange now centered in Europe.

• Europeans conveyed to the colonies some elements of their own modernizing process, including modern administrative and bureaucratic structures, communication and transportation infrastructure, schools, and modest provisions for health care.

• Nowhere in the colonial world did a breakthrough to modern industrial society of Japanese dimensions occur.

Q. *What impact did Western education have on colonial societies?*

• For an important minority, the acquisition of a Western education generated a new identity, providing access to better-paying jobs and escape from some of the most onerous obligations of living under European control, such as forced labor.

• It also brought them elite status within their own communities and an opportunity to achieve, or at least approach, equality with whites in racially defined societies.

• Education created a new cultural divide within Asian and African societies between the small number who had mastered to varying degrees the ways of their rulers and the vast majority who had not.

• Many of those who received a Western education saw themselves as a modernizing vanguard who were leading the regeneration of their societies, in association with colonial authorities. In India, Western-educated people organized a variety of reform societies, which sought a renewed Indian culture that was free of idolatry, child marriages, caste, and discrimination against women, while drawing inspiration from classic texts of Hinduism.

• But there was disillusionment among those who received a Western education as well, as Europeans generally declined to treat Asian and African subjects, regardless of their education, as equal partners in the enterprise of renewal.

Q. *What were the attractions of Christianity within some colonial societies?*

• Military defeat shook confidence in the old gods and local practices, fostering openness to new sources of supernatural power that could operate in the wider world now impinging on their societies.

• Christianity was widely associated with modern education, and, especially in Africa, mission schools were the primary providers of Western education.

• The young, the poor, and many women found new opportunities and greater freedom in some association with missions.

• The spread of the Christian message was less the work of European missionaries than of those many thousands of African teachers, catechists, and pastors who brought the new faith to remote villages as well as the local communities that begged for a teacher and supplied the labor and materials to build a small church or school.

• Christianity in Africa soon became Africanized, maintaining older traditions alongside new Christian ideas.

Q. *How and why did Hinduism emerge as a distinct religious tradition during the colonial era in India?*

• Only during the colonial era did leading intellectuals and reformers in India begin to define their region's endlessly varied beliefs, practices, sects, rituals, and schools of philosophy as a more distinct, unified, and separate religion that is now known as Hinduism.

• It was in part an effort to provide for India a religion wholly equivalent to Christianity, to create tradition and a sense of historical worth in spite of the humiliation of colonial rule.

• The idea of Hinduism gained in importance during the period because it provided a cultural foundation for emerging ideas of India as a nation, but it also accentuated a more conscious split between Muslims and Hindus.

Q. *In what way were "race" and "tribe" new identities in colonial Africa?*

• Before the colonial period, African peoples had long recognized differences among themselves based on language, kinship, clan, village, or state, but these were seldom sharp or clearly defined.

• The idea of an Africa sharply divided into separate and distinct "tribes" was in fact a European notion that facilitated colonial administration and reflected their belief in African primitiveness.

• But while Europeans may have created or sought to impose these categories, Africans increasingly found ethnic or tribal labels useful; this was especially true in rapidly growing urban areas, where migrants found it helpful to categorize themselves and others in larger ethnic terms.

ADDITIONAL RESOURCES FOR CHAPTER 20

Additional Bedford/St. Martin's Resources

FOR INSTRUCTORS

Computerized Test Bank

This test bank provides over thirty exercises per chapter, including multiple-choice, fill-in-the-blank, short-answer, and full-length essay questions. Instructors can customize quizzes, add or edit both questions and answers, and export questions and answers to a variety of formats, including WebCT and Blackboard. The disc includes correct answers and essay outlines.

Instructor's Resource CD-ROM

This disc provides instructors with ready-made and customizable PowerPoint multimedia presentations built around chapter outlines, maps, figures, and all images from the textbook, plus JPEG versions of all maps, figures, and images.

The following maps and images from Chapter 20 are available in both JPEG and PowerPoint format on the Instructor's Resource CD-ROM:

• Map 20.1: Colonial Asia in the Early Twentieth Century (p. 591)
• Map 20.2: Conquest and Resistance in Colonial Africa (p. 593)
• The Imperial Durbar of 1903 (p. 588)
• An Egyptian View of British Imperialism (p. 596)
• Colonial Violence in the Congo (p. 600)
• Economic Change in the Colonial World (p. 602)
• Women in Colonial Africa (p. 604)
• The Educated Elite (p. 608)
• The Missionary Factor (p. 609)
• Hinduism in the West (p. 610)

FOR STUDENTS

Documents and Essays from *Worlds of History: A Comparative Reader*, Third Edition (Volume 2)

The following documents, essays, and illustrations to accompany Chapter 20 are available in Chapter 8 of Volume 2 of this reader by Kevin Reilly:

• Jurgen Osterhammel, from *Colonialism*
• George Orwell, from *Burmese Days*
• David Cannadine, from *Ornamentalism*
• Joseph Conrad, from *Heart of Darkness*
• Chinua Achebe, *An Image of Africa: Racism in Conrad's* Heart of Darkness
• Rudyard Kipling, *The White Man's Burden*

Online Study Guide at bedfordstmartins.com/strayer

The Online Study Guide helps students synthesize the material from the text as well as practice the skills historians use to make sense of the past. Each chapter of the Online Study Guide contains specific testing exercises, including a multiple-choice self-test that focuses on important conceptual ideas; an identification quiz that helps students remember key people, places, and events; a flashcard activity that tests students on their knowledge of key terms; and two interactive map activities intended to strengthen students' geographic skills. Instructors can monitor students' progress through an online Quiz Gradebook or receive email updates.

Further Reading

Cannadine, David. *Ornamentalism: How the British Saw Their Empire.* Oxford: Oxford University Press, 2001. A highly original and interesting study that argues that, for the British, class was more important than race in defining relations with subjects.

Casahistoria: Imperialism, http://www.casahistoria.net/imperialism.htm. A good site to find out more about both historical and contemporary imperialism.

Chamberlain, M. E. *The Scramble for Africa.* 2nd ed. London: Longman, 1999. A short and useful overview of the subject.

Headrick, Daniel R. *The Tools of Empire: Technology and European Imperialism in the Nineteenth Century.* Oxford: Oxford University Press, 1981. A short, concise study of a very important topic.

Hochschild, Adam. *King Leopold's Ghost: A Story of Greed, Terror, and Heroism in Colonial Africa.* Boston: Houghton Mifflin, 1998. An excellent study not only of Leopold of Belgium's horrifying domination of the Congo but also of the human rights movement that came into creation in response to Leopold's atrocities.

Porter, Andrew, ed. *The Oxford History of the British Empire.* Volume 3, *The Nineteenth Century.* 2nd ed. Oxford: Oxford University Press, 2001. A major resource for the history of the British Empire around the world.

Samson, Jane. *Race and Empire.* London: Longman, 2005. An excellent comparative study of racism and imperialism.

Wesseling, H. L. *The European Colonial Empires, 1815–1919.* London: Longman, 2004. Perhaps the best overarching study of the imperial phenomenon in the nineteenth century.

Literature

Beames, John. *Memoirs of a Bengal Civilian.* 2nd ed. London: Eland, 2004. A firsthand account of life in British India after the Indian Rebellion.

Conrad, Joseph. *Heart of Darkness and Other Tales.* Rev. ed. Oxford: Oxford World's Classics, 2003. The four stories in this volume are set in Africa, Malaysia, and the East and explore colonial corruption and obsession.

Forster, E. M. *A Passage to India.* Orlando: Harcourt Brace & Co., 1952. A 1924 novel that explores the possibility of friendship between English newcomers in India and Indians.

Haggard, H. Rider. *King Solomon's Mines.* 2nd ed. New York: Modern Library, 2002. A gripping adventure tale, written in 1885, that gives a good sense of European fascination with Africa.

Halsall, Paul, ed. *Internet Modern History Sourcebook: Imperialism.* http://www.fordham.edu/halsall/mod/modsbook34.html. An interesting collection of short readings on the topic of imperialism.

Hayford, J. E. Casley. *Ethiopia Unbound: Studies in Race Emancipation.* London: Routledge, 1969. Written in 1911 by an African nationalist, this work combines fiction and political polemic to tell readers exactly what the author thinks of European exploitation.

Kipling, Rudyard. *Kim.* London: Penguin, 1987. An English vision of India (though the hero is actually Irish).

Orwell, George. *Burmese Days.* San Diego: Harcourt Brace & Co., 1962. A truly vivid portrait of life in colonial Burma.

Schreiner, Olive. *The Story of an African Farm.* 2nd ed. Oxford: Oxford World's Classics, 1999. Don't let the name fool you; this is a very rich book about the oppression of women and the injustices of imperialism in South Africa.

Tagore, Rabindranath. *Gitanjali*. Chennai: Macmillan India Ltd., 1974. This brief but moving collection of prose poems, originally published in 1913, was the first work by an Asian author to win the Nobel Prize for Literature.

Film

The Empire of Good Intentions, 1830–1925. BBC Home Video, 2000. 59 minutes. Simon Schama's well-produced account of the British Empire from Ireland to India during the empire's height and early decline.

The End of Empires. Films for the Humanities and Sciences, 1995. 49 minutes. A wide-ranging exploration of the end of European empires in Africa and Asia, including segments concerned with European empires at their height.

India: From Moghuls to Independence. Films for the Humanities and Sciences, 1993. 42 minutes. A survey of Indian history that includes important segments on British rule of India.

The Paths of Colonialism. Films for the Humanities and Sciences, 1991. 17 minutes. Places nineteenth-century colonialism in a long-term context stretching from the Spanish conquest of the Americas through Mussolini's invasion of Ethiopia.

The Scramble for Africa. Insight Media, 1986. 30 minutes. Examines the European partition of Africa between 1875 and 1900 and the motivations behind it.

The Wrong Empire, 1750–1800. BBC Home Video, 2000. 59 minutes. Simon Schama's well-produced account of the emergence of the British colonial empire.

PART SIX

THE MOST RECENT CENTURY, 1914–2008

Outline: The Big Picture: The Twentieth Century: A New Period in World History?

I. **The division of history into segments is necessary, but divisions are artificial and endlessly controversial.**

   A. The problem is especially pronounced with the twentieth century.

   B. Basic question: Does the twentieth century represent a separate phase of world history?

   1. giving the twentieth century "separate" status has become the norm in world history textbooks

   2. but it's unclear that future generations will view it the same way

   a. one hundred years is awfully short time in world historical terms

   b. we're suffering an information overload, which makes it hard to distinguish the forest from the trees

   c. we don't know if/when this period will end

   3. most historians start the twentieth century with the outbreak of WWI in 1914

II. **Old and New in the Twentieth Century**

   A. The twentieth century is marked by both continuities and changes.

   1. the world wars grew out of European inability to create a single state

   a. but the world wars were new in their mobilization of whole populations and enormity of destruction

   2. the communist revolutions also blended old and new

   B. The twentieth century is also distinguished by the disintegration of great empires and the creation of new nation-states.

   1. a new turn against the whole idea of empire

   2. by 2000, more than 200 nation-states existed

   C. The century's most fundamental process was explosive population growth: the human population nearly quadrupled between 1900 and 2000, and the earth's population is now over 6 billion.

1. such growth is unprecedented, but it was built on earlier achievements, especially improved food supplies, medicine, and sanitation

D. Industrial output increased fortyfold during the twentieth century.

1. such growth was novel, but it also built on earlier foundations, the Scientific and Industrial Revolutions

2. spread beyond the West to most of the world

3. human impact on the environment isn't new; it just has grown

E. Globalization also has very deep roots in the past.

1. has deepened and extended in the twentieth century

III. **Three Regions—One World**

A. Chapters 21, 22, and 23 tell the separate stories of three major regions.

1. the Western world

2. the communist world

3. the Third World

4. the histories of the three worlds frequently intersect and overlap

B. All are part of a larger story—globalization (Chapter 24).

IV. **Only the future will reveal how the twentieth century will be regarded by later generations.**

THE COLLAPSE AND RECOVERY OF EUROPE

1914–1970s

CHAPTER OVERVIEW

Chapter Objectives

• To examine the history of Europe between 1914 and the 1970s as an organic whole made up of closely interconnected parts

• To consider the repercussions of nationalism and colonialism in Europe and Japan

• To increase student awareness of the effects of the two world wars

• To help students imagine the appeal of totalitarian movements in the twentieth century

Chapter Outline

I. **Opening Vignette**
   A. The last veterans of World War I are dying.
      1. disappointment that it wasn't the "war to end all wars"
      2. but now the major European states have ended centuries of hostility
   B. The "Great War" (World War I) of 1914–1918 launched a new phase of world history.
      1. it was "a European civil war with a global reach"

   2. between 1914 and the end of WWII, Western Europe largely self-destructed
   3. but Europe recovered surprisingly well between 1950 and 2000
      a. but without its overseas empires
      b. and without its position as the core of Western civilization

II. **The First World War: European Civilization in Crisis, 1914–1918**
   A. By 1900, Europeans, or people of European ancestry, controlled most other peoples of the world.
   B. An Accident Waiting to Happen
      1. modernization and Europe's rise to global ascendancy had sharpened traditional rivalries between European states
      2. both Italy and Germany unified ca. 1870
         a. Germany's unification in the context of the Franco-Prussian War (1870–1871) had embittered French-German relations
         b. rise of a powerful new Germany was a disruptive new element
      3. by around 1900, the balance of power in Europe was shaped by two rival alliances
         a. Triple Alliance (Germany, Austria, Italy)
         b. Triple Entente (Russia, France, Britain)
         c. these alliances turned a minor incident into WWI

4. June 28, 1914: a Serbian nationalist assassinated Archduke Franz Ferdinand, heir to the Austrian throne
    a. Austria was determined to crush the nationalism movement
    b. Serbia had Russia (and Russia's allies) behind it
    c. general war broke out by August 1914
    [see Discussion Topic 1]
5. factors that contributed to the outbreak and character of the war:
    a. popular nationalism
        i. freedom movements like that of Serbia
        ii. intense nationalist competition between countries
        iii. gave statesmen little room for compromise
        iv. assured widespread popular support for starting war
    b. industrialized militarism
        i. military men had great prestige
        ii. all states had standing armies
        iii. all states but Britain relied on conscription
        iv. arms race, especially in warships
        v. all states had elaborate plans for what to do if war broke out
        vi. large number of new weapons had been invented (tanks, submarines, airplanes, poison gas, machine guns, barbed wire)
        vii. result: some 10 million people died in WWI, perhaps 20 million wounded
    c. Europe's colonial empires
        i. funneled colonial troops and laborers into the war effort
        ii. battles in Africa and South Pacific
        iii. Japan (allied with Britain) took German possessions
        iv. Ottoman Empire (allied with Germany) suffered intense military operations and an Arab revolt
        v. the U.S. joined the war in 1917 when German submarines harmed U.S. shipping
C. Legacies of the Great War
    1. most had expected WWI to be a quick war
    [see Lecture Strategy 1]
        a. Germany was finally defeated November 1918
    2. became a war of attrition ("trench warfare")
        a. some battles lasted months (Verdun, the Somme) and generated massive casualties
    3. became "total war"—each country's whole population was mobilized
        a. enormous expansion of government authority
        b. massive propaganda campaigns to arouse citizens
        c. women replaced men in factories
        d. labor unions accepted sacrifices
    4. the war left widespread disillusionment among intellectuals in its wake
        a. led to questioning of Enlightenment values
        b. led to questioning of the superiority of the West and its science
    5. rearrangement of the map of Central Europe
        a. creation of independent Poland, Czechoslovakia, Yugoslavia
        b. created new problems of ethnic minorities
        c. triggered the Russian Bolshevik revolution (1917)
    6. the Treaty of Versailles (1919) made the conditions that caused WWII
        a. Germany lost its colonial empire and 15 percent of its European territory
        b. Germany was required to pay heavy reparations
        c. Germany suffered restriction of its military forces
        d. Germany had to accept sole responsibility for the outbreak of the war
        e. Germans resented the treaty immensely
    7. dissolution of the Ottoman Empire
        a. the Armenian genocide
        b. creation of new Arab states
        c. British promises to both Arabs and Jews created a new problem in Palestine
    8. in Asia and Africa, many gained military skills and political awareness
        a. Britain promised to start the process of creating self-government in India in return for war help

b. Japan was strengthened by the war

c. Japan's assumption of German privileges and territory in China inspired some Chinese to adopt Soviet-style communism

9. the U.S. appeared as a global power

  a. U.S. manpower had been important in the defeat of Germany

  b. the U.S. became Europe's creditor

  c. many Europeans were fascinated by Woodrow Wilson's ideas

    i. Fourteen Points

    ii. League of Nations

    iii. but his vision largely failed, and the U.S. Senate refused to join the league

III. Capitalism Unraveling: The Great Depression [see Discussion Topic 2]

A. The war loosened the hold of many traditional values in Europe.

  1. enormous casualties promoted social mobility

  2. women increasingly won the right to vote

  3. flouting of sexual conventions

  4. rise of a new consumerism

B. The Great Depression represented the most influential postwar change.

  1. suggested that Europe's economy was failing

  2. worries about industrial capitalism

    a. it had generated individualist materialism

    b. it had created enormous social inequalities

    c. its instability caused great anxiety

  3. the Great Depression hit in 1929

    a. contracting stock prices wiped out paper fortunes

    b. many lost their life's savings

    c. world trade dropped 62 percent within a few years; businesses contracted

    d. unemployment soared; reached 30 percent in Germany and the U.S. by 1932

C. Causes of the Great Depression:

  1. the American economy boomed in the 1920s

    a. by the end of the decade, factories and farms produced more goods than could be sold

    b. Europe was impoverished by WWI and didn't purchase many American products

    c. Europe was recovering and produced more of its own goods

  2. speculative stock market had driven stock prices up artificially high

    a. with the stock market crash, the whole fragile economic network collapsed

D. Worldwide empires made the Great Depression a worldwide problem.

E. The Depression was a major challenge to governments.

  1. capitalist governments had thought that the economy would regulate itself

  2. the Soviet Union's economy had grown throughout the 1930s

  3. in response, some states turned to "democratic socialism," with greater regulation of the economy and more equal distribution of wealth

  4. the New Deal (1933–1942) in the U.S.

    a. Franklin Roosevelt's administration launched a complex series of reforms

    b. influenced by the British economist John Maynard Keynes

    c. Roosevelt's public spending programs permanently changed the relationship between government, the private economy, and individual citizens

     i. efforts to "prime the pump" of the economy

     ii. Social Security, minimum wage, and welfare as an economic safety net for the poor

     iii. creation of permanent agribusiness through farm subsidies

     iv. vast array of new government agencies to supervise the economy

    d. didn't work very well: the U.S. economy only improved with massive government spending because of WWII

  5. Nazi Germany and Japan coped the best with the Depression

IV. Democracy Denied: Comparing Italy, Germany, and Japan [see Classroom Activity 1]

A. Democratic political ideals came under attack in the wake of World War I.

  1. the challenge of communism

2. in the 1920s and 1930s, authoritarian, nationalist, anti-Communist regimes were a more immediate problem to victors in WWI
3. authoritarian states of Italy, Germany, and Japan allied with each other by 1936–1937
   a. 1940: formal military alliance (the Axis powers)

B. The Fascist Alternative in Europe
  1. new political ideology known as fascism became important in much of Europe in period 1919–1945
    a. intensely nationalistic
    b. exalted action over reflection
    c. looked to charismatic leadership
    d. against individualism, liberalism, feminism, parliamentary democracy, and communism
    e. determined to overthrow existing regimes
    f. conservative/reactionary: celebrated traditional values
  2. fascism appealed to dissatisfied people in all social classes
    a. fascist movements grew thanks to the devastation of WWI
    b. appeared in many Western European lands
    c. became important in Austria, Hungary, Romania, Spain
    d. achieved major power in Italy and Germany
  3. fascism first developed in Italy
    a. social tensions exacerbated by economic crisis
    b. Benito Mussolini (1883–1945) put together a private army, the Black Shirts, to use violence as a political tool
     i. won power in 1922
     ii. big business supported him because they feared communism and wanted social order
    c. Mussolini's movement took the ancient Roman *fasces* as symbol
    d. once in power, Mussolini built state power
     i. clamped down on opponents
     ii. created a "corporate state" economically

     iii. reached an accord with the papacy (1929)
     iv. women as domestic baby-factories
     v. invasion of Ethiopia (1935) to avenge defeat of 1896

C. Hitler and the Nazis
  1. German fascism was more important than that of Italy
  2. took shape as the Nazi Party under Adolf Hitler (1889–1945)
  3. many similarities to Italian fascism
  4. grew out of the collapse of the German imperial state after WWI
    a. a new government, the Weimar Republic, negotiated peace
    b. traditional elites were disgraced
    c. creation of myth that Germany had not really lost the war but had been betrayed by civilians (socialists, Communists, and Jews)
    d. 1920s: vigilante groups (the Freikorps) assassinated hundreds of supporters of the Weimar government
     i. gradually won support from middle class and landowners
    e. widespread economic suffering: massive inflation in 1923, then the Great Depression
    f. everyone wanted decisive government action
    g. the National Socialist (Nazi) Party won growing public support
  5. the Nazis had only 2.6 percent of the vote in 1928; 37 percent in 1932
    a. Hitler became chancellor of Germany in 1933
  6. as chancellor, Hitler suppressed all other political parties, arrested opponents, censored the press, and assumed police power
    a. successfully brought Germany out of the Depression
    b. by the late 1930s, had majority support
    c. invoked rural and traditional values
  7. used Jews as the ultimate scapegoat for the ills of society
    a. emphasis on a racial revolution
    b. Jews were increasingly excluded from public life

i. Nuremberg Laws (1935) forbade racial mixing of Jews with other Germans and forced Jews to wear the Star of David as identifier

ii. *Kristallnacht* (Nov. 9, 1938): massive destruction and looting of Jewish-owned shops

8. celebration of the superiority of the German race

a. Hitler as mystical Führer

b. rule by intuition and force, not reason

9. the rise of Nazism represents a moral collapse within the West

a. highly selective use of earlier strands of European culture

b. made use of modern science

D. Japanese Authoritarianism

1. Japan was also a newcomer to "great power" status

2. like Germany and Italy, moved to authoritarian government and territorial expansion

3. important differences:

a. Japan played only a minimal role in WWI

b. at Versailles, Japan was an equal participant on the winning side

4. 1920s: Japan was apparently moving toward democracy

a. expansion of education

b. creation of an urban consumer society

c. greater individual freedoms, including for women

d. lower-class movements worked for greater equality

5. elite reaction

a. Peace Preservation Law (1925): prison or death for anyone who organized against the imperial government or private property

6. the Great Depression hit Japan hard

a. led many to doubt that parliamentary democracy and capitalism could help resolve "national emergency"

b. development of Radical Nationalism (the Revolutionary Right)

i. extreme nationalism

ii. hostility to parliamentary democracy

iii. commitment to leadership focused around the emperor

iv. dedication to foreign expansion

v. but no right-wing party gained wide support or produced a charismatic leader

7. shift in Japanese public life in the 1930s

a. major government posts went to prominent bureaucrats or military figures, not to party leaders

b. the military became more dominant

c. free expression was increasingly limited

d. the government adopted many themes from the Radical Right

i. emphasis on loyalty to divinely descended emperor

ii. reflected long-standing respect for samurai values

e. major public works spending pulled Japan out of Depression rapidly

f. increasing government oversight of economic matters

8. Japan was less repressive than Germany or Italy

V. **A Second World War**

A. World War II was even more global than World War I. **[see Classroom Activity 2]**

1. independent origins in Asia and Europe

2. dissatisfied states in both continents wanted to rearrange international relations

B. The Road to War in Asia

1. Japanese imperial ambitions rose in the 1920s and 1930s

2. Japan had acquired influence in Manchuria after the Russo-Japanese War of 1904–1905

a. 1931: Japanese military units seized control of Manchuria

i. established the puppet state of Manchukuo

b. Western criticism led Japan to withdraw from League of Nations

c. by 1936, Japan was more closely aligned with Germany/Italy

3. 1937: major attack on the Chinese heartland started WWII in Asia

4. international opinion was against Japan; the Japanese felt threatened

a. growing belief that Western racism was in the way of Japan being accepted as an equal power

b. Japan was heavily dependent on foreign strategic goods, especially from the U.S.

c. imperialist powers controlled the resources of Southeast Asia

5. 1940–1941: Japan launched conquest of European colonies (Indochina, Malaya, Burma, Indonesia, and the Philippines)

a. presented themselves as liberators of their fellow Asians

b. the reality was highly brutal rule by the Japanese

c. December 1941: attack on Pearl Harbor

i. only after the U.S. imposed an oil embargo on Japan

ii. Japanese authorities couldn't see a way around U.S. hostility; saw no choice but war

6. Pearl Harbor joined the Asian and European theaters of war into a single global struggle

C. The Road to War in Europe

1. Nazis promised to rectify the injustices of Versailles

2. at first, Britain, France, and the USSR were unwilling to confront German aggression

3. war was perhaps actually desired by the Nazi leadership

a. Hitler stressed the need for "living space" in Eastern Europe

b. began rearmament in 1935

c. 1938: annexation of Austria and the German-speaking parts of Czechoslovakia

d. 1939: attack on Poland—triggered WWII in Europe

4. Germany quickly gained control of most of Europe

a. rapid defeat of France

b. air war against Britain

c. invasion of the USSR

5. Germany's new tactic of *blitzkrieg* was initially very successful

a. but was stopped by Soviet counterattack in 1942

b. Germans were finally defeated in May 1945

D. World War II: The Outcomes of Global Conflict

1. an estimated 60 million people died in WWII

a. more than half the casualties were civilians

b. the line between civilian and military targets was blurred

2. the USSR suffered more than 40 percent of the total number of deaths

a. massive destruction

3. China also suffered massive attacks against civilians

a. in many villages, every person and animal was killed

b. the Rape of Nanjing (1937–1938): 200,000–300,000 Chinese civilians were killed; countless women were raped

4. bombing raids on Britain, Japan, and Germany showed the new attitude toward total war

5. governments' mobilization of economies, people, and propaganda reached further than ever before

a. large numbers of women were drawn into industry and the military

6. the Holocaust: some 6 million Jews were killed in genocide

a. millions of others considered undesirable were also killed by the Nazis

7. WWII left Europe impoverished, with its industrial infrastructure in ruins and millions of people homeless or displaced

a. Europe soon was divided into U.S. and Soviet spheres of influence

8. weakened Europe could not hold onto its Asian and African colonies

9. WWII consolidated and expanded the communist world

a. Soviet victory over Germany gave new credibility to the communist regime

b. Soviet authorities played up a virtual cult of WWII

c. communist parties took power across Eastern Europe

d. communist takeover of China by 1949

i. Chinese Communist Party had led the fight against Japan

10. growing internationalism

a. creation of the United Nations (1945) as a means for peaceful conflict resolution

b. establishment of the World Bank and International Monetary Fund (1945)

11. the new dominance of the United States as a global superpower

VI. **The Recovery of Europe** [see Lecture Strategy 3]

A. Europe recovered in the second half of the twentieth century.

1. rebuilt industrial economies and revived democratic systems

2. the U.S. assumed a dominant role within Western civ. and in the world at large

B. How Europe recovered:

1. industrial societies are very resilient

2. the major states of Western Europe integrated their recovering economies

3. an extension of European civilization existed: the U.S.

a. the U.S. was a reservoir of resources for the whole West

b. by 1945, the center of gravity of Western civ. was the U.S.

c. the U.S. was the only major country not physically touched by WWII

d. by 1945, the U.S. accounted for 50 percent of all world production

4. the U.S. took the initiative to rebuild Europe: the Marshall Plan

a. magnificently successful

b. required the European recipients to cooperate with each other

c. 1951: creation of the European Coal and Steel Community

d. 1957: creation of the European Economic Community (Common Market)

e. 1994: transformation of EEC into the European Union

i. 2002: twelve member states adopted a common currency

f. political and military security against the Soviet threat

i. creation of the North Atlantic Treaty Organization (NATO)

C. Japan underwent a parallel recovery process.

1. U.S. occupation between 1945 and 1952

2. remarkable economic growth for two decades after WWII

a. assisted by U.S. economic aid

3. Japan depended on the U.S. for security, since it was forbidden to maintain military forces

VII. **Reflections: War and Remembrance: Learning from History** [see Classroom Activity 3]

A. Santayana said: "Those who cannot remember the past are condemned to repeat it."

1. but most historians are cautious about drawing particular lessons from the past

2. history is complex enough to allow different people to learn different lessons

B. Historians are skeptical of the notion that "history repeats itself."

C. The wars of the twentieth century led to unexpected consequences.

USING *WAYS OF THE WORLD* IN THE CLASSROOM

Lecture Strategies

Lecture Strategy 1

"From trench warfare to *blitzkrieg*."

The purpose of this lecture strategy is to examine the development of military technology and strategy in the twentieth century. Its objectives are:

- to understand the two world wars in the context of rapid developments in military technology
- to help students to understand what a shock World War I was to conventional military wisdom, and why
- to consider the major differences between World War I and World War II

A good place to begin is back in the nineteenth century, with the Crimean War and the U.S. Civil War, when breech-loading rifles and highly developed cannons made a mockery of the way war had been waged for two centuries—tightly packed ranks of men, unarmored, marching toward each other on open fields. (It is useful to cite the enormous casualty rates in the Battle of Gettysburg and the Charge of the Light Brigade when discussing this issue.)

From there, consider the arms race of the late nineteenth century and the limited opportunities that Western powers had to test out their arsenals before the outbreak of World War I. Thus, to a surprising extent, the beginning of that war saw the use of twentieth-century technology wedded to nineteenth-century tactics; the result was appalling casualties. Some new technologies to include when discussing World War I are:

- bolt-action infantry rifles
- machine guns
- rifled artillery
- hand grenades
- high-explosive shells
- flamethrowers
- poison gas
- the first use of military aircraft, tanks, and submarines

For World War II, the most important new technologies to stress are:

- much-improved aircraft, tanks, and submarines and how they made it possible to move beyond the trench warfare of World War I
- improvements in guns of all sorts
- communications systems, including field radios
- improvements in battlefield medicine
- and, of course, the atom bomb

It is useful to conclude this lecture with a discussion of what real differences these technological developments made to the face of war and to the societies that were at war.

Lecture Strategy 2

"Civilians and war."

In the "total wars" of the twentieth century, could anyone be regarded as "off-limits"? The issue of when it is justifiable (or at least expedient) to attack civilians is a very current one in our modern age of global terrorism. This lecture strategy proposes an examination of the history of civilians and war, the particular issues of the two world wars with regard to this topic, and the results in international law. The objectives of this lecture strategy are:

- to consider the ways in which attacks against civilians were different in World War I and World War II than in earlier history

- to investigate the logic of war atrocities
- to seek to understand massive bombing attacks in which whole cities were destroyed by discussing what those attacks accomplished and how they were justified

A good place to begin is with the evolution of international law to cover noncombatants in war zones. The key developments in this regard are the creation of the Hague Conventions (1899 and 1907) and the Geneva Conventions (1864 and 1949).

There are many directions one could go with this lecture. Some important points to consider are:

- the fact that civilians have almost always suffered in war (enslavement of populations; massacre of cities' inhabitants after sieges; casual looting, rape, and murder by troops passing through districts)
- the massive civilian casualties of the Thirty Years' War
- the Wounded Knee Massacre (1890)
- the first explicit international charge of a government committing a "crime against humanity"—the Allied statement issued in 1915 against the Armenian genocide strategic bombing (e.g., the London Blitz, the bombing of many German cities in World War II, and the dropping of atomic bombs on Nagasaki and Hiroshima) and the issue of attacking civilians because they contribute to the war effort
- the systematic use of terror to sap the enemy's will to fight (such as in the Rape of Nanjing)
- the behavior of troops toward civilians in occupied territories during World War II
- the issue of "victor's justice" (why some acts against civilians have *not* been regarded as war crimes, including the firebombing of Dresden and the use of atomic bombs on Hiroshima and Nagasaki)
- the Nuremburg Trials and the International Military Tribunal for the Far East, both convened by the Allied powers after World War II to prosecute war criminals

Lecture Strategy 3

"Recovery."

The purpose of this lecture strategy is to discuss Europe's and Japan's recovery after the Second World War. The lecture will be particularly effective with

PowerPoint or another means of image projection. Its objectives are:

- to make students aware of the massive destruction of World War II
- to consider the human cost of the war
- to investigate the Marshall Plan, including the U.S. policies behind it and the effect it had on Europe
- to study native efforts to recover from the war in both Europe and Japan

A good place to start is with a stark depiction of ravaged Europe and Japan in 1945. A great many photographs are readily available. Some particularly moving ones to include are:

- images of Hiroshima and Nagasaki
- images of Tokyo
- images of Dresden, Hamburg, and Berlin, among many other German cities
- images of London during and after the Blitz

It is also useful to include more specific views, including photos of structures that have been left in their war-ravaged state so as to remind people today of the horrors of war. Some good examples are:

- Coventry Cathedral in England
- the Kaiser Wilhelm Gedächniskirche (Memorial Church) in Berlin

Go on from there to consider how the task of rebuilding was done. Some points to include are:

- the vast number of refugees and displaced persons
- the difficulties in providing food and basic services
- excerpts from George Marshall's famous "Marshall Plan Speech," given at Harvard on June 5, 1947
- precisely what the Marshall Plan did
- how the United States helped recovery efforts in Japan
- careful consideration of what was done by European and Japanese people themselves
- a comparison to the cleanup on the Mississippi and Louisiana Gulf Coast after Hurricane Katrina, to help students imagine the sheer volume of rubble that had to be cleared away from many cities and towns

- choose a single structure (e.g., Coventry Cathedral, or, on a smaller scale, one of the lovely Romanesque churches of Cologne) and follow the timeline of reconstruction, including consideration of where the money and labor came from
- the rebuilding of industrial infrastructure, roads, and railroads

Things to Do in the Classroom

Discussion Topics

1. **Contextualization, large or small group.**
"Christmas in the Trenches."
Play for the class the John McCutcheon song called "Christmas in the Trenches" (also known as "My Name Is Francis Tolliver"), which movingly tells the story of the 1914 Christmas truce described in the chapter opening. Then ask the students to discuss the issues raised by the song. Please note that the song was written in 1984; could something similar have been produced in 1914?

2. **Comparison, large or small group.** "Could there be another Great Depression?"
Ask students to list important points about the Great Depression—the stock market collapse, massive unemployment, soup kitchens, etc. Then ask them to discuss whether something similar could happen today, or whether government interventions in the economy now make the occurrence of such an event very unlikely.

3. **Misconception/Difficult Topic, large or small group.** "The Holocaust killed only German Jews."
Leaving aside modern hate groups that claim, against all evidence, that the Holocaust never happened, many people have only a fuzzy notion of what was involved. A common misconception is that the Nazis' "Final Solution" only targeted Jews, and in particular only the Jews of Germany. To broaden students' perspective and to help them imagine the horrors of the Holocaust experienced by the much more numerous Jewish populations of Eastern Europe, as well as by Gypsies, homosexuals, and other groups, give the class one or two excerpts from Holocaust survivors' testimonies. The Fortunoff Video Archive for Holocaust Testimonies at www.library.yale.edu/testimonies/index.html includes a variety of testimony excerpts.

Classroom Activities

1. **Close-reading exercise, small group.** "Visualizing fascism."
The Mandeville Special Collections Library at the University of California, San Diego, has a very interesting collection of posters from the Spanish Civil War, available online at http://orpheus.ucsd.edu/speccoll/visfront/index.html. Show some of these posters, helping students to "read" them for their propaganda agenda.

2. **Map-analysis exercise, large or small group.** "The battles of World War II."
Using a large world map, show where the most important battles of World War II were fought. These battles include:

- the Atlantic
- Berlin
- Britain
- the Bulge
- El Alamein
- Guadalcanal
- Iwo Jima
- Kursk
- Leningrad
- Leyte Gulf
- Midway
- Milne Bay
- Normandy
- Okinawa
- Operation Barbarossa
- Operation Torch
- Pearl Harbor
- Philippine Sea
- Stalingrad

Then discuss the significance of their geographic distribution.

3. **Clicker question.** Which was a greater shock to Europe: World War I or World War II?

Key Terms

blitzkrieg: German term meaning "lightning war," used to describe Germany's novel military tactics in World War II, which involved the rapid movement of infantry, tanks, and airpower over large areas. (*pron.* BLITS-kreeg)

European Economic Community: The EEC (also known as the Common Market) was an alliance formed by Italy, France, West Germany, Belgium, the Netherlands, and Luxembourg in 1957 and dedicated to developing common trade policies and reduced tariffs; it gradually developed into the European Union.

European Union: The final step in a series of arrangements to increase cooperation between European states in the wake of World War II; the EU was formally established in 1994, and twelve of its members adopted a common currency in 2002.

fascism: Political ideology marked by its intense nationalism and authoritarianism; its name is derived from the *fasces* that were the symbol of magistrates in ancient Rome. (*pron.* FASH-iz-uhm)

flappers: Young middle-class women who emerged as a new form of social expression after World War I, flouting conventions and advocating a more open sexuality.

Fourteen Points: Plan of U.S. president Woodrow Wilson to establish lasting peace at the end of World War I; although Wilson's views were popular in Europe, his vision largely failed.

Franco-Prussian War: German war with France (1870–1871) that ended with the defeat of France and the unification of Germany into a single state under Prussian rule.

Franz Ferdinand, Archduke: Heir to the Austrian throne whose assassination by a Serbian nationalist on June 28, 1914, was the spark that ignited World War I.

Great Depression: Worldwide economic depression that began in 1929 with the New York stock market crash and continued in many areas until the outbreak of World War II.

Great War: Name originally given to the First World War (1914–1918).

Hitler, Adolf: Leader of the German Nazi Party (1889–1945) and Germany's head of state from 1933 until his death.

Holocaust: Name commonly used for the Nazi genocide of Jews and other "undesirables" in German society; Jews themselves prefer the term *Shoah*, which means "catastrophe," rather than Holocaust ("offering" or "sacrifice").

Kristallnacht: Literally, "crystal night"; name given to the night of November 9, 1938, when Nazi-led gangs smashed and looted Jewish shops throughout Germany. (*pron.* kris-TAHL-nakht)

League of Nations: International peacekeeping organization created after World War I; first proposed by U.S. president Woodrow Wilson as part of his Fourteen Points.

Manchukuo: Japanese puppet state established in Manchuria in 1931. (*pron.* man-CHEW-coo-oh)

Marshall Plan: Huge U.S. government initiative to aid in the post–World War II restoration of Europe that was masterminded by U.S. secretary of state George Marshall and put into effect in 1947.

Mussolini, Benito: Charismatic leader of the Italian fascist party (1883–1945) who came to power in 1922. (*pron.* ben-EE-toe moos-oh-LEE-nee)

Nanjing, Rape of: The Japanese army's systematic killing, mutilation, and rape of the Chinese civilian population of Nanjing in 1938. (*pron.* nahn-JING)

NATO: The North Atlantic Treaty Organization, a military and political alliance founded in 1949 that committed the United States to the defense of Europe in the event of Soviet aggression.

Nazi Germany: Germany as ruled by Hitler and the Nazi Party from 1933 to 1945, a fascist state dedicated to extreme nationalism, territorial expansion, and the purification of the German state.

Nazi Party: Properly known as the National Socialist Democratic Workers' Party, the Nazi party was founded in Germany shortly after World War I and advocated a strongly authoritarian and nationalist regime based on notions of racial superiority.

New Deal: A series of reforms enacted by the Franklin Roosevelt administration between 1933 and 1942 with the goal of ending the Great Depression.

Nuremberg Laws: Series of laws passed by the Nazi-dominated German parliament in 1935 that forbade sexual relations between Jews and other Germans and mandated that Jews identify themselves in public by wearing the Star of David.

Revolutionary Right (Japan): Also known as Radical Nationalism, this was a movement in Japanese political life ca. 1930–1945 that was marked by extreme nationalism, a commitment to elite leadership focused around the emperor, and dedication to foreign expansion.

total war: War that requires each country involved to mobilize its entire population in the effort to defeat the enemy.

Treaty of Versailles: 1919 treaty that officially ended World War I; the immense penalties it placed on Germany are regarded as one of the causes of World War II. (*pron.* vare-SIGH)

Triple Alliance: An alliance consisting of Germany, Austria, and Italy that was one of the two rival European alliances on the eve of World War I.

Triple Entente: An alliance consisting of Russia, France, and Britain that was one of the two rival European alliances on the eve of World War I.

United Nations: International peacekeeping organization and forum for international opinion, established in 1945.

Weimar Republic: The weak government that replaced the German imperial state at the end of World War I; its failure to take strong action against war reparations and the Great Depression provided an opportunity for the Nazi Party's rise to power. (*pron.* VIE-mahr)

Wilson, Woodrow: President of the United States from 1913 to 1921 who was especially noted for his idealistic approach to the end of World War I, which included advocacy of his Fourteen Points intended to regulate future international dealings and a League of Nations to enforce a new international order; although his vision largely failed, Wilson was widely respected for his views.

World War I: The "Great War" (1914–1918), in essence a European civil war with global implications that was marked by massive casualties, the expansion of offensive military technology beyond tactics and means of defense, and a great deal of disillusionment with the whole idea of "progress."

World War II in Asia: A struggle essentially to halt Japanese imperial expansion in Asia, fought by the Japanese against primarily Chinese and American foes.

World War II in Europe: A struggle essentially to halt German imperial expansion in Europe, fought by a coalition of allies that included Great Britain, the Soviet Union, and the United States.

zaibatsu: The huge industrial enterprises that dominated the Japanese economy in the period leading up to World War II. (*pron.* zye-BOT-soo)

ANSWER GUIDELINES FOR CHAPTER QUESTIONS

The two sets of questions that follow appear in the textbook at the end of the chapter and in the margins of the reading. They are also provided in the Computerized Test Bank with answer guidelines, for your convenience.

The Big Picture Questions

1. What explains the disasters that befell Europe in the first half of the twentieth century?

• A variety of factors lay behind the disasters: the numerous competitive states that were a force in driving Europe's expanding influence in the world over the previous four centuries became a liability as they turned on one another in devastating wars within Europe;

• the industrial production that underpinned Europe's wealth and power was used to fight destructive wars within Europe;

• the growing power of governments and the resources of their colonial empires were directed toward warfare between European powers;

• nationalism, communism, and fascism all provided ideological motivations for war;

• the Great Depression had an impact on all European economies, further destabilizing the region and adding to tensions within societies.

2. In what ways were the world wars a motor for change in the history of the twentieth century?

• The destructive national hostilities between European states that had led to the wars were dissipated following the Second World War.

• The world wars led to the collapse of European colonial empires;

• they also brought the United States to center stage as a global power.

• The needs of total war led to the expansion of government authority;

• the destruction wrought by the wars led to a widespread disillusionment among European intellectuals with their own civilization;

• the political map of the world was radically altered;

• communism emerged as an important political movement.

3. To what extent were the two world wars distinct and different conflicts, and in what ways were they related to each other? In particular, how did the First World War and its aftermath lay the foundations for World War II?

• They were distinct in that the Second World War was a more genuinely global conflict with independent origins in both Asia and Europe;

• new leaders, political structures, and ideologies underpinned the aggressive states in the Second World War.

• However, the aftermath of World War I did lay many of the foundations for World War II, including the Treaty of Versailles's humiliating terms for Germany, which created immense resentment in that country;

• the treaty imposed heavy reparation payments on Germany that made the economic crisis of the Great Depression even worse and thus strengthened the Nazi party.

• The aftermath of World War I also laid the basis for a series of naval treaties that Japanese leaders felt did not reflect Japan's status as a first-rank power;

• and it increased Japanese colonial ambitions.

• The Great Depression also strengthened the conservative forces in Japan.

4. In what ways did Europe's internal conflicts between 1914 and 1945 have global implications?

• They led to a decline of European influence on the world stage.

• They facilitated the decolonization movements in Asia and Africa after World War II.

• They facilitated the spread of communism.

• The decline of Western Europe due to the strains of these conflicts transferred leadership of the West to the United States.

Margin Review Questions

Q. *What aspects of Europe's nineteenth-century history contributed to the First World War?*

• Aspects of Europe's nineteenth-century history that contributed to the First World War include the emergence of Germany and Italy as unified states, which disrupted the fragile balance of power between Europe's major countries that had been established after the defeat of Napoleon in 1815;

- growing popular nationalism in Europe;
- industrialization and industrialized militarism;
- competition among European powers for colonial empires.

Q. *In what ways did World War I mark new departures in the history of the twentieth century?*

- The needs of total war led to the expansion of government authority;
- the destruction of life and property wrought by the war led to a widespread disillusionment among European intellectuals with their own civilization;
- the political map of Europe was radically altered with the collapse of the German, Russian, and Austrian empires, creating space for new nations in Central Europe, including Poland, Czechoslovakia, and Yugoslavia, all of which were formed around an ideology of national self-determination;
- in Russia, the strains of war triggered a vast revolutionary upheaval that launched world communism;
- the Treaty of Versailles, which brought the war to a close, also established the conditions that generated the Second World War;
- the massacre and deportation of one million Armenians by the Ottoman Empire set a precedent on which Nazi Germany later built;
- the collapse of the Ottoman Empire during World War I resulted in the political fragmentation of the Middle East and the emergence of the states of Turkey, Syria, Iraq, Jordan, and Palestine;
- conflicting promises made by the British to both Arabs and Jews concerning Palestine set the stage for an enduring struggle over that ancient and holy land;
- millions of colonial subjects who had participated in the war had gained new military skills and political awareness and returned home with less respect for their rulers and with expectations for better treatment as a reward for their service;
- in East Asia, Japan had emerged strengthened from the war, with European support for its claim to take over German territory and privileges in China;
- Japan's increased influence in China enraged Chinese nationalists and among a few sparked an interest in Soviet-style communism, for only the new Communist rulers of Russia seemed willing to end the imperialist penetration of China;
- World War I brought the United States to center stage as a global power.

Q. *In what ways was the Great Depression a global phenomenon?*

- Industrial production from Europe and especially the United States required foreign markets, and when those markets dried up, industrial production collapsed.
- Countries or colonies tied to exporting one or two commodities to industrial countries were especially hard-hit as the market for their exports dried up.

Q. *In what ways did fascism challenge the ideas and practices of European liberalism and democracy?*

- Where fascism arose, it sought to revitalize and purify the nation and to mobilize people for a grand task. Fascists condoned violence against enemies, exalted action rather than thought and reflection, and looked to a charismatic leader for direction. They condemned individualism, liberalism, feminism, and parliamentary democracy, all of which, they argued, divided and weakened the nation.

Q. *What was distinctive about the German expression of fascism? What was the basis of popular support for the Nazis?*

- In terms of the distinctiveness of German-style fascism, the Nazis were able to assume police powers more thoroughly than their Italian counterparts were able to achieve, which limited opposition;
- far more so than in Italy, Adolf Hitler and the Nazis used Jews as a symbol of the urban, capitalist, and foreign influences that were supposedly corrupting "true" German culture;
- emphasis on a racial revolution was a central feature of the Nazi program and differed from the racial attitudes in Italy.
- In terms of popular support for Nazism, war veterans who had felt betrayed by German politicians after World War I formed an important base of support;
- the Nazis also gradually drew support from the middle classes as well as from conservative landowners because of the ruinous inflation of 1923 and then the Great Depression;
- by the late 1930s, the Nazis apparently had the support of a considerable majority of the population, in large measure because their policies successfully brought Germany out of the Depression.

Q. *How did Japan's experience during the 1920s and 1930s resemble that of Germany, and how did it differ?*

- Their experiences were similar in that both countries were newcomers to great-power status;
- had limited experience with democratic politics;
- moved toward authoritarian government and a denial of democracy at home;

• launched aggressive programs of territorial expansion;

• and enacted policies that included state-financed credit and large-scale spending on armaments and public works projects to bring their respective countries out of the Depression quite quickly.

• Their experiences differed in that Japan remained, at least internally, a less repressive and more pluralistic society than Germany;

• no right-wing party was able to seize power in Japan;

• Japan produced no charismatic leader on the order of Mussolini or Hitler;

• Japanese conceptions of their racial purity and uniqueness were directed largely against foreigners rather than an internal minority.

Q. *In what way were the origins of World War II in Asia and in Europe similar to each other? How were they different?*

• In terms of similarities, both Japan and Germany were dissatisfied with their positions in the international power structure;

• both Japan and Germany expanded their territories through force, causing tensions with other powers.

• In terms of differences, Japanese leaders felt that they were not being treated as an equal power on the world stage because of racism, while Germans felt that they were being treated unfairly because of their defeat in World War I;

• Japan's initial conquests were driven primarily by a desire to acquire raw materials and other resources, whereas Germany's were driven primarily by strategic rivalries with neighboring powers.

Q. *How did World War II differ from World War I?*

• More than World War I, World War II was a genuinely global conflict with independent origins in both Asia and Europe;

• the Second World War was more destructive, with some 60 million deaths—six times the deaths in World War I.

• More than half the casualties of World War II were civilians, reflecting a nearly complete blurring of the traditional line between civilian and military targets as compared to World War I.

• In World War II, governments mobilized their economies, their people, and their propaganda machines even more extensively than in World War I.

• The Holocaust of World War II was an act of genocide that outstripped even the Armenian genocide of World War I in scale.

• World War II rearranged the architecture of world politics even more than had World War I. After World War II, Europe was effectively divided, with its western half operating under an American umbrella and the eastern half subject to Soviet control.

• In contrast to the aftermath of World War I, Europe's role in the world was greatly diminished in the decades that followed World War II, with European colonies in Asia and Africa achieving their independence.

• World War II allowed for the consolidation and extension of the communist world in a way that World War I did not.

• More effective worldwide organizations like the United Nations and the World Bank took shape after World War II, as compared to the League of Nations that was created after World War I.

• The United States took on a more dominant presence on the world stage after World War II as compared to the post–World War I era.

Q. *How was Europe able to recover from the devastation of war?*

• Europe's industrial societies proved to be resilient.

• The major Western European countries took steps to integrate their recovering economies.

• The United States was in a position to take a leadership role in the West and served as a reservoir of military manpower, economic resources, and political leadership for the West as a whole.

ADDITIONAL RESOURCES FOR CHAPTER 21

Additional Bedford/St. Martin's Resources

FOR INSTRUCTORS

Computerized Test Bank

This test bank provides over thirty exercises per chapter, including multiple-choice, fill-in-the-blank,

short-answer, and full-length essay questions. Instructors can customize quizzes, add or edit both questions and answers, and export questions and answers to a variety of formats, including WebCT and Blackboard. The disc includes correct answers and essay outlines.

Instructor's Resource CD-ROM

This disc provides instructors with ready-made and customizable PowerPoint multimedia presentations built around chapter outlines, maps, figures, and all images from the textbook, plus JPEG versions of all maps, figures, and images.

The following maps and images from Chapter 21 are available in both JPEG and PowerPoint format on the Instructor's Resource CD-ROM:

- Map 21.1: The World in 1914 (p. 626)
- Map 21.2: Europe on the Eve of World War I (p. 628)
- Map 21.3: Europe and the Middle East after World War I (p. 631)
- Map 21.4: World War II in Asia (p. 646)
- Map 21.5: World War II in Europe (p. 649)
- Map 21.6: The Growth of European Integration (p. 655)
- Over the Top (p. 624)
- Women and the Great War (p. 630)
- The Great Depression (p. 634)
- The Faces of European Fascism (p. 638)
- Nazi Hatred of the Jews (p. 640)
- Hiroshima (p. 651)

FOR STUDENTS

Documents and Essays from *Worlds of History: A Comparative Reader,* Third Edition (Volume 2)

The following documents, essays, and illustrations to accompany Chapter 21 are available in Chapters 10 and 11 of Volume 2 of this reader by Kevin Reilly:

From Chapter 10

- Sally Marks, *The Coming of the First World War*
- Erich Maria Remarque, from *All Quiet on the Western Front*
- Siegfried Sassoon, *Base Details*
- Wilfred Owen, *Dulce et Decorum Est*
- Rosa Luxemburg, *The Junius Pamphlet*
- V. I. Lenin, from *War and Revolution*
- Woodrow Wilson, *Fourteen Points*

From Chapter 11

- Joachim C. Fest, *The Rise of Hitler*
- Heinrich Himmler, *Speech to the SS*
- Jean-François Steiner, from *Treblinka*
- Iris Chang, from *The Rape of Nanking*

Online Study Guide at bedfordstmartins.com/strayer

The Online Study Guide helps students synthesize the material from the text as well as practice the skills historians use to make sense of the past. Each chapter of the Online Study Guide contains specific testing exercises, including a multiple-choice self-test that focuses on important conceptual ideas; an identification quiz that helps students remember key people, places, and events; a flashcard activity that tests students on their knowledge of key terms; and two interactive map activities intended to strengthen students' geographic skills. Instructors can monitor students' progress through an online Quiz Gradebook or receive email updates.

Further Reading

A-Bomb WWW Museum, http://www.csi.ad.jp/ABOMB/index.html. This Japanese site presents the story of the first atomic bombs from a Japanese perspective.

Dear, I. C. B., and M. R. D. Foot, eds. *The Oxford Companion to World War II.* New York: Oxford University Press, 2005. At 1,064 pages, this work is truly comprehensive.

Gilbert, Adrian, ed. *World War I in Photographs.* London: Macdonald Orbis, 1986. A very powerful collection of photographs that brings home the horrors of World War I.

Internet Resources for Jewish Studies, http://www2.lib.udel.edu/subj/jew/internet.htm. This site, maintained by the University of Delaware Library, provides a collection of resources on Jewish life and culture and on important subjects such as anti-Semitism and the Holocaust.

Keegan, John. *An Illustrated History of the First World War.* New York: Knopf, 2001. A very clear and thoughtful study.

Mills, Nicolaus. *Winning the Peace: The Marshall Plan and America's Coming of Age as a Superpower.* Hoboken, NJ: Wiley, 2008. A readable one-volume work on Europe's recovery after WWII.

The Nizkor Project, http://www.nizkor.org/. This site is dedicated to evidence of the Holocaust; the Hebrew word "nizkor" means "we will remember."

The Roaring '20s and the Great Depression, http://www.snowcrest.net/jmike/20sdep.html. A good collection of links on the 1920s and the Great Depression in the United States, arranged by topic.

Samuel, Wolfgang W. E. *The War of Our Childhood: Memories of World War II.* Jackson: University Press of Mississippi, 2002. This moving book relates the memories of twenty-seven Germans who were children during World War II.

World War I, "The Great War," http://members.aol.com/TeacherNet/WWI.html. An extremely thorough and well-crafted educational site on World War I.

World War II, http://www.donet.com/~mconrad/WW2.htm. An Internet museum of World War II, hosted by the Miami Valley Military History Museum.

Literature

Camus, Albert. *The Myth of Sisyphus and Other Essays.* New York: Vintage, 1955. This collection of stories, first published in French in 1942, is a classic statement of European hopelessness and despair.

Chang, Iris. *The Rape of Nanking.* London: Penguin, 1998. Based on interviews with survivors as well as on extant documents, this is a study of the horror of the Japanese conquest of Nanjing (Nanking) in 1937–1938.

Frank, Anne. *The Diary of a Young Girl.* New York: Bantam, 1993. This work, the tale of a Jewish girl and her family in hiding in the Nazi-occupied Netherlands, has been a classic ever since it was first published in 1947.

Hemingway, Ernest. *For Whom the Bell Tolls.* New York: Scribner, 1995. Hemingway's experience as a journalist covering the Spanish Civil War provided the basis for this work, one of the most powerful novels ever written about war.

Mauldin, Bill. *Bill Mauldin's Army: Bill Mauldin's Greatest World War II Cartoons.* Novato, CA: Presidio Press, 1983. A great collection of U.S. army cartoons.

Remarque, Erich. *All Quiet on the Western Front.* New York: Ballantine Books, 1987. This 1929 novel set during World War I is a profound critique of war.

Seghers, Anna. *The Seventh Cross.* Boston: Little, Brown, 1942. First published in 1942, this powerful novel about Germany under the Nazis tells of a communist's escape from a Nazi concentration camp.

Steinbeck, John. *The Grapes of Wrath.* London: Penguin, 2002. This classic novel, first published in 1939, gives a vivid look at the suffering and inhumanity of the American Dust Bowl migrations of the 1930s.

Wiesel, Elie. *After the Darkness: Reflections on the Holocaust.* New York: Schocken, 2002. Wiesel's first book, *Night* (1958), told of the author's survival of a Nazi concentration camp. *After the Darkness*, first published in 2002, is a short work that returns to the subject late in the author's life.

Film

There are any number of films available on the topics covered in this chapter; here are some that might be of particular use.

All Quiet on the Western Front. Universal Studios, 1930. 132 minutes. A film depiction of the classic novel by Erich Maria Remarque.

The Battle of the Somme. Films for the Humanities and Sciences, 1994. 94 minutes. An in-depth look at this seminal battle of World War I.

Between the Wars: The Economic Seeds of World War II. Films for the Humanities and Sciences, 1997. 25 minutes. Examines the economic origins of the Second World War.

Brother, Can You Spare a Dime? Films for the Humanities and Sciences. 20 minutes. Explores the global implications of the Great Depression, from the economic dislocation in the United States to the rise of the Nazi Party in Germany and Japanese expansionism.

Fascist Dictatorships. Insight Media, 1985. 36 minutes. Explores the historical and philosophical roots of fascism and traces the careers of both Benito Mussolini and Adolf Hitler.

Genocide in the First Half of the Twentieth Century. Films for the Humanities and Sciences, 2001. 57 minutes. Contextualizes the phenomenon of genocide, with segments on the Rape of Nanjing and the Holocaust.

Great Depression to Superpower: 1930–1990. Insight Media, 2000. 25 minutes. Traces the growing importance of the United States as a global power in the twentieth century.

The Hiding Place. World Wide Pictures, 1975. 134 minutes. The true and deeply moving tale of two women who helped hide Jews from the Nazis, and what happened when the Nazis found out.

Hirohito: Japan in the 20th Century. Insight Media, 1990. 58 minutes. Provides a good overview of Japanese history in the twentieth century.

How the Nazis Came to Power. Films for the Humanities and Sciences. 17 minutes. Traces the rise of the Nazi Party in Germany.

Testimony of the Human Spirit: Six Survivors of the Holocaust Tell Their Stories. Two episodes. Films for the Humanities and Sciences, 2003. 39 and 45 minutes. A moving documentary that draws on the experiences of Holocaust survivors.

World War I. Films for the Humanities and Sciences, 1990. 27 minutes. Provides a short overview of the course of the war, from its opening to the Treaty of Versailles.

World War II. Two episodes. Films for the Humanities and Sciences, 1999. 54 and 36 minutes. A two-part ABC News program anchored by Peter Jennings that surveys the course of World War II.

The Rise and Fall of World Communism

1917–Present

CHAPTER OVERVIEW

Chapter Objectives

- To examine the nature of the Russian and Chinese revolutions and how the differences between those revolutions affected the introduction of communist regimes in those countries
- To consider how communist states developed, especially in the USSR and the People's Republic of China
- To consider the benefits of a communist state
- To consider the harm caused by the two great communist states of the twentieth century
- To introduce students to the cold war and its major issues
- To explore the reasons why communism collapsed in the USSR and China
- To consider how we might assess the communist experience . . . and to inquire if historians should be asking such questions about moral judgment

Chapter Outline

I. **Opening Vignette**
   A. The Berlin Wall was breached on November 9, 1989.
      1. built in 1961 to seal off East Berlin from West Berlin

2. became a major symbol of communist tyranny
   B. Communism had originally been greeted by many as a promise of liberation.
      1. communist regimes had transformed their societies
      2. provided a major political/ideological threat to the Western world
         a. the cold war (1946–1991)
         b. scramble for influence in the third world between the U.S. and the USSR
         c. massive nuclear arms race
      3. and then it collapsed

II. **Global Communism**
   A. Communism had its roots in nineteenth-century socialism, inspired by Karl Marx.
      1. most European socialists came to believe that they could achieve their goals through the democratic process
      2. those who defined themselves as "communists" in the twentieth century advocated revolution
      3. "communism" in Marxist theory is the final stage of historical development, with full development of social equality and collective living
   B. At communism's height in the 1970s, almost one-third of the world's population was governed by communist regimes.
      1. the most important communist societies by far were the USSR and China

2. communism also came to Eastern Europe, North Korea, Vietnam, Laos, Cambodia, Cuba, and Afghanistan
3. none of these countries had the industrial capitalism that Marx thought necessary for a socialist revolution
4. communist parties took root in many other areas

C. The various expressions of communism shared common ground:
   1. a common ideology, based on Marxism
      a. an international revolutionary movement was more important than national loyalties
   2. inspiration of the 1917 Russian Revolution
      a. USSR provided aid and advice to aspiring revolutionaries elsewhere through Comintern (Communist International)
   3. during the cold war, the Warsaw Pact created a military alliance of Eastern European states and the USSR
      a. Council on Mutual Economic Assistance tied Eastern European economies to the USSR's
      b. Treaty of Friendship between the USSR and China (1950)
   4. but relations between communist countries were also marked by rivalry and hostility, sometimes war

III. **Comparing Revolutions as a Path to Communism**
   A. Communist revolutions drew on the mystique of the French Revolution.
      1. got rid of landed aristocracies and the old ruling classes
      2. involved peasant upheavals in the countryside; educated leadership in the cities
      3. French, Russian, and Chinese revolutions all looked to a modernizing future, eschewed any nostalgia for the past
      4. but there were important differences:
         a. communist revolutions were made by highly organized parties guided by a Marxist ideology
         b. the middle classes were among the victims of communist upheavals, whereas middle classes were chief beneficiaries of French Revolution

B. Russia: Revolution in a Single Year
   1. Russia's revolution (1917) was sudden, explosive
      a. Tsar Nicholas II was forced to abdicate the throne in February 1917
      b. massive social upheaval
   2. deep-seated social revolution soon showed the inadequacy of the Provisional Government
      a. it would not/could not meet the demands of the revolutionary masses
      b. refused to withdraw from WWI
      c. left opening for the rise of more radical groups
      d. most effective opposition group was the Bolsheviks, led by Vladimir Ulyanov (Lenin)
   3. Bolsheviks seized power in a coup (October 1917)
      a. claimed to act on behalf of the "soviets"
      b. three-year civil war followed: Bolsheviks vs. a variety of enemies
      c. by 1921, Bolsheviks (now calling their party "communist") had won
   4. during the civil war, the Bolsheviks:
      a. regimented the economy
      b. suppressed nationalist rebellions
      c. committed atrocities (as did their enemies)
      d. integrated many lower-class men into the Red Army and into local governments
      e. claimed to defend Russia from imperialists as well as from internal exploiters
      f. strengthened their tendency toward authoritarianism
   5. for 25 years, the new USSR was the only communist country
      a. expansion into Eastern Europe thanks to Soviet occupation at the end of WWII
      b. Stalin sought a buffer of "friendly" governments in Eastern Europe; imposed communism from outside
         i. there was also domestic support for communism
         ii. in Yugoslavia, development of a popular communist movement under Josef Broz (Tito)

C. China: A Prolonged Revolutionary Struggle
1. communism won in China in 1949, after a long struggle
   a. the Chinese imperial system had collapsed in 1911
   b. the Chinese Communist Party (CCP) was not founded until 1921
2. over the next 28 years, the CCP grew immensely and transformed its strategy under Mao Zedong
3. had a formidable enemy in the *Guomindang* (Nationalist Party), which ruled China after 1928
   a. Chiang Kai-shek led the Guomindang
   b. the Guomindang promoted modern development, at least in cities
   c. the countryside remained impoverished
4. the CCP was driven from the cities, developed a new strategy
   a. looked to the peasants for support, not city workers
   b. only gradually won respect and support of peasants
   c. given a boost by Japan's invasion of China
      i. destroyed Guomindang control of much of the country
      ii. meanwhile, the CCP grew enormously
      iii. CCP's People's Liberation Army waged vigorous war against Japanese invaders using guerrilla warfare tactics
      iv. the CCP instituted reforms in areas it controlled
5. the CCP addressed both foreign imperialism and peasant exploitation
   a. expressed Chinese nationalism and demand for social change
   b. gained a reputation for honesty, unlike the Guomindang

IV. **Building Socialism in Two Countries**
[see Lecture Strategy 1]
A. Joseph Stalin built a socialist society in the USSR in the 1920s and 1930s; Mao Zedong did the same in China in the 1950s and 1960s.
   1. first step: modernization and industrialization

2. serious attack on class and gender inequalities
3. both created political systems dominated by the Communist Party
   a. high-ranking party members were expected to exemplify socialism
   b. all other parties were forbidden
   c. the state controlled almost the entire economy
4. China's conversion to communism was a much easier process than that experienced by the USSR
   a. the USSR had already paved the way
   b. Chinese communists won the support of the rural masses
   c. but China had more economic problems to resolve
B. Communist Feminism
1. communist countries pioneered "women's liberation"
   a. largely directed by the state
   b. the USSR almost immediately declared full legal and political equality for women
   c. divorce, abortion, pregnancy leave, women's work were all enabled or encouraged
2. 1919: USSR's Communist Party set up *Zhenotdel* (Women's Department)
   a. pushed a feminist agenda
   b. male communist officials and ordinary people often opposed it
   c. Stalin abolished it in 1930
3. communist China also worked for women's equality
   a. Marriage Law of 1950 ordered free choice in marriage, easier divorce, the end of concubinage and child marriage, and equal property rights for women
   b. the CCP tried to implement pro-female changes against strong opposition
   c. women became much more active in the workforce
4. limitations on communist women's liberation
   a. Stalin declared the women's question "solved" in 1930
   b. no direct attack in either state on male domination within the family

  c. women retained burden of housework and child care as well as paid employment

  d. few women made it into top political leadership

 C. Socialism in the Countryside

  1. in both states, the communists took landed estates and redistributed the land to peasants

   a. Russia: peasants took and redistributed the land themselves

   b. China: land reform teams mobilized poor peasants to confront landlords and wealthier peasants

    i. 1 million–2 million landlords were killed in the process

  2. second stage of rural reform: effort to end private property in land by collectivizing agriculture

   a. in China, collectivization was largely peaceful (1950s)

   b. in the USSR, collectivization was imposed by violence (1928–1933)

    i. *kulaks* (rich peasants) were killed or deported

    ii. the result was a massive famine (around 5 million died)

   c. China's collectivization went further than the USSR's

    i. creation of huge "people's communes" during the Great Leap Forward (late 1950s)

    ii. the result was a massive famine (1959–1962) in which 20 million people or more died

 D. Communism and Industrial Development

  1. both states regarded industrialization as fundamental

   a. need to end humiliating backwardness and poverty

   b. desire to create military strength to survive in a hostile world

  2. China largely followed the model established by the USSR

   a. state ownership of property

   b. centralized planning (five-year plans)

   c. priority given to heavy industry

   d. massive mobilization of resources

   e. intrusive party control of the whole process

   f. both countries experienced major economic growth

    i. vast improvement in literacy and education

    ii. great increase in social mobility

    iii. rapid urbanization

    iv. development of a privileged bureaucratic and technological elite

  3. the USSR leadership largely accepted the social outcomes of industrialization

   a. gradual move away from revolutionary values

  4. China under Mao Zedong tried to combat the social effects of industrialization

   a. the Great Leap Forward (1958–1960) promoted small-scale industrialization in rural areas

    i. tried to spread technological education widely

    ii. hoped to bring full communism to the "people's communes" without waiting for industrial development

    iii. result: massive disruptions, accompanied by natural disasters, caused a massive famine

   b. the Great Proletarian Cultural Revolution (mid-1960s) **[see Discussion Topic 1]**

    i. intended to combat capitalist tendencies

    ii. effort to bring health care and education to the countryside

    iii. and to reinvigorate rural industrialization under local control

 E. The Search for Enemies

  1. the USSR and China under Stalin and Mao were rife with paranoia

   a. fear that important communists were corrupted by bourgeois ideas; became class enemies

   b. fear of a vast conspiracy by class enemies and foreign imperialists to restore capitalism

  2. USSR: the Terror (Great Purges) of the late 1930s

   a. enveloped millions of Russians, including tens of thousands of prominent communists

b. many were sentenced to harsh labor camps (the gulag)

c. nearly a million people were executed between 1936 and 1941

3. China: the search for enemies was a more public process

    a. the Cultural Revolution (1966–1969) escaped control of communist leadership

    b. Mao had called for rebellion against the Communist Party itself

    c. purge of millions of supposed capitalist sympathizers

    d. Mao had to call in the army to avert civil war

4. both the Terror and the Cultural Revolution discredited socialism and contributed to eventual collapse of communist experiment

V. East versus West: A Global Divide and a Cold War

A. Military Conflict and the Cold War

  1. Europe was the cold war's first arena

    a. Soviet concern for security and control in Eastern Europe

    b. American and British desire for open societies linked to the capitalist world economy **[see Classroom Activity 1]**

  2. creation of rival military alliances (NATO and the Warsaw Pact)

    a. American sphere of influence (Western Europe) was largely voluntary

    b. Soviet sphere (Eastern Europe) was imposed

    c. the "Iron Curtain" divided the two spheres

  3. communism spread into Asia (China, Korea, Vietnam), caused conflict **[see Lecture Strategy 2]**

    a. North Korea invaded South Korea in 1950

      i. bitter war (1950–1953), with Chinese and American involvement

      ii. ended in a standoff and a divided Korea

    b. Vietnam: massive U.S. intervention in the 1960s

      i. Vietnamese communists successfully united the country by 1975

4. major cold war–era conflict in Afghanistan

    a. a Marxist party took power in 1978 but soon alienated much of the population

    b. Soviet military intervention (1979–1989) met with little success

    c. USSR withdrew in 1989 under international pressure; communist rule of Afghanistan collapsed

5. the battle that never happened: Cuba

    a. Fidel Castro came to power in 1959

    b. nationalization of U.S. assets provoked U.S. hostility

    c. Castro gradually aligned himself with the USSR

    d. Cuban missile crisis (October 1962)

      i. Khrushchev deployed nuclear missiles in Cuba

      ii. the U.S. government detected the missiles

      iii. U.S. nearly invaded Cuba

      iv. Khrushchev and Kennedy reached a compromise

B. Nuclear Standoff and Third World Rivalry

  1. the USSR succeeded in creating a nuclear weapon in 1949

  2. massive arms race: by 1989, the world had nearly 60,000 nuclear warheads, with complex delivery systems

  3. 1949–1989: fear of massive nuclear destruction and even the possible extinction of humankind

  4. both sides knew how serious their destructive power was

    a. careful avoidance of nuclear provocation, especially after 1962

    b. avoidance of any direct military confrontation, since it might turn into a nuclear war

  5. both the U.S. and the USSR courted third world countries

    a. U.S. intervened in Iran, the Philippines, Guatemala, El Salvador, Chile, the Congo, and elsewhere because of fear of communist penetration

    b. the U.S. often supported corrupt, authoritarian regimes

    c. many third world countries resisted being used as pawns

d. some countries (e.g., India) claimed "nonalignment" status in the cold war

e. some tried to play off the superpowers against each other

   i. Indonesia received Soviet and Eastern European aid but destroyed the Indonesian Communist Party in 1965

   ii. Egypt turned toward the USSR when the U.S. wouldn't help build the Aswan Dam; turned back toward the U.S. in 1972

C. The United States: Superpower of the West, 1945–1975

1. the U.S. became leader of the West against communism

   a. led to the creation of an "imperial" presidency in the U.S.

   b. power was given to defense and intelligence agencies, creating a "national security state"

   c. fear that democracy was being undermined

   d. anticommunist witch-hunts (1950s) narrowed the range of political debate

   e. strengthened the influence of the "military-industrial complex"

2. U.S. military effort was sustained by a flourishing economy and an increasingly middle-class society

   a. U.S. industry hadn't been harmed by WWII, unlike every other major industrial society

   b. Americans were a "people of plenty"

   c. growing pace of U.S. investment abroad

3. American popular culture also spread around the world

   a. jazz, rock-and-roll, and rap found foreign audiences

   b. by the 1990s, American movies took about 70 percent of the European market

   c. around 20,000 McDonald's restaurants in 100 countries

D. The Communist World, 1950s–1970s **[see Lecture Strategy 3 and Classroom Activity 2]**

1. Nikita Khrushchev took power in the USSR in 1953; in 1956, he denounced Stalin as a criminal

2. the cold war justified a continuing Soviet emphasis on military and defense industries

   a. continuous government propaganda glorified the Soviet system and vilified America

3. growing conflict among the communist countries

   a. Yugoslavia rejected Soviet domination

   b. Soviet invasions of Hungary (1956–1957) and Czechoslovakia (1968) to crush reform movements

   c. early 1980s: Poland was also threatened with invasion

   d. brutal suppression of reform tarnished the image of Soviet communism, gave credence to Western views of the cold war as a struggle between tyranny and freedom

   e. sharp opposition between the USSR and China

     i. territorial disputes

     ii. ideological differences

     iii. rivalry for communist leadership

     iv. 1960: the USSR withdrew Soviet advisers and technicians from China

     v. China developed its own nuclear weapons

     vi. USSR and China were close to war by the late 1960s

   f. China went to war against a communist Vietnam in 1979

4. world communism reached its greatest extent in the 1970s

VI. **Comparing Paths to the End of Communism** [see Discussion Topic 2]

A. The communist era ended rapidly and peacefully between the late 1970s and 1991.

1. China: Mao Zedong died in 1976

   a. the CCP gradually abandoned Maoist socialism

2. Europe: popular movements overthrew communist governments in 1989

   a. USSR suffered political disintegration on Christmas Day, 1991

3. both cases show the *economic* failure of communism

   a. communist states couldn't catch up economically

   b. the Soviet economy was stagnant

    c. failures were known around the world

    d. economic failure limited military capacity

  4. both cases show the *moral* failure of communism

    a. Stalin's Terror and the gulag

    b. Mao's Cultural Revolution

    c. near-genocide in Cambodia

    d. all happened in a global climate that embraced democracy and human rights

B. China: Abandoning Communism and Maintaining the Party

  1. Deng Xiaoping came to power in 1976

    a. relaxed censorship

    b. released some 100,000 political prisoners

    c. dismantled collectivized farming system

  2. China opened itself to the world economy

    a. result: stunning economic growth and new prosperity

    b. also generated massive corruption among officials, urban inequality, pollution, and inequality between coast and interior

  3. the Chinese Communist Party has kept its political monopoly

    a. brutal crushing of democracy movement in late 1980s

    b. Tiananmen Square massacre

  4. China is now a "strange and troubled hybrid" that combines nationalism, consumerism, and new respect for ancient traditions

C. The Soviet Union: The Collapse of Communism and Country

  1. Mikhail Gorbachev became general secretary in mid-1980s

    a. launched economic reform program (*perestroika*, or "restructuring") in 1987

    b. was met with heavy resistance

    c. Gorbachev responded with *glasnost* ("openness") to greater cultural and intellectual freedoms

      i. effort to end the deep distrust between society and state

  2. glasnost revealed what a mess the USSR was (crime, prostitution, suicide, corruption, etc.)

    a. the extent of Stalin's atrocities was uncovered

    b. new openness to religious expression

    c. ending of government censorship of culture

  3. democratization—free elections in 1989

  4. move to end the cold war by making unilateral military cuts, negotiating arms control with U.S.

  5. but Gorbachev's reforms led to collapse of the USSR

    a. the planned economy was dismantled before a market-based system could develop

    b. new freedoms led to more strident demands

    c. subordinate states demanded greater autonomy or independence

    d. Gorbachev refused to use force to crush the protesters

  6. Eastern European states broke free from USSR-sponsored communism

  7. conservatives attempted a coup (August 1991)

    a. coup collapsed within three days, due to popular resistance

  8. fifteen new and independent states emerged from the breakup of the USSR

D. By 2000, the communist world had shrunk considerably.

  1. communism had lost its dominance completely in the USSR and Eastern Europe

  2. China had mostly abandoned communist economic policies

  3. Vietnam and Laos remained officially communist but pursued Chinese-style reforms

  4. Cuba: economic crisis in the 1990s, began to allow small businesses and private food markets

  5. North Korea is the most unreformed and Stalinist communist state left

  6. international tensions remain only in East Asia and the Caribbean

VII. Reflections: To Judge or Not to Judge: The Ambiguous Legacy of Communism

[see Discussion Topic 3 and Classroom Activity 3]

A. Many think that scholars shouldn't make moral judgments.

  1. but we can't help being affected by our own time and culture

2. it's more valuable to acknowledge the limits of cultural conditioning than to pretend to a dream of objectivity

3. judgments are a way of connecting with the past

B. Many continue to debate whether the Russian and Chinese revolutions were beneficial and whether the late twentieth-century reforms were good or bad.

1. communism brought hope to millions
2. communism killed and imprisoned millions

C. Is it possible to acknowledge such ambiguity?

USING *WAYS OF THE WORLD* IN THE CLASSROOM

Lecture Strategies

Lecture Strategy 1

"A tale of two communist leaders: Stalin and Mao." Both Joseph Stalin and Mao Zedong were denounced after their deaths for the brutality and harm inflicted by their regimes. The purpose of this lecture strategy is to consider the careers of the two men in greater detail, searching for positive as well as negative elements in their careers. Its objectives are:

- to explore how these two men rose to positions of power
- to examine the nature of that power, including the constitutional or other limitations, if any, within which they had to work
- to help students understand the realities of life under the rule of Stalin and Mao
- to present the massive death toll of both regimes, and to investigate the reasons for the widespread killing
- to consider the long-term legacies of Stalin and Mao

A good place to start is with the career of Stalin (1878–1953), since he is chronologically earlier than Mao. Some points to include are:

- what it meant to be general secretary of the Soviet Union's Communist Party
- the style of government that came to be known as "Stalinism"

- the goals of Stalin's programs to industrialize and collectivize the Soviet Union in the 1930s
- the reasons behind Stalin's political purges
- the gulag—who was sent there, what they did, the conditions of life there
- the role of the NKVD under Stalin
- to what degree the Soviet Union's eventual success in World War II was due to Stalin's leadership
- how much Stalin's policies can be blamed for the famine of 1932–1934
- the cult of personality during the Stalin regime (many great posters of Stalin can be found easily on the Internet)
- Soviet encouragement of advances in science
- moves to improve education, give equal rights to women, and improve health care
- Stalin's original burial in Lenin's Mausoleum, and the removal of his body in 1961
- how Stalin is regarded in Russia today

Mao Zedong (1893–1976), longtime chairman of the Chinese Communist Party, makes for an interesting contrast to Stalin. Some points worth emphasizing are:

- Mao's much more important leadership role in the revolution and the Chinese civil war
- Mao as writer and poet
- Mao's role in World War II
- the style of government that came to be known as "Maoism"
- the rationale behind, and the effects of, the Great Leap Forward (with comparison to Stalin's reforms; famine is an important consideration in both cases)
- the Hundred Flowers Campaign and its aftermath
- the Cultural Revolution of 1966–1969
- the cult of personality during Mao's reign
- the Chairman Mao Memorial Hall (mausoleum) in Tiananmen Square, Beijing
- what the Chinese think of Mao today

Lecture Strategy 2

"The 'hot wars' of the cold war era." Thanks to the History Channel, movies, and family stories, many students connect easily to the Korean and Vietnam wars (be aware that many people don't like to call U.S. involvement in either conflict a "war"). An exploration of these two East Asian conflicts can start with American involvement as the "hook" to engage students, going on from there to consider the two wars as important events in the history of the cold war. The objectives of this lecture strategy are:

- to educate students about the reasons underlying the Korean and Vietnam wars
- to consider the resources that China and the United States put into the war
- to examine the ways the wars were fought
- to investigate the costs of the wars for the people of the two countries
- to step back and examine the implications of the wars for the history of the cold war

Use a clip from a popular movie about the Vietnam War, something that shows the nasty reality of jungle fighting, as a beginning point to draw from students what they already know about the Korean and Vietnam wars. You will probably find that frighteningly few students know when or why the wars were fought. From there, it would be particularly useful to examine the two wars together, theme by theme, instead of discussing first one war and then the other. Major themes to consider for each war are:

- the extent of communism in each country before war broke out
- the role of Western colonialism in creating the conditions for war
- what caused the first shot to be fired
- how the United States got involved
- the *way* in which the United States was involved
- how and in what way other communist states became involved
- how deep the outside involvement was (it is very interesting, for example, to compare the percentage of their gross national product that China and the United States spent in Korea)
- the nature of the fighting that took place
- what the wars meant to the Korean and Vietnamese people
- how the wars ended
- long-term effects

Lecture Strategy 3

"Beyond the Iron Curtain: Life and death in communist Eastern Europe."
While communism had its problems in the USSR and China, at least it had developed organically from

perceived needs and a native response. Such was not the case in Eastern Europe, where Soviet occupation at the end of World War II led directly to the imposition of communism. This lecture strategy proposes to explore what communist rule and Soviet domination meant for Eastern Europe. More specifically, its objectives are:

- to examine the ways in which Eastern European governments were put in place after World War II
- to investigate ways in which communist rule improved life in East Germany, Poland, Czechoslovakia, etc.
- to examine ways in which communist rule was resented as a foreign imposition
- to explore the ways in which communists maintained control
- to consider why the communist regimes crumbled in 1989

A good place to begin is with a consideration of East and West Germany at the time they reunified in 1990. Compare the physical and ideological condition of the two regions, including industrial capability, condition of roads, public services, per capita income, attitude toward the government, and cultural life. Encourage students to discuss ways in which the two Germanies remained similar and ways that they diverged in the period 1949–1990.

From that point, consider the conditions of life in communist Eastern Europe more broadly. There are many possible approaches to this rich topic. Some points to consider for inclusion are:

- the condition of Eastern Europe in 1945
- Soviet reparations levied against the states of Eastern Europe
- how Yugoslavia managed to preserve relative freedom from the Soviet Union
- the Berlin Wall and its significance
- the Berlin airlift
- the Stasi and other police organizations and the nature of their repression
- anticommunist movements and rebellions and what the USSR did about them
- the Polish Solidarity movement
- sports (especially international sports)
- the education system
- the role of propaganda

- levels of economic development and prosperity and how they changed in the period 1945–1990
- the resettlement of millions of Poles (1945–1950)
- religious repression
- the "shortage economies" of the 1970s and 1980s
- what it meant to have a Polish pope (John Paul II)
- the Prague Spring of 1968
- the various ways in which communist rule was ended in 1989

Things to Do in the Classroom

Discussion Topics

1. Contextualization, large or small group.
"Cultural Revolution."
As briefly as possible, outline the major points and policies of the Chinese Cultural Revolution. Then ask students to discuss what effects such policies would have if imposed on modern America.

2. Comparison, large or small group.
"Communism goes bust."
Ask students to chart out the decline of communism in the USSR and China. First, have them decide on a number of categories for comparison (such as the source of reform ideas, government efforts to repress reformers, the revival of traditional ideas, etc.). Then ask them to list, in two columns, how each of these factors came into play during the breakup of communism in the USSR and China.

3. Misconception/Difficult Topic, large or small group.
"The communist 'experiment' was all bad."
While acknowledging that many bad things happened in the Soviet Union and China under communist rule, it is useful to remind students that few things are *all* bad. Ask various groups of students to focus on either the USSR or China, instructing them to discuss and make a list of main points about (1) conditions in that country before the communist revolution and (2) points that the text makes about real improvements for at least part of the population while under communism.

Classroom Activities

1. Analysis exercise, large or small group.
"President Kennedy at the Berlin Wall."
Play for the class a recording of John F. Kennedy's speech given in Berlin on June 26, 1963 (a recording of good quality is available at www.coug.com/kennedyinBerlin.htm). Then ask them to list the main points of the speech, and go on to discuss the speech's effectiveness as a propaganda masterpiece of the cold war. (Note: "Civis Romanus sum" is Latin for "I am a citizen of Rome." With the statement "Ich bin ein Berliner," the president intended to say "I am a citizen of Berlin." The fact that the phrase actually means "I am a jelly-filled doughnut" has been a matter of amusement among Germans for four decades; Kennedy *should* have said "Ich bin Berliner.")

2. Role-playing exercise, small group.
"An interview with the Stasi."
Select a small group of students to do research on the Stasi, the government police of communist East Germany. The rest of the class will play the role of applicants who want to be employed by this elite organization. Ask the "applicants" to reason out various methods the Stasi could have used to identify dissenters and maintain control of East Germany. It is the role of the experts to form a panel of Stasi officers who are weeding out applicants and who will tell the class if a suggested practice is one that the Stasi actually used or not.

3. Clicker question. Did communism do more harm than good to the people of the USSR and China?

Key Terms

Berlin Wall: Wall constructed by East German authorities in 1961 to seal off East Berlin from the West; it was breached on November 9, 1989.

Bolsheviks: Russian revolutionary party led by Vladimir Lenin and later renamed the Communist Party; the name "Bolshevik" means "the majority." (*pron.* BOWL-sheh-vik)

building socialism: Euphemistic expression for the often-forcible transformation of society when a communist regime came to power in a state.

Castro, Fidel: Revolutionary leader of Cuba from 1959 to 2008 who gradually turned to Soviet communism and engendered some of the worst crises of the cold war.

Chinese Revolution: Long revolutionary process in the period 1912–1949 that began with the overthrow of the Chinese imperial system and ended with the triumph of the Communist Party under the leadership of Mao Zedong.

cold war: Political and ideological state of near-war between the Western world and the communist world that lasted from 1946 to 1991.

collectivization: Process of rural reform undertaken by the communist leadership of both the USSR and China in which private property rights were abolished and peasants were forced onto larger and more industrialized farms to work and share the proceeds as a community rather than as individuals.

Comintern: In full, "Communist International"; Soviet organization intended to control the policies and actions of other communist states.

Cuban missile crisis: Major standoff between the United States and the Soviet Union in 1962 over Soviet deployment of nuclear missiles in Cuba; the confrontation ended in compromise, with the USSR removing its missiles in exchange for the United States agreeing not to invade Cuba.

Cultural Revolution: China's Great Proletarian Cultural Revolution was a massive campaign launched by Mao Zedong in the mid-1960s to combat the capitalist tendencies that he believed reached into even the highest ranks of the Communist Party; the campaign threw China into chaos.

Deng Xiaoping: Leader of China from 1976 to 1997 whose reforms essentially dismantled the communist elements of the Chinese economy. (*pron.* dung shee-yao-ping)

glasnost: Mikhail Gorbachev's policy of "openness," which allowed greater cultural and intellectual freedom and ended most censorship of the media; the result was a burst of awareness of the problems and corruption of the Soviet system. (*pron.* glaz-nost)

Gorbachev, Mikhail: Leader of the Soviet Union from 1985 to 1991 whose efforts to reform the USSR led to its collapse. (*pron.* MEE-ka-eel GORE-bah-CHOF)

Great Leap Forward: Major Chinese initiative (1958–1960) led by Mao Zedong that was intended to promote small-scale industrialization and increase knowledge of technology; in reality, it caused a major crisis and exacerbated the impact of a devastating famine.

Great Proletarian Cultural Revolution: Mao Zedong's great effort in the mid-1960s to weed out capitalist tendencies that he believed had developed in China.

Great Purges: Also called the Terror, the Great Purges of the late 1930s were a massive attempt to cleanse the Soviet Union of supposed "enemies of the people"; nearly a million people were executed between 1936 and 1941, and 4 million or 5 million more were sentenced to forced labor in the gulag.

gulag: Acronym for the Soviet government agency that administered forced labor camps. (*pron.* GOO-log)

Guomindang: The Chinese Nationalist Party led by Chiang Kai-shek from 1928 until its overthrow by the communists in 1949. (*pron.* gwo-min-dong)

Khrushchev, Nikita: Leader of the Soviet Union from 1953 to 1964. (*pron.* ni-KEE-tah KROOSH-chef)

Lenin: Adopted name of Vladimir Ilyich Ulyanov (1870–1924), the main leader of Russia's communist revolution and head of the Soviet state from 1917 until his death.

Mao Zedong: Chairman of China's Communist Party and *de facto* ruler of China from 1949 until his death in 1976. (*pron.* maow dzuh-dong)

McCarthyism: Wave of anticommunist fear and persecution that took place in the United States in the 1950s.

national security state: Form of government that arose in the United States in response to the cold war and in which defense and intelligence agencies gained great power and power in general came to be focused in the executive branch.

perestroika: Bold economic program launched in 1987 by Mikhail Gorbachev with the intention of freeing up Soviet industry and businesses. (*pron.* per-ih-STROY-kuh)

Russian Revolution: Massive revolutionary upheaval in 1917 that overthrew the Romanov dynasty in Russia and ended with the seizure of power by communists under the leadership of Vladimir Ilyich Lenin.

Stalin: Name assumed by Joseph Vissarionovich Jugashvili (1878–1953), leader of the Soviet Union from 1924 until his death; "Stalin" means "made of steel."

Warsaw Pact: Military alliance of the USSR and the communist states of Eastern Europe during the cold war.

Zhenotdel: Women's Department of the Communist Party in the Soviet Union from 1919 to 1930; Zhenotdel worked strongly to promote equality for women. (*pron.* zen-OHT-del)

ANSWER GUIDELINES FOR CHAPTER QUESTIONS

The two sets of questions that follow appear in the textbook at the end of the chapter and in the margins of the reading. They are also provided in the Computerized Test Bank with answer guidelines, for your convenience.

The Big Picture Questions

1. What was the appeal of communism, in terms of both its promise and its achievements? To what extent did it fulfill that promise?

 • In terms of its promises and achievements, communism promised a fairer distribution of society's wealth among the whole population;
 • modernization and industrialization of the economy;
 • and equality of all citizens, including women.
 • In terms of the extent to which it fulfilled these promises, communism can point to the redistribution and then the collectivization of land;
 • the impressive industrialization of communist countries;
 • and a substantial improvement in women's rights.
 • However, it must be noted that these accomplishments came at the cost of the creation of new elite classes.

2. Why did the communist experiment, which was committed to equality and a humane socialism, generate such oppressive, brutal, and totalitarian regimes?

 • An elastic concept of "enemy" came to include not only surviving remnants of the old prerevolutionary elites but also, and more surprisingly, high-ranking members and longtime supporters of the Communist Party who had allegedly been corrupted by bourgeois ideas. Refracted through the lens of Marxist thinking, these people became class enemies who had betrayed the revolution and were engaged in a vast conspiracy, often linked to foreign imperialists, to subvert the socialist enterprise and restore capitalism.
 • In an effort to combat capitalism and instill socialist values in society, communist regimes promoted the Communist Party's penetration of all levels of society in ways that some Western scholars have called totalitarian. As part of this process, the state came to control almost the entire economy; ensured that the arts, education, and the media conformed to approved ways of thinking; and controlled mass organizations for women, workers, students, and various professional groups.

3. What is distinctive about twentieth-century communist industrialization and modernization compared to the same processes in the West a century earlier?

 • The industrialization of communist countries was far more centrally planned than the same processes in the West were;
 • the capital and the factories were owned by the state in the Communist world but not in the West;
 • the Communist Party controlled industrialization in communist countries, whereas no political party controlled this process in the West;
 • unlike the West, a wealthy industrialist class did not emerge in communist countries, and the equivalent of the middle class in the West was dominated primarily by bureaucrats and the technological elite.

4. What was the global significance of the cold war?

 • The nuclear arms race that it spawned brought the threat of annihilation to the whole planet.
 • Regional wars and revolutionary insurrections, supported or opposed by one of the cold war superpowers, had an impact on regions across the globe.
 • In the postcolonial world, competition between cold war powers led to new relationships between third world countries and the global powers in which the United States and the Soviet Union both courted developing nations while those developing countries sought to define their relations with the superpowers to their advantage.

5.   "The end of communism was as revolutionary as its beginning." Do you agree with this statement?

• This question has no "right" answer and depends in large part upon how one defines "revolutionary."

• If one were to advocate the revolutionary nature of the end of communism, one could point to the profound changes that took place within communist countries following the abandonment of communism and argue that those changes were just as revolutionary for people living in those communist systems as the communist revolution was for those who lived in earlier capitalist systems.

• If one were to advocate the less revolutionary nature of the end of communism, one might emphasize that communist societies were in reality merely adopting aspects of their capitalist counterparts elsewhere in the world, and therefore the "revolutionary" nature of the transition away from communism was less pronounced than the original transition to a never-before-tried communist organization.

6.   In what different ways did the Soviet Union and China experience communism during the twentieth century?

• While many aspects of their experiences were similar, one critical difference was that, in the Soviet Union, the growth of a privileged bureaucratic and technological elite was largely accepted, whereas in China under Mao Zedong, there were recurrent attempts, including the Great Leap Forward and the Cultural Revolution, to combat these tendencies and revive the revolutionary spirit.

• As part of this process, Mao pushed several reforms, including the promotion of small-scale rural industrialization over urban industrialization, of widespread technical education, and of an immediate transition to communism in the "people's communes."

• The experiences of the Soviet Union and China also diverged dramatically after the mid-1970s, when Soviet communism failed to reform and ultimately collapsed completely, while Chinese communism reformed more slowly and without completely collapsing.

Margin Review Questions

Q.   *When and where did communism exercise influence during the twentieth century?*

• In 1917, Russia became the first country to embrace communism;

• communism also came to China, Eastern Europe, and the northern part of Korea in the wake of World War II;

• first the northern portion of Vietnam and then, after 1975, the whole of Vietnam became communist;

• communist parties took power in Laos and Cambodia in the mid-1970s;

• Cuba moved toward communism after Fidel Castro came to power in 1959;

• a shaky communist regime took power in Afghanistan in 1979, propped up briefly by the Soviet Union.

• After World War II, communist political parties also had influence in a number of nations, including Greece, France, and Italy.

• There was a small communist party in the United States that became the focus of an intense wave of fear and repression in the 1950s.

• Revolutionary communist movements threatened established governments in the Philippines, Malaya, Indonesia, Bolivia, Peru, and elsewhere.

• A number of African nations in the 1970s proclaimed themselves Marxist for a time and aligned with the Soviet Union in international affairs.

Q.   *Identify the major differences between the Russian and Chinese revolutions.*

• The revolution in China was a struggle of decades rather than a single year;

• unlike Russia, where intellectuals had been discussing socialism for half a century or more before the revolution, the ideas of Karl Marx were barely known in China in the early twentieth century;

• the Chinese communists faced a far more formidable political foe than the weak Provisional Government over which the Bolsheviks had triumphed in Russia;

• whereas the Bolsheviks in Russia found their primary audience among workers in Russia's major cities, Chinese communists increasingly looked to the country's peasant villages for support;

• Chinese peasants did not rise up spontaneously against their landlords, as Russian peasants had;

• Chinese communists ultimately put down deep roots among the peasantry in a way that the Bolsheviks never did;

• whereas the Bolsheviks gained support by urging Russian withdrawal from the highly unpopular First

World War, the Chinese communists won support by aggressively pursuing the struggle against Japanese invaders during World War II.

Q.   *Why were the Bolsheviks able to ride the Russian Revolution to power?*

• Impatience and outrage against the Provisional Government provided the Bolsheviks with an opening;
• the Bolsheviks' message—an end to the war, land for the peasants, workers' control of factories, and self-determination for non-Russian nationalities—resonated with an increasingly rebellious public mood;
• the Bolsheviks were able to seize power during an overnight coup in the capital city of St. Petersburg by claiming to act on the behalf of the highly popular soviets, in which they had a major presence;
• the Bolsheviks defeated their enemies in a three-year civil war.

Q.   *What was the appeal of communism in China before 1949?*

• The Chinese communists addressed head-on both of China's major problems—foreign imperialism and peasant exploitation.
• The Chinese Communist Party (CCP) expressed Chinese nationalism as well as a demand for radical social change.
• Chinese communists gained a reputation for honesty that contrasted sharply with the massive corruption of their opponents.
• The CCP gained a reputation for effective resistance against the Japanese invaders and offered a measure of security to many Chinese faced with Japanese atrocities.
• The CCP put down deep roots among the peasantry, making real changes in peasant lives in the areas it controlled, reducing rents, taxes, and interest payments for peasants and teaching literacy to adults.

Q.   *What changes did communist regimes bring to the lives of women?*

• In the Soviet Union, the communist government declared full legal and political equality for women;
• marriage became a civil procedure among freely consenting adults;
• divorce was legalized and made easier, as was abortion;
• illegitimacy was abolished;
• women no longer had to take their husbands' surnames;
• pregnancy leave for employed women was mandated;
• women were actively mobilized as workers in the country's drive to industrialization;
• the party set up a special organization called Zhenotdel (Women's Department), whose radical leaders, all women, pushed a decidedly feminist agenda in the 1920s by organizing conferences for women, training women to run day-care centers and medical clinics, publishing newspapers and magazines aimed at a female audience, providing literacy and prenatal classes, and encouraging Muslim women to take off their veils.
• In China, the Marriage Law of 1950 was a direct attack on patriarchal and Confucian traditions, decreeing free choice in marriage;
• relatively easy divorce;
• the end of concubinage and child marriage;
• permission for widows to remarry;
• and equal property rights for women;
• the Chinese Communist Party also launched a Women's Federation, a mass organization that enrolled millions of women, although its leadership was less radical than that of Zhenotdel.

Q.   *How did the collectivization of agriculture differ between the USSR and China?*

• In Russia, the peasants had spontaneously redistributed the land among themselves, and the victorious Bolsheviks merely ratified their actions. In China after 1949, it was a more prolonged and difficult process that featured "speak bitterness meetings" at which peasants were encouraged to confront and humiliate landlords. Ultimately the process resulted in the death of between 1 million and 2 million landlords.
• A second and more distinctively socialist stage of rural reform sought to end private property in land by collectivizing agriculture. In China, despite brief resistance from richer peasants, collectivization during the 1950s was a generally peaceful process. In the Soviet Union, peasant resistance to collectivization in the period 1928–1933 led to extensive violence.
• China pushed the collectivization process further than the Soviet Union did, particularly in huge "people's communes" during the "Great Leap Forward" in the late 1950s.

Q. *What were the achievements of communist efforts at industrialization? What problems did these achievements generate?*

• As far as achievements, both the Soviet Union and China experienced major—indeed unprecedented—economic growth;

• living standards improved;

• literacy rates and educational opportunities improved massively, allowing far greater social mobility for millions of people than ever before.

• As far as problems, industrialization brought rapid urbanization;

• exploitation of the countryside to provide for modern industry in the cities;

• and the growth of a privileged bureaucratic and technological elite intent on pursuing their own careers and passing on their new status to their children.

Q. *Why did communist regimes generate terror and violence on such a massive scale?*

• An elastic concept of "enemy" came to include not only surviving remnants of the old prerevolutionary elites but also, and more surprisingly, high-ranking members and longtime supporters of their respective communist parties who had allegedly been corrupted by bourgeois ideas. Refracted through the lens of Marxist thinking, these people became class enemies who had betrayed the revolution and were engaged in a vast conspiracy, often linked to foreign imperialists, to subvert the socialist enterprise and restore capitalism.

• Large-scale purges took place in light of these fears, including the Terror in the Soviet Union and the Cultural Revolution in China.

Q. *In what different ways was the cold war expressed?*

• The cold war was expressed in a number of ways: through rival military alliances known as NATO and the Warsaw Pact;

• through a series of regional wars, especially the "hot wars" in Korea and Vietnam and a later conflict in Afghanistan;

• in tense standoffs like the Cuban missile crisis;

• in a nuclear arms race;

• through competition for influence in third world countries across the globe;

• and by fomenting revolutionary groups across the world.

Q. *In what ways did the United States play a global role after World War II?*

• The United States spearheaded the Western effort to contain a worldwide communist movement that seemed to be on the move;

• deployed its military might around the world;

• became the world's largest creditor and its chief economic power;

• and became an exporter of popular culture.

Q. *Describe the strengths and weaknesses of the communist world by the 1970s.*

• In terms of strengths, communism had reached the greatest extent of its worldwide expansion in the 1970s;

• the Soviet Union had achieved its long-sought goal of matching U.S. military might.

• In terms of weaknesses, divisions within the communist world increased, especially between Eastern Europe and the Soviet Union, China and the Soviet Union, and China and Vietnam;

• the horrors of Stalin's Terror and the gulag, of Mao's Cultural Revolution, and of something approaching genocide in communist Cambodia all wore away at communist claims to moral superiority over capitalism.

Q. *What explains the end of the communist era?*

• Despite their early successes, communist economies by the late 1970s showed no signs of catching up to the more advanced capitalist countries.

• The horrors of Stalin's Terror and the gulag, of Mao's Cultural Revolution, and of something approaching genocide in communist Cambodia all wore away at communist claims to moral superiority over capitalism.

Q. *How did the end of communism in the Soviet Union differ from communism's demise in China?*

• The Soviet reform program was far more broadly based than that of China, embracing dramatic cultural and political changes that China refused to consider.

• Unlike what transpired in China, the reforms of the Soviet Union spun it into a sharp economic decline.

• Unlike Chinese peasants, few Soviet farmers were willing to risk the jump into private farming, and few foreign investors found the Soviet Union a tempting place to do business.

• In contrast to what occurred in China, the Soviet Union's reform program led to the political collapse of the state.

ADDITIONAL RESOURCES FOR CHAPTER 22

Additional Bedford/St. Martin's Resources

FOR INSTRUCTORS

Computerized Test Bank

This test bank provides over thirty exercises per chapter, including multiple-choice, fill-in-the-blank, short-answer, and full-length essay questions. Instructors can customize quizzes, add or edit both questions and answers, and export questions and answers to a variety of formats, including WebCT and Blackboard. The disc includes correct answers and essay outlines.

Instructor's Resource CD-ROM

This disc provides instructors with ready-made and customizable PowerPoint multimedia presentations built around chapter outlines, maps, figures, and all images from the textbook, plus JPEG versions of all maps, figures, and images.

The following maps and images from Chapter 22 are available in both JPEG and PowerPoint format on the Instructor's Resource CD-ROM:

- Map 22.1: Russia in 1917 (p. 663)
- Map 22.2: The Rise of Communism in China (p. 667)
- Map 22.3: The Global Cold War (p. 676)
- Map 22.4: The Collapse of the Soviet Empire (p. 686)
- Lenin (p. 658)
- Mao Zedong and the Long March (p. 665)
- Mobilizing Women for Communism (p. 669)
- Substituting Manpower for Machinery (p. 673)
- The Hydrogen Bomb (p. 677)
- Czechoslovakia, 1968 (p. 680)
- After Communism in China (p. 683)

FOR STUDENTS

Documents and Essays from *Worlds of History: A Comparative Reader,* Third Edition (Volume 2)

The following document to accompany Chapter 22 is available in Chapter 13 of Volume 2 of this reader by Kevin Reilly:

- *The Marriage Law of the People's Republic of China*

Online Study Guide at bedfordstmartins.com/strayer

The Online Study Guide helps students synthesize the material from the text as well as practice the skills historians use to make sense of the past. Each chapter of the Online Study Guide contains specific testing exercises, including a multiple-choice self-test that focuses on important conceptual ideas; an identification quiz that helps students remember key people, places, and events; a flashcard activity that tests students on their knowledge of key terms; and two interactive map activities intended to strengthen students' geographic skills. Instructors can monitor students' progress through an online Quiz Gradebook or receive email updates.

Further Reading

Cold War Hot Links: Some Cold War Web Resources, http://homepages.stmartin.edu/fac_staff/dprice/cold.war.htm. A very thorough collection of Internet resources on the cold war.

The Cold War Museum—Fall of the Soviet Union, http://www.coldwar.org/articles/90s/fall_of_the_soviet_union.asp. A useful site, with exhibits and a convenient timeline of events.

Davies, Norman. *God's Playground.* New York: Columbia University Press, 1982. An excellent one-volume history of Poland.

East & Southeast Asia: An Annotated Directory of Internet Resources: The Korean War, http://newton.uor.edu/Departments&Programs/AsianStudiesDept/korea-war.html. A fascinating collection of materials on the Korean War.

East & Southeast Asia: An Annotated Directory of Internet Resources: The Vietnam War, http://newton.uor.edu/Departments&Programs/AsianStudiesDept/vietnam-war.html. Another excellent site managed by the Asian Studies Department at the University of Oregon.

Fulbrook, Mary. *Anatomy of a Dictatorship: Inside the GDR, 1949–1989.* Oxford: Oxford University Press, 1995. An interesting study of the East German communist government.

Tiananmen, April–June 1989, http://www.christusrex. org/www1/sdc/tiananmen.html. A photo archive of the Chinese student protests in Tiananmen Square in 1989 and the ensuing massacre.

Literature

Akhmatova, Anna. *Selected Poems.* Trans. D. M. Thomas. London: Penguin, 1992. One of the greatest female poets of all time, Akhmatova (1889–1966) presents a magnificently chilling vision of Stalin's Great Purges.

Bulgakov, Mikhail. *The Master and Margarita.* New York: Vintage, 1996. Written in the 1930s, but not published until 1967—for reasons that become obvious while reading this allegorized indictment of Stalin's regime.

Carré, John le. *The Spy Who Came In from the Cold.* New York: Scribner, 2001. The first novel of a great writer who was himself a British agent in Berlin in the early stages of the cold war.

Fleming, Ian. Any of the author's James Bond novels—great tales of espionage in the cold war.

Ma Bo. *Blood Red Sunset: A Memoir of the Chinese Cultural Revolution.* Trans. Howard Goldblatt. London: Penguin, 1996. A particularly effective memoir by a supposed "counterrevolutionary" who survived the Cultural Revolution.

Mao Zedong (Tse-Tung). *Quotations from Chairman Mao Tse-Tung.* San Francisco: China Books & Periodicals, Inc., 1990. Used by millions of Chinese people during Mao's regime, this volume includes his thoughts on most aspects of communism and the future of China.

Orwell, George. *Animal Farm.* New York: Plume, 2003. Short enough for classroom use, this darkly comedic novel from 1945 tells of socialism gone awry.

Orwell, George. *1984.* New York: Plume, 2003. Perhaps the most chilling dystopia ever written, this 1949 novel is the classic tale of one man's search for freedom in a communist police state of the future.

Solzhenitsyn, Aleksandr. *One Day in the Life of Ivan Denisovich.* Trans. H. T. Willetts. 2nd ed. New York: Farrar, Straus and Giroux, 2005. First published in 1962, this short but painful novel based on the author's firsthand experience tells of life in a labor camp in Siberia.

Zamyatin, Yevgeny. *We.* Trans. Clarence Brown. London: Penguin, 1993. Originally published in 1920, this novel is a prophetic look at the future of Soviet communism.

Film

China at the Crossroads. Insight Media, 2000. 26 minutes. Examines contemporary China in the period of the reform program initiated by Deng Xiaoping.

China Through Mao's Eyes. Four-part series. Films for the Humanities and Sciences, 2005. 60 minutes each. An overview of the Chinese communist revolution, with a focus on the communist leader Mao Zedong; divided into four hour-long episodes: "1893–1945: Against the Tide—Mao's Early Years," "1945–1959: The Sorcerer's Apprentice—Founding the Republic," "1958–1969: Not a Dinner Party—The Cultural Revolution," and "1970 and Beyond: Mao Is Not Dead."

Communism. Films for the Humanities and Sciences, 1995. 49 minutes. Provides an overview of the rise and decline of world communism.

Communism: The Fall of the Romanovs and the Berlin Wall. Insight Media, 2003. 51 minutes. Focusing on two crucial moments in twentieth-century history, this film explores the birth and death of the Soviet Union.

The Cultural Revolution: Mao's Last Battle. Two-part series. Films for the Humanities and Sciences, 2003. 53 minutes each. Examines China's Cultural Revolution in two episodes: "No Rest for the Weary: The Cultural Revolution and Its Origins" and "The Unfortunate Generation: The Cultural Revolution and Beyond."

Eastern Europe: 1953–1991. Films for the Humanities and Sciences, 1991. 55 minutes. Provides an overview of Eastern Europe in the post-Stalin communist era.

Inside the Cold War with Sir David Frost. Two-part series. Films for the Humanities and Sciences, 1998. 48 minutes and 50 minutes. Examines the course of the cold war between the capitalist and communist worlds in two episodes: "Superpowers Collide" and "Powerplay: End of an Empire."

The Life and Times of Joseph Stalin. Films for the Humanities and Sciences, 90 minutes. Explores the life and career of this central figure in Soviet history.

The Nuclear Age. Films for the Humanities and Sciences, 1995. 49 minutes. Traces the development of nuclear weapons and their importance to the cold war.

October 1917: Lenin's Story. Two-part series. Films for the Humanities and Sciences, 2007. 52 minutes each. Two episodes ("The People's Revolution" and "Lenin's Revolution") that examine the course of the Bolshevik seizure of power in Russia and Lenin's role in it.

Soviet Disunion: Ten Years That Shook the World. Films for the Humanities and Sciences, 1995. 57 minutes. Focuses on the ten years of glasnost and perestroika that defined the Soviet reform efforts of the 1980s.

Independence and Development in the Global South

1914–Present

CHAPTER OVERVIEW

Chapter Objectives

• To explore the breakup of imperial systems in the twentieth century
• To consider, through the examples of India and South Africa, how the process of decolonization worked
• To examine the challenges that faced developing nations in the second half of the twentieth century
• To investigate the potential clash of tradition with modernity in the developing nations, especially considering the case of Islam in Turkey and Iran

Chapter Outline

I. **Opening Vignette**
  A. Nelson Mandela of South Africa spent 27 years in prison for treason, sabotage, and conspiracy.
    1. in 1994, he became South Africa's first black president

  B. Decolonization was vastly important in the second half of the twentieth century.
    1. the newly independent states experimented politically, economically, and culturally
    2. these states were labeled as the third world during the cold war
      a. now are often called developing countries or the Global South
      b. they include a large majority of the world's population
      c. suffer from enormous challenges

II. **Toward Freedom: Struggles for Independence**
  A. The End of Empire in World History
    1. India, Pakistan, Burma, Indonesia, Iraq, Jordan, and Israel won independence in the late 1940s
    2. African independence came between mid-1950s and mid-1970s
      a. more than 50 colonies won freedom
    3. imperial breakup wasn't new; the novelty was mobilization of the masses around a nationalist ideology and creation of a large number of new nation-states
      a. some comparison to the first decolonization of the late eighteenth and early nineteenth centuries

b. but in the Americas, most colonized people were of European origin, holding a common culture with their colonial rulers
4. fall of many empires in the twentieth century
   a. Austrian and Ottoman empires collapsed in the wake of WWI
   b. Russian Empire collapsed but was soon recreated as the USSR
   c. German and Japanese empires ended with WWII
   d. African and Asian independence movements shared with other "end of empire" stories the ideal of national self-determination
   e. nonterritorial empires (e.g., where U.S. wielded powerful influence) came under attack
      i. U.S. intrusion helped stimulate the Mexican Revolution (1910)
      ii. as in Mexico, Cuban revolution (1959–1960) included nationalization of assets dominated by foreign investors
   f. disintegration of the USSR (1991) was propelled by national self-determination (creation of 15 new states)
B. Explaining African and Asian Independence
   1. few people would have predicted imperial collapse in 1900
   2. several explanations for decolonization have emerged:
      a. emphasis on the fundamental contradictions in the colonial enterprise
         i. rhetoric of Christianity and material progress didn't fit the reality of racism, exploitation, and poverty
         ii. Europeans' increasingly democratic values were in conflict with colonial dictatorship
         iii. ideal of national self-determination was at odds with repression of the same in colonies
      b. historians use the idea of "conjuncture" to explain timing of decolonization
         i. the world wars had weakened Europe and undermined a sense of European superiority

      ii. the U.S. and USSR opposed older European colonial empires
      iii. the UN provided a platform for anticolonial moves
      iv. these factors helped create a moral climate in which imperialism was viewed as wrong
      v. by the early to mid-twentieth century, the colonies had multiple generations of Western-educated elites
   c. some scholars emphasize the role of specific groups and individuals—the issue of "agency"
      i. in many areas, colonial powers themselves planned for independence of colonies
      ii. pressure of nationalist movements
      iii. the leaders of some nationalist movements became the "fathers" of new states: Gandhi and Nehru (India), Sukarno (Indonesia), Ho Chi Minh (Vietnam), Nkrumah (Ghana), Mandela (South Africa)
      iv. millions of ordinary people joined in
   3. independence was contested everywhere
      a. independence efforts usually were not cohesive movements of uniformly oppressed people
      b. fragile coalitions of conflicting groups and parties

III. **Comparing Freedom Struggles**
   [see Lecture Strategy 1]
   A. The Case of India: Ending British Rule
      [see Classroom Activity 1]
      1. before 1900, few people of the Indian subcontinent thought of themselves as "Indians"
         a. cultural identity was primarily local
         b. diversity was enormous
      2. British rule promoted a growing sense of Indian identity
         a. unlike earlier foreign rulers, the British didn't assimilate; Indians shared more similarities to each other than to the rulers
         b. British communications and administrative networks, schools, and use of English bound India together
      3. 1885: establishment of the Indian National Congress (INC)

a. almost exclusively an association of English-educated, high-caste Hindus

b. made moderate demands; at first asked for a greater role in the life of British India

c. British mocked them and rejected their claim to speak for all Indians

d. the INC only began to gain a wide following after WWI

   i. in 1917, Britain promised future development of self-government

   ii. British attacks on the Ottoman Empire antagonized Muslim Indians

   iii. repressive actions by the British caused outrage

4. the role of Mohandas Gandhi (1869–1948)

a. had studied law in England but wasn't a very successful lawyer

b. in 1893, took a job in South Africa

   i. joined a movement to fight racial segregation there

   ii. developed a notion of India that included both Hindus and Muslims

c. developed the political philosophy of *satyagraha* ("truth force")

   i. active but nonviolent confrontation

d. back in India, Gandhi became a leader of the INC

   i. 1920s and 1930s: periodic mass campaigns that won massive public support

   ii. British responded with repression and concessions

   iii. Gandhi transformed the INC into a mass organization

   iv. won the name "Mahatma" (Great Soul)

e. attacked not just colonial rule but also mistreatment of India's untouchables and the evils of modernization

5. not everyone agreed with Gandhi

a. especially important was a growing Muslim/Hindu divide

b. 1906: creation of an All-India Muslim League

c. some Hindu politicians defined the nationalist struggle in religious terms

d. Muhammad Ali Jinnah, head of the Muslim League, argued that regions of India with a Muslim majority should be a separate state (Pakistan, the land of the pure)

6. independence in 1947 created two countries

a. Pakistan (Muslim, divided into two wings 1,000 miles apart)

b. India (secular but mostly Hindu)

c. process was accompanied by massive violence; some 1 million died, 12 million refugees relocated

7. 1948: a Hindu extremist assassinated Gandhi

B. The Case of South Africa: Ending Apartheid

1. South Africa won freedom from Great Britain in 1910

2. but its government was controlled by a white settler minority

a. so the black South African freedom struggle was against an internal opponent

3. white population was split between British descendants (had economic superiority) and Afrikaners (Boers) of Dutch descent (had political dominance)

a. Afrikaners had failed to win independence from the British in the Boer War (1899–1902)

b. both white groups felt threatened by any move toward black majority rule

4. by the early 1900s, South Africa had a mature industrial economy

a. by the 1960s, had major foreign investments and loans

b. black South Africans were extremely dependent on the white-controlled economy

c. the issue of race was overwhelmingly prominent

   i. policy of apartheid tried to keep blacks and white completely separate, while retaining black labor power

   ii. enormous repressive powers enforced social segregation

5. African National Congress (ANC) founded in 1912

a. like India's INC, it consisted of elite Africans who wanted a voice in society

b. for 40 years, the ANC was peaceful and moderate

c. 1950s: moved to nonviolent civil disobedience

d. the government's response was overwhelming repression

   i. 69 unarmed demonstrators were shot at Sharpville in 1960

   ii. ANC was banned and its leadership imprisoned

6. underground nationalist leaders turned to sabotage and assassination

a. opposition came to focus on student groups

b. Soweto uprising (1976) was the start of spreading violence

c. organization of strikes

7. growing international pressure

a. exclusion from international sporting events

b. economic boycotts

c. withdrawal of private investment funds

8. negotiations began in the late 1980s

a. key apartheid policies were abandoned

b. Mandela was freed and the ANC legalized

9. 1994: national elections brought the ANC to power

a. apartheid was ended without major bloodshed

b. most important threat was a number of separatist and "Africans only" groups

IV. Experiments with Freedom

A. New nations emerging from colonial rule confronted the problem of how to parlay independence into economic development and industrial growth, unification, and political participation.

1. already independent but nonindustrialized countries faced the same quest for a better life

2. all together = the third world (developing countries, the Global South)

3. 1950–2000: developing nations contained 75 percent of world population

a. accounted for almost all of the quadrupling of world population in the twentieth century

4. independence created euphoria, but optimism soon faded in light of difficulties

B. Experiments in Political Order: Comparing African Nations and India **[see Discussion Topic 1]**

1. common conditions confronted all efforts to establish political order:

a. explosive population growth

b. overly high expectations for independence

c. cultural diversity, with little loyalty to a central state

2. in the 1950s, British, French, and Belgians set up democratic institutions in their African colonies

a. few still survived by the early 1970s

b. many were swept away by military coups

c. some evolved into one-party systems

3. in India, Western-style democracy succeeded

a. the independence movement was more extended, and power was handed over gradually

b. many more Indians than Africans had administrative and technical skills at the time of independence

c. the Indian Congress Party embodied the whole nationalist movement, without too much internal discord

4. various arguments as to why Africans initially rejected democracy **[see Lecture Strategy 2]**

a. some argue that the Africans were not ready for democracy or lacked some necessary element

b. some argue that African traditional culture (communal, based on consensus) was not compatible with party politics

c. some argue that Western-style democracy was inadequate to the task of development

5. widespread economic disappointment discredited early African democracies

a. African economic performance since independence has been poor

b. widespread economic hardship

c. modern governments staked their popularity on economic success

6. the well-educated elite benefited most, obtaining high-paying bureaucratic jobs that caused resentment

7. economic resentment found expression in ethnic conflict
8. repeatedly, the military took power in a crisis
9. starting in the 1980s, Western-style democracy has resurfaced
    a. series of grassroots movements arose after authoritarian governments failed to improve economic situation

C. Experiments in Economic Development: Changing Priorities, Varying Outcomes **[see Discussion Topic 2]**
1. the belief that poverty isn't inevitable won out
    a. however, in many states, colonial rule had not provided much infrastructure for modern development
    b. most developing countries didn't have leverage in negotiation with wealthy nations and corporations
    c. African leaders got contradictory advice on how to develop successfully
2. general expectation in the developing world that the state would spur economic development
    a. most private economies were weakly developed
    b. Chinese and Soviet industrialization provided models
    c. but for several decades, there has been growing dependence on market forces for economic development
        i. many states privatized state-run industries
        ii. influenced by collapse of the USSR's state-dominated economy
        iii. Western pressures pushed developing countries toward capitalism
3. urban vs. rural development has been an important issue
    a. in some areas, the "urban bias" has been partly corrected
    b. women's access to employment, education, and birth control provided incentives to limit family size
4. debate over whether foreign aid, investment, and trade are good or bad
5. the degree of economic development has varied widely by region
    a. East Asia has been the most successful

b. 1990s: India opened itself more fully to the world market
c. several Latin American states developed industrially
d. most of Africa, much of the Arab world, and parts of Asia didn't catch up, and standards of living often declined
e. there is no general agreement about why such great variations developed

D. Experiments with Culture: The Role of Islam in Turkey and Iran **[see Lecture Strategy 3]**
1. the relationship between Western-style modernity and tradition has been an issue across the developing world
2. the case of Islam: Turkey and Iran approached the issue of how Islam and modernity should relate to each other very differently
3. Turkey: emerged in the wake of WWI, led by Mustafa Kemal Atatürk (1881–1938)
    a. major cultural revolution in the 1920s and 1930s
    b. effort to create a thoroughly modern, Western society
    c. much of the Islamic underpinning of society was abolished or put under firm government control
        i. effort to keep Islam personal, rather than an official part of public life
    d. men were ordered not to wear the *fez*; many elite women gave up the veil
    e. women gained legal rights, polygamy was abolished, and women got the vote (1930s)
    f. state-organized enterprises were set up
    g. government remained authoritarian, although a parliamentary system emerged after 1938
4. Iran: became the center of Islamic revival (1970s) **[see Discussion Topic 3 and Classroom Activity 2]**
    a. growing opposition to Shah Muhammad Reza Pahlavi's modernizing, secularizing, U.S.-supported government
    b. many of the shah's reforms offended traditional Islamic practices
    c. the mosque became the main center of opposition to the government

     i. the Shia ulama had stayed independent from the state

     ii. Shia leaders became the voice of opposition, especially the Ayatollah Khomeini

   d. the shah was forced to abdicate in 1979, and Khomeini assumed control of the state

     i. established the sharia as the law of the land

     ii. secular officials were purged

     iii. rejection of many Western practices as anti-Islamic

   e. the Islamic revolution in Iran wasn't revolutionary in social terms

     i. Iran also continued to work on economic modernity

V. Reflections: History in the Middle of the Stream [see Classroom Activity 3]

  A. It is difficult for historians to discuss more recent events and themes like those described in this chapter, because that history is still in the making.

   1. detachment is difficult

   2. we don't know what the final outcomes will be

  B. Historians know how unexpected and surprising historical processes can be.

   1. but still, history is our only guide to the possible shape of the future

   2. the history of modern events provides a useful reminder that people in earlier times didn't know the way things would turn out either

USING *WAYS OF THE WORLD* IN THE CLASSROOM

Lecture Strategies

Lecture Strategy 1

"Expanding independence."
Since this chapter focuses only on two sample cases of former colonies winning independence, this lecture strategy proposes casting the net rather wider, creating a comparative analysis of two or three more independence movements in addition to those included in the text. The objectives of this lecture strategy are:

- to encourage student understanding of the scope of decolonization in the twentieth century
- to give students a better idea of the common features of decolonization and some important regional variations
- to present the histories of Israel, Botswana, and Algeria as examples of important variants of the decolonization theme

It is convenient to begin with Israel, chronologically the earliest of the three independence movements to be discussed in this lecture. Some important points to include are:

- the Zionist movement and massive settlement of Jews in Palestine
- the Balfour Declaration and how it was interpreted
- British efforts to halt Jewish immigration
- the degree of British control in the Palestinian Mandate
- the partitioning of the mandate between Arab Palestine and a new state of Israel
- the creation of Israel in the context of the Holocaust
- Israel's wars for survival and territorial expansion

Algeria endured a very different kind of decolonization. The state won its independence from France only after considerable violence, and Algeria still struggles to find a clear national identity. Some major points are:

- French control of and settlement in Algeria
- major French investment in Algeria (especially in the oil industry)
- the war of independence and mass exodus of the *pieds-noirs* (French settlers in Algeria)
- the rise of militant Islam in Algeria
- the state of Algeria today

Finally, Botswana's peaceful progress to independence, political stability, and modest prosperity make a pleasant contrast to the otherwise depressing tale of decolonization in Africa. It would be useful to include the following points:

- the establishment of the Bechuanaland Protectorate by Great Britain

- Botswana's proposals for self-government, and Britain's acceptance of them
- the leadership of Seretse Khama
- the political stability of Botswana

Lecture Strategy 2

"Dictatorship and the new nations."

Africa has seen an extraordinary number of military coups and dictatorships since independence. This lecture strategy proposes examining the phenomenon of military dictatorship in third world countries in greater detail, focusing on Africa but pulling in examples from other developing nations. Its main objectives are:

- to help students understand why military dictatorships are so common in the Global South
- to explore the conditions that make dictatorship possible and sometimes even preferable
- to examine how dictators come to power and how they fall

A good place to start is with some consideration of what a dictator actually is. From there, go on to present a single "typical" dictator, establishing a base from which to explore the phenomenon more widely. Here is a list of dictators whom you might explore for this lecture:

- Idi Amin (Uganda)
- Suharto (Indonesia)
- Saddam Hussein (Iraq)
- Augusto Pinochet (Chile)
- Fidel Castro (Cuba)
- Robert Mugabe (Zimbabwe)
- Blaise Compaore (Burkina Faso)
- Joseph Kabila (Congo-Kinshasa)
- Charles Taylor (Liberia)
- Houari Boumedienne (Algeria)

Some themes to consider are:

- ethnic cleansing or genocide
- stability of the new military regime
- human rights abuses
- positive economic steps taken by the dictator
- alignment of the dictator in relation to other states

Lecture Strategy 3

"Religion and the third world."

The text provided the interesting example of how Islam has confronted modernization in Turkey and Iran. This lecture strategy is intended to expand the exploration of religion in the developing nations. Its objectives are:

- to encourage students to consider religion as both a unifying and a divisive factor in the third world
- to investigate the rapid spread of Islam and Christianity in the third world
- to consider what has become of traditional religions in the Global South

A good place to begin is with a map of the major religions of the world in 2000, such as can be found at www.justmaps.org/maps/thematics/religions.asp#. Go on from there to discuss the massive spread of evangelical and Pentecostal Christianity in Africa in recent decades and the Islamization of central Africa. Other related points include:

- the restoration of Russian Orthodoxy and the rapid spread of evangelical Christianity in parts of the former Soviet Union
- the revival of Confucianism in China
- the massive missionary enterprises of the Church of Jesus Christ of Latter-day Saints

More important is the question of what these religions mean to third world countries. Try to address the following points:

- Does religion provide some of the social and national glue that many third world countries do not receive from their governments?
- What is the texture of religious life in Roman Catholic South America? How does it differ from the practice of Islam in Nigeria or of Pentecostalism in Botswana?
- Which religions still maintain an active missionary presence in the third world, and what effect does a foreign presence have on those states?
- What is the relationship between religion and social services in the third world?
- What is the relationship between world religions like Christianity and Islam and the native religions of the developing nations?

Things to Do in the Classroom

Discussion Topics

1. **Misconception/Difficult Topic, large or small group.** "What's *wrong* with Africa?"
It is very common to hear the belief expressed that there must be something wrong with Africa to make most of the continent as impoverished, genocidal, and dictator-ridden as it is today. Ask your students to compile the evidence in the textbook that would support the argument that the new nations of Africa have been doing the best they could do in the face of the enormous social and economic challenges they inherited from the colonial era. Then ask them to discuss this evidence and how convincing they find it.

2. **Contextualization, large or small group.** "Africa in the news."
Ask students to collect all the news stories they can find about Africa for a week (hinting at extra credit for unusual news stories should assure a good selection). Go over the main news items in class, and then lead a discussion on the relationship between what's in the news today and the saga of Africa winning independence and struggling to develop economically.

3. **Comparison, large or small group.** "Islam's reaction to the West."
Ask students to outline the main points of this chapter's discussion of Iran's Islamic revolution. Then ask them to discuss similarities and dissimilarities between that movement and modern Islamic radical fundamentalism (as represented by the Taliban and al-Qaeda).

Classroom Activities

1. **Close-reading exercise, small group.** "Indian independence."
Distribute to the class Jawaharlal Nehru's "Speech on the Granting of Indian Independence," which he delivered on August 14, 1947 (a transcript of the speech can be found at http://www.fordham.edu/halsall/mod/1947nehru1.html). Ask students to identify the main themes of the speech, and go on to discuss how well they think India has lived up to this message of hope since 1947.

2. **Analysis exercise, large or small group.** "Islamic revolution in Iran."
A quick Google image search will provide you with a large number of images of the Iranian revolution. Pick some representative samples (e.g., a poster of Khomeini, mass rallies, American hostages, one of the many propaganda posters that shows the shah hanging on to Uncle Sam's coattails). Show them to the class and encourage discussion of the lessons that can be garnered from the images.

3. **Clicker question.** Do you believe that democracy is the ideal model of government and that it should be in place throughout the world?

Key Terms

African National Congress: South African political party established in 1912 by elite Africans who sought to win full acceptance in colonial society; it only gradually became a popular movement that came to control the government in 1994.

Atatürk, Mustafa Kemal: Founder and first president of the Republic of Turkey (1881–1938); as military commander and leader of the Turkish national movement, he made Turkey into a secular state. (*pron.* moo-STAH-fah kem-AHL at-ah-TURK)

Black Consciousness: South African movement that sought to foster pride, unity, and political awareness among the country's African majority and often resorted to violent protest against white minority rule.

Boers: Also known as Afrikaners, the sector of the white population of South Africa that was descended from early Dutch settlers. (*pron.* bores)

decolonization: Process in which many African and Asian states won their independence from Western colonial rule, in most cases by negotiated settlement with gradual political reforms and a program of investment rather than through military confrontation.

democracy in Africa: A subject of debate among scholars, the democracies established in the wake of decolonization in Africa proved to be fragile and often fell to military coups or were taken over by single-party authoritarian systems; Africa's initial rejection of democracy has sometimes been taken as a sign that Africans were not ready for democratic politics or that traditional African culture did not support it.

economic development: A process of growth or increasing production and the distribution of the proceeds of that growth to raise living standards;

nearly universal desire for economic development in the second half of the twentieth century reflected a central belief that poverty was no longer inevitable.

Gandhi, Mohandas K.: Usually referred to by his soubriquet "Mahatma" (Great Soul), Gandhi (1869–1948) was a political leader and the undoubted spiritual leader of the Indian drive for independence from Great Britain. (*pron.* moh-HAHN-dahs GAHN-dee)

Indian National Congress: Organization established in 1885 by Western-educated elite Indians in an effort to win a voice in the governance of India; over time, the INC became a major popular movement that won India's independence from Britain.

Jinnah, Muhammad Ali: Leader of India's All-India Muslim League and first president of the breakaway state of Pakistan (1876–1948). (*pron.* moo-HAHM-ad ah-LEE jee-NAH)

Khomeini, Ayatollah Ruholla: Important Shia *ayattolah* (advanced scholar of Islamic law and religion) who became the leader of Iran's Islamic revolution and ruled Iran from 1979 until his death in 1989. (*pron.* A-hat-ol-LAH ROOH-ol-LAH ko-MAY-nee)

Mandela, Nelson: South African nationalist (b. 1918) and leader of the African National Congress who was imprisoned for twenty-seven years on charges of treason, sabotage, and conspiracy to overthrow the apartheid government of South Africa; he was elected president of South Africa in 1994, four years after he was finally released from prison. (*pron.* man-DEL-ah)

Muslim League: The All-India Muslim League, created in 1906, was a response to the Indian National Congress in India's struggle for independence from Britain; the League's leader, Muhammad Ali Jinna, argued that regions of India with a Muslim majority should form a separate state called Pakistan.

Nehru, Jawaharlal: The first prime minister of independent India (1889–1964). (*pron.* jaw-WAH-harlal NAY-roo)

Pahlavi, Muhammad Reza: Born in 1919, Pahlavi was shah of Iran from 1941 until he was deposed and fled the country in 1979; he died in 1980. (*pron.* moo-HAHM-ad RAY-zah pah-LAV-ee)

satyagraha: Literally, "truth force"; Mahatma Gandhi's political philosophy, which advocated confrontational but nonviolent political action. (*pron.* sah-TYAH-grah-hah)

Soweto: Impoverished black neighborhood outside Johannesburg, South Africa, and the site of a violent uprising in 1976 in which hundreds were killed; that rebellion began a series of violent protests and strikes that helped end apartheid. (*pron.* sow-WAY-toe)

ANSWER GUIDELINES FOR CHAPTER QUESTIONS

The two sets of questions that follow appear in the textbook at the end of the chapter and in the margins of the reading. They are also provided in the Computerized Test Bank with answer guidelines, for your convenience.

The Big Picture Questions

1. In what ways did the colonial experience and the struggle for independence shape the agenda of developing countries in the second half of the twentieth century?

• Colonization and decolonization created a new national identity, which took shape in opposition to the imperial power. Central to this agenda was the establishment of stable governing institutions and a new civil society.

• Economic development provided the second critical element in the agenda as newly free states sought both to increase production and to distribute the fruits of that growth to raise living standards, a central promise of independence movements.

2. To what extent did the experience of the former colonies and developing countries in the twentieth century parallel that of the earlier "new nations" in the Americas in the eighteenth and nineteenth centuries?

• All sought to define their states following periods of dominance by European powers;
• they claimed international status equivalent to that of their former rulers;
• they often secured freedom through revolutionary struggle;
• they sought to develop their economies, which were heavily influenced by their past and continued interactions with the industrial nations of the West.

3. How would you compare the historical experience of India and China in the twentieth century?

• In the early part of the century, both India and China found themselves under considerable Western influence, with India being part of the British Empire and China partially occupied by several European powers;

• both secured their independence in the 1940s, but China did so through revolutionary struggle, while India did so through more peaceful means;

• India in the second half of the century maintained a democratic government, while China adopted a communist government.

• India maintained private property, even if the state provided tariffs, licenses, loans, subsidies, and overall planning; the Chinese adopted a communist approach to industrialization before slowly shifting to a more capitalistic approach.

• Both grew rapidly in the final decades of the century to emerge as economic powers.

4. How has the experience of modern development in the third world differed from that of the capitalist West and the communist East?

• The third world drew on both capitalist and communist economic models rather than coalescing around one or the other.

• Unlike the capitalist West and, to a lesser extent, the communist East, the third world had to contend with a colonial legacy that often left its societies with few of the resources needed to modernize, as they possessed low rates of literacy, few people with managerial experience, a weak private economy, and transportation systems oriented to export rather than national integration.

Margin Review Questions

Q. *What was distinctive about the end of Europe's African and Asian empires compared to other cases of imperial disintegration?*

• Never before had the end of empire been so associated with the mobilization of the masses around a nationalist ideology;

• nor had earlier cases of imperial dissolution generated such a plethora of nation-states, each claiming an equal place in a world of nation-states.

Q. *What international circumstances and social changes contributed to the end of colonial empires?*

• In terms of international circumstances, the world wars weakened Europe, while discrediting any sense of European moral superiority;

• both the United States and the Soviet Union, the new global superpowers, generally opposed the older European colonial empires;

• the United Nations provided a prestigious platform from which to conduct anticolonial agitation.

• In terms of social circumstances, by the early twentieth century in Asia and the mid-twentieth century in Africa, a second or third generation of Western-educated elites, largely male, had arisen throughout the colonial world. These young men were thoroughly familiar with European culture, were deeply aware of the gap between its values and its practices, no longer viewed colonial rule as a vehicle for their peoples' progress as their fathers had, and increasingly insisted on independence now;

• growing numbers of ordinary people also were receptive to this message.

Q. *What obstacles confronted the leaders of movements for independence?*

• Leaders had to organize political parties, recruit members, plot strategy, develop an ideology, and negotiate both with one another and with the colonial power to secure the transition to independence;

• in some regions—particularly settler-dominated colonies and Portuguese territories—leaders also directed military operations and administered liberated areas;

• beneath the common goal of independence, anticolonial groups struggled with one another over questions of leadership, power, strategy, ideology, and the distribution of material benefits.

Q. *Was India's freedom struggle a success? Consider the question from several points of view.*

• The freedom struggle was a success in that India secured political independence from Britain.

• However, it was not a complete success for Gandhi, as his vision of one India was thwarted by religious divisions between Muslims and Hindus.

• Those killed or displaced during the partition of India also must have seen the freedom struggle as less than a complete success.

Q. *What was the role of Gandhi in India's struggle for independence?*

• He pioneered active and confrontational, though nonviolent, strategies of resistance that underpinned the Indian independence movement;

• he became a leader in the Indian National Congress during the 1920s and 1930s;

• he played a critical role in turning the INC into a mass organization.

Q. *What conflicts and differences divided India's nationalist movement?*

• Gandhi opposed industrialization, but his chief lieutenant, Jawaharlal Nehru, supported it.

• Not all nationalists accepted Gandhi's nonviolence or his inclusive definition of India.

• Some militant Hindus preached hatred of Muslims.

• Some saw efforts to improve the position of women or untouchables as a distraction from the chief task of gaining independence from Britain.

• There was disagreement about whether to participate in British-sponsored legislative bodies without complete independence.

• A number of smaller parties advocated on behalf of particular regions or castes.

• There was a growing divide between India's Hindu and Muslim populations, which led to arguments that India was really two nations rather than one.

Q. *Why was African majority rule in South Africa delayed until 1994, whereas the overthrow of European colonialism had occurred much earlier in the rest of Africa and Asia?*

• Black South Africans' freedom struggle was against their country's white settler minority, rather than against a European colonial power;

• the intransigence of the sizable and threatened settler community played a role in the delay;

• the extreme dependence of most Africans on the white-controlled economy rendered individuals highly vulnerable to repressive action, though collectively the threat to withdraw their essential labor also provided them with a powerful weapon;

• race was a much more prominent issue in South Africa, expressed most clearly in the policy of apartheid, which attempted to separate blacks from whites in every conceivable way while retaining their labor power in the white-controlled economy.

Q. *How did South Africa's struggle against white domination change over time?*

• In the opening decades of the twentieth century, the educated, professional, and middle-class Africans who led the political party known as the African National Congress sought not to overthrow the existing order but to be accepted as "civilized men" within that society. They appealed to the liberal, humane, and Christian values that white society claimed. For four decades, the leaders of the ANC pursued peaceful and moderate protest, but to little effect.

• During the 1950s, a new and younger generation of the ANC leadership broadened its base of support and launched nonviolent civil disobedience.

• In the 1960s, following the banning of the ANC, underground nationalist leaders turned to armed struggle, authorizing selected acts of sabotage and assassination, while preparing for guerrilla warfare in camps outside the country;

• the 1970s and 1980s saw an outbreak of protests in sprawling, segregated, and impoverished black neighborhoods as well as an increasingly active black labor movement.

• The South African freedom struggle also benefited from increasing international pressure on the apartheid government.

Q. *Why was Africa's experience with political democracy so different from that of India?*

• The struggle for independence in India had been a far more prolonged affair, thus providing time for an Indian political leadership to sort itself out.

• Britain began to hand over power in India in a gradual way well before complete independence was granted.

• Because of these factors, a far larger number of Indians had useful administrative or technical skills than was the case in Africa.

• Unlike most African countries, the nationalist movement in India was embodied in a single national party, the INC, whose leadership was committed to democratic practice.

• The partition of India at independence eliminated a major source of internal discord.

• Indian statehood could be built on cultural and political traditions that were far more deeply rooted than in most African states.

Q. *What accounts for the ups and downs of political democracy in postcolonial Africa?*

• Some have argued that Africans lacked some crucial ingredient for democratic politics—an educated electorate, a middle class, or perhaps a thoroughly capitalist economy.

• Others have suggested that Africa's traditional culture, based on communal rather than individualistic values and concerned to achieve consensus rather than majority rule, was not compatible with the competitiveness of party politics.

• Some have argued that Western-style democracy was simply inadequate for the tasks of development confronting the new states;

• creating national unity was more difficult when competing political parties identified primarily with particular ethnic or "tribal" groups;

• the immense problems that inevitably accompany the early stages of economic development may be compounded by the heavy demands of a political system based on universal suffrage.

• Widespread economic disappointment weakened the popular support of many postindependence governments in Africa and discredited their initial democracies.

Q. *What obstacles impeded the economic development of third world countries?*

• The quest for economic development took place in societies divided by class, religion, ethnic groups, and gender and occurred in the face of explosive population growth.

• colonial rule had provided only the most slender foundations for modern development to many of the newly independent nations, which had low rates of literacy, few people with managerial experience, a weak private economy, and transportation systems oriented to export rather than national integration;

• development had to occur in a world split by rival superpowers and economically dominated by the powerful capitalist economies of the West;

• developing countries had little leverage in negotiations with the wealthy nations of the Global North and their immense transnational corporations;

• it was hard for leaders of developing countries to know what strategies to pursue.

Q. *In what ways did thinking about the role of the state in the economic life of developing countries change? Why did it change?*

• At the opening, people in the developing world and particularly those in newly independent countries expected that state authorities would take major responsibility for spurring the economic development of their countries, and some state-directed economies had real successes.

• But in the last several decades of the twentieth century, the earlier consensus in favor of state direction largely collapsed, replaced by a growing dependence on the market to generate economic development.

• At the dawn of the new millennium, a number of Latin American countries were once again asserting a more prominent role for the state in their quests for economic development and social justice.

Q. *In what ways did cultural revolutions in Turkey and Iran reflect different understandings of the role of Islam in modern societies?*

• The cultural revolution in Turkey sought to embrace modern culture and Western ways fully in public life and to relegate Islam to the sphere of private life. With that in mind, almost everything that had made Islam an official part of Ottoman public life was dismantled, and Islam was redefined as a modernized personal religion, available to individual citizens of a secular Turkish state.

• The cultural revolution in Iran cast Islam as a guide to public as well as private life. With this goal in mind, the sharia became the law of the land, and religious leaders assumed the reins of government. Culture and education were regulated by the state according to Islamic law.

ADDITIONAL RESOURCES FOR CHAPTER 23

Additional Bedford/St. Martin's Resources

FOR INSTRUCTORS

Computerized Test Bank

This test bank provides over thirty exercises per chapter, including multiple-choice, fill-in-the-blank,

short-answer, and full-length essay questions. Instructors can customize quizzes, add or edit both questions and answers, and export questions and answers to a variety of formats, including WebCT and Blackboard. The disc includes correct answers and essay outlines.

Instructor's Resource CD-ROM

This disc provides instructors with ready-made and customizable PowerPoint multimedia presentations built around chapter outlines, maps, figures, and all images from the textbook, plus JPEG versions of all maps, figures, and images.

The following maps and images from Chapter 23 are available in both JPEG and PowerPoint format on the Instructor's Resource CD-ROM:

- Map 23.1: The End of European Empires (p. 694)
- Map 23.2: South Africa after Apartheid (p. 704)
- Map 23.3: The "Worlds" of the Twentieth Century (p. 705)
- Map 23.4: Political Life in Postindependence Africa (p. 709)
- Nelson Mandela (p. 690)
- Mahatma Gandhi (p. 697)
- Independence in Kenya, East Africa (p. 702)
- Microloans (p. 712)
- Westernization in Turkey (p. 716)
- Women and the Iranian Revolution (p. 718)

FOR STUDENTS

Online Study Guide at bedfordstmartins.com/strayer

The Online Study Guide helps students synthesize the material from the text as well as practice the skills historians use to make sense of the past. Each chapter of the Online Study Guide contains specific testing exercises, including a multiple-choice self-test that focuses on important conceptual ideas; an identification quiz that helps students remember key people, places, and events; a flashcard activity that tests students on their knowledge of key terms; and two interactive map activities intended to strengthen students' geographic skills. Instructors can monitor students' progress through an online Quiz Gradebook or receive email updates.

Further Reading

African Studies Center: Africa: Country Pages, http://www.africa.upenn.edu/Home_Page/Country .html. A good collection of Internet resources on Africa, arranged by country.

Clark, Nancy L., and William H. Worger. *South Africa: The Rise and Fall of Apartheid*. London: Longman, 2004. A clear and readable account of the history of apartheid.

Daniel, E. Valentine. *Charred Lullabies*. Princeton, NJ: Princeton University Press, 1996. An important study of nationalist violence.

Darwin, John. *The End of the British Empire: The Historical Debate*. Oxford: Wiley-Blackwell, 2006. A nice short look at the historiography of why the British Empire came to an end.

Davidson, Basil. *The Black Man's Burden: Africa and the Curse of the Nation-State*. New York: Times Books, 1992. A thought-provoking book about nationalism and its discontents in Africa.

India Virtual Library, http://www.southasianist.info/india/index.html. An interesting collection of resources on India.

Mahatma Gandhi Album, http://www.kamat.com/mmgandhi/. A collection of materials on Gandhi, including a nice selection of photographs.

Literature

Achebe, Chinua. *Things Fall Apart*. New York: Anchor, 1994. This first novel by acclaimed author Chinua Achebe was published in 1958, two years before Nigeria won its independence. It tells of life in an Ibo clan and how the clan's traditional life unravels.

Dangarembga, Tsitsi. *Nervous Conditions*. Seattle: Seal Press, 1988. This novel tells the story of a girl coming of age in colonial Rhodesia of the 1960s and conveys the enormous cultural strains on that society.

Gandhi, Mohandas. *Gandhi: An Autobiography: The Story of My Experiments with Truth*. Boston: Beacon, 1993. A selective autobiography that provides a great deal of food for thought.

McCall Smith, Alexander. *The No. 1 Ladies' Detective Agency*. New York: Anchor Books, 2002. The first volume of an immensely popular, gentle, and thoughtful series showing the rhythms of life in modern Botswana.

Paton, Alan. *Cry, the Beloved Country*. 2nd ed. New York: Vintage, 2002. First published in 1948, this is a moving depiction of life under apartheid in South Africa.

Sadat, Jehan. *A Woman of Egypt*. New York: Simon & Schuster, 2002. An autobiographical account by the widow of Egyptian leader Anwar Sadat, with much useful material about the changing role of women in Islam and the tension between Islam and modernity.

Singh, Khushwant. *Train to Pakistan*. New York: Grove, 1956. A powerful novel about the partition of India in 1947.

Tutu, Desmond. *No Future without Forgiveness*. New York: Doubleday, 1999. A fascinating look at the healing of South Africa in the wake of apartheid, written by the Anglican archbishop of Cape Town and chair of the Truth and Reconciliation Commission.

Film

Africa: In Defiance of Democracy. Films for the Humanities and Sciences, 2001. 56 minutes. Explores the history of democracy in postcolonial Africa.

The Battle for Islam. Insight Media, 2005. 63 minutes. An up-to-date exploration of the tension within Islamic societies between secular and religious forces, including a segment on Turkey.

India after Independence. Films for the Humanities and Sciences, 1991. 21 minutes. A short film that focuses on the crucial years following independence in 1947.

India of the Gandhis. Insight Media, 2004. 52 minutes. This film explores the influence of Gandhi and his followers and family on the history of postindependence India.

Iran. Films for the Humanities and Sciences, 2003. 37 minutes. Explores contemporary Iran with reference to the impact of governing the country using Islamic principles.

Mahatma Gandhi: The Great Soul Lives. Films for the Humanities and Sciences, 1998. 60 minutes. A biography of Gandhi's life, including his training in London and his time in South Africa.

Mandela: From Prison to President. Films for the Humanities and Sciences, 1994. 52 minutes. A biography of this important leader of the African National Congress who became president of South Africa.

A New South Africa. Insight Media, 2001. 60 minutes. Examines the emergence of a postapartheid South Africa.

Spear of the Nation: The Story of the African National Congress. Films for the Humanities and Sciences, 1986. 52 minutes. Explores the history of the African National Congress from its foundation.

The Third World: An Introduction. Insight Media, 1983. 21 minutes. A short introduction to the third world and its postcolonial history.

Accelerating Global Interaction

Since 1945

CHAPTER OVERVIEW

Chapter Objectives

- To consider the steps since 1945 that have increasingly made human populations into a single "world" rather than citizens of distinct nation-states
- To explore the factors that make it possible to speak now of a true "world economy"
- To explore the debate about economic globalization
- To raise student awareness of global liberation movements, especially feminism, and their implications for human life
- To investigate the "fundamentalist" religious response to aspects of modernity
- To consider environmentalism as a matter that cannot help but be global because the stakes are so high for all humankind
- To step back and ponder the value of studying history

Chapter Outline

I. **Opening Vignette**
   A. The discussion of Barbie and Ken dolls shows the power of global commerce today.
      1. but it also shows reaction to the values portrayed by Barbie/Ken elsewhere in the world, e.g., Iran
      2. Iran created new dolls (Sara and Dara) that displayed Iranian Muslim values and practices
      3. but the Sara/Dara dolls and the Barbie/Ken dolls were all made in China
   B. Throughout the twentieth century, a dense web of political relationships, economic transactions, and cultural influences increasingly bound the world together.
      1. by the 1990s, this process of accelerating engagement was known as globalization
      2. globalization has a long history upon which twentieth-century globalization was built
      3. pace of globalization increased rapidly after WWII

II. Global Interaction and the Transformation of the World Economy [see Classroom Activity 1]

A. Most commonly, "globalization" refers to international economic transactions.
   1. has come to seem inevitable to many since 1950
   2. global economic linkages contracted significantly in the first half of the twentieth century, especially between the two world wars
   3. the capitalist winners of WWII were determined not to repeat the Great Depression
      a. Bretton Woods (New Hampshire) agreements (1944):
         i. established the World Bank and the International Monetary Fund
         ii. laid the foundation for postwar globalization
         iii. the "Bretton Woods system" promoted relatively free trade, stable currencies linked to the U.S. dollar, high levels of capital investment
      b. technology also helped accelerate economic globalization
   4. 1970s: major capitalist countries dropped many controls on economic activity; increasingly viewed the world as a single market
      a. this approach was known as neo-liberalism
      b. favored reduction of tariffs, free global movement of capital, a mobile and temporary workforce, privatization of state enterprises, less government regulation of the economy, tax and spending cuts
      c. neo-liberalism was imposed on many poor countries as a condition for giving them loans
      d. the breakdown of communist state-controlled economies furthered the process

B. Reglobalization **[see Discussion Topic 1]**
   1. global economic transactions quickened dramatically after WWII
   2. world trade skyrocketed ($57 billion in 1947; over $7 trillion in 2001)
   3. money became highly mobile globally
      a. foreign direct investment (FDI), especially after 1960
      b. short-term investment in foreign currencies or stocks
      c. international credit cards, allowing easy transfer of money to other countries (e.g., in 2003, MasterCard was accepted in 210 countries or territories)
   4. central to the process are transnational corporations (TNCs), huge global businesses that operate in many countries simultaneously
      a. some TNCs have greater economic clout than many countries
      b. by 2000, 51 of the world's 100 largest economic units were TNCs, not countries
   5. large numbers of workers, both laborers and professionals, have moved all over the world from poor countries to richer ones
      a. millions more people have sought refuge in the West from oppression or civil war at home
      b. hundreds of millions of short-term international travelers and tourists

C. Disparities and Resistance
   1. economic globalization accompanied, and maybe helped generate, the greatest economic growth spurt in world history; immense creation of wealth
      a. life expectancies rose nearly everywhere; infant mortality declined
      b. literacy rates increased
      c. great decline in poverty
   2. massive chasm has developed between rich industrialized countries and everyone else
      a. ratio between the income of the top and bottom 20 percent of world's population was 3:1 in 1820; 86:1 in 1991
      b. the great disparity has shaped almost everyone's life chances
         i. provided the foundation for a new kind of global conflict
         ii. new fights over rules for world trade, foreign aid, representation in international economic organizations,

indebtedness, and environmental and labor standards

   c. growing disparities between the developing countries made common action difficult

3. growing economic inequality within individual states, both rich and poor

   a. the U.S. lost millions of manufacturing jobs, forcing factory workers into lower-paying jobs, while others prospered in high-tech industries

   b. northern Mexico (with links to the U.S.) became much more prosperous than southern Mexico

     i. reflected in the Chiapas rebellion, which began in 1994

   c. in China, urban income by 2000 was three times that of rural income

4. growing popular movement against globalization emerged in the 1990s

   a. involves people from both rich and poor countries

   b. they argue that free-trade, market-driven corporate globalization:

     i. lowers labor standards

     ii. is bad for the environment

     iii. keeps poor countries from protecting themselves

     iv. ignores local cultures and human rights

   c. attracted global attention with massive protest at World Trade Organization meeting in Seattle (1999)

   d. 2001: alternative globalization activists created the World Social Forum to coordinate strategy and share experiences

D. Globalization and an American Empire **[see Lecture Strategy 1]**

1. for many, opposition to corporate free-trade globalization = opposition to growing U.S. power and influence in the world

   a. often seen as an "American Empire"

   b. most Americans deny that America is an empire

   c. perhaps best described as an "informal empire" like those exercised by

Europeans in China and the Middle East in the nineteenth century

     i. marked by economic penetration, political pressure, and periodic military action, not direct governance

     ii. use of immense wealth to entice or intimidate

     iii. "soft power" of cultural attractiveness

2. the collapse of the Soviet Union and the end of the cold war left the U.S. without any equivalent power in opposition

   a. the U.S. was able to act unilaterally against Afghanistan and Iraq after being attacked by Islamic militants on September 11, 2001

   b. establishment of a lasting peace is more elusive

   c. the U.S. is in a new global struggle, to contain or eliminate Islamic "terrorism"

3. the U.S. has faced growing international economic competition since about 1975

   a. U.S. share of overall world production: about 50 percent in 1945; 20 percent in the 1980s

   b. sharp reversal of U.S. trade balance: U.S. imports now far exceed its exports

4. armed struggle against U.S. intervention in Vietnam, Cuba, Iraq, etc.

   a. during the cold war, some states turned toward the USSR to limit U.S. influence; France even withdrew from NATO in 1967

   b. intense dislike of American "cultural imperialism"

   c. by 2000, widespread opposition to U.S. international policies

     i. U.S. refused to accept International Criminal Court jurisdiction

     ii. U.S. refused to ratify the Kyoto protocol on global warming

     iii. U.S. doctrine of preemptive war used in Iraq

     iv. U.S. use of torture

5. the global exercise of American power has also caused controversy *within* the U.S.

   a. the Vietnam War split the country worse than anything since the Civil War

   b. the U.S. invasion of Iraq provoked similar protests and controversies

III. The Globalization of Liberation: Comparing Feminist Movements [see Lecture Strategy 2]

A. The idea of liberation traveled around the world in the twentieth century.

   1. the 1960s in particular saw a convergence of protest movements around the world, suggesting a new global culture of liberation

      a. U.S.: civil rights, youthful counterculture, antiwar protests

      b. Europe: protests against unresponsive bureaucracy, consumerism, middle-class values (especially in France in 1968)

      c. communist world: attempt to give socialism a human face in Czechoslovakia ("Prague spring," 1968)

         i. movement was crushed by the Soviet Union

      d. China: Cultural Revolution

   2. development of the idea of a third world

      a. dream of offering an alternative to both capitalism and communism; cultural renewal

      b. third world ideology exemplified by Che Guevara (d. 1967): effort to replicate the liberation of the Cuban revolution through guerrilla warfare in Africa and Latin America

   3. among all the liberation movements, feminism had the most profound potential for change

      a. rethinking of basic relationships between men and women

      b. began in the West in the nineteenth century (suffrage)

B. Feminism in the West

   1. organized feminism revived in the West (1960s) with a new agenda

      a. against historic understanding of women as "other" or deviant

      b. demanded right of women to control their own bodies

      c. agenda of equal rights in employment and education

   2. "women's liberation": broad attack on patriarchy as a system of domination

      a. consciousness raising: becoming aware of oppression

      b. open discussion of issues involving sexuality

   3. black women emphasized solidarity with black men, not separation from them

C. Feminism in the Global South

   1. women had been welcomed in communist and revolutionary movements but were sidelined after movements' success

   2. many African feminists (1970s) thought Western feminists were too individualistic and too focused on sex

      a. resented Western feminists' interest in cultural matters like female circumcision and polygamy

      b. many African governments and many African men identified feminism with colonialism

   3. not all women's movements dealt explicitly with gender

      a. Kenya: women's group movement supported individual women and communities

      b. Morocco: feminist movement targeted law defining women as minors; women finally obtained legal equality in 2004

      c. Chile: women's movement during Augusto Pinochet's dictatorship (1973–1990) crossed class and party lines, helped groups survive economically, exposed human rights abuses

      d. South Korea: women joined a mass popular movement that brought democracy by the late 1980s

         i. drew heavily on the experience and exploitation of young female workers in the country's export industries

D. International Feminism

   1. the "woman question" became a global issue in the twentieth century

      a. patriarchy lost some of its legitimacy

      b. UN declared 1975 as International Women's Year

      c. and declared 1975–1985 as the Decade for Women

      d. UN sponsored a series of World Conferences on Women

      e. by 2006, 183 nations had ratified the UN Convention to Eliminate Discrimination against Women

2. sharp divisions within global feminism
    a. Who has the right to speak on behalf of women?
    b. conflict between developed and developing nations' interests
    c. third world groups often disagreed
3. global backlash
    a. view that feminism had undermined family life

IV. **Religion and Global Modernity**
  A. Modernity presented a challenge to the world's religions.
    1. "advanced" thinkers of the eighteenth–twentieth centuries believed that supernatural religion was headed for extinction
    2. sharp decline in religious belief and practice in some places
    3. spread of scientific culture convinced small minorities that the only realities worth considering were those that could be measured scientifically
    4. but the most prominent trends of the last century have been the further spread of major world religions, their resurgence in new forms, and their attacks on elements of a secular and global modernity
    5. Buddhist ideas and practices were well received in the West
      a. Christianity spread even further; majority of Christians are no longer in Europe and the U.S.
      b. Islam also spread widely
      c. religious pluralism on a level never before seen
  B. Fundamentalism on a Global Scale
    [see Discussion Topic 2]
    1. "fundamentalism" is a major reaction against modernization and globalization
      a. a militant piety, defensive and exclusive
      b. has developed in every major religious tradition
    2. many features of the modern world appear threatening to established religion
      a. have upset customary class, family, and gender relationships
      b. nation-states (often associated with a particular religion) were undermined by the global economy and foreign culture

      c. disruption was often caused by foreigners from the West
    3. fundamentalists have responded with selective rejection of modernity
      a. actively use modern communication technology
    4. the term "fundamentalism" comes from U.S. religious conservatives in the early twentieth century; called for a return to the fundamentals of Christianity
      a. many saw the U.S. on the edge of a moral abyss
      b. in the 1970s, began to enter the political arena as the religious right
    5. another fundamentalism, called *Hindutva*, or Hindu nationalism, developed in India in the 1980s
      a. formed a political party (Bharatiya Janata Party)
      b. opposed state efforts to cater to Muslims, Sikhs, and the lower castes
      c. BJP promoted a distinct Hindu identity in education, culture, and religion
  C. Creating Islamic Societies: Resistance and Renewal in the World of Islam
    [see Classroom Activity 2]
    1. Islamic fundamentalism is the most prominent fundamentalism of the late twentieth century
      a. Osama bin Laden and the attack on the World Trade Center on September 11, 2001
      b. WTC destruction is only one sign of a much bigger phenomenon
    2. great disappointments in the Muslim world by the 1970s
      a. new states (e.g., Egypt, Iran, Algeria) pursued basically Western and secular policies
      b. new policies were largely unsuccessful
      c. foreign intrusion continued
        i. Israel, founded in 1948, was regarded as an outpost of the West
        ii. Israel defeated Arab forces in the Six-Day War (1967)
        iii. Western cultural penetration
    3. growing attraction of an Islamic alternative to Western models

a. foundations laid early in the century (e.g., Mawlana Mawdudi, Sayyid Qutb)

    i. insistence that the Quran and the sharia provide a guide for all life

    ii. decline and subordination of Islamic world caused by departure from Islamic principles

b. effort to return to true Islam was labeled "jihad"

4. penetration of fundamentalist thought in the Islamic world

    a. increase in religious observance

    b. many women voluntarily adopted modest dress and veils

    c. many governments used Islamic rhetoric and practice as anchor

    d. series of Islamic organizations were formed to provide social services

    e. Islamic activists became leaders in unions and professional organizations

    f. entry into politics

        i. the Algerian Islamic Salvation Front was set to win elections (1992), but the military government canceled elections; led to 10 years of civil war

5. some groups sought overthrow of compromised regimes

    a. the Egyptian Islamic Jihad assassinated Anwar Sadat in 1981

    b. in 1979, a radical Islamic group in Mecca tried to overthrow the Saudi government

    c. Islamic movements took power in Iran (1979) and Afghanistan (1996); implemented radical Islamization

6. attacks on hostile foreign powers

    a. Hamas (Palestine) and Hezbollah (Lebanon) targeted Israel

    b. response to Soviet invasion of Afghanistan (1979)

        i. Osama bin Laden founded al-Qaeda ("the base") to funnel support to the Afghan resistance

        ii. bin Laden was disillusioned by the stationing of U.S. troops in Arabia

    c. in 1998, al-Qaeda issued a *fatwa* (religious edict) declaring war against America

d. attacks on Western interests in East Africa, Indonesia, Great Britain, Spain, Saudi Arabia, and Yemen

e. the "great enemy" was irreligious Western-style modernity, U.S. imperialism, and economic globalization

D. Religious Alternatives to Fundamentalism

1. militancy isn't the only religious response to modernity

2. considerable debate within the Islamic world

3. other religious traditions responded to global modernity

    a. e.g., Christian groups were concerned with the ethical issues of economic globalization

    b. "liberation theology" (especially in Latin America) advocated Christian action in areas of social justice, poverty, human rights

    c. growing movement of "socially engaged Buddhism" in Asia

4. World Peace Summit (2000): more than 1,000 religious and spiritual leaders explored how to confront conflicts in the world

V. **The World's Environment and the Globalization of Environmentalism**

[see Lecture Strategy 3]

A. The Global Environment Transformed

1. three factors have magnified the human impact on the earth

    a. world population quadrupled in the twentieth century

    b. massive use of fossil fuels (coal in the nineteenth century, oil in the twentieth)

    c. enormous economic growth

2. uneven spread of all three over the world

    a. but economic growth came to appear possible and desirable almost everywhere

3. human environmental disruptions are now of global proportions

    a. doubling of cropland and corresponding contraction of forests and grasslands

    b. numerous extinctions of plant and animal species

    c. air pollution in many major cities and rivers

d. chlorofluorocarbons (CFCs) thinned the ozone layer

4. by 2000, scientific consensus on the occurrence of "global warming" as the result of burning of fossil fuels and loss of trees

B. Green and Global

1. environmentalism began in the nineteenth century as a response to the Industrial Revolution

   a. did not draw a mass following

2. environmentalism only became a global phenomenon in the second half of the twentieth century **[see Discussion Topic 3]**

   a. began in the West with Rachel Carson's *Silent Spring* (1962)

   b. impetus for action came from the grassroots and citizen protest

   c. in Germany, environmentalists entered politics as the Green Party

3. environmentalism took root in developing countries in 1970s–1980s

   a. tended to be more locally based, involving poorer people

   b. more concerned with food security, health, and survival

   c. more focused on saving threatened people, rather than plants and animals

   d. environmentalists sometimes have sought basic changes in political and social structure of their country (e.g., Philippine activism against foreign mining companies)

      i. some movements have included guerrilla warfare ("green armies")

4. environmentalism became a matter of global concern by end of twentieth century

   a. legislation to control pollution in many countries

   b. encouragement for businesses to become "green"

   c. research on alternative energy sources

   d. conferences on global warming

   e. international agreements on a number of issues

5. sharp conflicts between the Global North and South

   a. Northern efforts to control pollution and global warming could limit the South's industrial development

   b. developing countries perceive the developed ones as unwilling to give up their extravagance and really help matters

      i. e.g., U.S. refusal to ratify the Kyoto protocol

   c. controversy over export of hazardous wastes by rich countries

6. nonetheless, global environmentalism has come to symbolize focus on the plight of all humankind

   a. it's a challenge to modernity itself, especially commitment to endless growth

   b. growing importance of ideas of sustainability and restraint

VI. **Final Reflections: Pondering the Uses of History** [see Classroom Activity 3]

A. What's the good of studying history?

1. many have used history to explore the significance of human experience

2. most contemporary historians are skeptical of grand understandings of the past, especially those that claim to discern a "purpose" in human history

B. It *is* possible to detect some general "directions" in the human story.

1. growing populations, linked to greater control over the environment

2. growing complexity of human societies

3. increasing pace of change

4. greater global connections

C. But human changes didn't happen smoothly, evenly, or everywhere.

1. numerous ups and downs, reversals, and variations

2. "direction" is an observation; "progress" is a judgment

D. Political authorities have used the past to inculcate national, religious, civic, patriotic, or other values.

E. Studying history is a way to ponder matters of the heart and spirit.

1. e.g., history provides vast evidence of human suffering

2. perhaps historical study can foster compassion
3. the historical record offers encouragement, with examples of those who have fought to rectify injustice, sometimes successfully
F. Studying history helps prevent insularity.
    1. opens people up to a wider world

USING *WAYS OF THE WORLD* IN THE CLASSROOM

Lecture Strategies

Lecture Strategy 1

"The United States and the world: An evil empire?" This is a sensitive lecture topic. Many Americans have a strong inclination to bristle at any hint of criticism of U.S. policies. Nonetheless, helping students to understand why many people throughout the world hate the United States, and exploring the justice or injustice of their complaints, is a very valuable service you can provide to your students. The objectives of this lecture strategy are:

- to encourage understanding of the United States as an economic as well as a political/military force in the modern world
- to explore the roots and development of America's understanding of itself as the policeman of the world
- to consider what aspects of American culture are most offensive to people in other parts of the world
- to examine why the United States waged the Gulf War and the Iraq War
- to investigate what the implications of those two wars have been in perceptions of the United States abroad

A good place to start is at the simplest level: the stereotype of the "ugly American." Travel anywhere beyond the boundaries of the United States, and you'll see dirty looks aimed at the American tourist, who is perceived as being loud, intrusive of other people's space, critical, pushy, certain that everyone can understand English if it's spoken loudly enough, and just generally obnoxious. Of course, all American tourists aren't like that, but it has become such an integral part of the experience of American tourists that if you *don't* behave like that abroad you're likely to be singled out for praise. Explore this stereotype (a Google image search will produce some interesting illustrations) as a starting point to consider American attitudes toward the rest of the world, or, more importantly, how Americans are *perceived* abroad.

After this point, there's a wide range of material that could be included, depending on your interests and those of your class. Some points to consider are:

- how large an impact a multinational corporation can have on a developing nation (e.g., sweatshops, environmental impact, interference in governments)
- the effect on the United States of its being the only superpower left in the world
- the sort of American culture that is being exported, and the question of whether the most visible exports (the Barbies mentioned in the text, popular music, Hollywood movies, McDonald's, etc.) actually reflect the reality of American culture or whether they give a distorted picture
- the United States' role in the United Nations as host and as a member of the Security Council, and whether or not the United States regards itself as bound by UN decisions
- the United States' extraordinary record of giving massive amounts of money and manpower to charitable causes throughout the world
- what caused the Gulf War, and how that war affected perceptions of the United States abroad
- what the Iraq War has done to change foreign attitudes about the United States (including such issues as the UN's vote not to support the war, the failure to find weapons of mass destruction in Iraq, and the ongoing violence in Iraq)

A balanced and evenhanded approach is key to making this lecture work. The United States, both as a nation and in the form of its many citizens, has done a great deal of good in the modern world; don't forget to include that in the picture you develop. Also be careful not to engage in direct attacks on a political leader or party—especially with a topic like this, it's important to remember objectivity.

Lecture Strategy 2

"The other sex: Making women visible."
The purpose of this lecture strategy is to develop the history of global feminism that was briefly covered in this chapter. Its objectives are:

- to help students understand the revolutionary nature of the current women's movement
- to examine how far the movement has gone in various parts of the world
- to consider problems the movement has faced and continues to face in the modern world

A good place to begin is with the typical household in the developed world. Encourage your students to discuss things invented within the past century that have made it easier for women to work outside the home or have significantly reduced the amount of work that has to be done inside it. It is particularly useful to bring along a list of inventions that includes the year each item was invented, to add to the discussion and to help emphasize the extreme modernity of frozen foods, microwave ovens, vacuum cleaners, myriad processed foods that can be bought ready to eat, and so on. It's also useful to consider that reliable feminine hygiene products and the availability of aspirin make it easier for women to work consistently outside the home, as does day care. Get your students to consider the percentage of time housework takes now compared to even a century ago.

From there, go on to examine the second wave of feminism. Some issues to consider are:

- the relationship between the feminist movement and the civil rights movement in the United States
- the leaders of the movement in the Western world and their goals
- whether the sexual liberation preached by the women's movement is new in world history or just new for the female of the species
- what the role of biology is in all this—the fact that women and men are anatomically and genetically different, and that women have the babies
- homosexuality, both female and male

Move beyond the Global North to consider in greater detail some of the issues of international feminism raised by the textbook. Some specific points you might care to consider are:

- how female political leaders (Margaret Thatcher, Indira Gandhi, Sonia Gandhi, Benazir Bhutto, Golda Meir, etc.) have managed to gain and retain power
- traditional strictures that prevent men from regarding women as equals
- the issue of women's spheres and men's spheres of work that have proven hard to overturn

Lecture Strategy 3

"Re-greening the world."
The modern environmental movement is a tale of desperate worry about the fate of the planet, but it also shows human resilience and hope at many levels. The objectives of this lecture strategy are:

- to consider the factors that have caused the earth's current environmental fears
- to examine the role of both governments and nongovernmental organizations in taking responsibility for the environment
- to raise student awareness of environmental issues

A good place to begin is with Nobel laureate Wangari Maathai of Kenya, the first environmental activist to win the Nobel Peace Prize (in 2004). Her Green Belt Movement planted 30 million trees in Africa, aiming to slow deforestation and help poor people gain access to firewood and building materials. Move from the case of Maathai to the problem of deforestation around the world and what is being done to combat it.

Beyond that point, there are many possible approaches you could take. Perhaps the most straightforward approach is a thematic one. Some possible themes are:

- protection of endangered plants and animals (including legislation like the Environmental Protection Act in the United States, NGOs like the World Wildlife Fund that buy and preserve habitats, and direct-action groups like Greenpeace, with their history of throwing themselves between whaling ships and threatened whales)
- advocacy for environmentally friendly products (detergents, recycled products, etc.)
- efforts to force or convince corporations to adopt environmentally friendly policies

(protests against specific polluters and legislation such as the U.S. Environmental Protection Act)

- fear of global warming (including discussion of what is going on and efforts to combat it, such as bans on CFCs and greenhouse gases; the Kyoto protocol and why the United States refused to ratify it; and international conferences on the subject)

Things to Do in the Classroom

Discussion Topics

1. Comparison, large or small group.
"Reglobalization."
Ask students to examine the Snapshot on page 728 entitled "Indicators of 'Reglobalization.'" Ask them in particular to discuss the *significance* of three of the statistics found in the Snapshot: What differences does it make to the world and our experience in it that these vast waves of growth have taken place? Conclude by having each student write a paragraph on the significance of one item, and then share their statements with the whole class.

2. Misconception/Difficult Topic, large or small group. "Religious extremism is a Muslim matter."
Students usually regard the militant religious extremism of groups like al-Qaeda as a unique phenomenon that in some way shows the basic irrationality of Islam. Ask students each to come to class on discussion day with an example they have found of non-Muslim religious extremism, either historical or contemporary (e.g., ancient Jewish zealots, or cults like Heaven's Gate or Aum Shinrikyo in Japan). Discuss their examples, going on to consider the dividing line between fundamentalism and extremism.

3. Contextualization, large or small group.
"Thinking green."
How far have environmental concerns penetrated into *your* community? Ask students to discuss the ways environmentalism has had an impact on their own lives.

Classroom Activities

1. Analysis exercise, large or small group. "A global economy."
Ask students to identify the country of origin of the objects around them in the classroom, including their own clothing and any snacks they might have in their backpacks. Mark the sources on a projected map, and then encourage discussion of *why* goods are brought such long distances instead of being produced closer to home.

2. Close-reading exercise, small group. "The letter to America."
Predistribute to the class copies of Osama bin Laden's "Letter to America" of November 24, 2002 (readily available on the Internet). Ask students to list the major complaints against the United States contained in the letter. Then ask them to discuss the text in light of what they know about the history of the United States and the world in the twentieth and early twenty-first centuries. Do they think the charges are fair? Do the charges have an element of truth but not the complete truth? Do any of your students believe the charges are entirely false? Make sure that students discuss the evidence, not just their feelings.

3. Clicker question.
Are you in general optimistic or pessimistic about the future of the human species?

Key Terms

al-Qaeda: International organization of fundamentalist Islamic militants, headed by Osama bin Laden. (*pron.* al-KIGH-dah *or* al-KAHY-dah)

antiglobalization: Major international movement that protests the development of the global economy on the grounds that it makes the rich richer and keeps poor regions in poverty while exploiting their labor and environments; the movement burst onto the world stage in 1999 with massive protests at a meeting of the World Trade Organization in Seattle.

bin Laden, Osama: The leader of al-Qaeda, a wealthy Saudi Arabian who turned to militant fundamentalism. (*pron.* oh-ZAHM-ah bin LAWD-n)

Bretton Woods system: Named for a conference held at Bretton Woods, New Hampshire, in 1944, this system provided the foundation for postwar economic globalization, including the World Bank and the International Monetary Fund; based on the promotion of free trade, stable currencies, and high levels of capital investment.

environmentalism: Twentieth-century movement to preserve the natural world in the face of spiraling human ability to alter the world environment.

fundamentalism: Occurring within all the major world religions, fundamentalism is a self-proclaimed return to the "fundamentals" of a religion and is marked by a militant piety and exclusivism.

globalization: Term commonly used to refer to the massive growth in international economic transactions from around 1950 to the present.

global warming: A worldwide scientific consensus that the increased burning of fossil fuels and the loss of trees have begun to warm the earth's atmosphere artificially and significantly, causing climate change and leading to possibly catastrophic results if the problem is not addressed.

Guevara, Che: Ernesto "Che" Guevara was an Argentine-born revolutionary (1928–1967) who waged guerrilla war in an effort to remedy Latin America's and Africa's social and economic ills. (*pron.* chay gah-VAHR-ah)

Hindutva: Fundamentalist Hindu movement that became politically important in India in the 1980s by advocating a distinct Hindu identity and decrying government efforts to accommodate other faith groups. (*pron.* hin-DOOT-vah)

Islamic renewal: Large number of movements in Islamic lands that promote a return to strict adherence to the Quran and the sharia in opposition to key elements of Western culture.

jihad: Term used by modern militant Islamic groups to denote not just the "struggle" or "striving" that the word originally meant but also the defense of authentic Islam against Western aggression. (*pron.* ji-HAHD)

Kyoto protocol on global warming: International agreement to reduce greenhouse gas emissions in an effort to slow global warming; as of November 2007, 174 countries had subscribed to the agreement, but the United States' refusal to ratify the protocol has caused international tensions.

liberation theology: Christian movement that is particularly active in Latin America and that argues the need for Christians to engage in the pursuit of social justice and human rights.

neo-liberalism: An approach to the world economy, developed in the 1970s, that favored reduced tariffs, the free movement of capital, a mobile and temporary workforce, the privatization of industry, and the curtailing of government efforts to regulate the economy.

North/South gap: Growing disparity between the Global North and the Global South that appears to be exacerbated by current world trade practices.

Pinochet, Augusto: Military dictator of Chile from 1973 to 1990 who was known for his widespread use of torture and for liquidating thousands of opponents of his regime. (*pron.* ow-GOOS-toe pin-oh-SHAY)

Prague spring: Sweeping series of reforms instituted by communist leader Alexander Dubcek in Czechoslovakia in 1968; the movement was subsequently crushed by a Soviet invasion.

reglobalization: The quickening of global economic transactions after World War II, which resulted in total world output returning to the levels established before the Great Depression and moving beyond them.

religious right: The fundamentalist phenomenon as it appeared in U.S. politics in the 1970s.

second-wave feminism: Women's rights movement that revived in the 1960s with a different agenda than earlier women's suffrage movements; second-wave feminists demanded equal rights for women in employment and education, women's right to control their own bodies, and the end of patriarchal domination.

socially engaged Buddhism: A growing movement in Asia that addresses the needs of the poor through social reform, educational programs, and health services.

transnational corporations: Huge global businesses that produce goods or deliver services simultaneously in many countries; often abbreviated as TNCs.

World Trade Organization: International body representing 149 nations that negotiates the rules for global commerce and is dedicated to the promotion of free trade.

ANSWER GUIDELINES FOR CHAPTER QUESTIONS

The two sets of questions that follow appear in the textbook at the end of the chapter and in the margins of the reading. They are also provided in the Computerized Test Bank with answer guidelines, for your convenience.

The Big Picture Questions

1. To what extent did the processes discussed in this chapter (economic globalization, feminism, fundamentalism, environmentalism) represent something new in the twentieth century? In what respects did they have roots in the more distant past?

• Economic globalization was a long-term process that began early in human history. It increased in scope and intensity after 1500 as a new global network anchored in Europe took shape and industrialization further spurred economic contact between regions. Nonetheless, after a decline in global trade during the Great Depression, developments after World War II—including population growth, technological advances, and the fostering of global trade by the leading powers of the capitalist world—have all led to further rapid economic globalization.

• Feminism in the twentieth century had its roots in the ideals of the Atlantic revolutions and the first feminist movements of the nineteenth century. However, the spread of feminism outside the Western world and the emergence of the women's liberation movement within the Western world during the twentieth century mark important new developments.

• Fundamentalism at its core was a reaction to the modernity that took shape during the nineteenth century, and elements of this reaction can be found in that century. Nonetheless, fundamentalism in the twentieth century became better defined and more widespread than before.

• Environmentalism began in the nineteenth century as Romantic poets like William Blake and William Wordsworth denounced the "dark satanic mills" of the industrial era, which threatened the "green and pleasant land" of an earlier England. The "scientific management" of nature, both in industrializing countries and in European colonies, represented another element of emerging environmental awareness among a few. So did the "wilderness idea," which aimed to preserve untouched areas from human disruption. But none of these movements attracted the mass following or provoked the global response that the environmental movement of the twentieth century achieved.

2. In what ways did the global North/South divide find expression in the twentieth century?

• Global economic development has increased the divide between a rich North and poor South;

• it has resulted in a "brain drain" from the Global South to the Global North;

• it has found expression in differing priorities in otherwise international feminist and environmentalist movements.

3. What have been the benefits and drawbacks of globalization since 1945?

• In terms of benefits, globalization brought economic growth;

• and it put the peoples of the world in closer contact.

• In terms of drawbacks, it left a world deeply divided;

• made it more unequal;

• and has led to violence.

4. Does the twentieth century as a whole confirm or undermine Enlightenment predictions about the future of humankind?

• The twentieth century confirmed some Enlightenment predictions, though these ideas were taken in new directions, including the continued effort of women in feminist movements to make all humankind equal;

• the potential of scientific and technological developments continued to prove important;

• the idea of self-determination continued to have an impact in the twentieth century.

• Nevertheless, the twentieth century also undermined Enlightenment predictions as the idea of steady progress toward a more democratic world was challenged by the emergence of fascism and communism;

• environmental problems and growing disparities between the rich and poor muddied for some the meaning and perceived positive nature of the Enlightenment concept of progress.

5. "The twentieth century marks the end of the era of Western dominance in world history." What evidence might support this statement? What evidence might contradict it?

• In support of the statement, one might note the end of European colonial empires and the emergence of national self-determination;

• the weakening of European powers because of the two world wars;

• the rise of a number of developing nations, including India and China;

• the reaction against Western cultural influences, especially in the Islamic world;

• the emergence of communism as a rival system to the Western capitalist model.

• In opposition to the statement, one might note the continued influence of Europe and the United States as political and military powers;

• the continued influence of Europe and the United States on the world economy;

• the continued cultural influence of Europe and the United States;

• the collapse of communist states in the final decades of the twentieth century.

6. To what extent do you think the various liberation movements of the twentieth century—communism, nationalism, democracy, feminism, internationalism—have achieved their goals?

• Communism achieved a great deal before the 1970s, but it has since largely disintegrated as a movement.

• Nationalism continues to flourish, with national self-determination still accepted as an idea in the international community. That said, the rise of globalization decreased the centrality of the nation-state as an identity.

• Democracy has enjoyed mixed results, having an important impact in places like India while failing, at least initially, elsewhere (such as Africa). However, the democratic movement has gained in strength, especially over the last several decades with the disintegration of the communist world and the expansion of democracy in Africa.

• Feminism grew as a movement in the twentieth century. In the West, it developed distinctive new strands, including women's liberation and a movement among women of color. Perhaps more importantly, feminism moved beyond the Western world, with distinctive strands developing across the globe.

• Internationalism certainly increased over the century alongside globalization, with new organizations like the United Nations emerging and with new mass organizations that cross borders (like Greenpeace) taking shape.

7. Based on material in Chapters 21, 22, and 24, how might you define the evolving roles of the United States in the history of the twentieth century?

• In Chapter 21, the United States emerged as the preeminent power in the capitalist West. It cast off its isolationist tendencies, especially after World War II, to take a leading role in the world. One of its key contributions was its role in the revival of Western Europe after World War II, both through its willingness to maintain troops in Europe and through the Marshall Plan, which contributed to the revival of Western European economies.

• In Chapter 22, the United States emerged as one of two world superpowers and as the leader of the capitalist West in a global competition with the communist East known as the cold war. Ultimately, the United States emerged as the sole superpower in the world following the collapse of the Soviet Union in the early 1990s.

• In Chapter 24, the United States established an "informal empire" by using economic penetration, political pressure, and periodic military action to create societies and governments compatible with the values and interests of the United States, but without directly governing large populations for long periods of time. A central means of accomplishing this was through economic muscle, creating an "empire of production" that drew on the United States' immense wealth to entice or intimidate potential collaborators. Another form of power that critics cite is the "soft power" of the United States' cultural attractiveness, its political and cultural freedoms, the economic benefits of cooperation, and the general willingness of many to follow the American lead voluntarily.

Margin Review Questions

Q. *What factors contributed to economic globalization during the twentieth century?*

• The capitalist victors in World War II were determined to avoid a return to Depression-era conditions.

• They forged a set of agreements and institutions (the World Bank and the International Monetary Fund) that laid the foundations for postwar globalization. This "Bretton Woods system" set the rules for commercial and financial dealings among the major capitalist countries, while promoting relatively free trade, stable currency values linked to the American dollar, and high levels of capital investment.

• Technology also contributed to economic globalization; containerized shipping, huge oil tankers, and air express services dramatically lowered transportation costs, while fiber optic cables and later the Internet provided the communication infrastructure for global interaction.

• Population growth, especially when tied to growing economies and modernizing societies, further fueled globalization as dozens of new nations, eager for modern development, entered the world economy.

• In the 1970s and after, major capitalist countries like the United States abandoned many earlier political controls on economic activity as their leaders and businesspeople increasingly viewed the entire world as a single market. Powerful international lending agencies imposed similar free-market and pro-business conditions on many poor countries if they were to qualify for much-needed loans.

• The collapse of the communist world only furthered such unrestricted global capitalism.

Q. *In what ways has economic globalization linked the world's peoples more closely together?*

• World trade skyrocketed in the second half of the twentieth century;

• money as well as goods achieved an amazing global mobility through foreign direct investment, the short-term movement of capital, and the personal funds of individuals;

• companies have become increasingly transnational;

• workers have been on the move more than ever.

Q. *What new or sharper divisions has economic globalization generated?*

• It has increased the gap between rich and poor in the world.

• It has also increased gaps in many other areas, including educational and employment opportunities and access to medical care and the Internet.

• It has created important disparities among developing countries, which are dependent in large part on their role in the world economy.

• It has also generated economic inequalities within individual countries, both rich and poor ones.

• It has created a split between those who support globalization and those who oppose it.

Q. *What distinguished feminism in the industrialized countries from that of the Global South?*

• In the industrialized countries, feminism focused on questions of equal rights (especially in employment and education) and women's liberation (which took aim at patriarchy as a system of domination), and a distinctive strain emerged among women of color that focused on racism and poverty.

• Many feminists in the Global South felt that feminism in the industrialized countries was too individualistic, overly focused on sexuality, and insufficiently concerned with issues of motherhood, marriage, and poverty to be of much use.

• In the Global South, the feminist movement took up a variety of issues, not all of which were explicitly gender-based, including the creation in East Africa of small associations of women who supported one another in a variety of ways. In Morocco, the feminist movement targeted the changing of the Family Law Code. In South Korea, women's mobilization contributed to a "mass people's movement" that brought a return to democracy by the late 1980s.

• The differences between the Northern and Southern movements sometimes surfaced at international conferences such as the Mexico City gathering in 1975; the United States attempted to limit the meeting's agenda to matters of political and civil rights for women, while delegates from third world and communist countries wanted to include issues of economic justice, decolonization, and disarmament.

Q. *In what respect did the various religious fundamentalists of the twentieth century express hostility to global modernity?*

• In the United States, fundamentalists at first sought to separate themselves from the secular world in their own churches and schools, but from the 1970s on, they entered the political arena as the religious right, determined to return America to a "godly path."

• In India in the 1980s, a Hindu fundamentalist movement known as *Hindutva* entered the political arena, seeking to counter efforts by secular governments to cater to the interests of Muslims, Sikhs, and the lower castes.

• In the late twentieth century in the Islamic world, fundamentalist Muslims expressed hostility in a number of ways, including the adoption of more observant forms of Islam, the foundation of Islamic organizations that operated legally to provide social services that the state offered inadequately or not at all, violent opposition to foreign powers that encroached on the Islamic world, and the launching of terrorist attacks on Western interests—defining the enemy not as Christianity itself or even Western civilization but as irreligious Western-style modernity, U.S. imperialism, and an American-led economic globalization.

Q. *From what sources did Islamic renewal movements derive?*

• There were several factors that gave strength to Islamic activism. Political independence had given rise to major states such as Egypt, Iran, and Algeria that pursued essentially Western and secular policies of nationalism, socialism, and economic development, often with only lip service to an Islamic identity. These policies were not very successful, with many states beset by endemic problems that ran counter to the great expectations that had accompanied the struggle against European domination.

• Foreign intrusion also played a role. Israel, widely regarded as an outpost of the West, had been reestablished as a Jewish state in the very center of the Islamic world in 1948. Broader signs of Western cultural penetration also appeared frequently in the Muslim world.

• Islamic alternatives to Western models of modernity provided inspiration; in particular, the teachings of Mawlana Mawdudi and Sayyid Qutb asserted that the Quran and the sharia provided a guide for all of life and a blueprint for a distinctly Islamic modernity not dependent on Western ideas.

Q. *In what different ways did Islamic renewal express itself?*

• At the level of personal life, many people became more religiously observant, attending mosque, praying regularly, and fasting. Substantial numbers of women, many of them young, urban, and well educated, adopted modest Islamic dress and the veil quite voluntarily. Participation in Sufi mystical practices increased.

• Many governments sought to anchor themselves in Islamic rhetoric and practice.

• Across the Muslim world, renewal movements spawned organizations that operated legally to provide social services that the state offered inadequately or not at all. Islamic activists took leadership roles in unions and professional organizations of teachers, journalists, engineers, doctors, and lawyers. Such people embraced modern science and technology but sought to embed these elements of modernity within a distinctly Islamic culture.

• Some sought the violent overthrow of what they saw as compromised regimes in the Muslim world, succeeding in both Iran and Afghanistan.

• Islamic revolutionaries also took aim at hostile foreign powers, targeting Israel and, after the Soviet invasion of 1979, Afghanistan.

• Others sought to attack Western interests, defining the enemy not as Christianity itself or even Western civilization but as irreligious Western-style modernity, U.S. imperialism, and an American-led economic globalization.

Q. *How can we explain the dramatic increase in the human impact on the environment in the twentieth century?*

• The dramatic increase in the human impact on the environment can be attributed to the explosion in the human population;

• the new ability of humankind to tap the energy potential of fossil fuels;

• phenomenal economic growth as modern science and technology immensely increased the production of goods and services.

Q. *What differences emerged between environmentalism in the Global North and that in the Global South?*

• Both activists and governments in the developing countries have often felt that Northern initiatives to address atmospheric pollution and global warming would curtail their industrial development, leaving the North/South gap intact.

• Another North/South difference arose over the export of hazardous wastes generated in rich Northern countries to disposal sites in the developing countries.

ADDITIONAL RESOURCES FOR CHAPTER 24

Additional Bedford/St. Martin's Resources

FOR INSTRUCTORS

Computerized Test Bank

This test bank provides over thirty exercises per chapter, including multiple-choice, fill-in-the-blank,

short-answer, and full-length essay questions. Instructors can customize quizzes, add or edit both questions and answers, and export questions and answers to a variety of formats, including WebCT and Blackboard. The disc includes correct answers and essay outlines.

Instructor's Resource CD-ROM

This disc provides instructors with ready-made and customizable PowerPoint multimedia presentations built around chapter outlines, maps, figures, and all images from the textbook, plus JPEG versions of all maps, figures, and images.

The following maps and images from Chapter 24 are available in both JPEG and PowerPoint format on the Instructor's Resource CD-ROM:

- Map 24.1: Globalization in Action: Trade and Investment in the Early Twenty-first Century (p. 726)
- Map 24.2: Global Inequality: Population and Economic Development (p. 729)
- Map 24.3: Two Faces of an "American Empire" (p. 732)
- Map 24.4: The Islamic World in the Early Twenty-first Century (p. 743)
- Map 24.5: Carbon Dioxide Emissions in the Twentieth Century (p. 750)
- One World (p. 722)
- A World Economy (p. 725)
- Che Guevara (p. 735)
- Mothers of Missing Children (p. 738)
- Hamas in Action (p. 744)
- Environmentalism in Action (p. 751)

FOR STUDENTS

Documents and Essays from *Worlds of History: A Comparative Reader,* Third Edition (Volume 2)

The following documents, essays, and illustrations to accompany Chapter 24 are available in Chapter 14 of Volume 2 of this reader by Kevin Reilly:

- Sherif Hetata, *Dollarization*
- Philippe Legrain, *Cultural Globalization Is Not Americanization*
- Miriam Ching Yoon Louie, from *Sweatshop Warriors: Immigrant Women Workers Take On the Global Factory*
- Benjamin Barber, from *Jihad vs. McWorld*

- *Global Snapshots*
  1. Cartogram of Global Warming
  2. Satellite Photo of the Earth at Night
  3. Population Density of the World, 2004
  4. GNP per Capita Growth, 1990–2001
- John Roach, *By 2050 Warming to Doom Million Species, Study Says*
- Andrew C. Revkin, *Climate Data Hint at Irreversible Rise in Seas*
- Larry Rohter, *With Big Boost from Sugarcane, Brazil Is Satisfying Its Fuel Needs*

Online Study Guide at bedfordstmartins.com/strayer

The Online Study Guide helps students synthesize the material from the text as well as practice the skills historians use to make sense of the past. Each chapter of the Online Study Guide contains specific testing exercises, including a multiple-choice self-test that focuses on important conceptual ideas; an identification quiz that helps students remember key people, places, and events; a flashcard activity that tests students on their knowledge of key terms; and two interactive map activities intended to strengthen students' geographic skills. Instructors can monitor students' progress through an online Quiz Gradebook or receive email updates.

Further Reading

Armstrong, Karen. *The Battle for God.* New York: Ballantine, 2000. A brilliant and readable study of fundamentalism in world religions.

Basu, Amrita, ed. *The Challenge of Local Feminisms: Women's Movements in Global Perspective.* Boulder: Westview Press, 1995. An interesting collection of articles, highlighting the fact that feminism varies widely from region to region.

Best Environmental Directories, http://www.ulb.ac.be/ceese/meta/cds.html. A great collection of Internet resources on the world environment and on ecological activism.

Cohen, Daniel. *Globalization and Its Enemies.* Trans. Jessica B. Baker. Cambridge, MA: MIT Press, 2006. An insightful study by a major French economist.

Freedman, Estelle. *No Turning Back: The History of Feminism and the Future of Women.* New York: Ballantine, 2002. A thought-provoking and very readable study.

Gore, Al. *An Inconvenient Truth: The Planetary Emergency of Global Warming and What We Can Do About It.* Emmaus, PA: Rodale Press, c. 2006. An essential introduction to the topic of global warming.

Guha, Ramachandra. *Environmentalism: A Global History.* London: Longman, 1999. A very good (and short) overview of the environmental movement.

Hannam, June. *Feminism.* London: Longman, 2006. Part of Longman's Short Histories of Big Ideas series, this is a useful overview of the subject.

McNeill, John R., and Paul Kennedy. *Something New Under the Sun: An Environmental History of the Twentieth-Century World.* New York: W. W. Norton, 2001. An engrossing study that is written objectively and compellingly.

Rivoli, Pietra. *The Travels of a T-Shirt in the Global Economy: An Economist Examines the Markets, Power, and Politics of World Trade.* Hoboken, NJ: Wiley, 2005. A very readable and eye-opening introduction to the complications of the global economy.

Ruthven, Malise. *Fundamentalism: A Very Short Introduction.* Oxford: Oxford University Press, 2007. A clearly written and insightful study.

Literature

Beauvoir, Simone de. *The Second Sex.* Trans. H. M. Parshley. New York: Bantam, 1961. Still an eye-opening work, in which the author confronts head-on assumptions about women's "proper" place that have been held for a very, very long time.

Carson, Rachel. *Silent Spring.* Boston: Houghton Mifflin, 2002. This book, first published in 1962, made the world aware as never before of damage done to the environment.

Friedan, Betty. *The Feminine Mystique.* New York: W. W. Norton, 1963. One of the seminal works of the late-twentieth century feminist movement.

Hosseini, Khaled. *A Thousand Splendid Suns.* New York: Riverhead Books, 2007. A moving novel set against the backdrop of the Taliban in Afghanistan that tells the story of two women.

Ibrahim, Raymond, ed. *The Al Qaeda Reader.* New York: Broadway, 2007. A disturbing collection of writings from the al-Qaeda movement.

Schneir, Miriam, ed. *Feminism in Our Time: The Essential Writings, World War II to the Present.* New York: Vintage, 1994. This collection focuses on feminist writings of the 1960s and 1970s.

Film

Che Guevara: A Guerrilla to the End. Films for the Humanities and Sciences, 1999. 51 minutes. Biographical documentary centered on Che Guevara and his role in the liberation struggles of Latin America.

Global Jihad. Insight Media, 2004. 22 minutes. ABC news program that examines al-Qaeda style fundamentalism in Southeast Asia.

Power to the People. Films for the Humanities and Sciences, 1995. 49 minutes. Traces the people-power movements of the twentieth century, from the Russian Revolution through the civil rights movements of the 1960s.

Rachel Carson: Nature's Guardian. Films for the Humanities and Sciences, 2007. 58 minutes. Bill Moyers explores the career and impact of Rachel Carson.

Times Are A-Changin'. Insight Media, 2005. 30 minutes. Explores the political and social changes that took place in the United States in the 1960s and 1970s, including segments dedicated to feminism and Latino movements.

A World without Borders: What Is Happening with Globalization. Insight Media, 2000. 26 minutes. A broad overview of the impact of globalization on political and environmental issues.

The First Half of World History

A Class Plan

The first thirteen chapters of *Ways of the World* deal with material usually covered in the first semester of a world history survey course. How does one organize all that material, integrating what's in the textbook with your own points of particular interest and the issues your department might want to highlight? To a considerable extent, every world history course is a unique product in which the instructor crafts a balance between her or his strengths, programmatic needs, and the materials s/he has available. The following is an example of how such a class might be crafted, suggesting ways in which the Instructor's Resource Manual could be incorporated into a syllabus. It is provided more as food for thought for a new world history instructor than as a blueprint. It assumes that the instructor will have about forty classroom days in an average semester, if teaching a 50-minute course on Mondays, Wednesdays, and Fridays. It could easily be modified for a Tuesday and Thursday course with 75-minute class meetings. Note that it is based on the assumption that students will read the textbook for themselves; while reviews are included, no space is included for instructors simply to cover the material in the textbook.

Day 1: Introduction to the course. Go over grading policies, reading expectations, and, especially, your own *objectives* for the course. Do as much as you can to provide a roadmap for the students, and go over the Prologue to *Ways of the World*.

Chapter 1

Day 2: Give the lecture "Looking at the 'losers'" outlined in Chapter 1 of the Instructor's Resource Manual. Incorporate a short clip from the *Nova* episode entitled "In Search of Human Origins" to help students visualize the material you are discussing.

Day 3: Give a five-minute quiz (three fill-in-the–blank questions and one short-answer question) to test how much students actually took in from the first lecture and their first reading. This should drive home the point that students should (1) take good notes and (2) review their notes regularly. In the following lecture, take advantage of every possible opportunity for teaching moments about note taking and how to remember material. Give the lecture "The world of the last Ice Age" outlined in Chapter 1 of the Instructor's Resource Manual, utilizing the map-analysis exercise included in the Classroom Activities section of that chapter.

Day 4: Review the main points covered in Chapter 1 of the textbook as interactively as possible. Move on from there to the discussion question of your choice. If time allows, show a short clip from the film *First Contact* to drive home the point that there are still Paleolithic peoples in the world. Conclude with Chapter 1's clicker question.

Chapter 2

Day 5: Start with the role-playing exercise "How to domesticate a plant" from Chapter 2 of the Instructor's Resource Manual. Go on from there to present the lecture "The Fertile Crescent then and now" outlined in the Instructor's Resource Manual as a way to highlight both the Agricultural Revolution and its long-term effects on the environment.

Day 6: Give a five-minute quiz to see if students are working on their note-taking and learning skills. Go on to show a short film clip from the options listed in the Film section of Chapter 2 of the Instructor's Resource Manual. Finish with the map-analysis exercise outlined in this chapter of the manual.

Day 7: Lecture on whichever of the two remaining lecture strategies outlined in Chapter 2 of the Instructor's Resource Manual interests you most, incorporating a review of the textbook's main points. Use as many images as possible, to provide variety to your classroom presentation. Finish with the chapter's clicker question.

Chapter 3

Day 8: Students should have read Chapter 3 before this meeting. Review the material covered in the chapter, going on from there to the map-analysis exercise outlined in Chapter 3 of the Instructor's Resource Manual. If time allows, move on to the role-playing exercise, or show a clip from one of the films listed in the Film section of this chapter of the manual.

Day 9: Give the lecture "The monumental nature of First Civilizations" outlined in Chapter 3 of the Instructor's Resource Manual. Include a clip from the film *Mari, Part 2: The Palace of Zimri-Lim* to help students visualize the matters discussed.

Day 10: Give the lecture "Unification in the First Civilizations" discussed in Chapter 3 of the Instructor's Resource Manual. Incorporate into the lecture the map-analysis exercise provided in the Instructor's Resource Manual. Conclude with Chapter 3's clicker question.

Day 11: Divide the class time into two parts. In the first part, give a short exam testing students on Part One of the textbook and on the related lectures and discussions they have experienced. In the second half of the class, encourage classroom discussion of two of the issues laid out in Chapter 3 of the Instructor's Resource Manual.

Chapter 4

Day 12: Use the map-analysis exercise included in Chapter 4 of the Instructor's Resource Manual as a basis from which to review the material covered in Chapter 4 of the textbook. If time allows, go on to discussion of the topic "Government of the people, by the people, and for the people" included in Chapter 4 of the manual.

Day 13: Give the lecture "The shadow of the Parthenon" outlined in Chapter 4 of the Instructor's Resource Manual. Go on from there to class discussion of the topic "The Persians were a bunch of barbarian savages" included in the manual.

Day 14: Give the lecture "The conquests of Alexander the Great" laid out in Chapter 4 of the Instructor's Resource Manual, if possible going on to compare Alexander's empire with that of the Mauryans of India.

Day 15: Give a five-minute quiz to check that students are keeping up with their studying, and go on from there to deliver the lecture "Tying it all together: Identity and governance in classical empires" outlined in Chapter 4 of the Instructor's Resource Manual. Be sure to provide plenty of Chinese material for comparison. Spend the last few minutes of class with a report from the students acting as Chinese officials in the role-playing activity for Chapter 4. Finish with Chapter 4's clicker question.

Chapter 5

Day 16: It is useful to begin the classroom presentation of Chapter 5 with frank discussion of religion's place in world history, including what historians do that departments of religious studies *don't* do. One way to approach this issue is by giving the lecture "Religion and government" (provided in Chapter 5 of the Instructor's Resource Manual), which has discussion elements built into it.

Day 17: Show an extended clip from the film among those listed in the Film section of Chapter 5 of the

Instructor's Resource Manual that you think will be most useful for your purposes. Then encourage class discussion of one or two of the discussion topics included in the manual.

Day 18: Give a lecture on whichever of the two remaining lecture strategies in Chapter 5 of the Instructor's Resource Manual suits you best. Make the lecture brief, reserving enough time for the role-playing exercise sketched out in this chapter of the manual. Finish with the chapter's clicker question.

Chapter 6

Day 19: Give a five-minute quiz. Then review the material covered in Chapter 6, working it as much as possible into the context of the lecture strategy "Women . . . and men . . . of the classical world" outlined in Chapter 6 of the Instructor's Resource Manual.

Day 20: Show the film *Ancient China* (listed in the Film section of Chapter 6 of the Instructor's Resource Manual). Stop the film occasionally to highlight points covered in the textbook.

Day 21: Give the lecture "A closer look at Greco-Roman slavery," which is laid out in Chapter 6 of the Instructor's Resource Manual. Reserve enough time to discuss at least two of the discussion topics provided for this chapter. Finish with the chapter's clicker question.

Chapter 7

Day 22: Incorporate a review of the textbook material on Africa into the lecture "How we know: Rewriting African history" outlined in Chapter 7 of the Instructor's Resource Manual. Show one or two clips from the film *Wonders of the African World* (PBS, 2003) to give variety to your lecture, and also make some use of the map-analysis activity included in Chapter 7 of the manual to help students to think spatially about the issues involved.

Day 23: Deliver the lecture "Diversity in the Americas" included in Chapter 7 of the Instructor's Resource Manual. In conjunction with the lecture, introduce the contextualization discussion topic on Teotihuacán.

Day 24: Give the lecture "Life among the Maya" included in Chapter 7 of the Instructor's Resource Manual. At the appropriate point in the lecture, encourage discussion of Maya writing as laid out in the Chapter 7 discussion topic "Maya writing." Ask the clicker question for Chapter 7. Then conclude with a discussion of the midterm exam, covering the types of questions that will be included and grading expectations.
Day 25: Midterm examination

Chapter 8

Day 26: Go over the basic points laid out in the introduction to Part Three of the textbook. Then devote the rest of the class time to a consideration of long-distance trade, including a brief version of the lecture "World transport among the third-wave civilizations" included in Chapter 8 of the Instructor's Resource Manual and discussion of at least two of the discussion topics outlined for this chapter in the manual.

Day 27: Show a clip from one of the films included in the Film section of Chapter 8 of the Instructor's Resource Manual. Then encourage students to consider the realities of travel in the premodern world by giving the lecture "The world of merchants" detailed in the manual, culminating with a discussion of this chapter's close-reading exercise, "A Chinese traveler to India."

Chapter 9

Day 28: Give a five-minute quiz. Then begin reviewing the major elements of Chapter 9 through a discussion of the topic "China never changed" as outlined in Chapter 9 of the Instructor's Resource Manual. Spend the rest of the available time by giving the lecture "China's golden age" that is sketched out in the manual.

Day 29: Give the lecture "Medieval Japan: Why unification failed" that is developed in Chapter 9 of the Instructor's Resource Manual. Include the close-reading exercise "The Seventeen Article Constitution" in the context of the lecture.

Day 30: Present the lecture "Is geography destiny? The case of East Asia" that appears in Chapter 9 of the Instructor's Resource Manual. Conclude with the analysis exercise "The big picture" that appears in the manual and with the clicker question for Chapter 9.

Chapter 10

Day 31: Give the lecture "The fall of Rome and creation of the Germanic successor states" described in Chapter 10 of the Instructor's Resource Manual. Incorporate the map-analysis exercise for this chapter into your lecture.

Day 32: Give a five-minute quiz. Then give the lecture "Charlemagne and the last wave of 'barbarian' invasions" outlined in Chapter 10 of the Instructor's Resource Manual. Include a clip from the film *Charlemagne and the Holy Roman Empire*.

Day 33: Give the lecture "The medieval expansion of Europe" detailed in Chapter 10 of the Instructor's Resource Manual, incorporating a review of Chapter 10's main points into your lecture. Follow that up with a discussion of the misconception that "the era of the Middle Ages in Europe was a 'Dark Age,'" one of the discussion topics listed in the Instructor's Resource Manual, and conclude with Chapter 10's clicker question.

Chapter 11

Day 34: Divide the class time into two parts. In the first part, give a short exam on the material covered since the midterm. For the remainder of the class, briefly lecture on "The Arab conquests" as outlined in Chapter 11 of the Instructor's Resource Manual.

Day 35: Spend a whole day on discussion, including the close-reading exercise and at least two of the discussion topics suggested for this chapter in the Instructor's Resource Manual.

Day 36: Lecture on "The golden age of Islam" as outlined in Chapter 11 of the Instructor's Resource Manual. Include a film clip from at least one of the films suggested in the Film section of this chapter of the manual. And don't forget the clicker question!

Chapter 12

Day 37: Review the main points in Chapter 12 of the textbook, using the discussion topics and the map-analysis exercise outlined in Chapter 12 of the Instructor's Resource Manual to help reinforce student understanding of the issues.

Day 38: Give a five-minute quiz. Then give the lecture "Disease in human history" described in Chapter 12 of the Instructor's Resource Manual. Also show a clip from one of the films listed in the Film section of this chapter of the manual. Conclude with Chapter 12's clicker question.

Chapter 13

Day 39: Examine life in the Americas before the European invasion, using elements of the lectures "North America in 1500" and "Aztecs and Incas" that are outlined in Chapter 13 of the Instructor's Resource Manual. If possible, include the close-reading exercise described in this chapter of the manual.

Day 40: Move from a brief exposition of the Ottoman Turks as potential world dominators in the next historical era (see the lecture strategy entitled "An ascendant society: The Ottoman golden age" in Chapter 13 of the Instructor's Resource Manual) to the more basic question of where the world stands in the year 1500—and how to cope with the upcoming final exam. Several of the discussion topics and classroom activities were written with a review for the exam in mind; use whichever suggestion you think will work best for your class. Finish with Chapter 13's clicker question—the most important one of the course.

The Second Half of World History

A Class Plan

Chapters 14–24 of *Ways of the World* deal with material usually covered in the second semester of a world history survey course. How does one organize all that material, integrating what's in the textbook with your own points of particular interest and the issues your department might want to highlight? To a considerable extent, every world history course is a unique product in which the instructor crafts a balance between her or his strengths, programmatic needs, and the materials s/he has available. The following is an example of how such a class might be crafted, suggesting ways in which the Instructor's Resource Manual could be incorporated into a syllabus. It is provided more as food for thought for a new world history instructor than as a blueprint. It assumes that the instructor will have about forty classroom days in an average semester, if teaching a 50-minute course on Mondays, Wednesdays, and Fridays. It could easily be modified for a Tuesday/Thursday course with 75-minute class meetings. Note that it is based on the assumption that students will read the textbook for themselves; while reviews are included, no space is allocated for instructors to simply cover the material in the textbook.

Day 1: Introduction to the course. Go over grading policies, reading expectations, and, especially, your own *objectives* for the course. Do as much as you can to provide a roadmap for the students, and go over the Prologue to Volume 2 of *Ways of the World*.

Chapter 14

Day 2: Start by discussing "The Big Picture" laid out in the introduction to Part Four of the textbook. Then review the main points of Chapter 14 of the textbook, using the map-analysis exercise provided in Chapter 14 of the Instructor's Resource Manual as a framework.

Day 3: Give the lecture "The quest for human rights in the Americas" outlined in Chapter 14 of the Instructor's Resource Manual. Incorporate into the lecture a clip from either *Conquistadores* or *The Conquest of Mexico* (both films are listed in the Film section of Chapter 14 of the manual).

Day 4: Give a five-minute quiz. Proceed to the lecture "A tale of two colonies" detailed in Chapter 14 of the Instructor's Resource Manual, incorporating lessons on note-taking skills into your lecture. Conclude with a discussion of the topic "The New World as Europeans saw it" as suggested in the manual.

Day 5: Present the lecture "Spain at the center" outlined in Chapter 14 of the Instructor's Resource Manual. Proceed from there to the discussion topic "Exploration and colonization happened only in the Atlantic world," and conclude with Chapter 14's clicker question.

Chapter 15

Day 6: Begin with the lecture "Of ships and the sea: The mechanics of a new world order" described in Chapter 15 of the Instructor's Resource Manual. It may prove useful to show short clips from one of the films listed in the Film section of this chapter that deal with exploration and trade. Move from there to the analysis exercise entitled "Find the ports."

Day 7: Make this "slavery day" with a clip from one of the films listed in the Film section of this chapter that deal with slavery, the comparative discussion topic "Slavery, old and new," and the role-playing exercise "Justifying slavery."

Day 8: Give a five-minute quiz. Then deliver the lecture "The companies" outlined in Chapter 15 of the Instructor's Resource Manual.

Day 9: Give the lecture "The Tokugawa shogunate" detailed in Chapter 15 of the Instructor's Resource Manual, and proceed from there to a brief review of the main points of Chapter 15. Conclude with the chapter's clicker question.

Chapter 16

Day 10: Give the lecture "The Reformations and their global significance" outlined in Chapter 16 of the Instructor's Resource Manual. Expand your treatment to include world missionary work by incorporating the role-playing exercise "Matteo Ricci in China."

Day 11: Expand the lecture "Asia and the individual" suggested in Chapter 16 of the Instructor's Resource Manual to consider the issue of individualism more generally. This is a good opportunity to mention that Europe had a Renaissance (and what the significance is of a renaissance), but be sure not to shortchange Asia.

Day 12: Give the lecture "Science and the world" that is detailed in Chapter 16 of the Instructor's Resource Manual, including a clip from the film *The Age of Reason* to provide variety in instructional method. Go from there to the contextualization discussion topic "What did we get from the Scientific Revolution?" which can also serve as a review of material covered in this chapter. Conclude with Chapter 16's clicker question.

Chapter 17

Day 13: Divide the class time in half. In the first half, give a short exam on the material covered in Part Four of the textbook (Chapters 14–16). Spend the rest of the class time with the timeline exercise for Chapter 17, "Revolutions and ideas."

Day 14: Give the lecture "What makes a successful colonial revolution? Looking at the Americas—and Ireland" outlined in Chapter 17 of the Instructor's Resource Manual. Integrate into it the discussion topic "The American Revolution was 'revolutionary.'"

Day 15: Show the short film *The Nationalists* (listed in the Film section of Chapter 17 of the Instructor's Resource Manual). Spend the rest of the class time presenting a short version of the lecture "One nation under God: Revolutions and nationalist movements" outlined in the manual.

Day 16: Give the lecture "At last—a woman's voice" described in Chapter 17 of the Instructor's Resource Manual. As time allows, review the chapter's main points. Ask the clicker question for Chapter 17.

Chapter 18

Day 17: Give the lecture "Imagining the Industrial Revolution" described in Chapter 18 of the Instructor's Resource Manual. Work a review of the chapter's main points into the context of the lecture, as well as a brief clip or two from the film *The Growth of Towns and Cities* (see the Film section of Chapter 18 of the manual for details).

Day 18: Give a five-minute quiz. Then proceed with the lecture "Socialism" outlined in the Instructor's Resource Manual. You might find it helpful to show a clip from one of the films listed in Chapter 18's Film section. Ask the chapter's clicker question.

Day 19: Give the lecture "Economic imperialism" detailed in Chapter 18 of the Instructor's Resource Manual. It might be a good corrective to the notion of Europeans as a whole oppressing other peoples as a whole if you include some discussion of the analysis exercise for Chapter 18, "Life in an industrial city, ca. 1850."

Day 20: Midterm examination

Chapter 19

Day 21: Begin with a good long look at a map, to make sure that students are spatially grounded in the chapter's materials; this is a good opportunity for a quick review of major points. Spend the rest of the class time with the lecture "Confronting racism" outlined in Chapter 19 of the Instructor's Resource Manual.

Day 22: Present the lecture "The nineteenth century and the millennium" that appears in Chapter 19 of the Instructor's Resource Manual. Include a short reading from one of the millennial movements of the era for classroom discussion.

Day 23: Give the lecture "The Meiji restoration and the Young Turks" described in Chapter 19 of the Instructor's Resource Manual. Include a film clip that presents the Meiji period of Japanese history (see the films listed in the Film section of Chapter 19 of the manual). Conclude with the clicker question for Chapter 19.

Chapter 20

Day 24: Begin the class with a five-minute quiz. Then give the lecture "Creating a communication and transportation infrastructure" outlined in Chapter 20 of the Instructor's Resource Manual. In this context, a discussion of the topic "The deep corruption of colonial rule" may prove useful.

Day 25: Give the lecture "The scramble for Africa" detailed in Chapter 20 of the Instructor's Resource Manual, incorporating the map-analysis exercise "Scrambling for Africa" to make the lecture more interactive.

Day 26: Show a clip from the film *The Empire of Good Intentions* (see the Film section of Chapter 20 of the manual for details) that discusses British rule in India. Proceed from there to the lecture "The Raj" described in the manual.

Day 27: Begin the class with the close-reading exercise "The White Man's Burden" described in Chapter 20 of the Instructor's Resource Manual. Go on to undertake at least one of the discussion topics for this chapter included

in the manual. If time allows, show another film clip that exemplifies the main themes of this chapter. Conclude with the clicker question for Chapter 20.

Chapter 21

Day 28: A good place to begin work on the issues covered in this chapter is with the contextualization discussion topic "Christmas in the Trenches" provided in Chapter 21 of the Instructor's Resource Manual. Go on from there to the lecture "From trench warfare to *blitzkrieg*" outlined in the manual.

Day 29: Give a five-minute quiz. Then continue the class with a review of the main issues of the Great Depression, asking the comparison discussion question "Could there be another Great Depression?" Show a clip from the film *Brother, Can You Spare a Dime?* (see the Film section of Chapter 21 of the manual) to help students visualize Depression-era issues.

Day 30: Begin the class with the close-reading exercise "Visualizing fascism" suggested in Chapter 21 of the Instructor's Resource Manual. From the point of fascism actively mobilizing all the people of a country behind the cause of nationalism, go on to the lecture "Civilians and war" detailed in the manual.

Day 31: Give the lecture "Recovery" suggested in Chapter 21 of the Instructor's Resource Manual. If time allows, include a clip from the film *Great Depression to Superpower: 1930–1990* that shows the United States' role in the years after World War II. Ask the clicker question for Chapter 21.

Chapter 22

Day 32: Divide the class time in half. In the first half, give a short exam on materials covered since the midterm. In the remaining time, give a brief version of the lecture "A tale of two communist leaders: Stalin and Mao" outlined in Chapter 22 of the Instructor's Resource Manual, using the lecture as a way to review the main points about the early Soviet Union and communist China given in the textbook.

Day 33: Begin with a review of the main ideological conflicts of the cold war, going on to deliver the lecture

"The 'hot wars' of the cold war era" outlined in Chapter 22 of the Instructor's Resource Manual.

Day 34: Show a clip from either *China at the Crossroads* or *Soviet Disunion* (details provided in the Film section of Chapter 22 of the Instructor's Resource Manual). Move from there to engagement with two of the discussion topics provided for this chapter. Conclude by asking the clicker question for Chapter 22.

Chapter 23

Day 35: Give a five-minute quiz. Then present the lecture "Expanding independence" outlined in Chapter 23 of the Instructor's Resource Manual, incorporating as much as possible a review of the chapter's main points about decolonization.

Day 36: Show extensive clips from the film *Africa: In Defiance of Democracy* (see the Film section of Chapter 23 of the Instructor's Resource Manual for details). Go on from there to present a brief lecture on the topic "Dictatorship and the new nations" as outlined in the Instructor's Resource Manual.

Day 37: Start the class with the analysis exercise "Islamic revolution in Iran" from Chapter 23 of the Instructor's Resource Manual. From that point, expand your scope to the lecture topic "Religion and the third world" detailed in the manual. Don't forget to ask the clicker question!

Chapter 24

Day 38: Begin the class with the close-reading exercise "The letter to America" laid out in Chapter 24 of the Instructor's Resource Manual. From there, segue into the lecture "The United States and the world: An evil empire?" outlined in the manual.

Day 39: Give the lecture "Re-greening the World," including the contextualization discussion topic "Thinking green" detailed in Chapter 24 of the Instructor's Resource Manual. Finish with a clip from the film *Rachel Carson: Nature's Guardian* (see the Film section of Chapter 24 of the manual for details).

Day 40: Review both what's in the chapter and your expectations for the final exam. Be sure to spend some time going over the major points of the feminist movement, and make sure that students are clear on the issues of globalization that were covered in Chapter 24. Finish with the final clicker question.

Discussing *Ways of the World*:
A Survival Guide for First-Time Teaching Assistants

Contents

Introduction

All education is a continuous dialogue — questions and answers that pursue every problem to the horizon. That is the essence of academic freedom.

—William O. Douglas

The Role of a Teaching Assistant

Reflect for a moment on the best teachers you have encountered in your educational career. Like most great teachers, they were probably fired up by some seldom-expressed idealism, a conviction that teaching is the ultimate form of subversion, capable of touching the lives of the young and permanently undermining complacency. The most effective teaching often appears effortless, but it is in fact the product of a lifetime's commitment to helping others and years of practice and preparation. It is also probable that one of these great teachers inspired you to want to teach, and you may hope to emulate your mentor's example. But you also have to write a thesis or dissertation. This survival guide seeks to (1) diminish stress, (2) save you time, and (3) increase your self-confidence as a teacher. Taken together, these three goals should make your job a lot easier while making space for your own research.

Teaching and Scholarship

A teaching assistantship is for most graduate students the introduction to teaching, a wonderful opportunity to develop skills you will use later in your career. Your TA-ship raises a justifiable fear: Will it interfere with the completion of your thesis or dissertation? The answer is no, for the opposite should be the case. There are many reasons why being a teaching assistant should enhance the development of your scholarship, especially if you look to your colleagues, your fellow TAs, and the professor for help and guidance. This survival guide intends to promote this idea, making a difficult task simpler and saving you from having to reinvent the wheel.

Getting to Know *Ways of the World*

In *Ways of the World*, Robert Strayer has produced a brief, comparative text for the world history survey course that privileges big ideas over extensive detail. As such, it is ideally suited to the types of classroom discussion that teaching assistants most often lead. Every chapter of the book is driven by questions, themes, and sustained comparisons that are well suited to debate

and discussion. Moreover, teaching assistants can productively draw on several helpful features of the text to organize and facilitate classroom discussion. When organizing discussion sections, keep the following features in mind:

"Big Picture" part openers provide engaging, question-driven introductions to each large section that place the chapters of each part into a larger context.

The prominence of **sustained comparison** sections, like that between the San and the Chumash in Chapter 1, provide students with the material needed to examine and explore central themes of the book in class.

Every **chapter-opening vignette** reveals the contemporary relevance of the material under discussion, providing a readily accessible and engaging avenue into a discussion of the ongoing importance of the topic today.

Margin Review questions provide carefully formulated questions that are ready-made for classroom discussion and designed to draw crucial themes out of the text.

Snapshots that summarize or highlight particular material in graphic, bulleted, or tabular form can provide ideal opportunities for class analysis and discussion.

In the **Reflections** section at the conclusion of each chapter, Strayer ponders the larger implications of historical analysis in a manner well suited to discussion and debate.

The Instructor's Resource Manual provides further classroom ideas, including **Discussion Topics** and **Classroom Activities**, in the Using *Ways of the World* in the Classroom section of each chapter.

1. Working with a Professor

Defining Your Roles

Make no mistake, a TA-ship is not easy. Most likely, you neither designed this class nor selected the readings, and you will not deliver the lectures. Your position is essentially that of an apprentice, learning the craft not simply by being shown the tools and their use but by observing someone who has mastered the skill.

The boundaries between professors and teaching assistants differ with the institution, its size and traditions, and the people involved. At one extreme, a class may have hundreds of students and as many as twenty TAs. In this sort of context, as is the case at most large research institutions, it is possible that the professor initially does not know most of his or her graduate TAs, and vice versa. The professor's primary role is to supervise and inspect the work of TAs. Such a situation often generates a formal relationship, especially since the TAs know that the professor will be writing a letter for their files. By contrast, at other institutions, a professor will typically have just one or two TAs in a class, and more informal associations result. But in either context, yours is a slightly anomalous position. Most of the time, you are entirely free to conduct your section as you see fit, though within a context set by the professor. The professor selects the readings and topics, but you determine how to address the material. In class discussion, the initiative is entirely yours; aiding students with their writing and grading their work will probably also be your responsibility. But you should not forget that the first and the final word always belong to the professor, who sets the syllabus and signs the grade sheet. It is wise to follow the tone he or she sets. The professor will quickly make it obvious whether you are a colleague or an assistant. If the latter, you may need to adhere more closely to the formalities; but whatever the case, take advantage of the opportunity to work closely with an experienced instructor to learn the art of teaching.

Disagreeing: What to Do

TAs often agonize over occasions when the professor contradicts the textbook or presents views with which they do not agree. Such situations are, in fact, likely to happen, as historical interpretation is full of such disagreements; the lack of uniformity is what gives history its life and excitement. The best tactic is to speak with the professor about such perceived inconsistencies, though not everyone is comfortable with the direct approach. While it would be inappropriate to tell your students that the professor's point of view is wrong, it is legitimate to raise the question of alternative perspectives in your discussion sections and to use it as an exercise in historical method. *Ways of the World* will prove helpful in such a situation. The professor has assigned this book and so should have no objection to your making use of its contents. Highlighting various interpretations does not contradict statements by the instructor. Rather it allows the students to come to terms with the difficulty of the historian's task, while helping them to construct their own informed judgment. The text is your anchor, upon which you can rely in any classroom situation.

You can take further advantage of working with a professor by observing his or her teaching style. Decide for yourself what are valuable methods in the classroom. If it is not part of your TA program to have the professor speak with you about pedagogical issues, join with your fellow TAs to invite him or her to do so. Most professors welcome the opportunity to talk about teaching itself, and you may find that the invitation opens a number of doors onto other ways to learn and acquire teaching skills. For instance, if your professor invites you to deliver a guest lecture to the class, leap at the opportunity, as it is great practice and can figure prominently in a future letter of recommendation from that professor. Likewise, consider asking your professor or graduate adviser to sit in on one of your sections. When the time comes to enter the job market, you will benefit enormously by having letters of recommendation that speak knowledgeably about your teaching experience. In short, the TA-ship is your route to ensuring that you get to teach even more after you have finished your thesis or dissertation.

2. Working with Students

Classroom Atmosphere

Teaching assistants naturally want to work with their students in the friendliest fashion possible. Students, in turn, generally respect TAs and respond well to a relaxed atmosphere. Nonetheless, students also know that the TA is not a professor, and some will occasionally try to exploit the situation. Over the years, instructors have heard every imaginable excuse and plea for special consideration, as well as some that defy the imagination. Your best defense can be a stern offense, clarifying both your accessibility and your professionalism. There are no hard-and-fast rules on how to achieve this balance in the classroom, and every class has its own dynamic. What follows are a number of suggestions on how to establish a professional distance while retaining a sense of camaraderie.

Avoiding Pitfalls

Some aspects of teaching can only be learned the hard way. It may seem unlikely, but some students feel betrayed if they think of you as a close friend and get less than an excellent grade. Other students may turn to you as a personal confessor and share their most private confidences, leading to embarrassment and the lessening of your professional standing with both the other students and your professor. Most dangerous of all, a student may misunderstand your friendliness as an invitation to intimacy. An accusation of sexual harassment can have dire consequences for your professional and personal life.

How you respond to, say, an excess of friendliness, depends on your personality; however, there are three rules that one should keep in mind:

1. No overloads (that is, never increase the size of your class; it is already too large).
2. No sarcasm (students hate it!).
3. No private meetings with students behind closed doors.

Always leave your door open when a student is in your office. Some TAs will only meet students in the middle of the quad; others hold their office hours together. One should not have any trouble saying to a student intent on telling stories that are far too personal, "I'm sorry, but that is none of my business." Some will turn the conversation back to the textbook. But sometimes there is no way of avoiding the student who tearfully tells you of some desperate family trauma and begs for your understanding. Always keep at hand the phone number of the counseling center, and make sure you know where the center is located.

From experience then, most professors discover the need to maintain a friendly but critical distance. The challenge is to remember that working as a TA is part of the process of becoming a professional and therefore requires an appreciation for the trust placed in any teacher. When a student tells you of a personal crisis, it is best to take it seriously and offer sympathy; it is also best to let those better qualified than you deal with the problem.

Finally, there is a tendency among many professors and graduate student instructors to treat their students with disdain, to make fun of their ignorance and belittle their writing skills. While it certainly can relieve tension to get together with other TAs to compare classroom confusions, making fun of your students will quickly take the joy out of teaching and make you question your commitment. Also, undergraduates usually notice a negative attitude. Try to recall your own undergraduate experiences. Indeed, if you have one, read a paper that you wrote in your first year at college.

It is a sobering experience, and one that makes you appreciate even more how much you have gained from a college education.

3. Leading Discussions

For most TAs, the majority of class time is spent conducting discussions based on the lectures, the readings, or both. In terms of effective teaching, discussions are preferable to lectures. It is easier to keep students' attention when they are part of the discussion. Their involvement helps to ensure that they are absorbing information and alerts the instructor to what is working and sinking in and what is not. As John Stuart Mill noted, "The interests of truth require a diversity of opinions." And a highly interactive class is just more fun.

The key to a great discussion is preparation—not the sort of intricate organization that force-marches the students through the material but a thorough understanding of the topic and a conception of the key issues that need to be addressed. Advance preparation will make it all look easy to the students while allowing you the confidence to respond with flexibility to the flow of the discussion.

This guide is directed at aiding the TA in getting started. Examples are therefore drawn from the first chapters of *Ways of the World* that you are likely to use in the first month of classes. While these particular examples are just suggestions, their logic should be transferable to other chapters and other periods in world history.

The First Day of Class

Your first task is to ease your students' tension and anxieties. They are generally nervous about taking a history class that requires them to synthesize both lectures and readings at the college level. Often they do not know anyone else in the section and are scared to voice opinions in front of peers. Even though this is an introductory world history course, you may be surprised to learn how many of your students disliked high school history and learned little of what we understand history to be. Many students think of history as the memorization of dates. You therefore need to reassure your students that there is a lot more to history than dates and that it will be worth their time to give it a second chance. If you are comfortable doing so, you may want to introduce both yourself and the subject by talking a bit about the origins of your own fascination with history and what sustains that interest. *Nothing*—heavy emphasis—makes an introductory course more successful than the enthusiasm of the instructor for the material.

Icebreakers

Before addressing the subject matter, turn to your students. If you can establish even the loosest sense of community on the first day, you will find the weeks ahead far more pleasant, as your students will be a little less hesitant to share their judgments and far more receptive to your leadership. So get acquainted quickly, indicating that they are among friends and that what they have to say will be heard and respected. It is usually not sufficient to go around the room and ask the students to give their names. You must instead try to get a sense of their identities. One way is to ask each student to relay the standard information—name, academic year, major, where he or she is from—and then add something unique, such as a favorite record or the last book he or she read for pleasure. You may even want to write this information down on index cards as a way of helping yourself to learn each student's name over the first few weeks. Alternatively, try some version of the "name game," for instance by pairing off students and asking them not simply to tell one another their names but to say something about the history of that name; what it means, where it came from, whether it originally belonged to someone else, like a grandparent. After a few minutes of letting the students talk and relax, one can go around the room and ask each student to tell the whole class about his or her neighbor. By the end of this exercise, one can be fairly confident that the students will not refer to one another as "that guy" and that they will get a sense of the personal power of history.

After spending some time getting to know one another, you may want to share with your students your goals for the semester. Even here, though, it is best to keep the tone light. When students first hear about an essay assignment, they often start worrying almost immediately about what they are going to write. It is better to frame the discussion of the paper assignment within the context of questions or doubts they may have about world history. Ask them what event in world history most bothers them or most intrigues them. The events you write on the board form a range of possible research and discussion topics.

Before the students leave the classroom, make certain that they know how to reach you, and vice versa. With email, this task has become easier. Circulate a list and ask them to record their electronic addresses. If you have the time, make up a list of email addresses so you can send reminders to your students of upcoming assignments. They will certainly appreciate the extra effort on your part. You can also send out a message the day after the first class just reminding everyone of your office hours and their first reading assignment. Students generally welcome any indication that their teachers care. Whatever you do on the first day, it is appropriate and advisable to keep it light and informal; a friendly atmosphere pays long-term dividends in the classroom. It is for that reason that you might consider having your students use your first name in class. They know you are the teacher and calling you by your first name need not diminish respect. But if you want to be called Mr. or Ms. TA, it is best to make that clear up front by introducing yourself that way.

Preparing to Teach a Section

A common initial response is despair over the seeming ignorance of the majority of the undergraduates. Teaching assistants enter their first classes with high expectations of the stimulating conversations before them, only to discover that even those college students that took world history in high school have retained very little. While it is therefore safe—and helpful—to assume that you know a great deal more world history than most of your students, it is a grievous error to treat those students with contempt. You can have confidence that your greater knowledge allows you to avoid the hurdles of overpreparation for a fifty-minute discussion. But remember also that it is a mistake to denigrate students for their lack of preparation; it will only make your job harder. Effective teachers, like all great craftspeople, work with the materials at hand. Your task is to teach *your* students, not some idealized version of what a student should be. And you can feel rather comfortable that you will not be boring your students with well-known material; it is most likely new to them.

There is no rule on how much time to devote to preparing for your class. If you are discussing a theme with which you are personally very familiar, you may find yourself simply walking in to lead the discussion. On the other hand, if you have never studied, for instance, the emergence of First Civilizations, you may find yourself spending about four hours preparing for a single hour of class time. Half that preparation time may be devoted to rereading the text and any supplemental works assigned, while it will probably take you about an hour to outline the direction in which you would like the conversation to go, with all the main points and page references arranged in a logical order.

The Instructor's Resource Manual can provide assistance in the preparation of class plans. Each chapter of the textbook is outlined in the manual; and while you may not want to proceed simply, point by point, through the textbook, you can certainly pull out a section of the outline for ideas on organizing your own class. For instance, look at the outline for Chapter 3. Section III–C of the outline forms a cohesive framework for a discussion of the emergence of patriarchy in the First Civilizations. How you use the Instructor's Resource Manual depends on what additional reading might be assigned. If the class is reading source documents such as, for instance, Hammurabi's law code, then the above suggestions would work very well, and you could easily plug this additional reading into the Instructor's Resource Manual outline. Moreover, in the Using *Ways of the World* in the Classroom section of each chapter of the Instructor's Resource Manual, we have provided nine concrete suggestions for exploring the chapter's themes in the classroom. The suggestions included under the headings "Discussion Topics" and "Classroom Activities" are specifically designed for discussion-based classes and can provide you with a place to start your lesson planning. Thus, for example, Discussion Topic 3 and Classroom Activity 2 from Chapter 3 of the Instructor's Resource Manual provide ways of contextualizing the question of patriarchy in class.

You should, however, avoid overdoing it. It is very easy to overprepare, even for a topic with which you are unfamiliar. There is no rule you can follow on how much preparation is enough. If you don't feel comfortable talking with the other TAs about a subject *after* you have read the textbook, ask the professor for a recommendation of an article or a book that might deepen your understanding of the theme under discussion. If you have read the textbook and just one other book on the subject, you are way ahead of your students. By the way, should you feel the need to read a supplementary text, bring it to class with you. Not only will you find its presence comforting, but most students will be impressed with your diligence when you tell them you

were reading the book the night before and found a great passage.

But you are not really prepared for a class just because you have read and outlined the chapter and stuck some bookmarks into the textbook. Class discussions rarely follow logical schematics of discourse, and your job is not just to summarize what the students read. You need to devote at least another hour before class imagining the types of questions you are likely to receive and considering how you will demonstrate the larger issues under consideration. It is very helpful in this context to get together with at least one other TA and compare notes. You will probably notice that you and your fellow TAs have outlined the material in very different ways. Of course, this divergence is inherent in the very nature of history. Historians do not select the same facts or events for their interpretations of the past, nor do they structure their arguments similarly. But just as we learn from reading scholars with whom we disagree, so you can enhance your scholarship and develop your scholarly voice in the classroom by getting a sense of how other educated people address the same subject. In that regard, your premier source for intellectual comparison should be your professor. Listen closely to the lectures, and talk to him or her about your understanding of the subject under discussion.

Getting Started

At first thought, nothing is more difficult than starting a lively conversation with twenty or thirty students—many of whom may not want to talk about a historic topic of little apparent relevance to modern life. But teachers have developed a number of very effective techniques over the years from which you are free to borrow—a few of them are described below. Observe good teachers and note their techniques, appropriating whatever works for you.

An effective discussion should not only clarify the meaning of the lectures and texts but also provide a network of ideas that, by connecting the material, will allow students to see the big picture. The key is to get your students' attention early on and maintain it. An energetic beginning will make a strong impression on your students, allowing you to keep their interest, and provide the framework for the entire discussion.

You will quickly notice that many of your students have not yet learned the necessary analytical skills to make connections between the lecture and the assigned reading or to formulate independent interpretations. It would be wise for you to get in the habit of discussing the texts from the start and explaining to students the importance of substantiating their comments with evidence from the textbook or lectures. At the very first meeting, turn to the first page of the textbook. Even if you have reason to believe that no one has done the reading, or rather precisely *because* you think no one has done the reading, draw everyone's attention to the opening passages of the book. Why does a history of the world begin with creation myths from around the world? Stories are often an effective way of unpacking a whole range of larger issues. In the Prologue, students are introduced to billions of years of history in just a few pages, in some ways offering the modern equivalent of the earlier creation myths. Strayer also includes in the Prologue a clear statement of what world history is and how it differs from other approaches to history. In this short introduction, the textbook provides the context in which the course should be considered and also shows that students should be drawing on information gleaned from the lectures and the textbook to construct their own understanding of historical development; your role will be more that of a moderator than an instigator.

Effective Methods

There are, of course, a number of different methods for getting off to a quick and successful start. Try using the chapter-ending Reflections sections, which ask students to consider the larger implications of historical analysis in a manner well suited to discussion and debate. Alternatively, you might use the chapter-opening vignettes, which emphasize the contemporary relevance of the topic explored in each chapter. These sections are structured in such a way that they require students to respond personally to the topic in hand, which can facilitate getting discussion started. The issues raised in these sections seek to convey a certain contemporary resonance for students, an attribute to be encouraged, as it will carry your class conversations beyond the classroom.

Likewise, the snapshots and maps in each chapter can also provide fertile ground for opening classroom discussion. For instance, as suggested in Discussion Topic 1 from Chapter 5 of the Instructor's Resource Manual, the passages about love included in Snapshot 5.2 (p. 145

of the textbook) provide an excellent starting point for students to consider both common ground among, and differences between, the classical cultural systems. Another example, as suggested in Classroom Activity 2 from Chapter 4, uses the maps in Chapter 4 and could provide an excellent opening to a class dedicated to a comparison of classical empires. A final possibility would be to return in Chapter 6 to a theme like patriarchy or slavery that has already been explored in Chapter 3. Reference back to a previous discussion can provide an easy and fruitful comparison with which to open a new class.

Explaining Historiography

One of the most difficult yet exciting lessons of history for undergraduates is the discovery that the discipline of history changes constantly. The facts of a given event can be altered to suit some later purpose, only to be "discovered" decades later. *Ways of the World* is particularly good at presenting multiple schools of thought about key developments in a manner that is accessible to students and ripe for discussion. In Chapter 3, for instance, Strayer offers multiple possible interpretations to both the question of why some chiefdoms developed into civilizations and the question of why patriarchy developed in the First Civilizations. These passages can easily be expanded upon in class by bringing in further evidence for students to consider. In pursuit of historiographical understanding among your students, it may be useful to begin the class with a reading from an old history text that will shock students' sensibilities about issues like the place and role of women in ancient societies. But beyond shocking students, these older passages show students how interpretations change through time and how much we have learned in just the past few decades. Students will gain a noticeable confidence in formulating their own historical perspectives through an appreciation of history as a work in progress.

Sustaining Focus

The easiest way to sustain a focused discussion is to require the students to do most of the work. There are a number of short assignments that can help you attain this end. For example, have students select a single passage in the reading that most captures their attention, have them bring a single question to class, or have them write a hypothesis on a theme covered in the lecture with one piece of supportive evidence drawn from the text. These assignments will lay the basis for deeper discussion, as will both the innovative exercises described below and the numerous suggestions in the Using *Ways of the World* in the Classroom section of each chapter of the Instructor's Resource Manual.

Role-Playing Exercises

One of the most successful routes to a lively conversation is to have the students take sides in a debate. Some of the Discussion and Classroom Activity suggestions in the Instructor's Resource Manual suggest possible debates. Many others could easily be modified for debate—for instance, Discussion Topic 3 from Chapter 3, which asks students to discuss a central theme of that chapter: the deep-seated assumption that civilization was necessarily a good thing in human history.

Alternatively, role playing can be a useful and engaging tool. Many role-playing possibilities are offered in the Classroom Activities sections of the Instructor's Resource Manual. For instance, Classroom Activity 2 from Chapter 1 suggests a simple role-play that could be conducted on the spur of the moment in class by asking students to split into small groups, pick a climate area, and decide what items they absolutely need for survival as gatherers and hunters in the Paleolithic period. Alternatively, Classroom Activity 2 from Chapter 5 suggests a more complex role-playing scenario that would require preparation by some of the students in small groups outside of class. In this scenario, the class is a group of Ethiopian royal counselors in the third century C.E., while three groups drawn from the class play the roles of Buddhist, Christian, and Zoroastrian missionaries. Have each group make a short presentation on why the king of Ethiopia should convert to *their* religion, then allow the rest of the class to vote, based on the quality of the presentations.

Making Connections

Students will undoubtedly find some issues more difficult than others and will need help in making sense of what seems to them a very complicated connection. For instance, students used to studying regions in history courses may find Chapters 5 and 6 confusing, as cultural traditions and social hierarchies in the classical period are explored comparatively. It is important to spot these potential problems ahead of time, as doing so allows one to deal with the problems head-on at the start of the class session. In this case, it would be helpful to ask students why the author chose to look at such very different belief systems or social hierarchies together. If they appear baffled, draw their attention to the opening pages of the chapter, where the author explains his thinking. Here lies both the explanation for your question and a way of reading the textbook that will come in useful for students in later chapters. Careful preparation in highlighting the textbook's argument will save you a great deal of time and forestall any mounting confusion that may derail discussion.

It is also vital to remain aware of gaps in your students' understanding. Students are often largely ignorant of the time periods under study, particularly in Volume 1. If your class does not grasp the foundation of a specific historical sequence, students will not be able to follow its development. Thus, without an understanding of what drove humans to settle down to an agricultural lifestyle, a discussion of the emergence of First Civilizations will be completely muddled. This is not to say that you should move at a stately pace, page by page, through the text. Rather, touch on the key passages to ensure that vital concepts are grasped and that your students are constructing the historical causality. For example, prepare for your discussion of the emergence of the First Civilizations in Chapter 3 by making sure that students fully understand the key characteristics of agricultural village societies and chiefdoms explored in Chapter 2. You can help students make causal connections by returning to Chapter 2 before moving on.

Attention-Getting Devices

Occasionally, you will get the sense that the students' collective attention is lagging. There are varieties of effective attention-getting devices available—voicing an outrageous assertion or quotation, calling on students by name, or even the old classic: "This will be on the final." (The latter can induce a bit of anxiety, which some say reduces attention, so it may best be used as an obvious joke.) One can also be less dramatic and play on the desire of students to generalize about world history by culling examples, metaphors, and analogies from the textbook and then asking students to expand on their representative value. Alternatively, you might want to draw on the "Misconception/Difficult Topic" discussion ideas offered in the Using *Ways of the World* in the Classroom section of each chapter of the Instructor's Resource Manual. For instance, the "Misconception/Difficult Topic" from Chapter 6 is the idea that only women are "oppressed" in a patriarchy. A topic like this offers an engaging subject closely associated with the central themes of the chapter with which to revive classroom discussion. If none of these approaches works, you may just want to try a complete change of pace, telling the students that you will return to these questions later (be sure to do so) and attack the issue from a completely different direction. If you resort to the latter tactic, it is useful to flip back a page or two and get a running start. Try asking about something that you are sure the students must know as a way of building momentum and getting opinions out in the open. Often the students themselves will then return to your earlier question with a loud "I get it!" (For further ideas, see "Dealing with Problems" on page 411 of this guide.)

The purpose of using these exercises in discussion building is to link the knowledge available in the textbook and lectures with the students' reasoning powers. Students often read through textbooks and sit through lectures without pausing to consider the broader implications of statements. Until you ask what is meant by "the Columbian exchange," a student might not comprehend the powerful impact of Columbus's voyages on the Atlantic world.

4. Testing

Standards

Generally, TAs work with the materials the professor prepares. You may therefore encounter many different types of tests. Objective midterm and final exams have the advantage of being straightforward; an answer is either correct or incorrect, and you just have to mark it as such. Short essays and even short identifications are a different matter, and the standards of grading are generally the same as those which apply to papers, as discussed below. But it is important to note that, since you will be reading responses to questions you did not write, and since those answers are often based more on the lectures than the text, it would be wise to spend some time getting a sense of the professor's expectations. Most professors will hold a meeting for this purpose on their own initiative. If such a discussion is not forthcoming, you should request it. Ask the professor to outline what she or he considers the essential material to be covered in an exam essay. Determine if the professor expects the exam to be based largely on the texts, the lectures, or both. Are students to be judged on the quality of their writing or solely on their ability to touch on several key facts and arguments? Is there a specific scale for grading (for example, is an A equivalent to a score of 90 and above or to a score of 95 and higher)? What should you do if a student misses a test and then shows up in your office demanding to take the exam at that time? (The answer from the professor should be "Send that student to see me.") And perhaps most important, what does the professor expect of you in assisting the students to prepare for the exam? Are study sessions with your participation encouraged, tolerated, or forbidden? You must be clear on these standards before you devote time to helping your students and evaluating their work.

Preparing Students

Given the enormous stress that most students feel over finals, they will appreciate any help you can offer them. But keep in mind that you will also be making your job easier in preparing the students for the exam, if only because it will prevent complaints later. You can meet with individual students or groups of students during your office hours, though you will quickly find yourself repeating the same advice. The most efficient way to help is to moderate a study session. Note my choice of the word "moderate." You are doing your students an enormous favor in holding a study session, but you should not get carried away and essentially do their work for them.

The best approach, once you have gotten the approval of your professor, is to hand out, at your last discussion meeting before the exam, a number of sample identifications or essay topics (and note that many professors routinely make such lists available anyway). Divide up the list among those interested in attending a study session, and make each student responsible for outlining—and only outlining—a useful answer or identification. If you have prepared well, you have already reserved a classroom and a time for the review session. At that session, you may want to begin with a few general rules for students to follow during the exam—essentially a summary of the expectations of the professor. For instance, you may tell students to avoid rhetorical flourishes and padding. It is not the length of the answer that matters but its precision. Add that they must write neatly; if you cannot read what is written, you will assume that it is incorrect. (One of the oldest tricks of test taking, dating back to classical Greece, is to deliberately obscure one's writing in the hope that the grader will assume the answer is correct.)

Now comes the heart of the review session. Ask the student or students who tackled the first problem to write their outline(s) on the board and to explain the logic of their structure. Your task at this point is simply to question the comparative worth of details. By this time in the semester, students should be talking fairly freely with one another, and you can count on the other students to point out errors or failures of logic. More substantively, students may debate the relative merit of certain facts for an identification or essay question. At this point, you can intervene and suggest that the particulars each student selects depend on the larger argument he or she is trying to make.

Once you have moved through all the problems in turn and covered the boards with sample outlines, you may want to repeat the basic expectations for the exam. Specifically, you can remind students what is considered an excellent answer and what constitutes a barely acceptable one. If students are convinced that they understand the nature of the exam, they will be much more comfortable taking it and will produce better work. It is vital that you remember how important it is for students to do well on the final. With a review session, you not only allow students to provide one another with sample outlines but also encourage them to think about the problems before them. When you come to grade your exams, you will certainly find some recapitulations from your review, but you will also be surprised by the multiplicity of responses you receive to the same question.

5. Paper Assignments

Helping Students Generate Topics

Most professors supply paper assignments. As you already know, these assignments take many forms. Some draw entirely on the assigned reading, which reduces your responsibilities substantially. Others require the students to go to the library. At this point, many students will need your help. Your first task is often to clarify the difference between primary and secondary sources. Explain that primary sources are the building blocks of history and that each historian is capable of reading these sources differently, often in dramatically distinctive ways. This would be a good time to distribute the "Guidelines for Writing a Good History Essay" and "The Use of Sources in Writing Research Papers" handouts (on pp. 407 and 408), should you be using them. Unless your library has an especially good tour of its resources, it is well worth the time to take your section to the library yourself and show them how you use the resources. After all, you are a historian, and, at least for this paper, your students are historians as well.

Should you have the chance to craft your own essay assignment, you may want to use your professor's previous assignments as models. You will probably note that many professors operate on the assumption that, at least in introductory courses, there is a difference between first and later assignments. With the first essay—often the student's first college paper—it is best to offer topics with precise alternatives, such as: "Did peoples settling down to agriculture in the Fertile Crescent have advantages compared to those peoples who pioneered agriculture in Mesoamerica? Were those advantages significant?" In such instances, you can draw attention to very specific parts of the textbook as starting points for discussion. While such categorical assignments posed as questions (rather than phrased with the deadly "explain" or "describe") do not determine the individual student's essay, they do provide a clear sense of alternatives on which the student can build his or her analysis. And students will proceed more logically in their research if they perceive the need to answer a historical question and take a definite position on a scholarly question. By the time they receive the final paper assignment, students should be able to construct an independent thesis without needing such blatant directional markers.

The Writing Process

Most of your work as a TA outside the classroom will be devoted to guiding and grading essay assignments. It is advisable to offer extra office hours during the week before a paper is due. In these consultations, many students will essentially ask you for their thesis. Avoid the impulse to provide one. You will need to ask many leading questions (for example, "What role does race play in the institution of slavery?" or "Do you think that patriarchy in Egypt was less severe than in Mesopotamia?"), and you may think the student's thesis lacks depth, but you do not want to be accountable for the paper when it comes time to grade it. And remember, many students try to distance themselves from responsibility for the final product. Do not let them say "*your* paper"; it is "*my* paper."

The single most common gripe about history classes is this: "It was not an English class, and yet I was graded on my grammar." You therefore need to explain, in the strongest possible terms, that writing clearly is an absolute necessity. A history course requires the same level of writing as that required in any composition class. History papers are not the regurgitation of facts but the expression of a mode of

analysis. It does not matter how good an idea is if no one can understand it. If a student seems to be struggling with writing, make sure to let her or him know what resources are available on your campus, such as writing centers and tutoring services.

Make clear your expectations for student writing assignments. You may want to establish certain recommendations for the preparation of a superior essay. Generally, it is wise to keep such guidelines brief so that students will actually read them (please see the handout "Guidelines for Writing a Good History Essay" below for an example, which you are free to use). The particulars of your guidelines are going to reflect your own sense of good writing.

The very last point in the handout references plagiarism and may require further guidelines. Some of the most common student defenses include: (1) "The

---

Guidelines for Writing a Good History Essay

1. **Preparation.** Good history papers begin with effective reading. Your work will be based on your understanding of primary and secondary literature. If you cannot summarize the point of either sort of document in a sentence or two, go back and read the document again.

2. **Thesis.** Your essay should be driven by a clear, comprehensible, and sustained thesis. Your first paragraph should state that thesis and indicate how you plan to substantiate it.

3. **Organization.** Every paragraph should clarify, demonstrate, expand, or build on your thesis. An outline is a handy tool for ensuring the coherence of your essay.

4. **Evidence.** Every generalization should be supported with specific evidence.

5. **Chronology.** Historians like dates; we use them to organize information and demonstrate intellectual and social developments over time. Be clear in your chronology, using dates to structure your arguments.

6. **Conclusion.** A good essay goes somewhere; it does not simply circle back to repeat the opening statement. Your conclusion should indicate the

direction of your thoughts, briefly summarizing your argument, for instance, while indicating its wider historical significance.

7. **Editing.** All good writers rewrite, and often. Proofread your essay. Do not hesitate to rewrite if you find flaws in its content, logic, or style. With spell checkers, there is no longer any excuse for spelling errors. Reading your work aloud or having a friend do so is a good way to catch errors of grammar and reasoning.

8. **Style.** The key to effective nonfiction writing is clarity. Therefore, avoid the passive voice like the plague. "Poland was invaded" avoids the unpleasant fact that Germany invaded Poland. Passive voice obscures, which is why bureaucrats love it. Similarly, "this" and "these" should always be followed by a noun so that your reader knows what you are talking about.

9. **References.** All quotations must bear some form of citation, such as a footnote or an endnote. These citations should allow your reader to find your sources easily. Be aware that a writer's facts, ideas, and phraseology are the property of that individual. Anyone using a writer's ideas or phraseology without due credit is guilty of plagiarism.

The Use of Sources in Writing Research Papers

A writer's facts, ideas, and phraseology should be regarded as his or her property. *Any person who uses a writer's ideas or phraseology without giving due credit is guilty of plagiarism.*

Information may be put into a paper without a footnote or without some kind of documentation only if it meets the following conditions: It may be found in several books on the subject and therefore belongs to common knowledge; it is written entirely in the words of the student and is not paraphrased from any particular source.

Generally, if you write while looking at a source or while looking at notes taken from a source, a footnote or an endnote should be given. Instructors encourage students to explore, appreciate, and use the ideas of others, but we expect proper attribution for those ideas. Even when written entirely in your own words, the opinions of others must be credited.

All direct quotations should be cited. Brief phrases and even key words that are used as they appear in a source should be in quotation marks.

Summaries and paraphrases are expressions of another writer's words and ideas. You cannot simply substitute a few synonyms and call the idea your own. You must express summaries and paraphrases using your own language. Even within a summary or paraphrase, any direct quotes of phrases, however small, should be accompanied by quotation marks.

On page 704 of *The Bedford Handbook,* Seventh Edition (2006), Diana Hacker suggests how to avoid plagiarism while summarizing or paraphrasing: "Set the source aside, write from memory, and consult the source later to check for accuracy."

A primary source is a document or artifact written or created during the period you wish to study. Secondary works are books or articles written after the fact.

Proper Source Citation and Plagiarism Examples

In reading Linda Kerber, *Women of the Republic* (1980), you come across the following sentences on page 23:

> Rousseau is well known for his sharp criticism of contemporary society and his vision of radical social change. His statements about women, however, usually reinforced the existing order .... Rousseau's conservatism about women may well have served to make his radical comments about men's behavior more palatable.

Quotation:

The writer has used a direct quotation from the source material and has correctly applied quotation marks and an in-text citation crediting Kerber's work.

> Kerber questions Rousseau's reputation as a social critic, noting that his "statements about women .... usually reinforced the existing order" (23).

Paraphrase:

The writer has taken an idea from the source material and put it into her own words, using an in-text citation to credit Kerber's ideas.

> Kerber questions Rousseau's reputation as a social critic, noting that he always endorsed conventional views of women's roles (23).

No need to cite:

This sentence draws on common knowledge and does not require a citation.

> Rousseau was a prominent Enlightenment philosopher.

Plagiarism:

Here the writer plagiarized by failing to use quotation marks and by not inserting the proper citation, even though she directly quoted part of the source material.

> Rousseau was a prominent Enlightenment philosopher whose statements about women usually reinforced the existing order.

> Or

The writer presents paraphrased material but plagiarizes by failing to include a proper citation.

> Rousseau is generally perceived to have been a radical social thinker. Yet because of his traditional views on the role of women, his more extreme criticisms of male society may have been more acceptable.

Note that rearranging a sentence or using a thesaurus search is still plagiarism, as is the failure to use quotation marks.

teacher did not explain plagiarism," (2) "My culture/former school/other professors permit copying directly from the book," and (3) "I printed the wrong file from my computer." None of these is a good excuse, which does not prevent students' repeated attempts to use them. Many professors therefore hand out precise explanations of plagiarism in a hopeful effort to prevent problems. There is an example of such an explanation on page 408 of the Instructor's Resource Manual. Feel free to plagiarize it.

Plagiarism is usually fairly easy to discern, as you will note the complete absence of grammatical errors or the use of obscure archival sources. Proving plagiarism can be a very difficult and time-consuming task, unless the miscreant plagiarizes from the textbook (a great deal more common than you might think). Quite often, though, a simple Web search of a distinctive phrase will within minutes find the source from which the student copied. Recent innovations like www.turnitin.com make it even more difficult for a student to plagiarize with impunity. If you suspect plagiarism, inform your professor immediately.

Being proactive with your students' essays is time-efficient, as it takes less time to read and grade a good essay than a bad one. So do not hesitate to welcome, or demand, outlines and rough drafts. You know from your own experience that good writing is the product of several drafts; demand the same of your students. The fifteen minutes required to go over an outline and/or rough draft with a student can save hours of explanation and defense based on an easily avoided misunderstanding.

6. Grading Tests and Papers

Avoiding Uncertainty

Grading is a form of communication. The greatest complaint of students is the uncertainty of grading. You will almost always see more students in your office in the first few hours after the first grade has been awarded than at any other time during the semester; and what they will most want explained to them is why they received the exact grade they did—why they got a C+ and not an A. If you cannot explain the distinction, students will very often move on to the professor with bitter criticisms of incompetence on the part of the TA. The more you can make the subjective process of grading appear objective, the more useful and congenial the conversation will be with your students.

Choosing a Grading System

With grading, it is best to provide the answer before the question is even framed. One approach is to define the structure of your grading system in the professor's course syllabus. Some instructors supply general rules of grading, emphasizing the characteristics they expect in a good paper. Others attempt to break down the exact parameters of grading, as much as that is possible, assigning definitions to each aspect of the grading process. Others try "blind grading," having students use numbers instead of names on their papers. Blind grading has its drawbacks. Each student is different—each has specific needs and backgrounds, convictions, and problems, all of which should be considered when grading a paper. Blind grading allows no opportunity to note improvement, let alone praise and reward it. Think very carefully about your understanding of the process of teaching before adopting such a procedure.

There is simply no way that anyone can provide hard standards for grading. Page 410 of the Instructor's Resource Manual has an example of such a grading chart, which you are free to use if you like. This chart attempts to clarify the component parts of an essay and define the grade equivalent. Such a chart not only gives students a sense of the seriousness of your approach to grading but also provides the basis for any discussions about grading—if it does not forestall such conversations entirely. Obviously, this chart works on the assumption of an absolute standard rather than on some sort of modified bell curve, as is still used in a few colleges.

Two obvious points: (1) Particulars of this or any other such standard of grading will need some precise explanation; (2) by being very rigorous in your statement on grading, you allow yourself room for generosity when appropriate. Nonetheless, if you use a grading chart like this one, stick to it and use it as the basis for all conversations with students about their grades. If, in such a discussion, a student begins to wander to peripheral issues like the font he or she used, bring him or her back to the chart with the question, "Did I establish that as a necessary quality of your essay?" Similarly, if a student complains that you graded primarily on grammar and not enough on "my ideas" (a very common complaint), point out the importance you attached to language skills and make clear that the best

Grade	Thesis	Analysis	Development and Support	Structure	Grammar
A	Essay is based on a clear, precise, well-defined, and original thesis that goes beyond ideas discussed in class or the assigned readings.	Essay contains cogent analysis that demonstrates a command of interpretive and conceptual task required by assignment and course material.	Essay includes well-chosen examples, persuasive reasoning consistently applied, and solid evidence directly applicable to the thesis.	Essay moves easily from one point to the next with clear, smooth, and appropriate transitions, coherent organization, and fully developed paragraphs.	The author employs sophisticated sentences effectively, chooses words aptly, and observes all the conventions of English grammar to craft an eloquent essay.
B	A clear, specific thesis, central to the essay.	Demonstrates a solid understanding of the texts, ideas, and methods of the assignment.	Pursues thesis consistently, clearly developing a core argument with well-defined component points and appropriate supportive detail.	Clear transitions and the development of coherent, connected ideas in unified paragraphs.	A good command of English, though with occasional stylistic or grammatical problems.
C	A general thesis, central to the essay.	Shows an understanding of the basic ideas and information involved in the assignment, though with some errors of fact or confusion of interpretation, and a tendency toward recapitulations or narration of standard chronology.	Incomplete development of core argument; weak organization or shallow analysis, insufficiently articulated ideas, or unsupported generalizations.	Some awkward transitions and weak or undeveloped paragraphs not clearly connected to one another.	A tendency toward wordiness, unclear or awkward sentences, imprecise use of words, grammatical errors, and a vagueness of meaning brought on by the passive voice.
D	Vague or irrelevant thesis.	Inadequate command of course material with significant factual or conceptual errors. Fails to respond directly to the assignment.	Discursive and undeveloped, a mere narration that digresses from one topic to another.	Simplistic and discursive, tending to vague summations and digressions from one topic to another.	Major grammatical problems such as subject-verb disagreement, obscure pronouns, and sentence fragments. Language marred by clichés, colloquialisms, repeated inexact word choices, and gross spelling errors.
F	No discernible thesis.	Failure to understand class materials. Essay is not a response to the assignment.	Little or no development; a listing of the vaguest generalizations or misinformation.	No transitions and incoherent paragraphs.	Unreadable owing to the violation of the basic rules of grammar.

ideas in the world are useless if no one can understand them. Suggest that your students think of the grading chart as the "rule book"; you do not argue with the umpire to switch to four strikes just this once.

Commenting on Student Papers

All this preparation will be wasted if you cannot convey to your students your judgments of their work. In other words, grading is not only the assignment of a grade but also an indication of the reasons for that grade. Do not just append a grade to the end of a student essay; write out a paragraph explaining your understanding of the reasons for that grade. Again, it saves time to be as precise as possible in these comments. It is vital that you leave the student with his or her self-respect intact, but you must also be completely clear as to what problems the paper has. The key here is to treat the final comments as a series of recommendations for improvement. Rather than saying something sarcastic, suggest that the student seek assistance at the college writing center. Rather than saying "You did not understand this book," recommend that the student look again at the author's thesis as presented in the introduction. In short, work on the assumption that your students will want to go back and correct their errors in order to improve future essays.

You will no doubt feel the urge to correct every error of grammar, organization, and logic that you perceive while reading the essay. Avoid this impulse. It takes up far too much of your time and quite simply can depress a student to the point where he or she feels there is no hope. Highlight key problems with the essay, or circle examples of common errors. The student can then realistically tackle the major hurdles. An added advantage of this approach is that, should the student complain about his or her grade, you can go back and point out further problems, demonstrating the full level of your prior compassion and the justice of your generous grade.

Finally the day arrives when you must calculate a class grade for each student. Avoid sudden gifts, such as last-minute extra credit or forgiveness for some component of a grade for a specific student. Word will get out, and other students will demand similar treatment, even after grades have been turned in. Set a standard and stick to it. The course syllabus should state precisely the relative values of class assignments (for example, each essay equaling 25 percent of the class grade). The one place where you can allow yourself a little leeway in determining final grades is in class participation. Here is where you can reward those students who made positive contributions to the class over the term and penalize those who slept through class. If you have prepared well, no student will be surprised by his or her final grade. Still, it is wise to attach a clear calculation of the class grade to each student's final, reiterating the percentages assigned to each class assignment and recording every grade received by the student—for instance, "1st essay (25%): C+; 2nd essay (25%): B+; final exam (40%): B; class participation (10%): B+; final grade: B."

7. Dealing with Problems

Teaching carries with it problems large and small. Keep the distinction between large and small problems clear and avoid making those problems easily solved into complicated situations that drain you of time and energy. An overly aggressive student whose conduct borders on sexual harassment is a large problem. A student who comes to you with tales of woe may become a large problem. Do not—repeat, DO NOT—attempt to deal with these large problems yourself. Every college employs people who are trained to handle these kinds of problems. At the very least, it is your professor who should address any complicated issues or threatening situations. Report any such matters to the professor immediately, and let others with more authority or professional preparation cope with them. Careers have been cut short by a TA's conviction that a major confrontation or talk of suicide was a joke. Disengage yourself as quickly as possible from an undergraduate's personal problems and let people with more experience and resources take over.

What *is* of concern to you are the little problems that arise as you learn any skill. No one is a born teacher any more than anyone is a born bicycle rider. Every teacher makes mistakes and confronts roadblocks; recognize them as part of your training, identify the problem, and work on it. Talk with your fellow TAs and professors about a specific difficulty and learn how they dealt with it. While students are most creative in inventing new crises for teachers, there are a few common difficulties you may encounter that we should consider.

You may not suffer from this trauma, but many students have a deep fear of speaking in public. You may observe a student who is a blabbermouth in the cafeteria yet clams up in your classroom. Usually, these students are just afraid of making fools of themselves. There are several ways of getting a shy student, or most of a quiet class, to participate. The first step is to avoid phrasing questions in a manner that implies only one answer (factual questions aside). Having the class write their responses to a specific question and then read them out loud in class is very effective; even shy people feel safe reading aloud something they have already written. Breaking the class into smaller groups responsible for developing reactions to a historical problem also draws quieter students into the conversation, though you need to be particularly alert to the dynamic of each group.

At the other extreme are those who participate too much. A private conversation during your office hours is the best way to let a student know that, while you appreciate his or her contributions to the class discussion, you would like his or her help in drawing out some of the quieter students. All but the dimmest students will get the hint.

Often in the course of the day, you will find your class getting bogged down. Petty debate over minor details or a frustrating inability to understand the larger issues can prevent your making steady progress. Worse still, you may discover that none of the students has done the assigned reading. It is important on these occasions not to lose your temper. Try, literally, to focus students' attention on something different. Illustrations in the textbook are especially effective for changing direction in a conversation or bringing home a point. Ask questions about the illustrations that require students to reflect on specific issues raised in the text or lectures. For instance, if you are talking about the spiritual world of the Paleolithic era and the discussion is starting to drag, turn to the illustrations in Chapter 1 and ask the students to examine the paintings and sculptures. Encourage the students to speculate about what these pieces of art might tell us about the spiritual lives of the people who made them. Bring in crucial details, for instance, about what the Venus figurine pictured in the photo on page 22 of the textbook is thought to represent.

Illustrations have a way of waking up students and inspiring those who are most disengaged. Even a picture lacking obvious drama can bring forth deep passions and insights. For instance, the photo on page 101 depicting the ruins of Persepolis will mean little to

students at first glance, but it will engage the students' imaginations as you decode with the class the meaning of the sculpted figures, in particular the figure of Ahura Mazda at the top. The textbook allows you to bring history to life and ensures that your class discussions reflect that drama.

There may be occasions when none of these methods works or when the problem persists class after class. One approach is that of outstaring students. Students, like most people, hate extended silences. Or one can take the silence itself as a point worthy of discussion: "OK, my friends, why doesn't anyone want to talk today?" Students may laugh and finally admit that they just don't get it or that none of them has done the reading. For those who don't get it, one can go back to the book, open it up, and start parsing a passage. To deal with students who simply fail to do the work, never forget—and this rule applies to all teaching problems— that you have the power of the grade. Sometimes it may just be appropriate to remind a particular student or the entire class that "F" is an option. A pop quiz can clarify this fact efficiently.

Better still, though, you can avoid such confrontations through careful preparation. It is important to remember that students want to resolve the intellectual problem under consideration. Begin by reaching an agreement on the nature of the topic under discussion, and keep clarifying that issue and where you are in the process—for instance, defining, suggesting hypotheses and evidence, evaluating alternatives—while involving the students as much as possible. If you get a sense that many students are overwhelmed by the reading, provide them with questions beforehand to guide them through the material. It is vitally important to make sure students have done the reading, even if you are not confident of their level of understanding. Thus, it is important never to denigrate an initial interpretation; rather, build on it. Find something positive to say about every comment, rephrase silly comments (and yes, there are dumb questions), write key phrases spoken by students on the board to encourage a sense of responsibility and pride in one's words, and link the comments of one student with those of another to get them to talk to one another and not just to you. Expending such extra energy early on will convince students that they can master the material and offer something of value. Nourish that confidence, as it is the very foundation of education.

8. Effective Teaching: Polishing Your Skills

Combine your enthusiasm for teaching with a practical appreciation for future employment. A TA-ship is the first step in building an academic career—every one of your professors was once a TA. The point of teaching is to be effective, to impart a body of information and a mode of analysis. The better you teach, the clearer your own perception of the workings of history, an insight that cannot but improve your dissertation.

And the accumulation of teaching experience will make any graduate student more attractive on the job market.

There are several ways of improving your teaching while building a supportive portfolio, which includes recommendations, evaluations, and references that you will show prospective employers. Ask your students for written evaluations, and read them carefully. With time, you may find these evaluations valuable components of a job application. Be honest with yourself in identifying weaknesses, and work to correct flaws. Some methods of self-examination are more attractive than others; videotaping your class is valuable but painful. Just as you encourage your students to show their rough drafts to friends, invite your adviser and any other professors with whom you are comfortable into your classroom so that they can suggest improvements and later attest to your teaching abilities in letters of recommendation.

Much of what is offered in this brief guide is given to you in the spirit of exploration. A great deal can be learned from talking with and observing experienced teachers, but that does not mean you should try to become some ideal type of college professor. You will quickly discover your own voice and style as a teacher, and you should have no trouble retaining your sense of humor in the process. Do not hesitate to experiment—and abandon an idea if it flops. Some approaches work for some teachers and not for others. Do not be afraid to try something new. It is your classroom, your career—and teaching should be fun. With music, as Duke Ellington said, "If it sounds good, it is good." With teaching, if it works for you, it is good teaching.

The New World Civilization Instructor:

Thirty Books to Get You Started

Graduate school forces most of us into a narrower and narrower research field, so it can be a rude awakening when we land that first job and discover that we'll be teaching a lot of world history. Lucky new instructors have at least had experience as teaching assistants in world history classes, but for most world history instructors, the task can at first seem overwhelming.

Teaching world history courses is an additive process; most painstaking teachers will work on deepening their knowledge of various fields and developing their own interpretations for years (if not forever!). The following list is not for them. Rather, it is intended for the *new* world history instructor who is overwhelmed to the point of paralysis at the daunting task before her or him. This is a list of thirty readily available general books that will at least introduce you to most of the regions and issues of world history, providing a starting point for your own research. The books chosen are not, in most cases, the most profound books available—profundity takes space, and the goal of this list was above all to provide a manageable reading plan for people who might have a single summer before stepping behind a world history lectern for the first time. Read the books on this list and take good notes, and you'll find that, while you certainly don't know everything there is to know about world history, at least you'll have the resources to write many lectures without further research, to answer most student questions, and to not feel completely lost as you start exploring world history in your classroom.

Armstrong, Karen. *Islam: A Short History*. New York: Modern Library, 2000. A short and sensitive introduction to the history of Islam as both a religious and a political entity.

Barber, Elizabeth W. *Women's Work: The First 20,000 Years*. 2nd ed. New York: W. W. Norton, 1995. A highly readable and insightful book that deals with women and textile production.

Bentley, Jerry H. *Old World Encounters*. Oxford: Oxford University Press, 1993. A readable book of modest length that deals well with the theme of cross-cultural encounters before 1492.

Brogan, Hugh. *The Penguin History of the USA*. 2nd ed. London: Penguin, 2001. Written from a British perspective, this book is a surprisingly easy read for its size and gives comprehensive coverage of U.S. history that's particularly useful for the non-Americanist teaching world civ. for the first time.

Chasteen, John C. *Born in Blood and Fire: A Concise History of Latin America*. 2nd ed. New York: W. W. Norton, 2005. A very deftly written work that goes far beyond the feeling of a textbook.

Chaudhuri, K. N. *Trade and Civilization in the Indian Ocean: An Economic History from the Rise of Islam to 1750*. Cambridge: Cambridge University Press, 1985. Reading this book will make sure that you never shortchange the importance of the Indian Ocean again.

Christian, David. *Maps of Time*. Berkeley: University of California Press, 2004. In this work, David Christian, a leading world historian and an advocate of "big history," places human history firmly in the context of the history of the universe.

Crosby, Alfred. *Ecological Imperialism*. Cambridge: Cambridge University Press, 1986. A discussion of the impact of biological exchange between the Old and New worlds.

Curtin, Philip D. *Cross-Cultural Trade in World History*. Cambridge: Cambridge University Press, 1984. A far-reaching and thought-provoking study.

Davidson, Basil. *Africa in History*. 4th ed. London: Orion Books, 1991. An excellent one-volume overview of African history.

Davies, Norman. *Europe: A History*. Oxford: Oxford University Press, 1996. This book is an amazing *tour de force* of European history from the Ice Age to the fall of the Iron Curtain. At 1,365 pages, it's not a light read, but the author's lucid interpretations give a very good overview of European history.

Diamond, Jared. *Guns, Germs, and Steel: The Fates of Human Societies*. New York: W. W. Norton, 1997. A good read, this book provides an overarching explanation—one that centers on geography, demography, and ecological happenstance—for why Western Europe became such an important force in world history after 1500.

Dunn, Ross E. *The New World History: A Teacher's Companion*. Boston: Bedford/St. Martin's, 2000. A collection of helpful articles on the problem of teaching world history, this book also provides a good introduction to the field.

Ebrey, Patricia Buckley. *The Cambridge Illustrated History of China*. Rev. ed. Cambridge: Cambridge University Press, 1999. An excellent and beautifully illustrated overview of Chinese history and culture.

Frank, Andre Gunder, and Barry Gills, eds. *The World System: Five Hundred Years or Five Thousand?* London: Routledge, 1993. An important collection of articles arguing that the economic interconnectedness of the world goes back 5,000 years.

Fredrickson, George M. *Racism: A Short History*. 2nd ed. Princeton, NJ: Princeton University Press, 2003. Although this book focuses on views of Africans and Jews, it is also useful in raising consciousness of racial issues more generally.

Hughes, Sarah S., and Brady Hughes, eds. *Women in World History*. 2 vols. Armonk, NY: M. E. Sharpe, 1995. A collection of readings, both primary and secondary, that is particularly useful at suggesting ways to include women in a world history survey.

Keegan, John. *A History of Warfare*. New York: Alfred A. Knopf, 1993. Face it: a lot of students like war, so war is a good "hook" to draw them in to consider other topics. This book provides a great deal of information in a short space.

Kehoe, Alice Beck. *America before the European Invasions*. London: Longman, 2002. An excellent study that especially examines the variety of Indian societies in the time before Columbus.

McNeill, William H. *Plagues and Peoples*. New York: Anchor, 1976. A balanced overview of the role of disease in human history.

Mills, Nicolaus. *Winning the Peace: The Marshall Plan and America's Coming of Age as a Superpower*. Hoboken, NJ: Wiley, 2008. An interesting and insightful work on how the United States assumed a position of world dominance.

Murphey, Rhoads. *A History of Asia*. 5th ed. London: Longman, 2005. A textbook, but a good one that will give you an overview of Asian history from prehistoric times to the present.

Pacey, Arnold. *Technology in World Civilization*. Cambridge, MA: MIT Press, 1990. A very interesting history of technology over the past 1,000 years.

Parkyn, Neil, ed. *The Seventy Wonders of the Modern World*. London: Thames & Hudson, 2002. An extraordinary look at architectural feats of the past 1,500 years from around the world.

Roberts, J. M. *The Penguin History of the Twentieth Century*. London: Penguin, 2004. An astonishing overview, monumental at 928 pages but food for thought—and fodder for many lectures in the latter part of the course.

Rudgley, Richard. *The Lost Civilizations of the Stone Age*. New York: Touchstone, 1999. A readable, well-illustrated book about Paleolithic, Mesolithic, and Neolithic societies.

Scarre, Chris, ed. *The Seventy Wonders of the Ancient World*. London: Thames and Hudson, 1999. Seventy wonderful vignettes of how various ancient societies actually did things, complete with illustrations and measurements.

Scarre, Christopher, and Brian M. Fagan. *Ancient Civilizations*. 2nd ed. Upper Saddle River, NJ: Prentice Hall, 2003. This wonderful book provides short presentations on Mesopotamia, Egypt, the Indus Valley civilization, early Chinese civilizations, Near Eastern kingdoms, early states in northeast Africa, early civilizations of the Americas, and more.

Stearns, Peter N. *The Industrial Revolution in World History*. 3rd ed. Boulder, CO: Westview Press, 2007. This book examines the impact of industrialization on several major societies.

Wesseling, H. L. *The European Colonial Empires, 1815–1919*. London: Longman, 2004. A very fine, overarching study of the imperial phenomenon in the nineteenth century.

A World History Reference Library

The following is a list of resources that will be useful for anyone teaching world history classes. Ideally, every history department that offers world history courses should have these or similar books readily available for instructors preparing lectures; at the least, your university library should have such a collection.

Allen, Larry. *Encyclopedia of Money*. Santa Barbara, CA: ABC-Clio, 1999.

Bartlett, John. *Bartlett's Familiar Quotations*. 17th ed. Boston: Little, Brown, 2002.

Bowker, John, ed. *The Oxford Dictionary of World Religions*. Oxford: Oxford University Press, 1997.

Boyer, Paul S., ed. *The Oxford Companion to United States History*. Oxford: Oxford University Press, 2001.

Buisseret, David, ed. *The Oxford Companion to World Exploration*. 2 vols. New York: Oxford University Press, 2007.

Carnes, Mark C., et al., eds. *Past Imperfect: History According to the Movies*. New York: Henry Holt, 1995.

Daniels, Patricia S., and Stephen G. Hyslop. *National Geographic Almanac of World History*. Washington, DC: National Geographic, 2003.

Davis, Paul K. *100 Decisive Battles: From Ancient Times to the Present*. Santa Barbara, CA: ABC-Clio, 2000.

Fagan, Brian M., ed. *The Oxford Companion to Archaeology*. New York: Oxford University Press, 1996.

Farrington, Karen. *Historical Atlas of Religions*. New York: Facts on File, 2002.

Holmes, Richard, ed. *The Oxford Companion to Military History*. Oxford: Oxford University Press, 2001.

Kohn, George C. *Dictionary of Historic Documents*. Rev. ed. New York: Facts on File, 2003.

Leeming, David. *The Oxford Companion to World Mythology*. Oxford: Oxford University Press, 2005.

McColl, R. W. *Encyclopedia of World Geography*. 3 vols. New York: Facts on File, 2005.

McNeese, Tim. *Political Revolutions of the 18th, 19th, and 20th Centuries*. New York: Facts on File, 2005.

O'Brien, Patrick, ed. *Oxford Atlas of World History: Concise Edition*. New York: Oxford University Press, 2002.

Page, Melvin E., ed. *Colonialism: An International Social, Cultural, and Political Encyclopedia*. 3 vols. Santa Barbara, CA: ABC-Clio, 2003.

Palmer, Alan W. *The Penguin Dictionary of Twentieth-Century History*. 5th ed. London: Penguin, 1999.

Roquemore, Joseph H. *History Goes to the Movies: A Viewer's Guide to the Best (and Some of the Worst) Historical Films Ever Made*. New York: Main Street Books, 1999.

Teeple, John B. *Timelines of World History*. London: DK Publications, 2002.

Waldman, Carl, and Alan Wexler. *Encyclopedia of Exploration*. New York: Facts on File, 2004.

Wright, Edmund, and Jonathan Law, eds. *Oxford Dictionary of World History*. 2nd ed. New York: Oxford University Press, 2007.

Useful Web Sites for the World History Instructor

The following is an up-to-date list of Web sites that are likely to be particularly useful to a world history instructor. These Web sites are chosen to complement the more specific Web sites suggested in the Further Reading section of each chapter of the Instructor's Resource Manual.

Annenberg Media: Teacher Resources and Teacher Professional Development Programming across the Curriculum, http://www.learner.org/. This site includes a free-access world history Web course designed by leading figures in the field. Within each subject are video clips of lectures, a gallery of visual materials for use in the classroom, and a set of full text readings.

Art History Resources on the Web, http://witcombe .sbc.edu/ARTHLinks.html. This site, maintained by Christopher L. C. E. Witcombe, is a wonderful source for art from all periods and from around the world.

BBC: History, http://www.bbc.co.uk/history/. An interesting range of materials.

Best of History Web Sites, http://www.besthistorysites.net/. An award-winning portal with annotated links to over 1,000 history Web sites as well as history lesson plans, teacher guides, games, quizzes, and more.

The Biographical Dictionary, http://www.s9.com/. A still-growing compendium of brief biographies of over 33,000 notable people.

The Center for Teaching History with Technology, http://www.thwt.org/. Although this site was created with an eye toward teaching K–12 history and social studies, it has much valuable information for college instructors, too. Hints on PowerPoint, podcasts, blogs, and online teaching are practical and useful.

EuroDocs: Online Sources for European History, http://eudocs.lib.byu.edu/index.php/Main_Page. A rich collection from all periods of European history.

Exploring Ancient World Cultures: An Introduction to Ancient World Cultures on the World Wide Web, http://eawc.evansville.edu/. An excellent site, maintained by the University of Evansville, that includes basic information, primary sources in translation, and Internet links for the ancient Near East, India, Egypt, China, Greece, Rome, Islam, and Europe.

History Museums and Memorials in the Yahoo! Directory, http://dir.yahoo.com/Arts/humanities/history/museums_and_memorials/. An impressive collection of museum sites.

History Research Online, http://members.aol.com/historyresearch/. A useful portal to resources that supply basic information about many regions and periods of world history, including maps, statistics, and timelines.

HyperHistory Online, http://www.hyperhistory.com/online_n2/History_n2/a.html. An interesting site with uneven coverage but with a great deal of material that would be useful in world history lectures.

Internet History Sourcebooks Project, http://www.fordham.edu/halsall/. An extremely useful site assembled by Paul Halsall, with primary source readings on most periods of world history for which sources are available in English translation, many of them one- or two-page excerpts that are particularly handy for classroom use.

National Geographic, http://www.nationalgeographic.com/. This site contains links to many interesting National Geographic Society programs and projects.

National Geographic's Map Machine, http://plasma.nationalgeographic.com/mapmachine/index.html. This must be seen to be believed.

Outline Maps, http://www.eduplace.com/ss/maps/. A great selection of world maps, U.S. maps, regional maps, and historical maps—all in outline form for

class map quizzes and available for free for personal or classroom use.

Web Gallery of Art, http://www.wga.hu/index1.html. A great collection of European art from 1100 to the present.

World History Connected, http://worldhistoryconnected.press.uiuc.edu/. This open-access ejournal offers articles and reviews specifically designed to help world history teachers improve their courses and stay current in the field.

World History Matters, http://worldhistorymatters.org/. This important Web portal hosted by George Mason University includes links to an extensive set of world history sources along with ideas and case studies on how to use world history sources effectively in the classroom. It also includes a second site, Women in World History, with extensive source readings and scenarios for bringing the history of women into the classroom.